UNDERSTANDING EDUCATIONAL RESEARCH

UNDERSTANDING EDUCATIONAL RESEARCH

AN INTRODUCTION
ENLARGED/REVISED

DEOBOLD B. VAN DALEN PH.D.
University of California
Berkeley

With Two Chapters By
WILLIAM J. MEYER PH.D.
Syracuse University

McGraw-Hill Book Company
New York/St. Louis
San Francisco
Toronto
London
Sydney

McGRAW-HILL SERIES IN EDUCATION

Harold Benjamin, *Consulting Editor-in-Chief*

Arno A. Bellack *Teachers College, Columbia University*
CONSULTING EDITOR, CURRICULUM AND METHODS IN EDUCATION

Harold Benjamin *Emeritus Professor of Education*
George Peabody College for Teachers
CONSULTING EDITOR, FOUNDATIONS IN EDUCATION

Harlan Hagman *Wayne State University*
CONSULTING EDITOR, ADMINISTRATION IN EDUCATION

Nicholas Hobbs *George Peabody College for Teachers*
CONSULTING EDITOR, PSYCHOLOGY
AND HUMAN DEVELOPMENT IN EDUCATION

Walter F. Johnson *Michigan State University*
CONSULTING EDITOR, GUIDANCE, COUNSELING,
AND STUDENT PERSONNEL IN EDUCATION

PSYCHOLOGY AND HUMAN DEVELOPMENT IN EDUCATION

Nicholas Hobbs, *Consulting Editor*

Frandsen *Educational Psychology*

Ginott *Group Psychotherapy with Children*

Haring and Phillips *Educating Emotionally Disturbed Children*

Hildreth *Introduction to the Gifted*

Van Dalen *Understanding Educational Research*

Preface

Progress is an evolutionary process, but today the pace is brisk. Since this text was first published, the entire climate in the field of educational research has changed. Support and pressure from fund-granting agencies and the activities of professional organizations are upgrading the quality of the work being done and the caliber of the training required. In the past, writing a scholarly paper and taking an elementary statistics course were the only "research" experiences that many educators received. In the research-oriented world of today in which revolutionary developments in investigative tactics, strategy, and tools are taking place, we must train a new breed of researchers.

The communication gap between educators and scientific investigators cannot be closed in one leap, but the first edition of this text gave some momentum to the movement; this comprehensive revision should accelerate it. Although the general structure of the text remains unchanged, not a single chapter remains the same. All chapters, the appendix, and the bibliography have been revised to keep educators abreast of advances in the field.

The chapter on experimental research has been revised and expanded extensively. The statistical chapters have been simplified, more extensive explanations have been given, and some of the more complex content has been eliminated. Chapter 5, Printed Resources for Problem Solving, has been brought up-to-date and an introduction to bibliographical and informational retrieval systems has been added. Other examples of new materials that have been included are an explanation of the use of computers and modern data processing techniques, an expanded discussion on how to judge the validity of research tools and designs, an introduction to factorial designs, and an explanation of the difference between the research hypothesis and the null hypothesis.

The objectives stated for the first edition of the text are the same for the revision. The formidable "foreign" language of research causes many teachers to shy away from reading about new studies, and the resulting paucity of teacher-researcher communication impedes professional progress. Hence, helping classroom teachers to comprehend the terminology and tactics of the research world is of paramount importance to society.

Popularized and oversimplified accounts of scientific endeavors spark interest, but students who wish to further investigate the research are hindered. More technical books provide a firmer foundation for understanding the complexities of scientific studies, but many novices plunge enthusiastically into these works only to become perplexed because the language is unintelligible to them.

In this text the viewpoint of the readers who are approaching the systematic study of research for the first time is constantly kept in mind. To aid the students who have a limited background in psychology, logic, and mathematics, the text links scientific terminology and tactics to their everyday experiences. Through illustrations of commonplace activities in classroom and life situations, the text explores techniques that men have devised to solve problems. With a minimum of technical jargon and some carefully constructed steppingstones of understanding, the text introduces students to the psychological and logical foundations of scientific investigation. Readers gradually become acquainted with the goals, basic assumptions, limitations, and language of scientists—with the way researchers talk and how their minds work in getting results. The text imparts what Conant calls for in *Science and Common Sense*: some knowledge of "tactics and strategy" and of "what science can and cannot accomplish."

The text then gives some insight into how scholars tackle investigations; how they locate problems; some of the methods, procedures, and indispensable tools that they employ; the general sequence of events that occurs during an investigation; the skills and knowledges required to undertake various types of studies; the library and research tools that are available; and the study habits and attitudes that are conducive to fruitful

work. Readers are reminded that many of these tools and procedures can also help them improve their term papers and
professional reports.

The objective of this book is to imbue students with a
respect for the scientific spirit of inquiry and to acquaint them
with problem-solving techniques that will prove useful in their
academic, personal, and professional lives. The discussion is
designed to help readers understand and appreciate the complexity of social science phenomena, the difficulties investigators
encounter, the importance of promoting sound research projects,
and the need for applying the findings of significant studies in
the classroom.

The discussion emphasizes *understanding* research and presents varied viewpoints rather than a single school of thought.
Experimental research is given extensive treatment, but historical and descriptive research are also fully discussed. The importance of the theoretical framework of an investigation and
the formulation of hypotheses receive as much attention as
research designs and statistics. The needs and views of the
classroom teacher and the administrator are considered as well
as those of the psychologist, statistician, sociologist, and logician.

The text strives to encourage and enable teachers to locate
and read some research reports in their field, to evaluate with
more discrimination the research reports that are found in professional periodicals, and to cooperate more intelligently with
experts in the field. Perhaps this volume will also give some
students the confidence and impetus to undertake modest investigations, to broaden and deepen their knowledge in this
field, and eventually to prepare themselves for professional
research work.

The text is designed to reach a broader reading public than
may exist in any one institution. Some professors may utilize
all of the materials; some professors may emphasize research
designs and statistics and utilize the remaining chapters of the
book as a supplementary reference; other professors may confine their attention to the nonstatistical chapters. The text is
suitable for any novice interested in research, but it is written
expressly for an introductory course in educational research
for mature upperclassmen, graduates pursuing their master's
degree, and doctoral candidates who have had only a limited
exposure to the scientific method. It leaves the task of exploring
the specific academic areas necessary to train professional
workers to more advanced and specialized books.

The author wishes to express his deepest appreciation to the
professors and students who offered constructive suggestions
that have been incorporated in this revised version of the text.

The author also wishes to acknowledge his indebtedness to the individuals whose names appear in the bibliography and to the publishers who generously gave permission to quote or use materials from their publications. Special thanks go to Prof. C. Mauritz Lindvall and Prof. William J. Asher of the Department of Educational Research, University of Pittsburgh, for their trenchant and penetrating analysis of Chapter 11; and to Miss Hazel Johnson, reference librarian at the University of Pittsburgh, for her many valuable and constructive suggestions for the improvement of Chapter 5. Special thanks also go to Prof. William J. Meyer for rewriting the chapters on statistics. My greatest personal indebtedness is to my wife, Marcella Madison Van Dalen, who has done much to clarify the exposition.

Deobold B. Van Dalen

Contents

1

Research and Social Progress

Research has moved during this century from the periphery to the center of our social and economic life. What is the nature of this force? Why is it gathering momentum? You hear the word "research" almost daily. A manufacturer proudly announces that after years of research his company has produced a new fabric. A stock analyst claims that his market forecasts are products of sound research. When in need of help, teachers, housewives, farmers, politicians, and military men turn to research laboratories for aid. Yes, "research" is a common word, a magic word. But what does it mean? What contributions do research workers make to our society?

Research workers engage in a systematic search for solutions to the problems that plague and puzzle mankind. An awareness of ignorance and an abundance of curiosity spark their ventures, and an intense yearning to acquire knowledge, to achieve intellectual order, and to improve our society sustain their efforts. Down through the decades, a succession of scientists have paved the road to social betterment. Their work has improved men's physical well-being, standard of living, and military security. Their efforts have provided people with better quality, quantity, and variety of food; more attractive and diverse clothing; and innumerable comforts and conveniences that ease men's burdens and enliven their lives. Ideas conceived in research laboratories have increased the speed and ease of transportation; replaced the muscle-straining pick, plow, and shovel with powerful machines; and created complicated automatic devices to assume many monotonous duties. On every front, scientists have attacked drudgery and disease. As a result of their efforts, people live longer, possess better health, enjoy more leisure, see more of the world, endure less suffering, and experience less arduous labor.

Attitudes toward Research

Having observed a parade of astonishing advances and having become increasingly indebted to science, citizens should have the greatest respect for research work. But many people, unfortunately, do not have an intelligent understanding of the nature and value of research and its relationship to their lives. Consequently, they have developed attitudes that impede scientific progress. While reading the following paragraphs, perhaps you will recognize points of view expressed by some of your classmates or teaching colleagues.

Repressing Research/ Because of vested interests in the *status quo* or from a fearful distrust of new ideas or developments, some individuals and groups do not want scientists to jar people out of their traditional patterns of thought and behavior. To them, change is unnecessary and undesirable; hence, they rudely reject or ruthlessly repress researchers who present ideas or inventions that depart too far from prevailing beliefs or practices. Historians have repeatedly related tales of the severe measures taken by authorities to prevent scientists from advancing knowledge. Copernicus was excommunicated for publishing *On The Revolutions of the Celestial Orbs.* Tycho Brahe, the astronomer, was burned at the stake. Galileo was persecuted by the Inquisition. Darwin was severely censured for his *Origin of Species.* The discovery of the basic principle of genetics by Mendel was ignored by society for thirty-five years after it was published. Dewey and his disciples, who sought to make education more scientific, were vigorously attacked. Not uncommonly, a crown of thorns rather than an olive wreath has been the reward of research workers.

Ridiculing Research/ Because of inertia, ignorance, or the belief that further advances in knowledge cannot be made, some people ridicule the efforts of research workers. They dismiss scientists as peculiar fellows who putter with rats, chemicals, or books rather than attacking problems in the practical world of affairs. These critics contend that all the important discoveries have already been made and that our society can best be preserved by following the good old ways of the good old days. They believe that scientists busy themselves with trivial problems, stud their research reports with technical jargon and mounds of statistics to camouflage the insignificance of their work, and foist upon society foolish, newfangled theories that never work.

Worshiping Research/ Indiscriminate admiration of scientists can also hamper social progress. Some educators and other citizens place research on the highest pedestal and blindly worship it. They believe scientists are gifted geniuses—a different species of humanity—who engage in grueling hours of work utilizing complicated procedures that ordinary men cannot possibly comprehend. Standing in absolute awe of science, they accept all research reports as revolutionary, reliable solutions to problems. With great enthusiasm they adopt each new drug, gadget, and remedy on the market. Digging deep into their pockets, they generously donate to any project labeled research. They swallow, hook, line, and sinker, whatever a research worker tells them. Desiring to identify themselves as alert and progressive, they eagerly grasp and apply new theories whether they have an intelligent understanding of them or not. Abandoning all critical caution, they conclude that whatever is proclaimed to be a product of research is good.

Assuming a Superior Aptitude for Research/ Having witnessed a succession of dramatic scientific transformations, some men accept such progress as automatic. Many Americans assume that we are world leaders because we instinctively possess the know-how to solve problems. Earlier in the century, a similar nationalistic pride caused German chemists to proclaim that their successes resulted from the possession of special "moral qualities." To assume that any nation has a monopoly on scientific aptitude is naïve. Many shocked Americans discovered this fact when the Russians put the first satellite in orbit. This incident precipitated an agonizing reappraisal of their smug attitudes and awakened them to the necessity of providing our scientists with better training, equipment, facilities, and financial support.

Accepting Applied Rather than Pure Research/ Laymen tend to sanction some types of research more readily than others. Most of them approve of applied research that produces plainly practical and immediately useful findings—a polio vaccine, a television set, or a hearing aid. But they are less enthusiastic about supporting basic or pure research that strives to ferret out new knowledge about the fundamental laws of nature. Many men, for example, would contribute generously to an applied research program for the development of an anticancer pill or an arithmetic-teaching machine. But they might balk at supplying funds for a basic study on cellular growth or the nature of learning that did not guarantee to produce a product of immediate social and economic value. Yet the study on cellular growth might eventually throw light on the prevention not only of cancer but of a host of other diseases. Likewise, a study on the nature of learning might provide a major breakthrough that would lead to improvement in teaching not only arithmetic but also many other subjects. Basic research may ultimately lead to more fruitful developments than applied research, but the public is less willing to support it. Many people cannot easily see how pure research will better their lives. They are leery of projects that do not promise specific and quick returns on their investments.

Accepting Natural Science Research More Easily than Social Science Research/ Society has exerted considerable effort to promote research in the natural sciences, but it has assumed a more skeptical and antagonistic attitude toward supporting research in the social sciences. Many people are quite willing to accept changes in physics and technical fields, but they are rather reluctant to alter their social institutions. Citizens who quickly turn to scientists for aid in solving industrial problems rely on do-it-yourself and trial-and-error techniques for improving educational practices. Men who would not think of providing for national defense by returning to the military hardware of World War I confidently claim they can solve all educational problems by returning to the practices of the McGuffey reader era. Manufacturers and politicians who continually increase research expenditures to produce more comfort gadgets and deadly weapons are not equally eager to earmark funds for educational research. Seeking better means of developing the potentialities of our children does not command as much attention as creating a new model car. Technologically, the attitude of society toward research is in the Space Age; educationally, it is hardly beyond the Horse and Buggy Age.

Acquiring Better Understanding of Research

Many undesirable attitudes toward research have developed because the public is not well informed about scientific procedures and objectives. Our country must take steps to fill this intellectual vacuum. If citizens remain ignorant of research, they may impede social development and endanger national survival. In a democracy, all men play a part in determining policies. If they do not appreciate the value of scientific investigations, they will not make intelligent decisions when asked to support research projects. Scientific understanding, therefore, cannot remain the exclusive privilege of an intellectual elite. If citizens acquire sufficient knowledge of research to see the relationship between scientific findings and their individual and national well-being, they will be more willing to assume the responsibilities necessary to promote investigations.

Scientifically informed citizens will appreciate that social progress is not inevitable, but must be won by a serious search for answers to problems. They will insist upon recruiting talented youths for research work, supplying the selected scholars with superior training, and granting scientists the prestige due them. They will support educational as well as natural science research and will finance basic as well as applied research. On no occasion will they permit social, political, economic, or religious bodies to curb the scientists' freedom of inquiry and right to question existing funds of knowledge. Nor will they allow individuals and institutions to pervert research efforts so as to obtain findings favorable to selfish interests. Rather than gullibly accepting claims made for new theories and products, they will evaluate critically whether the assertions are based upon sound research. Rather than ignoring reliable research findings or forcing sound scientific theories to remain locked in laboratories, they will apply each advance in knowledge to everyday life.

Education and Research

Despite the rather apathetic attitude of the general public toward educational research, a few lay and school leaders have developed agencies and organizations to promote it. Their progress has been slow and laborious, for winning public support takes time. But some day society may feel as deeply indebted to the men who have founded educational research as it now does to the pioneer workers in the natural sciences.

Establishing Agencies of Research

Lively sparks of interest in solving educational problems through research began to stimulate men's minds in the late nineteenth century. Some seeds of the research movement sprouted at Leipzig in 1879 when Wilhelm Wundt established the first psychological laboratory. In England, about the same time, Francis Galton and Karl Pearson were developing statistical methods that were later to be used in educational research. After the turn of the century, the French scholar Alfred Binet initiated his studies in mental testing. During these decades, the American students who streamed to Europe for advanced study caught the scientific fever and returned home burning with enthusiasm for research.

Developing Research Institutions/ Having been deeply impressed with the leadership, laboratories, and libraries provided by European universities to help students engage in research, outstanding American educators agitated for the founding of similar institutions in this country. Francis Wayland of Brown University and Henry P. Tappan and James B. Angell of Michigan were among the early leaders who recommended sweeping educational reforms. Charles W. Eliot of Harvard, Andrew Dickson White of Cornell, and Frederick A. P. Barnard of Columbia also participated in the movement. In 1869, a committee of the National Teachers' Association strongly urged the nation to establish a "real university" that would push back the frontiers of knowledge by means of research.

Harvard, Yale, Columbia, Michigan, and other schools made some effort to offer advanced instruction fairly early. Real graduate schools did not exist, however, until the establishment of the Johns Hopkins University in 1876, Clark University in 1888, and the University of Chicago in 1890 with Daniel Coit Gilman, G. Stanley Hall, and William Rainey Harper as their respective presidents. In the pioneer universities, scholars such as Cattell, Judd, Hall, Thorndike, Pintner, Courtis, Terman, and others initiated research studies and inspired their students to carry on the work.

As the research movement gained momentum, a number of agencies began to further scientific investigations. Colleges established psychological laboratories and research centers, such as the child study laboratories at Yale, Iowa, Columbia, and Minnesota. By 1924, twenty-two institutions had established research bureaus. Private and public experimental schools and teacher-training laboratory schools planned special programs to study children and to apply research findings. Public school authorities selected particular schools or classes in which to conduct investigations or to try out new procedures. Foundations, such as the W. K. Kellogg Foundation, the Ford Foundation, and the Russell Sage Foundation, gave substantial grants for research studies. City, state, and national educational authorities added directors of research to their staffs. In 1922, the National Education Association (NEA) established the Research Division which now collects considerable data and conducts many studies of concern to its members. In recent decades, agencies promoting educational research have multiplied, and most institutions have expanded their facilities and programs.

Developing Research Periodicals and Organizations/ Distinguished leaders in the research movement also founded many organizations and publications to disseminate information and advance their work. In 1876 the first psychological journal, *Mind,* appeared in England. G. Stanley Hall started *The American Journal of Psychology* in 1887 and *Pedagogical Seminary* in 1891. Binet's work on intelligence appeared in *L'Année Psychologique,* which he founded in 1894. After the *Teachers College Record* was founded in 1900, it presented many of Thorndike's studies. *The Journal of Educational Psychology,* established in 1910, became a valuable publication. Taking note of the importance of research, many universities established bureaus to publish research monographs, and educational associations added research sections to their organizations and publications.

In 1915, pioneer research workers established the National Association of Directors of Educational Research. In 1930, this group became the American Educational Research Association (AERA), a department of the NEA. The AERA has exerted a wide influence on the research movement and has founded several publications: the *Educational Research Bulletin* in 1920, the *Review of Educational Research* in 1931, and the *American Educational Research Journal* in 1964. The AERA has also produced the *Encyclopedia of Educational Research* to aid scholars.

In addition to the AERA, a number of other organizations have contributed to modern research. The American Council on Education and the National Society for the Study of Education have served as stimulating agencies. Phi Delta Kappa, a graduate fraternity of students interested in education and research, has initiated over 100,000 members. Dozens of other educational organizations have established research sections and have produced periodicals and yearbooks that are devoted wholly or partly to research. During the past two decades, an increasing number of research textbooks have been published.

Expanding Areas of Research

At the turn of the century, a relatively small group of men became dissatisfied with the traditional trial-and-error and intuitive methods of solving educational problems. Realizing that guesswork was an unsatisfactory method of obtaining reliable knowledge about educational phenomena, these inspired leaders tried to establish more efficient and objective methods. For two or three decades, only a few men joined the intellectually disciplined ranks of research workers. But by mid-century, an army of investigators was conducting scientific studies to determine the educational effectiveness of the curriculum, school plant, teaching methods, guidance programs, and administrative practices. Down through the years, the research workers have greatly expanded the scope of their activities and have gradually exerted an influence on the practices in every area of education.

Developing Tests/ Measurement formed the cornerstone of the research movement. "For there cannot be a science without fairly precise quantification: not that science is measurement, but that traits which are devoid of any reasonably definite quality simply do not have the required specificity for entering into the careful thinking essential to science. When quantities are disregarded almost any generalization is true" (111:253 –254).[1] Recognizing this fact, Thorndike designed his famous battle banner for research workers: "Whatever exists at all exists in some amount" (133:16). Following his advice, scholars soon began to employ quantitative methods of inquiry to obtain precise facts about various areas of education.

Devising tests to measure intelligence was a major concern of Binet, Terman, Otis, Pintner, Paterson, Wechsler, and other able investigators. Developing aptitude tests also received considerable attention. The Seashore Test of Musical Talent appeared in 1915. Thereafter, investigators developed many other tests to measure specific types of capacity. Edward L. Thorndike and his students constructed most of the early tests and scales for measuring academic achievements of children. The Stone Arithmetic Test appeared in 1908 and the Thorndike Handwriting Scale in 1910. About this time, Stuart A. Courtis, who was also active in developing standardized tests, was invited to New York City where he conducted the testing in the first formal school survey in which such tests were employed. Within a few years, many other investigators published com-

---

1/ The figure before the colon is the citation number in the Bibliography at the end of the text. The figures following the colon are page numbers in the work cited.

position, spelling, language, and arithmetic scales. Research workers also became interested in devising tests to measure personality, attitudes, and interests of students. The information provided by the tests developed during the past fifty years has led to many improvements in educational and vocational guidance programs, curriculum construction, and administration.

Investigating the Learning Process/ In an endeavor to push back the frontiers of educational knowledge, psychologists have raised the fundamental question: How do children learn? Prior to this century, teachers had rather vague concepts of the learning process. Many of them believed that learning would take place automatically if sufficient drill and discipline were administered. Upon becoming acquainted with the various theoretical explanations of learning that psychologists were constructing, educators began to appreciate that learning was a more complex process than they had thought. Throughout the nation, instructors began to change their teaching practices to conform with some of the findings that research studies revealed played a part in learning.

Investigating the Nature of Children/ Some research workers collected data about the nature of children and the processes by which they grow and develop into mature personalities. Hundreds of investigators followed in the footsteps of G. Stanley Hall, the founder of the child study movement. The findings reported by Gesell, Baldwin, Dearborn, Rothney, Ilg, Ogg, Olson, and other workers have considerably influenced the practices that teachers and parents employ when guiding the development of boys and girls.

Developing the Curriculum/ Curriculum research has challenged some existing school practices, confirmed the desirability of continuing others, and encouraged the adoption of new practices. During the early decades of the century, research workers who had doubts about the traditional educational objectives and curriculum began to ask pertinent questions: What knowledges and skills are most useful in society? Can educational objectives be stated in observable terms to provide for the subsequent evaluation of the curriculum? What subject matter should be chosen as the basis of instruction? How should subject matter be integrated? What types of learning experiences should be included in the curriculum? How can the school provide for a longitudinal sequence of learning experiences? What kind of daily and weekly schedule of activities should be adopted? By proposing answers for some of these questions Bobbitt, Charters, Tyler, Caswell, Alberty, and many others made significant contributions to curriculum construction. The Eight-year Study, the Southern Association Study, and various state curriculum studies played a part in encouraging schools to depart from some of their traditional practices. In the past two decades, the explosion of knowledge, social pressures, and the renewed communication between educators and members of related disciplines has given rise to many curriculum studies. As a result, new courses of study in the sciences, mathematics, languages, and other fields have been developed which are quite different from those they superseded. Pilot projects and studies relating to television teaching, team teaching, programmed learning, flexible scheduling and grouping, and enriched and accelerated learning programs have also commanded the attention of many investigators. Current research will undoubtedly quicken the rate of curriculum change in the future.

Improving School Administration and Evaluation/ School administrators have encouraged investigators to conduct studies concerning taxation, budgeting, purchasing, class size, grouping of pupils, school-community relations, selection of teachers, and other problems. Administrators also have made an effort to translate research findings into practice. Since 1910, many school authorities have had experts survey their school systems and suggest how to improve them. Early surveyors based their judgments on personal opinion, but leaders of the research movement soon began to objectify the appraisals through the use of the newly devised standardized tests, scales, and measuring devices. To clarify and define their evaluative judgments in specific areas, surveyors developed new rating scales and scorecards, such as the Strayer-Engelhardt Score Card for Junior High School Buildings and the Mort-Cornell Guide for Self-appraisal of School Systems. As the survey movement developed, administrators began to recognize the need for continuous self-evaluation. Consequently, they established their own bureaus of research to administer testing programs, to interpret research findings to classroom teachers, and to apply the products of research in the schools. Foundations and the Federal government are now providing financial support that is enabling administrators and research workers to collaborate on a number of promising pilot projects. In recent years, the development of systematic administrative theories and studies of administrative roles and behavior have also commanded the attention of many research workers.

Improving the Quality of Research

Having been nourished by the enthusiasm and effort of forward-looking educators, the infant educational research movement has experienced considerable growth. Dedicated men have extended our knowledge in the field of education, but much work remains to be done. The growing pains, problems, and weaknesses common to other sciences in the early days of their development have also plagued educational research. Platoons of well-trained investigators did not spring up overnight to present the world with flawless solutions to educational problems. Each generation of research scholars has had to build upon the work of its predecessors—correcting errors when possible, filling in gaps, and gradually constructing a body of concepts that are more useful than the guesswork of laymen in solving educational problems. Under the leadership of able men, the research movement has made slow but promising progress. Today, a strenuous effort is being made to attract intelligent young people to the field and to provide the type of training that will enable them to improve the quality of educational research.

Developing a Higher Caliber of Research Personnel/ In the past, many research workers lacked the necessary foundations in the basic sciences, mathematics, psychology, languages, and logic. Some of them were not thoroughly familiar with the literature in their field and had only the basic rudiments of training in statistics and research procedures. To meet the demand for higher-caliber and better-prepared research workers, graduate schools have raised admittance standards and have developed extensive educational programs and instructional materials to prepare students specifically for research work. Compact information and useful guides for workers in the field, which once were obtainable only through the most laborious individual effort, now appear in textbooks, periodicals, and other publications.

Rather than relegating research to one-shot doctoral dissertation projects or a spare-time hobby for professors carrying a full teaching load, many institutions are developing divisions of research which are staffed with well-trained specialists who devote all their energies to scientific investigations and to helping other people design studies. In addition, many colleges are now providing released time for other staff members who wish to pursue postdoctoral studies.

Developing Higher Standards for Research Work/ The early decades in the scientific movement were primarily devoted to accumulating descriptive data which concerned educational phenomena and to developing testing instruments. By 1935, a tremendous quantity of research had been done, but leaders in the field were beginning to question the quality of the studies. Much of the work was localized, repetitive, trivial, biased, fragmentary, and defective in design and methodology; most studies made little, if any, contribution to a body of organized scientific knowledge concerning education.

Today, research workers are making searching appraisals of their technical shortcomings and of the gaps that exist in the overall production of educational studies. They are concerned about weaknesses in research designs, the indiscriminate use of the questionnaire as a research tool, and the fetish of counting cases and statistical manipulation. The reluctance to move from the more tangible fact-collecting stage of research to the more fundamental types of probes and controlled experiments is under attack. The failure to press on until the findings of research are translated into a context in which they can be tested in practical school situations is creating a demand for more developmental engineers. Attention is also being focused on the need to evaluate critically the varied and conflicting explanations of phenomena, to test them in a wide variety of situations, to reject the weaker ones, and to synthesize the stronger ones.

The self-criticism that is taking place in the field of educational research denotes the emergence of greater maturity. The research movement is passing from infancy to a more sophisticated stage of development. The successful work produced by educators and psychologists during the war years, the growing public recognition of the need for inquiry in all fields, and the current critical examination of our schools are winning recognition and financial support for research work. As a result of the development of highly imaginative research tools and the refinement of data-gathering devices, research designs, and statistical analysis, educators are beginning to tackle complex, fundamental problems that once had to be ignored. The current resurgence and reorientation of our research efforts will undoubtedly play a dynamic role in changing the character of American education in the years that lie ahead.

Financing Educational Research

Tremendous impetus has been given to the educational research movement during the last decade as a result of the substantial financial support that, for the first time in history, has been granted to educators. The Cooperative Research Program (CRP) of the Office of Education, the National Defense Education Act of 1958, the Fund for the Advancement of Education, and the Ford Foundation are the best-known sources of funds. When the CRP got under way in the fiscal year 1957, 1 million dollars was made available to implement it; in 1962 the CRP budget was 5 million dollars, and in 1964 it was 11.5 million dollars. Grants for some large-scale projects that involve teams of researchers are in excess of a million dollars. Small grants for short-term projects are made available to professors, young instructors, and graduate students under Title VII, NDEA. Large grants have been given to test educational approaches that have been suggested by previous research, and a number of pure research projects are also under way. The Elementary and Secondary Education Act of 1965 amended the CRP budget. One result of this act is the provision of 100 million dollars over the next five years for the establishment of national and regional educational laboratory facilities, some of which are now under way at Harvard, Wisconsin, Oregon, and Pittsburgh.

Teachers and Research

Educational research is as important to you as a classroom teacher as it is to leaders in the profession. Acquiring some understanding of research work will broaden and deepen your general fund of knowledge, will give you some appreciation of the part research plays in fashioning our lives, and will help you improve your methods of solving personal and instructional problems. An introduction to research will open up an interesting new world in which you will have opportunities to experience continuous personal and professional growth.

Offering Student Guidance/ As an educator, you must be sufficiently informed about research to help pupils gain an understanding of the role scientific investigations play in promoting social progress. Since the better instructional procedures today are organized around problem-solving activities rather than around rote memorization, you must also help students acquire skill in scientific methods of solving problems. In addition, society holds you responsible for helping exceptionally able youths to become interested in a career in research, and for guiding them in the selection of academic experiences needed to realize their aspirations. You cannot perform these services satisfactorily unless you become well acquainted with research.

Improving Classroom Practices/ Reading research studies to keep abreast of educational developments will help you acquire new interests, new motives, and new insights that will replenish your enthusiasms and revitalize your instructional procedures. Research will awaken your curiosity, will shatter some pet entrenched ideas and attitudes, and will make you question traditional practices. If your teaching is confined to regurgitating yesterday's facts, you may ignore research. But if teaching is concerned with searching for new truths, adding to our knowledge about educational phenomena and practice, and preparing youngsters for tomorrow's world, you must venture into the world of research. Embarking on a quest for new viewpoints and better ways of planning and guiding children's learning experiences will spur the development of your potentialities and will give you the satisfaction that comes from exercising your mind and maintaining a high level of professional competence.

Reducing Lag in Application of Research Findings/ A twenty-five-year lag between research findings and their application is commonplace in our schools, and some studies never receive proper consideration. This situation suggests that teachers are unaware of educational investigations made by competent scholars, unwilling to apply the outcomes of research in the schools, or unable to put the knowledge into effect owing to inadequate facilities and restrictive administrative policies. Some delay between the discovery of knowledge and the application of it is inevitable, but the present lag appears to be unjustifiably long.

If you and your fellow teachers are ignorant of research studies or do not apply the findings in the classroom, you can nullify the efforts of the most brilliant research workers. Of what value, for example, is the development of reliable measures of child aggressiveness and submissiveness and methods of dealing with them, if teachers fail to utilize this information when working with children? Of what value is the development of reading-readiness measures, if teachers continue to organize reading instruction groups on an age- or grade-level basis rather than on the pupil's readiness to read? As a classroom teacher, you play a key role in translating educational research findings into practice. If you do not perform this function, the seeds of understanding that researchers develop will never bear fruit.

Strengthening the Profession/ Teachers retard the professionalization of education if they regard research as an expendable academic appendage. Research workers provide the structural foundations upon which practitioners build. Ingenious theories precede successful practices. Doctors cannot make medical decisions without referring to well-confirmed theories. Nor can you make the best educational judgments on the basis of whim, expediency, or habit. In the classroom, you behave in terms of sound or unsound theories without realizing it. To make wise choices, you must make decisions on the basis of reliable knowledge. Research provides the means of obtaining such knowledge. Education cannot make advances similar to those that have been made by medicine or gain public recognition as a full-fledged profession unless a body of competent research is built up.

As a classroom teacher you should not only develop a respect for research but also learn how to discriminate between faulty, trivial studies and well-grounded, fundamental investigations. If you become a blind idolator of research and stuff your instructional cabinets with every nostrum on the market, some of the wonder drugs you dispense will fail to cure students' ills and some may produce harmful side effects. If you put into practice only the more significant and reliable research findings, not only will you increase your effectiveness in the classroom and youngsters' opportunities to develop their talents but also you will encourage the public to hold teachers in higher esteem, to look to them for leadership, and to grant them greater financial reward.

Developing an interest in research will also help you establish better relationships with colleagues, administrators, and parents. Your enthusiasm for finding better ways of working will have a stimulating effect on your associates. Your willingness to appeal to facts for answers to problems will create a hopeful, healthful working climate. Rather than becoming involved in emotionalized arguments with associates and the public concerning educational practices, you will ask questions such as the following to direct the discussion into more productive channels: Have these practices been put to a rigorous scientific test? What does the observable evidence reveal about them?

Participating in Research Projects/ Although most classroom teachers are appliers rather than producers of research, instructors play a role in some investigations. To assist research workers, you may be requested to offer your classroom for observational purposes, to supply information about students, to administer tests, or to recruit students as subjects for experimental programs. You may play a part in the research movement that encourages classroom teachers to attack local problems under the supervision of specialists. You may cooperate with research workers who translate new theories and scientific findings into practical programs and conduct pilot programs in public schools to test them.

In the future, more and more teachers will be called upon to play a role in research. Certainly you will be a more interested and intelligent participant if you possess some knowledge of scientific investigative procedures. To introduce you to this aspect of your professional life, the following chapters present a simple explanation of the researcher's work—his objectives, methods, problems, and limitations. The discussion will illuminate your understanding of what a researcher does and what he cannot do, will enable you to read reports or summaries of research more intelligently, and will help you acquire knowledges and skills that are required for advanced study. This entrée into the world of research may interest you in preparing yourself as a specialist in this field where the profession desperately needs qualified workers. Whatever role you play in research will enrich your life, for participating in the perpetual process of discovery, achieving order, and structuring meaningful patterns where none have existed before satisfy man's curiosity and desire to know. Research is an intrinsically rewarding and gratifying activity.

2

Methods of Acquiring Knowledge

Man is a curious animal who has sought to enlarge his understanding of himself and the world about him in hope of improving his way of living. To lighten his burdens, early man discovered the wheel, the sail, and the lever. Babylonian scholars gazed into the heavens and formulated explanations for what they saw that enabled them to predict eclipses as early as the sixth century B.C. The yearly flooding of the Nile and the repeated task of mapping out fields caused the Egyptians to create a calendar and to acquire knowledge of geometry. From ancient times to the present day, man has encountered a never-ending succession of puzzling phenomena and disturbing difficulties. To solve his problems, he has drawn upon various sources of knowledge: (1) authority, (2) personal experience, (3) deductive reasoning, (4) inductive reasoning, and (5) the scientific method.

Older Methods of Acquiring Knowledge

When his habitual method of dealing with situations produced discouraging results, man resorted to crude trial-and-error methods of seeking solutions. Through centuries of experience with problem solving, he was able to refine his knowledge-seeking methods. Periods of complacency and retardation periodically halted cultural progress, but exciting leaps forward also occurred, and the long-term trend was characterized by an extension of knowledge.

Authority

Seeking advice from an authority was a well-established method of solving problems even in the earliest civilizations. Preliterate man appealed to the medicine man to relieve him of pain and plied the tribal chieftain with questions about the elements. When floods, famine, lightning, or leprosy terrified him, he blindly accepted the ancestral explanations that his elders imparted, and appealed to supernatural powers for help. Rather than attempting to determine truth independently, modern man may also seek advice from authorities. A trial lawyer may ask a psychiatrist to testify concerning the sanity of the defendant, a ballistic expert to give opinions concerning weapons, and a handwriting specialist to compare signatures. A housewife may consult a child care book or a doctor concerning the spots on her son's chest. Turning to authorities to obtain knowledge often saves time and effort, but care must be employed in choosing authorities and evaluating their pronouncements.

Tradition/ In many situations modern man does not evaluate the truth or falsity of his beliefs any more than his forefathers did. He unconsciously or unquestioningly accepts many traditions of his culture, such as the customary modes of dress, speech, food, worship, and etiquette. In the world of practical affairs this automatic acceptance of approved patterns of behavior is often necessary, for one cannot question *all* things. But one should not make the mistake of assuming that everything that has customarily been done is right or that appealing to the accumulated wisdom of the ages will always ascertain the truth.

Historical records reveal that man has not only solved many problems and accumulated much wisdom but has also formulated many erroneous explanations of phenomena. Many long-revered educational, medical, and scientific theories have been proved false. For instance, man once believed that children differed from adults only in size and dignity, that asafetida bags warded off disease, and that the planets revolved around the earth. Truth is not a guaranteed product of a popularity contest: a statement is not true merely because "everyone knows it" or "everybody has always believed it." Age, alone, is not sufficient to establish the truth or falsity of a belief.

Church, State, and Ancient Scholars/ Preliterate man turned to tribal leaders when seeking knowledge. In medieval times, man believed that ancient scholars and churchmen had discovered the truth for all times and their pronouncements could not be questioned. The Scholastics, for example, accepted Aristotle's conjecture that women have more teeth than men as absolutely true, even though simple observation and enumeration would have provided evidence to the contrary. When invited by Galileo to view the newly discovered moons of Jupiter, one scholar refused to look through the telescope. He was convinced that the moons could not possibly be seen because Aristotle had not mentioned them in his discussions on astronomy. Like most scholars of that era, the man who declined Galileo's invitation clung blindly to faulty Grecian theories and attacked any new idea that contradicted the accepted authorities.

With the rise of strong secular states after the Middle Ages, man began to turn to kings, legislatures, and courts as sources of information. Today, many citizens also expect government officials to solve problems concerning agricultural surpluses, international trade, and labor-management difficulties. Some people appeal to the courts for interpretations on basic issues confronting them, such as the validity of Darwin's theory of natural selection, segregated school practices, and the use of prayers in public schools. From the earliest times to the present, man has sought guidance and information from his oracles, leaders, and rulers.

Man often prefers to rely on the judgment of outstanding authorities whose beliefs have withstood the test of time, because he fears that if he himself searched for answers to difficult questions he might make errors. But if modern man can make errors when searching for knowledge, his ancestors must have been subject to the same weakness. If tradition, the church, and the state are to be the source of all reliable information, what happens when these institutions render opinions that conflict with one another? The authorities in different churches and states do not always agree, and traditions of cultures vary. Man may encounter perplexing problems when he turns to the multiplicity of existing authorities in a search for answers to his questions. Ignoring the cultural cumulations of the centuries is imprudent, for little progress will occur if each generation rejects the judgment of the ages and starts from scratch to accumulate knowledge. On the other hand, refusing ever to question any accepted belief—total reliance on dogmatic authority—will result in social stagnation.

Expert Opinion/ When searching for knowledge, man sometimes seeks the testimony of experts who because of their intellect, training, experience, or aptitudes are better informed than other people. Experts are necessary in a complicated culture such as ours. An effort must be made, however, to find out whether the experts are recognized by other authorities in the field and whether they are in a position to know the facts about the particular problem under consideration. One should check not only the credentials of experts but also the arguments and evidence upon which they base their claims to knowledge. Accepting experts' opinions unconditionally and for all time is a dubious if not a dangerous practice.

Personal Experience

When confronted with a problem, man often tries to recall or to seek a personal experience that will help him reach a solution. When searching for food, ancient nomads probably remembered that certain berries always made them ill, that fish were more plentiful in some streams than others, and that grains ripened at particular times of the year. When trying to determine the quickest route to work, modern man may time himself on different roads. When deciding where to plant seeds, a gardener may try to remember in what part of the yard flowers grew best last year. When given a handful of coins to divide with his brother, a small boy may recall that selecting the biggest piece of candy on a plate is usually a wise choice; because of his previous experience with candy, he may decide to keep the big nickels and give his brother the little dimes.

Appealing to personal experiences is a useful and common method of seeking knowledge. An uncritical use of personal experience, however, may lead to incorrect conclusions, as the boy who selected the nickels with his "candy measuring stick" discovered. A person may make errors when observing or when reporting what he has seen or done. He may (1) omit evidence that does not agree with his opinion, (2) use measuring instruments that require many subjective estimates, (3) establish a belief on insufficient evidence, (4) fail to observe significant factors relating to a specific situation, or (5) draw improper conclusions or inferences owing to personal prejudices. To avoid dangerous pitfalls, the modern research worker exercises many precautions when he turns to experience in his search for reliable knowledge.

Deduction

To obtain more reliable knowledge, Aristotle developed the syllogism, a deductive argument which provides a means of testing the validity of a particular conclusion. A syllogism consists of three statements or propositions. The first two statements are called "premises," since they furnish the evidence or grounds for the conclusion, which is the statement standing last. Aristotle defined the syllogism as "a discourse in which certain things being posited, something else than what is posited necessarily follows from them." The following *categorical syllogism* is an example of such a discourse:

(Major premise)	All mammals are mortal.		If all *M* are *P,* and
	(middle) *M*	(major) *P*	
(Minor premise)	All men are mammals.		all *S* are *M,*
	(minor) *S*	(middle) *M*	then
(Conclusion)	All men are mortal.		all *S* are *P.*
	(minor) *S*	(major) *P*	

A valid syllogism contains terms referring to three and only three classes[1] of things. In the above argument the classes are mortals, mammals, and men. Each statement in the categorical syllogism contains two terms. Each term appears twice in the syllogism. The subject term *S* of the conclusion (men), which is called the "minor term," also appears in the minor premise. (See above.) The predicate term *P* of the conclusion (mortal), which is known as the "major term," is also found in the major premise. The third or middle term *M* occurs once in each premise and *does not* appear in the conclusion. The function of the middle term is to establish the relationship between the minor term and major term which is asserted in the conclusion.

In the argument above, "mammals" is the middle term or mediating factor which brings the minor term "men" in the conclusion into the asserted relation with the major term "mortal." The function of the middle term will become clearer if you examine Figure 2.1 as you read the following review of the argument. If the class of mammals *M* is included in the large class of mortals *P* as the major premise stipulates, and the class of men *S* is included in the class of mammals *M* as the minor premise stipulates, then it follows logically that the class of men *S* is included in the class of mortals *P.* Thus, this argument is valid, for the premises are related to the conclusion in such a way that the conclusion must be true if the premises are true. If a person accepts the premises, he must agree to the conclusion that follows, because the conclusion

---

1/ A logical class is a collection of particulars—things, persons, qualities—which are all alike in some defining respect. Consequently, one can infer with confidence knowledge about members of the class from knowledge of the class. Whatever can be asserted or denied of a whole class can be asserted or denied of any member of that class.

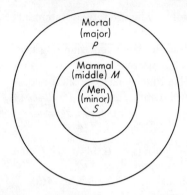

Figure 2.1/ A schematic representation of a valid argument.

merely states explicitly or reformulates information which is already implicit in the premises.

Categorical syllogisms may be cast in various forms. The position of the terms *M, P,* and *S* may be ordered in four different ways in the premises. These four forms are known as figures of the syllogism.

M-P	*P-M*	*M-P*	*P-M*
S-M	*S-M*	*M-S*	*M-S*
S-P	*S-P*	*S-P*	*S-P*

The nature of the categorical statements in a syllogism may also vary. The four types of categorical statements are (1) universal affirmative (Example: All students are white), (2) universal negative (Example: No students are white), (3) particular affirmative (Example: Some students are white), and (4) particular negative (Example: Some students are not white). A categorical syllogism may contain any three of these four types of statements in various combinations. By varying the types of statements used in the four figures, one can state arguments in 256 forms, but most of them are invalid. From two negative premises or from two particular premises, for example, no conclusion can be inferred.

A syllogism does not have to be composed exclusively of categorical statements. As the examples reveal, arguments may involve *hypothetical, alternative,* and *disjunctive* propositions.

Hypothetical.
> If the school is on fire, the children are in danger.
> The school is on fire.
> Therefore, the children are in danger.

Alternative.
> Either I will get a passing mark on this test, or I will flunk the course.
> I will not get a passing mark on this test.
> Therefore, I will flunk the course.

Disjunctive.

It is not the case that it is both a rainy day and a good day
to present the school pageant outdoors.

It is a rainy day.

Therefore, it is not a good day to present the school pageant
outdoors.

As you note in the examples, each syllogism is labeled according to the type of proposition occurring in the major premise. Each type of syllogism is used in different stages of assurance concerning knowledge. Let us examine when the various types of syllogisms are used.

Categorical propositions represent a certain settled stage of our
knowledge, and conclusions validly drawn from categorical syllogisms are unconditional. Hypothetical or conditional propositions,
however, represent an unsettled stage in thinking and knowing. Hypothetical thinking proceeds on various levels, from the solution
of simple problems of daily life, and the detection of crime, to
the technique of identification and classification in science, and the
search after scientific laws by means of the statement and testing
of hypotheses. Likewise alternative arguments represent an unsettled state of knowledge, but within limits; the alternative often being quite well within the possibility of progressive elimination or
verification. The disjunctive syllogism is a combination of knowledge and ignorance, like the alternative, but is an advance upon
the alternative in the direction of more definite knowledge, and
reaches a conclusion by means of what is known and can be asserted in the minor premise (115:114–115).

In personal and professional life, you use deductive reasoning
when solving problems. The lawyer, doctor, soldier, and detective often resort to deductive argument. In investigating a
murder case, a prosecuting attorney may search through piles
of evidence—existing knowledge—select previously unconnected facts, and combine them in such a way that they logically
imply a hitherto unsuspected conclusion. Deductive reasoning
enables him to organize premises into patterns that provide
conclusive evidence for the validity of his particular conclusion.

The modern research worker also utilizes deductive reasoning to carry out certain phases of his work. Some men
scoff at the role of reason in research and contend that an investigator is only concerned with facts he can obtain through
observation and experiment. But collecting facts is not
sufficient. Without deduction "most of our preoccupation with
facts would be fruitless, since we could not fit them into the
increasingly deductive systems which we call sciences. The latter are man's most economical instruments" (84:113). The sci-

entist frequently tries to pigeonhole a particular instance under an already established principle from which the instance can be deduced. Through the use of the tools of deduction, he hypothetically manipulates and explores possibilities that may open up new areas of inquiry.

In daily discourse many assertions are deductive in nature and may be logically correct without appearing in a syllogistic form. Outside of logic texts one rarely finds arguments set off in the middle of the page and explicitly labeled. The premises may or may not precede the conclusion, and some premises may be missing. The conclusion may come first, last, or even in the middle of the argument. One must be able to recognize arguments that appear in prose or discourse; locate the premises and conclusion; supply the missing premises, if necessary; restate the argument in a complete and explicit form; and then apply logical standards to determine whether the argument is logically correct or fallacious.

When analyzing a deductive argument, one must pay close attention to language. Words may have more than one meaning; consequently, language may play tricks that lead thinking astray. A syllogistic argument is not valid unless each term is used in the same sense throughout the argument. A shift in the meaning of any term leads to an error in reasoning. Examine the following syllogism:

Only man can talk.
No woman is a man.
All women cannot talk.

The above argument would be valid if the term "man" had the same meaning in each premise, but in the major premise the term "man" means "human being," and in the minor premise it means "human male." Since the meaning of the middle term "man" has been changed during the course of the argument, there is no mediating term which links the two premises together so that they yield a logical conclusion.

The categorical syllogism has severe limitations. The content of the conclusion of the syllogism cannot exceed the content of the premises. A categorical syllogism deduces the consequences of preexisting knowledge; it does not enable man to gain new knowledge or to make new discoveries. A second weakness of deductive reasoning lies in the possibility that one or more of the premises is not materially true. When the validity of a deductive argument is checked, questions are not raised about the content (truth or falsity) of the statements but about

the forms of the arguments. One asks: Are these premises related to the conclusion in such a way that a person cannot
accept the premises and reject the conclusion? The formal
reasoning in an argument may be sound even if the argument
is based on false premises. Consider the following as an example:

All professors of education hold doctoral degrees.
All men in this meeting are professors of education.
Hence, all men in this meeting hold doctoral degrees.

The conclusion "All men in this meeting hold doctoral degrees" is valid, for it necessarily follows from the premises
given. But the conclusion is not true in fact, for some professors
in the meeting hold only masters' degrees. In this instance
the major premise was not true in fact. The conclusion reached
by a deductive argument produces reliable knowledge only if
it is deduced from true premises and the premises are properly
related to the conclusion. Deductive logic, therefore, cannot be
relied upon exclusively in searching for the truth, because it
is not a self-sufficient means of securing dependable knowledge.

Induction

If the conclusions reached by deductive reasoning are true
only if derived from true premises, man must find some way
of determining whether his premises are true. Consequently, he
has devised inductive reasoning to complement deductive reasoning as a means of searching for knowledge. In inductive
reasoning, an investigator initiates his inquiry by observing particular instances (concrete facts). From his examination of
these facts, he establishes a general conclusion about the whole
class to which these particular instances belong. If an investigator arrives at general conclusions through induction, he may
use them as major premises for deductive inferences.

Perfect Induction/ One form of induction is complete enumeration. In this form of induction, one simply counts *all* the instances in a given class and announces his results in a general
conclusion. In other words, a conclusion about all instances of
a class is drawn from premises which refer to the observed instances of the class. For example, to determine the occupations
of the members of a club, one questions each member, tabulates
the results, and announces the conclusion: All twenty-five mem-

bers of this club are teachers. Perfect induction obtains reliable information. But how often does one have an opportunity to examine all the instances to which a conclusion refers? This type of enumeration cannot be employed as a method of investigation in the solution of most problems.

Baconian Induction/ Francis Bacon (1561–1626) severely criticized the medieval practice of deducing conclusions from self-evident or authoritative premises. He held that man should not enslave himself to other men's thoughts. Rather than accepting the premises (generalizations, theories) handed down by authorities as absolute truths, Bacon believed the investigator himself should study nature closely and establish general conclusions on the basis of direct observation.

The system Bacon recommended for arriving at generalizations was laborious. He advised the investigator to tabulate all the facts concerning nature and to study these facts for their "forms," that is, for the underlying essence of the phenomena. To accomplish this task, the investigator was to compile three tables: (1) positive instances—instances where certain phenomena appeared, (2) negative instances—instances where certain phenomena did not appear, and (3) instances where certain phenomena appeared in varying degrees and where the form varied accordingly. The purpose of the tables was to determine what properties were invariably connected with certain forms. Bacon cautioned against formulating any solution to a problem until all the facts had been gathered. His demand that the investigator first search for the facts was justified, but the exhaustive collection of facts he required was beyond the realm of human capacity.

Imperfect Induction/ Whereas perfect induction establishes a conclusion by an exhaustive enumeration of all instances that are subsumable under it, imperfect induction arrives at a generalization by observing only *some* instances that make up the class. The research worker utilizes imperfect induction more often than perfect induction, for in most investigations he cannot examine all of the instances to which a conclusion refers. From observing some instances, however, he can draw a general conclusion regarding all similar instances, some of which he has not observed.

When examining all the instances of a class under consideration is not practical, the investigator does the next best thing: he arrives at a generalization by observing an adequate and representative sample from the entire class. To check on the purity of the water in a swimming pool, for instance, a health officer may take a single sample of water, test it, and draw a conclusion about the purity of the water in the entire swimming pool. Perhaps on the same day his friend, a restaurant owner, purchases 500 steaks. To ascertain whether they are of choice quality without examining each steak, he selects at random a few steaks and finds that they are choice grade. From his selective observations he draws the conclusion that all the steaks are probably of choice quality.

Drawing an inference about a whole class of things after sampling a few of its members does not necessarily yield absolutely certain knowledge. The size and representativeness of the instances observed determine whether one arrives at a sound conclusion. If the material observed is homogeneous, one or a few samples may be adequate for arriving at a reliable generalization. If the material is not homogeneous, the same number of samples probably will yield a less reliable generalization. The conclusion drawn from one sample of water, for example, may be more satisfactory than one drawn from several samples of steak. Previous knowledge of the composition of water gives the health officer greater assurance that all the water in the pool is like the small sample, than his friend can expect from a larger number of instances taken from cattle of different breeds and environments.

Both deductive and inductive arguments have advantages and disadvantages. A deductive argument does not guarantee that the conclusion is true, but if the two premises are true, the deductive argument arrives at a conclusion that is necessarily true. The conclusion of the deductive argument, however, does not probe beyond that which is already known, already present, at least implicitly, in the premises. In an imperfect inductive argument, the conclusion does contain information that is not present, even implicitly, in one of the premises (the observed instances). This type of argument is absolutely necessary if man is to extend his knowledge. Through imperfect induction, however, an investigator merely arrives at conclusions of varying degrees of probability. If all the premises (observed instances) are true, the conclusion is probably true but not necessarily true. The possibility always exists that some unexamined instance of the class does not agree with the conclusion. To summarize, the inductive argument expands the content of the premises at the expense of achieving absolutely certain knowledge; the deductive argument arrives at absolutely certain knowledge (if the premises are true) by sacrificing any expansion of the content (109:15).

Modern Method of Acquiring Knowledge

About the seventeenth century, man developed a new method of acquiring knowledge and as a result gave birth to the modern scientific movement. Francis Bacon planted the seeds of the scientific method when he attacked the deductive method of reaching conclusions on the basis of authoritative premises, and recommended reaching general conclusions on the basis of observed facts. As was previously noted, Bacon's method of gathering random facts produced masses of unwieldy information. To construct a more practical method of attaining reliable knowledge, such men as Newton, Galileo, and their successors eventually combined the inductive and the deductive thought processes. This synthesis of reason and observation produced the modern scientific method of research.

Steps in the Scientific Method

In the scientific method, purposeful fact gathering replaces unsystematic fact gathering, and premises are tested probabilities rather than assumed truths. When using the scientific method, man shuttles back and forth between deduction and induction; he engages in reflective thinking. In 1910, John Dewey in *How We Think* analyzed the stages of activity involved in the act of reflective thinking. The following discussion distinguishes five stages in the act of problem solving:

1/ A felt difficulty.
Man encounters some obstacle, experience, or problem that puzzles him.
    a He lacks the *means* to get to the *end* desired.
    b He has difficulty in identifying the character of an object.
    c He cannot explain an unexpected event.

2/ Location and definition of the difficulty.
Man makes observations—gathers facts—that enable him to define his difficulty more precisely.

3/ Suggested solutions of the problem—hypotheses.
From his preliminary study of the facts man makes intelligent guesses about possible solutions of the problem. The conjectural statements—generalizations he offers to explain the facts that are causing the difficulty—are called hypotheses.

4/ Deductively reasoning out the consequences of the suggested solutions.
Man deductively reasons that if each hypothesis is true, certain consequences should follow.

5/ Testing the hypotheses by action.
Man tests each hypothesis by searching for observable evidence
that will confirm whether or not the consequences that should
follow actually occur. By this process, he finds out which hypothesis
is in harmony with observable facts and thus offers the most reliable solution to his problem.

These steps in the act of reflective thinking reveal how induction and deduction serve as opposing blades of the scientific
shears that cut out segments of truth. "Induction provides the
groundwork for hypotheses, and deduction explores the logical
consequences of the hypotheses, in order to eliminate those that
are inconsistent with the facts, while induction again contributes
to the verification of the remaining hypothesis" (115:4). The
research worker continually shifts among collecting facts; making generalizations (hypotheses) to explain facts; deducing the
consequences of his hypotheses; and seeking additional facts
to test the hypotheses. By employing both induction and deduction, he is able to arrive at reliable knowledge.

The scientific method of thinking presented above gives an
insight into the procedures that are involved in conducting an
investigation. Listing these steps, however, may give an inaccurate impression of the research process. These steps do not provide a rigid pattern into which a scientist must force his thinking, for thinking simply cannot be scheduled. Investigators
rarely follow a prescribed sequence of procedures. Research is
a confused, floundering process rather than a logical, orderly
one. An investigator does not tackle one step at a time, complete that process, and then move on to the next step. He may
tackle the steps out of order, shuffle back and forth between
steps, or work on two steps more or less simultaneously. Some
steps may require little effort; other steps may absorb a disproportionate amount of time and effort. When the investigator reports his findings to the scientific community, however, he structures his presentation in a precise and logically arranged form
which closely parallels the steps of the scientific method listed
above.

Illustration of the Scientific Method

The five steps or processes in reflective thinking will be discussed in greater detail in later chapters. For the time being,
the following homely illustration may give you a better insight
into the scientific method of securing knowledge:

A man returns from his vacation and discovers that his
garden is destroyed (felt difficulty—step 1). He examines the

garden and finds a twisted fence, flattened flowers, and uprooted stakes (concrete facts that enable him to define the precise nature of the difficulty—step 2). While searching for an explanation of these facts, he considers whether the neighbors' children may have deliberately destroyed the garden (hypothesis or generalization explaining the facts—step 3). His hypothesis goes beyond existing knowledge, for he did not see the children perform the act. He also thinks of a second hypothesis which may explain the facts—a bad storm may have wrecked the garden. Consequently, he suspends judgment and searches for proof.

By deduction, the man reasons out the consequences of his first hypothesis (step 4): If the children wrecked the garden, they had to be at home during the time he was on his vacation. To test his hypothesis (step 5), he questions the neighbors and learns that the children were away at camp while he was on vacation. Thus, he must reject his first hypothesis, for it is not in harmony with the verifiable facts. He then reasons out deductively the consequences of his second hypothesis (step 4): If a severe storm destroyed the garden, it probably wrecked other nearby gardens. To test this hypothesis (step 5), he observes other gardens and finds they have also been destroyed. He checks in newspapers and finds an account of a storm which destroyed many gardens in his section of the city. A neighbor tells him he watched the hail and wind uproot the garden. The man concludes that his second hypothesis is a reasonable explanation of the facts.

Thus, by reflective thinking man moves from particular facts to general statements of explanation about these facts, and from his general statements of explanation to a search for facts that will support them. He continues to shuttle between inductive and deductive approaches to the problem until he establishes a defensible explanation of the facts. Research workers follow procedures similar to those of the garden owner, but they carry them out in a more systematic manner.

Applicability of the Scientific Method

The scientific method is a tool that investigators use to solve diverse types of problems. A worker engaged in pure research uses this method to ferret out new knowledge about the mysteries of the universe. A worker engaged in applied research uses it to develop a new product that will improve some existing condition. As J. R. Angell, former president of Yale University, pointed out, "The objects of research in pure science and the motives inspiring the work may be appreciably different from those encountered in the field of applied science. But the technique of the procedure in the two cases may be all but indistinguishable" (5:27). The scientific method provides a key to advances in both pure and applied research.

Progress Made in Acquiring Knowledge

Man has made considerable progress in developing better methods of seeking knowledge through the ages and, in so doing, has learned to approach the unknown with greater humility. Man once believed that he possessed a body of absolutely reliable knowledge that enabled him to give authoritative answers to questions. The modern research worker is less dogmatic, for he knows that the revolutionary advances made by science within the past century have overthrown some long-standing theories. His awareness of the tentative, evolutionary status of knowledge makes him more willing to challenge accepted theories when he becomes suspicious about their validity. After carrying out an investigation, he makes no claim that his conclusions are infallible; rather, he invites others to confirm, modify, or refute them. If his hypothesis is found to be incompatible with reliable evidence produced in later experiments, he knows that the scientific community will abandon or alter it. A modern researcher is cognizant of the notorious fallibility of knowledge. He exposes his ideas to critical examination, because he knows that only through testing, rechecking, and refining our concepts concerning the nature of phenomena will uncertainty be reduced and knowledge become cumulative.

The scientific method does not lead to absolute certainties, but Cohen and Nagel point out that this method of obtaining knowledge is more reliable than some methods that claim they do.

The other methods . . . are all inflexible, that is, none of them can admit that it will lead us into error. Hence, none of them can make provision for correcting its own results. What is called *scientific method* differs radically from these by encouraging and developing the utmost possible doubt, so that what is left after such doubt is always supported by the best available evidence. As new evidence or new doubts arise, it is the essence of scientific method to incorporate them—to make them an integral part of the body of knowledge so far attained. Its method, then, makes science progressive because it is never too certain about its results (32:195).

The scientific method is a powerful and practical torchlight for man to use in lighting the way to the discovery of new knowledge. Searching for knowledge in this manner is a slow process, but the tentative solutions to problems that are found may be accepted with greater confidence than definitive answers that are based on arbitrary assumptions and pontifical pronouncements which preclude any further investigation.

Despite the improvements man has made in searching for knowledge, he has not yet arrived at a perfect method for seeking answers to his questions. Authority, experience, and both inductive and deductive reasoning have certain limitations as research tools. The scientific method has proved to be an especially useful means of seeking knowledge in the natural sciences, and it has also helped educators to probe into problems. But the scientific method is not a suitable instrument for seeking answers to certain types of questions. James B. Conant declares that "only an occasional brave man will be found nowadays to claim that the so-called scientific method is applicable to the solution of almost all the problems of daily life in the modern world" (33:10). The many lively debates that appear in scholarly periodicals reveal that authorities have not reached a common agreement concerning the breadth of the applicability of the scientific method.

Some critics contend that the scientific method cannot be used except in the natural sciences. Others question whether the scientific method follows a *single* method of investigation. They believe that no rigid set of logical rules can be established for physical scientists, archaeologists, mathematicians, psychologists, sociologists, educators, and historians to follow in their respective undertakings. These critics argue that since sciences differ from one another, each science requires a different method. When questioned about the existence of a general scientific method, other scholars note the numerous common features in scientific inquiries conducted in different fields and suggest that

. . . on a highly conceptual level science may be considered a general method. When scientists study specific problems, however, this general method is modified in numerous ways, and many of these adaptations are of sufficient importance and sufficiently general in nature to be considered methods within themselves. Science, then, is a very general method, modified in various ways into many less general methods that are utilized in the study of specific problems (17:5).

Controversy exists concerning the nature and use of the scientific method, but most scholars regard this intellectual tool as one of the most promising instruments that man possesses for pushing back the frontiers of human understanding and increasing the accumulation of tested and verified knowledge. Thus, you will want to become better acquainted with this disciplined and scholarly method of investigation.

3

General Concepts Concerning the Scientific Method

The scientific method has evolved down through the years out of the various methods scientists have devised for solving problems. Particularly since the beginning of this century, scholars have critically examined the scientific method, and the steps listed in the last chapter summarize one well-known analysis that materialized. This simplified account provides a thumbnail sketch of the activities involved in scientific investigations. But to comprehend the conceptual framework upon which the scientific method is founded, one must also examine the goals that scientists hope to achieve and the assumptions they make about the universe that enable them to hope for success in their ventures.

Assumptions Underlying the Scientific Method

The scientific method rests upon certain fundamental assumptions about nature and the psychological processes. These assumptions directly influence all a researcher's activity: they form the basis for his procedures, influence his methods of executing them, and affect the interpretation of his findings. Probing the validity of these assumptions falls within the domain of the philosophy of science. The researcher merely accepts them on a common-sense basis because he cannot proceed in his quest for scientific knowledge without assuming that they are valid.

Assumption of the Uniformity of Nature

Most of the assumptions about natural phenomena can be classified under the heading "the uniformity of nature." The principle of the uniformity of nature means that "there are such things in nature as parallel cases; that what happens once, will, under sufficient degree of similarity of circumstances, happen again, and not only again, but always" (93:184). The scientist must accept the assumption that nature is so constituted that whatever is true with any one case is probably true in all cases of a similar description, that what has been found to be true in many instances in the past will probably continue to hold true in the future. In other words, nature is orderly; events in nature are not purely random or unrelated occurrences. Assuming that nature is absolutely uniform in all respects is not necessary; but science is only possible to the extent that nature is reasonably uniform.

If the assumption of the uniformity of nature is divided into individual postulates, each can be examined in greater detail. Thus, the following paragraphs discuss the postulates of (1) natural kinds, (2) constancy, and (3) determinism.

Postulate of Natural Kinds/ When man observes natural phenomena, he notices that some objects and events possess a number of striking likenesses. Consequently, he examines phenomena to determine their essential properties, functions, or structures. After finding several objects or events that have common characteristics, he places them in a group and gives them a class name, such as thermometers, administrators, visual aids, or achievement tests. The resemblances he notes may be of color, size, shape, function, structures, occurrences, or varied combinations of associations between these resemblances. Thus, an investigator may group people by the color of their hair; or he may observe structural resemblances, such as an association between blond hair and delicate skin, or functional resemblances, such as poor muscular coordination and poor mechanical skills; or he may correlate structural and functional resemblances, such as a cleft palate and difficulty in pronunciation. Resemblances between phenomena intrigue the scientist: he looks continually for factors that objects or events have in common; then he groups like things, and finally searches for and expects to find additional resemblances among these phenomena.

Pigeonholing like events and objects is one of the first steps scientists take to arrive at useful knowledge. Man has always turned to grouping similar phenomena when searching for answers to problems. In the interest of survival, early man learned to classify berries as edible or poisonous, animals as dangerous or harmless, and his neighbors as friendly or unfriendly. For generations children have appealed to classification when searching for answers in the ancient game "Animal, Vegetable, Mineral." Classification is characteristic of the early developmental stage of any science. The research worker must have some knowledge of the resemblances and regularities in nature before he can discover and formulate scientific laws.

By classifying phenomena in accordance with their resemblances, scientists organize masses of information into a coherent and unified structure that is useful to man. Three men, for example, devised classification systems to help investigators identify, understand, and evaluate new phenomena in their respective fields. In the eighteenth century, Linnaeus, the Swedish botanist, devised a grouping system based on the number and arrangement of stamens. This system, despite its weaknesses, led to the development of better schemes for classifying plant life. In the nineteenth century, Mendeleev worked out a periodic table of chemical elements which proved invaluable to men doing research in the field. The international system of fingerprinting proposed in 1823 by J. E. Purkinje enabled law-enforcement agencies to classify millions of fingerprints under the heads of arches, loops, whorls, and composites. When strange plants, chemical elements, or criminals' fingerprints are discovered, these classification systems simplify location and identification.

Educators have also attempted to classify phenomena in their field. They have classified educational objectives within the affective domain (82) and within the cognitive domain (14). The major classes in the latter taxonomy are knowledge, comprehension, application, analysis, synthesis, and evaluation. Subclassifications are clearly defined for each of these classes; analysis, for example, is subdivided into analysis of elements, analysis of relationships, and analysis of organizational principles. This classification scheme was devised to ensure greater accuracy of communication about phenomena in the field, to aid research workers in formulating hypotheses about the learning process, and to provide a guide for the development of curricula, tests, and instructional techniques.

By looking for resemblances between things and classifying the things into groups, a researcher can increase his knowledge about them. But if he attributes importance to resemblances that are of no significance, his classification scheme is of little value. If several girls flunk chemistry in a given class, the professor may observe that they all wear the same shade of lipstick, but this resemblance is not the key factor causing their failure. If an alcoholic notes that he always adds soda to his bourbon, gin, or scotch, he has recognized a resemblance among his drinks, but giving up soda will not cure his drunkenness. Classification schemes that prove most useful penetrate to the underlying key characteristics of phenomena. These characteristics are not usually the most obvious ones; they are discovered through intensive and devious examination rather than casual and superficial observation.

Postulate of Constancy/ The postulate of constancy assumes that relatively constant conditions exist in nature; that is, some phenomena do not appreciably change their basic characteristics in a given period of time. The postulate of constancy does not demand absolute conditions of fixity, persistency, or permanency, nor does the postulate deny that rates of change vary for different phenomena. Some phenomena remain substantially unchanged over the years; other phenomena exhibit relatively marked rates of change. The sun, planets, and diamonds display exceptionally enduring qualities down through the decades. The walls, stoves, and plumbing in a home economics laboratory may change slightly from year to year, but in general these things remain quite the same. But a dish of ice cream, a dozen eggs, or a fruit fly in the same environment will exhibit less permanency over an extended period of time. In other words, different types of phenomena have different rates of change.

Classroom teachers expect children to exhibit about the same characteristics from day to day. Peripheral personality traits may change considerably as youngsters react to certain kinds of experiences, but youngsters possess a central core of personality traits that does not vary appreciably even when subjected to radical environmental changes. In some respects John and Mary remain more or less the same throughout grade school; in other respects they change rapidly. Society, likewise, may enjoy relatively long eras of peace and tranquility and then may suddenly experience devastating wars, financial crises, horrendous epidemics, or technological advances that cause revolutionary changes.

The postulate of constancy is a prerequisite for scientific advancement. Absolute constancy is not required, but changes must take place slowly enough for scientists to draw valid generalizations concerning phenomena that will hold true for a given period of time. The period must be long enough for other men to confirm the findings and for society to apply the knowledge before subsequent events render it useless. If phenomena were not consistent for a given period of time, all inquiries into the innermost secrets of nature would be fleeting, fruitless, historical accounts. The knowledge gained in one study could never be applied when dealing with the same phenomena in the future. Without some permanence of phenomena, science cannot carry out its primary function, the accumulation of verified and predictable knowledge. If science denies the postulate of constancy, its predictions possess little value, for they merely rest on blind speculations and chance occurrences.

Postulate of Determinism/ The postulate of determinism denies that the occurrence of an event is the result of chance or an accidental situation, and that it is purely a spontaneous incident. Rather, the postulate affirms that natural phenomena are determined by antecedent events. If water is to boil, a definite set of conditions must exist before the event will take place. If an explosion occurs, man is certain that sufficient and necessary circumstances existed before this event happened, and whenever these conditions occur he can be certain that an explosion will follow. The postulate of determinism assumes that the occurrence of a given phenomena is invariably preceded by the occurrence of other events or conditions.

Man has been aware of orderliness in nature since earliest times. He noticed regularities in nature: day followed night and seasons came in a regular order. To understand nature, he also searched for antecedent conditions that appeared to be related to events, but often concluded that supernatural forces or whatever immediately preceded an event was the cause of it. Hence, he reasoned that the floods were caused by the thunder of angered gods and that a good day of hunting was the result of finding a rare flower at dawn. By attacking problems more systematically and searching more deeply to find functional relationships, the modern research worker has been able to discover regularities in nature that are not detected through casual observation.

Determinism is a necessary and fundamental concept that underlies all scientific enterprises. Yet, rigidly interpreted determinism, belief in eternal natural stability and absolute certainty of uniformity, is questioned as a result of modern developments in physics. Scientists no longer assume that they deal with absolute certainty, but only with levels of probability. This revised version of determinism continues to play a role in research, for the scientist requires lawfulness in the events of nature. If any phenomena fall outside the postulate of determination, they are also outside the realm of scientific investigation.

If a scientist must consider each phenomenon as a capricious rather than a determined event, he is deprived of a means of attacking problems that enables him to formulate laws capable of explaining large bodies of phenomena. No pattern or scheme for setting up and controlling an experiment can be established and no predictions about what will happen in the future can be made if the assumption that what has happened in the past will happen again is false. The best that the scientist can do in an indetermined situation is to describe the character of an isolated incident.

Assumptions Concerning the Psychological Process

Every research worker accepts the assumption that he can gain knowledge of the world through the psychological processes of perceiving, remembering, and reasoning. The scientific method cannot operate without utilizing these processes. Perceiving, remembering, and reasoning, however, are subject to error. If inaccurate processes are at work, they subsequently reflect their unreliability in the results of the investigation and invalidate it. The research worker, therefore, must acquaint himself with the nature of these psychological processes and must take the necessary steps to obtain the highest possible degree of accuracy when employing them.

Postulate of the Reliability of Perceiving/ In the laboratory the investigator routinely records the information he has experienced through his senses. Yet he knows that the human sense organs are limited in range and in fineness of discrimination. His dog can hear the high tones of a whistle that are inaudible to him. His colleagues may be able to hear a greater range of sounds than he can. His sense perceptions may differ not only from those of his friends, but also in successive observations he makes himself. Because his senses are subject to fatigue and adaptation, he may experience varied perceptions when exposed repeatedly to the same sound, taste, or odor.

Errors in visual perception are as commonplace as errors in auditory perception. Through illusions and shifts of attention, a chic dress designer, a deft magician, a war camouflage expert, a football strategist, or a clever advertiser can lead people to make false judgments and inferences. Recently, for example, twenty subjects in a psychological experiment viewed a line drawing of a man's expressionless face on a screen. After seeing the word "happy" intermittently flashed beneath the picture, they thought the face gradually became happier even though it had not changed.

Everyone experiences visual deceptions. On her annual August vacation, an elementary school teacher may encounter several perceptual puzzles. At the railroad station, she may have the illusion that her train is pulling out, when it actually is standing still but the train on the next track is beginning to move in the opposite direction. At the beach, she may notice that her vertically striped swimming suit makes her appear thinner than the one with horizontal stripes. When she looks down the road, her eyes will tell her that it converges at a point in the distance.

The scientist has no more natural immunity to faulty perception than the elementary school teacher. When working on a problem, he may make inaccurate observations because of momentary distractions, strong intellectual biases, personal prejudices, emotional sets, and inaccurate discriminations. Sometimes he may see what he expects to see whether it is there or not, or he may fail to perceive relevant factors. History is studded with stories of scientists who failed to track the trail of truth because they were guilty of making perceptual blunders. Despite the untrustworthiness of the perceptual processes, the scientist assumes that one can obtain reliable knowledge through his sense organs. But he familiarizes himself with the common errors made in observation and takes the necessary precautions to prevent them from creeping into his work.

Postulate of the Reliability of Remembering/ Remembering, like the activity of perceiving, is subject to error. Everyday experiences indicate the frailties of man's mental processes. A teacher may be unable to recall where he parked his car, or the name of a former student. An individual often recalls only those things he wants to recall. A boy may remember that his mother promised to take him to the circus, but forget that she asked him to mow the lawn. A scientist may remember things that support his beliefs rather than those that do not.

Despite the weaknesses of the human memory, the research worker accepts the assumption that one can obtain fundamentally reliable knowledge from this source. He must accept this assumption, for progress would terminate if man questioned the accuracy of every single fact. But since forgetting information or recalling it inaccurately is easy, a scientist develops systematic methods of recording information; periodically reviews these data; and sometimes takes photographs, movies, recordings, or X rays of conditions or events for future reference.

Adopting such practices enables him to improve the range, accuracy, and completeness of his memory.

Postulate of the Reliability of Reasoning/ Reasoning, like perceiving and remembering, is subject to errors. Reasoning, even by exceptionally intelligent individuals, is beset by many potential pitfalls. Mistakes in reasoning occur because of use of false premises, violation of the rules of logic, presence of intellectual biases, failure to grasp the exact meanings of words, and faulty judgments made regarding the suitability and use of statistical and experimental techniques.

Despite the limitations of the reasoning process, the scientist recognizes its value as an implement of research. He resorts to reasoning when selecting and defining his problem, when framing a solution, when deciding what observations to make, when devising techniques for obtaining data, and when determining whether to accept, modify, or reject his hypothesis. Without mentally manipulating ideas, the scientist cannot make much progress in any investigation. Therefore, he accepts reasoning as a generally reliable tool of research. He takes many precautions, however, to detect and to check errors in his thought processes. He examines the premises on which his reasoning is based to determine whether they are true, and he subjects his arguments to the rules of logic that govern correct reasoning. Since confused reasoning can stem from the slovenly use of language, he endeavors to assign clear, correct, consistent, and specific meanings to words, phrases, and terms. Because personal prejudices and wishes may cause him to ignore facts and to reason illogically, he deliberately searches for and gives fair consideration to evidence that does not conform to his hypothesis.

Goals of Science

The goals of science are not unlike those of man down through the ages. A craving for knowledge of the world about him caused man to construct crude explanations for phenomena centuries ago. Longing to know what the future held in store for him, he turned to wise men, fortune tellers, prophets, and astrologers for answers. His deepest desire was to acquire knowledge that would enable him to control floods, famines, diseases, and other forces impinging upon his life. With more refined methods, the modern scientist also seeks to understand the phenomena he observes. Discovering order in the universe, comprehending the laws of nature, and learning how to master the forces of nature are his objectives. The goal of the scientist is to improve his ability and success in explaining, predicting, and controlling conditions and events.

Explanation as a Goal of Science

The essential purpose of research is to go beyond mere description of phenomena and provide an explanation for them. A scientist is not completely satisfied with naming, classifying, or describing phenomena. Rather than terminating his investigation with simple observations, such as that apples fall down, balloons rise, some children stutter, or certain diseases kill, he probes more deeply to find reasons for the occurrence of these events. Going behind casually observed factors to search for some underlying pattern that explains them is his objective. After discovering a possible relationship between antecedent factors and the particular event or condition, he frames a verifiable generalization that explains how the variables involved in the situation behave. Explanation—not mere description—is the product of his effort.

Science does not want to know only *what* phenomena are, but also *how* phenomena act as they do. A man may notice, for example, that on a hot summer day a steel cable expands as do streetcar tracks and metal beams. From his observation of these particular incidents, he may propose the generalization that heat expands metal. This low-level explanation is useful information for it describes what happens to heated metals, but it does not reveal how metals expand when heated.

When scientists tried to find some underlying principle to account for the fact that heat expands metal, they framed the following explanation: all heat is caused by the motion of molecules of matter; the greater the motion of the molecules, the greater is the heat of a body. The agitation of the molecules makes them jostle one another apart; hence, they take up more space. Thus, an increase in temperature results in expansion. This generalization gave man a better understanding of the phenomena observed, for it revealed the causes of the expansion of metal.

Once man understood and confirmed this scientific principle, he was able to apply it to other facts. Thereafter, upon encountering any phenomena involving expansion, he looked for heat as a possible cause; whenever heat was present, he considered expansion as a possible effect. Thus, the principle not only helped him to understand a particular phenomenon, but also enlarged his capacity to explain a large range of natural events. Basically, science seeks to explain phenomena by locating their place in a larger body of systematic coherent relations.

Formulating generalizations—conceptual schemes—that explain phenomena is a major goal of science. A generalization which explains a limited body of phenomena is useful, but the objective of science is to develop ever more far-reaching conceptual schemes. Hypotheses, theories, and laws are generalizations of gradually increasing generality. Since the generalization that offers the most comprehensive explanation is of the greatest value, a law is of greater importance than a theory or hypothesis. A generalization that explains the movement of one planet is useful, for example, but a law that explains the movement of all planets is of considerably greater value.

Science aims at the progressive unification of its generalizations. The ultimate goal of science is to seek laws of the highest generality—laws of the utmost comprehensiveness. Newton's theory of gravitation is an example of a comprehensive explanation. Before Newton was born, Galileo formulated his law of falling bodies which explained the motion of bodies on the surface of the earth. About the same time that Galileo proposed his explanation for terrestrial motion, Kepler formulated the laws of celestial motion. When Newton came upon the scene, he devised a more comprehensive generalization that applied to all massive bodies, whether terrestrial or celestial. His new theory performed the work of the two generalizations it replaced. Thus, Newton helped science take a giant stride in its continuous campaign to construct generalizations that explain a wider and wider range of phenomena. Since his time, a procession of creative geniuses has been endlessly "lifting science from problem to problem and adequate theory to more adequate theory with greater and greater generality" (99:29). Their successively more comprehensive theoretical explanations have given mankind important keys to understanding the universe.

Prediction as a Goal of Science

An explanation that does not increase man's power over nature is useful, but it is not as valuable as one that enables him to predict events. A scientist, therefore, is not satisfied merely with formulating generalizations that explain phenomena; he also wants to make predictions concerning the way a generalization will operate in new situations. His objective is to take known data and accepted generalizations and from them to predict some future event or hitherto unobserved phenomena. By noting gaps in the periodic table that classified the known chemical elements, Mendeleev was able to predict in 1871 the existence of a new element, germanium, fifteen years before it was discovered. By studying the data, theories, and laws available in their fields, modern research workers also make rather accurate forecasts concerning the coming of an eclipse, future weather conditions, or the probable scholastic success individual members of the freshman class will attain in college.

The natural scientist has been able to make predictions in many fields, and some of them possess such a high degree of probability that they are almost absolutely certain. Making predictions has been much more difficult for social scientists, and the predictions they have proposed are of an approximate character or are confined to relatively simple problems. Because of the difficulty of the feat, making an accurate prediction is a satisfying and spectacular achievement.

Control as a Goal of Science

Scientists strive to attain such a thorough understanding of the laws of nature that they are able not only to predict but also to control an increasing range of events. "Control" refers to the process of manipulating certain of the essential conditions that determine an event so as to make the event happen or prevent it from occurring. A doctor, for example, knows that if the pancreas fails to secrete insulin the body is unable to utilize properly the carbohydrates in the body. The doctor can predict what will happen to a patient when this condition—diabetes—exists, and he can control diabetes by giving the patient injections of insulin. When a doctor predicts and controls a diabetic condition he is actually demonstrating his understanding of the nature of the disease.

Scientists do not restrict the term "control" to conditions and events of a practical nature, such as the diabetic condition of the patient in the above example. The pure scientist, particularly, uses the term in an abstract and theoretical sense. He must show logically how a particular outcome can be obtained by controlling conceptual situations according to the implications of his theory. Einstein, for example, in the development of the theory of relativity, utilized the concept of control in the abstract and theoretical sense rather than in a sense of controlling a practical situation.

Controlling natural forces is the deepest desire of the scientist. Assuming that constancy and consistency exist in nature to a degree that will enable him to predict that what has happened once will probably happen again, he digs deeply into the nature of phenomena to discover the specific factors and relationships that cause a particular condition or event. After acquiring a thorough and intimate knowledge of his subject matter, he gains an insight into the particular factors that he must manipulate to produce a desired event or to prevent an undesired condition. Such knowledge has enabled man to harness rampaging rivers and to convert their power into a rich resource for mankind. Diseases, such as tuberculosis, diphtheria, malaria, and poliomyelitis, which once took their terrible toll upon society, have come under effective control in many parts of the world as a result of the research work done in scientific laboratories.

Psychologists and educators have long been investigating the skills and aptitudes that lead to success in particular vocations. They hope that sufficient understanding of the conditions necessary to become a superior dentist, teacher, doctor, or electrician will enable them to construct aptitude tests that will predict the caliber of work an individual will do in a given field. If such knowledge is obtained and predictions are made with a sufficiently high degree of accuracy, these vocational guidance instruments will prevent square pegs from trying to force themselves into round holes. If the selection of students trained in each field is controlled through an aptitude testing program, the nation will be assured of a more effective utilization of the human potentialities in our society.

The goal of science is to control nature, but this objective is difficult to achieve. Man can predict but cannot control many natural events. Qualified individuals are able to predict, with varying degrees of success, the weather, the coming of a comet, or the course of cancer, but they are unable to control the conditions causing these phenomena. Scientists can neither predict nor control some events. They cannot predict, for example, when and where earthquakes will take place, nor can they control them. In general, scientists have made greater progress in learning to control natural than social phenomena. One of the desperate demands of society today is to discover means of controlling phenomena such as destructive wars, juvenile delinquency, human oppression, and group intertensions that weaken our social structure.

Differences between the Social Sciences and the Natural Sciences

As we have noted, the natural sciences have made considerable progress in achieving some of the aims of science. The social sciences, such as history, economics, and education, have lagged far behind. A few leaders believe that the social sciences never can become "scientific." Some men contend that the social sciences will gradually make some progress but will not reach the high level of the natural sciences. Other authorities admit that the social sciences are on an immature level, but they claim that research in these areas eventually will become as "scientific" as in the natural sciences. A number of obstacles, however, will prevent the ready realization of this objective. In the endeavor to obtain a better understanding of the fundamental factors underlying human behavior so that they can explain, predict, and control social phenomena, the social scientists encounter many difficulties. The following paragraphs discuss some of their problems.

Complexity of Subject Matter

Social science phenomena are more complex than natural science phenomena. The natural scientist deals with phenomena on one level—the physical. Social facts have physical elements, but something other than the laws of physics or biology is usually needed to explain social phenomena. If a teacher spanks a child, the laws of chemistry, physics, and physiology partially explain the event, but they fail to account for some significant aspects of the act: Why did the teacher punish the child? How did the child feel about the punishment? What was the reaction of the parents or the school board to this act?

The natural scientist is concerned with phenomena on the gross physical level. His studies involve a comparatively small number of variables (the set of conditions required for an event) that can be measured quite precisely. Because the social scientist is concerned with man as an individual and as a member of a group, he must disentangle much more complex systems of interaction. Social problems may involve such a large number of variables that they overwhelm the investigator with possibilities to consider.

When a natural scientist investigates a chemical explosion, a *relatively few physical factors* will account for the event. When a social scientist investigates a social explosion—a riot or a crime—*innumerable factors,* some of them not physical, may be involved: a switchblade knife, the force and direction of the blow, blood vessels severed, the intoxicated condition of the murderer, the strength of the adversary, biological heredity, gang social pressures, the lack of police protection, the hot and humid evening, rejection by parents, poverty, and strained race relations.

A number of physical explanations may be given for a crime or any other social phenomenon. Moreover, social phenomena may be observed not only on the physical level, but also from the sociological, psychological, or biological point of view, or from any combination of these. They can be explained in patterns of—just to mention a few—growth, time, type, place, activities, motivation, or trends. This state of affairs creates many difficulties for the social scientist. He is always plagued with the problem of what points of view and what variables he must select to explain phenomena satisfactorily.

Observability of Subject Matter

Direct observation of phenomena is more difficult in some respects for the social scientist than for the physical scientist. A social scientist cannot see, hear, touch, smell, or taste phenomena that existed in the past. An educator studying colonial schools cannot personally view the children, teachers, and instructional procedures of that early era in American history. A chemist or physicist can set up the same desired conditions again and again and directly observe what takes place, but a psychologist cannot put ingredients into a test tube and conjure up the exact events of an adult's childhood. The nature of past social phenomena precludes direct and repeated observation.

The social scientist can observe some present social phenomena directly but he cannot bring others into the open for scrutiny. In a child study laboratory, an investigator may observe when John Jurk slaps a companion, how many words he reads in a minute, and what range of sounds he can hear. But some social factors, such as Johnny's preferences, motives, and dreams, are matters of inner consciousness and are not accessible to direct public examination. The investigator must either (1) interpret that "inner state" himself, which he can do only in light of his own life experience, a process that leaves room for error, or (2) accept his subject's description of his inner state, which may be inaccurate.

Social facts are more variable than physical facts. For most purposes in chemistry, an observation of any cubic centimeter of sulfuric acid will be as good as another. But observations of 30 seventh-grade pupils in one city will not necessarily coincide with the observations of a like number and age of pupils in another city. The height, weight, size of vocabulary, play participation, and arithmetic achievement of one 10-year-old may vary widely from those of his age-mates. In some situations a social scientist may treat all individuals alike, such as in the

tabulation of births. But because of the wide range of differences in humans, attributing to a whole class what is true of
selected samples is dangerous.

Non-repeatability of Subject Matter

Social phenomena are less repeatable than natural phenomena. Many phenomena of the natural sciences are highly uniform and recurrent; they lend themselves to abstraction and
the precise, quantitative formulation of generalizations and universal laws. Social problems usually deal with specific historical
happenings; they are concerned with singularities, with events
that occur but never reoccur in exactly the same way. Some
generalizations may be made about social life and human behavior. Generalizations may be formulated, for example, about
certain features that wars, raids, and revolutions or adults, adolescents, and infants have in common. Yet a social phenomenon
has its unique and non-repeatable character that needs to be
comprehended in its entirety if it is to be understood. Thus,
abstracting factors that are common to several social events so
as to formulate a generalization cannot be carried too far without falsifying the material. Because social phenomena are less
uniform and recurrent than natural phenomena, establishing
and verifying social laws are more difficult.

Relationship of Scientists
to Their Subject Matter

Physical phenomena such as chemical elements are impersonal. The natural scientist does not have to consider the purposes or motives of planets or oceans. But social science phenomena are concerned with man, who is a purposeful creature.
Man seeks certain desirable ends and possesses the capacity
to make choices, which enables him to modify his conduct.
Since social science subject matter is strongly influenced by
human will and human decision, social phenomena are constantly changing as a result of action taken by human beings.

The natural scientist inquires into nature's processes and formulates general laws governing these processes. He does not
expect to alter nature or to approve or disapprove of its processes. He merely hopes his knowledge of physical phenomena
will enable him to make better use of nature's processes. When
the natural scientist constructs a hypothesis to explain a physical phenomenon, he knows that his generalizations will not
cause the phenomenon to modify its character. If an astronomer
formulates a generalization to explain the orbits of planets, he

does not expect the planets to react to his theory in any way. The celestial bodies will remain unchanged by his pronouncements. They will not call a celestial congress to campaign for the adoption of new patterns of movement.

Because the social sciences are integrally interwoven with the social fabric, they present a different situation. Generalizations made to explain social phenomena may affect social events and conditions. If men accept an explanation of social phenomena, they may decide to readjust social patterns in view of this knowledge and thereby create conditions which make the generalization invalid. Consequently, accurate prediction is more difficult in economics and education than in astronomy or physics. If a social scientist states that 600 people will die in automobile crashes over the Memorial Day holiday, his prediction may not come true. The public may become alarmed by his pronouncement and conduct nationwide safety campaigns that reduce the anticipated highway slaughter. The findings in natural science lose their strength only when they are replaced by better insight into the phenomena. But findings in the social sciences may lose their value if the knowledge they provide causes humans to change the social conditions.

The social scientist is not an impartial observer who stands outside society to watch its processes. He is an integral part of the subject matter he observes. Man may impartially observe physical phenomena such as the structure of protoplasm, but his own interests, values, preferences, and purposes influence his judgment when he observes social phenomena. Man is much less capable of remaining objective about human reactions in school segregation incidents than about chemical reactions in test tubes, about social stress in slum areas than about physical stress in physics, about the Communistic system in society than about the solar system in nature. Emotional attachments to particular systems of values tend to make the social scientist approve or disapprove of particular social processes. Eliminating personal biases when observing social science phenomena is difficult.

The natural scientist is concerned with problems of fact; he confines his investigations to the conditions that exist in nature. The social scientist is also interested in problems of fact. To ascertain what conditions exist in society, he studies the characteristics and causes of poverty, juvenile delinquency, reading failure, or a similar problem. But the social scientist is interested not only in society as it is, but also in developing theories to designate what ought to be—what is socially desirable. Some social scientists contend they are not concerned with social ends, but they may unconsciously accept the prevailing order as the ideal. Some researchers may ignore social ends but the findings of their studies may cause others to seek the development of an ideal social order. Because social science subject matter is intimately related to man, who is a purposeful, value-seeking creature, it presents types of problems that the natural sciences do not present.

Social scientists must overcome many obstacles if they hope to make significant advances in explaining, predicting, and controlling human conduct. Progress can be made only by persistent and patient probing. Because of the phenomenal advances the natural scientists have made in unleashing the secrets of the physical world in the past century, social scientists must attack human problems with renewed energy. The development of atomic energy, high-speed transportation, and automation processes has produced a multiplicity of complex social problems that must be solved if society is to survive. In our modern world a most urgent necessity for psychological, educational, sociological, and economic research exists. A concentrated effort must be made to train scholars who can bring social progress abreast of the progress of the physical sciences.

4

Nature of Observation

Observation is fundamental in research, for it produces one of the basic elements of science—facts. Observing is an activity the research worker engages in throughout the several stages of his investigation. By utilizing his senses of hearing, sight, smell, feel, and taste, he gathers facts that help him locate a problem. Through alert and skillful observation he discovers clues that enable him to construct a theoretical solution for his problem. When conducting an experiment to determine whether there is evidence that will support his solution, he again makes careful and accurate observations. From the inception of an inquiry to the final confirmation or rejection of his proposed problem solution, a research worker relies on observation to keep him on the trail to truth.

Because observation, facts, and theories are closely related factors that play a significant role in scientific investigations, understanding their nature, function, and relationship is important. The layman is familiar with these terms, but his concept of their meaning is usually quite different from the definition a scientist would give. This chapter, therefore, will explore the following questions: What is the nature of scientific observation? What is the nature of a fact? What is the nature of theories? What is the relationship between theory and fact in research?

50

Conditions Necessary for Observation

Everyone uses his sensory capacities to become aware of phenomena in his environment. The act of "recognizing and noting some fact or occurrence" can be of a very simple nature or it can involve the most complex modern research techniques. The simplest kind of observation is an uncritical report by a casual observer of something he has experienced through the use of his senses. If you ask a friend whether it is snowing outside, he replies in the affirmative. How does he reach this conclusion? His answer is simple: "I know it is snowing because I have just *seen* snowflakes land on the window sill." Scientific problems may be solved by making direct and simple observations, but quite commonly, complex and indirect types of observation are required. Scientific observation involves the deliberate selection of some significant aspect of the phenomena in a certain situation and at a definite time, a close scrutiny of them which may require the use of precision procedures and instruments, and the presentation of the results in a form that is suitable for public verification. Thus, although observations can be made by anyone, accurate and fruitful ones are usually the product of considerable practice and training.

Since observation is essential in scientific inquiry, a neophyte should learn how to establish the conditions within himself and his working environment that will enable him to obtain reliable facts with maximum efficiency. Involved in observation are four psychological factors to which he must give due consideration: attention, sensation, perception, and conception.

Attention

Attention is a necessary condition for successful observation. This condition is characterized by a mental set or a state of alertness which an individual assumes so as to sense or perceive selected events, conditions, or things. Being bombarded constantly by a multiplicity of stimuli, the nervous network of the human organism cannot simultaneously channel all of them to the cortex for interpretation. Hence, an observer sifts out the specific ones from which he wants to receive messages. This process of selection is "attention." Adequate attention is imperative if one is to acquire clear, concise, and detailed information about phenomena. If thoughts about the weekend dance or the attractive girl across the aisle are flashing through your mind at the moment, you are probably receiving blurred messages from this printed page. Indeed, you may "read" the whole page without acquiring any knowledge of its contents, for your attention is elsewhere: you are not ready to receive the stimuli of the printed word.

The observational powers of man are limited. He may fail to perceive phenomena accurately when his attention is not intentionally concentrated upon them. Observing several things at once is beyond his capacity; he can give specific attention only to one thing at a time. If a researcher attempts to observe too many things, he often overlooks significant events that occur because at the moment his attention is elsewhere. A competent investigator, consequently, directs his attention toward a portion of phenomena that is pertinent to his purpose, yet small enough to be encompassed.

Learning to "pay attention" is an important part of observational training. One must acquire the habit of placing himself in a state of readiness to perceive the specific segment of phenomena that relates to his problem and to ignore other factors. By cultivating a deep interest in a particular point of view, one may concentrate more intensively upon the details that are relevant to a problem. Interest helps one watch things with an active, inquiring mind; interest rivets one's attention on the stimuli that can supply the desired data. By exercising a high degree of self-control, one can keep strong and interesting extraneous stimuli from capturing his attention and can curb any natural restlessness that might permit his attention to wander. Sustained and selective attention becomes gradually so habitual a method of working, that an observer is less easily distracted by those factors that are not absolutely essential to his investigation.

Although attention is necessary in observation, it can lead to certain errors that the scientist must guard against. By becoming too obsessed with his hypothesis—too set on looking for facts that support his proposed solution to a problem—one may observe only what he wants to find and ignore facts that do not agree with his theory. To eliminate such biases, an experienced investigator is extremely critical of his observation. When concentrating his attention on specific phenomena, he not only looks for facts that support his theory, but he is also alert to detect unsuspected facts that tend to disprove it. When making observations, he strives to notice all the significant aspects of the situation—the unanticipated as well as the anticipated events and conditions.

The scientist controls not only personal factors that interfere with attention, but also characteristics of subject matter that prohibit effective observation. Man cannot successfully fix his attention upon objects or events that are exceptionally unstable or elusive. Thus, phenomena too big, too small, too fleeting, or too chaotic to be perceived with the senses and special instruments are not suitable subjects for an investigation. A researcher must study phenomena that are sufficiently stable, constant, and manageable that others can view them at the same time or check them at a later date.

Sensation

Man becomes aware of the world about him through his senses or their extension by appropriate "sensing" apparatus. When changes occur in a man's internal or external environment, they stimulate his sense organs which in turn excite his sensory nerves. When these sensory nerve impulses reach his brain, he experiences the event: a smell, a shape, or a sound. A man can experience thousands of different visual and auditory qualities; he can feel pressure, pain, warmth, and cold; he can taste sweet, sour, salty, and bitter qualities; and he can distinguish different odors.

Yet, the sense organs have definite limitations. Man's senses are not reliable tools for making exact measurements of distance, speed, size, or intensity and they are poor instruments for making comparisons. Because sense organs have a limited scope of sensitivity, they do not enable one to hear many tones, to see all the colors of the spectrum, or to feel the difference between distances that fall within a certain magnitude. Any defect of the senses, of course, reduces the possibility of observing phenomena accurately. Factors that can distort observations include congenital imperfections, such as color blindness and tone deafness; temporary impairments due to fatigue, drugs, or emotional status; and gradual deterioration because of age or illness. Steps can be taken to avoid or compensate for some of these conditions; the researcher can also employ specially devised instruments, such as the microscope, amplifying tube, and polygraph, to extend the range and clarity of his observations.

In addition to checking whether his senses are operating efficiently, a scientist also makes certain that he is getting clear, undistorted signals from his phenomena. Strong competing stimuli or a confusion of extraneous ones may make it difficult for his senses to isolate the significant stimuli. A foreign or distracting medium that comes between him and his subject matter can create many problems. A dirty test tube, for example, or undetected biases of subjects cooperating in an experiment can cause him to make startling but faulty observations. When investigating human phenomena—for example, in a classroom or a metropolitan slum—an investigator often finds that his mere presence on the scene makes subjects modify their behavior. Consequently, when studying the home life of Puerto Rican pupils, a social worker may assume some normal neighborhood role that will permit him to mingle with the people without arousing their suspicions and causing them to change their customary patterns of behavior. An educator studying cheating practices of pupils may take the precaution of observing them from a concealed position. By locating himself in the most favorable vantage point for observation, removing competing sensory stimuli, if possible and desirable, and checking to make certain he has an unobstructed, normal view of his subject matter, a scientist is able to make more accurate observations.

Perception

Observation is more than experiencing sensations. Observation is sensation plus perception. Sensation is the immediate result of stimulating the sense organs: a sound, a smell, or a visual experience. This information is not useful unless it is interpreted. One can hear a sound, but it remains a mere noise until he learns to identify it with the ringing of the telephone, rumbling of a streetcar, or mewing of the cat. Perception is the art of linking what is sensed with some past experience to give the sensation meaning. When the Hontoon family is at the park, tiny baby Tim notices a moving object; his four-year-old brother Dale recognizes that it is a bird, for he has seen them in his storybooks; his mother explains that a recent magazine called these small yellow birds warblers; and his father, an ornithologist, identifies the bird as a Nashville warbler. Aside from the baby, each member of the family linked up what he had seen with his past experience; each engaged in perception.

Meanings are in men's minds rather than in the objects themselves. Hence, when looking at the same object, everyone does not "see" the same thing. One person, moreover, may see the same object in different ways at different times. One may look at a line drawing of a cube, for example, and see that it is an open box at one moment, a solid cube of ice at another time, and a square wire frame at a later date. The drawing does not change, but the observer's organization of what he sees does.

Perceptions may be relatively simple or highly complex. They may involve a single sense organ, such as when one identifies the color of an object. On the other hand, several senses, a wide background of experience, and prolonged training may be required to give a detailed interpretation of the sensations contributing to a given experience. The perceptions of a novice in any field—science, education, music—are apt to be vague, meager, and uncritical. Those of an expert are more definite, detailed, and discriminate.

Obstacles to Accurate Observation/ Man interprets his sensations in terms of his past experiences. All too frequently he quickly associates a sensory signal with some previously acquired knowledge and jumps to the conclusion that he has seen or heard something he really has not. When a small, dark object travels across a picnic table, he may immediately associate this occurrence with his storehouse of picnic information and conclude that the object is an ant, when it actually is a crumb that has rolled off the chocolate cake. Anticipation of an event can also cause him to make a faulty inference. Newspaper stories concerning flying saucers usually bring a rash of reports from readers who have seen a moving object and have concluded that it is a spaceship. The possibility of perceptual error is always present when the observer makes inferences on the basis of scanty sensory cues.

Strong personal interests tend to make the research worker see only those things he wants to see. After having reviewed many scientific studies made of animal learning, Bertrand Russell noted that

. . . all the animals have behaved so as to confirm the philosophy in which the observer believed before his observations began. Nay, more, they have all displayed the national characteristics of the observer. Animals studied by Americans rush about frantically, with an incredible display of hustle and pep, and at last achieve the desired result by chance. Animals observed by Germans sit still and think, and at last evolve the solution out of their inner consciousness (106:32–33).

Because man can choose to interpret or ignore stimuli impinging upon him, his private passions and preconceptions can often serve as stumbling blocks to impartial observation.

Perceptions are subject to distortions because of the observer's emotions, motivations, prejudices, mental sets, sense of values, physical condition, and errors of inference. Psychology professors often demonstrate the unreliability of human observation by staging a well-rehearsed mock shooting and asking students to write a description of what they have seen. The results are amazing! Not uncommonly students fail to agree on the

size, age, dress, and number of participants in the incident, as
well as the order of events and the type and number of weapons
used. They not only miss seeing some important things, but
also report details that are pure fabrications. When lawyers collect evidence for trials involving an accident, they encounter
similar situations.

A person tends to see what he knows. If a teacher, doctor,
and architect inspect a school building, each will see the things
that are of special interest to him and other matters will escape
his attention. The teacher will notice the instructional situations,
the doctor the health conditions, and the architect the structure
and design of the building. If an individual knows little about
a particular subject, he usually does not "see too much" when
he observes it. If a Texan who knows nothing about ice hockey
attends a game, he merely sees a number of padded players
lining up in peculiar formations, skating swiftly with sticks in
hand, pursuing a little black disk, bumping into one another,
flaring into fist fights, and entering and leaving the field of play
at frequent intervals. But the game does not make much sense
to him because he does not know enough about the rules, the
players' responsibilities, and the play formations to understand
what is going on. He does not perceive as many details as the
veteran hockey fan or a rival coach scouting the game, because
he does not possess the knowledge needed to interpret the
events transpiring before him.

Efforts to Objectify Observations/ To increase the range, richness, and accuracy of his observations and to guard against errors in perception, a scientist takes a number of precautions.
First, he acquires a broad background of knowledge in the field
wherein his problem lies. This knowledge helps him to determine what facts to look for and where and when he may find
them. If relevant data from these funds of knowledge are linked
with his sense experiences, they may help him interpret his observations. Becoming thoroughly familiar with what to expect
in a given situation places him in a better position to identify
significant events that occur, as well as any conditions that are
unusual or that do not conform to his beliefs or the accepted
theories. Like the veteran hockey fan, he is able to perceive
the relevancy of what takes place in a given situation because
of his extensive knowledge about the subject.

To sharpen his perceptive powers, a scientist acquires abundant practice in the art of examining phenomena with an alert
and questioning mind. He studies the special observational instruments and procedures designed to gather facts and strives
to become proficient in employing them. Like the proofreader,

piano tuner, teataster, or airplane spotter, he trains himself to discriminate between similar stimuli that workers encounter in his field. Since emotional and intellectual biases can prevent accuracy of observation, he takes positive action to counteract them. During an investigation, he makes a serious study of views that differ from his own, deliberately searches for facts that will explode his pet theories, compares his observations with those made by others, and invites colleagues to check his findings. Whenever possible, he repeats experiments to see whether the results will be the same on each occasion. Through the exercise of rigorous self-discipline, the establishment of systematic work methods, and the identification and elimination of recurring mistakes, a researcher improves his receptivity to sensory stimuli and learns to detect more and more details about phenomena.

Because human frailties and biases may introduce errors into data gathering, a scientist often employs movie cameras, recordings, oscillographs, or similar instruments to make a permanent record of the occurrences in an investigation. These devices provide firsthand evidence that he and others can study immediately and can recheck as often as necessary in the future. Even the most delicate and expensive instruments, however, cannot record certain factors and do not have the varied observational powers of human beings. Instruments are of little value, of course, unless the investigator knows how to use them skillfully, understands their limitations, and checks their operational performance for precision and accuracy.

To avoid errors in perception that arise because of faulty recall, a researcher records his data as soon after making an observation as possible in an exact system of notation. Delaying the compilation of his notes may cause him to forget relevant data, or to have blurred, distorted, or incorrect impressions of what happened. When recording data, he includes every significant detail about the phenomena, equipment, procedures, and difficulties encountered. To avoid overlooking important facts, he may construct a list of items to be noted during each observation. A novice observer may err in keeping too few and too scanty notes. Experience teaches the trained scientist to record comprehensive, complete notes, and to make detailed drawings of all pertinent incidents that transpire during an investigation, for these items prove to be invaluable possessions when the time comes to analyze and interpret the data or to explain and defend his findings.

Scientific descriptions are written in precise, concrete terms. One employs words and symbols that mean the same thing to other investigators as they mean to the writer. Because vague generalizations and haphazard guesses are the products of sloppy thinking and provide useless information for problem solving, they are culled from reports. Rather than recording general impressions, one writes an exact account of each smell, sight, and sound. Rather than stating that children in a class are disobedient, one lists the specific disobedient acts they perform, the number of children participating, and the frequency or duration of the acts.

A research worker soon learns that words that seem to be specific may carry more than one meaning. As one man suggests, "age" of the subject may refer to present age, age at last birthday, or age at next birthday. Consequently, in scientific work one defines his terms and checks to make certain that each sentence describes exactly what he observes, and that no other interpretation can be placed upon his words. These systematic, precise, and thorough methods of work may seem pedantic, but they are essential if the collected data are to be of any value in solving problems.

Whenever possible, an investigator describes his data quantitatively: in terms of height, distance, duration, speed, or number of units. Rather than describing pupils as large boys, he gives their anthropometric measurements. Rather than recording that pupils look at television programs frequently, he records the number of minutes per day they view them. Rather than describing his subjects as "a group of students," he states the exact number of pupils of each sex in the group and the range in their ages. Numerical measures are more precise than word descriptions and may make possible further analysis of the problem by statistical procedures. Whenever a scientist uses questionnaires, ratings, or lists to gather data, he tries to put them in a form that requires quantitative answers.

Conception

Perception is extremely important, yet its deficiencies become apparent when an investigator relies upon it exclusively. On some occasions one is confronted with a puzzling situation and is not able to perceive all its relevant elements. To liberate oneself from such a dilemma and to understand the character of a problem, one is compelled to act on the basis of conception—to make various guesses about what is occurring in a given situation. One circumvents the limitations of perceptual experiences through the construction of imaginary concepts—hypotheses and theories—that visualize what one cannot perceive directly. These concepts provide one with new orientations for observing his problem. After constructing a conceptual scheme, one reobserves his puzzling situation to see whether he can find facts that fit into this framework. Concepts are mental constructs that suggest what one might observe to solve his problem. To see how concepts function as part of the process of the scientific method, the reader must await a detailed discussion of it in the latter half of this chapter and in Chapter 8.

Nature of Facts

The scientist makes observations to get at facts. But what are facts? Facts mean different things to different people. When a layman speaks of wanting the facts, he may have a rather narrow concept of their nature. He may believe that their meanings are self-evident and that their nature is precise and permanent. To the scientist, facts are not something that is self-evident, but rather data he discovers through purposeful probing. A scientist does not claim that facts possess everlasting validity; he believes that they are subject to reinterpretation or revision whenever man gains a better insight into phenomena.

The scientist is not dogmatic about the certainty of facts. He emphasizes their usefulness, but is constantly critical of them. He does not expect all facts to be equally stable, precise, and accessible. His prolonged pursuit of facts has taught him that some can be expressed quantitatively, others can be expressed only in words, and some do not readily lend themselves to either mathematical or language descriptions. To the scientist, a fact is any experience, change, occurrence, or event that is sufficiently stable and supported by enough evidence to be counted on in an investigation.

Accessibility of Facts

Not all facts are equally accessible to the observer. Personal or private facts, such as dreams, memories, fears, preferences, feelings, and revelations, lie hidden deep within the individual. They may be very real to him and pass his personal tests of reliability, but they are not accessible for examination by others. Pink elephants are real to the alcoholic and horrible dreams are real to a child, but these specific facts cannot be verified empirically by someone else. One cannot observe these inner, personal phenomena directly to see whether he draws the same conclusions about them as other observers or the individual having the experience. If he relies on the individual's description of a personal experience, inaccurate information may be obtained. Tommy may tell the doctor that his stomach hurts when the pain is actually located in his chest or when he feels good but has an intense longing to stay home from school.

A research worker may infer that the private experience of an individual is like one he himself has had under similar circumstances, but this may not be true. In daily life people often make such errors. Joe Adams assumes that his wife gets as much pleasure out of witnessing a boxing match as he does. An English teacher expects her nephew to experience the same enjoyment from reading *David Copperfield* as she always has. Investigators studying people of a culture, social status, or era different from their own may fall into error if they conclude that their subjects experience the same reaction to given stimuli as they do. Raw fish eyes served at a puberty rite feast may be a nauseous form of nourishment to an American anthropologist but a delightful delicacy to the natives. Watching a child being flogged will not arouse the same response in a modern educator as it did in a teacher of ancient Sparta. When seeking reliable information, it is always dangerous for a scientist to equate another man's inner experiences with his own.

Because of the hidden nature of personal facts, social scientists often have difficulty in interpreting a commonplace event. If a student takes the smallest piece of cake at a tea, for example, different observers may conclude that he is trying to be polite, doesn't like chocolate cake, or thinks the hostess is a poor cook. The student may report that his doctor has placed him on a diet to conceal the fact that he has just eaten two candy bars and is not hungry. Personal, inner facts are one man's knowledge, and that man may not be willing or able to analyze his experience accurately.

Public facts—those which can be observed and tested by everyone—are relatively impersonal knowledge. They do not depend on the peculiarities of a single individual for verification. Because they are open to inspection by everyone and are agreed upon by a number of independent observers, public facts are much more reliable than inner, personal facts. If one man asserts that an object weighs ten pounds, for example, it is not necessary to take his word for it. Any normal person can test the validity of that statement by reference to evidence which is independent of the observers. If many men use their senses and special instruments to test the weight of the object and they all reach approximately the same conclusion, their findings can be accepted as being quite reliable. In time, public facts win common acceptance as the most trustworthy knowledge available to mankind.

Natural scientists deal primarily with public facts, but some of the most pressing problems demanding solution in the social sciences involve personal, inner facts or a mixture of public and personal facts. Natural scientists have devised a number of reliable instruments that enable men to weigh, measure, and time phenomena in their field. When social scientists attempt to create similar instruments, they are confounded by the concealed, elusive nature of private facts. Because of the nature of their subject matter, social scientists encounter much more difficulty than natural scientists when they observe phenomena.

Levels of Facts

Some facts are derived directly from the impact of stimuli upon the senses, others are reached by conceptual manipulations. For purposes of summarization, the following paragraphs discuss three levels of facts that range (1) from those that man becomes aware of through immediate sense experiences, (2) to those that man identifies by describing or interpreting his immediate experiences, (3) to those he identifies by engaging in a highly abstract reasoning process.

Facts of immediate experience are pure sensations without any names or labels. They represent raw experiences because no attempt is made to identify, interpret, or assign meaning to them. These facts are known by immediate apprehension alone. They are sometimes called "pure facts" or "the most factual of facts" because they have not been changed in any way by the individual's intellectual process. When facts of immediate experience undergo intellectualization, they no longer retain their pure character. It is doubtful that people other than babies can have such raw experiences, for human beings early in life begin to name or assign meaning to experiences.

The second level of facts, those describing or interpreting immediate experience, is not just raw experience. When man describes or interprets a sensation as a sound of a jet engine, he engages in perception or a low level of conceptualization. Through an intellectual process, he associates the raw sensation with his past experiences and identifies it with that class of things he calls "sounds from jet aircraft." Facts describing immediate experiences are relatively close to sensory experiences. They are not highly conceptualized. Some, however, are more conceptual than others. Facts which are primarily sensory in nature, such as sound or smell, are less conceptual than those derived from thought or reasoning experiences, such as memories or ideas.

The third level of facts is highly abstract and conceptual in nature. These facts are remote from sensory experiences. They are derived primarily from human reasoning processes and cannot be observed directly by the senses. Although they are highly conceptual in nature, they are supported by enough empirical evidence to prove they exist and, therefore, are acceptable as facts. Through an involved reasoning process, for example, man constructs the proposition: The world is "round."[1] Man cannot see that it is round with his naked eye, but he can provide sufficient evidence traceable to various forms of sensory experience to confirm this proposition. He may point out that a ship disappears over the horizon progressively—hull, cabins, and finally, smokestack. Another example of a fact derived from abstract reasoning is one that shows the relationship between two concepts. That reading ability is closely related to arithmetic ability is accepted as a fact. This relationship cannot be observed directly by an individual; it can only be experienced on the conceptual level. Since this concept can be traced to empirical referents, it receives indirect substantiation as a fact. Most people do not realize how little of what they accept as facts is given by raw experience alone. Theorizing plays a major role in obtaining facts.

Nature of Theories

The average man thinks that the philosopher is concerned with theories and the scientist deals with facts. A scientist is envisaged as a disciplined, dedicated man who searches for the "true" facts, rather than as an unconventional, intellectual adventurer who creates imaginative structures. Many men dismiss theories as mere speculations or daydreams, but they respect facts. They believe that facts are definite, real, and concrete, and that their meaning is self-evident.

Many educators also scoff at theories and demand that researchers provide them with "practical facts" that will help them in the classroom. Yet, every act a teacher performs is based to some extent on a theory. An elementary teacher may select textbook A rather than B because the larger print is more suitable for younger students, or he may plan a field trip to a farm because varied sensory experiences aid the learning process. Without realizing it, perhaps, he has made these choices on the basis of theories. Indeed, an educator would flounder fu-

1/ Studies of the orbital flight of Vanguard I show the earth to be slightly pear-shaped rather than a bulging sphere.

tilely if no theories were available to guide him in making choices.

Construction of Theories

What are theories? They are statements that explain a particular segment of phenomena. These statements, which may be called "guesses," "hunches," "principles," "empirical generalizations," "models," "hypotheses," "theories," or "laws," differ in explicitness, scope, depth, and fertility of explanation. They range along a continuum from nonscientific to scientific, from the simple to the complex. Some theories, for example, deal with practical classroom problems, such as methods of teaching addition. More sophisticated theories may seek to explain learning, retention, or transfer, which apply to all school subjects and to all ages of humans. In a later chapter, the differences among various levels of theoretical explanation will be discussed in detail.

How and why are theories formulated? A researcher soon discovers that gathering masses of isolated facts is not an efficient way of solving problems. Consequently, he engages not only in induction (observing and accumulating facts) but also in deduction (theorizing about facts). Because facts do not speak for themselves, he tries to see relationships between them, to structure imaginative concepts that supply missing links, and to keep manipulating ideas until he stumbles upon a key concept that enables him to order many facts into a meaningful pattern. Through arduous reasoning, he builds a theoretical structure that explains facts and the causal interrelationships among them. Thus, theories and facts are reciprocally interdependent. Theories are not mere speculations, for they are built upon facts; isolated facts are useless unless someone structures a theory that will make them fall into a meaningful pattern. Theories provide logical explanations for facts.

Little scientific progress would be made if researchers rejected reasoning and accepted only those facts that the senses could immediately apprehend. Conceptual fertility—the capacity to structure bold and radical guesses about how facts are ordered—is the greatest gift a scientist can possess. Although science stresses objectivity, it is to a large degree concerned with the subjective act of theorizing. Science is "objective in that it is verifiable, within assignable limits of probability, but it is subjective in that the facts observed are immediately interpreted in terms of some pattern which enables man to make sense out of them" (110:33). Theorizing is not an ornamental instrument that men toy with in their "ivory towers"; it is a practical tool that enables them to explore the underlying mechanisms of their phenomena. Theorizing provides the road maps for research; without it new knowledge cannot be discovered.

Types of Theories

The things, events, or relationships that a researcher chooses to observe are dictated by some theory. He cannot proceed without a theory, but he may proceed without clearly identifying his theory. His theory may be a vague hunch, an informed guess, a set of inconsistent assumptions, or a logically structured explanation. When structuring theories, not all scientists give equal emphasis to the fact-gathering inductive procedures and the theory-formulating deductive procedures, nor do they move from one procedure to the other in the same order (91:4–46).

Hypothetical-Deductive Theory/ Some researchers emphasize the explicit and logical formulation of explanatory propositions even when the observational evidence is known to be inadequate. Their motto is: Theorize first and then make empirical checks to correct the theory. The hypothetical-deductive theory consists of (1) a set of definitions of the critical terms, (2) a set of hypothetical statements concerning the presumptive relationships among the phenomena represented by the critical terms, and (3) a series of deduced consequences that are logically derived from the hypothetical statements.[2] These elements are tied together in the form of a conditional "if-then" statement which stipulates: If such and such antecedent condition exists, then such and such consequences will be observable (see Appendix G). The validity of a hypothetical-deductive theory is dependent upon the extent of the agreement between the deduced consequences, on the one hand, and the observation of phenomena to which it refers, on the other.

Functional Theory/ Some theories are evolved in a less formal manner. Many investigators believe that an undue, premature concern with ordering facts and structuring highly formalized theories may cause them to terminate their exploratory activities too soon and may blind them to other facts and ordering possibilities. To them, a theory is a provisional tool. They place less emphasis on elegant conceptualizations and logical-deductive procedures and more explicit emphasis upon observation

2/ Hypothetical statements may be referred to as "postulates" or "axioms," and deduced consequences may be called "theorems."

and data-oriented explanations. They believe that the interaction of observational and conceptual processes is necessary for scientific progress and that, therefore, the two processes should proceed simultaneously and should be given more or less equal emphasis.

Inductive Theory/ The inductive theory emphasizes after-the-fact explanation. Facts are established first, and theory emerges from a careful consideration of these facts. Factual acquisition is maximized and the hypothetical-deductive process is minimized. The theory is no more than a summarizing statement about specific, concrete observations. Some highly imaginative and productive researchers claim that this is the procedure that they follow. But they do not merely make chance observations. Their minds are not virgin receptacles and their observations are not completely unbiased. They start out with some expectations; some informal theory governs the choices they make. They cannot keep these hunches private forever; eventually, they must communicate them effectively. Critics of the radical empiricists also believe that a reluctance to utilize deductive procedures makes it more difficult to deal with the intricacies of complex phenomena.

Model/ The term "model" (paradigm) has become quite fashionable in the literature, and a bewildering array of models has been developed. Essentially, models are simplified or familiar structures which are used to gain insights into phenomena that scientists want to explain. (See Appendix H for an educational model.)

Models may be drawings or physical replicas that represent the real thing, or they may be more abstract. Mathematical equations, verbal statements, symbolic descriptions, graphic presentations, or electromechanical devices may be used to represent objects and relationships that are being modeled. Some investigators locate a structure about which much is known and use it to gain insight into a field about which little is known. A researcher who wishes to study how rumors spread, for example, may wonder whether they spread in the same way as diseases. In other words, he may utilize the laws of epidemiology, about which much is known, as a model for a theory about rumor transmission. Well-known laws in the areas of physics, chemistry, biology, etc., are employed frequently as models for constructing theories about psychology and education.

Some scholars contend that models and theories are one and the same thing, but other scholars make the following distinction (91:104–129): Both theories and models are conceptual schemes that explain the relationships of the variables under consideration. But models are analogies (this thing is like that thing), and therefore can tolerate some facts that are not in accord with the real phenomena. A theory, on the other hand, is supposed to describe the facts and relationships that exist, and any facts that are not compatible with the theory invalidate the theory. In summary, some scholars argue that models are judged by their usefulness and theories by their truthfulness; models are not theories but tools that are used as a basis for formal and rigorous theory construction.

Functions of Theories

Theories serve as tools and goals, as means and ends. As goals, they provide explanations for specific phenomena with maximal probability and exactitude. As tools, they provide a guiding framework for observation and discovery. The following paragraphs explain how theories help researchers examine and explain phenomena and thereby contribute to the advancement of knowledge.

Indentification of Relevant Facts/ Theories govern the kind of phenomena that investigators study. Theories provide frameworks within which and against which investigators observe, test, and interpret their observations. Scientists cannot collect facts about everything. They must narrow the area of their interest to limited segments of phenomena and give these segments their undivided attention. Investigators, for example, may study the game of baseball in the sociological framework of play, in the physical framework of stress and velocity, in the economic framework of supply and demand, or in many other ways. But a multiplicity of facts are associated with any one of these problem areas. Not until researchers construct theoretical solutions for their problems do they know precisely what facts to observe. After theorizing that there is a relationship between A and B, they know which specific facts to locate; those that will provide the empirical evidence necessary to confirm or disconfirm their theory. The theory determines the number and kinds of facts that are relevant to a study. Facts do not identify themselves as relevant; only a theory can tell an investigator what to observe and what to ignore.

Classification of Phenomena/ Every science develops a structural foundation to facilitate research. Scientists cannot work efficiently and effectively with masses of assorted facts; they need some scheme for ordering the data in their fields. Therefore, the first stage in any science consists in constructing theoretical frameworks for classifying facts. The older sciences have been quite successful in devising these systematic conceptual schemes. Geologists have developed systems for classifying rocks and botanists have developed systems for classifying plants. The younger behavioral sciences have also striven to locate the key characteristics of their subject matter that will enable them to construct the most useful classification systems.

Educators have devised some classification schemes for the phenomena in their field. The classification of educational objectives in the cognitive domain has been mentioned previously. An attempt to place in a single table all the functions of administration is known as "POSDCORB." The table includes planning, organizing, staffing, directing, coordinating, reporting, and budgeting. Many of the classification systems that educators have constructed have been crude. But as more and more investigators describe the complex and diverse facts relating to their subject matter, note the similarities, differences, and relationships among them, and structure frameworks to categorize them, they should gain a deeper and clearer insight into teaching, learning, and children. If educators fail to develop theoretical structures to order and describe phenomena in their field, they will be handicapped in their work and unable to advance knowledge appreciably.

Formulation of Logical Constructs/ Reliable knowledge can be acquired through direct observation and measurement, but many factors that contribute to educational phenomena are not observable directly. Consequently, investigators often create imaginative concepts to account for behavior or effects that they observe. These concepts are called "logical constructs," "hypothetical constructs," "intervening variables," or just "constructs." These constructs are not directly observable, but through logical arguments the investigator ties them to empirical referents. Knowledge, for example, is not an observed entity; it is merely inferred from using instruments which sample subject behavior. Reading readiness, cooperative attitude, and conditioned reflex cannot be observed directly; they are only observable indirectly as they manifest themselves in behavior. Concept development and the precise description of referent behavior are of utmost importance in research, for these shorthand symbols are the major elements of theories, and they guide theoretical and experimental thinking. They convey considerable compact information to scientists and make it easier for them to manipulate facts and to communicate findings.

Summarization of Facts/ Theorization is used to summarize knowledge within a given field. These summaries are stated with varying degrees of comprehensiveness and precision. They may range from relatively simple generalizations to exceedingly complex theoretical relationships. A summarization may describe a limited range of events, such as when an educator makes a generalization about the practice of granting varsity letters to high school athletes. This low level of summarizing is not usually referred to as a "theory." But the educator might construct a more complex generalization, one that describes the relationship between phenomena. After observing such phenomena as honor societies, varsity letters, and certificates of achievement, for example, he may note a relationship among them and draw the generalization that public recognition rewards are a means of motivating pupils. Summarization on a high scientific level, of course, involves integrating the major empirical generalizations into a more comprehensive theoretical framework. In the natural sciences, Einstein strove for this in the unified field theory. Social scientists are endeavoring to summarize knowledge about human behavior with the hope that they may someday construct comprehensive generalizations that will explain the great motivating force of human nature. Thus, theorizing integrates pertinent facts into compact frameworks of knowledge that give man a better understanding of phenomena. A more comprehensive theory, anchored in verified observations, denotes a more mature science.

Prediction of Facts/ A generalization about data—a theory—enables one to predict the existence of unobserved instances conforming to it. For instance, investigators have made the following generalization: When children learn a baseball-throwing skill, much improvement occurs during the initial learning stages. On the basis of this theory, one can anticipate that a class of elementary pupils learning this skill or any similar skill will experience an achievement spurt during the early practice periods. Correspondingly, one can expect that where children have acquired proficiency in these skills, the pattern of their improvement will have conformed to this theory. Similarly, if the generalization that a high rate of truancy is associated with slum areas has been confirmed, one can look for and expect to find this pattern in a slum area where no truancy statistics have been compiled. Theory enables one to predict what should be observable where data are not available. Theory serves as a powerful beacon that directs man in his search for facts.

Revelation of Needed Research/ Since theories generalize about facts and predict facts, they also indicate areas where knowledge is deficient. Theories, particularly in the social sciences, may lack supporting evidence in one or more aspects. Such theories need further supporting evidence to provide the maturity and vitality essential for their proper functioning. Because theories suggest where evidence is lacking, they are an excellent source to turn to when in search of research problems.

Even a rather low level of theorization can point out the need for further research. An investigator, for example, may find evidence that supports the following generalization: A rather high correlation exists between the physical endowments and proficiencies of students in a suburban junior high school and the frequency, duration, and nature of their play activities. This generalization suggests where to search for additional facts and raises the following questions: Does the general relationship above hold true for elementary and high school children? Does this pattern hold true for rural groups or youths in other countries? Is there any difference in the general relationship between the sexes? Does grouping the junior high school children according to their intelligence reveal any difference in the magnitude of the correlations between the groups? Does grouping the children in accordance with their body builds (ectomorphy, mesomorphy, and endomorphy) influence the general relationship in any way? To what extent do children of low physical abilities prefer to indulge in other activities because they are barred from successful competition by their age-mates who are better endowed physically? Theorization on any level tends to open up new avenues of inquiry even as it did in this instance.

Relationship of Facts to Theories

In pushing back the frontiers of knowledge, scientists are very dependent upon the process of theorization, but they cannot construct or confirm any theory without the aid of facts. Throughout a scientific investigation, facts and theories interact constantly; one depends upon the other; they are inextricably interwoven.

Stimulation of Theorization by Facts/ The scientist does not theorize in a vacuum. The history of science is replete with instances of simple observation of facts that have led to the formulation of important theories. When Archimedes observed water overflowing while he was taking a bath, he grasped the principle of displacement. When Newton saw an apple fall, he developed the principle of gravitation. When Watt watched steam escape from a teakettle, he envisioned the principle of steam power. Facts are prods that stimulate the theorizing process.

Of course, not everyone is capable of leaping from a fact to a theory; many men made the same observations as Newton, Watt, and Archimedes without being intellectually stimulated. Several scientists noticed the inhibition of bacterial growth by molds before Fleming saw the significance in this fact that led to the discovery of penicillin. As Pasteur pointed out, when men make observations "chance favors the prepared mind." A scientist must have a broad background of knowledge if he is to recognize an unusual fact and utilize this sudden insight to structure an explanation for the nature of the phenomena. Facts cannot initiate theorization unless an alert, disciplined, and imaginative mind observes them and mentally constructs a possible explanation for them.

Confirmation of Theories by Facts/ Facts are essential for the establishment of a scientific theory: they determine whether a theory can be confirmed or should be rejected or reformulated. Facts may not be available immediately for the confirmation or rejection of a theory, but they are necessary for the eventual acceptance or abandonment of it. The discovery of pertinent facts that support a theory strengthen it. But, if facts are found that do not substantiate the theory, one must reject or reformulate the theory to fit the new evidence. Theories must be tailored to fit the facts and remodeled whenever new facts reveal the need for such action.

Theoretical formulations do not necessarily retain their original structures. New evidence being unearthed in laboratories may lead to the revision of old theories or may spur the formulation of new explanations for phenomena. Theoretical explanations of learning, for example, have undergone revolutionary changes within the past several decades. The association and behavioral psychologists formulated some of the earlier theories of learning. When their work had come to be accepted almost as definitive, dramatic developments occurred as a result of investigations made by the Gestalt and the topological psychologists. These field psychologists challenged both the basic assumptions and the research techniques of their predecessors. Facts revealed by their laboratory experiments and clinical studies caused them to formulate a new explanation of the learning process.

Clarification of Theories by Facts/ Theories are refined and clarified as knowledge accumulates. New theories in the social sciences are apt to be elusive and ill-defined; they often give a rather crude, general explanation of phenomena. Further observation and experimentation may reveal, however, facts that not only agree with the theory, but also specify in detail and with precision what the theory states in a general way. For instance, modern psychologists have developed the so-called "field theories of learning" which contribute to our general understanding of the learning process. Yet, investigations conducted by Tolman, Lewin, Anderson, Murphy, and many others have added considerable substance and depth to these general theories of learning. Their work illustrates how additional facts can give greater specificity and breadth to a theory.

Interdependence of Facts and Theories/ The marriage of facts and theories produces many advances in science. Man is forever searching for a more abundant life and better understanding of the world in which he lives. Finding answers to his questions entails a persistent search for facts that will aid him in building mental constructs capable of explaining phenomena. Facts supply the raw building materials; man's imagination and intellect supply the theoretical framework—the blueprint that describes the known and unknown facts and relationships that presumably produce the phenomena under consideration. Facts alone are a rather useless pile of bricks, and theories must rely on facts as the building blocks for their construction. Facts contribute to both the conception and the confirmation of theories. In science, man puts his trust, "not in facts as such, but rather in the interaction of many minds observing similar facts, projecting these facts against different conceptual backgrounds, testing the divergent interpretations by means of further observation, and seeking explanations of any final differences" (110:34) Science rests on facts and on ideas; it is both objective and subjective; it is a product of empirical knowledge and imaginative mental constructs; it advances under the power of inductive and deductive thought processes.

5

Printed Resources for Problem Solving

A few centuries ago the scholar aspired to acquire an encyclopedic education that would acquaint him with all available knowledge. This goal is no longer attainable, for knowledge is growing much faster than man's ability to assimilate it. Keeping abreast of the vast and complex developments in a specialized field is difficult today, for more than 2,000 pages of books, newspapers, or reports are being published every minute of the twenty-four-hour day, and 30,000 scientific journals present 600,000 new papers each year. This explosive expansion of knowledge makes it imperative for an educator to become proficient in locating, selecting, and utilizing the references that appear in an ever-increasing variety of printed resources.

An educator can save months of time during his professional life if he prowls through the library and thumbs through books and indexes until he becomes thoroughly familiar with the available resources. When locating library materials is as automatic a process as finding the light switches in his home, a researcher has acquired a professional tool that carries a lifetime guarantee of usefulness. To aid you in achieving such skill, this chapter provides a study guide for surveying (1) the types of available references, (2) the nature of information that each contains, and (3) how to use them.

Reference Books

Utilizing the reference room facilities is a satisfying experience for an expert investigator who possesses the tools and techniques to mine the various sources for "pay dirt" information. But it is a frustrating experience for a neophyte who wanders in the endless tunnels of facts and does not know how to dig out the gems he wants. Since locating specific facts or compact overviews is frequently necessary, one should become well acquainted with reference books—such as encyclopedias, dictionaries, yearbooks, and directories—that can help him.

To facilitate the search for a reference book, one may consult the following carefully compiled volumes: *Guide to Reference Books* by Constance M. Winchell (145), which has biennial supplements to bring the information up-to-date, describes and evaluates over 5,000 references. *Basic Reference Sources* by Louis Shores, 1954, covers fewer references but gives more detailed descriptions. *Reference Books: A Brief Guide for Students and Other Users of the Library,* by Mary N. Barton and Marion V. Bell, 1962, is a helpful but considerably shorter guide. *How and Where to Look It Up* by Robert W. Murphey, 1958, is a comprehensive bibliography of basic reference works. It also offers guidance in the preparation and style of research papers. The *International Guide to Educational Documentation (1955–1960)*, UNESCO, 1963, is a one-volume international guide to educational books, pamphlets, periodicals, occasional papers, film and sound recordings, etc. *How to Locate Educational Information and Data* by Carter Alexander and Arvid Burke provides an excellent introduction to literature in the field.

If the reader desires more detailed bibliographic information about the sources listed in this chapter, he may find them in the preceding guides. Even after becoming thoroughly familiar with various reference books, it is advisable to check Winchell or the other guides occasionally to discover whether any useful new references are available or whether any changes have been made in the author, editor, title, publisher, or scope of material covered by the older references. If an educator fails to take such precautions, he may continue to search for items in a periodical index long after the information that interests him has been dropped; moreover, he may never discover that materials that were once published in one journal or index are now being presented in another source or under a new title.

Encyclopedias

Encyclopedias may be used to check a fact or to obtain a brief overview of a topic. These storehouses of information usually contain well-rounded discussions and selected bibliographies that are prepared by specialists. To make the most efficient use of encyclopedias, one should check dates of issue, consult the annual supplements that bring the materials up-to-date, and scan the indexes. To discover which general encyclopedia presents the best treatment of subjects in his field, one should examine some of the better-known ones, such as *Encyclopedia Americana, Encyclopaedia Britannica, Encyclopaedia International,* and the useful one-volume *Columbia Encyclopedia.*

Every educator finds the comprehensive *Encyclopedia of Educational Research,* Chester W. Harris (ed.), 1960, an invaluable reference. This book is arranged alphabetically by subject and for each field of research it (1) presents a critical evaluation and summary of the work that has been done, (2) suggests needed research, and (3) includes a selective bibliography. Other volumes that can be consulted are *Encyclopedia of Modern Education,* Harry N. Rivlin and Herbert Schueler (eds.), 1943, and *The Educator's Encyclopedia,* E. W. Smith, S. W. Krouse, and M. A. Atkinson (eds.), 1961. In addition, there are many special-field encyclopedias available, such as *The New Encyclopedia of Sports,* Frank G. Menke (ed.); *Encyclopedia of Child Guidance,* Ralph B. Winn (ed.); and *Encyclopedia of Vocational Guidance,* Oscar J. Kaplan (ed.).

The following list gives samples of other types of encyclopedias that educators might use: *International Encyclopedia of the Social Sciences, Van Nostrand's Scientific Encyclopedia, Catholic Encyclopedia, Jewish Encyclopedia, International Cyclopedia of Music and Musicians, Encyclopaedia of World History,* and *Encyclopaedia of Religion and Ethics.*

Dictionaries

Dictionaries that provide information concerning the spelling, pronunciation, derivation, syllabication, and correct usage and meaning of words are the constant companions of a researcher. In general, dictionaries that are unabridged, of recent date and compilation, responsibly edited, and specialized are better for investigative purposes than older, less comprehensive, and more general works. Among the better-known general dictionaries are: *Oxford English Dictionary,* 12 vols.; *Dictionary of American English on Historical Principles,* 4 vols.; *Funk and Wagnalls*

New Standard Dictionary; and *Webster's New International Dictionary of the English Language.*

Because a researcher must define educational terms with precision, a researcher in this field usually owns a copy of the *Dictionary of Education,* Carter V. Good (ed.), 1959. He also has a good abridged dictionary on his desk as well as Henry Fowler's *Dictionary of Modern English Usage* or Margaret Nicholson's *Dictionary of American-English Usage* and Peter Roget's *Thesaurus of English Words and Phrases.* Some of the special-field dictionaries he may use are: *Dictionary of Sociology,* Henry P. Fairchild (ed.); *Dictionary of Social Sciences,* John T. Zadrozny, (ed.); *Comprehensive Dictionary of Psychological and Psychoanalytical Terms,* H. B. English and Ava C. A. English; and *Dictionary of Statistical Terms,* Maurice G. Kendall and William R. A. Buckland.

Almanacs and Yearbooks

A wealth of current information may be found in almanacs and yearbooks. Up-to-date statistics and data concerning events, progress, and conditions in a wide variety of social, educational, industrial, political, financial, and religious fields appear in the *World Almanac,* 1868—,[1] and *Information Please Almanac,* 1947—. Statistics on population, standard of living, prices, labor, and business are presented in the *Economic Almanac,* 1940—. *The New York Times Sports Almanac,* 1965—, provides a record of all sports during the preceding year and brings all-time records up-to-date.

Educational Handbooks and Yearbooks/ The *Handbook of Research on Teaching,* N. L. Gage (ed.), contains scholarly materials concerning theoretical orientations, methodologies in research on teaching, and research on teaching various grade levels and subject matters. The *Rand McNally Handbook of Education,* Arthur W. Foshay (ed.), 1963, is a convenient, one-source compilation of the most important facts about education in the United States, and a quick-reference comparison of education in England, France, and Russia.

Recent statistics and discussions on educational problems, thought, and practices are found in several outstanding yearbooks. Some yearbooks cover a new topic of current interest each year, others give more general reviews of events. One of the most valuable yearbooks has been put out since 1902 by

1/ Interpret reference of this nature as follows: published from 1868 to the present.

the National Society for the Study of Education. Each year-book in this series is now issued in several parts; thus, a reference to this source must indicate the part as well as the year. Other important yearbooks are sponsored by the American Council on Education, the Fund for the Advancement of Education, and the NEA Educational Policies Commission.

About fifteen departments of the NEA publish yearbooks or annual reports. Some of them, such as those compiled by the American Association of School Administrators, have made major contributions to education. The *NEA Handbook for Local, State, and National Associations,* 1945—, lists its publications, gives accounts of its work, and includes facts about education in general. A report of the programs, meetings, and activities of the NEA and its departments, commissions, and committees has appeared in the annual volume of *Addresses and Proceedings* since 1857.

Many worthwhile yearbooks are also published in special fields. Educators may consult the *Mental Measurements Yearbook* (title and years of publication vary—1938, 1941, 1949, 1953, 1959, 1965) which is compiled by Oscar K. Buros. It lists all commercially available educational, psychological, and vocational tests published during the period covered by the volume and gives price, publisher, grade level, and evaluations. *The Yearbook of School Law,* edited by M. M. Chambers, 1932 to 1942, and by Lee O. Garber, 1950—, presents abstracts of important court cases dealing with education as well as a few feature articles.

Statistical Information/ Statistics concerning public and private schools on all levels appear in the indispensable *Biennial Survey of Education in the United States* for the years 1916 to 1918—. This work contains data on such things as personnel, enrollment, receipts, expenditures, salaries, attendance, buildings, and per-capita costs. The U.S. Department of Health, Education, and Welfare, Office of Education,[2] publishes a compilation of significant statistical material in the *Digest of Educational Statistics,* 1962—. The NEA publication, *Research Bulletin,* which is issued four times a year, is an excellent source for recent statistics and discussions on topics such as salaries, working conditions, educational practices, and teacher supply and demand.

The United States Census Bureau's ten-year reports and its *Census Abstract* are reliable and detailed. The *Statistical Abstract of the United States,* 1878—, is the annual authoritative

---

2/ Hereafter, the shorter term Office of Education will be used to designate this agency.

summary of statistics on the political, social, industrial, and economic organization of the nation. *Historical Statistics of the United States,* a supplement to the *Statistical Abstract,* contains more than 8,200 time series, mostly annual, on American social and economic development covering the periods from 1610 to 1957. Since 1947, UNESCO has published international economic statistics in the *Statistical Yearbook* and population and social statistics in the *Demographic Yearbook.*

International Information/ International surveys and descriptions of educational systems in many countries are found in the *Year Book of Education,* 1932 to 1940, 1948—. The early volumes reviewed educational developments in the major European and English-speaking nations. Since 1953, each annual edition has examined at length a particular aspect of education in many countries of the world. The theme of the 1963 edition, for example, was "The Education and Training of Teachers." The *International Yearbook of Education,* which is issued jointly by UNESCO and the International Bureau of Education, 1948—, reviews the educational developments of approximately eighty-six countries, including the United States and Canada. Prior to 1948, this yearbook was published in French. The three-volume *World Survey of Education:* vol. I, *Handbook of Educational Organization and Statistics,* 1955; vol. II, *Primary Education,* 1958; vol. III, *Secondary Education,* 1961, is issued by UNESCO.

Directories

Directories are as valuable in professional life as a personal address book is in private life. An educator uses them to locate the names and addresses of persons, periodicals, publishers, organizations, or firms when he wants to obtain information, interviews, a grant from a foundation, or research materials and equipment. By consulting directories, he may find people or organizations who have similar professional interests or who are qualified to answer his questionnaires or help solve his problems. To locate an appropriate directory, he may use the *Guide to American Educational Directories* which assembles in one volume over 1,200 educational and allied directories. The directories are listed alphabetically and are arranged under subject headings.

The Education Directory, published by the Office of Education, is a widely used reference. It has five parts and includes the following data: part I, state and territorial school officials; part II, county and city school officials, including some parochial superintendents; part III, higher educational institutions —enrollment, curricula, officers, accrediting agency, and statistical tables; part IV, officers of educational associations, religious and international organizations, and educational foundations; part V, Federal educational officials. Similar information appears in *Patterson's American Education*. The *NEA Handbook* lists the NEA departments and affiliated associations and their officers. Many educational associations include membership lists in their yearbooks.

Information about educational institutions is presented in *Patterson's American Education* and the *Education Directory*, part III, which were cited above. The following guides published by the American Council on Education are also useful: *American Universities and Colleges, American Junior Colleges,* and *Universities of the World Outside U.S.A.* Other references in this field include *The College Blue Book*, C. E. Burckel; *A Guide to Graduate Study,* Frederic W. Ness (ed.), American Council on Education; *Handbook of Private Schools,* Porter Sargent. *Index Generalis* lists institutions of higher learning, academies, libraries, gardens, museums, and observatories throughout the world.

An educator might also have the occasion to consult specialized directories, such as the *Directory of Special Libraries and Information Centers*, the *Directory of University Research Bureaus and Institutes,* and the *National Register of Educational Research Personnel*. The following directories also contain information that is frequently sought by educators: *American Foundations and their Fields* and the *Encyclopedia of Associations*.

Biographical Sources

When carrying out a research study, one may have to obtain a specific fact about a person, such as his birthdate, degrees, publications, present position, or professional affiliations. This type of information, as well as general information concerning the background, competency, prestige, or biases of a person, may be found in encyclopedias or in one of the following sources:

The *Biography Index,* 1947—, provides a comprehensive guide to biographical materials appearing in current books, periodicals, and *The New York Times*. This quarterly index, which has annual and three-year cumulations, indexes items by profession and occupation as well as by name. It includes persons both living and dead, lists obituaries, and indicates which articles include portraits (see Figure 5.1). Winchell (145)

DEWEY, John, 1859-1952, philosopher
Nathanson, J. John Dewey. (In Mason, Gabriel Richard, ed. Great American liberals. Starr King press '56 p 143-53)
Pillsbury, W. B. John Dewey, 1859-1952. (In National academy of sciences. Biographical memoirs. Columbia univ. press '57 p 105-24) bibliog por autograph

DE WINT, Peter, 1784-1849, English painter
New York (city). Museum of modern art. Masters of British painting, 1800-1950. The museum '56 p52-3 bibliog il

DEWITT, Anna (Drury) 1884?-1957, political leader
Obituary
N Y Times p29 Ja 17 '57

DIONNE, Cecile, 1934- one of the Dionne quintuplets
First of the quints to say mais oui. il pors Life 42:57 Ap 8 '57

DIOR, Christian, 1905- French costume designer
Dictator by demand. il pors Time 69:30-4+ Mr 4 '57
Dior stages a dress rehearsal. il pors Look 21:88-9 Ap 2 '57
Pictorial works
Dior celebrates a decade at the very top. Life 42:129-32+ Mr 4 '57

DIRKS, Rudolph, 1877?- cartoonist
Dirks's bad boys. il por Time 69:48 Mr 4 '57

Figure 5.1/ Typical entries in the *Biography Index.* (*The H. W. Wilson Company.*)

describes some useful earlier guides to biographical materials by Marian Dorgan, Edward H. O'Neill, and the co-compilers Helen Hefling and Jessie Dyde.

Reference books that contain biographies of notable personalities both living and dead are *Webster's Biographical Dictionary,* which gives brief sketches, and the comprehensive *National Cyclopaedia of American Biography.* Deceased notables are found in the reliable and scholarly *Dictionary of American Biography,* and in *Who Was Who in America.* Notable contemporaries are listed in sources, such as *World Biography; Who's Who in America,* a biennial with monthly supplements; *Who's Who in the East* (volumes are also published for other sections of the United States); and similarly named publications in other countries. *Current Biography,* gives lively sketches of recent newsworthy names throughout the world. Some educators are included in the *Directory of American Scholars* and the *American Men of Science* and many are listed in *Leaders in Education* and *Who's Who in American Education.* Similar references have been compiled to cover art, music, government, industry, and many other fields.

Bibliographical Sources

Compiling a bibliography is one of the first and one of the last things a researcher does in conducting a study. This essential task is less arduous and time consuming if he is well acquainted with the various laborsaving devices at his disposal. He may find books and periodicals in the library that will help him locate bibliographies that have already been compiled. Of course, the bibliographies will vary in type and quality; some will be exhaustive and others selective or brief; some will be annotated and others not. If the bibliographies are compiled by experts in the field and give clues to the content, general

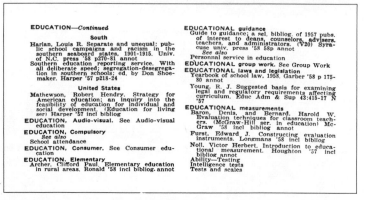

EDUCATION—*Continued*

South

Harlan, Louis R. Separate and unequal; public school campaigns and racism in the southern seaboard states, 1901-1915. Univ. of N.C. press '58 p270-81 annot

Southern education reporting service. With all deliberate speed; segregation-desegregation in southern schools; ed. by Don Shoemaker. Harper '57 p218-24

United States

Mathewson, Robert Hendry. Strategy for American education; an inquiry into the feasibility of education for individual and social development. (Education for living ser) Harper '57 incl bibliog

EDUCATION, Audio-visual. See Audio-visual education

EDUCATION, Compulsory
See also
School attendance

EDUCATION, Consumer. See Consumer education

EDUCATION, Elementary
Archer, Clifford Paul. Elementary education in rural areas. Ronald '58 incl bibliog. annot

EDUCATIONAL guidance
Guide to guidance; a sel. bibliog. of 1957 pubs. of interest to deans, counselors, advisers, teachers, and administrators. (V20) Syracuse univ. press '58 58p annot
See also
Personnel service in education

EDUCATIONAL group work. See Group Work

EDUCATIONAL laws and legislation
Yearbook of school law, 1958. Garber '58 p 175-80 annot

Young, R. J. Suggested basis for examining legal and regulatory requirements affecting curriculum. Educ Adm & Sup 43:415-17 N '57

EDUCATIONAL measurements
Baron, Denis, and Bernard, Harold W. Evaluation techniques for classroom teachers. (McGraw-Hill ser. in education) McGraw '58 incl bibliog annot

Furst, Edward J. Constructing evaluation instruments. Longmans '58 incl bibliog

Noll, Victor Herbert. Introduction to educational measurement. Houghton '57 incl bibliog annot
Ability—Testing
Intelligence tests
Tests and scales

Figure 5.2/ Typical entries in the *Bibliographic Index*. (*The H. W. Wilson Company.*)

value, scholarship, and significant features of the publications, they may save the researcher weeks of searching time.

Since 1937, the excellent *Bibliographic Index* has provided a guide to bibliographies in all fields (see Figure 5.2). Under subjects only, it lists bibliographies that are published as separate books or pamphlets as well as those appearing in books, pamphlets, and periodicals, both in English and foreign languages. This semiannual subject index has annual and larger cumulations. For materials published earlier than 1937, an educator can consult Winchell (145) under the heading Bibliographies.

For locating educational bibliographies published since 1928, the best source is the *Education Index*. In this guide, bibliographies are listed as a subhead under a main head subject (i.e., main head Social Sciences, subhead Bibliography). Earlier bibliographies can be found in *Bibliographies and Summaries in Education to July 1, 1935* by Walter S. Monroe and Louis Shores. Bibliographies also appear in the *Cumulative Book Index*.

Excellent educational bibliographies also may be found in the *Encyclopedia of Educational Research* and issues of the *Review of Educational Research*. Books or articles in special fields, such as *Guide to Research in Educational History* (Brickman), *Handbook of Research on Teaching* (Gage), *Handbook of Research Methods in Child Development* (Mussen), and *Tests in Print* (Buros) often include a list of bibliographies. An educator sometimes finds that the *Art Index, Agriculture Index,* or similar publications are the best source to consult for his purposes. Textbooks, some professional magazines, and various organizations also provide bibliographies. The U.S. Department of Health, Education, and Welfare publishes a number of bibliographies; for example, *Administration of Higher Education: An Annotated Bibliography,* bulletin 1960, contains 2,708 studies and *Research Relating to Mentally Retarded Children,* 1960, includes 458 studies.

Books and Monographs

Books and monographs are major research resources. Unless a student can quickly ascertain what publications the local library has on his subject and knows how to find the titles and locations of those that are available elsewhere, he cannot make much progress with an investigation. Examining everything that has been written on a subject either will be impossible or will consume an exorbitant amount of time; consequently, one must master the art of selecting books discriminatingly. To judge which books are most useful for his purpose, one must learn how to locate and interpret the information provided by the card catalog, book lists, and reviews.

Card Catalog

The card catalog is the key to the local library's collection of books and some other items. The "dictionary-type" catalog contains (1) author, (2) title, and (3) subject cards arranged alphabetically. An author card is filed last name first. A title card is filed under the first principal word in the title of the book (initial articles—"a," "the," "an"—are disregarded). A subject card has a heading, usually typed in red, which indicates what a book is about. If a book falls under several subjects, it is filed under each pertinent subject heading. Subject headings that have several entries are subdivided and the division headings are listed alphabetically; for example, the subject heading Education may be followed by the division headings Aims, Bibliographies, History, and Philosophy. Cross-reference cards which carry the notation "see" or "see also" are inserted in the catalog when the information sought can be located under other subject headings or when the author uses a pseudonym.

A library may use its own typed cards in the catalog or those published by the Library of Congress or the H. W. Wilson Company. Some libraries are now dividing their card catalog into two sections—one for authors and title cards and the other for subject cards. They also may have separate catalogs for dissertations, reserved books, and other special collections.

The wealth of information that appears on the cards in the catalog can be exceedingly helpful if the researcher knows how to interpret it. Merely by checking the author card, which carries the most detailed data about a book, he may find a number of valuable clues that will indicate whether the book will meet his needs. Besides the title of the book and the name of the author, the card will list the birthdate of the author, the edition, the publication date, the number of pages, and the name and location of the publisher. Other items sometimes noted on cards are bibliographies, maps, portraits, illustrations, tables or tabulations if given, series if any in which a book appears, a brief description or quoted evaluation of the book, whether the book is a translation and who did the translation, and whether the author uses a pseudonym.

Books Not Located in the Local Library

What does an educator do if he needs information about a book that is not available in the local library? How can he determine whether a book has been published on a given subject? How can he get data to correct or complete a reference listed in his bibliography? How can he obtain information about a book that was published by an author in 1940? How can he find out which libraries have a copy of the book he wants? By becoming familiar with some of the following guides, one usually can answer such questions.

Books from Other Libraries/ If a book is not in the local library, it may be available in another institution. The *National Union Catalog* and other national and regional catalogs, which contain entries of works cataloged by many libraries, give such information. By consulting them, an educator can discover what institution has a particular book and request the local reference librarian to obtain it for him on an interlibrary loan. By checking the *Union List of Microfilms,* an educator can ascertain whether any institution has a microfilmed copy of a nonlendable book. For a small fee, the larger libraries will prepare a photocopy of a few pages in a book. Before requesting any of these services, of course, one must obtain complete bibliographic information about the book and must make certain that it is not available locally.

General Lists of Books/ A number of sources may be consulted to find the title, author, or publisher of a book. The most recent books published in the United States are listed in *The Publishers' Weekly.* Books published in the past months or years

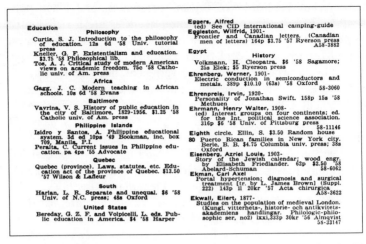

Education

Philosophy

Curtis, S. J. Introduction to the philosophy of education. 12s 6d '58 Univ. tutorial press

Kneller, G. F. Existentialism and education. $3.75 '58 Philosophical lib.

Tos, A. J. Critical study of modern American views on academic freedom. 75c '58 Catholic univ. of Am. press

Africa

Gagg, J. C. Modern teaching in African schools. 10s 6d '58 Evans

Baltimore

Vavrina, V. S. History of public education in the city of Baltimore, 1829-1956. $1.25 '58 Catholic univ. of Am. press

Philippine Islands

Isidro y Santos, A. Philippine educational system. 3d ed 10ps '49 Bookman, inc, box 709, Manila, P.I.

Peralta, C. Current issues in Philippine education. pa 4ps '55 Advocate

Quebec

Quebec (province). Laws, statutes, etc. Education act of the province of Quebec. $13.50 '57 Wilson & Lafleur

South

Harlan, L. R. Separate and unequal. $6 '58 Univ. of N.C. press; 48s Oxford

United States

Bereday, G. Z. F. and Volpicelli, L. eds. Public education in America. $4 '58 Harper

Eggers, Alfred
(ed) See CID international camping-guide

Eggleston, Wilfrid, 1901-
Frontier and Canadian letters. (Canadian men of letters) 164p $3.75 '57 Ryerson press
A58-3882

Egypt

History

Volkmann, H. Cleopatra. $6 '58 Sagamore; 25s Elek; $5 Ryerson press

Ehrenberg, Werner, 1901-
Electric conduction in semiconductors and metals. 389p $10.10 (63s) '58 Oxford
58-3060

Ehrenpreis, Irvin, 1920-
Personality of Jonathan Swift. 158p 15s '58 Methuen

Ehrmann, Henry Walter, 1908-
(ed) Interest groups on four continents; ed. for the Int. political science association. 316p $6 '58 Univ. of Pittsburg press
58-11146

Eighth circle. Ellin, S. $3.50 Random house

80 Puerto Rican families in New York city. Berle, B. B. $4.75 Columbia univ. press; 38s Oxford

Eisenberg, Azriel Louis, 1903-
Story of the Jewish calendar; wood engr. by Elisabeth Friedlander. 62p $2.50 '58 Abelard-Schuman
58-6062

Ekman, Carl Axel
Portal hypertension; diagnosis and surgical treatment [tr. by L. James Brown] (Suppl. 222) 143p il 20kr '57 Acta chirurgica
A58-3622

Ekwall, Eilert, 1877-
Studies on the population of medieval London. (Kungl. vitterhets-, historie- och antikvitetsakademiens handlingar. Philologic-philosophic ser, no2) lxxi,333p 30kr '56 Almqvist
58-33147

Figure 5.3/ Typical entries in the *Cumulative Book Index.* (*The H. W. Wilson Company.*)

are indexed soon after their publication in a monthly issue of the *Cumulative Book Index,* 1928—, and in its larger cumulations. This world list of books in the English language includes most publications, but omits pamphlets, government documents, and maps. Entries in the *Cumulative Book Index* are cataloged by author, title, and subject in one alphabetical list; the author entries give the complete bibliographical information (see Figure 5.3). Older books can be found in the *United States Catalog* which lists books in print 1899 to 1928 and the *American Catalogue of Books* which covers the 1876 to 1910 period.

Books in Print/ Sometimes it is necessary to know whether a book is in print. If the author or title of the book is known, it may be found in *Books in Print;* otherwise, it may be found in *Subject Guide to Books in Print.* Paperbacks may be located in *Paperback Books in Print.* Out-of-print books may sometimes be found through the columns of the weekly *Antiquarian Bookman.*

Educational Publications/ Current textbooks are listed in *Textbooks in Print, Books in Print,* and the *Cumulative Book Index.* Most educational organizations compile lists or catalogs of the publications that they produce or that may be obtained from other sources. The NEA, for example, annually puts out *Publications,* a list of over a thousand books, pamphlets, periodicals, research reports, and audio-visual materials. Many lists such as this one may be obtained upon request from publishers and the national headquarters of educational organizations.

Government Publications/ Books, pamphlets, and other publications from various governmental agencies are a rich source of information, for they include statistical data, research studies, official reports, laws, and other materials that are not always available elsewhere. Locating government documents may be difficult, especially if one does not know that librarians index government publications under the name of the official body responsible for them rather than under the author's name. If one reads the brief overview concerning government publications written by Louis Shores (118) and the chapter of detailed suggestions presented by Alexander and Burke (1:267–283), he will find it easier to locate government materials.

The publications of the Office of Education are listed in the *Education Index* under the main heading United States. A list of items that are for sale, which is entitled *Education,* Price List 31, may be obtained by writing to the Superintendent of Documents, Government Printing Office, Washington, D.C. *The 1937–1959 Publications,* Office of Education, presents a more comprehensive single list, and the annual supplements keep the list up-to-date. Alexander and Burke (1:247–266) present a detailed guide on how to locate Office of Education publications. To find publications of other government agencies, an educator may refer to the two general source books: the *Monthly Catalog of United States Government Publications,* which lists entries by departments and has a subject index, and the *Monthly Checklist of State Publications* issued by the Library of Congress.

Book Lists and Reviews

How can an educator decide which books are the most useful and reliable souces? From experience he learns that some authors and publishers maintain higher standards than others and the information given in the card catalog provides him with some clues. In addition to these guides, he may consult book lists, book reviews, and editorial comments to evaluate the worthiness of the book.

Book Lists/ Since carelessly prepared book lists are worthless, a researcher should become acquainted with reputable ones, such as those compiled by the competent staff members of *School and Society,* the Research Division of the NEA, the American Library Association, and the Enoch Pratt Free Library. The staff of the Pratt Library compiles a comprehensive list on a single topic which appears in the spring issues of *Educational Horizons* and a list of outstanding educational books of the year which appears in the May issue of the *NEA Journal*. Current educational book lists are found in the *Education Index* under the main headings Reading Lists, Books and Reading with the subhead Best Books, and Education with the subhead Bibliography. Many lists may also be found in the *Bibliographic Index* under the following headings: Reading Lists, Book Lists, Books and Reading, Bibliography, and Education.

Book Reviews/ More detailed information about books may be obtained from book reviews, but if they are used to evaluate books, due consideration must be given to the special interests, biases, and competencies of the reviewers as well as the standards of the periodicals that printed them. Book reviews may be located in several sources. Every month the *Book Review Digest* gives condensed reports of book reviews appearing in a wide variety of sources. This publication lists entries alphabetically by the author of the book reviewed. An entry describes the purpose and scope of the book, notes where reviews are located, indicates whether they are favorable or unfavorable by the use of a plus or minus sign, and may include excerpts from some reviews. The *Technical Book Review Index* is a useful guide to reviews in technical, scientific, and trade journals. The *Index to Book Reviews in the Humanities,* 1960—, covers over 600 English-language journals.

Periodicals and Other Serials

Information about new ideas and developments often appears in periodicals long before it appears in books. Periodicals also publish articles of temporary, local, or limited interest that never appear in book form. Current periodicals are the best source for reports on recent research studies, and the older volumes provide a priceless record of past proposals, accomplishments, conflicts, attitudes, propaganda, ideas, and events.

Periodical Indexes

What a hopeless task a researcher would face if he had to leaf through all the periodicals in the library to find the articles he needed! Fortunately, expertly compiled indexes are available that serve as guides to the contents of periodicals just as card catalogs serve as guides to books. These periodical guides usually list the selected magazines they index on the inside covers or near the front of each issue. This list changes occasionally when new periodicals are added or old ones are dropped. An experienced researcher always checks whether a periodical guide indexes the magazines that are likely to answer his problems. Before writing out a call slip for a periodical, he also checks whether the local library has a copy of it. In the reference or periodical room, he may find a list or file which will provide him with the names and volume numbers of the periodicals that the library has available.

Educational Indexes/ One of the greatest worksaving devices ever created for educators is the *Education Index.* Since 1929, it has provided the most extensive and detailed guide to professional literature in the field. It lists all articles in outstanding educational journals and many educational articles in nonprofessional periodicals. In addition, it lists many pamphlets, monographs, government documents, important yearbooks, courses of study, tests and scales, bibliographies, biographies, and reports. Almost all the publications of the NEA and the Office of Education are in the *Education Index.* This valuable guide is published monthly, except for June and August, and is cumulated frequently. All main entries in the *Education Index* are listed alphabetically with appropriate subheadings. The plan of indexing (prior to September, 1961) was by author and subject, and the author entries gave full bibliographic data. Now, the plan of indexing is by subject only. By utilizing the "Key to Abbreviations" and the "List of Periodicals Indexed" which are located at the front of each issue or cumulation, it is easy to interpret an entry.

If a novice researcher wants further information on how to use the *Education Index,* he will find that Alexander and Burke provide an excellent guide (1:106–122). To locate articles that were published before the *Education Index* was established in 1929, he can examine a number of other guides: The *Record of Current Educational Publications* compiled by the Office of Education covers the period from January, 1912, to March, 1932; indexes have also been compiled for the early NEA publications (1:231, 145), and the *Ohio State University Periodical Index* (Ohio File) which includes articles published between 1919 and 1929 and, thereafter, specializes in local and state journals.

Readers' Guide/ Since 1900, the *Readers' Guide to Periodical Literature* has served as a faithful servant to library patrons. This semimonthly (monthly in July and August) subject and author index lists general-interest articles in more than 130 magazines, but rarely duplicates those that appear in the *Educa-*

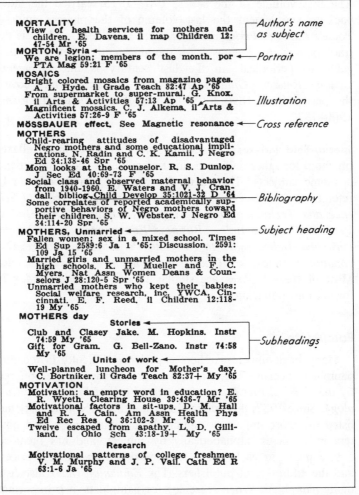

MORTALITY
View of health services for mothers and
children. E. Davens. il map Children 12:
47-54 Mr '65 ———— Author's name as subject

MORTON, Syria ————
We are legion; members of the month. por ←— Portrait
PTA Mag 59:21 F '65

MOSAICS
Bright colored mosaics from magazine pages.
A. L. Hyde. il Grade Teach 82:47 Ap '65
From supermarket to super-mural. G. Knox.
il Arts & Activities 57:13 Ap '65 ———— Illustration
Magnificent mosaics. C. J. Alkema. il Arts &
Activities 57:26-9 F '65

MÖSSBAUER effect. See Magnetic resonance ←— Cross reference

MOTHERS
Child-rearing attitudes of disadvantaged
Negro mothers and some educational impli-
cations. N. Radin and C. K. Kamii. J Negro
Ed 34:138-46 Spr '65
Mom looks at the counselor. R. S. Dunlop.
J Sec Ed 40:69-73 F '65
Social class and observed maternal behavior
from 1940-1960. E. Waters and V. J. Cran-
dall. bibliog Child Develop 35:1021-32 D '64 ———— Bibliography
Some correlates of reported academically sup-
portive behaviors of Negro mothers toward
their children. S. W. Webster. J Negro Ed
34:114-20 Spr '65 ———— Subject heading

MOTHERS, Unmarried ←————
Fallen women; sex in a mixed school. Times
Ed Sup 2589:6 Ja 1 '65; Discussion. 2591:
109 Ja 15 '65
Married girls and unmarried mothers in the
high schools. K. H. Mueller and F. C.
Myers. Nat Assn Women Deans & Coun-
selors J 28:120-5 Spr '65
Unmarried mothers who kept their babies;
Social welfare research, inc. YWCA, Cin-
cinnati. E. F. Reed. il Children 12:118-
19 My '65

MOTHERS day
   Stories ←————
Club and Clasey Jake. M. Hopkins. Instr
74:59 My '65
Gift for Gram. G. Bell-Zano. Instr 74:58
My '65 ————— Subheadings

   Units of work ←————
Well-planned luncheon for Mother's day.
C. Bortniker. il Grade Teach 82:37+ My '65

MOTIVATION
Motivation: an empty word in education? E.
R. Wyeth. Clearing House 39:436-7 Mr '65
Motivational factors in sit-ups. D. M. Hall
and R. L. Cain. Am Assn Health Phys
Ed Rec Res Q 36:102-3 Mr '65
Twelve escaped from apathy. L. D. Gilli-
land. il Ohio Sch 43:18-19+ My '65

   Research
Motivational patterns of college freshmen.
V. M. Murphy and J. P. Vail. Cath Ed R
63:1-6 Ja '65

Figure 5.4/ Typical entries in the *Education Index.* (*The H. W. Wilson
Company.*)

tion Index. Prior to 1929, it is one of the best indexes to
educational literature.

International and Early Indexes/ When searching for technical
articles concerning education prior to 1929, the *International
Index to Periodicals* is the most helpful source to consult. This
excellent guide to scholarly articles, which covers many more
periodicals than the *Readers' Guide,* indexes articles concerning
the social sciences, humanities, and subjects of general interest.
Prior to 1955, it covered some foreign and scientific periodicals.

This index is published quarterly and cumulated periodically. Prior to 1920, it was called the *Readers' Guide Supplement*. The first volume of the series, 1907–1915, carried the index back to supplement the last volume of the pioneer guide— *Poole's Index to Periodical Literature*, 1802–1907, which is the traditional source to consult for the nineteenth century. Another guide to periodicals in the last century is the *Nineteenth Century Readers' Guide to Periodical Literature* which covers the period from 1890 to 1899, with *Supplemental Indexing,* 1900–1922.

Special-field Indexes/ Educators find that specialized indexes prepared for other fields are superior guides for locating articles on some subjects. They may, for example, have occasion to refer to such sources as: the *Agricultural Index, Applied Science and Technology Index* (formerly, *Industrial Arts Index,* 1913–1957), *Art Index, Business Education Index, Catholic Periodical Index, Index to Religious Periodical Literature, Occupational Index,* or *Quarterly Cumulative Index Medicus.* Most of these indexes are similar to the *Education Index* in format and publication.

Pamphlets

Many beginning researchers experience difficulty in locating pamphlets because they are not aware of the services offered by the *Vertical File Index* (formerly, *Vertical File Service Catalog*). Since 1932, this publication (monthly except August) has listed the more important pamphlets, bulletins, maps, and posters in all fields, alphabetically by subject, and has included a title index in each issue. It gives descriptive notes, prices, and the addresses of publishers. The *Education Index* also lists many pamphlets. When searching for pamphlets, it is important to remember that they usually are available only a short time after publication and some are produced for advertising or propaganda purposes.

Periodicals not Available Locally

Since the local library cannot subscribe to all periodicals that are printed each year, an educator sometimes must locate a publication elsewhere. The following books will advise him which libraries have what volumes of a given publication. The old *Union List of Serials in Libraries of the United States and Canada* and its two supplements, 1941–1943 and 1944–1949, list alphabetically by title the publications held in over 600 libraries. The publication of this work was terminated in 1949.

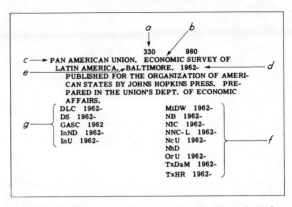

Figure 5.5/ Typical entries in the *New Serial Titles:* (*a*) Dewey decimal classification, (*b*) serial title, (*c*) issuing body, (*d*) initial publication date, (*e*) place of publication, (*f*) holdings of the library (volumes), (*g*) participating libraries, coded, i.e., DLC is the Library of Congress. A key on the inside cover of the work interprets the symbols used. (*Library of Congress.*)

As a continuing supplement to the *Union List of Serials,* the Library of Congress publishes a guide which is now known as *New Serials Titles* (see Figure 5.5). This work lists the new serials received by the Library of Congress and many participating libraries. It is published monthly and is cumulated periodically. In this guide, titles are listed alphabetically; but a related monthly, noncumulative publication, *New Serial Titles—Classed Subject Arrangement,* contains the same entries arranged by the Dewey decimal classification numbers which reflect the subject contents of the serials. A key to the code used in the entries makes it possible to interpret which libraries have a periodical and whether they loan serials or furnish photocopies and microfilms.

Educators may find the *Union List of Technical Periodicals* helpful. It lists publications in 200 libraries that are concerned with science and its application in various fields. If a researcher wants to purchase back issues of a periodical for his private library, he may try the publisher, the Periodical Clearing House of the H. W. Wilson Company, or dealers who specialize in such service.

Newspapers

Current newspapers provide up-to-date information on speeches, reports, conferences, new developments, personalities, and a host of other topics. Old newspapers, which preserve a record of past events and the evolution of movements and ideas,

EDITOR & Publisher (Pub). See Ad—US, newspaper par S 26
EDITORS (Orgns). See other key words
EDMUNDS, Larry M. See Philatelic Americans Soc
EDUCATION (Orgns). See also other key words
EDUCATION, Council for Financial Aid to. See Colls—US, finances par S 28
EDUCATION, Institute of International. See Art—Shows—Gen S 17,21
EDUCATION and Schools. See: Athletics. Colls. Mental Tests. Scholarships. Teachers. Vocational Training. Mass educ media, eg, TV & Radio. Profession and sport names. State and locality names (for educ bds and depts). Private school names. Subjects taught

Foreign Study and Travel: 7½-mos round-world trip with study abroad for 12th graders offered by new Internatl School of Amer, NYC, S 20,38:2. General: Pope says Cath schools fail to get as much support from govts as they merit, s to RC teachers group; urges broad study of Cath schools role, S 17, 4:8. Germany, West: Population rise poses challenge to system of selectivity; more schools being built but requirements and programs kept same as decades ago; enrollment figures; other data, S 21, 27:1

Great Britain
Sussex County Council orders merger of Bognor Regis Secondary Boys School and Secondary Girls School; 50 girls march in protest against co-educ, S 28,87:4
Labor party annual conf debates pub schools; schools scored as sign of class privilege; motion to

ENROLLMENT: total hits record 3,436,000, with 2.64 million in pas, 4% above yr ago; Comr Allen comments; notes rate of growth is uneven; repts '54-58 rise in NYC is 6%, in Suffolk County 72%; other data, S 20,8:7
FINANCES (gen): Comr Allen says NYS must provide more funds, s, School Supts Council; urges Legis study state and local tax structure to provide funds, S 22,1:2; ed, S 23,32:2; Assemblyman Carlino cites Allen views, scores Harriman for failing to suggest tax structure revision, S 26,17:1; comment on issue; charts, S 28,IV,9:1
HANDICAPPED STUDENTS: Gov Harriman breaks ground, W Seneca, for state school for mentally retarded, S 27,12:1. STATE AID: See: adult educ par S 25. Colls—NYC ▲ Educ Dept repts '57-58 aid totaled $508,204,218; sees $88 million rise, '58-59; details, S 26,19:2

Poland. W Gomulka urges tying school system more closely with production needs and Communist ideology; apparently impressed with USSR proposals for revision, S 28,27:1

USSR
Khrushchev says school system will be overhauled to teach respect for physical labor and prepare youth for useful work, discourse on educ reptdly approved by Communist party Presidium; says current system produces elementary and has grads unfit for anything but further study even though higher learning is available only to 25-33% of grads; repts grads and their families regard physical labor as fate of failures; says influence of parents often counts for more than student ability in selection of candidates

NJ School Supts back Dr Co[n]prehensive hs can fill needs of educ, S 26,53:4
AIMS AND CURRICULUM: P subject matter traditional, mett Psychological Assn; urges 'qu S 21,IV,9:4
STUDENT ACTIVITIES ANI Rock, Ark, School Bd bars all vities in strict interpretation o: closing schools to bar racial ir (see also subhead US—Racial I 1st S 16 par)
US—Junior High Schools: § cial Integration ▲ 2 youths sei: to Maplewood, NJ, NHS; implic all 3 charged with arson, S 19, Schools: See subhead US—Gen,
US—Racial Integration
Little Rock, Ark; all 4 hss s Faubus orders as fall term oper concern; notes lack of plan to r private basis with assurance of som repts parents worried; Bd i program; plans full term whenev to maintain accreditation; Asst confs with Judge Miller; Mayor Faubus pledge for state police Faubus denies widespread pres schools; finds wide resentment S 16,1:6; teachers rept to empty their, parents, students reaction rept for extracurricular activitie

Figure 5.6/ Typical entries in *The New York Times Index*. (*a*) heading: Education; (*b*) cross references; see Council for Financial Aid to Education under main heading Colleges, subhead United States, paragraph on finances, September, 28, (*c*) cross references: suggests other headings under which to look for information, (*d*) entry: (summary of story) i.e., "Population rise poses . . ."; (*e*) date, page, column: Sept. 21, page 27, column 1. (*The New York Times*.)

are particularly useful in historical inquiries. The larger metro-politan Sunday editions, such as *The New York Times* and *New York Herald Tribune,* have special sections devoted to weekly news reviews and to educational affairs. Current events and educational news are also reported in periodicals such as *Time, Newsweek, Current History,* and *Foreign Affairs.* The loose-leaf encyclopedia of current events, *Facts on File,* which is usually found in the reference room of a library, gives a weekly digest of world news in a few pages. *Keesing's Contemporary Archives,* 1931—, provides similar information. Some general periodicals and many educational journals also have special sections devoted to news digest of educational events.

To locate articles in a newspaper, a reader can refer to *The New York Times Index,* a semimonthly publication with annual cumulations (see Figure 5.6). Since 1913, it has classified all important items in the paper alphabetically by subject, personality, and organization. Since most news events of wide public interest are published immediately, *The New York Times Index* gives a reader clues concerning the dates when a particular item may have appeared in other newspapers.

Lists of early American newspapers and the location of existing files are found in Clarence S. Brigham's *History and Bibliography of American Newspapers, 1690–1820,* and Winifred Gregory's *American Newspapers, 1821–1936.* The *New York Daily Tribune Index,* 1875–1906, is useful for the dates it covers. Some libraries, state historical associations, and universities prepare lists of the newspapers and existing files in their local areas. Two English indexes that cover a span of many years are *The Official Index to The Times* (London), 1906—, and *Palmer's Index to the Times Newspaper* (London), 1790—. Ayer's *Directory of Newspapers and Periodicals* has listed sectional or local American newspapers since 1880.

Directories to Periodicals and Newspapers

Sometimes a researcher has to find what publications are available in a particular field or geographical area. To proceed with some phases of his work, he may need the name, address, price, circulation figures, or date of origin of a periodical. To evaluate a magazine or newspaper, he may want to know the name of the publisher or editor, the political bias of a publication, or where it is indexed. By consulting one or more of the following directories, he can usually find answers to such questions.

America's Education Press: A Classified List of Educational Periodicals Issued in the United States of America is published in odd-numbered years in the yearbook of the Educational Press Association of America. This list classifies periodicals under a number of educational subject headings and indexes them alphabetically by title. The twenty-sixth yearbook differs from earlier works in that it was published jointly with UNESCO and carries international as well as domestic educational periodicals. Later editions also include the international list. *Ulrich's Periodicals Directory* covers a list of about 20,000 foreign and domestic periodicals in all fields. N. W. Ayer's annual *Directory of Newspapers and Periodicals* gives an extensive coverage for newspapers and periodicals. It contains several lists, such as agricultural; college; Negro; religious; and trade, technical, and class publications. The main catalog list of over 1,000 pages is arranged geographically, first by state, and then by city or town of publication.

Microforms and Audio-Visual Aids

Through the means of microforms, the modern researcher can examine copies of the Bay Psalm Book[3] of 1640, a colonial or modern newspaper, an 1898 educational periodical, rare books in foreign libraries, or a recent doctoral dissertation. The local library may own some microforms and may help patrons obtain copies from other institutions or agencies.

A few guides have been published to help locate microforms. *Newspapers on Microfilm,* Library of Congress, is a source for many foreign and domestic newspapers. *Guide to Microforms in Print,* 1961—, is an annual guide to microforms, except theses and dissertations, that can be obtained from United States publishers. Since 1942, the *Union List of Microfilms* and its later editions and supplements has listed thousands of periodicals and other titles reported by many institutions in the United States and Canada. Since 1953, it has limited coverage to serials other than newspapers. This publication is provided by the Philadelphia Bibliographical Center and the Union Library Catalogue. Any student engaged in research will have occasion to refer to *Dissertation Abstracts* (formerly *Microfilm Abstracts.* 1938–1952) and *Master's Abstracts,* 1962—, which are put out by the University Microfilms, Ann Arbor, Michigan.

Articles concerning audio-visual aids have multiplied rapidly in recent decades. The *Education Index* lists many articles. The H. W. Wilson Company publishes *Filmstrip Guide* and *Educational Film Guide.* Educators Progress Service, Randolph, Wis-

---

3/ The correct title is *The Whole Book of Psalms Faithfully Translated into English Metre.*

consin, puts out *Educators Guide to Free Films; Educators Guide to Free Tapes, Scripts, and Transcriptions;* and *Educators Guide to Free Slide Films.* The National Union Catalog, Library of Congress, now has two parts in special subject areas available: *Motion Pictures and Filmstrips* and *Music and Phonorecords.* An annual *Blue Book of Audio-Visual Materials* presents a list of films, filmstrips, and recordings. It was previously issued separately, but since 1955 it has been a special issue of *Educational Screen.*

Educational Research

An educator cannot engage in research successfully unless he becomes adept at locating theses, dissertations, and the reports of studies that embody the bulk of the work done in his field. One may begin searching for this literature in the previously discussed *Education Index, Encyclopedia of Educational Research, Handbook of Research on Teaching* (Gage), and *Bibliographies and Summaries in Education to July, 1935.* As soon as possible, one should form the habit of examining the following sources regularly.

Review and Abstracting Journals

An educator is usually well acquainted with the general periodicals in his field, but he may need to become more familiar with review and abstracting journals. These journals give brief summaries of research studies reported in a wide variety of periodicals; hence, they are great timesavers. They enable one to keep abreast of the work being done in his own field and also in related fields.

Review journals vary in content. Some give brief summaries of individual studies and others go into greater detail. Some summarize all the work being done in an area rather than individual studies; in addition, they may trace trends, discuss new techniques, point out gaps in research, and present bibliographies. Abstracts of research reports naturally lag considerably behind the original publication of the studies.

The *Review of Educational Research* gives an educator an excellent overview of the work that has been done in the field and helps him keep up with recent developments. In this publication, which has been issued five times a year since 1931, one may find reviews of the following eleven subdivisions of

TELEVISION/EDUCATIONAL
FOR ASTRONAUTICAL FLIGHT
TRAINING 4766
DEPENDING RESPONSES TO, IN
COLLEGE CLASS 4666
EFFECTIVENESS OF 9202
LEARNING BY 9208
PSYCHOLOGY SERIES TN 4802
REPETITION IN, EXACT VS. VARIED
6389
IN SCIENCE, EFFICIENCY OF 9203
SPANISH ACHIEVEMENT, &
VIEWER LOCATION 3135
STUDENT ATTITUDES ON 3141

9202. **Rottman, Leon H., & Kepers, George L.**
(U. Minnesota) **The effectiveness of television
instruction in science.** *New Mexico Society for the
Study of Education educ. Res. Bull.*, 1963, 1–6.—All
9th grade pupils in Albuquerque studied science either
by television (experimental group) or by the regular
way. Analysis of convariance disclosed that the experimental group learned more than the controls as
measured by standardized tests (ITED, 2 and 6).
However, the control groups revealed consistently
more favorable attitudes toward science, the method
of instruction, and the teacher.—*J. G. Cooper.*

Figure 5.7/ Typical entries
in subject index of the *Psychological Abstracts*, 38
(December, 1964) 1269.
(*The American Psycho-
logical Association.*

Figure 5.8/ A typical abstract taken from
Psychological Abstracts, 38 (October,
1964) 1005. (*The American Psychological Association.*)

education: Administration; Curriculum; Educational Measurement; Educational Psychology; Educational Sociology; Guidance and Counseling; Mental and Physical Development;
Language Arts, Fine Arts, Natural Sciences, and Mathematics;
Research Methods; Special Programs; and Teacher Personnel.

Each of these eleven subdivisions is reviewed about every
three years. Curriculum, for example, was reviewed in I:1 (January, 1931); IV:2 (April, 1934); VII:2 (April, 1937); XII:3
(June, 1942); XV:3 (June, 1945); XVIII:3 (June, 1948);
XXI:3 (June, 1951); XXIV:3 (June, 1954); XXVI:2 (April,
1956); XXVII:3 (June, 1957); XXX:3 June, 1960); and
XXXIII:3 (June, 1963). The back page of the *Review of Educational Research* presents a similar list of the recent issues that
have reviewed each of the other subdivisions in the series. The
extensive bibliographies in each issue give the researcher additional leads to literature in the field.

Psychological Abstracts, 1927—, is a bimonthly work which
contains abstracts of articles (see Figure 5.8) appearing in over
530 journals—many of them predominately educational periodicals. In this publication, the sections relating to educational psychology (learning, interests, attitudes, guidance,
measurement, personnel, etc.), developmental psychology
(childhood, adolescence, maturity, old age), and social psychology (cultural relations, social status, communication, etc.) are
of particular interest to educators. The December issue contains
both an author and a subject index (see Figure 5.7) of all articles abstracted during the year. Where the *Education Index* and
Psychological Abstracts cover the same topics, the latter
resource should be checked first because it provides an abstract
that will help the researcher decide whether a given article per-
tains to his problem.

Perhaps there is no better way to become acquainted with

research techniques and progress than by reading several periodicals devoted primarily to abstracts and reviews. In addition to the *Review of Educational Research* and *Psychological Abstracts,* a student may examine the quarterly *Education Abstracts,* which Phi Delta Kappa will probably begin publishing in 1966, and some of the following publications: *Annual Review of Psychology,* 1950—; *Child Development Abstracts and Bibliography,* 1927—; *Dissertation Abstracts,* 1952—; *Education Abstracts* (UNESCO publication, title varies), 1949—; *Psychological Bulletin,* 1904—; *Sociological Abstracts,* 1952—; *Biological Abstracts,* 1926—; *Chemical Abstracts,* 1907—; *Historical Abstracts,* 1775–1945, 1955—; *Mathematical Reviews,* 1940—; and *Nutrition Abstracts and Reviews,* 1931—.

Many other professional periodicals and yearbooks include some reviews of research progress, abstracts of studies, lists of dissertations, statistical information, and scholarly discussions of educational problems in one or all of their issues. Some of the sources that an educator may profitably consult are:

Educational research.
Journal of Educational Research, NEA Research Bulletin, Educational and Psychological Measurement, Journal of Experimental Education, Research Quarterly, Journal of Research in Music Education, American Educational Research Journal, and *Speech Monographs.*
Psychology.
Journal of Educational Psychology, Journal of Psychology, Journal of Social Psychology, and *Journal of Applied Psychology.*
Sociology.
Sociology of Education, American Journal of Sociology, American Sociological Review, Social Forces, and *Sociology and Social Research.*
General and specific fields.
Harvard Educational Review, Educational Record, School Review, Educational Leadership, Teachers College Record, Religious Education, Catholic Educational Review, Journal of Negro Education, Journal of Home Economics, National Business Education Quarterly, Elementary School Journal, Vocational Guidance Quarterly, Journal of Teacher Education, History of Education Quarterly, and *Educational Forum.*

Dissertations and Theses

Theses and dissertations, which embody the bulk of present-day educational research, are usually housed by the institutions that award the authors their advanced degrees. Sometimes these studies are published in whole or in part in educational journals.

Because many graduate studies are never published, a check of the following specialized guides is necessary for a thorough coverage of the research literature.

Bibliographical Guide/ The entry "Dissertations, Academic" in each issue of the *Bibliographic Index* is the most comprehensive listing of sources to theses, dissertations, research in progress, etc.

General Guides/ Doctoral dissertations in all fields, including education, can be found in sources compiled by various agencies. For the period 1912 to 1938, the Library of Congress provided the annual *List of American Doctoral Dissertations* for published studies. From 1933–1934 to 1954–1955, the Association of Research Libraries sponsored the annual *Doctoral Dissertations Accepted by American Universities*. This service was continued by the *Index to American Doctoral Dissertations, 1956—,* which is published as an additional issue of *Dissertation Abstracts*.

The *Index to American Doctoral Dissertations* gives a comprehensive list of the dissertations from a number of universities. Many of these studies are summarized in the monthly *Dissertation Abstracts*. By reading these abstracts, a researcher may often glean enough information to satisfy his needs. Moreover, in this one source, he may quickly scan not only education theses but also those from related fields. If he wants to read a complete study of a dissertation that is presented in *Dissertation Abstracts,* he may purchase a microfilm or Xerox copy from University Microfilms. The order number and price are given in the abstract. In addition to these sources, a researcher may consult various graduate schools' lists and abstracts of their students' dissertations.

Educational Guides/ Lists of studies that are devoted exclusively to educational research are found in *Ten Years of Educational Research, 1918–1927* by Walter S. Monroe. Similar lists were compiled annually by the Office of Education from 1926 to 1940 under the title *Bibliography of Research Studies in Education*. Since 1941, this work has been continued by Phi Delta Kappa under the title *Research Studies in Education*. This series classifies studies by subject fields and now includes dissertations under way as well as those that have been completed. Prior to 1953, educational dissertations under way were published in the January *Journal of Educational Research 1931–1946,* and in the spring issues of *Phi Delta Kappan, 1947–1952.* Master's theses for many institutions are listed in the annual *Master's Theses in Education,* 1951—, now edited by H. M. Silvey.

Special Field Guides/ Most of the departments of the NEA and many educational societies annually or occasionally publish lists of research studies in progress or completed. Dr. T. K. Cureton, for example, compiled "Doctorate Theses Reported by Graduate Departments of Health, Physical Education, and Recreation, 1930–46," for the *Research Quarterly,* March, 1949, and later he prepared a list for master's theses. Yearly supplements by the Research Council of the AAHPER have kept these compilations up-to-date. Walter C. Eells prepared *American Dissertations on Foreign Education* (1884–1958) for the NEA Committee on International Relations. *The Research on Programed Instruction* was published in 1964 by the U.S. Department of Health, Education, and Welfare. The *Journal of Research in Music Education* (Spring, 1964), presented "Doctoral Dissertations in Music and Music Education." Educators may also locate pertinent special field studies in *Speech Monographs, Religious Education, Journal of Home Economics,* and many other professional journals.

Bibliographical and Information-retrieval Systems

Because of the vast quantities of knowledge that are being accumulated, the classical methods of locating information are being supplemented by new techniques. Innovations are now appearing on the educational horizon that record, organize, store, retrieve, and transmit new information more effectively than the traditional procedures. The more highly developed knowledge-storage and knowledge-retrieval systems require that a bibliography, abstract, or entire article be coded so that retrievable words or phrases can be stored on magnetic tape for use by an electronic computer. When a research worker wants to locate abstracts or bibliographical data that are related to a specific problem, he contacts a "documentation center" which locates the pertinent materials quickly and provides copies inexpensively. The development of codes and documentation centers for educational literature is just getting under way. Some less sophisticated information-retrieval systems which index collections up to 10,000 items on IBM, Royal McBee Keysort, or other cards, are being used to locate information in special areas of interest, such as comparative education. Every educator should keep himself informed about the development of retrieval systems and should learn how to use these tools.

Values of Searching the Literature

Mastering the guides to the literature that are presented in this chapter may seem a time-consuming task. But an educator who remains ignorant of these professional tools encounters insurmountable obstacles when he wades into the ever-expanding volume of literature. Skimming a few sources and dismissing the literature search as an unimportant research routine is a form of self-deception that can only lead to failure. Reviewing the literature with a high level of professional skill is a demanding but a rewarding experience that provides the inspiration for undertaking a study and lays a sound foundation for the entire investigation.

Exploring the literature moves the educator to the frontiers of knowledge where he can examine new findings in his field, spot gaps in knowledge, note contradictory findings, and identify needed research. While examining the work of other scholars, he becomes acquainted with methods of attack, facts, concepts, theories, and bibliographies that may prove useful in his own investigation. After examining the strengths and weaknesses of many research reports, he is less likely to produce a shallow and naïve work himself or to plunge into the procedural pitfalls that plagued his predecessors.

6

Library Skills
for Problem
Solving

The number of reading hours and the amount of notes you log do not provide a reliable measuring stick of your problem-solving productivity. Time and motion studies of your work may reveal an enormous waste of effort. Perhaps you are laboring at a low level of efficiency because you have not mastered the library searching, reference reading, and note-taking techniques needed for carrying out an investigation.

Improving Library Searching

Locating the best available sources pertaining to a problem and extracting the essential information from them is of such importance in research that you should make every effort to improve your techniques. The following discussion suggests some worthwhile habits for you to form.

Knowing the Library and Its Regulations/ Before using a new library, familiarize yourself with its layout, facilities, services, and regulations. First, inquire whether there is printed material available to guide you on an orientation tour, and then proceed as follows:

1/

Locate the card catalog, check how it is organized, and find out whether the library classifies books according to the Dewey or the Library of Congress system.

2/

Note the call number symbols under which most books in your field fall, and locate them in the stacks. Browse through the shelves, and familiarize yourself with the nature and number of books available for various areas in your field.

3/

Examine the type and placement of materials in the reference, periodical, reserve book, rare book, and special collection rooms, and discover where most of the government and educational publications are kept.

4/

Locate the microtext readers, picture files, recording library, coin typewriters, and other services.

5/

Procure a copy of the hours and regulations observed in various sections of the library, and plan your work to conform with them.

6/

Acquaint yourself with the procedures for withdrawing books for overnight or extended use, for reserving a book that is now in circulation, and for obtaining back issues of periodicals, interlibrary loans, microfilms, records, or pictures.

Constructing a Guide to the Literature/ The acquisition of a personal library and the construction of tailor-made guides to educational source materials will ease your investigative labors. If you select items discriminatingly and organize them in an orderly fashion—in private files and on bookshelves—you will have a reliable corps of research assistants at your command. Many questions that might cause frustrating delays and repeated trips to the library may be answered quickly if you obtain or construct some of the following guides:

1/

Compile a personal who's who—include names of leaders in your field and note their positions, publications, professional training, special interests, biases, and standing in the professional world.

2/

List the research agencies and the chief collectors of statistics in your field; note the nature and quality of their staffs, work, and facilities; the frequency of their publications and the issuing agencies; and the headings under which indexes and the card catalog list their publications.

3/

Compile a list of libraries, museums, and individuals that have special collections in your field.

4/

Obtain copies of the best bibliographies for your files; list the titles, natures, and locations of others; and note which periodicals regularly, or occasionally, print such lists and the dates of the issues in which they appear.

5/

Keep a list of the best reference books, indexes, handbooks, historical studies, and legal references in your area of specialization.

6/

List the publishers and manufacturers who specialize in books and equipment you may need.

7/

Purchase the more important reference books, textbooks, periodicals, and pamphlets in the field for your personal library. If you intend to make research a lifework, collect the pertinent back issues of outstanding professional periodicals that relate to your work.

8/

List the official names of the leading periodicals, organizations, and government agencies serving the field, and the titles, addresses, and procedures to use when requesting information from them. Note also which periodical indexes cover their publications and under what headings.

9/

Keep a record of the present and previous names of periodicals, organizations, and government agencies and the dates when changes in the names were made. This information is often important, for you do not want to use the present name of an organization when referring to the work it did under another name, or to search for a 1920 publication under its current name which was adopted in 1960, or to become confused when reading because the same organization has had three different names during various stages of its development.

Developing Skill in Heading Searching/ Searching for references in a card catalog or index can be a discouraging experience or an exciting adventure. Is it arduous labor for you to perform the mental gymnastics required to recall topical headings under which materials may be located? If you cannot find a reference listed under the heading Grading, for example, do you give up in disgust, or do you begin to look under topics such as Evaluation, Testing, Marking Systems, Student Achievement, or Report Cards? If associational poverty paralyzes your progress, take some of the following steps to overcome this handicap:

1/

Familiarize yourself with typical headings used in the field: study the indexes of textbooks, card catalogs, *Education Index, Encyclopedia of Educational Research, Review of Educational Research,* and some abstracting journals.

2/

Search for references on a particular topic under synonymous titles or larger-area classifications. Office of Education publications, for example, may be indexed under United States or under Department of Health, Education, and Welfare; aptitude tests under Mental Measurements; and a speech educational association under NEA, Teachers, or Education.

3/

Keep notes concerning commonly experienced classification difficulties to help you eliminate recurring problems. You may note, for example, that government publications are usually indexed under the name of the issuing agency and not the name of the author; older indexes are more apt to use the heading Teacher Training, and the more recent ones, Teacher Education; the *Education Index* does not cover certain periodicals in which you are particularly interested; Federal government documents are listed under the main head United States, and then under the subhead for the issuing department.

4/

Utilize references that give numerous suggested subject headings to help you locate materials. Near the card catalog, some libraries keep a copy of *Subject Headings Used in the Dictionary Catalogs of the Library of Congress,* Marguerite V. Quattlebaum (ed.). The larger cumulations of the *Education Index* give promising headings for the various topics covered. For example, in one two-year cumulative issue under the topic Tests and Scales appears the note "See also" which is followed by approximately 150 cross references. Extensive lists of headings for education are presented by L. Belle Voegelein in *List of Educational Subject Headings,* 1928, and by Clyde Pettus in *Subject Headings in Education: A Systematic List for Use in a Dictionary Catalog,* 1938. A number of professional leaders have also written guides to the literature in their special fields. The Bookwalters, for example, have compiled a suggestive list of headings for materials in the areas of health, physical education, and recreation (2:32–34).

5/

Develop a good "date sense" to aid you in locating materials. Recalling the years in which a subject was of national interest may help you locate more references than looking in current sources or searching blindly in older ones. Articles on teacher shortages, for example, usually appear during inflationary periods; academic freedom was an issue during the era of intensive Communistic investigations; and science education articles peppered periodicals after the Russians launched the Sputnik.

6/

Recognize that styles change in educational terminology, and become familiar with the older as well as the modern terms used in headings. Topics that are now classified under School Health Services, for example, probably would have appeared under Health Inspection earlier in the century; School Desegregation under Civil Rights or Negro; and Exceptional Children under Handicapped, Blind, Deaf, Hard of Hearing, Crippled, Mentally Retarded, Speech Defective, or Gifted Children.

Planning Library Work Procedures/ To avoid frittering away precious time on random reading and source searching, outline your work before going to the library and plan how to accomplish each task most efficiently.

1/

After constructing a work list, keep revising it until the statements pinpoint the precise information to be located. If your note reads "Get some information on teachers' salaries," probe further, asking: What do I want to find out about salaries? How are salary schedules constructed? Do I want up-to-date, last-year, or last-century data? Am I interested in local, state, national, or international salary information? Determining the specific type and amount of data required for your purpose will narrow the search for references, and hence will hasten the location of pertinent materials.

2/

After stating each question as concretely as possible, jot down the best sources to consult and some alternative references to consider if the first choices are unavailable or do not produce answers. Also prepare an alphabetical list of appropriate headings (key words) to look under for each topic. This list will enable you to save time and will reduce the likelihood of overlooking important studies.

3/

After grouping your questions in accordance with areas in the library where answers may be found, schedule the most logical order to follow in pursuing your library work. Give due consideration to the availability of microtext readers and to the accessibility of references, i.e., reserve books in great demand, overnight books, and two-week loan books.

4/

After checking the schedule of library hours, note the peak patronage periods, and then plan to study when there is the least noise and competition for resources and services.

Acquiring Library Work Skills/ What woes an inexperienced scholar can encounter in the library! When entering the building, you may be fired with enthusiasm about a topic. After floundering from one section of the library to the other, you may become mired in unpleasant bogs that dampen your spirits: The books you need are not available. The reserve book room is closed. A call slip is returned because some "insignificant item of information" is lacking. When the books eventually arrive, you do not have enough time left to read them. Tensions mount and fatigue sets in as obstacles keep arising to impede progress. But many of these irritating delays may be avoided if you observe the following practices:

1/

Arrange to spend a block of time in the library that is sufficient to accomplish a specific task. When little time is available, clear up questions that can be answered quickly in references that are readily accessible. The value of budgeting time and work units carefully cannot be overemphasized. The practice increases work productivity and produces a pleasant feeling of satisfactory accomplishment at each library session which heightens one's interest and stimulates further intellectual effort.

2/

Read reserved books first or when they are in least demand and then move on to more accessible materials.

3/

Obtain all references on your list that are located in one part of the library before moving elsewhere.

4/

Copy on a call slip *all* information that the librarian needs to obtain a reference for you. Before closing the periodical index or card catalog, carefully *recheck* and *rectify* any errors or omissions. Such precautions pay dividends. Nothing is more annoying than a prolonged wait at the circulation desk that is rewarded by the return of the call slip rather than the desired publication. If you fail to copy down the volume number of a periodical, the title of a yearbook, or the name of the government issuing agency, or if you spell the author's name Roberts instead of Robbins, you will experience many such disappointments.

5/

Anticipate delays and the possibility that some source materials will not be available. Make out call slips for all or most of the books needed in one session. While waiting to receive the books, have a list of other work to do—perhaps reviewing notes, reading other materials, or checking items in the card catalog, index, encyclopedia, or dictionary.

6/

Send for interlibrary loans and reserve microtext readers when you have sufficient time to use them profitably.

Improving Reading

When locating research problems, reviewing the literature, and selecting investigative procedures, you devote many hours to reading. To keep abreast of the activities in education, you scan the titles of hundreds of the books and articles that appear each year, decide which ones to ignore, which ones to skim, and which ones to read critically. Since a great proportion of your time is spent screening source materials and examining printed pages, you will profit from forming the following habits:

Screening Reading Materials

Prior to writing out a call slip for a book or periodical, squeeze as much information about it as you can from the card catalog, a periodical index, a bibliography, or a book review. Check whether the reference includes maps, tables, illustrations, or a bibliography that may prove helpful. Do not write out a call slip for a reference if the date indicates that it is too old or too recent for your purpose; if the number of pages reveals that the discussion is too comprehensive or too limited to serve your needs; or if the title or subtitle suggests that the reference covers the social aspects of the subject rather than the political information you want. If the periodical, publisher, or author does not have a reputation for maintaining high scholarly standards, refrain from giving the reference further consideration.

After selecting the most promising materials relating to a problem, do not engage immediately in a cover-to-cover, word-at-a-time perusal of the references. If you work customarily in this manner, jar yourself out of this unprofitable habit. No researcher can afford this luxury. Before reading a book or an article, leaf through the pages: obtain a critical bird's eye view of the contents; note the scope, purpose, bias, and distinctive features of the reference as you skim through the preface, foreword, and introduction; and examine the table of contents, figures, bibliography, and appendix. If the reference presents the type of information you are seeking, reexamine the table of contents and the index to locate the particular sections that may be useful to you. Read carefully the topical headlines, lead sentences, and summary paragraphs on these pages. As you read, jot down the numbers of the pages or lines that warrant a more detailed analysis at a later date.

Some novice researchers have a guilt complex about surveying source materials. To them, skimming is a careless work
habit, if not a form of cheating. They are convinced that a
complete, conscientious reading of all references is essential
in research. Careful reading is required, but plodding
purposelessly through every page in a book is a wasteful practice. Page-by-page reading may include much irrelevant material and may leave you in a confused maze of details. A quick
survey of a reference enables you to locate the pertinent passages and provides you with a key for interpreting the entire
discussion. Grasping the meaning of isolated passages is much
easier if you skim through a book or article before reading it
and reexamine the table of contents and topic headings
periodically.

Mastering Reference Utilization Guides

Before using a reference, investigate whether the author or
publisher has included any mechanical aids or special information to help the reader. Seek answers to several questions: Is
the reference organized alphabetically, chronologically, or topi-
cally? Are summary paragraphs provided at the end of the
chapter? Is a table of contents and a subject or author index
provided to facilitate the location of information? Are any
keys, codes, statements of explanation, pages of directions, or
other conventions provided that interpret abbreviations, symbols, and other data in the reference? Are these guides located
on the inside covers, in the introductory pages, at the end of
chapters, in the appendixes, or immediately after the items mentioned in the work? To benefit from the full potential of printed
resources, you must learn how to locate and to use these guides.

Investigating the Scope of References

Have you ever wasted considerable time examining a reference before you discovered that the desired information was
purposely omitted from the work? To avoid such discouraging
experiences, ask pertinent questions about source materials before you use them. Do the authors or editors state the delimita-
tions of the reference in the subtitle, preface, introduction, or
elsewhere? (For example, a book or periodical may state that
it lists printed but not unpublished dissertations, doctoral but
not master's studies, or American but not foreign research reports.) Does the publisher indicate whether the periodical is
indexed in each issue, in an annual issue, or in a standard pe-

riodical index? Does a periodical cover certain features monthly, annually, or at other stated intervals? Does a particular cumulation of the periodical index cover the years in which the desired data will appear? Is the publication issued monthly, annually, or biennially? Are there any supplements that bring a reference up to date? Knowing the scope of the services and information that various resources offer saves precious time and energy when you are searching for answers to questions.

Reading Selectively

Reading only those materials that are pertinent to one's purposes and in proportion to one's needs is a skill the novice must master. Plodding through an entire chapter to find a fact that can be located quickly in an encyclopedia, almanac, or dictionary cannot be justified. You do not have to read an entire biography to find where Horace Mann was born. When making a definitive study of a man or a problem, however, you should expend most of your effort on primary rather than secondary source materials, for reading about a publication is never as satisfactory as reading the work itself. A translation or summary of a book may satisfy your needs in some instances, but a secondary source may contain errors or misinterpretations and may not retain the literary taste and tang of the original version.

Reading simple explanations of topics before tackling more comprehensive discussions may be helpful. To explore a new or difficult topic, procure an encyclopedia or elementary textbook that gives a brief overview of it. If possible, read discussions on the topic in several textbooks, for each one will explain some things more thoroughly or clearly than the others. After acquiring some background knowledges in the field, select more advanced references; elementary textbooks will usually direct you to the better sources.

To initiate an investigation, check recent bibliographies and from them select four or five key references that give a well-rounded overview of the subject. Skim through these sources and note the large natural divisions of the problem. On the basis of this information, construct a crude outline for your investigation and compile a working bibliography that will give a well-balanced coverage for each topic. If you fail to get a picture of the whole problem before studying special aspects of it, you may read volumes on some phases of a subject, ignore other equally important topics, and get bogged down in masses of details. Close scrutiny of detail after detail while reading is of little value if the facts are not fitted into the mosaic of the total problem picture.

Learning to Concentrate

Before beginning to study, select a place and time to read that invites the fewest interruptions and distractions. Approach your work with eager anticipation and give concentrated attention to the specific problem at hand. If getting a brief overview of a book is the objective, devote yourself exclusively to skimming its contents—refrain from reading paragraphs and chapters. When you read a chapter for the first time, concentrate on grasping the author's ideas—do not stop to take detailed notes, do not get sidetracked in any way. A researcher cannot fragmentize his attention and read intelligently. If during the one hour that is available for work, you read, take notes, check questionable points, and look up references the author mentions, you will become irritated with the slowness of your progress and will get a confused concept of the author's ideas. You cannot do everything at once; concentrate on one task at a time.

Checking Comprehension

An intelligent reader makes certain that he is getting the exact meaning that the author is trying to convey. Because of unfamiliar terminology, you may not be able to follow or to understand an author's discussion. As soon as you become confused, begin to construct vocabulary cards or lists and refer to them as you read. On these cards or lists, place the definitions of key terms and the common terms which the author uses in a particular sense.

An experienced reader, like an experienced automobile driver, judges his speed in accordance with the situations he meets. You can skim some materials, but must analyze other passages with great care. Whenever you fail to grasp the meaning of a paragraph, try to locate the difficulty immediately: Is it vocabulary? Did you fail to spot a key transitional sentence or word, the topic sentence, or the author's signal that something was to follow? Did you fail to relate the material to the topic headline or the overall chapter organization? Did the author subsequently modify a definition or statement that he made earlier in the work? Accurately assimilating the author's ideas is vital in investigative work.

Reading Critically

Accepting unquestioningly the words on a printed page is a dangerous practice. Reference materials vary in reliability;

consequently, you must test them. As you read, evaluate critically the merit of each fact, sentence, and argument. Keep asking questions: What does this information contribute to my problem needs? Is this statement true? Does this author agree with other authorities? Did he borrow this idea from someone else? Does this statement contradict what he wrote earlier? Does he use this term in the same sense that Dewey did? From what source did he obtain these statistics? How were they derived? Has he arrived at this conclusion by a sound reasoning process? Do the statements that he presents as supporting evidence justify his conclusions? The more probing and the more pointed these questions are, the more productive your reading sessions will be. Critical analysis rather than passive absorption is required when reading for research purposes.

Developing Sound Study and Health Habits

Chronic fatigue, frequent colds, and other health problems cut down tremendously on your working efficiency. Reading without needed glasses, in insufficient light, and when tired is unproductive. Doing unselective reading and note taking, making more professional and social commitments than you can meet, and loafing until it becomes necessary to plunge into work orgies drain physical reserves and impede an investigation. To achieve success in research, you must schedule sensible working hours; establish timesaving routines; get adequate food, rest, relaxation, and medical attention; and change activities to refresh and to relax your mind and body. These practices will keep you in tip-top physical condition for intensive intellectual effort.

Improving Note Taking

Note taking, like reading, is not an end in itself, but a means of furthering the whole investigative process. Note taking is a servant, not a master; a stimulus to thought, not mere copy work. Taking notes properly keeps you alert mentally—making comparisons, noting discrepancies, seeing relationships, analyzing arguments, and evaluating data. Carefully composed notes enable you to review and to reconsider ideas encountered months previously in light of those read recently.

Critical note taking is an exciting, challenging experience; passive note taking is a monotonous, boring activity. A nonselective, unsystematic method of recording notes usually piles up tangled masses of data that are a greater obstacle than an aid to a researcher who is working on a problem. An effective note-taking system preserves the most significant ideas in a form that facilitates shifting, comparing, grouping, and ordering items. Pertinent, precise, and flexible notes are organized and synthesized into original thought patterns more easily than continuous pages of rambling, jumbled information. Any note-taking system that serves your needs is acceptable, but the following well-tested bibliographical and subject note procedures are worthy of consideration.

Bibliographical Notes

Bibliographical notes are made for several purposes: (1) to have the complete bibliographical information available for each reference that may contribute to an investigation, (2) to facilitate the relocation of a reference in the local library, (3) to preserve a brief record of the general nature and value of a reference, and (4) to have the information necessary for constructing a formal bibliography.

Information on Bibliographical Notes/ A bibliographical note carries all the data necessary for the writer, reader, or librarian to relocate the reference. The following information is the minimum needed for a book bibliographical card: (1) full name of the author (two initials if the first name is not given, or issuing agent if author is not given); (2) full title of the work, underlined;[1] (3) place, publisher, and the publication date of the book; (4) edition if given; (5) the total pages and/or the particular pages used may be included; and in some instances (6) the volume and part numbers may be needed to locate the reference. A bibliographical card for a periodical or newspaper article is somewhat different. It includes (1) the full name of the author; (2) the full title of the article in quotation marks; (3) the name of the publication, underlined; (4) the volume number; (5) date of issue; and (6) the number of the initial page or the range of the pages the article covers.

To help you relocate a reference quickly, place on the front or back of the bibliographical card, but always in the same place and set conspicuously apart from the other information, (1) the library call number; (2) the name of the library, if you patronize more than one; and (3) the room, department, division, or section that houses the work (see Figure 6.1).

1/ In a typewritten manuscript, underlining indicates the material is to be italicized.

```
                                          CuLL  No.
      O. K.

      Brodbeck, May, "The Philosophy of Science and
         Educational Research."

         Review of Educational Research,
         27 (December, 1957): 427.

                                            U. of Pitt.
                                            Educ. Lib.
                                            Section D
```

Figure 6.1/ Front of a bibliography card for a periodical.

After using several references, an investigator may become confused about what information is in the various volumes. Writing brief notes on the back of the bibliographical card concerning the nature, scope, special features, or chief strengths and weaknesses of the book and the page numbers of the most pertinent topics (see Figure 6.2) will help you recall what contributions the reference may make to your study. When compiling an annotated bibliography for the final research report, these notes will provide you with much useful information.

How to Take Notes/ To economize on time and effort, establish efficient bibliographical note-taking habits. Screen references before copying a single item so as to avoid accumulating many useless cards. Refrain from scribbling partial bibliographical in-

```
      Excellent review of literature (1948-1957) on:

         Operationalism          427
         Nomological Network     429
         Causation               433
         Theories                435
         Models                  439

      Gives appropriate examples and implications
         for education.
      Cites pertinent bibliography.
      Points out criticisms of operationalism.
      Draws attention to the form of operational
         definition—conditional or "if-then" sentence.
```

Figure 6.2/ Back of the same bibliography card.

formation on notebook covers, backs of letters, class notes, or any available scrap of paper. Scattered, fragmentary notes that are written on assorted sizes of paper are easy to lose, difficult to relocate and file, and hard to interpret.

Copying each reference in full, once and for all, on a *separate* standardized-size card or sheet of paper is a prudent practice. Cards are more durable and easier to handle, to sort, and to file than lists of sources on sheets of paper. A three- by five-inch card is convenient to carry, but some researchers prefer larger cards. If you keep a few blank cards in your purse or pocket at all times, recopying bibliographical information will not be necessary.

Before compiling your bibliography, investigate the form and content of the entries that you will be required to use in the final report. Different professors, institutions, and publishers establish style standards that vary slightly. If they do not have their own style manual, they require that scholars conform to some other recognized style manual (28, 47, 135).

If you form the habit of recording bibliographical notes in conformity with a recommended style manual, you can type the final bibliography directly from these cards without reorganizing the data. This practice eliminates the tedious task of shifting items on cards and avoids the errors that may creep into a bibliography during the recopying process. Always carry sample style cards for a book, periodical, and newspaper with you and refer to these samples when you write bibliographical notes. To save time and to eliminate errors, you may prefer to purchase printed bibliographical cards or to mimeograph cards that provide blanks for required items.

If you keep a style manual accessible while working, you can check the correct bibliographical form when special problems arise, such as how to write up the entry when an organization is the author; when a pseudonym is used; when a translator or editor is noted; or when the article comes from an encyclopedia, a chapter of a yearbook, or a newspaper. When you do not have a style manual available, copy all the essential information from the reference; reorganize these items in accordance with the approved style before you include them in the formal report.

Before taking a single note from a reference, make out a bibliographical card neatly and legibly in ink. Procure the information for books from the title page rather than from the cover of the book. After completing the task, check carefully whether you have omitted any necessary data—an item, word, letter, punctuation mark, or number—and check the correctness of the spelling, punctuation marks, and call number. When you are finished, make an "OK" notation on the card so that no doubts concerning its accuracy will arise later. The extra minutes expended in recording bibliographical information accurately is time well invested, for careless errors may later cause you to spend hours searching for missing items, recopying cards, and retyping entire bibliographies. Merely omitting the pages covered by an article on an entry may force you to make a special trip to the library, and if the volume is out, a return trip and more wearisome waiting at the circulation desk will be necessary.

How to File Notes/ After collecting a number of bibliographical notes, one must organize them into some meaningful order. An alphabetical arrangement by authors' surnames—or the first important word of the title if there is no author given—proves satisfactory in most studies. Some workers file their bibliographical cards under subject headings and then alphabetize them by authors' surnames. They make out duplicate or cross-reference cards for a work that is used in more than one section of the report, annotating its usefulness for each section. In some studies, researchers classify cards under primary and secondary sources; under types of references, such as books, periodicals, and pamphlets; or under a chronological arrangement. Because elaborate filing systems are cumbersome, experienced writers employ simple systems.

Subject Notes

Subject and bibliographical notes serve different purposes. Each type of note possesses its individual characteristics. From a practical standpoint, mongrel notes (part bibliographical and part subject) are useless. Copying full bibliographical data on each subject note would be excessively time consuming; failing to put full data on mongrel notes would cause difficulties; therefore, keeping the two types of notes separate is advisable.

The information that you record on subject notes depends upon the nature of your problem and your experiential background. During an investigation, you may (1) copy many specific facts from references, such as dates, places, names, statistics, formulas, and definitions, (2) summarize or copy arguments, questions, explanations, illustrations, or descriptions, (3) write comments about your reactions to reference materials, (4) state relationships, conclusions, or interpretations that come to mind during the contemplative phases of your work, and (5) jot down items that require further checking.

Subject notes usually make up the bulk of the notes taken

in any study; they form a reservoir of facts. When writing a report you may draw upon them to (1) support a particular position, (2) illustrate a point of view, (3) make comparisons, (4) weave a web of logical evidence, or (5) buttress arguments by passages from recognized authorities. Discriminatingly selected subject notes provide the building blocks that you need to solve a problem; haphazardly collected notes may cause your investigation to collapse.

Taking Notes after Evaluating Items/ Copying notes about every item that remotely relates to your problem is an unprofitable practice. To avoid wasting time writing, filing, reexamining, and culling many worthless subject cards, form the following habits: Before taking any notes, skim quickly through a few of the best references and record the location of the important facts or passages. If you own the book, underline these items; if not, list the location of them on a card in an abbreviated form, such as 198:2, 4–6 (page 198: paragraph 2, lines 4 to 6). Photocopying some materials may save considerable time. After you have skimmed the references, reevaluate the underlined, listed, or photocopied passages, and copy or paraphrase the most pertinent ones.

Taking Flexible, Durable Notes/ A system of note taking that produces permanent, easy-to-handle notes lessens the labor involved in assembling the final report. Writing notes consecutively in bound books or on pages of paper is an unwise practice, for the items will later have to be relocated, reclassified, and either recopied or indexed elaborately. A note is of the greatest value if it is a complete unit that can be found quickly in a sheaf of notes, traced readily to the original source, and transferred easily from one position in your outline to another.

If each item is placed on a separate card or page, you can run through notes taken from many sources and at different times, slip out those cards that pertain to the same subject, and reorganize them quickly in a logical sequence for your report. When several items of information are placed on one card, problems arise. If the items fall logically into different sections of the report, the process of shuffling cards and ordering them into the proper report sequence is a confusing and arduous task. You may overlook important information that is buried among other data on a card, or you may combine unrelated facts in a report merely because they were on the same card.

Writing Intelligible Notes/ Since smeared penciled notes or illegible pen scratchings that are crammed with complicated abbreviations will impede your progress, always type notes or write them in ink. Make an effort to form each letter and figure perfectly and to use a simple abbreviation system consistently. After taking a note, check to make certain that you or a secretary can decipher each word accurately now and in the future.

Using Uniform-size Note Sheets/ Because assorted shapes of note sheets are clumsy to organize and easy to lose, write all subject notes on paper or cards of the same size. Some workers prefer to use note paper because it is not as bulky as cards, provides more space for writing, and is more convenient to use when typing; others prefer cards because they are more durable and easier to sort and arrange. The nature of the study and the idiosyncrasies of the writer determine what size card or paper is most serviceable. Subject notes may require a larger-size card than bibliographical notes.

Using One Side of Paper/ Writing notes on both sides of a paper is a mistake. If you must flip papers constantly when organizing notes into a logical order, you may become confused and overlook items. Have you ever searched desperately for a note, only to find it much later tucked away on the back of a page you assumed was blank? If an entire note cannot be placed on one side of a page, complete it on a second card. Write "to be continued" on the first card and "continued from card one" on the second card, and staple them together.

Using Topic Headings That Conform with the Report Outline/ To give clues concerning the content of the notes on cards, place suitable topic headings, or slugs, consistently at the top left-hand or right-hand side of the subject cards. If these slugs are the same as the topics and subtopics in your tentative report outline, they will facilitate the locating, sorting, and classifying of the cards and the writing of the report. If you encounter materials in a reference that suggest a new or more effective topic heading, use it and revise your outline accordingly. When you cannot decide where to file a note, study its relationship to the subject and determine whether your outline contains overlapping, vague, or insufficient subject headings. Your initial outline and the headings you assign to topics will not be perfect. You will discover weaknesses in them as you work and ways to improve them.

Noting Location in Reference/ On each subject card place the source from which the information was obtained, either on the

```
Brodbeck, Phil. of Sci.,              Operationalism, Nature of

    Concept formation in science is operational:  The mean-
 ings of terms are not defined by listing the observable attri-
 butes of objects — shape of chair — but by reference to more
 abstract properties — IQ — obtainable by dividing M.A. by
 C.A.  Operationalism holds that concepts derive their mean-
 ings from the techniques employed in observation or investi-
 gation —their operations.  427-428

   *Check: Bridgman, P.W., Logic of Modern Physics for his ex-
 planation.
   **Sometimes called operationism, why?
   ***Does this definition have application to historical research?
```

Figure 6.3/ A summary subject note with comments.

bottom of the card or opposite the topic heading at the top
of the card. Since bibliographical cards carry the complete data
for references, the subject card may merely identify the source
by author, or by author and an abbreviated title, but it must
indicate the exact page or pages from which the note is derived
(see Figure 6.3). Since each footnote in your final report will
have to state the complete bibliographical information for the
reference, forgetting to record the source and page of a note
may cause discouraging delays when you are ready to write
up the study. Days may be spent in obtaining a reference again
and rereading it to locate a quotation—and the search may not
always culminate in success!

Quoting References Properly/ After locating pertinent material
in a reference, you may decide to copy it verbatim, paraphrase
it, or summarize it. Your decision will determine the type and
form of the note you make. Never copy a statement word for
word unless it is especially significant and vitally important to
your study. Enclose a copied statement in quotation marks at
once so that you will not later assume these are your own words
and commit an act of plagiarism unwittingly. Copy quoted passages exactly as they appear in the original. Permit errors to
stand, but call attention to them by adding the notation [sic]
immediately after their occurrence in a passage. If you insert
a word or phrase to clarify a quotation, enclose the addition
in brackets. For example, "A former department head [James
Damber] wrote the report." To inform the reader that words
have been omitted, insert ellipses—three periods with alternat-
ing spaces—for example, "Professor Thomas Wood . . . first
outlined the program in 1910." If you omit something from

the end of a sentence or delete more than one sentence, add an additional period—making four periods in all. After copying a quotation, recheck each word, punctuation mark, and capital letter to make certain that you have not made a mistake or omitted anything.

Learning to Paraphrase/ Refrain from copying pages of direct quotations. Get the full meaning out of the author's ideas, and then paraphrase his ideas into notes that can be woven into the first draft of your report with little or no recasting. Stringing quotations together to form a research report is an indication of sloppy, superficial thinking; such compilations make dull reading and no significant contribution to the advancement of knowledge. A worthwhile report is a product of critical thinking: it presents the investigator's own ideas and is written in his own words. Copying notes verbatim merely postpones the time when you must analyze and synthesize the source materials.

Paraphrasing and summarizing are skills that require practice. Copying phrases, words, or partial sentences usually produces unsatisfactory notes, for after a lapse of time these isolated items may not convey significant meanings and the partial quotes may be mistaken for one's own words or may be easily distorted. You cannot assimilate an author's ideas if you merely copy fragments of his sentences or change a word or two. Assimilation requires effort: you must concentrate on passages until you eliminate unessential details, single out the significant ones, and recast these ideas into sharply coined, original sentences that reproduce the exact intent of the author. A few carefully drafted notes are invaluable; an abundance of inaccurate, ambiguously stated notes is useless.

Recording Reactions to References/ Disturbing doubts and challenging questions may seep into your mind as you read a reference. You may ask: Did the author use primary sources? Is this definition of "hypothesis" different from that given by Professor Jones? Is Galileo not spelled differently in the *Encyclopaedia Britannica?* Are the author's conclusions based on facts? Did he observe these conditions himself? Critical reading will produce many questions such as these. Keeping a record of them and seeking answers to them will prod your investigation toward a successful solution. Personal reactions to reference materials may be written on separate notes or below a summary or quotation note. If you register a personal reaction to a source material directly on a subject note, distinguish your words from those of the author by enclosing them in brackets or by placing an asterisk or some similar symbol beside them (see Figure 6.3).

Recording Temporary Notes/ Brief notes may be made of items that vie for your attention when you are trying to concentrate on something else. While reading, note taking, or engaging in some other pursuit, you may encounter a worthwhile reference, see a desirable method of classifying some facts, question a point, or become concerned about a personal problem. To avoid becoming sidetracked and to prevent worthwhile ideas from escaping you, jot these thoughts down quickly in abbreviated form to preserve them for later consideration. Once recorded, they are less likely to keep intruding on your train of thought and interrupting the work at hand.

Notes of a temporary nature may be listed in a notebook and those of a more permanent nature on cards. Divide your temporary notes into research and personal items. For example, Research: "Good bibliography on Russian education, Staley, p. 322. Check average salary of Russian high school teachers last year. How long did Mr. Sach observe Russian Schools? Did he speak the language?" Personal: "Obtain a copy of *The New York Times*. Ask Professor Jacks for a conference on Thursday. Get stamps." Each day scan these questions and during spare moments try to answer some of them. Set aside definite blocks of time periodically to clear up any unfinished business. When you finish an item, cross it off your list.

Filing Notes/ To prevent materials from getting lost during the collection of data, file your notes regularly in a convenient depository. Use vertical files, letter files, accordian files, work organizers, or large manila folders and a cardboard box of the proper size. To speed the filing of notes and to order them in a manner that will facilitate writing the final report, label the file guide cards with the main topics and subtopics in your report outline. Keep your filing system up to date. If a category that was once important is no longer useful, place the notes under other topics, or place them in an inactive file until the study is completed. When you must add new topics, fit them properly into the organizational scheme of the report.

7

Analysis of
the Problem

An overview of the scientific method of solving a problem was presented in Chapter 2. The next two chapters will present a more detailed consideration of the processes involved in (1) discovering and defining a problem and (2) constructing and testing hypotheses. From previous discussions you will recall that planning an investigation is a fumbling, flexible process: the various steps in problem solving are not necessarily well delineated one from another or taken in successive order.

In the beginning, while groping in the dark, a research worker may follow many false clues, pursue fruitless ideas, collect irrelevant data, and try faulty techniques. During an investigation, he moves back and forth from one problem-solving task to another—searching, evaluating, changing, and clarifying. He tackles a problem like an artist who works constantly on his whole composition rather than first perfecting an eye, then a nose, and then a mouth. Research work is inventive and individualistic rather than mechanical. No two investigators work alike. Research is not a completely haphazard undertaking, however, for all creative work entails necessary disciplines and procedures. Some of the activities that researchers engage in are presented in this chapter to give you a deeper insight into their work.

Development of a Problem

Finding and analyzing a problem is a prerequisite for conducting a research study, but an inexperienced investigator often overlooks this fact. Quite commonly, he has an unrealistic, glamorized conception of his work. The excitement of executing an investigation completely commands his attention and causes him to engage in frenzied activity on the superstructure of the study before he has constructed a firm foundation upon which the investigation can rest. The laborious task of analyzing a problem does not intrigue him; he dreams of playing the starring role in a dramatic experiment that culminates in an earthshaking discovery. In this imaginative drama, he visualizes himself manipulating intriguing technical procedures, complicated questionnaires, electric computers, batteries of tests, or intricate statistics while the public observes with awe and admiration.

A novice investigator is usually as anxious as a child to leap to the answer stage of problem solving. He listens impatiently to advisers who ask: "Have you defined your problem clearly? Do you know what variables are involved? Do you possess the basic skills to conduct the investigation? Have you constructed a sound theoretical framework for this problem?" Without giving these questions serious consideration, the novice plunges headlong into gathering copious notes and setting up an elaborate experiment. Since he is employing sophisticated terminology, statistics, and research procedures, he assumes that the solution to his problem will automatically materialize. But the elation he experiences while conducting this pseudo-scientific experiment is quickly extinguished when critics attack his problem design.

Competent research does not consist in playacting with scientific paraphernalia and techniques to produce a senseless stack of statistics, a grab-bag gathering of facts, and a casual collection of glossy generalizations unsubstantiated by acceptable evidence. Solutions to problems are not produced by toying with laboratory tools. Research tools are means to an end; they must be employed purposefully to be of value; and they cannot be used intelligently unless an investigator knows what problem he is trying to solve. The analysis of the problem—isolating the variables that are involved and their relationships—may consume more time than any other single aspect of an investigator's study. Planning the investigation in advance down to the finest detail is what counts in research; carrying out the plan—making observations and collecting the data—is largely a mechanical process which requires more persistence than profundity.

Identification of a Problem

Locating and analyzing a problem is a crucial step in research, yet many novices grasp at any straw and label it a problem. They spend months or years gathering data that relates to vague topics without ever defining a specific problem. The end result of their furious figuring and fact finding is a formless, frustrating fund of data. Having never decided precisely what to solve, they roam rudderless in a sea of facts with their chartless voyage committed to failure.

Since identifying the exact nature and dimensions of a problem is of major importance in research, an investigator must learn how to recognize and define a problem. How does one locate problems? What conditions give rise to them? John Dewey answered these questions by suggesting that a problem arises out of some felt difficulty. Something puzzles or disturbs an individual; a gnawing dissatisfaction nibbles at his peace of mind until he can locate precisely what is bothering him and find some means of solving it.

Suppose that late at night the sound of rushing water awakens and alarms you. Having been plunged into a problematic situation, you immediately strain to pinpoint the difficulty. Is the water rushing from the eaves? Is the creek flooding? Has a water pipe burst? What is the precise nature of your problem? Not only household but also scientific problems spring from puzzling experiences. A problem materializes when a scholar senses that something is not right or needs further explanation. Perhaps he fails to produce the customary results when carrying out a familiar experiment, finds some facts that do not agree with accepted theories or beliefs, notes that the results of several investigations are contradictory, detects inconsistencies between his observations and those made by other investigators, or observes something he cannot explain. When a scientist has an inkling that something is wrong or needs to be explained, and is anxious to obtain a clearer concept of the factors causing this puzzling or commonplace occurrence, he has established some of the conditions necessary for identifying a problem.

A vague feeling that something is wrong or that some theory is not adequate does not constitute a problem, but these suspicions or doubts indicate an area in which a problem may exist. If a doctor examines a patient with a fever and a rash, he knows that a problem exists. But, before he can cure the patient, he must diagnose the exact nature of the difficulty. If a teacher becomes disturbed about the amount of time correcting test papers consumes, he is aware of a problematic situation but has not identified the specific difficulty. To bring the causes of his problem into clearer focus, he may ask several probing questions. Do I correct tests when I am too tired or experience too many interruptions? Is the form of the test difficult to correct? Would a shorter test serve the purpose equally well? Until the teacher and the doctor locate the key to their difficulties, they cannot solve their problems. Recognizing a general problematic situation provides a starting point for an investigation, but before proceeding too far, one must isolate, sharpen, and clarify the pertinent points that give rise to the problem.

Analysis of a Problem

Problem analysis in research may be quite complex. Perhaps you will gain a better understanding of the procedures involved if you first examine the analysis of a practical classroom problem made by Miss White, an elementary school teacher (132). Her investigation will give you some insight into the inductive and deductive procedures that are employed to identify the factors that give rise to a problem.

Developing an Inquiry from a Felt Difficulty/ Miss White's investigation originates from a felt difficulty—as all problems do. She is dissatisfied with the reading progress of her pupils and wants *to solve the reading retardation problem.* But this initial problem statement is too vague to serve as a guide for formulating a solution. Unless Miss White delimits the inquiry to a more specific situation and probes deeply into it, she may fish facts forever out of the vast reservoirs of reading data. In desperation, she may blindly accept a superficial generalization or a personally favored explanation for reading retardation without analyzing whether these facts and explanations are biased or are related to the difficulties of her particular pupils. Miss White cannot profitably search for a solution until she identifies the dimensions and clarifies the nature of the problem.

Collecting Information That May Relate to the Problem/ To help her locate the specific factors that gave rise to the difficulty, Miss White compiles a list of (1) known and suspected factual items of information and (2) possible explanations that may have a bearing on the problem:

Number of retarded readers	Size of textbook print
Sex of retarded readers	Amount of vocabulary drill
Speed of reading	Phonics background
Comprehension	Enunciation of teacher
Hour of day that class is taught	Classroom noise

Intelligence of students
Time devoted to reading
Foreign language spoken exclusively at home
Broken or unhappy home conditions
Children's experiential background
Attitude of parents toward reading development of their children

Dietary problems
Hearing impairment
Visual impairment
Lack of sleep
Class too large for effective instruction
Class too heterogeneous for effective instruction
Textbook materials not sufficiently varied to meet different interests

The more known and suspected facts and possible explanations that Miss White can think of, the better are the chances that she will locate the causes of the children's reading difficulty. Undue haste in analyzing a problem may impair the entire investigation. Crude guesswork produces answers quickly, but the answers seldom lead to successful solutions even though the most sophisticated methods are employed in executing the subsequent phases of the investigation. No magic elixir can quicken the process of analyzing a problem. Teasing out the relevant variables and their relationships requires painstaking care and thought. Probing into the simplest educational problem usually reveals that the phenomena are enormously complex. Obtaining a picture of all of the factors involved consumes considerable time—but unless this work is done the problem cannot be solved.

Deriving Meanings from the Information/ To squeeze as much meaning as possible out of the listed constituents of the problem, Miss White looks for relationships between facts and facts, explanations and explanations, and facts and explanations. She may inquire whether a relationship exists among hearing impairment, classroom noise, and the teacher's poor enunciation that reveals a key to the difficulty. Facts and explanations that first come to mind may yield more precise knowledge of the difficulty if she probes them for more detailed information. Upon becoming suspicious that a dietary problem exists, for example, she may ask: Is the real cause a lack of a balanced diet, conditions under which meals are eaten, or improper preparation of the food? Is there empirical evidence available to confirm that a relationship exists between the nature of the breakfast consumed by children and their work capacity?

As she digs more deeply into the problem, Miss White may discover that conditions that first appeared to be important causes of the difficulty are not the specific factors responsible. If the class is taught late in the morning, she may begin to question whether the late hour or some associated factor is responsible for the reading retardation. She may wonder whether the children are restless and uninterested because they do not get enough sleep, do not eat breakfast, or are distracted by the school band which practices outside the classroom during that period. Factors that may seem most important when the analysis first gets under way may merely be clues that lead to the real causes of the difficulty.

Searching for Facts to Clarify the Problem/ After listing the items she thinks might be relevant to the problem and trying to see relationships among them, Miss White searches for facts to determine whether these items are relevant to her problem; whether there are flaws in her reasoning regarding the nature of the problem; and whether there are additional facts, explanations, or relationships that play a determinate role in the reading retardation of her pupils. To obtain the required facts, she observes her pupils while they are reading, studying, and playing; checks their health records, intelligence tests, and reading tests; and studies the information volunteered by pupils, parents, other teachers, and the school nurse. To learn what variables other scholars have found to be related to reading retardation, she examines professional literature and research studies.

Examining Assumptions Underlying the Suggested Constituents/
After Miss White adds new clues to her list of constituent elements and eliminates those items that appear to be irrelevant, she makes a thorough examination of the assumptions underlying the remaining facts, explanations, and relations. Has she jumped to any faulty conclusions? Have preconceived notions, hidden beliefs, or false basic assumptions caused her to ignore the real source of the problem? Is she about to travel down a dead-end alley for a solution? If certain methods of teaching or grouping students seem to account for the reading-retardation problem, and adopting alternative methods seems to be a logical solution, she rigorously examines these assumptions: Will vocabulary practice sessions improve reading progress? What kind of practice? How often? How much? Can such practice have adverse effects? Does homogeneous grouping of pupils guarantee greater reading progress than heterogeneous grouping? Is reading retardation associated with the sex, race, or socioeconomic status of pupils? What evidence have researchers produced to support these contentions? Have they found evidence to disprove them? The assumptions underlying Miss White's suggested constituent elements of the problem may be sound, but she must examine them carefully and assemble

evidence to support them before proceeding too far with the investigation.

Delineating the Dimensions of the Problem/ As a result of her investigation, Miss White discovers that ten boys and two girls are not making satisfactory progress. They miss basic sight words, stumble over easy words, call "wrong" words, attack unfamiliar words without confidence, and read word by word; they ignore thought sequences, picture and context clues, and punctuation. They exhibit an indifference toward reading, daydream, or engage in disruptive activities during reading periods. When someone reads to them their comprehension is much better than when they read to themselves. Most of the children come from modest homes in which English is spoken; only two of them have divorced parents. The pupils have little reading material in their homes and they have not had varied or extensive home, community, travel, and educational experiences. Although some of the students are shy, none of them gives evidence of being emotionally disturbed. In mental ability they range from an IQ of 82 to one of 129.

This detailed analysis gives Miss White a clearer picture of the problematic situation. When she discovers that only twelve of the thirty pupils are retarded readers, she can limit further study to them. When facts reveal that some of her "guessed-at" explanations for unsatisfactory reading progress—mental, emotional, and visual conditions—are not the causes of the difficulty, she can eliminate these irrelevant items from the investigation. Through the prolonged process of listing possible constituents of the problem, collecting reliable information that justifies eliminating or adding items, and continuing to trace the relationships among the remaining items, Miss White brings her problem into clearer and clearer focus. In the beginning she asked a rather vague question: Why aren't my pupils making more satisfactory progress in reading? When she concluded her analysis, she asked a more specific question: Are twelve children in my class retarded in reading because they lack varied sensory and oral experiences to help them associate printed symbols with words and ideas?

Summarizing Problem-analysis Procedures/ The preceding discussion reveals that an investigator engages in many activities when analyzing a problematic situation. The following list summarizes these tasks:

1/
Accumulating the facts that might be related to the problem.

2/

Settling by observation whether the facts are relevant.

3/

Tracing any relationships between facts that might reveal the key to the difficulty.

4/

Proposing various explanations (hypotheses) for the cause of the difficulty.

5/

Ascertaining through observation and analysis whether they are relevant to the problem.

6/

Tracing relationships between explanations that may give an insight into the problem solution.

7/

Tracing relationships between facts and explanations.

8/

Questioning assumptions underlying the analysis of the problem (see Figure 7.1).

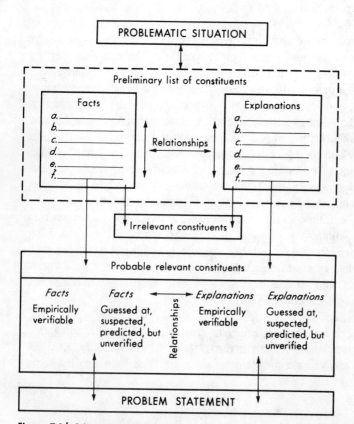

Figure 7.1/ Schematic analysis of a problem.

This painstaking probe eliminates irrelevant ideas and forces into view the pertinent facts and explanations involved in the difficulty.

Examples of Problem Analysis

Two problems that were undertaken by experienced investigators may give you a clearer comprehension of the problem-identification and problem-analysis aspects of research work.

Definition of Force

Several centuries ago, Galileo observed a phenomenon that did not seem to conform to the accepted theories of his time. When shooting off a projectile, he noticed that its movement did not conform to Aristotle's explanation of motion. By mentally mulling over this projectile phenomenon, Galileo sought to put his finger on the source of the difficulty. He examined the traditional assumptions about what causes motion and finally decided that the difficulty was not located in the flight of the projectile, but rather in Aristotle's definition of force. Having somewhat identified the nature of the problem, he did no further fact collecting about the projectile but concentrated his attention instead on the definition of force.

According to Aristotle, force is that which produces movement; it follows, then, that when force ceases to act on a body, the body will stop moving. Aristotle's definition gives a reasonable explanation of force that holds true in most instances. If you push a box, it moves; when you stop pushing a box, it stops moving. In case of the projectile, however, the force stops acting the moment the explosion takes place, but the projectile continues to move for some time and distance after the explosion. As Galileo discovered, the projectile phenomenon contradicts Aristotle's definition.

Having identified his difficulty as a need for an all-embracing definition of force, Galileo began to search for the facts required to construct a new definition. To analyze the problem, he selected the most elementary example of a force acting on a moving object he could—a ball falling freely under the force of gravitation. While closely observing the ball fall to the floor, he tried to determine what factors might be involved in the relationship between force and motion. Some scientists had concluded previously that temperature, smell, color, and shape of bodies were irrelevant to the problem. The ancient scientists had also assumed that distance and duration of the fall were irrelevant. But Galileo's mathematical, physical, and philosophical background, and his familiarity with the works of certain contemporaries and predecessors, caused him to reject the latter assumption.

After making observations, collecting facts, recalling previous experiences, reviewing scholarly studies, and searching for the relationships that might be involved in the difficulty, Galileo concluded that there were three factors upon which the fall might depend: (1) the weight of the object, (2) the distance it traveled, and (3) the time required for the fall. His extensive analysis of the problem had enabled him to locate and describe the precise factors that had to be investigated before an acceptable definition of force could be formulated. The next chapter will reveal how Galileo tested each of these factors so as to arrive at an adequate explanation of force.

Assessment of Teacher Effectiveness

Skipping a few centuries, let us turn our attention to a recent analysis of an educational problem (94). The investigator was disturbed about a long-standing educational problem—how to determine the effectiveness of teachers and to predict the degree of success a potential teacher will achieve in a classroom. Before reading further, jot down some of the factors that you think may contribute to teacher effectiveness, and try to trace the relationships among these factors. After you have explored this problem for a short time, you may have a greater appreciation of the effort that the investigator expended when he analyzed the problem. He decided that four major factors were involved in teacher effectiveness. To bring these four types of variables and their interrelationships into clear focus, he constructed a paradigm or model (see Figure 7.2). Study this paradigm as you read the following explanation of it.

Type I variables are composed of an almost inexhaustible number of human characteristics [personality and training factors] on which teachers differ and which can be hypothesized to account, in part, for differences in teacher effectiveness. Ideally some Type I variables ought to be estimated before young people begin training as teachers, others by their very nature must be deferred until training is underway or completed.

Type II variables are contingency factors [school environment and pupil variables] which modify and influence the whole complex of behaviors that enter into the educational process. If Type II variables play a commanding role in the achievement of educational objectives, then we will be required to replicate studies of teacher

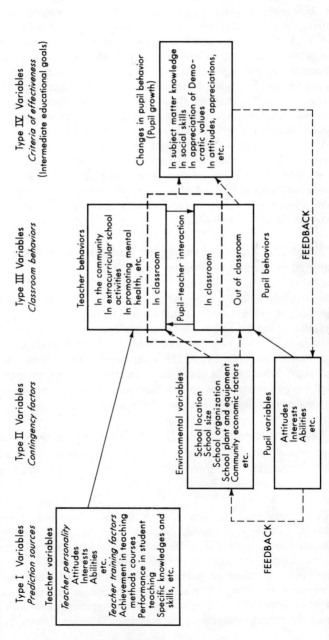

Figure 7.2/ Generalized schema for research in teacher effectiveness.

effectiveness in a great many different situations, and predictions of teacher success from Type I variables will have to be contingent upon Type II variables. Some Type II environmental variables are undoubtedly inaccessible to measurement and to manipulation; these must be controlled or their effects minimized by appropriate experimental designs.

Type III variables, or behaviors [teacher-pupil behavior] . . . are of crucial significance in the process of assessing effective teaching. The classroom provides the focal point wherein the personality and training of the teacher are translated into actions. Likewise school and background influences on pupils determine in part pupils' classroom behavior. It is primarily out of the interaction of these elements that we expect educational goals to be attained. Or, as Ryans has indicated, the behavior of the teacher that ought to be studied is social behavior. Considering that classroom behaviors bear such heavy responsibilities in determining educational outcomes, remarkably little is known about them or their effects.

Type IV variables [pupil growth] are the criteria or standards against which the whole of educational effort must be judged. We have subtitled them intermediate educational goals, meaning measurable outcomes at the end of a period of instruction to distinguish them from the ultimate criterion which might be phrased as "a better world in which to live."

The interrelationships among the four types of variables are indicated by connecting lines on Figure 7.2.

In general, solid lines are indicative of direct effects and dotted lines suggest indirect or tangential effects. In such a scheme teacher variables (Type I) and pupil variables (Type II) are direct determinants of teacher behavior and pupil behavior respectively. Environmental variables (Type II) indirectly influence both teacher and pupil behaviors. In the view presented here the complex of pupil-teacher interactions in the classroom is the primary source to which one must look to account for pupil growth.

The investigator in this study (94) also explored the assumptions underlying his conceptual assessment scheme of teacher effectiveness. He recognized that it rested upon at least two fundamental assumptions.

First, there must be some stability in human personality which exerts a consistent governing or modifying effect on a teacher's behavior in the classroom. If the behaviors of a teacher are wholly, or even largely, determined by the environmental and pupil variables operating at any given time, then prediction of behavior seems foredoomed to failure. The second assumption is that the teacher (or more precisely, the teacher's behavior) as contrasted with the home, the school equipment, the principal, or other factors, is the primary causative factor in accounting for pupil growth toward the goals of the school. It is on this premise that the whole structure of professional education of teachers is based. Intuitively, we tend to feel that teachers are important, even though we do not yet possess the evidence to show what it is about their behavior that is crucial to children's learning.

The general conceptual framework presented in Figure 7.2, delineating the factors involved in teaching effectiveness, evolved out of a thorough analysis of the problem. By searching for facts and explanations relating to teacher effectiveness, and by tracing their relationships, the investigator brought the relevant factors into focus. By constructing the paradigm, he placed this information into meaningful relationships that presented a unified picture of the problem in all of its dimensions. The paradigm provided a useful backdrop against which many investigations could be projected.

Observe, for example, how the paradigm guided the investigator in conducting a longitudinal study beginning with the 1953–1954 class of student teachers in the municipal colleges in New York City. He explained the project as follows:

Of these approximately 1,800 young persons, biographical and test data were initially obtained from about 1,600 of them. In order to study their persistence in teaching we have maintained correspondence with more than 90% of these teacher education graduates. To be able to assess their effectiveness as teachers from the basic group, we chose a sample of 75 who had accepted their first-year positions in the New York City public schools, teaching grades three through six. . . .

During October and November the pupils in 56 teachers' classes were tested with a reading test, an arithmetic test, a group-solving test, and a test of mental ability for a control variable. During the early spring months of the school year six observers working in teams each made two half-hour visits in the classrooms of these beginning teachers. Thus a total of 588 half-hour classroom visitations were made to observe the teacher and pupil behaviors occurring in the classrooms. . . . A carefully designed objective observation schedule . . . was employed by the observers to record classroom behaviors. This schedule was constructed after a review of the papers by Cornell on measurement of individualities of schools and classrooms, by Withall on social-emotional climate and by Harold Anderson on dominative and integrative behavior of kindergarten teachers. . . .

During the months of April and May of 1955, 904 pupils were retested with equivalent forms of the achievement instruments used in the previous fall. With these procedures we laid the basis for the development of pupil growth criteria in reading ability, in arithmetic skills, and in group problem-solving ability. Two less crucial criterion variables, a measure of teacher-pupil rapport and a measure of classroom disorder, were obtained from a 47-item pupil reaction inventory given to the youngsters and entitled *My Class*. Gross controls on mental ability levels and school effects were provided in the design. Furthermore, we obtained detailed classroom behavior records for 49 teachers which are being analyzed and combined into meaningful descriptive dimensions (94).

This briefly sketched description of an investigation gives you some insight into the value of exploring the factors involved in a problematic situation before trying to define and delimit a particular problem for investigation. It reveals how a general problem analysis aids in locating potential problems and in determining what information to search for when conducting the study.

Description and Statement of the Problem

The first draft of a problem statement may be revised several times during the analysis of a problem. While searching the literature, conducting a pilot study, or utilizing models to refine his thinking, a researcher often gains insights into phenomena that make him dissatisfied with his problem statement and motivate him to reformulate it. The problem statement that a researcher places in his final report is rarely the same one he formulated originally.

Limiting the Scope of the Investigation

If a researcher describes a problem and narrows its boundaries before his imagination has had an ample opportunity to view it from varied vistas, he may overlook the most promising approach to it. But he must eventually trim his investigation to a manageable size which may be difficult. Having experienced a felt difficulty about the "world situation," classroom discipline, children's attitudes, or religious education, a student may think that he has located a problem. But he may collect data on these broad subjects for years without unearthing all the relevant materials. If he investigates religious education, he will accumulate unmanageable mounds of information about the training of infants, adolescents, and adults among Jews, Christians, Mohammedans, ancient Romans, and modern suburbanites. Where does he stop? This grandiose religious problem and its multiplicity of variables will keep him engaged in an interminable investigation that never will arrive at a solution. If he delimits his study, however, to an investigation of the religious education programs provided for teen-age youths by Ohio Methodist churches since 1900, and explores this segment of phenomena, he may be able to formulate and answer a specific question regarding it.

To trim an investigation to a manageable size, the original question that is raised may be broken down into various subquestions. If the researcher raises a question concerning the effectiveness of programmed learning, subquestions may be raised concerning the effect of this teaching tool on academic achievement, attitudes of students, staff morale, etc. Sometimes two or more subquestions are incorporated in one study, but because of time, cost, or other considerations a researcher may have to reduce the scope of his investigation. The subquestions of the original question may provide the basis for separate studies. Perhaps several studies will have to be conducted to answer the original generalized question.

Specifying the Nature of the Problem

Problems may be expressed in the form of questions or in the form of statements. The hypothesis, which is discussed in the following chapter, is one of the most useful tools to use in expressing problems. Regardless of the form in which a problem is cast, the objective is to present the exact dimensions of the problem in a concrete and explicit statement.

When the investigator describes his problem, he presents the background of the study, the theories on which it is based (see Appendix I), and the assumptions underlying the statement of the problem. He stipulates specifically what persons, materials, situations, factors, and causes will and will not be considered. An adequate statement of the problem encompasses the sum total of all the facts, relations, and explanations that the analysis of the problem indicated were relevant. These factors are not listed in an encyclopedic fashion; they are placed in relationship to one another. They are framed in a descriptive statement or question which clearly indicates what information the investigator must obtain to solve the problem.

Defining the Terms

A vaguely or ambiguously stated problem confuses the investigator rather than guiding him to the sources of information

necessary for its solution. When constructing a problem statement, therefore, he tries to clarify precisely what phenomenon
is being considered and to evaluate whether each term and symbol will call up the same core of meaning to all competent
workers in the field. If a word fails to meet this requirement,
he substitutes a more specific term—one that relates directly
to an observable event—or retains the word and adds a definition that will convey the same idea to everyone. When writing
up his research report, he includes the definition of this term
as well as the statement of the problem.

Definition by Example/ Various kinds of definition are possible.
Examples are useful means of connecting words with the concrete world. Definition by demonstration is the most direct route
of closing the gap between a symbol and a sensory experience.
To define the term "teaching machine" by demonstration, one
would point to the object or introduce a specimen of it. In
many instances, however, the phenomenon that one wishes to
define may not be readily available or may be more abstract
than a simple object to which one can point. An educator cannot define "IQ," "self-concept," or "mechanical ability," for example, by pointing to something.

Instead of demonstrating by pointing to an object, one may
try to bring it to mind by a number of illustrative instances.
To describe audio-visual aids, for example, one may state that
they are teaching tools, such as movies, slides, maps, charts,
etc. This denotative type of definition may make the meaning
of terms clear, but unless all instances are enumerated, the
boundaries of the definition are ambiguous.

Definition by Genus and Differentia/ A definition is adequate
if it states enough essential characteristics so that through them
the term in question is clearly related to the intended referent
and distinguished from all other referents. Stating the "essence
of a thing" can be done by indicating its *genus,* the larger class
of things in which the referent is included, and then by indicating how it differs from other subclasses of the same genus. To
define "full professor," one moves up first to the next larger
class, teacher, and then states the essential *differentia* to eliminate all teachers who are not full professors. One might state,
for example, that "full professors" are teachers of the highest
academic rank in institutions of higher education. This definition distinguishes full professors from teachers of lower rank
in institutions of higher learning and from teachers in secondary

schools and other institutions. Definition by genus and differentia is especially useful in areas where phenomena have been structurally classified and a number of large-class terms have been established whose meanings are not in serious dispute.

Definition by Stipulation/ Sometimes a researcher wishes to convey an idea to others and finds no established way of expressing it. In such instances, he may coin a term, such as "social distance," "self-concept," etc., and stipulate the sense in which he proposes to use it. In one study (53), for example, the investigators classified the elements which appear to be related to all human movement as structural, perceptual, and conceptual. They invented three words to use when referring to these general aspects of human movement by combining the root of the Greek word *kinein* (to move) with the general word forms. The three words they formulated—kinestruct, kinescept, and kinesymbol—were then defined. "Kinestruct," for example, was defined as "a dynamic somatic form constructed by body masses in motion."

An investigator soon discovers that commonplace words can cause as much confusion as coined, figurative, or unusual ones. Educational terms such as "student" and "school day" are not unfamiliar, but what do they mean? Does a school day begin when the building is unlocked, when the first child or teacher arrives, or when the first class starts? Does the word "student" in the study refer to a nondegree, a degree, a full-time, or a graduate student? The simpler a term is, the more meanings it may have acquired; consequently, the greater may be the need for defining it. When a researcher uses a word that is familiar but whose meaning is not a matter of universal agreement, he stipulates the sense in which he will use it. He may state, for example, that in his study "junior high school" refers to grades seven and eight or that "unemployed youth" refers to a person between the ages of eighteen and twenty-five years of age who is out of work, able to work, and wants to find work. One must always be on guard when reading and comparing research reports, for the findings may be based on familiar terms that different researchers have defined differently.

Definition by Operational Analysis/ To make the observational basis of terms that are employed in the study as explicit as possible, a researcher must specify the empirical referent for his terms. Operational definitions attempt to achieve this objective by providing a set of instructions regarding the operations—the manipulations and observations—necessary to produce the phenomenon. In a child development study, for example, the investigator may define "chest girth" by specifying the kind of apparatus needed, describing the manner in which to use it, locating the body landmarks for measurement, and indicating how (preferably in what units) the phenomenon is measured.

Many phenomena in education are not directly observable, but rather are inferred from behavior. Anxiety, motivation, frustration, and knowledge are constructs that have been created to stand for something that we presume to be inside the child. They are not "realities." We cannot point to them. Only through logical arguments can we tie such presumed phenomena to empirical referents. To make his logical arguments clear, a researcher may stipulate precisely how and what he will measure to make inferences about the presumed characteristics. He may say, "When I am talking about arithmetic achievement, I am talking about something that is produced by administering and scoring standardized test X according to the directions specified by the test constructors, and by noting the results." In order to be quite clear about what he means by the word "prejudice," or "conservative," he may state that a person is prejudiced, or conservative, if he gives a certain pattern of responses to a given battery of questions.

Since different operations may measure similar concepts, but not necessarily the same concepts, considerable stress has been placed on defining terms in this way. When an investigator defines the terms he employs by describing precisely how the phenomenon is measured, the following objectives are accomplished: The gap between the term and the experience of direct observation is closed; the phenomenon can be agreed upon and reproduced by others; and the possibility of cumulative research is facilitated.

Aids in Locating and Analyzing Problems

Problems spring from felt difficulties, but one cannot expect to remain idle and aloof waiting for a formal introduction to a difficulty. An impoverished intellect has little opportunity to meet or to recognize difficulties. Problem ideas do not germinate in barren brains but rather in minds enriched by varied experiences and fertile layers of knowledge. Reading extensively in educational and scientific publications will help you prepare an intellectual soil in which ideas are likely to sprout.

Steeping Yourself in the Literature

When searching for a problem, explore the literature in a particular area of interest, construct an overview of the theories[1] that have been developed by others, and examine studies that have been designed to test various aspects of these theories. You may be able to make deductions from these theories that can be tested in respect to phenomena in your field. Fine (56), for example, examined Eysenck's theory concerning the introversion-extroversion dimensions of personality. Fine decided to test the hypothesis that extroverts would have more automobile accidents and traffic violations than introverts.

While studying the theories regarding particular phenomena, you may note weaknesses, inconsistencies, or gaps in knowledge that point to problem possibilities. When Gross and his co-workers (66) were investigating the role of school superintendents, for example, they noted that other scholars ignored the question of the sources of role expectations. In their studies, they employed the concept of role consensus as a variable and developed other concepts to bridge a gap in theory. When Stogdill (131) developed his input-output "middle-range theory" of administration, he felt that previous theories had ignored such factors as group purposes and norms, expectations as an input variable, and group achievement.

If you obtain an extensive background in a special field, you may challenge existing theories. Ausubel (6), for example, challenged the assumption that tension and emotional disturbances must result from sex repression, as Dollard and Miller's aggression-frustration hypothesis and Freud's theory of repression suggest. If you begin to question the basis on which an existing theory has been conceptualized, you may be able to construct a new theory. To develop a group of interrelated hypotheses that would account for delinquent gangs in our society, for example, Cohen (31) drew on his own experience with such gangs, prior research on delinquency, and psychological and sociological theories. His theory suggests that investigators need to collect data in a different manner than has been done in the past and that different kinds of information should be sought. Researchers may use his theory not only to study juve-

1/ You may be able to locate a book or article that discusses theories that relate to phenomena that interest you. For example, Muuss in *Theories of Adolescence* (96) presents an overview of existing theories concerning adolescence and summarizes the contemporary issues; Filby (55) in "Teaching Machines: A Review of Theory and Research," presents empirical principles from learning theories that are applicable to automated teaching.

nile gangs but also to gain a better understanding of other sub-cultures, such as fraternities.

Contradictory findings that are reported in the literature may alert you to the existence of a problem. If three men study the effect that teachers' praise has on students' achievement and their reports present conflicting results, you may question whether an uncontrolled extraneous factor is producing the difference in the results. You may wonder whether different types of students were used in the studies and may decide to investigate whether pupils who differ in intelligence, socioeconomic status, or other factors react differently to praise.

Promising problem seeds lie dormant in professional periodicals awaiting your discovery. You should form the habit of scanning pertinent research literature (see pages 93 to 97). These publications directly or indirectly point to unsolved problems in (1) reports of current research, (2) articles that discuss or question assumptions, procedures, techniques, and generalizations commonly accepted in the field, and (3) surveys that summarize the frequency of investigation in various areas, thereby indicating where gaps exist and further research is needed. In one source, for example, Martin Trow suggests that, "For all that has been said about the supposed advantages of one counseling program or another, very little is really known about the effects of various counseling programs on the careers of students" (40:258). Trow also suggests that there is a need for research in the areas of teacher recruitment and retention, the cultural climate of schools, and policies concerning the choices of majors by college students.

Doctoral dissertations and technical papers published by workers in education and allied fields—particularly the concluding paragraphs of such studies—may provide you with suggestions for follow-up studies. After reading them, you may undertake similar studies to challenge, to verify, or to extend the findings reported. A familiarity with the periodic bibliographies, interpretative summaries, and critical reviews of research will also help you locate problems in the field.[2] In *Self-concept*, for example, Wylie (147) makes an exhaustive and scholarly re-

2/ Doris V. Gunderson, *Research in Reading Readiness*, bulletin 1964, no. 81. Washington, D.C.: U.S. Department of Health, Education, and Welfare, 1964.

Erwin R. Steinberg, *Needed Research in the Teaching of English*, Cooperative Research Monograph, no. 11. Washington, D.C.: U.S. Department of Health, Education, and Welfare, 1963.

Children's Bureau, *Research Relating to Children*. Washington, D.C.: U.S. Department of Health, Education, and Welfare, published periodically since 1950.

view of research on the self-concept. Sweitzer (40:199) assesses two theories of administration in one article and suggests questions raised by these theories that can keep researchers busy for years. In *New Teaching Aids* (113) several authorities discuss the state of research in instructional television and tutorial machines and suggest areas of needed research.

Exposing Yourself to Professional Stimulation

Placing yourself in a dynamic research environment increases your opportunities for finding and solving problems. Spirited intellectual intercourse in which ideas are presented, explained, analyzed, and challenged is a rich source of inspiration. Graduate courses, seminars, professional meetings—particularly those in which papers are read and criticized—conferences with stimulating professors, lectures by eminent men in education, "gabfests" with fellow research workers, visits to laboratories, and part-time jobs in research centers often give birth to ideas worthy of investigation or provide clues needed for the solution of problems. Engaging in research produces many ideas, for one investigation usually points up other problems that need to be solved.

Examining Everyday Experiences

Since all problems spring from life situations, a practitioner in the field of education is in a favorable position to locate problems. Every day you encounter difficulties with students, equipment, tests, textbooks, guidance, discipline, parents, curriculum, supervision, or administration. If you are a superintendent, you may wonder whether the chain-of-command organization is the best type of administrative structure. If you are a supervisor, you may wonder whether the traits approach in studying success in teaching is the best approach. If you are a teacher of exceptional children, you may wonder whether it is disadvantageous for deaf children to learn to communicate manually (sign language) before they are taught to communicate orally. Throughout your career, you will experience dissatisfaction with some conditions—wonder how or why they developed—and will notice things or relationships for which you know of no satisfactory explanation. Seize upon these felt difficulties and explore them thoroughly; discover whether they have been or can be solved. An alert mind, sensitively studying classroom situations, serves as an excellent detector of research problems.

Keeping Notes

Keeping systematic notes prior to and throughout an investigation stimulates critical thinking and leads to the discovery of new ideas. Flashes of insight that identify problems or that marshal facts concerning a problem into a logical chain of evidence may come to you at any time. Fruitful ideas may snap into focus when you are deliberately trying to put tangled thoughts into some meaningful order, or they may pop up unexpectedly while you are talking with friends, listening to a lecture, teaching a class, reading a book, or relaxing at home. These mercurial ideas may produce crucial clues that at the moment appear to be crystal clear and too important to forget. Weeks may pass before you want to use them in your investigation, however, and by that time they may have escaped your memory. When a kernel of thought first sprouts in your mind, jot it down immediately and indicate what implications it has for your investigation.

Adopting a Critical Outlook

Problems are neither discovered nor solved by complacent educators who are habitually subservient to traditional authority, smugly satisfied with the *status quo,* or perpetually parroting pedagogical jargon. Knowledge is advanced by creative minds filled with curiosity. A research worker cannot afford the comforts of conformity. You must experience the difficulties and delights of challenging existing theories and practices. While reading, conversing, teaching, observing, and attending classes, seminars, and professional meetings, you must adopt a critical attitude toward the information, generalizations, assumptions, and procedures you encounter. Question them; challenge their validity; look for deficiencies and contradictions; maintain a healthy skepticism. Keep asking questions: Is it true? Did the investigator interpret the results of the experiment accurately? Is there a better explanation for this phenomenon? Follow Francis Bacon's advice: "Read not to contradict and confute, nor to believe and take for granted . . . but to weigh and consider."

Evaluation of a Problem

When you first become aware of a problematic situation, begin to evaluate whether investigating it will be feasible and worthwhile. Whenever you encounter evidence that indicates expending further effort would be imprudent, either drop the problem or refashion it into a more acceptable form. Delaying this evaluation process too long or terminating it too soon may cause you to waste months of valuable time conducting a useless investigation or one that you cannot complete.

A thorough evaluation of a major research study requires a familiarity with many complex methodological techniques, but you can understand some of the elementary considerations that are involved. Because problems in education are multiform and multipurpose, the advisability of undertaking a particular study depends upon two factors: (1) who is doing the investigating and (2) what is being considered for solution. Problems that are worthy of investigation vary somewhat for classroom teachers, curriculum committees, research staffs of public and private agencies, and graduate students. No matter what problem is being evaluated, however, both personal and social factors must be taken into consideration.

Personal Considerations

Blustering boldly into an investigation is foolhardy if one lacks the necessary qualifications, support, or facilities to complete it. To avoid making such an error, an intelligent investigator explores questions such as the following:

1/
Is the problem in line with my goal expectations and the expectations of others?
2/
Am I genuinely interested in this problem but free from strong biases?
3/
Do I possess or can I acquire the necessary skills, abilities, and background knowledge to study this problem?
4/
Do I have access to the tools, equipment, laboratories, and subjects necessary to conduct the investigation?
5/
Do I have the time and money to complete it?
6/
Can I obtain adequate data?
7/
Does the problem meet the scope, significance, and topical requirements of the institution or periodical to which I will submit my report?

8/
Can I obtain administrative support, guidance, and cooperation for the conduct of the study?

Since interest is a tremendous stimulus to work in any form of endeavor, an investigator should select a problem that he has a consuming desire to solve. Maintaining the prodigious effort required in research is difficult if one feels that his topic is meaningless and boring. An insatiable curiosity about a subject gives the investigator the extra enthusiasm and drive necessary to withstand the prolonged period of exacting work.

Avoiding a problem may be advisable, however, if one is strongly biased in favor of a particular viewpoint, for he probably will be unable to maintain an objective attitude. Common sense also demands that one work within the framework of the social milieu and his personal potentialities. Before undertaking any study, therefore, a researcher should raise several pertinent questions: Am I willing to do the background reading and study which will lift me to the level of sophistication that is acceptable to individuals who are knowledgeable in this area? Is the foundation, school administrator, or professor who is sponsoring my work opposed to this problem? Are my advisors capable of offering competent guidance in this area? Are the necessary equipment, subjects, or facilities available? No matter how enthusiastic one is about a study, these stubborn actualities may prevent him from making any progress. A problem may require, for example, that an investigator read Russian scientific journals, travel to various private libraries for data, obtain access to classified government documents, procure the correspondence of a deceased man from his uncooperative family, possess a knowledge of physiology, and use specialized equipment that is only available at a distant university. If one is unable to do these things, he must face reality and reject the problem—at least for the present.

Social Considerations

Social as well as personal factors must be carefully evaluated when selecting a problem, for a researcher works not only to achieve personal satisfactions, but also to advance knowledge for the good of mankind. When evaluating a problem, therefore, questions such as the following must be raised:

1/
Will the solution of this problem advance knowledge in the field appreciably?

2/
Will the findings be of practical value to educators, parents, social workers, or others?

3/
What will be the breadth of the application of the findings in terms of range of individuals, years of applicability, and areas of coverage?

4/
Will the investigation duplicate the work that has been or is being done adequately by someone else?

5/
If this topic has been covered, does it need to be extended beyond its present limits?

6/
Is the topic sufficiently delimited to permit an exhaustive treatment yet sufficiently significant to warrant investigating it?

7/
Will the conclusions of the study be of doubtful value because the tools and techniques available to conduct the inquiry are not adequately refined and sufficiently reliable?

8/
Will the study lead to the development of other investigations?

When a research worker becomes interested in a topic, he locates and evaluates all studies relating to it that have been completed or are under way. If this survey reveals that his proposed problem has already been thoroughly explored, he usually abandons it. He may pursue the problem, however, if he doubts the validity of the conclusions reached by others, discovers contradictory findings, believes new evidence or better techniques have been discovered that require a new investigation, or thinks that there are gaps to fill or extensions to be made in the organized body of educational knowledge.

A more detailed discussion of the social and methodological questions that a research worker evaluates before undertaking an investigation is presented in succeeding chapters. But perhaps some mention should be made here of another evaluative technique that may be employed. After making an extensive analysis of his problem and formulating a plan to carry out the investigation, a research worker may set up a pilot study so that he can see more clearly how the variables in the situation work. During this small-scale study, which precedes the main investigation, he discovers whether adequate tools and the required type and number of subjects are available, whether he can obtain the necessary cooperation to carry out the study, and where difficulties may arise in establishing controls and making measurements. He finds out where changes should be made in data-collecting methods; in questionnaries or interview schedules; and in directions to subjects, observers, or interviewers. Pilot studies are particularly important when the subjects are children, for the ability to establish rapport with youngsters and convey directions clearly to them cannot be taken for granted. The pilot study helps a research worker evaluate the feasibility of launching into a full-scale investigation.

Serving society is the ultimate objective of scientists. Thus, competent workers examine their personal limitations and endeavor to overcome them so that they can undertake challenging problems. But some graduate students, driven by a strong desire to obtain an advanced degree as quickly as possible, utilize expediency rather than excellency as their problem-selection measuring stick. They circumvent any investigation that requires them to become proficient in utilizing a difficult statistical procedure, to interview people in distant cities, to master a new field of knowledge, or to do considerable detective work in locating primary source materials. Rather than searching for ways to make the most significant contribution to research, they hunt myopically for a problem that will demand the least possible effort on their part. The insignificant inquiries undertaken by these easy-degree seekers are neither challenging nor interesting; consequently, completing them is the dullest drudgery. Society also suffers, for mankind profits little from surface-skimming investigations. When a profession has a multitude of pressing problems to solve, its members cannot afford to waste precious time and talent on trivial studies. Neither the educational profession nor its practitioners will experience satisfactory growth and a sense of significance by sidestepping difficult problems.

8

The Solution of
the Problem

Problems are solved by a complex creative process that involves unique forms of conceptualization similar to those employed in producing great works of art and music. Creative thought is not a step-by-step process that one can master by following directions in a "how-to-do-it" manual. A successful scientist may appear to pluck problems magically out of the academic atmosphere, but months or years of patient plodding may precede the exciting moment when he describes the precise nature of the particular event or condition that requires explaining. And no blinding flash of intuition immediately illuminates his mind with a brilliant solution; a long period of arduous intellectual activity may ensue before he evolves an adequate explanation.

Constructing Hypotheses

When attacking a problem, an educator, chemist, or detective gathers many facts. But he is not interested in "facts and nothing but the facts," for much speculation—bold, imaginative guesswork—is required to solve problems. If undirected observation were the only tool an investigator possessed, he might gather data for years without unearthing the particular facts and relationships that are required to solve his problem. To overcome this difficulty, a competent investigator structures possible explanations for the puzzling condition or event that concerns him (Dewey's step 3). These explanations—hypotheses—are the most useful tools in his "detective kit." A hypothesis suggests where he can search most profitably for facts and how to detect relevant relationships between them. Facts must be obtained to solve a problem; facts, however, "never speak for themselves but only *to* someone who has an hypothesis which he wishes to test" (103:123–124).

Nature of Hypotheses

When an investigator begins to analyze a problem—a murder, an airplane crash, or some form of pupil behavior—he may notice that some data are vague or incomplete, that some elements do not appear to be related to other known elements or to fit into any particular order, or that no adequate explanation can be given for some phenomena. He is disturbed and keeps asking how he can complete the data, systematize the information, or give some interpretation that will explain the unknown factors. When an educator reaches this agitated mental state, he is standing on the threshold of research. If he can imagine some unknown fact and combine it with observed facts and an existing body of theory to form a reasonable explanation or solution for the problem, he will take a giant step forward. Leaping beyond the known facts and constructing hypotheses—intelligent guesses that offer possible solutions to the problem—may enable him to push back the frontiers of knowledge.

Man uses hypotheses to solve simple as well as complex problems. If the lamp on your desk does not light, you may immediately combine this "known fact" with the following "unknown facts" that you imagine, suspect, or predict may explain the occurrence of this phenomenon: (1) the bulb is burned out, (2) the cord is not plugged in the outlet, or (3) the cord is severed. These hypotheses help you locate and pattern the facts needed to solve the problem. If you put the bulb in another lamp and it lights, you know that hypothesis 1 is not the solution to your problem. After testing the other hypotheses, you may find that hypothesis 3 fits all the evidence and satisfactorily explains why the desk light is out. Hypotheses "are your eyes as you try to approach problems in a scientific manner. Through them you look into the disorder that is a problem and see the possibilities of order" (69:120).

To summarize, hypotheses are suggested problem solutions which are expressed as generalizations or propositions. They are statements consisting of elements expressed in an orderly system of relationships which seek to describe or to explain conditions or events that have not yet been confirmed by facts.

Some elements or relationships in hypotheses are *known facts* and others are *conceptual*. The conceptual elements are products of the research worker's imagination. Thus, hypotheses include facts and transcend the known facts to give plausible explanations for unknown conditions. They may provide the conceptual elements that complete the known data, conceptual relationships that systematize unordered elements, or conceptual meanings and interpretations that explain the unknown phenomena. By logically relating known facts to intelligent guesses about unknown conditions, hypotheses are able to extend and enlarge our knowledge.

Conditions Conducive to Creativity

Hypotheses are calculated guesses, but these guesses are not merely "happy accidents," as some scientists modestly suggest. No precise rules can be given for formulating hypotheses, but some conditions are more conducive to their construction than others. The quality and quantity of the hypotheses you construct will be governed by (1) the range and richness of the knowledge you bring to bear on a problem and (2) the versatility and discrimination with which you select facts, create concepts, trace relationships, and organize them into new and meaningful explanatory patterns.

Background Knowledge/ A scientist cannot be an isolated rebel who relies on personal observation alone to create fruitful hypotheses. His work will be hopelessly hampered if he is not thoroughly familiar with established facts, existing theories, and previous research relating to his problems. While manipulating relevant raw materials drawn from these sources, he may locate the key associations or missing data needed to explain puzzling phenomena. Supplying the imaginative concepts—missing pieces—needed to solve a problem is his ultimate objective, but these concepts may be produced more readily if he is familiar with the known facts and orders them imaginatively.

Familiarity with the literature in the field relating to a problem gives the trained person a tremendous advantage over the neophyte or outsider in arriving at a successful solution. Complete slavery to traditional thought and excessive specialization in a field, however, may crush creativity. After accumulating masses of educational information, some students can no longer see the forest for the trees; they cannot abstract the data necessary to formulate a solution. Intensive preoccupation with the literature may fix traditional thought patterns so firmly in their minds that they cannot see problems from fresh viewpoints.

To keep from being shackled to the thought patterns of their predecessors, some scientists give their imaginations free reign and refrain from perusing the literature when they first search for solutions. To help research teams see problems through "virgin eyes," some industrial concerns place an intellectually able man who is unfamiliar with the particular field of inquiry on each team. Approaching a problem from a fresh or foreign viewpoint may lead to the solution of a problem, but ignorance is never a useful tool for attacking problems. Significant hypotheses may spring into the consciousness of cultivated minds that are not trained in the particular branch of knowledge, but the creators of these hypotheses bring a varied background of knowledges and skills from their own fields to bear on the problems. Before testing any hypothesis, of course, researchers always evaluate it in light of the existing body of theory.

Investigators who confine their attention exclusively to a narrow field of interest reduce their problem-solving potential, for provincial minds tend to see problems from limited and prejudiced viewpoints. Liberally educated minds are more likely to look at problems from the multiple angles suggested by their myriad experiences. Educators find that diverse knowledges from related or even distant fields sometimes provide them with the keys to problem solutions that extensive knowledge of their own field fails to produce. Perhaps one of the most productive means of creating hypotheses is to examine conceptual schemes developed by the other disciplines and to decide whether they provide insights that would help explain educational phenomena. Kurt Lewin, for example, drew on the concept of force in physics to help him explain human behavior.

Imagination/ To strip off stereotyped blinders that might prevent him from originating useful hypotheses, a scientist obtains a broad experiential background in his own and other fields, employs safeguards to minimize his emotional and intellectual biases, and strives to increase the range, richness, and accuracy of his observations. These precautionary measures are of little value, however, unless he also flexes his imagination. Science relies heavily upon imagination. According to Einstein, "Imagination is more powerful than knowledge."

Imagination, the magic catalyst in research, is the product of an adventuresome attitude and an agile intellect. When an experienced investigator encounters a problem, he assumes that the traditional and obvious explanations for the phenomena may be inaccurate or inadequate. Stubborn skepticism stimulates him to search for flaws in old theories. To break from traditional thought patterns, he views the puzzling phenomena from unorthodox positions or fragmentizes previous knowledge concerning it and combines the elements into new patterns. To stimulate his imagination, he keeps asking questions: What else is like this phenomenon? What can I copy? Does something need to be added, subtracted, enlarged, combined, divided, or rearranged? Can I invent some logical construct that will account for the occurrence of this phenomena? In many instances a reversal of viewpoint helps him stumble upon the most effective solution for a problem. When strange ideas pop momentarily to the surface of his mind, he does not dismiss them. Any "happy accident" that gives him insight into a situation and kindles a creative flame in his mind is entertained. With intensive concentration, he selects, shifts, and combines seemingly unlike and previously unconnected known and imaginary facts until he constructs a simple, coherent explanation for a phenomenon.

Higher-quality hypotheses are produced if investigators prolong the solution-searching process, separate it from the solution-evaluation process, and delay the solution-selection process. After discovering one possible explanation for a phenomenon, some problem solvers hurry along this promising pathway and away from possible alternatives. They crystallize their thinking prematurely. After making heavy ego-effort investments in their proposed solution, they are reluctant to start over again or to entertain other solution possibilities which may be better. Because quantity tends to breed quality, experienced investigators first concentrate on piling up alternative hypotheses. Because critical evaluation and concern about practical considerations depress flights of the imagination and inhibit the construction of hypotheses, they refrain from weighing the merits of each idea as it occurs to them. During the "idea-getting" stage of research, caution is abandoned. Radical ideas are entertained; wild experimental associations are made; risks are taken—they must be taken, for discoveries are not made by jogging along in ruts of past experience. Unconventional thinking is not unconditionally guaranteed to produce problem solutions, but it holds greater promise of advancing knowledge than does clinging credulously to traditional patterns of thought.

Order and Analogy

Most scientists agree that inspiration is a product of perspiration. Jarring oneself loose from the emotional and intellectual ties of traditional thought requires a stronger will power and a richer imagination than the average person possesses. Following hundreds of hunches that lead up blind alleys before finding one that leads in the right direction requires more patience and persistence than most men ever develop.

In each investigation the researcher is faced with a puzzle—a disordered, disturbing situation—and a crude trial-and-error method of attack is unlikely to provide a solution. Trying to perceive a pattern or a deviation from a known pattern in the phenomena may help him find an explanation for it. To learn why a teacher is ineffective, why Johnny can't read, or why a student manifests aggressive behavior, an educator usually begins to look for factors that are associated with the phenomena, the frequency of their occurrence, the order in which they occur, and the relationships among them. During a prolonged and thorough analysis of the problem, he strives to structure disordered items of information into a pattern that will explain the occurrence of the condition or situation that is puzzling him.

Analogy is an ancient "order-searching" tool that man uses to build bridges from the known to the unknown. When faced with a problem, a researcher may look for a successful previous ordering of nature that might illuminate his present difficulty. Upon spotting some similarity between a new situation and an old one, he wonders whether the old situation which he knows a lot about will provide him with any clues that will help him solve his present problem. He reasons that if these two situations have some resemblances in common, they may be analogous in other as yet unknown respects.

1/
If A (new situation) resembles B (old situation) in regard to X factor,

2/
and he knows from previous experience that B is related to Y and Z as well as to X,

3/
then perhaps A is also related to Y and Z.

Thus, the analogy leads the investigator to clues he might not otherwise stumble upon and hints at hypotheses that he might profitably test.

Analogies are useful but not foolproof tools for finding solutions to problems. They may lead to error, for the assumed similarities may not actually exist. If any essential dissimilarity prevails, the analogy is false, as Miss Wilson, an elementary school principal, discovered to her dismay. When the poor attendance at the afternoon PTA meeting disturbed her, she recalled that young matrons had doubled the weekly attendance in her Sunday school class by organizing a nursery to care for members' children during their meetings. Miss Wilson reasoned that since the PTA and the Sunday school class both had young mothers as members and similar attendance difficulties, the same solution might work in both cases. But Miss Wilson failed to detect an important difference in the two situations: the school children's mothers were career women and could not leave their jobs to attend afternoon meetings even if a nursery were provided. Miss Wilson's experience indicates that problem solvers must be not only exceptionally adept at noting similarities between things, but also meticulously careful about detecting differences between them that might make the analogies false. Despite the danger of mistaking an analogy for evidence, scientists favor using it with caution. They recognize that the reliability of analogical reasoning is restricted, but with proper safeguards it is one of the more helpful means of discovering hypotheses.

Other Practices/ Research workers find they are more apt to devise hypotheses if they allot sufficient blocks of time—uninterrupted by distractions—to mull over, organize, and reorganize their collected data. After periods of intensive work on a problem, they sometimes abstain temporarily from conscious intellectual effort and direct their attention to other work or just relax. In moments of relaxation their subconscious minds may continue to consider the problem and pop up with a useful hypothesis when they least expect it. Dropping a problem periodically permits them to escape from unprofitable ruts of thought they have been following and to return to their labors later with fresh and more objective viewpoints. Conversations with colleagues and authorities from different fields may help them detect errors in their reasoning and may stimulate them to venture up new avenues of thought. Lecturing or writing about the puzzling phenomena may clarify their thinking and force the "key clue" to the surface. Drawing diagrams, constructing models, or forming mental images of the factors involved in the problem may also help them "break through" to a plausible explanation for the phenomena.

Examples of Hypothesis Construction

Hypotheses range from relatively simple to highly sophisticated statements. The schoolboy devises elementary hypotheses to explain ordinary life or classroom occurrences which puzzle him. The genius creates elaborate theories concerning complex physical, social, or psychological phenomena. You engage in hypothesis construction every day when searching for solutions to problems such as: Where did I leave my glasses? Why won't my car start? Why did so many students fail the last English test? Perhaps the following illustration will help you recall the mental processes involved in making a constructive attack on a problem.

Personal Problem/ If you experience periodically symptoms similar to a cold—dripping nose, watering eyes, annoying sneezes—and yet never develop a cold, the situation is unpleasant and puzzling. You have a problem and want to obtain some explanation for the repeated occurrence of this phenomenon. To initiate the inquiry, you collect empirically verifiable facts about when, where, and how frequently it occurs. At the same time you begin to think of explanations for the phenomenon. From your previous experiences—reading, conversations with friends, observations of people with similar problems—you cull some of the following possible solutions: Does dust cause it? Do I eat, wear, or become exposed to something that is irritating? Am I allergic to wool or feathers? Do the chemicals I use at work cause it? Do some flowers or plants cause it? Do I have hay fever? These hypotheses are mere hunches at this stage. They must be analyzed and developed. Empirically verifiable facts must be found to support them.

By examining and reexamining the facts and explanations and tracing relationships between them, you try to determine which hypothesis is in agreement with all the facts in the case and gives a better explanation of the phenomenon than any of the others. If dust causes the phenomenon, you should suffer the most during the spring and fall housecleaning seasons. Since you experience the greatest difficulty in August and December, the dust hypothesis does not stand up under analysis. If chemicals used at work cause it, you should sneeze more at work than at home. But this is not true, for the greatest discomfort occurs during the August and December vacation weeks. Could it be hay fever? The December facts negate this possibility. Could it be a wool allergy? The August facts negate this possibility. Just what is the relationship between August and December? After probing this possibility further and searching for additional facts, you recall that the phenomenon occurs most frequently outdoors in August and indoors in December.

In one magic moment at an August beach party, a reasonable solution springs into your mind. Because the miserable cold symptoms have recurred, the whining questions your daughter Janie keeps asking irritate you. But one of those unwelcome questions suddenly supplies the missing clue that solves your problem. Janie complains, "There are too many old cedar trees around the porch. Why don't we cut them down for our Christmas decorations instead of always taking trees from the clump down by the lake?" Sitting up—suddenly tingling with excitement—you pounce upon her words. Do they supply the missing link to your puzzle? Cedar trees grow around the cottage where you stay in August; during the Christmas holidays you use them for decorations in your city apartment. Is cedar the cause of your difficulty? This explanation is a more concise and testable hypothesis than the original vague explanation that some plant, dust, chemical, wool, or flower caused your suffering. The hypothesis still has to be tested to determine whether cedar is actually the cause of the difficulty. But you have an informed guess to work on that has a reasonable chance of being the correct answer to the problem.

Educational Problem/ If you will recall, Miss White, whom you met in Chapter 7, went through many of the same steps in hypothesis construction. She was disturbed by a problematic situation: her pupils were not making satisfactory progress in reading. With this glimmering of a problem as a prod to action, she made observations and gathered facts to clarify it: Which children were having difficulty? How many? What sex were they? What difficulties did they have? At the same time she began to recall from her previous experiences—working with children, reading professional literature, conversations with colleagues, doctors, nurses, parents—some theories or explanations for reading difficulties.

Miss White mulled over various explanations and asked: Are these particular children having difficulty because of their low intelligence level, impaired hearing or vision, inadequate sensory experiences, or emotional instability? Through further observation and analysis she endeavored to trace the relationship between her accumulated facts and explanations. When new questions arose, she had to search for additional data. By adding, subtracting, and reorganizing materials in this manner, she obtained a clearer and clearer picture of the facts and explanations that were relevant to the problem. Facts produced by intelligence tests caused her to dismiss low intelligence as an explanation for the difficulty. After obtaining verifiable evidence relating to the other hypotheses, she was able to reject some and to retain others for further consideration.

Through this thorough analysis of the problem, Miss White removed many ambiguities and uncertainties. She crystallized the following hypothesis which seemed to agree with all the facts in the case and to offer the most logical explanation of the problem: Twelve third-grade pupils are retarded from one year, seven months, to two years, six months, in reading because they lack varied sensory experiences to help them associate printed symbols with words and ideas.

Testing Hypotheses

A hypothesis is a provisional or possible explanation which accounts for the factors, events, or conditions that the research worker is trying to understand. But even after a hypothesis is analyzed critically for logical consistency and completeness, it is not acceptable as an explanatory device. A hypothesis remains a mere guess—and possesses little explanatory value—until empirically verifiable evidence is produced to support it. Thus, after formulating a hypothesis, an investigator must (1) deduce its consequences (Dewey's step 4), (2) select or develop tests that will determine through experiments or sense observations whether these consequences actually occur, and (3) carry out these tests (Dewey's step 5), thereby collecting facts that will either confirm or disconfirm the hypothesis.

Deducing the Consequences

Some hypotheses may be tested directly, but many scientific explanations must be tested indirectly. If a man guesses that a noise is caused by rain beating on the roof, he looks outdoors and confirms or disconfirms his hypothesis by direct observation. If he guesses that Mr. Jones shot Sally Lake, that the world is "round" rather than flat, or that the professor applying for a job is an impostor, he cannot directly observe these facts or conditions, but he may test them indirectly. After studying the hypotheses to see what they logically imply, he may deduce consequences that must occur if these hypotheses are true. He may reason: If these hypotheses are true, then certain consequences are observable and may be tested directly.

Perhaps a fictitious example will clarify this process. Suppose Dean Henry is suspicious of the college training and degree records that Professor Silnatch has included in his application for a job. Since the dean cannot tell whether the man is an impostor merely by looking at him or his application, he proposes the following hypothesis and deduces the consequences that it logically implies.

/ *If* job applicant, Professor Stanley Silnatch, received a doctorate from Jones University in 1938,

/ *then* (1) Jones University will have a record of awarding him the degree;

/ *then* (2) his doctoral project will be listed in *Doctoral Dissertations Accepted by American Universities;*

/ *then* (3) he will recall the names of the members of his doctoral dissertation committee;

/ *then* (4) his signature will be similar to the one on college records;

/ *then* (5) college health records and photographs of student Stanley Silnatch will reveal a number of facts that are characteristic of the job applicant (general height, bone structure, color of eyes, and physical handicaps).

These five consequences may be tested directly. If Dean Henry finds empirically verifiable evidence that agrees or disagrees with these consequences, he indirectly confirms or disconfirms the hypothesis. Thus, the deduced consequences of a hypothesis rather than the hypothesis itself are tested in a scientific investigation.

Deducing consequences from hypotheses that can be empirically verified cannot be a hurried or casual procedure. In major research projects the indirect method of attacking problems may lead through extremely intricate and remote channels of reasoning. In any investigation one must check his reasoning to make certain that the consequences are logically implied by the hypothesis, for there is no point in testing them if they are not. The consequences must also be expressed in clear, precise terms, for testing ambiguously stated ones is a difficult if not an impossible task.

Imaginative and disciplined intellectual effort is required in the deductive elaboration of hypotheses. When a significant hypothesis is proposed, the process may go on for years with a number of scientists deducing and testing various consequences. Thus, in many investigations the researcher does not originate his hypothesis, but rather tests consequences deduced from other men's explorations of phenomena.[1] Through this process he obtains additional evidence that either strengthens the confirmation of the hypothesis or disconfirms it (also see Appendixes D and G).

1/ When reading research literature, you may become confused because some workers refer to the proposed solutions to problems as "theories" and to the deduced consequences of a theory as "hypotheses." Even the present author sometimes resorts to the shorthand statement, "One tests the hypothesis," rather than using the longer but more accurate statement, "One tests the deduced consequences of the hypothesis." Whatever language may be used to explain the process, the important thing to keep in mind is that the researcher presents an explanation for phenomena that he or someone else has originated, deduces the consequences that must occur if that explanation is accurate, and then conducts tests to determine whether these conditions or events do occur.

Selecting Test Procedures

Having determined what consequences are logically implied by the hypothesis, the researcher next devises a factual situation that will test them. A study by Durkheim (49) may give you an insight into this three-step procedure. (1) He proposed the hypothesis that although the progressive division of labor increases material wealth, it decreases group cohesiveness and hence personal happiness. (2) If this hypothesis were correct, he deduced that the following consequences should be observable: Suicide rates would be (a) higher in nations with greater material wealth, (b) higher in city than in farming areas, (c) higher in some types of occupations than in other types, and (d) higher among religious groups requiring little cohesiveness than in those requiring more cohesiveness. (3) To test whether these deduced consequences were observable, he examined international records on suicides.

Selecting and perfecting suitable testing procedures requires the most careful consideration. Weak, unreliable, or inappropriate tests will produce results of questionable value. A foolish error made when structuring a questionnaire, selecting subjects, controlling experimental conditions, or checking the authenticity of a document may prove to be a fatal flaw in an investigation. If tests do not measure precisely what one wishes to measure, they are of no value. A 100-yard dash, for example, cannot measure the maximum running speed of six-year-old children, for it tests endurance rather than speed of youngsters of that age. Nor does an English version of an intelligence test ascertain the IQ of children with little or no command of the language. The appropriateness of the empirical test depends upon the nature of the deduced consequence; to be acceptable, a test must factually fulfill the specific requirements of the consequence. Hence, one must always make certain that there is logical consistency between a test and the deduced consequence it is supposed to check.

In his stiff appraisal of testing procedures, a competent researcher asks: Do these tests correctly and adequately represent the particular factors, conditions, or relationships of the consequences? Are they valid, reliable, and objective? Will they enable me to collect the necessary evidence with a minimum of effort? Since improper administration of a test or improper interpretation of the data will cause critics to reject his findings, he also exercises every precaution during these stages of his investigation.

Keeping accurate records of testing procedures is also essential in research. Writing a complete description of what he intends to do before initiating the full investigation makes it possible for the researcher to spot and correct obvious weaknesses. Keeping a diary of all procedures employed during the testing process places him in a better position to compile an account of them at the conclusion of the investigation. When the researcher presents his study to other scholars for consideration, he must include a detailed and accurate description of the subjects selected, statistical techniques employed, apparatus used, controls established, and any factor, condition, or event that played a part in the testing situation. If any procedure is based on some assumption, he states that fact also. When presenting the test results, he exercises similar care and precision, for the omission of data or an ambiguous account will create a mystery rather than solve a problem.

Because tests are needed to meet a variety of demands, hundreds of them have been developed. A more detailed discussion of them is presented in later chapters, but this text merely provides an introduction to the subject. To pursue research work as a career, you must attain proficiency in employing a wide variety of test procedures. A limited familiarity with investigative techniques will limit the range of the work you can do.

Confirming the Hypothesis

At this point, let us review the problem-solving process. After analyzing a felt difficulty and drafting a specific problem statement, the researcher formulates a hypothesis—a proposed solution for the problem—and deduces certain logical consequences that should be observable if the hypothesis is to be confirmed. His hypothetico-deductive argument is usually stated in an "if-then" form: If hypothesis H_1 is accurate, then the consequences C_1, C_2, C_3, etc., should be observable. To test whether these previously unexamined phenomena actually occur in the way H_1 predicts, he conducts appropriate empirical tests. On the basis of the factual evidence obtained from the tests, he draws a conclusion—an inductive inference—about whether the hypothesis is confirmed or disconfirmed (see Figure 8.1).

The success of an investigation rests not only on the problem, hypothesis, deduced observable predictions, tests, evidence, and conclusions, but also on the cogency of the logic with which these elements are connected. The hypothesis must provide a logical explanation for the specific problem that is raised. The deduced consequences must be logically implied by the hypothesis, the test situation must adequately represent the essential factors expressed in the consequence, and the conclusions must be based on the factual evidence collected in the empirical tests.

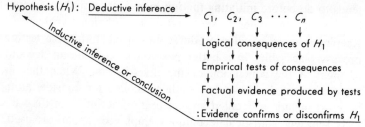

Figure 8.1/ Representation of the procedure for testing a hypothesis.

Requirements for Confirmation/ A hypothesis is not confirmed unless the test results produce evidence that agrees with the consequences implied by the hypothesis. When Dean Henry endeavored to confirm whether the job applicant, Prof. Stanley Silnatch, had been awarded a doctorate degree by Jones University in 1938, he found considerable evidence to support some deduced consequences. The published list of doctoral dissertations indicated that Stanley Silnatch had produced a study in 1938. The Jones University records revealed that in 1938 a doctorate had been awarded to Stanley Silnatch. Dean Henry was almost convinced that his suspicions were unjustified, when he noticed that the student's signature on college records was quite different from the job applicant's signature. This observation puzzled him. When checking Stanley Silnatch's college health records and photographs, he discovered the key evidence that solved the problem. According to the 1938 records, Mr. Silnatch was over six feet tall, has blue eyes, and had lost three fingers on his left hand. Obviously the job applicant was an impostor for he was five and a half feet tall, had brown eyes, and possessed all his fingers. Dean Henry had discovered evidence that contradicted a deduced consequence; hence, he had definitely disconfirmed his hypothesis. The job applicant was merely masquerading as one of his former classmates who had been an outstanding student at Jones University.

To confirm a hypothesis, the researcher must provide factual evidence that agrees with every consequence logically implied by it. If Dean Henry had claimed that the hypothesis was confirmed merely because a number of facts fitted the theory perfectly, he would have been in error. Whenever *any evidence* produced by a test flatly contradicts one or more consequences and no errors have been made in test procedures, the researcher must abandon or modify his original hypothesis. No matter how much evidence is obtained to support a hypothesis, a single item of contradictory evidence can disprove it. A hypothesis is not confirmed unless all the factual evidence collected in the empirical tests corresponds with the consequences.

Strength of Confirmation/ A scientist confirms rather than proves or verifies a hypothesis. The term "prove" carries the connotation of finality and absolute certainty. The term "verification" often appears in research literature, but the word literally means "to prove true" which is not an exact description of what the testing process produces. Hypotheses are never *proved* by producing factual evidence that is in harmony with the consequences; they are established only as *possessing a degree of probability*.

An educator may make the mistake of assuming that he has found the real cause of some phenomena because he has found empirical evidence that supports one or more consequences of his hypothesis.

He may argue:
Major premise: If H_1 is true, then C_1, C_2, C_3 . . . will follow.
  (antecedent)   (consequent)
Minor premise: But C_1, C_2, C_3 do follow.
  (empirical evidence affirms the consequent)
Conclusion: Therefore, hypothesis H_1 is true.
  (inferred fact)

This argument does not confirm conclusively that H_1 is true, for it involves the "fallacy of affirming the consequent."

Formal logic rules that if a minor premise affirms the consequent, as it does in this instance, the hypothetical argument is not valid. The educator's argument may show that C_1, C_2, C_3, supports H_1 or confirms it to some extent, but other hypotheses may also account for these consequences. Moreover, when a wider range of phenomena is examined, some fact related to the problem may turn up that can be explained by a rival hypothesis and not by this hypothesis. The educator may have argued that low intelligence causes juvenile delinquency, and he may have found empirical evidence that showed that a disproportionate number of children with criminal records obtain low intelligence test scores. But has he proven that low intelligence causes juvenile delinquency? Perhaps low intelligence is associated with juvenile delinquency, but many other factors may also be associated with it. Perhaps low intelligence is merely associated with heredity, early environment, or some other factor or combination of factors which may be the true cause of juvenile delinquency. Perhaps low intelligence is as frequent among law-abiding youths as among juvenile delinquents who come from the same environment.

After conducting an investigation, the conclusion—inductive

inference—that is drawn from the empirical evidence may support the hypothesis. The hypothesis, however, is not accepted as being logically fully verified. From the standpoint of formal logic, an investigator cannot prove that exceptions to his hypothesis will never occur. An investigator does not establish an everlasting truth. He cannot state with "absolute certainty" that his hypothesis is the only hypothesis that can explain the phenomena, but he tries to come as close to this goal as possible. To show that no rival hypothesis can account for the known facts relating to the problem as adequately as his hypothesis, he obtains experimental evidence to support consequences in a number of widely scattered areas. The wider the range of consequences his hypothesis can account for, the fewer is the number of rival hypotheses that can account for the same consequences.

The affirmation of one consequence cannot prove that a hypothesis is true. The affirmation of several consequences cannot prove it is true either, but building a web of evidence makes the hypothesis "more probably true." If little evidence is produced to substantiate the consequences of H_1, the hypothesis is poorly or weakly confirmed. If considerable factual evidence is produced to support several deduced consequences of H_1, the degree of probability that the hypothesis offers a satisfactory explanation approaches greater certainty. But remember, a well-confirmed hypothesis is held only tentatively and provisionally. If the predictions that are made on the basis of H_1 turn out to be correct when empirical evidence is examined, then H_1 has "stood up to trial," but it remains on probation and is subject to modification or abandonment whenever new factual evidence demands it. Empirical support merely confirms, strengthens, or substantiates the hypothesis; it does not *prove* something is absolutely true for all time.

Reformulation or Abandonment of a Hypothesis/ An inexperienced research worker often has such an intense desire to confirm his hypothesis that he disregards evidence that will disconfirm it. After formulating the hypothesis "All geniuses exhibit antisocial behavior," he may search eagerly for data concerning drunkenness, dope addiction, riotous living, and immorality among great painters, writers, scientists, and musicians, but may fail to investigate the lives of Einstein, Pasteur, and other "well-behaved geniuses." Incandescent infatuation with his hypothesis may blind him to its faults and cause him to ignore evidence that may explode it.

Parting with a pet hypothesis is a painful experience for a man who is intellectually impoverished. An imaginative investigator, who can originate a number of alternative solutions, is less reluctant to abandon an untenable hypothesis. The wastebasket of a successful scientist is usually filled with rejected ideas. W. Stanley Jevons pointed out that a great discoverer is not a man who "seizes at once upon the truth, or has any unerring method of divining it. In all probability the errors of the great mind exceed in number those of the less vigorous one. Fertility of imagination and abundance of guesses at truth are among the first requisites of discovery" (74:577). Before formulating a fruitful hypothesis, an experienced investigator may explore and discard dozens of hopeless hunches.

Advances in knowledge are never made by clinging tenaciously to disconfirmed hypotheses. Hypotheses are not sacred slogans to be preserved at all costs. Darwin once declared that he could not remember ever formulating a hypothesis that he did not modify greatly or abandon. Einstein observed that ninety-nine out of a hundred of his conclusions were false. Hypotheses are mere guesses, and the vast majority of them prove to be wrong. Most hypotheses go quickly to their graves, some experience a short life, and only a select few are handed down from generation to generation.

An investigator has no alternative but to abandon or to revise a disconfirmed hypothesis, but he does not abandon a hypothesis merely because finding supporting evidence is difficult. Some scientists have conducted hundreds of tests and endured years of frustration before they were able to produce evidence confirming their hypotheses. A research worker must be capable of judging when he has no choice but to reject a hypothesis and when he should persevere with it. If the tools or techniques needed to obtain confirming evidence have not been devised, he may have to set aside the investigation. If the conditions required to test the hypothesis do not exist, he may have to wait until they do. One of the consequences of the theory of relativity could not be tested, for example, until a total eclipse of the sun occurred.

Types of Confirmation/ The social sciences encompass many specific subject fields with a wide variety of problems in each area. Each social science problem is distinctive, but most of them fall into two broad categories: (1) problems of fact and (2) problems of value. Each type of problem raises a different kind of question. Many scholars believe that the scientific method cannot deal with problems of value; others argue that it can (61, 99, 129). Some of the difficulties involved can best be understood by reviewing the nature of problems of fact and value.

1/ Problems of fact.

Problems of fact propose questions that ask: What is the actual state of affairs in a given society? These problems raise questions which require the determination of facts. An educator, for example, might propose that the ratio of left-handed to right-handed children who stutter is 3 to 1. To confirm this hypothesis, the educator must find factual evidence in the existing culture that corresponds exactly with it. For the solution of his factual problem, he resorts to the scientific method of inquiry.

2/ Problems of value.

Problems of value raise questions that ask: What kind of society should man aim to achieve? Normative social theories answer these problems by defining the ideal society. Different people have different concepts of the social norms at which they aim. The Russians and Americans, for example, do not envisage the same form of ideal social organization. Problems of value differ sharply from problems of fact, for they question what the ideal society ought to be like, not what the facts of the situation are in any given culture. The democratic or Christian ideal, for example, is not realized completely in practice, but this lack of conformity with the theory does not make the theory invalid. Yet, this is the conclusion an investigator would have to draw if he confirmed *normative* social theories and *factual* social theories by the same method.

To be valid, a factual theory must be absolutely in accord with the facts in a given society. Since a normative social theory is formulated to change the status of society rather than to coincide completely with the existing facts, an investigator cannot solve problems of value by the same method as problems of fact. Different types of problems require somewhat different methods of solution.

Some scholars argue that some value as well as fact problems may be attacked by the scientific method, but the method of confirmation in the two types of problems differs. To verify factual theories, an investigator checks his theory against the *conditions in society,* and if they agree completely, his theory is confirmed. According to Northrup, an investigator may verify a normative social theory, not by checking it against the *facts in society,* now or in the future, but by checking it with the *facts of nature.* For example, American educators believe that a "good" educational system is one that provides for individual differences. This theory, if checked against the facts of society, will not be verified empirically, for many schools do not provide for individual differences. But this theory will be confirmed when checked against the facts of nature, for empirical evidence is available to verify that children differ in capacities.

To solve problems of value, man does not stand aloof from science and the scientific method. Scientific data may help him determine which hypotheses regarding *what is* and *what is not* "good" for children are based on observative evidence. The various sciences may supply facts about the likely outcome of courses of action that are based on different value judgments. The most scientifically correct and adequate normative social theory, in the opinion of some scholars, is the one that can care for the widest range of empirically verified facts concerning man and nature.

Examples of Testing Hypotheses

Many steps are involved in the process of solving a problem. Perhaps a brief review of two investigations will refocus your attention on the totality of the hypothetico-deductive argument.

Galileo's Experiment/ You will recall that Galileo constructed three hypotheses that might offer satisfactory explanations for the phenomenon, motion, that he was trying to understand. These hypotheses were merely proposed solutions; they lacked confirmation. To determine whether any one of them could be confirmed, he had to deduce and test the consequences of each hypothesis.

Galileo as well as others before him gave consideration to the relationship of weight and the motion or velocity of falling bodies. Thus, he first examined this ancient hypothesis: The velocity with which bodies fall is proportional to the weight of the body. From this hypothesis he could deduce the following consequence: If this hypothesis is true, then when bodies of different weights are dropped simultaneously from the same height, they will reach the earth at different times. Common sense would seem to indicate that the heavier objects would hit the ground before the lighter ones. But Galileo was not willing to accept this explanation merely because it was logical; he insisted upon putting it to an empirical test. In the Tower of Pisa experiment (or if this tale is mythical, some similar test), he discovered that except for differences caused by the resistance of air, objects of different weights fall at the same speed (and in a vacuum they would hit the ground at the same time). Hence, Galileo had disconfirmed the hypothesis that the velocity with which a body falls depends on the weight.

Galileo next examined his second hypothesis: Velocity is proportional to the distance through which the body travels. But he rejected this hypothesis because he thought he had demonstrated mathematically that one of its consequences presented an impossibility. Thus, he turned to consider his third hypotheses: Velocity is proportional to the length of time during which the body falls. In other words, he proposed that the acceleration or change in velocity during any unit interval of time is constant.

Galileo's third hypothesis could not be tested directly. But Galileo deduced that if this hypothesis were true, the distance covered by free-falling bodies was proportional to the square of the time of their fall. Thus, if a body fell one unit of time and covered one unit of distance, in two units of time it would travel four units of distance, and in three units of time it would cover nine units of distance. If such evidence could be found, it would strengthen his hypothesis that the acceleration of falling bodies is constant.

To obtain empirical evidence that would confirm or disconfirm his hypothesis, Galileo set up an experiment. He placed a metal ball on an inclined plane which allowed the ball to move down freely, but relatively slowly, and observed how many units of time the ball consumed in covering different units of distance. As a result of this experiment, he was able to present empirical evidence that the relation between distance and time was in accord with his hypothesis. Therefore, Galileo's third hypothesis possessed empirical support and provided the basis for a new understanding of motion.

Having acquired a better understanding of motion, Galileo was able to construct a more satisfactory definition of force. According to Galileo's definition, force was not that which produces motion or velocity as Aristotle had described it, but that which produces a change of velocity—acceleration of movement. Thus, an object, such as a projectile, experiences continuous acceleration as long as it is being acted upon by force. According to Aristotle's definition, it does not stop moving when the explosion ends, it merely ceases to change velocity. It would continue to move with a constant velocity if the force of gravitation did not draw it toward the earth. By solving the problem that had puzzled him, Galileo was able to present the world with a new, all-embracing definition of force that applied to any motion whatever.

Educational Investigation/ If you examine educational research studies, some of the discussion in the reports may be unintelligible to you at the present time. But in many instances, such as in the Balows' study which appears in Appendix I, you can follow the general nature of the arguments that are presented.

The Balows were concerned with the following problem: Is there a significant relationship between lateral dominance and reading achievement in the second grade? Workers in reading clinics had suggested that there might be a relationship between reading disability and left-eye dominance, crossed dominance (opposite eye-hand preference), mixed dominance (mixed-hand preference), and delayed establishment of consistent hand dominance. Although the investigators do not present a formal statement of their hypothetico-deductive argument, they probably reasoned as follows:

/ *If* the above deviations from what is accepted as normal ocular and manual dominance are related to reading achievement in the second grade,

/ *then,* when second-grade children are classified according to normal, crossed, and mixed dominance, the crossed-dominance and mixed-dominance groups will score significantly below the other group in reading achievement;

/ *then,* when second-grade children are classified in terms of strength and direction of hand dominance, the mixed-hand-dominance group will score significantly below the other groups in reading achievement;

/ *then,* when second-grade children are classified according to strength and direction of eye dominance, the left-eyed group will score significantly below the other groups in reading achievement;

/ *then,* when second-grade children are classified according to time of establishing hand dominance, the group that is late in establishing hand dominance will score significantly below the other groups.

The investigators in their report defined the terms normal, crossed, and mixed dominance. They named the specific tests that were administered to measure reading achievement, lateral dominance, and intelligence. They stipulated what subjects were used, how they were selected, and how they were classified to test each deduced consequence of the hypothesis. After collecting the empirical evidence that was required to test each deduced consequence, and applying appropriate statistical procedures to these data, the investigators examined their findings. Since their data did not conform to the consequences implied by their hypothesis, they concluded that their *research hypothesis* was disconfirmed. They advised other research workers that "lateral dominance does not seem to be a fruitful area for seeking out determiners of individual differences in reading achievement" (7:143).

Research Hypothesis and Null Hypothesis/ The type of hypothesis that we have been discussing is often referred to as the "research hypothesis" (H_1), or the "general," "empirical," "problem," or "substantive" hypothesis. To test this hypothesis statistically, an investigator must transform the research hypothesis into a statistical or null hypothesis (H_0). In the lateral-dominance reading study, for example, the hypotheses that were actually tested were null hypotheses. Presenting detailed information concerning statistical tools at this time seems to be a premature and imprudent procedure, for many considerations are involved. But the brief discussion that follows will give you some concept of the difference between a research hypothesis and a null hypothesis. A more extensive discussion of the null hypothesis will be presented later (Chapter 14).

The research hypothesis usually states a relationship between two or more variables that the experimenter predicts will emerge (for example, that left-eyed children will score significantly below other children in reading achievement). The null hypothesis does not necessarily reflect the researcher's expectation concerning the outcomes of the experiment—indeed, it is usually diametrically opposed to the research hypothesis—but the null hypothesis form is used because it is more suitable for the application of statistical tests. The null hypothesis (statistical test of no difference) states that *no relationship exists between the variables concerned*. (For example, there is no difference between the reading achievement of left-eyed children and other children.) The null hypothesis is usually formulated with the expectation that it will be rejected. If it is rejected, the research hypothesis is accepted.

Evaluating Hypotheses

Some hypotheses are more satisfactory than others. But how does a scientist determine whether a hypothesis is worthy of serious consideration? When two hypotheses seem to explain the same facts, how does he decide which is the more desirable? The following criteria may help him make judgments.

Plausibility of Explanation

One of the first questions that a researcher asks is: Does this hypothesis present a relevant and logical possibility? An explanation that does not pertain to the problem under consideration or that contains contradictory terms is not acceptable. Nor does an explanation that suggests a physical impossibility provide a satisfactory solution to a problem. Suppose that someone suggests that the government can cut expenditures for military uniforms by controlling the growth of young men so that they all require the same size garments. This hypothesis presents a physical impossibility; hence, it is worthless. To suggest that the fall of the French government caused twenty pupils in a particular Muskegon, Michigan, school to fail an algebra test is an unacceptable explanation. The failure of the students is not logically implied by the hypothesis. The explanation has nothing to do with the problem; it is irrelevant. To repeat, a properly structured hypothesis is logically consistent, pertinent to the question under consideration, and does not contradict the laws of nature (see Appendix F).

Testability of Explanation

Another question that a researcher asks when evaluating the worth of a hypothesis is: Can its consequences be tested empirically at the present time or in the foreseeable future? Unless a hypothesis implies consequences that can be checked by observational tests, it can never pass from the status of a guess to that of a confirmed fact. Some problems that are of the greatest interest to educators cannot be attacked, unfortunately, because the techniques for testing the proposed solutions are not yet available.

Regarding a hypothesis that states that evil spirits cause the children of Xandu tribesmen to steal chickens, educators would quickly point out that this hypothesis lies beyond the range of empirical tests. But some hypotheses that educators cherish contain variables that cannot be measured or observed any more easily than evil spirits. Inexperienced investigators often make the mistake of constructing hypotheses that will require years to test or that state relationships which cannot be measured by available tests. An untestable hypothesis or a grandiose hypothesis that requires such prolonged and complicated testing procedures that it can never be completed is not a practical tool for prying loose reliable knowledge. A hypothesis that can be neither confirmed nor disconfirmed cannot advance science; it remains a mere guess; and genuine knowledge rests upon more than guesses.

A hypothesis cannot be tested if it is stated in vague language and the terms employed are not clearly defined. Examine this hypothesis: Modern pupils' failure to read is due to insufficient practice in the use of phonics. Whom, what, and how much would you observe to check this hypothesis? What constitutes "modern pupils," "failure," and "insufficient"? These vague concepts fail to indicate exactly what evidence you must locate and measure to confirm the hypothesis. Embedding value terms, such as "good," "poor," "bad," "ought," and "should" in hypotheses also causes problems. Consider the following hypothesis: Poor students view television more than good students. What constitutes "good," "poor," and "more"?

A hypothesis cannot consist of ambiguous, obscure, and emotionally spiced prose passages. Clear and precise terms are required—if possible, terms should be operationally defined in a manner that enables the investigator to count, weigh, measure, time, or in some way quantify the factors to be checked by direct observation. If "poor students" are students in Cedar Falls High School who failed two or more stipulated subjects in the past semester, any investigator can count them and arrive at the same answer. A hypothesis must state a specific condition that can be empirically examined, such as in the following example: Water temperature does not affect the performance of or the physiological stress (heart beat and body temperature) on University of Pittsburgh varsity swimmers. This hypothesis provides a satisfactory basis for research because the variables (water temperature, performance, heart beat, body temperature) are definitely stated, the relationship between water temperature and the other variables is clearly cited, and the variables are measurable.

Adequacy of Scope

The most useful hypotheses explain all the facts that are relevant to their respective problems and contradict none of them. Many hypotheses explain some phenomena relating to a problem, but lack the power to explain other factors. One reason for the unsatisfactory situation in educational psychology today is the limited scope of the several hypotheses explaining the nature of learning. Each hypothesis accounts for some phenomena of learning but ignores factors that other hypotheses explain.

In the early stages of development in any field, the hypotheses are apt to be limited in scope. This situation is natural, for men cannot leap to the pinnacle of thought in one jump. Innumerable limited explorations are usually made before some genius creates a hypothesis that represents a major breakthrough in knowledge. Modest hypotheses make necessary and valuable contributions to science, but investigators work continuously toward the formulation of more adequate and more comprehensive ones.

The more consequences that a hypothesis yields, the greater

is its fruitfulness. If H_1 (hypothesis one) explains A and B, H_2 explains A, B, and C, and H_3 explains A, B, C, and D, H_3 is preferable. A hypothesis is of greater value if it establishes a generalization that can be applied in many areas of education or in many fields. If a geographer develops a hypothesis that enables zoologists, historians, and geologists to explain phenomena that have been puzzling them, the hypothesis is of greater worth than if it accounted only for phenomena in one discipline. Theories formulated about gravitation, atoms, and evolution are examples of hypotheses that possess extensive explanatory powers. As science advances, investigators strive to devise more and more comprehensive concepts to account for phenomena that were previously explained by different, rival, or unrelated theories. In the unified field theory, for example, Einstein attempted to bring gravitation, light, and electricity—all of them manifestations of energy—into one grand formula. The highest goal of any science is to develop a few comprehensive explanations that will account for all the facts that come within its scope.

The most satisfactory hypotheses not only explain all the known facts that gave rise to the original problems, but also enable scientists to make predictions about as yet unobserved events and relationships. If H_3 explains A, B, C, and D, and also predicts successfully E, F, and G—previously undiscovered phenomena—it will be greatly strengthened. The heliocentric theory acquired added weight, for example, because it enabled scientists to predict the existence of Neptune long before they sighted the planet through a telescope. Whenever predictions projected from a hypothesis are confirmed, the hypothesis gains tremendously in stature.

Usefulness of False Hypotheses

Hypotheses need not be the correct answers to problems to be useful. In almost every inquiry a scholar constructs several hypotheses and hopes that one will provide a satisfactory solution to the problem. By eliminating the false hypotheses one by one, he keeps narrowing the field in which the answer must lie. If a doctor, for example, tries to determine why students became ill after a school picnic, he may theorize that the potato salad, cream pie, chicken, or drinking water made them ill. If his tests indicate that the first three items were not responsible, he is on his way to finding that the water was the causative agent. A researcher makes a contribution to science even though none of his hypotheses solve a problem. Pointing out lines of inquiry that are unprofitable lightens the task of his successors. The testing of false hypotheses is also of value if it directs the attention of the investigator or other scientists to unsuspected facts or relations that eventually help solve the problem. History is sprinkled with stories of investigators who have stumbled upon clues leading to a successful hypothesis while testing a false one.

Roots in Existing Theories

Science develops by building cumulatively on the existing body of facts and theories. A useful educational hypothesis, therefore, adds something to previously established knowledge by supporting, qualifying, refuting, or enlarging upon existing theories. A hypothesis that is compatible with well-attested theories is in a favorable position to advance science. It does not have to agree with all the established facts, but should be consistent with a substantial body of them. Science cannot build sound, well-knit theoretical structures with isolated and conflicting hypotheses. If progress is to be made, new hypotheses must fit into the framework of existing theories and transform them into more perfect explanatory schemes.

Hypotheses that are incompatible with established theories have a low probability of being true; hence, they are regarded with suspicion. Occasionally, however, radical ideas that have little support from what is known about phenomena spark spectacular advances in science. Hypotheses proposed by Newton, Darwin, and Einstein, for example, upset bodies of theory and led to the reorganization of knowledge in their fields. Concepts introduced by Dewey, Thorndike, Köhler, and Lewin revolutionized educational thought. But scientists do not readily relinquish well-established theories. The discoverers of new knowledge rarely discard all older knowledge as they move forward; they usually correct errors in existing theories, extend the coverage of theories, or reconcile conflicting theories. If a new theory explains phenomena previously explained by two or more hypotheses, the new proposal usually receives careful consideration in scientific circles. Hypotheses that overthrow existing theories win support if they eliminate contradictions in the existing ones. Einstein accomplished this feat when he constructed the theory of relativity which eliminated conflicts in the basic laws of classical mechanics and electrodynamics. In his unified field theory, he attempted to reconcile conflicts in the relativity and quantum theories. Thus, even the more revolutionary theories are not completely disassociated from the existing body of knowledge.

Suitability for Intended Purpose

Several hypotheses may explain the same phenomenon, and each may be acceptable. If fifty children lose their lives in a school fire, an architect, pathologist, psychologist, and fire chief may offer different but not necessarily mutually exclusive explanations of the event. Each hypothesis will reflect the past experience, special branch of knowledge, and particular frame of reference of its creator. Obviously, an explanation for the loss of life that satisfies the fire chief will not be the same as that which satisfies the pathologist. But each hypothesis that offers a satisfactory explanation of what it intends to explain is useful for that purpose. The various explanations cannot contradict each other, of course, and they may be mutually supportive. But each hypothesis serves a particular purpose and must be adequate for the purpose it claims to serve.

Simplicity of Explanation

If two hypotheses are capable of explaining the same facts, the simpler one is the better. Simplicity in this instance does not imply ease of comprehension or a low level of significance. Rather, it means that the hypothesis explains the phenomena with the least complex theoretical structure. The theory of relativity, for example, is not easy to comprehend, but it is admired and accepted, in part, because of its logical compactness. The classic example of simplicity is in the field of astronomy. Both the heliocentric theory and the geocentric theory explain the movements of the sun, moon, and planets. Both theories introduce epicycles to account for the positions of heavenly bodies, but the heliocentric theory introduces fewer epicycles. Because the heliocentric theory offers a less elaborate and less complex explanation, it is more satisfactory. The hypothesis that accounts for all the facts with the fewest independent or special assumptions and complexities is always preferable.

Place in Hierarchy of Knowledge

Perhaps the value of hypotheses can best be comprehended by tracing their relationship to facts, theories, and laws. Through inductive and deductive methods of searching for truth, scientists build gradually a hierarchy of knowledge: (1) hypotheses, (2) theories, and (3) laws. Since not everyone employs the same language when referring to these levels of knowledge, students often become confused. In the research literature, for example, the terms "law" and "theory" and the terms "theory" and "hypothesis" are sometimes used interchangeably, and theorizing may refer to the formulation of hypotheses, theories, or laws. The following discussion will distinguish among these levels of knowledge by using the more commonly accepted terminology.

Hypotheses and Facts/ A hypothesis is the first step beyond random suggestions in the direction of scientific truth. In the hierarchy of scientific knowledge, it is the lowest on the scale. This temporary working principle requires testing to determine its worth. If empirical evidence can be found to support the hypothesis, it gains the status of a fact. It retains this status thereafter unless evidence is discovered later to discredit it. Whether or not a hypothesis possesses the status of a fact depends upon the supporting evidence it can secure and hold.

Forget

Hypotheses and Theories/ A theory may contain several logically interrelated hypotheses, and the term "postulate" may be used as a synonym for hypothesis. Hypotheses and theories are alike in that they are both conceptual in nature and in that both seek to explain and to predict phenomena. A theory usually offers a more general or higher-level explanation than a hypothesis. One hypothesis may predict that there is a relationship between A and B, and other hypotheses may predict that there is a relationship between C and B, D and B, and E and B. A theory may present an underlying principle that will explain or account for all these phenomena. After reading the literature relating to phenomenon B, a research worker may ask the question: What common thread runs through these four hypotheses? He may conclude that X is present in each instance, and hence is the key factor that is responsible for the occurrence of B. Because a theory usually presents a comprehensive conceptual scheme that explains diverse phenomena, considerable empirical evidence is needed to support it. This mass of evidence makes the probability of the certainty of a theory greater than that of an isolated, weakly confirmed hypothesis. But no matter how wide a variety of confirming data is obtained, the theory is not established as an absolute truth.

Hypotheses and Laws/ Some hypotheses receive sufficient confirmation to become or lead to the formulation of theories; some lead to the establishment of laws. Laws usually utilize highly abstract concepts, for they offer the most comprehensive type of explanations. A law may be applied to a great number and wide variety of phenomena; a law may explain phenomena that have been explained previously by two or three theories. Because laws are developed and verified by a long, painstaking process, during which they receive extensive empirical confirmation in many areas, they represent the highest level of scientific certainty and are accepted with little question. A law retains its lofty scientific status, however, only as long as it continues to explain every instance which it claims to explain. If new evidence arises that does not conform to its tenets, the law is either reconstructed to conform to the new evidence or abandoned, depending on the nature of the data that are discovered.

Importance of Hypotheses

Hypotheses are indispensable research tools, for they build a bridge between the problem and the location of empirical evidence that may solve the problem. A hypothesis provides the map that guides and expedites the exploration of the phenomena under consideration.

Pinpointing of Problems by Hypotheses

Without a hypothesis to guide him, a research worker often wastes time making a superficial or generalized attack on a problem. To chisel out a hypothesis, he must examine thoroughly the factual and conceptual elements that appear to be related to a problem, trace their relationships and isolate and combine the relevant information into an all-encompassing statement. The process of formulating a hypothesis, deducing its consequences, and defining the terms employed clarifies the issues involved in the inquiry and crystallizes the problem for investigation. The research worker is no longer fumbling with nebulous ideas.

Using Hypotheses to Determine the Relevancy of Facts

Scientific knowledge rests not on *the* facts, but on *selected* facts. The selection of facts is a matter of crucial concern in an investigation. Aimlessly collecting a mass of data on a given subject is futile, for the infinity of possibilities prohibits any rational manipulation of them. The strategic facts needed to solve a problem do not automatically label themselves as relevant to it. The hypothesis helps the investigator ascertain what facts to collect and enables him to decide how many facts are required to test its consequences adequately. Without a hypothesis the research worker drifts into an unfocused trial-and-error inquiry in which he may become hopelessly confused by a welter of irrelevant facts and may never stumble upon a successful problem solution. A hypothesis directs an investigator's efforts into productive channels.

Research Design Indicated by Hypotheses

The hypothesis indicates not only what to look for in an investigation but also how to obtain the data. The hypothetico-deductive argument points up the pertinent issues at stake in a manner that rules out many testing methods as irrelevant. A well-constructed hypothesis suggests what research design or mode of attack will meet its specific demands. A hypothesis may suggest what subjects, tests, or tools are needed, what operations must be performed, what statistical methods are appropriate, and where to locate the events, facts, or circumstances that it predicts are observable.

Explanations Presented by Hypotheses

Modern scientific inquiry goes beyond the amassing of facts or the describing and classifying of them in accordance with their superficial properties. Rather than merely tabulating symptoms of diseases, characteristics of aggressive behavior, or facts about juvenile crime, a serious research worker seeks to determine the underlying pattern of factors that account for the occurrence of phenomena. To leap across gaps in knowledge, he artfully welds known facts and relationships with imaginative constructs to create provisional explanations for phenomena. These hypotheses—constructed from established facts and flights of fancy—provide the investigator with the most efficient instrument for exploring and explaining the unknown.

The Framework for Conclusions
Provided by Hypotheses

If an investigator initiates an investigation with a hypothetico-deductive argument, he has a tailor-made framework available for stating his conclusions. He reasons: If H_1 is true, then these facts are observable; empirical tests reveal that these facts are or are not observable; therefore, the conclusion can be drawn that H_1 is confirmed or disconfirmed. Merely collecting facts on a subject and citing them per se or classifying them according to one's whim in the conclusions of the study may produce a fuzzy, biased, or indecisive interpretation of the findings that does not advance knowledge appreciably. A hypothesis provides a framework for interpreting the findings in a sharp and meaningful manner. If a prediction is not hypothesized in advance, the facts do not have a chance to confirm or disconfirm anything. In the "scientific game," as Kerlinger points out (80:24), an investigator bets first and then rolls the dice; he does not roll the dice and then bet; and he cannot change his bet after the data are in.

Further Research Stimulated by Hypotheses

A well-conceived hypothesis not only explains a given phenomenon, but also may serve as an intellectual lever by which investigators can pry loose more facts to be fitted into other or more inclusive explanations. One report on teacher characteristics (108:399), for example, lists seventeen of the many suggestions that could be put forward about further research needed in this area. The Salk poliomyelitis vaccine, which stemmed from hypotheses relating to tissue culture and viruses that had been established by many earlier investigators, in turn opened up the following questions: Can safer strains be produced? For how long can immunity be achieved? Can effective vaccines be developed for measles, encephalitis, common colds, etc.?

A hypothesis is not advanced as a final statement; as Max Weber said, "it asks to be outdated and surpassed." It is our passkey to the unknown, leading us from one problem to another, from modest explanations to more adequate conceptual schemes that successively open up exciting new areas on the frontiers of knowledge.

9

Strategy of Historical Research

Because educational research embraces segments of many related disciplines and utilizes a great variety of procedures, it is somewhat difficult to obtain an overview of the work. Educators undertake studies in all phases of education; they investigate phenomena in the areas of curriculum, administration, guidance, methods, and teacher preparation; and they probe fundamental problems concerning the nature of learning and of child development. Several volumes would have to be written to explore the work being done, and the discussion would become repetitive because investigators in the various fields employ somewhat similar techniques and procedures. The remainder of this text, therefore, discusses (1) the three general methods that educators utilize to solve problems—the historical, descriptive, and experimental methods, (2) the tools that researchers employ, and (3) the manner in which they write and evaluate research reports.

This chapter will examine the investigative procedures that are employed by historians. Obtaining knowledge about the past has always intrigued men, but the purpose and scope of historical writing have changed down through the ages. Most of the early writers sought to achieve literary rather than scientific objectives; they preserved beloved folk tales or created stirring epics to entertain or inspire the reader. A few ancient Greek scholars, however, envisioned history somewhat as a science—a search for truth. Thucydides, who wrote his famous historical accounts in the fifth century B.C., aspired to be more than an imaginative storyteller. His objective was to present an accurate account of the past in order to aid "in the interpretation of the future." To achieve this goal, Thucydides based his writings on his own observations or the reports of eyewitnesses that he subjected to detailed tests of reliability. For centuries most historians ignored the exacting methods and lofty aims of Thucydides; many of them wrote history to glorify the state or church rather than to arrive at objective truth. Some historians were disciplined, however, by rigorous critical standards of research, and this practice became more commonplace particularly after the vigorous academic discussions of the historical method that took place shortly after the turn of the century.

Today, historians strive to recreate the past experiences of mankind in a manner that does no violence to the actual events and conditions of the time. They collect, examine, select, verify, and classify facts in accordance with specific standards, and endeavor to interpret and present those facts in an exposition that will stand the test of critical examination. They apply the same scholarly standards whether the problem is concerned with the history of a nation, the evolution of American universities, the life of an outstanding educator, or the history of an educational association. Modern historical research is a critical search for truth.

The historical method of investigation may be applied not only to subject matter that is commonly referred to as history, but also to ascertain the meaning and reliability of past facts in the natural sciences, law, medicine, religion, or any other discipline. Even if a researcher is not engaged in a historical study, he may employ the critical standards established by historians to help him evaluate previous studies relating to his problem, the tools and procedures utilized by his predecessors, and the circumstances that conditioned the results of the previous studies. Every researcher should be familiar with this method of investigation.

When undertaking a historical study, a scholar engages in some activities that are common to all investigations, but the nature of his subject matter presents him with some peculiar problems and requires him to apply some special standards and techniques. In general, a historian becomes involved in the following procedures: (1) formulating the problem, (2) collecting source materials, (3) criticizing source materials, (4) formulating hypotheses to explain events or conditions, and (5) interpreting and reporting the findings. These are not necessarily separate or successive processes, but for the sake of convenience and clarity, they will be considered separately in the following discussion. After reviewing these steps, the chapter will conclude with an evaluation of the historical method.

Formulating the Problem

Historical inquiry begins when some event, development, or experience of the past is questioned. The resulting uncertainty leads the investigator to a consideration of the nature and dimensions of the questions for which he seeks an answer. Beginning with a rather general, diffused, or even confused notion of the problem, he isolates one by one the crucial points that are giving rise to the uncertainty, and then formulates a simple, clear, complete description of the problem. Before proceeding further he checks whether this problem is answerable by available methods of inquiry and by the available sources of data.

Earlier chapters in this text, as you recall, discussed the various sequential stages through which the investigator progresses to formulate the problem. Repeating these stages in this chapter is unnecessary, because the general considerations for selecting, delimiting, and doing the background reading remain the same regardless of the type of investigation one undertakes. It is sufficient, therefore, to state that historical research, like any scientific inquiry, stems from a problematic situation which starts the investigator on his quest for a solution.

Collecting Source Materials

Obtaining the best data available to solve a problem is an initial and important task of a historian. Thus, early in any study, he sifts through the vast and varied traces of human activity that testify about past events, and from these he selects evidence that is relevant to his problem. Although he may begin his search by examining secondary sources, his ultimate objective is to locate primary sources. Hence, he must be able to distinguish between the two types of source materials and must become adept at locating them.

Primary and Secondary Sources

Since a historian cannot observe past events for himself, he endeavors to obtain the "best evidence" available from *primary sources:* (1) the testimony of able eye and ear witnesses to past events, and (2) actual objects used in the past that can be examined directly. The importance of these sources cannot be overemphasized: through these surviving traces of men's thoughts and activities a historian can gain some understanding of the past; without them he is helpless—"Without them history would be only an empty tale, signifying nothing" (146:185). Primary sources are the basic materials of historical research.

Because a historian knows the worth of "firsthand" evidence, he makes every effort to locate it. But sometimes he finds it necessary to consult *secondary sources:* information provided by a person who did not directly observe the event, object, or condition. These summaries appear in encyclopedias, newspapers, periodicals, and other references. Some secondary source materials are actually based on fourth- and fifth-hand information. The more interpretations that come between the past event and the reader, the less trustworthy is the evidence, for the facts may become changed and distorted in transmission.

A rigid classification of source materials is not always possible, for both first- and second-hand information may appear in the same report. A principal's report of a school fire, for example, may describe incidents that he observed personally as well as those that other people described to him. In some instances, an item may be classified as either a primary or a secondary source, depending upon how it is used. A general history of education textbook, for example, is many times removed from the original events, and is, therefore, a secondary source. If a scholar is studying how authors organized history of education textbooks and the emphasis they placed on various topics, however, it is a primary source.

A reputable historian obtains evidence from the closest witness to the past events or conditions. A newspaper account of what transpired at an NEA executive meeting would not satisfy him if he could obtain a copy of the official minutes of the meeting. A translation of an educational document would not satisfy him if he could obtain and read the original document. Whenever possible, he would visit an old school building or laboratory rather than study pictures of it. Primary sources are highly prized by a historian. Secondary sources are never trusted completely, but they do serve useful purposes. They may acquaint a neophyte with work that has been done in an area that he is exploring, may suggest problem possibilities and working hypotheses, and may introduce him to important primary sources. An investigator may use secondary sources to obtain an overview of the problem area, to accumulate background information for his study, and to develop the general setting for his problem. During the investigation, he will alter his problem outline, of course, whenever firsthand information indicates it is imperative to do so.

Records and Remains

For the most part the historian's source materials are *records that have been preserved with the conscious intent of transmitting information.* Diverse types of records of past ideas, conditions, and events are available in written, pictorial, and mechanical forms, for example:

1/ Official records.
Legislative, judicial, or executive documents prepared by Federal, state, or local governments, such as constitutions, laws, charters, court proceedings and decisions, tax lists, and vital statistics; the data preserved by churches, such as baptismal, marriage, financial, and board meeting records; the information compiled by Federal and state education departments, special commissions, professional organizations, school boards, or administrative authorities, such as the minutes of meetings, reports of committees, administrative orders or directives, school surveys, annual reports, budgets, courses of study, class schedules, salary lists, attendance records, health records, safety and accident reports, and athletic records

2/ Personal records.
Diaries, autobiographies, letters, wills, deeds, contracts, lecture notes, and original drafts of speeches, articles, and books

3/ Oral traditions.
Myths, folk tales, family stories, dances, games, ceremonies, reminiscences by eyewitnesses to events, and recordings

4/ Pictorial records.
Photographs, movies, microfilms, drawings, paintings, and sculpture

5/ Published materials.
Newspaper, pamphlet, and periodical articles; literary and philosophical works that convey information about education

6/ Mechanical records.
Tape recordings of interviews and meetings, phonograph records of pupils' speech or reading efforts

In some instances, the historian does not have to rely on the records, reports, or words of others, for he can actually handle objects of the past that have been preserved. *These remains or relics which are handed down from the past without the specific intent of imparting facts or information constitute an unconscious testimony of incidents in the lives of people.* The toys, weapons, and implements found on a burial site, for example, may convey considerable information about the past. Remains sometimes reveal the actual practices and conditions better than official documents. A law may be found, for example, stating it was compulsory for children to remain in school until they were sixteen years of age. But youthful skeletons that are found at isolated working sites where catastrophes occurred and other unpremeditated evidence may reveal that many pupils left school before that age.

Various types of remains a historian might find are:

1/ Physical remains.
Buildings, facilities, furniture, equipment, costumes, implements, awards, and skeletal remains
2/ Printed materials.
Textbooks, record blanks, contracts, attendance forms, report cards, and newspaper advertisements
3/ Handwritten materials.
Pupil manuscripts, drawings, and exercises

Since relics and remains are tangible evidence that the researcher can examine personally, they are more trustworthy as sources than records. The historian can measure, weigh, and describe an ancient instrument that was once used to punish children. To interpret how, when, or why it was used, however, he usually must search for clues in reports made by men in the past.

Source materials do not necessarily fall into exclusive categories. An item may be either a record or a relic depending upon the purpose for which it is used and the intention of the producer of the document or relic. A blank form for recording academic studies and achievements, for example, is a remain. But, if someone writes the courses, the grades, credits earned, and the name of the student on it, the form conveys information intentionally; thus, it is a document. Similarly, a recording may be made of a pupil's speech merely to test the equipment and with no intention of conveying information; or it may be made to have a record of the pupil's speech patterns for future analysis.

Location of Source Materials

In a preliminary search for historical data, the card catalog, periodical indexes, bibliographies, historical reviews, dissertations, and research journals provide helpful leads. Useful materials may be located in the local library, but during an investigation the search usually extends to other institutions and to specialized depositories that have business, government, or private papers relating to his problem.

Some individuals and agencies have exerted considerable effort to collect educational records and remains and have established a number of historical depositories to preserve them. The types of resources and completeness of the accumulations in the various depositories vary greatly: some contain extensive collections of a particular kind of material and others have fragmentary collections of items from different fields. Owing to the wide expanse of time and the broad scope of educational endeavors, no one depository, however excellent, can possibly house all the available materials.

The Library of Congress, the New York Public Library, and some universities and specialized libraries have valuable collections in particular educational areas. The Museum of the City of New York and similar institutions in other communities possess local educational remains. Some state and local historical societies have museums that contain important remains, newspaper files, and documents. Educational organizations have preserved documents and relics pertinent to their interests, for example, the American Association for Health, Physical Education, and Recreation has established a depository at Queens College and more recently at Ohio State University. A few universities have kept libraries, equipment, and effects of outstanding educators who have served on their staffs. Private citizens and prominent educators have also accumulated exceptional collections, such as the 8,000 old school textbooks that Dr. John Nietz acquired and presented to the University of Pittsburgh.

Not all source materials are collected for the convenience of a researcher. Private probing expeditions may turn up much valuable evidence. Important data may be discovered by talking with "old-timers" in the profession; exploring secondhand stores, bookshops, and attics; visiting school sites, getting permission to examine the correspondence, lecture notes, manuscripts, and files of retired teachers; or studying court, town, church, school, and institutional reports and records.

Criticizing Source Materials

A historian does not assume that a remain is genuine or that a record presents an authentic account of past happenings. He examines each one meticulously and attempts to determine how trustworthy it is. Detecting whether a document contains unintentional errors or is a deliberate deception is an essential part of his work. Any investigator who fails to take this precaution is foolhardy, for research based on unreliable sources is labor lost. "In historical studies doubt is the beginning of wisdom" (75:50). To give mankind a credible account of past events, a historian subjects his source materials to rigorous external and internal criticism.

External Criticism

Through external criticism the historian checks the genuineness or, more accurately, the validity of the document or relic—whether it is what it appears or claims to be—to determine whether it is admissible as evidence. To discover the origins of source materials, he asks many questions: When or why was the document produced? Who was the author or creator? Did the credited author write the material? Is this the original or an accurate copy of the author's work? If not, can the original text of the document be restored? Questions, questions, questions—the researcher keeps asking them until he can ascertain when, where, why, and by whom a document or relic was produced.

Establishing authorship is a common test performed by a historian, for some documents do not carry the name of the writer, conceal his identity with a pseudonym, or present a man as the author who wrote little or none of the work. Educational committees and school administrators, for example, may issue reports that do not clearly identify the writer. Although three committee members may sign a report, only one of them may have written it—or a subordinate of one member may have compiled it. To ascertain the authorship of a superintendent's annual report, a historian may have to investigate several things: Did the superintendent or one of his assistants write it, or was it a compilation of reports made by various school administrative heads? If the superintendent used other people's materials, did he correct, alter, omit, suppress, or expand parts of their reports?

Enterprising and exacting detective work is often required to establish authorship, trace anonymous and undated documents, ferret out forgeries, discover plagiarism, spot incorrectly identified items, or restore a document to its original form. When sleuthing for clues, the historian examines items attentively and asks pertinent questions, such as: (1) Are the language, style, spelling, handwriting, and printing of the document typical of the author's other work and the period in which it was written? (2) Did the author exhibit ignorance of things a man of his training and time should have known? (3) Did he write about events, things, or places that a man of that period could not have known? (4) Did anyone alter the manuscript—intentionally or unintentionally—by copying it incorrectly, adding to it, or deleting passages? (5) Is this an original draft of the author's work or a copy? If it is a copy, is it reproduced in the exact words of the original? (6) If the manuscript is undated or the author unknown, are there any internal clues in the document that reveal its origins?

When cross-examining his silent witnesses to determine the genuineness of a document or relic, a researcher experiences greater success if he possesses a rich fund of historical and general knowledge. He also needs a good "chronological sense," a versatile intellect, good common sense, an intelligent understanding of human behavior, and plenty of patience and persistence. To solve some problems, he must be familiar with philology, chemistry, anthropology, archaeology, cartography, numismatics, art, literature, paleography, or various modern and ancient languages. A historian cannot have a knowledge of everything, of course, but he usually acquires special training in auxiliary fields that are most closely related to his educational problem. If he is not qualified to undertake certain aspects of textual criticism, he seeks the help of competent experts in the field.

Internal Criticism

After completing the external criticism of a source material, the historian engages in internal criticism. External criticism is concerned with establishing the time, place, and authorship of the document and restoring the original form and language employed by the author. Internal criticism is concerned with ascertaining the meaning and trustworthiness of the *data within the document*. When checking the content of a source material, the historian probes for answers to the following questions: (1) What did the author mean by each word and statement? (2) Are the statements that the author made credible? The intent of internal criticism is to determine the conditions under which a document was produced, the validity of the intellectual premises upon which the writer proceeded, and the correct interpretation to be placed upon data.

Determining the meaning of a statement, technical term, or archaic word can be a complicated task requiring considerable knowledge of history, laws, customs, and languages. Many words in older documents do not mean the same thing today that they did in earlier times. Interpreting words and statements in recent publications is a less arduous task, but some words do not convey the same meaning to all people. When English and American writers use the word "football" or "public school," for example, they are not referring to the same thing. Nor do all authors have identical meanings in mind when they use the term "progressive education" or "juvenile delinquent."

Reading a document "through the author's eyes" is easier if one is familiar with the geographical, social, religious, and economic environment that the writer experienced. If one knows why an author wrote a report, he is able to interpret its meanings more accurately. The possession of such background information helps an investigator detect whether the author is writing seriously, humorously, ironically, or symbolically. It helps him determine whether the author is voicing his real sentiments or pious, polite, or conventional phrases for public consumption. Whenever a researcher uses a translation of a historical document or does the work himself, he makes certain that the translated materials convey exactly the same meaning as the original. Accurate analysis and interpretation of the author's meaning is of paramount importance if a scholar is to recreate a reliable account of past events.

A historian remains skeptical of statements made in source materials until he investigates whether the author was willing and able to tell the truth in each instance. When conducting this probe, he asks some of the following questions: (1) Is the author accepted as a competent observer and reliable reporter by other authorities in this special field? (2) Were his facilities, technical training, and location favorable for observing the conditions he reported? (3) Did emotional stress, age, or health conditions cause him to make faulty observations or an inaccurate report? (4) Did he report on direct observations, hearsay, or borrowed source materials? (5) Did he write the document at the time of observation or weeks or years later? (6) Did he write from detailed notes of observations or from memory? (7) Did he have biases concerning any nation, region, race, religion, person, political party, social or economic group, professional body, period of history, teaching method, or educational philosophy that influenced his writing? (8) Did anyone finance his research work with the hope of securing a report favorable to a specific cause? (9) Did the author write under any economic, political, religious, or social condition that might have caused him to ignore, misinterpret, or misrepresent certain facts? (10) Was he motivated to write by malice, vanity, or a desire to justify his acts? (11) Was his objective to win the approval of succeeding generations or to please or antagonize some group? (12) Did the author distort or embellish the truth to achieve colorful literary effects? (13) Did the author contradict himself? (14) Do accounts by other independent, competent observers of different backgrounds agree with the report of the author?/

Examples of Criticism

Many questions arise when one engages in historical criticism. To give you some insight into typical problems that a researcher encounters, the following discussion presents a case of (1) determining authorship, (2) identifying an unknown manuscript, (3) assessing authenticity, (4) restoring a document, (5) determining an event, (6) ascertaining meaning, (7) finding the correct spelling, and (8) checking origin.

Determining Authorship/ Sometimes a man will be credited as an author of a work for years and in many reputable references before anyone questions the fact. A book on gymnastics that was used in some early American schools, for example, has the name of Salzmann on the title page. Scholars who traced the origins of this text, found that Johann C. F. Guts Muths, a teacher in Salzmann's school, was actually the author of the original book *Gymnastik für die Jugend,* which was published in 1793. In 1800, an English publisher translated Guts Muths's book and placed Salzmann's name on the title page. A footnote explained that there was no doubt that Salzmann wrote it, for his name was subjoined to the advertisement in which it was announced (85:80). This error of authorship was repeated in the American work of 1802. A comparison of the original Guts Muths edition with the translated versions also reveals that the later editions were altered and condensed.

Identifying an Unknown Manuscript/ An interesting story of tracking down the author, time, place, and purpose of a document has been told by Thomas Woody (146:188–189). In the University of Pennsylvania Archives, an old manuscript was found with other original manuscripts relating to the University. It was in relatively good condition, apparently free from alteration and mutilation, but devoid of any external indication of its origin.

After examining the manuscript carefully for clues, Woody was able to formulate the following hypotheses: (1) the document was all or part of an original document or a translated account of the rules and operation of *Pädagogium Regii,* a school established by Francke at Halle, Germany; (2) the appearance of certain awkward expressions suggested that the writer or translator was unfamiliar with the English language; (3) the reference to money in terms of Pennsylvania currency suggested that the author expected the information to be used in that locale; and (4) a reference made to 1726 indicated that the manuscript was probably produced sometime after that date.

To test his hypotheses, Woody turned to the most promising source—the Trustees' Minutes—for supporting evidence. In the minutes, he found that the Trustees in 1750–1751 appointed a committee to draw up regulations for the new institution that had been established and placed under their care. The committee, wishing to be better informed about institutional regulations, requested "the Trustees to get a Translation made of a Pamphlet written in the German Language, recommended by the Revd. Mr. Whitefield, containing the Rules and Orders observed by the celebrated . . . School at Hall [Halle]" (146:189). The minutes stated that the Trustees agreed unanimously to the committee's proposal.

Woody suggested that, "from the foregoing, it seems reasonably certain, but the proof is not complete, that the English manuscript *may be the translation* of a document which, presumably, Mr. Whitefield had in his possession" (146:189). This conclusion was also supported by the fact that many of Mr. Whitefield's letters express admiration for the institutions established by Francke. Woody concluded "Further search would probably lead to discovery of the original pamphlet, or a copy of the same, from which this MS. translation was made, and many other matters" (146:189). But his discussion is sufficient to reveal some of the steps and techniques involved in tracing an unknown manuscript.

Assessing Authenticity/ Historians are curious about whether a document actually is what it claims to be. Hoaxes and intentional falsifications are not common in educational literature, but doubts sometimes arise concerning the real nature of a document. This happened in the case of *A Young Girl's Diary* (71), an anonymous work that was claimed to be a genuine and unedited diary of an early adolescent. This book, which Freud described as a "gem" in a brief introductory letter, gained wide recognition in psychological circles as a revelation of the beginning of sexual consciousness, its development, and its incorporation into maturer thought patterns.

When a few readers (20) began to suspect that the diary was not the work of an early adolescent, they suggested that it might be a reproduction of childhood experiences by an adult. To support their position they pointed out that the style of writing and the sustained logical thinking were too mature for an eleven- to fourteen-year-old girl. The length of the entries aroused their suspicions, for they thought that writing 2,000 words a day was too taxing a task for a child. The critics held that the continuity, coherence, and clarity of the diary were extraordinary, particularly because it had to be kept secret from an anxious mother and an inquisitive sister. Unexplained allusions and unconnected incidents did not impede the reader's understanding of the passages as would be expected. One did not need editorial notes to explain who characters were and each incident reported contributed to building the main dramatic theme. Inconsistencies were noted when checking the girl's references to the weather on certain days, visits to places that were nonexistent at the time, and other items (83). Some men concluded, therefore, that the diary probably was not written by a young girl during the years the events took place.

Restoring a Document/ An author's words are not necessarily preserved in print exactly as he wrote them. *The Autobiography of St. Thérèse of Lisieux* (81), for example, was published after her death and became a best seller. When she was canonized, the original script of her autobiography was located and analyzed. In comparing it with the printed work, scholars noted many differences. During the process of restoring the autobiography, they discovered that 7,000 changes had been made in the manuscript!

Determining an Event/ In some widely used reference books, Boston University has been given credit erroneously for granting the first bachelor of music degree in 1876. The report of the United States Commissioner of Education for 1873 indicates that such action had been taken by Adrian College, and the Trustees' Minutes of the College dated June, 1873 (52:35), confirm that the degree was conferred on a student that year.

Ascertaining Meaning/ When men want to settle questions, they may turn to traditional sources of authority for guidance. In recent years, for example, some citizens have urged that sectarian religious instruction be fostered in public schools and that public funds be made available to private and parochial schools. Their opponents claim that such action would violate the principle of the separation of church and state expressed in the First Amendment, which reads: "Congress shall make no law respecting an establishment of religion, or prohibiting the free exercise thereof. . . ." The question raised is: "Does the ban on 'establishment of religion' prohibit 'co-operation' between church and state in education or is greater 'co-operation' than we now have both permissible and desirable? Does 'co-operation' amount to an alliance or fusion of church and state?" (21:xiii). To reach any decision, it is necessary to determine what the principle of separation of church and state means.

Professor Butts tried to discover the authentic meaning of "establishment of religion" by sifting through the available historical evidence. To trace what the term has meant in America from colonial days to the mid-twentieth century, he examined the deliberations and constitutions of colonial, state, and national bodies; the writings of outstanding leaders; and the school laws, legislative acts, and judicial decisions that had a bearing on the problem. Butt's analysis extended over 200 pages, and his conclusions concerning the meaning of the term "separation of church and state" for education were summarized in ten statements (21:209–210). His study reveals the tremendous amount of labor that is sometimes involved in determining what a statement means.

Finding the Correct Spelling/ Standard works of reference generally possess their quota of mistakes. The *Encyclopaedia Britannica,* for instance, refers to the wife of the fourth president of the United States as Dorothy; the *Encyclopedia Americana* states that she is Dolly; the *Reader's Encyclopedia* says she is Dorothea. When a group of scholars examined letters from Mrs. Madison to friends, a note to a minister, her will, and her mother's letters, they found evidence which indicated that Mrs. Madison's first name was Dolley—not Dolly.

Checking Origin/ Our national pastime of baseball has also been the subject of historical criticism. Modern literature commonly credits Abner Doubleday as the inventor of the game. How he won this reputation and the historical criticism of the claim is an intriguing story that reveals how a picture of the past may be distorted.

When baseball became a popular sport in this country at the turn of the century, enthusiastic fans claimed that the game was of American origin. A British-born sportsman, Henry Chadwick, challenged this theory, for he believed the sport was a direct descendent of the English game of "rounders." A. G. Spalding, a popular baseball figure who supported the American theory, sought to settle the issue in "some comprehensive and authoritative way, *for all time*" (67:173) by establishing a commission of six public-spirited men to investigate.

The public was invited to send pertinent information to the commission. Two years later the members accepted the testimony submitted in a letter by Abner Graves, who wrote that his boyhood friend, Abner Doubleday, originated the game.

Without any additional supporting evidence, they announced that Doubleday invented and named the game "Base Ball" in 1839 when he marked off a diamond-shaped field and diagramed the location of players at Cooperstown, New York. This report remained unchallenged by most people for years and was copied in a number of textbooks, newspapers, and sports' books.

When Henderson examined the evidence, he presented some interesting conclusions (67:170–196). The report was primarily the work of the chairman of the commission, A. G. Mills, who was a military friend of Doubleday. Mills based his findings apparently on a letter written by Abner Graves, for no documents by any other person and no contemporary records were presented to support the Graves story. Henderson points out that when Doubleday originated the game in Cooperstown, he was actually in West Point and did not return to Cooperstown on leave. After retiring from the army, Doubleday wrote many articles for publication but none about baseball, and when he died in 1893, his obituary notice did not mention that he invented the game.

A critical examination of the commission's report revealed many other weaknesses. The name "Base Ball," illustrations of a baseball diamond, and rules of the game that were invented supposedly in 1839 had appeared in print before that time. Although it was claimed that Graves was present when Doubleday traced the first baseball diamond in the dirt, the original Graves letter did not mention this incident. A later letter that appears to have been written by Graves disclosed that he did not know "where the first game was played according to Doubleday's plan." Comparisons of the two Graves letters revealed some inconsistencies, which was not surprising, for the man wrote from memory almost seven decades after the event.

Henderson believes that certain personal factors may have caused members of the commission to accept the report. Because of the pressure of other duties, they probably did not check the facts thoroughly. Perhaps patriotic prejudices also influenced their decision. Some of the men were anxious to prove that baseball was of American rather than British origin. The possibility that General Doubleday, a famous Civil War soldier, invented the great American game must have appealed to them.

General Principles of Criticism

The examples given of historical criticism reveal that researchers make many judgments when evaluating records and relics. Not all the principles of criticism can be fully discussed in this text, but the following suggestions made by Woody will serve as a general guide.

(1) Do not read into earlier documents the conceptions of later times; (2) do not judge an author ignorant of certain events, necessarily, because he fails to mention them (the argument *ex silentio*), or that they did not occur, for the same reason; (3) underestimating a source is no less an error than overestimating it in the same degree, and there is no more virtue in placing an event too late than in dating it too early by the same number of years or centuries; (4) a single true source may establish the existence of an idea, but other direct, competent, independent witnesses are required to prove the reality of events or objective facts; (5) identical errors prove the dependence of sources on each other, or a common source; (6) if witnesses contradict each other on a certain point, one or the other may be true, but both may be in error; (7) direct, competent, independent witnesses who report the same central fact and also many peripheral matters in a casual way may be accepted for the points of their agreement; (8) official testimony, oral or written, must be compared with unofficial testimony whenever possible, for neither one nor the other is alone sufficient; (9) a document may provide competent and dependable evidence on certain points, yet carry no weight in respect to others it mentions (146:190).

For a more detailed discussion of the problems and principles involved in external and internal criticism, the reader may consult the excellent discussions and interesting examples presented by outstanding authorities in the field (13, 16, 64, 68, 75). One must keep in mind that criticism of documents yields only isolated information and fails to meet the legitimate goals of the scientific method.

Formulating Hypotheses

Historians do not aimlessly collect records and relics, subject them to intensive criticism, and then present the mass of facts—names, events, places, and dates—to the public like "beads on a string." Unrelated bits of information do not advance knowledge appreciably. Even if scholars group their facts and arrange their groups in a logical order, they produce a narrative that is little more than a series of disconnected and unexplained events. Isolated facts lack meaning; consequently, research workers go beyond the amassing of data or merely describing and classifying them in accordance with their superficial properties. To produce works of value, they formulate tentative hypotheses that explain the occurrence of events and conditions. They seek the hidden connections, underlying patterns, or general principles that explain or describe the structural interrelations of the phenomena under study. After constructing hypotheses, they search for evidence that will confirm or disconfirm them.

When Woody traced the origin of a manuscript, you recall, he first hypothesized that it might be a copy of the regulations observed in a German school and then searched for evidence to test this reasoned guess. Other historians follow a similar procedure. After examining raw materials in some area of interest they (1) formulate a precisely stated hypothesis about the nature of a past event and (2) note any assumptions that underlie the structuring of their problem. Thus, a reader is informed of their objectives and of any political, philosophical, social, etc., views they hold that may influence the selection of data. Since a previous chapter discussed the structuring and testing of hypotheses in detail, perhaps the best way of gaining a deeper understanding of the process is to examine some concrete examples.

Principle of Separation of Church and State

When Butts undertook the task of determining the meaning of the principle of "establishment of religion," he observed the standards of sound scholarship. In the introduction of the study, he expressed his objective simply

This book is an effort to state as clearly, as briefly, and as objectively as possible what the weight of historical evidence means concerning the American principle and practice of separation of church and state. . . . In the pages that follow, a portion of the available historical evidence is presented in order to help the American people decide whether or not the principle of separation of church and state is an authentic and valid tradition in America (21:5–6).

Because his selection of evidence is necessarily conditioned by his beliefs, Butts frankly states that his work is written

. . . in a framework of values which includes the following assumptions: that religious freedom is a foundation stone of American liberty, that the preservation of the equal rights of religious conscience is a necessity for genuine religious freedom, that the guarantee of religious freedom is an essential function of our constitutional form of government, that public education is a bulwark of our common democratic values, that private education has a legitimate and desirable function to serve in American society, and that "an establishment of religion" (as defined in Chapters 2, 3, and 4) is a threat to religious freedom and to the American tradition of democracy. This all means, by and large, that the historic principle of separation of church and state as defined in 175 years of American history is a desirable tradition to maintain in American education (as outlined in Chapters 5 and 6). These are the working hypotheses upon which the investigation in this book has been undertaken. Whether or not the conclusions reached are justifiable depends in the last analysis upon public judgment (21:xiii–xiv).

Early Roman Education

A study of early Roman education caused Chiappetta to formulate a hypothesis concerning the period, "namely, that the Romans did not accept formal education or use it as a reliable or effective behavior changing device" (29:155). He noted that aside from the writing of Quintilian there were practically no reliable reports on educational practices during this period and there was also a "curious lack of archaeological remains which would indicate the existence of schools in any great number" (29:155). To test his hypothesis, Chiappetta examined "some of the events which occurred, or more importantly, did *not* occur" and reported the following conclusions:

The scanty evidences indicate that only a small segment of the population attended schools. In general, the sons of the senatorial class became the next senators or patricians, and at no time did the schools become a vehicle for social mobility. . . . Further, while the Romans . . . built not only an empire, but all the appurtenances that go with a complicated society—a language, a priesthood, commercial systems, an architecture, roads, bridges, sanitation systems, armies, navies, *ad infinitum*—at no time do we hear of schools which prepared the Romans to do these outstanding deeds. Apparently there was no institutional educational attempt to prepare people for the vast range of employments required in the constantly enlarged Roman-dominated area. The attempts at secondary and higher education seemed to concentrate on the production of the orator, and . . . the tyranny of the Roman emperors was in the process of becoming so absolute that Rome no longer needed statesmen, educated or not. . . . Finally, the late entry of the state into the support of education seems to indicate that the Romans thought lightly of such matters (29:155–156).

Early New York Schools

Errors may appear in educational literature and be repeated for years before someone challenges them. About the turn of the century, for example Andrew S. Draper stated that "all the English schools in the province [New York] from 1700 down to the time of the Declaration of Independence, were maintained by a great religious society . . . called the society for the propagation of the gospel in foreign parts [SPGFP]" (46:29–30). Other educational historians agreed.

Years later, Professor Seybolt (117), apparently after reading a doctoral dissertation by Kemp (79) on the work of the religious society, began to doubt Draper's generalization. Kemp stated that from 1710 to 1776 the SPGFP supported continuously from five to ten elementary schools in New York. Seybolt got the notion that there were probably many "English Schools" in New York during those years that were not maintained by the religious society. To test his hypothesis, he examined eighteenth-century records and found evidence that there were at least 200 schools not maintained by the SPGFP. Thus, Seybolt had produced facts to refute Draper's generalization and to support his own. In brief, he noted a conflict in the literature, proposed a working hypothesis, collected data that supported his position, and thus confirmed his hypothesis.

Early American Textbooks

Sister Marie Léonore Fell formulated a hypothesis to guide her study of *The Foundations of Nativism in American Textbooks, 1783–1860*. Previous studies had indicated that considerable opposition to minority groups existed in the United States at this time, but the "contribution of biased text-books to political nativism" remained unknown. She examined more than a thousand reading, history, and geography texts to test the hypothesis that during the formative years of our country the compilers of textbooks "laid the foundations of the anti-Catholic and anti-foreign attitudes, which had their political conclusions in the Nativist movements of the 1830's and 1840's and in the Know-Nothing party of the 1850's" (54:vi). In reporting her findings, she stated that the study "reveals not so much an anti-foreign slant as an anti-Catholic attitude on the part of the compilers of the texts" (54:224). Thus, Sister Fell had established a hypothesis, examined primary source materials to test it, and announced her conclusions that the evidence revealed "intentional" anti-Catholic indoctrination in textbooks.

Origin of Sport

Because the recreations of people reveal much about the period in which they live, some men are interested in tracing the development of sports. After studying various ball games and wondering about their origins, Henderson formulated the hypothesis that "all modern games played with bat and ball descend from one common source: an ancient fertility rite observed by Priest-Kings in the Egypt of the Pyramids" (67:4). To test his hypothesis, he examined the religious ceremonies and folk customs of ancient man and traced the evolution of games played with a ball. Henderson reported finding evidence in rituals, customs, and tombs to support his thesis that the modern bat-and-ball games are vestigial remains of ancient rites.

Reporting the Findings

After completing their investigations, historians write well-organized reports of their work. Chapter 15 gives a detailed discussion of the processes involved in reporting research. It is sufficient to state here that an investigator's exposition includes a statement of the problem, a review of the literature, the basic assumptions underlying the hypothesis, the statement of the hypothesis, the methods employed in testing the hypothesis, the results obtained, the conclusions reached, and a bibliography.

The hypothesis helps the historian determine what is relevant and irrelevant to a study and provides a framework for stating the conclusions of the study in a meaningful manner. Within the framework of the hypothesis, of course, the historian will pattern his material in some systematic order, such as chronological, geographical, topical, or a combination of these. He will also make judgments concerning the amount of emphasis or space to give to various evidence. Considerable information may be collected on relatively minor points in a study and little evidence on more significant events. Reporting everything would produce a distorted picture of the past. Determining which data are most significant and how many of them to include requires a reappraisal of the hypothesis and the study as a whole.

Weaving raw data into a cohesive, well-proportioned, colorful exposition requires painstaking labor. To achieve the twin objectives of maintaining accuracy and interest, a historian refrains from embellishing narratives with dramatic flourishes that distort the truth, but strives for literary excellence. Stretching or supplementing the existing evidence to create a more spirited narrative is not permissible. Fitting the pieces of established evidence into a simple, vivid mosaic that delineates past events dramatically is the difficult but desired ideal. History is life—and it deserves better than a drab description. The historian cannot sacrifice accuracy for eloquence; but by developing his creative and critical skills he can learn to write lucid, lively, logical accounts without violating the rigorous rules of historical scholarship.

Evaluating Historical Research

Historical research is an exciting and satisfying pursuit, but a proper perspective of its achievements and limitations is important. Some people credit historians with accomplishing more than is possible; others believe they cannot possibly produce scientifically reliable data. The truth probably lies somewhere between these two extreme positions. By reading the following arguments, you may get a better insight into the problem and draw your own conclusions.

Nature of Historical Knowledge

Adulators of historical writing sometimes assume that the researchers present the totality of past actuality. The historian cannot possibly do this; he can give only a fragmentary picture of the past. Historical knowledge is never complete; it is derived from the surviving records of a limited number of events that took place in the past. As Gottschalk points out,

. . . only a part of what was observed in the past was remembered by those who observed it; only a part of what was remembered was recorded; only a part of what was recorded has survived; only a part of what has survived has come to the historians' attention; only a part of what has come to their attention is credible; only a part of what is credible has been grasped; and only a part of what has been grasped can be expounded or narrated by the historian (64:45).

Because historical knowledge is partial, not total, knowledge of the past, how closely written history represents past actuality is always a matter of conjecture.

Need for Documents

Historical knowledge is no better than the availability of "bits and pieces" of past actuality. Yet the education profession has been negligent about preserving these "bits and pieces." Each year important source materials are lost permanently to mankind. Valuable letters, documents, and other materials are discarded from the files of retiring professors; records of embryonic educational organizations are tossed away; old textbooks, school records, and equipment are cleared from attics and storerooms and destroyed. Educators can make an important contribution to the profession by rescuing these primary source materials from oblivion and establishing depositories for their preservation.

Application of the Scientific Method

Some men believe that historical researchers can adhere to the same principles and purposes that the physical scientists do. Other scholars contend that history embraces a different kind of subject matter than science and that it therefore requires a different method and interpretation. Men from both schools of thought usually agree that the historical method is scientific in some respects, but they do not agree that it is in other respects.

Hockett has described the scientific method as "consisting of three processes: observation, hypothesis and experiment" (68:58). He and others argue that modern historians are scientific in that they (1) examine their source materials critically and (2) formulate hypotheses carefully. But Hockett and other scholars recognize that historians encounter greater difficulty than physical scientists in applying the scientific method of research. Some of the problems that arise are concerned with (1) critical examination of sources, (2) construction of hypotheses, (3) observation and experimentation, (4) technical terminology, and (5) generalization and prediction.

Critical Examination of the Sources/ Myriads of historical facts are established as scientifically as are facts of the physical sciences. Examining documents and checking the testimony in these sources against one another enables a historian to report the time and place of a particular event with almost the same certainty that a physical scientist reports that mixing two chemicals under given conditions will produce a certain precipitate. But not all facts that interest a historian are concrete, single historical incidents that have been reported by reliable eyewitnesses.

Ascertaining the facts scientifically becomes difficult or impossible for the researcher if he cannot locate adequate reports of firsthand observations, or if he is interested in causes, motivations, influences, generalizations, or value judgments. After examining available records, for example, a researcher can de-

UNDERSTANDING EDUCATIONAL RESEARCH

termine whether or not Superintendent Hayes made a particular
speech at a certain time or place, but he cannot ascertain with
the same assurance that the speech caused 80 per cent of the
voters to support the school bond issue. Within limits, historical
research is scientific, for an investigator's results can be verified by other scholars. But in some instances, investigators cannot isolate and measure pertinent facts.

Construction of Hypotheses/ Like the physical scientist, the historian formulates hypotheses. He also collects and analyzes relevant evidence to ascertain whether his hypothesis gives a more
satisfactory explanation for an event than rival hypotheses. But
the types of hypotheses and procedures for testing used by the
historian usually differ from those that are used by the physical
scientist.

Because his subject matter is more complex than that of the
physical scientist, a historian experiences greater difficulty in
ascertaining the causes of events. As you know, scientists hold
that an event is dependent upon and conditioned by its causes,
that is, certain conditions must exist before an event can take
place. Since the physical scientist deals with relatively stable
elements solely on the physical level, he is able to speak of
"the cause"—the precise and exclusive factor or factors that
account for an occurrence. When a historian attempts to select
the probable antecedent conditions that precipitated an event,
and to test whether one or more of them caused it, he may
encounter many obstacles. Some factors that were associated
with a past event may be difficult to discern, unmeasurable,
or unrecorded; consequently, he is never certain that he is giving
consideration to all pertinent antecedent factors. Historical
phenomena may have a greater number of antecedents and a
more complicated pattern of interaction among them than physical science phenomena.

Since no single cause explains most historical events, an investigator resorts to multiple hypotheses. He presents a group
of explanations for a given occurrence, or establishes some hierarchy of causes which indicates their relation to one another.
If a historian speaks of "the cause," he means "not the only
cause but 'the most important cause' . . . among a complex of
causal conditions, or the condition which was most decisive to
what occurred, or which made the difference between what occurred and what would probably have occurred in its absence"
(103:111). Because of the complexity of his subject matter
and the limited quantity of his data, the historian is unable to
draw conclusions about causes that are as conclusive and decisive as those of his colleagues in the physical sciences.

Observation and Experimentation/ Unlike physical scientists, educational historians cannot test their hypotheses by experimentation—controlled observation. They cannot recreate personalities and conditions as they once were for the purpose of further examination and manipulation. Historians cannot set up an experiment in which they control all essential factors, remove or add particular factors, and measure their effect on the situation. Because each past event is unique and cannot be repeated under laboratory conditions, research workers confine their examinations to whatever relevant data are available, and attempt to gain a better understanding of them through historical comparisons and hypothetical constructs. They may compare and contrast an event with similar events in the past to detect likenesses and differences. Sometimes they visualize what would have taken place if a particular antecedent event had not occurred and give an answer, "of varying degrees of probability, in terms of approximate regularities observable in other instances" (103:113). But no matter how carefully this work is done, it is not as satisfactory as actual observation.

Since historians cannot personally view the educational practices of hundreds of years ago, they must rely on observations made by others in bygone days and on the examination of relics. Secondhand observations, of course, are not as satisfactory as the direct observations that physical scientists make. But the authenticity and credibility of historical source materials may be checked by subjecting them to intensive external and internal criticism. Ascertaining whether every fact is absolutely true is not possible, for the most reliable witness to an event may have erred in perception or memory. The credibility of relics and testimony is determined in degrees of confidence—from confidence that is approximately certain at one end of the scale to confidence that is mingled with considerable doubt on the other end. Because the reliability of data is dependent on the character, circumstances, and competence of the creators and interpreters, historians are extremely cautious about accepting any artifact or report.

The reliability of a historical research report is determined not only by how critically the investigator examined his source materials but also by how well informed he is about the past and present. The historian delineates events of yesteryear in as much detail as surviving evidence permits and in terms of his knowledge about occurrences, peoples, and institutions. His interpretation of early Greek education, for example, will be conditioned by how much he knows about Grecian society, his conceptions of psychology and human behavior, and his familiarity with the present as well as the past. Block points out that "misunderstanding of the present is the inevitable consequence of ignorance of the past. But a man may wear himself out just as fruitlessly in seeking to understand the past, if he is totally ignorant of the present" (13:43). If a historian acquires a comprehensive understanding of both the past and the present, he is less likely to ignore, to distort, or to misinterpret important evidence and more likely to produce an accurate account of past events.

Technical Terminology/ Educational historians are handicapped because they lack the precise technical vocabulary that physical scientists possess. Many educational terms do not have clearly assigned and commonly understood meanings. When words such as "democracy," "education," "curriculum," and "discipline" are used by different workers in the field, they may stand for slightly or radically different things. In contrast, the technical terms in the exact sciences, such as meter, ampere, light-year, and calorie are instruments of great exactitude. Because a "one-to-one correspondence between symbols and meanings" (84:249) exists, variations due to their use by different physical scientists are kept at a minimum. The absence of a clearly defined technical vocabulary is a distinct weakness in the discipline of educational history, for conceptual vagueness blocks the communication of ideas and information.

Generalization and Prediction/ Some historians dispute whether history can be classified as a science on another basis. Science seeks to generalize. Both scientists and historians may start with propositions about unique events, but the scientist's ultimate objective is to establish broad generalizations—universal laws and theories that will explain many unrelated, singular events or conditions. Scientists strive to establish laws that have precise predictive power.

Constructing laws by generalizing about repetitive and common factors relating to past events is entirely outside the province of historical research in the opinion of some authorities. They acquire richly detailed knowledge of a particular event or condition that occurred at a specific time and place in the past and trace what preceded and succeeded it. But they are not concerned about what always, typically, or generally happens, about similarities between events, or about repeatable aspects of events. The unique factors associated with a specific occurrence that differentiate it from other events are what interest them. In their opinion, as soon as a fact becomes an instance of a general rule or law, it has lost its identification with the past and therefore is no longer a historical fact. Historians of this school show causal relationships between parts of an event or between the conditions existing before and after it, but they do not seek to generalize about the qualities one occurrence has in common with similar ones. They leave the establishment of generalizations or laws that will predict what will recur under certain conditions to sociologists and psychologists.

Historians with a "particularist passion" are challenged by other scholars who contend that historians must go beyond the description and interpretation of particular events in the past. These scholars are convinced that broad generalizations or laws can be derived from a study of historical facts and that the past should be studied for the lessons it teaches. Like Thucydides, they want to tell "what has happened and will hereafter happen again according to human nature" (134). They believe that historians can discover and formulate the fixed laws that explain human events just as scientists have discovered natural laws that explain phenomena in the physical world.

A more modest role is accepted by most historians. Some believe it is their responsibility to make generalizations about *past events* but that it is not within their power to predict *future events*. Others contend that by drawing historical analogies and tracing historical trends they may suggest in some instances various possible outcomes "one or more of which may be anticipated with a high degree of probability" (103:139). They provide us with a basis of knowledge for choosing alternative courses of action, but do not construct comprehensive generalizations that possess the precise predictive power of laws in the physical sciences. "Historical analogies present us most often with clues to *possible* rather than *probable* behavior, with the ability only to *anticipate* rather than to predict, to *take precautions* rather than to *control*" (64:269).

The possibility that man may someday establish historical laws continues to intrigue many scholars. When critics attack this view as unscientific they ask whether "it is more scientific to assume that the development of man as a social being has been casual, fortuitous, uncontrolled by law?" (112:166–167). But entertaining the idea that historical laws may be constructed does not blind these scholars to the overwhelming difficulties that must be surmounted.

Among the reasons that have been given for the lack of success in constructing historical laws as exact as those developed in the physical sciences are:

. . . (1) the apparent impossibility of using certain modern scientific methods, notably experimentation and the use of instruments to aid the senses; (2) the greater complexity of social data as compared to physical: as seen in the circumstance that history presents unique personalities who seem to affect the course of history (or events) and from time to time emergent phenomena not apparently explicable by preexisting phenomena; (3) the paucity in the social and psychological sciences of adequate generalizations which might be applied in historical studies; (4) the changing character of social phenomena from one age to the next, in comparison with the relatively constant character of the data of the physical sciences; and (5) the circumstance that many potentially pertinent data are lost beyond recall (103:138–139).

The compilers of this list question whether these difficulties can be overcome, but suggest that some of them may be eventually. In the meantime, the historian must recognize his limitations and must make his work as exact as possible.

10

Strategy of Descriptive Research

Before much progress can be made in solving problems, men must possess descriptions of the phenomena with which they work. Early developments in educational research, therefore, as in other disciplines, have been concerned with making accurate assessments of the incidence, distribution, and relationships of phenomena in the field. To solve problems about children, school administration, curriculum, or the teaching of arithmetic, investigators ask the question: What exists—what is the present status of these phenomena? Determining the nature of prevailing conditions, practices, and attitudes—seeking accurate descriptions of activities, objects, processes, and persons—is their objective. But descriptive research is not confined to routine fact gathering. Predicting and identifying relationships among and between variables is the goal of competent investigators.

General Overview of Descriptive Studies

The nature of descriptive research is easier to comprehend if one first obtains some knowledge of the various steps involved in an investigation as well as the different methods employed to collect and express data, and the general categories under which studies may be classified. Thus, the following brief overview presents skeletal information concerning these topics.

Steps in an Investigation

In descriptive studies researchers do not merely present private convictions and data based on casual or cursory observations. As in any investigation, they (1) examine their problematic situation, (2) define their problem and state their hypotheses, (3) list the assumptions upon which their hypotheses and procedures are based, (4) select appropriate subjects and source materials, (5) select or construct techniques for collecting the data, (6) establish categories for classifying data that are unambiguous, appropriate for the purpose of the study, and capable of bringing out significant likenesses, differences, or relationships, (7) validate the data-gathering techniques, (8) make discriminating, objective observations, and (9) describe, analyze, and interpret their findings in clear, precise terms. Investigators seek more than bare description: they are not—or should not be—mere tabulators. Competent researchers collect evidence on the basis of some hypothesis or theory, tabulate and summarize the data carefully, and then analyze the results thoroughly in an endeavor to draw meaningful generalizations that will advance knowledge.

Collection of Data

When presenting a descriptive research report, one must identify not only what data were obtained but also the exact nature of the population from which the data were obtained. The population, sometimes called the universe or aggregate, is a *whole*. The units that constitute a population may be people, items, events, or objects; thus, all the arithmetic books published in this country between 1930 and 1940 or all the children in Haven High School may constitute a population. After identifying the population, one must decide whether to collect data from (1) the total population or (2) a representative sample of the population. The nature of the problem and the use to be made of the findings determine which method is employed.

Total Population / Obtaining information from every unit of a small population is not difficult in most instances, but the findings are not applicable to any population other than the group studied. After collecting information from every teacher in Jones School, an investigator may draw generalizations from his data about the average salary, training, and age of the staff members in Jones School, but he cannot claim that these generalizations would hold true for teachers in any other school—now, in the past, or in the future.

Sample Population/ Obtaining information from a large population, such as all the teachers in the state, is often impractical, impossible, or exorbitantly costly. Contacting, observing, measuring, or interviewing every unit in the group may absorb so much time that the data become obsolete before the study is completed. To overcome these difficulties, investigators often collect information from a few *carefully selected* units drawn from a population. If these sample units represent accurately the characteristics of the population, generalizations based on the data obtained from them may be applied to the entire group. But selecting a representative sample is a difficult task, as you will discover when reading this chapter and the discussion on sampling in Chapter 12.

Expression of Data

Descriptive data may be expressed (1) *qualitatively*—in verbal symbols—or (2) *quantitatively*—in mathematical symbols. A study may consist almost exclusively of one form or may contain both forms. If an investigator is comparing the guidance programs of selected schools, he may present qualitative data—word descriptions—concerning the organization of the program, the duties of counselors, and the board of education decisions regarding the program. But he may also include considerable quantitative data, such as the amount of money spent on guidance, the number of children served by each counselor, and the amount of specialized training staff members have received.

Qualitative Symbols/ Qualitative data[1]—word descriptions—may predominate in studies that examine the general nature of phenomena. Pioneer studies in a field are usually expressed in verbal terms. The qualitative statements made by Freud, for example, laid the foundation for clinical psychology. Arnold Gesell wrote descriptions of the changes in motor and perceptual skills that take place as children mature. In *Changing the Curriculum,* Alice Miel presented verbal observations of the factors that hinder or foster change in the school curriculum. Verbal data have been used extensively in comparative educational studies to describe objectives, administration, philosophy, and other factors.

Qualitative studies give social scientists much useful information, but verbal symbols lack precision: words do not hold the

1/ Some verbal symbols, such as "few," "small," "near," "light," and "seldom," possess quantitative characteristics.

same meaning for all people, for all times, and in all contexts. Great leaps forward are not usually made until countable units of measurement are used. But qualitative studies need not be deprecated, for they help workers identify the significant factors to measure. Until these general explorations are made, measurement cannot be utilized fruitfully. If researchers can devise tools to measure the key factors that are identified in qualitative studies, they can describe data with numerical rather than verbal symbols. But years, decades, or a century may elapse before workers in a field pass from the qualitative to the quantitative stage of research, and at present, in some areas of social science, this objective appears to be unattainable.

Quantitative Symbols/ Characteristics and examples of quantitative studies are discussed later in this chapter and in other chapters. But a few introductory remarks may serve a useful purpose at this point. The numerical symbols used to describe data may be the products of counting or measuring. Researchers may *count* the occurrence or nonoccurrence of discernible units, items, or categories of elements. Frequency-of-occurrence data, for example, may reveal the number of teachers in the city schools with B.A., M.A., and Ph.D. degrees; the number of people who do and do not favor consolidating the schools in a district; or the number of guidance counselors who have or have not had specialized training. Sometimes researchers are interested in measuring amounts rather than counting items. They may, for example, *measure* the amount of practice required to type thirty words per minute, the weight of twelve-year-old girls, the mental age of nonreading first-grade pupils, or the amount of space devoted to playgrounds.

Types of Descriptive Research

Writers are not in agreement on how to classify descriptive studies. This text will utilize the following convenient but arbitrarily selected categories: (1) survey studies, (2) interrelationship studies, and (3) developmental studies. These categories are not rigid. Some studies fall exclusively within one of these areas, but others have characteristics of more than one.

Survey Studies

When trying to solve problems, men in educational, governmental, industrial, and political organizations often conduct surveys. They collect detailed descriptions of existing phenomena with the intent of employing the data to justify current conditions and practices or to make more intelligent plans for improving them. Their objective may be not only to ascertain status, but also to determine the adequacy of status by comparing it with selected or established standards. Health examination procedures, for example, may be compared with "best practices" as defined by authorities, and children's reading scores may be compared with norms established for specific groups. Educators who wish to improve existing status may survey how others have solved similar problems. Some men collect all three types of information: (1) data concerning existing status, (2) comparisons of status and standards, and (3) means of improving status. Others confine their studies to one or two of these types.

Surveys may be broad or narrow in scope. They may encompass several countries or may be confined to one nation, region, state, city school system, or some other unit. Survey data may be gathered from every member of a population or from a carefully selected sample. Data may be collected concerning a large number of related factors or a few selected items. The scope and depth of the study depend primarily upon the nature of the problem.

Survey studies will be discussed under the following headings in this chapter: (1) School Surveys, (2) Job Analysis, (3) Documentary Analysis, (4) Public Opinion Surveys, and (5) Community Surveys. No presumption is made that this classification is universally accepted or that a sharp dividing line separates these categories.

School Surveys

Early in this century, members of the profession began to conduct school surveys. On the basis of their findings, they formulated plans for improving educational efficiency and effectiveness. Down through the years, their successors have continued to gather facts through observations, questionnaries, interviews, standardized tests, scorecards, rating scales, and other data-gathering techniques. Analyses of such information have enabled educators to make recommendations that have transformed many administrative, instructional, financial, and curricular practices in our schools.

Types of School Surveys/ Three ways of making school surveys have evolved since 1910, when one of the first modern studies was conducted at Boise, Idaho. All three patterns—(1) the *out-*

side expert survey, (2) the *self-survey,* and (3) the *cooperative survey*—are still employed. But there is a definite trend away from the pioneer type of outside expert survey that is conducted exclusively by the research staff of a university or state department of education. The self-survey which is undertaken by members of the local school organization appeared more frequently in the 1920's when schools began to add research specialists to their staffs who could offer competent leadership. The self-survey remains popular today, but since 1935 the cooperative survey has been gaining ground. Cooperative surveys are of two types: outside consultants join with a local staff to conduct a study, or lay citizens and school staff members—with or without consultants—undertake the survey.

Cooperative surveys have certain advantages over one-shot or periodic surveys that are made exclusively by outside experts. Visiting specialists who are well trained in survey techniques may have a limited knowledge of the local scene. To design the most appropriate survey for a particular school, they need the assistance of educators and laymen who are intimately familiar with the local community. If local staff members do not participate in surveying the strengths and weaknesses of the schools, they may not understand why a change is needed and the means by which the experts advise to effect it. Under such circumstances, they may ignore recommendations for change or may resist placing them into effect. Many administrators, therefore, favor utilizing experts to guide, supplement, and stimulate the work done by the local teachers and citizens. Rather than conducting surveys at infrequent intervals, they carry on more or less continuous survey activities.

Coverage of Surveys/ Most school surveys have been done on the local level. By 1938, a total of 3,022 public school surveys were listed in bibliographies prepared by Smith and O'Dell (124, 125). Since that time a multiplicity of published and unpublished reports have appeared. Some state-wide surveys have been made, such as the studies done in Flordia and Indiana. On the national level the Office of Education has conducted the *National Survey of Secondary Education* (138) and the *National Survey of the Education of Teachers* (139).

Data Sought in Surveys/ The information sought in most surveys falls into the following categories: (1) the setting for learning, (2) the characteristics of educational personnel, (3) the nature of the pupils, and (4) the nature of the educational process. Studies may explore extensively one or more of these areas or they may examine intensively specific aspects of one area.

1/ The setting for learning.

Some surveys are concerned with the legal, administrative, social, or physical setting for learning. Studies may seek information about the enabling acts. state regulations, local council ordinances, board of education rulings, or boards of health and recreation regulations that affect education. Studies may investigate the composition, responsibilities, and interrelationships of school boards, councils, commissions, and associations that are related to educational enterprises. Questions about school finance, such as the amount of taxable wealth, present basis of taxation, bonded indebtedness, and per-pupil costs, may be asked. Not uncommonly, surveys seek descriptions of various aspects of the school plant, such as the location, heating, lighting, ventilation, floor space per pupil, health and safety conditions, play areas, cafeteria, and library. Questions are sometimes asked about equipment and supplies, such as the number and kinds of library books or the amount and types of laboratory, athletic, or audio-visual equipment. Some studies are concerned with the size, length, and frequency of classes. Other studies investigate aspects of the social structure in the classroom, home, or community that may influence learning.

2/ The characteristics of educational personnel.

Many surveys gather information about teachers, supervisors, and administrators. Questions may be raised concerning their sex, age, education, degrees, socioeconomic background, group memberships, or income. An effort may be made to ascertain where school personnel live; the adequacy of their dwellings; or their certification, tenure, and retirement status. Numerous surveys study the behavior of instructional personnel in the classroom, the department, and the community, with the objective of assessing or improving teaching effectiveness. Determining the physical fitness of educators; their attitudes on various questions; the nature and number of their contacts with colleagues, students, and the community; and the levels of expectation they hold for themselves, students, and the school are the objectives of some surveys. Studies are also made of the responsibilities and interrelationships of administrators, department heads, teachers, and nonteaching personnel.

3/ The nature of pupils.

Acquiring information about the behavior patterns of pupils in classrooms, with peers, at home, and in the community is the purpose of many surveys. Descriptions of the socioeconomic status of the family may be sought. Researchers may ask questions about pupils' health attitudes, knowledges, skills, academic achievements, intelligence, aptitudes, work or study habits, and likes and dislikes. Some studies inventory extracurricular activities, work or travel experiences, or play and recreational activities. Questions about reading habits, health practices, or diet may be asked. Some investigations are concerned with attendance and dropout records, the number and type of handicapped or other exceptional students, or the number and nature of disciplinary or delinquency incidents.

4/ The nature of the educational process.

The educational programs, processes, and outcomes may come under scrutiny. Researchers may investigate what is and is not included in the curriculum. Time allotments for activities and for various aspects of each activity, such as the amount of time given to literature, grammar, and composition in the English classes, may be studied. The nature and amount of the content in textbooks and instructional materials may be appraised. The nature and number of school services, such as health, library, guidance, research and adult education services may be described. Some investigators seek information about the kinds and degrees of acceleration or retardation among students in various subjects and on different academic levels.

Job Analysis

Sometimes job analysis—a technique borrowed from business and government—is employed to study administrative, teaching, and noninstructional positions. In these investigations information may be collected about the general duties and responsibilities of workers, the specific activities that they engage in on a job, their status and relationships in the administrative organization, their working conditions, and the nature and type of their facilities. Descriptions of the education, specialized training, experience, and salaries of workers and the knowledges, skills, habits, health standards, and behavioral traits that they possess also may be sought. The data gathered help investigators describe the current practices and conditions of employment and the competencies and behavioral traits that personnel possess or should possess to carry out their work effectively and efficiently. Obtaining an analytical knowledge of job components helps administrators and scholars (1) detect weaknesses, duplications, or inefficiency in the present work procedures, (2) establish uniform classifications for similar work, (3) determine wage or salary schedules for jobs entailing various levels of skill or responsibility, (4) identify the competencies to seek when employing personnel, (5) assign workers to jobs in a manner that will achieve the best utilization of the available manpower, (6) set up training programs and prepare instructional materials for prospective or inservice employees, (7) establish requirements for promotion, (8) make decisions concerning the transfer or retraining of personnel, and (9) develop a theoretical framework for studying administrative functions and structures.

Various procedures are employed by those who conduct job-analysis studies (63:343). From personal observations and judgments obtained from authorities in the field, they may compile a list of the broad functions involved in administrative, supervisory, or teaching positions. They may examine documents, such as state laws, school district regulations, or court decisions, to obtain information concerning the duties, responsibilities, and rights of personnel holding a given position. They may question workers concerning the nature of their duties, training, or professional activities. Bryant and Deloach (19), for example, studied music instructors in Negro high schools in South Carolina. Wade (141) described the work load and class size of high school English teachers in New York. The Research Division of the NEA (98), sent a questionnaire to over 2,000 teachers asking them to report the number of hours given per week to various duties. Similar time studies have been made to describe the work load of principals, college teachers, and other workers.

Educators who undertake job-analysis studies should be aware of the difficulties involved in obtaining accurate descriptions. If a study breaks down a job into many specific activities, for example, the sum of these quantitative or mechanical considerations gives only a partial picture of the job. If the qualitative or creative characteristics which are necessary for successful job performance, such as ideals and attitudes, resourcefulness and cooperativeness, dependability and tact, are not appraised, the study will not produce a full job description. But obtaining objective and reliable data concerning these personal characteristics is extremely difficult. A job analysis that gives equal weight to all activities, functions, and personal characteristics associated with a particular position also presents a distorted picture, for each factor does not contribute equally to work performance. Some method of weighing the relative importance of the various job components is needed, but devising an objective method of making such judgments is difficult.

Documentary Analysis

Documents and records may be dull reading to laymen, but researchers often unearth exciting and pertinent data from these sources. Documentary analysis—which is sometimes referred to as "content," "activity," or "informational analysis"—is closely akin to historical research. Both methods of investigation require that workers examine existing records, but historical research is primarily concerned with the more distant past and descriptive research with the present.

Types of Analyses/ A wide variety of documentary surveys are made. Some scholars analyze judicial decisions, state laws, and school board rulings. They count and classify specific items in these sources that relate to their problems, such as information about salary schedules, certification, liability for school accidents, and district organization. Researchers may also gather data describing existing school practices, processes, and conditions from administrative records, forms, and reports; committee reports and minutes of meetings; budgets and financial records; and cumulative attendance and health records.

University catalogs or bulletins may provide information about curriculum offerings, content of particular courses, entrance or graduation requirements, and tuition. Syllabi, courses of study, reading lists, school schedules, lesson plans, textbooks, or pupils' work may help investigators determine what is and is not taught, the grade placement of particular materials, and the amount of time devoted to them. When analyzing textbooks, researchers may count the kind and frequency of concepts, the errors and distortions, or the number of pictures or tables. They may measure the length of sentences, the allotment of space to certain topics (44), or the vocabulary level. This information enables them to determine where, when, and how much is being taught about specific topics and helps them detect prejudices and beliefs of the writers. Sometimes they find that personal documents, such as diaries, expense accounts, and letters, provide them with valuable data. Scholars may also analyze the contents of reference works, newspapers, periodicals, and films. Sometimes they examine the cumulative health records of students to determine the prevalence of particular diseases (35).

Classroom teachers often complain, "We can't teach everything! What are the most important skills and knowledges that children should attain?" To answer this question, many educators have turned to documentary research. In the field of mathematics, they have conducted studies to discover what arithmetic processes are most commonly employed in business and social usage. Wilson and Dalrymple (144) examined 102,000 uses of fractions which they obtained from business records and concluded that 90 per cent of ordinary adult usage of fractions was confined to halves, thirds, and fourths. To determine what content should be included in the curriculum, investigators have also analyzed the types of errors made by pupils in oral and written communication, arithmetic, and other subjects. Educational textbook writers have been aided by studies that have ascertained the basic vocabulary that children possess at different ages. To determine what facts, topics, issues, and generalizations are most frequently used in adult life, social scientists have tabulated the frequency of their mention in newspapers, periodicals, motion pictures, cartoons, and other sources. Studies such as these have lead to important curriculum revisions.

Early documentary research was rather superficial and mechanical; workers read written or printed materials and tabulated the frequency of the occurrence of items; they used convenient categories that did not reveal particularly significant meanings. About 1950, more subtle and plastic methods of categorizing items were introduced in order to force significant qualitative factors to the surface. These qualitative studies were concerned with more complex themes than the quantitative studies. They asked questions such as: How accurately are cultural settings outside the United States represented in stories found in basal readers (123)? How are minority ethnic groups treated in elementary social studies textbooks? How do the values in Boy Scout literature in the United States differ from the values in the youth organization literature in other cultures? When conducting this qualitative type of study, the researcher is "relatively less concerned with the content as such than with content as a 'reflection' of 'deeper' phenomena" (11:123). His work may be semiqualitative in nature, but it is "often based upon presence-absence of particular content (rather than relative frequencies)" (11:119), and it usually contains "a higher ratio of non-content to content statements than quantitative analysis" (11:122).

Advantages and Limitations/ Documentary analysis may help educators (1) describe specific conditions and practices that exist in schools and society, (2) spot trends, (3) detect weaknesses, (4) trace the development of a student's or a writer's work, (5) discover differences in the practices that prevail in various areas, states, or countries, (6) evaluate the relationships of stated objectives and what is being taught, and (7) detect the biases, attitudes, interests, values, and psychological states of people.

Documentary research produces much valuable information, but the method has certain limitations, and investigators may draw faulty conclusions from the data. An analysis of the errors made on test papers, for example, may reveal what difficulties pupils encounter, but this information is of limited usefulness for it does not reveal why they made the errors. Through frequency-of-occurrence studies investigators may discover the existing status of interests or activities, but these facts may be too fleeting or too temporary in nature to serve as a basis for planning long-term educational policies. Counting the frequency of occurrence of particular contents or activities and measuring the amount of time or space devoted to them may not reveal the cruciality or importance of the item being analyzed. The position of content in a record or document and the emotional terms with which it is described are factors that also must be considered.

Some documentary research findings are of little value because the investigators failed to analyze a representative sample of source materials. Many studies do not provide information concerning the adequacy of the sample size or the conformity of the sample to the universe. If an analysis is made of newspaper editorials concerning school segregation, the reading of the Bible in public schools, or teachers' labor unions, for example, the reader must judge for himself whether the newspapers selected represent the opinions in different parts of the country, different-size cities, and different social, religious, economic, or political groups.

Another weakness found in some documentary studies is the failure to analyze the trustworthiness of source materials. Printed and written materials are not necessarily accurate. Sometimes clerks make errors in recording information; committee members conceal their real convictions when writing reports; official records are altered or slanted to make conditions appear better than they are; different types of data are classified under the same category by various institutions; courses listed in college catalogs are not always taught; personal documents such as diaries, autobiographies, or letters are forgeries or are attributed to the wrong author. When engaged in documentary analysis, a researcher must submit his source materials to the same careful criticism that a historian does to establish the authenticity of documents and the validity of their contents.

Public Opinion Surveys

Industrial, political, educational, and other leaders must make many decisions. Rather than formulating policies on the basis of private hunches, blind guesses, or pressure-group demands, some leaders seek knowledge of the public's opinions, attitudes, and preferences. Business firms, for example, often conduct public opinion polls—market surveys—to determine what types of products, packaging, or advertising appeal to purchasers. Politicians conduct polls to ascertain how people will vote or what programs they favor. Educators make public opinion surveys to find out how people feel about school issues (92).

Public opinion surveyors usually employ questionnaires or interviews to gather their data, and the able ones select their subjects with care so that the views of each segment of a speci-

fied population are represented. To predict the outcome of a
national election, for example, they first identify the variables
that will affect how individuals vote, such as economic status,
religion, party affiliation, age, rural-urban residence, education,
and sex. After making these determinations, they evaluate how
much weight to give each variable when selecting the sample.

Public opinion surveys have limitations. Careful consideration must be given to how, when, where, and from whom data
are obtained. Information that is elicited from a readily available group will not always reflect the opinion of the total population. Suppose a superintendent passes out questionnaires concerning a school bond issue at all public school PTA meetings.
The results of his survey may not correspond with the vote
of election day, for PTA members are usually much more interested in obtaining new schools than retired citizens, childless
couples, and people who send their children to nonpublic
schools. The environment in which a poll is taken may also
affect the reliability of the data. Suppose students are asked
to express their attitudes toward mathematics. If they do not
like their present teacher or have taken a difficult test that day,
they may record these reactions rather than their more permanent attitudes toward the subject. Other questions may also
arise concerning the reliability of the answers gathered in surveys. If people have given considerable thought to an issue,
they may have a definite opinion about it; if they are unin-
formed concerning the topic, they can only make arbitrary decisions or snap judgments. Measuring the intensity or depth of
opinion is also difficult. If two women answer a questionnaire,
each may indicate that she is opposed to teaching about the
United Nations in the schools, but one of them may easily be
convinced to change her opinion and the other may be intensely
opposed and adamant in her conviction.

Community Surveys

Because of the close relationship between the schools and
the community, educators often collect data concerning the
local setting and particular aspects of life in it. Sometimes they
join social scientists in fact-finding projects known as "community surveys," "social surveys," or "field studies." These
community surveys are closely akin to school surveys; they
may contain data concerning the schools, and conversely school
surveys may analyze many aspects of the community.

History of Surveys/ The "muckraking" articles that appeared at
the turn of this century gave impetus to the community survey

movement in this country. These dramatic descriptions of slums and sweatshops aroused a demand for social reforms and caused some social foundations and government agencies to undertake community surveys. A precedent for compiling detailed bodies of exact, verifiable facts about a community as a means of instigating social reforms had been set by men abroad. Some of the early surveyors were John Howard (1726–1790), who made a detailed study of English prisons; Frédéric Le Play (1806–1882), who studied French working people; and Charles Booth (1840–1916), who surveyed the impoverished East Side of London.

One of the first extensive community surveys (1909 to 1914) in the United States was conducted by Paul Kellogg and a group of professional workers in Pittsburgh. Other surveys of American cities, many of which were limited to particular phases of community life, soon followed. *A Bibliography of Social Surveys* (50) listed 2,775 that were completed by the end of 1927. Not only local but also regional surveys were conducted. Between 1927 and 1931, *The Regional Survey of New York and Its Environs* (eight volumes) and *The Regional Plan of New York* (two volumes) were published. Other communities also initiated studies to gather data that would enable them to plan for the future development of their regions. Such surveys have been repeated at intervals or have been conducted on a continuing basis by some communities. Another *New York Metropolitan Region Study* (nine volumes) for example, was published in 1959–1960 under the direction of Raymond Vernon.

Some researchers conduct surveys to obtain detailed scientific knowledge about community life. The pioneers in this movement, Robert S. and Helen M. Lynd, painstakingly studied and restudied Muncie, Indiana. Their sociological reports, *Middletown* (1929) and *Middletown in Transition* (1937), vividly portrayed the changing culture in an average-size Middle Western town over a period of several decades. Since the appearance of the Lynds' studies, several similar ones, such as *Plainville, USA* and *Hollow Folk* have been produced, and many improvements in survey techniques have been devised.

Scope and Depth of Community Surveys/ Some community studies focus sharply on a particular condition, such as health services, employment, juvenile delinquency, housing, or racial discrimination. Other studies present data concerning a specific segment of society, such as Puerto Ricans, Negroes, or trailer-camp residents. Comprehensive surveys, on the other hand, cover many aspects of community life and may give approximately equal weight to each phase. The scope and depth of a survey are determined by the nature of the problem, the amount of time, money, and qualified leadership available, and the willingness of community agencies to cooperate.

Investigators who make comprehensive surveys gather information concerning many factors that contribute to the character of community life. To obtain data, they ask questions such as the following:

1/ History.
What facts are available concerning the origin and development of the community? Who were the first inhabitants and the early leaders? What institutions and economic activities did they develop? What developments have taken place since that time? What factors caused these changes?

2/ Government and law.
What is the legal or regulative basis for the existence and present operation of the community? How do enabling acts, charters, state regulations, and local ordinances define the rights, duties, and relationships of the various agencies and officials? What political organizations exist? What factions dominate them and who are the leaders? What methods of levying taxes are employed? What laws govern the right to raise taxes? What is the taxable wealth of the community? What is the nature, quality, and extent of the services offered by governmental agencies?

3/ Geographical and economic conditions.
How does the geography of the area affect transportation, communication, business, occupations, health, land values, recreation, distribution of the population, and social history? What economic activities exist in the community? What men, cliques, or organizations represent the interests of the various business, labor, or farm groups? What influence do they have in the community? What is the economic status of the people?

4/ Cultural characteristics.
Is the community isolated from other communities? What are the causes and effects of this condition? Does evidence of cooperative efforts and group solidarity exist? Do class, color, religious, or nationality cleavages and conflicts exist? What are the general moral standards of the community? What cultural activities, services, and facilities exist, such as churches, libraries, museums, and parks? What agencies and organizations provide these services? What are their relationships with one another? What antisocial activities or conditions exist, such as blight, crime, and delinquency, and who is responsible for them? To what extent and how do various groups, agencies, and conditions enrich or endanger community life?

5/ Population.
What is the composition of the population on the basis of age, sex, race, color, nationality, education, occupation, home language, political affiliation, and type and location of residence? How mobile is the population? What is the size of the population? Is it increas-

ing or decreasing and why? What do the birth, death, and disease rates reveal about the population?

Community survey investigators employ research methods from various fields and draw upon many different sources of information. They use questionnaires, interviews, and direct observation as well as statistical, ecological, and other techniques to gather data from public officials, social agencies, ministers, children, teachers, and various documents. Their interdisciplinary approach enables them to utilize multiple, interrelated methods of ferreting out information concerning the nature and role of various social processes.

Interrelationships Studies

Some educators do not merely collect facts to obtain an accurate description of existing status; they endeavor to trace interrelationships between facts that will provide a deeper insight into the phenomena. Three types of these studies will be discussed in this section: case studies, causal-comparative studies, and correlation studies.

Case Study

In a case study, an educator makes an intensive investigation of a social unit—a person, family, group, social institution, or community. He gathers pertinent data about the present status, past experiences, and environmental forces that contribute to the individuality and behavior of the unit. After analyzing the sequences and interrelationships of these factors, he constructs a comprehensive, integrated picture of the social unit as it functions in society.

Nature of Case Studies/ Social workers and guidance counselors conduct case studies with the intent of diagnosing a particular condition and recommending therapeutic measures. Their interest is confined to the individual as a unique personality. Research workers, on the other hand, are interested in individuals as representative types. They gather data about a carefully selected sample of subjects with the intent of deriving valid generalizations about the population that the sample represents.

Case studies probe in depth; they may examine the total life cycle of a social unit or may focus attention on a specific phase of it. An investigator may make a detailed study of the relationships of boys with members of their gang or the relationships of teachers with their administrators. On the other hand, if he wants to ascertain what has contributed to the social maladjustment of hardened criminals or to the success of teachers, he may investigate almost every aspect of their lives—their childhood, home, school, work, and social experiences, and many of their behavioral traits.

A case analysis is cast within an adequate social framework, and the nature of the case determines the dimensions of the framework. To discover what conditions or forces cause youths to commit crimes, for example, the investigation must go beyond the incidents themselves—the time, place, nature, and immediate cause of the acts. Case studies that are confined to an isolated fragment of a man's life are superficial and meaningless; they do not produce the data necessary to probe the fundamental cause-effect relationships. Since human beings function in a dynamic social setting, a case study must include considerable information about the people, groups, and conditions that the subjects contact and the nature of their relationships with them. Human beings interact constantly with diverse environmental factors; consequently, their behavior cannot be understood without examining these varied relationships.

Case study data may come from numerous sources. An investigator may ask subjects to recall past experiences or to express present wishes in interviews or on questionnaires. Personal documents, such as diaries and letters, and various physical, psychological, or sociological measurements may yield valuable information. (These tools are discussed in Chapter 12.) Data may be obtained from parents, brothers, sisters, and friends, or from court, school, hospital, business, social agency, or church records.

A case study is similar to a survey,[2] but instead of gathering data concerning a few factors from a large number of social units, the investigator makes an intensive study of a limited number of representative cases. A case study is narrower in scope but more exhaustive and more qualitative in nature than a survey. Because word descriptions reveal a wealth of enlightening information that a quantitative study might not be able to produce, the case study is often used to supplement the survey method. Young claims that "the most meaningful numerical studies in social science are those which are linked with exhaustive case studies describing accurately the interrelationships of factors and of processes" (148:230). Case studies may re-

---

2/ Some studies of communities, for example, are classified as case studies by some writers and as surveys by others.

veal relevant factors in a given situation that the surveyor can measure quantitatively. Statistical surveys, on the other hand, may provide a guide for selecting representative subjects for case studies. Thus, the two methods are more or less interdependent.

Contributions and Limitations/ Case studies make useful contributions to research, but they have certain limitations that the investigator must keep in mind. The expansive, exploratory nature of a case study may provide insights that will help him formulate a fruitful hypothesis, for knowledge that a particular condition exists in a unique instance suggests a factor to look for in other cases. But a generalization drawn from a single case or a few casually selected ones cannot be applied to all cases in a given population. Evidence derived from one case study cannot be generalized to a universe, but a negative piece of evidence produced in a single case will alert the investigator to the possibility that he may need to modify his hypothesis. Case study data also prove useful when the researcher needs to illustrate statistical findings, for concrete examples drawn from individual cases may help readers understand statistical generalizations more readily.

Are case study data too subjective to be of scientific value? Some data, such as those concerning height and weight, are as objective as data collected by other research methods. But elements of subjectivity may enter into a report, particularly when judgments are made about a subject's character and motives. An investigator must guard against permitting personal biases and standards to influence his interpretation. Facts must be reported precisely and objectively and judgments must be suspended until adequate evidence supports a conclusion. When collecting evidence from records, interviews, and questionnaires, one must exercise every possible precaution to detect data that are the product of faulty perception, deliberate deception, a poor memory, unconscious biases, or the reporter's or subject's desire to present the "right" answer. The tendency to overemphasize unusual events or to distort them for dramatic effect must also be kept in mind.

Causal-comparative Studies

Some investigators try to discover not only *what* a phenomenon is like, but, if possible, *how* and *why* it occurs. They compare the likenesses and differences among phenomena to find out what factors or circumstances seem to accompany or contribute to the occurrence of certain events, conditions, or practices.

Need for Causal-comparative Method/ When scientists study causation they prefer to employ the experimental method, but sometimes the causal-comparative method[3] is the only feasible way to attack a problem. In a laboratory experiment, the investigator controls all variables except the independent variable or variables which he manipulates to see what happens. But because of the complexity and nature of social phenomena, an educator cannot always select, control, and manipulate the factors neccessary to study cause-effect relations. An investigator, for example, cannot manipulate home background, social class, teacher personality, or intelligence. When an experimenter attempts to control variations in all but a single independent—experimental—variable, he may prevent the simultaneous functioning of variables that normally are found operating together and thus may free the independent variable from the influence of other variables (17:336). In such instances an analysis of what happens in a natural rather than a laboratory situation may be a more satisfactory way to study causes.

Employing the experimental method is impractical or prohibitively costly in time, money, and effort in some instances, such as studies of riots or "life as it is lived." Ethical considerations may proscribe experimentation. One cannot justify, for example, placing emotionally stable children in controlled environments to determine whether various psychoses can be produced. Respect for living things prevents an investigator from inflicting unnecessary pain, hardship, or harm on others, or from interfering in any way with the normal growth and development of an individual.

Nature of Causal-comparative Studies/ When researchers cannot manipulate the independent variable and establish the controls that are required in "true experiments," they may conduct a causal-comparative study. In an experiment, the researcher may hypothesize: If students have experience A, then result B will be observable. He then manipulates the independent variable A: he exposes an experimental group to experience A, withholds the experience from a control group, and observes the result. In a causal-comparative study, the investigator reverses this procedure. He observes phenomena B which already exists and searches back through a multiplicity of possible

---

3/ Sometimes referred to, particularly by sociologists, as the "ex post facto design."

causes for the factors—independent variables—that are related
to or contribute to the occurrence of the phenomena.

In a causal-comparative investigation, a researcher studies a
life situation in which subjects have experienced what he wants
to investigate. To study school integration riots, for example,
rather than setting up a controlled experiment to test whether
various factors will cause a riot, he compares a community that
has experienced a riot with one that has not. After studying
the likenesses and differences between the two situations, he
describes the factors that appear to account for the riot in one
instance and for its lack in the other.

Likewise, if an investigator wants to study emotional instability, he does not place children in a situation where all factors
are kept constant except one variable which is manipulated to
determine what causes a particular type of emotional distur-
bance. Rather, he chooses children who according to a selected
criterion are "disturbed" and compares them with emotionally
stable children. After searching for factors or conditions which
seem to be associated with one group and not the other, he
may present a possible explanation of the underlying causes
of the emotional problem.

The causal-comparative type of investigation stems from
John Stuart Mill's method of discovering causal connections.
Mill's Method of Agreement rules that, "If two or more instances of the phenomenon under investigation have only one
circumstance in common, the circumstance in which alone all
the instances agree, is the cause (or effect) of the given phenomenon" (93:224). A concrete illustration of this principle
may make it more comprehensible. Suppose that six
students—A, B, C, D, E, and F—went to a debating tourna-
ment, and subsequently, three of them—A, B, and C—became
ill. To find out the cause of their illness, the doctor questioned
A, B, and C about what food they had eaten and discovered
that every item they had selected differed except for strawberry
cream pie. In other words, the only food consumed by all those
who became ill was the pie. In conformity with the Method
of Agreement, the doctor concluded that the illness was caused
by the pie, for it was this, and only this, item on the menu
that the ill students had experienced in common.

To make more certain of his diagnosis, the doctor could have
employed Mill's Joint Method of Agreement and Difference
which rules that, "If two or more instances in which the phenomenon occurs have only one circumstance in common, while
two or more instances in which it does not occur have nothing
in common save the absence of that circumstance; the circumstance in which alone the two sets of instances differ, is the

effect, or cause, or necessary part of the cause, of the phenomenon" (93:229). To apply this rule, the doctor would have had to determine that strawberry cream pie was the only food that all the ill students consumed, and he also would have had to question members of the group who did not become ill—*D, E,* and *F.* If he found the only item common to those who suffered no ill effects was the absence of pie, he would have strengthened his conclusion that strawberry cream pie was causally related to the illness of the students. Thus, this method gives the researcher a double check on his conclusions concerning causality. Life situations, however, are rarely as simple as this illustration.

Types of Problems/ Many educational processes, practices, programs, and products have been analyzed by the causal-comparative method. The problems range from relatively simple, nonmathematical designs to moderately complex studies in which control groups and some characteristics of the experimental method are employed. A few representative studies are a differential analysis of the play of adolescent boys (140), the differences between conforming and nonconforming senior high school boys (101), the differential achievement among boys in algebra (149), the differences in the personality patterns of gifted children and "normal" children (100), and a comparison of the achievement of multigraded and single-graded rural school children (57). In these studies, the investigators searched for likenesses and differences among their subjects to obtain clues about what might cause or contribute to the occurrence of a particular phenomenon.

Difficulties Encountered/ When educators seek to explain phenomena, they often conduct causal-comparative studies. But this method of research has limitations.

1/
Lack of control is the greatest weakness of the causal-comparative method of research. Suppose that a researcher observes phenomenon *B* and hypothesizes that *A* causes the occurrence of *B.* If his descriptive study produces data which indicate that *A* is related to *B,* he cannot be certain that some other factor, *C, D,* or *E* (rival hypotheses) might not be the real cause of the occurrence of *B.* If he conducts an experiment in which all factors are controlled except *A,* which is manipulated, he can be more certain that *A* is related to *B.* The best that he can do to gain some measure of control in a descriptive study is to test and rule out as many rival hypotheses for the occurrence of *B* as he can.

2/

If the relevant factor causing a particular condition is not included among the items being considered when studying the problem, the cause cannot be ascertained. But how does one determine what is relevant? If certain factors seem to accompany a certain condition, one or more of them may be the cause of it; but on the other hand, things may go together without having a cause-effect relationship. The three ill debaters in our previous illustration may have had certain common experiences aside from eating strawberry pie—drinking coffee, taking the same type of pills, or swimming in the same pool—that did not play any part in their illness. A scholar must have considerable general knowledge of his phenomena and must plan his observational procedures with care if he is going to spot possible relevant causes and to ignore chance associative factors.

3/

The joint method of agreement and disagreement requires that a single critical factor must be responsible for the occurrence or nonoccurrence of the phenomenon. But this condition is rarely found when working with complex social phenomena, for events usually have multiple rather than single causes. What, for example, is the decisive factor responsible for the instructional effectiveness of a teacher? Is it the amount of college education, quality of scholarship, nature of nonschool experiences, attitudes toward children, or type of personality? The phenomenon of effective teaching does not seem to stem from a single definable factor, but from the interaction of several relevant factors.

4/

A phenomenon may result not only from multiple causes but also from one cause in one instance and from another cause in another instance. The three ill debaters, for example, all experienced one factor in common—eating strawberry cream pie—but this factor may not have caused their illness. Student *A* may have become ill because of overexertion, *B* because of inhaling automobile gas fumes, and *C* because of overeating. Thus searching for likenesses associated with conditions or events may lead an investigator up blind alleys and may prevent him from detecting the real cause involved in the situation.

5/

When a relationship between two variables is discovered, determining which is the cause and which is the effect may be difficult. If a study notes a relationship between low academic marks and automobile ownership among high school boys, the question arises: Does automobile ownership cause the low marks or do boys who get low marks feel insecure and seek status by purchasing automobiles? Even though two factors may always appear together, the one may not necessarily be the cause of the other, for both of them may be caused by a third factor or a complex of factors. Studies reveal, for example, that older women in the general population bear more intelligent children than younger women. This relationship exists, true. But can one conclude that middle age is the best time to bear intelligent children, or does this relationship exist because women with high intelligence and ability tend to marry later in life?

6/

Classifying subjects into dichotomous groups for the purpose of comparison also presents problems, for social phenomena are not alike except within broad limits. They do not automatically fall into exclusive categories. Typists, swimmers, teachers, or spellers may range from those who possess few skills to those who are highly skilled. Even the ill debaters previously mentioned may vary from one who experiences a slight headache to one who is critically ill. Comparing one vague variable with another may produce a precise statistic, but the findings may provide little useful knowledge about the phenomena one is trying to explain. If comparisons between successful and unsuccessful students, ill and well debaters, or any other subjects are made to ascertain what causes or contributes to the factor under consideration, the phenomena and categories must be defined with great care.

7/

In comparative studies of natural situations, the researcher does not have the same careful control over the selection of subjects as he does in well-designed experimental studies. Locating existing groups of subjects who are similar in all respects except for their exposure to one variable is extremely difficult. The danger always exists that the groups differ in some other way—health, intelligence, home background, previous experience—that will affect the findings of the study. Suppose that an investigator decides to test a hypothesis about the effects of a new health textbook on specific practices of children. If he compares the hygienic habits of students who have read the book with those who have not, the possibility exists that the group that did read the book had better hygienic training in the home than the former group. In an experiment, extraneous variables such as home background can be controlled by assigning subjects to groups at random and assigning the experimental treatment to groups at random. But in causal-comparative studies, the subjects may "select themselves" into the groups and some difference in the character of these subjects other than the experimental treatment may account for the findings of the study. If health were not a required subject, for example, the students who enrolled in the course were probably more interested in health and more highly motivated to improve their health practices than the nonenrollees. The textbook, therefore, might not have the same effect on nonenrollees as it had on the enrollees.

Causal-comparative studies have many limitations, and they often do not produce the precise, reliable knowledge that can be gained through rigorous experimental studies. But they do provide a means of tackling problems that cannot be probed in laboratory situations, and they do yield valuable clues concerning the nature of phenomena. As the techniques, tools, and controls used in conducting causal-comparative studies have been improved, this method of inquiry has gained greater respect.

Correlation Studies

To obtain descriptions of phenomena, some investigators employ correlation techniques. The mathematical processes involved in these procedures will be discussed in Chapter 13, but the following general explanation and illustrations will indicate how these techniques help researchers detect the magnitude of relationships between data.

Correlation techniques are used to ascertain the extent to which two variables are related, that is, the extent to which variations in one factor correspond with variations in another. Suppose that you want to know whether any connection—and how much—exists between the IQ scores and algebra marks of ninth-grade students in attendance at the Lincoln School during the last academic year. On the basis of general impressions, you may have arrived at the hypothesis that the higher the student's IQ score, the higher his algebra mark. The following procedures will enable you to test this hypothesis and to determine the magnitude of the relationship.

First, obtain the IQ scores and algebra marks for the ninth-grade students from their cumulative folders. After recording the IQ scores in order of increasing size—from the lowest to the highest score—place each pupil's algebra mark beside his IQ score. Now note whether the algebra marks increase in correspondence with the IQ scores. If the two orders correspond exactly, a perfect positive correlation exists between the IQ and algebra scores. If the two orders coincide in part, some relationship between the two scores may exist, but the intensity of the relationship between the variables can only be determined by applying certain mathematical procedures.

Variables may be closely related, moderately related, or completely unrelated. In general, the magnitude of a correlation depends upon the extent to which an increase or decrease in one variable is accompanied by an increase or decrease in the other—whether in the same direction or the opposite direction. For example, a *high positive correlation* exists if, in general, a high rank in one set of scores is accompanied by a high rank in the other (high IQ—high school marks) and a low rank in one set is accompanied by a low rank in the other (low IQ—low school marks). A *high negative correlation* exists if, in general, a high rank in one set of scores corresponds with a low rank in the other (high IQ—low school marks), and if a low rank in the first set corresponds with a high rank in the other (low IQ—high school marks). *No or little correlation* exists if, in general, a high score in one set is just as likely to correspond with a low as with a high score in the other set. (Students with high IQ scores, for example, are as likely to have high as low school marks). In other words, no discernible correspondence prevails between the high and low ranks of the sets of scores. Correlations, therefore, range over a scale which extends from a perfect negative correlation to no correlation to a perfect positive correlation.

Correlation techniques serve a number of different purposes. Social scientists find them particularly useful in studies of prediction. Researchers are often asked to find a means of predicting whether pupils or employees will be successful on the job or in mastering particular skills or subject matter (36). When faced with a problem of predicting scholastic success, for example, the staff of an educational research bureau may design a test to measure "academic aptitude" and administer it to all freshman students entering college in September. At the close of the academic year, the staff members may correlate the students' scores on the academic aptitude test with their quality-point averages. If a high positive correlation between the two variables exists and if the youths taking the academic aptitude test are representative of the succeeding freshman students, the researchers may assume that the test will be of value in predicting the scholastic success of future students. They may, therefore, plan to use the test as a basis for screening and counseling students. The possibility exists, of course, that the relationship found between the variables is due to mere chance or to some irrelevant factors.

In studies analyzing cause and effect, the correlation technique may be used in the following manner. Suppose that from observing typing classes you have decided that the amount of time spent in glancing away from the copy is inversely related to typing speed. To test this hypothesis, you have all ninth-grade typing students in Jones school type the same copy. After recording the typing speed of each student and the amount of time spent in glancing away from the copy, you compare the speed scores with the glancing-away time and discover that a high negative correlation exists—that is, the lower the typing speed a student achieves, the more time he spends glancing away from his copy. This correlation suggests, but does not prove conclusively, that time spent in glancing away from the copy is an important factor relating to the speed of typing. The findings of the study suggest that speed of typing may be improved by decreasing the amount of time spent glancing away from the copy.

The correlation technique is a valuable research tool. But a coefficient of correlation merely quantifies the extent to which two variables are related; it does not imply that a cause-effect relationship necessarily exists. Interpreting the meaning of the relationship is accomplished by logical analysis rather than by statistical computation. This interpretation is subject to all the pitfalls and limitations discussed in the previous section on causal-comparative studies.

Developmental Studies

Developmental studies are concerned not only with the existing status and interrelationships of phenomena, but also with changes that take place as a function of time. In these studies, investigators describe variables in the course of their development over a period of months or years. The following sections discuss two types of developmental studies: growth studies and trend studies.

Growth Studies

To teach effectively, one must have knowledge of the nature and rate of changes that take place in human organisms. One must know what interrelated factors affect growth at various stages of development and when various aspects of growth are first observable, spurt forward, remain rather stationary, reach optimal development, and decline.

Growth-study Techniques/ Human development can be studied by two methods: the longitudinal and the cross-sectional techniques. In both types of studies a series of planned and systematic observations are made. In the *longitudinal* studies, the growth states of the *same children* are measured at *different ages.* You might, for example, test and measure the same group of students on a number of variables when they are twelve, thirteen, fourteen, and fifteen years of age and plot their individual growth patterns for these factors during these years. But when conducting a *cross-sectional* study, rather than repeatedly measuring the same children, you make one set of measurements of *different children from each age level.* Then you calculate the averages for the variables for each group and plot these averages to depict the general growth patterns of each variable for children from twelve to sixteen years of age.

Cross-sectional studies usually include more subjects, but describe fewer growth factors than longitudinal studies. In a cross-sectional study, you might record the weight and some length, girth, and breadth measurements of several thousand students between twelve and sixteen years of age. To obtain the "norms" of growth for these phenomena, you would calculate the central tendency of the items measured for each of the five years. Thus, you could state the average weight of children on each age level and the average for each of the other measurements taken.

In a longitudinal growth study, you would probably observe fewer subjects and measure more variables. For example, a study described in *Development in Adolescence* by Jones (77) and his associates at the University of California traced the development of a boy, "John Sanders," for a period of years. Among the many factors studied were (1) home, neighborhood, and family background, (2) entry into adolescence, (3) reactions of teachers and classmates, (4) membership in social groups, (5) physical development—health records, physical growth, skeletal maturing, growth curves relative to the group, physiological changes, (6) motor and mental abilities—strength record, achievement tests, aspects of learning ability, and various physical, manual, and mental abilities, (7) interests and attitudes, (8) underlying tendencies—analyses of drive patterns, projective materials, voice records, Rorschach records, and emotional trends, and (9) John as he saw himself and as he judged himself and others.

Evaluation of Growth-study Techniques/ The longitudinal technique is the most satisfactory method of studying human development, but the cross-sectional technique is more commonly used because it is less expensive and less time consuming. If an educator employs the cross-sectional technique, he can gather and analyze his data in a relatively short time; he does not have to test the subjects year after year or wait until they mature before he can complete his study.

Sampling problems occur in the use of both techniques. In cross-sectional studies, the different subjects measured at each age level may not be comparable. If the strength and intelligence of males between fifteen and sixty-five years of age are measured, for example, the data collected for the youngest and oldest age group are not comparable for two reasons. The older men are presumably representative of those who at fifteen possessed the physical and intellectual capacity to survive until sixty-five years of age. The fifteen-year-old group undoubtedly contains some boys who will not survive until they are sixty-five years of age. Even if the age spread in a cross-sectional study is not great, errors may be made in comparing the average growth of different groups. A researcher may want to obtain a description of the average strength and intelligence of American children between the ages of six and eighteen. But testing the students in Irontown schools between these ages will give him a distorted picture of older youths' capacities, for in this mining town many brighter students go away to school after the ninth grade and many stronger boys go to work.

Longitudinal studies also have sampling weaknesses. The data in these studies are usually obtained from a limited number of subjects and hence do not experience the corrective influence of many samples. When subjects are selected from a community with a stable population for the sake of keeping track of them throughout the years of the study, the low mobility of the group introduces a bias that will influence the findings. Longitudinal studies may give accurate measurements for the growth of the individuals studied, but these descriptions are not necessarily representative of the total population. Can findings, for example, concerning the growth and development of students in a laboratory school at the University of Michigan be applied directly to students in a rural Mississippi community or children of migrant Mexican laborers?

Another complication of the longitudinal method is that the researcher usually cannot make improvements in his techniques as his study develops without disrupting the continuity of procedures. If he discovers a new and better instrument for measuring a particular aptitude after the study has been under way for a year or two and decides to use it, the data he collects with the different tests are not likely to be comparable.

Because longitudinal studies usually include a relatively small number of subjects from one locality, they do not give as accurate a picture of the great range of individual differences that exist among children as cross-sectional studies do. But individual variability of growth and development is revealed better in longitudinal than in cross-sectional studies. At best, cross-sectional studies provide approximations about the individuality of growth with time, for they give the average growth status of an age group which tends to minimize or blot out individual variability. Thus, the growth spurt during adolescence may not be revealed in a cross-sectional study, because the combination of late-maturing and early-maturing subjects tends to smooth out the curve. When studying the physical growth patterns of children, for example, Shuttleworth (119) found that late-maturing and early-maturing girls exhibited different growth curves which were not apparent when age cross-sectional data were used. Children mature at different rates, and their growth patterns reflect the influence of illness and environmental experiences that they encounter. Hence, the longitudinal method is the best way of obtaining accurate descriptions of individual growth.

When utilizing the longitudinal technique, however, a researcher may encounter other difficulties. Obtaining complete data for all subjects over the years may be impossible because some of them may die, become ill, move, or lose interest in participating. The conditions that made the subjects unavailable may have a bearing on the growth patterns being studied, which, of course, cannot be reflected in the last stages of the study results. If strength is being measured, for example, the weaker boys may lose interest in the study and "just go through the motions" or even refuse to take the tests after the first few years. If all data for subjects with incomplete measurements are discarded, as some investigators suggest should be done (4), the size of the sample may be reduced to a point of little value. The alternative, of course, is to start with a group considerably larger than will be reported in the final results, which is costly and time-consuming and does not resolve the sampling problems that arise when a particular type of subject drops out.

Because longitudinal studies require extensive facilities, considerable financial support, and continuity of personnel over a number of years, child welfare stations connected with the larger universities have exerted most of the leadership in this field of research. Graduate students and professors who have small grants or no financial assistance usually pursue cross-sectional studies. But no real antagonism exists between cross-sectional and longitudinal methods: each method possesses values and each tends to supplement the information concerning growth and development provided by the other.

Trend Studies

Obtaining social, economic, or political data and analyzing them to identify trends and to predict what is likely to take place in the future is the objective of some descriptive studies. Researchers who engage in this work either repeat the same status study at intervals over a period of years, or gather information from documentary sources that describe present events or conditions and those that occurred at different times in the past. After comparing the data—studying the rate and direction of change—they predict the conditions or events that may prevail in the future. This type of study may combine the historical, documentary, and survey techniques.

Before formulating policies and plans for the future of an industry, community, or school system, administrators often conduct or examine trend surveys. Leaders from many fields undoubtedly will peruse the *New York Metropolitan Region Study* (nine volumes), which examines jobs and wages; shift of residential areas; population growth and decline; conditions affecting business, industry, and trade; transportation; finance; labor; and education. On the basis of current trends, the study projects probable developments through 1985. To plan future courses of action intelligently, school authorities must possess considerable information about trends. Studies of home-building trends in the community and the age of the new residents, for example, give them some idea of when and where to build future schools. Studies of migrations inform them of the population gains and losses to expect, so that they can adjust school budgets, instructional programs, classroom construction, and teacher-recruitment programs accordingly.

After World War II, several studies (98,102,136) warned educators to prepare for enormous increases in secondary school and college enrollments. These predictions were based on trend analyses that revealed a skyrocketing increase in births and a higher proportion of students completing their high school education and going on to college. These studies alerted college officials to the need for accelerating their building programs, attracting more youths to college teaching as a profession, and conducting vigorous campaigns for the funds needed to expand their programs.

Among other examples of educational trend studies are the interesting and complex analyses of population changes that have been reported by Edwards and Richey (51) and the Research Division of the NEA (see issues of the *Research Bulletin*). These studies raise questions about the educational implications of trends, such as the rising level of schooling attained by the population, the changing age structure of the population, and the differential fertility of the racial, socioeconomic, and educational groups in the population. For several years, analyses have been made of birthrate trends, enrollments in schools of education, and other factors, to make predictions about teacher supply and demand in various fields. Studies in occupational trends have also provided school administrators with information that aids them in planning future educational programs.

Making predictions from social trend data is a precarious venture because economic conditions, technological advances, wars, personal wants, and other unforeseen events may suddenly modify the anticipated course of events. Long-range population predictions, for example, have usually proved wrong. Malthus foresaw mass starvation because of overpopulation, but he did not foresee the productivity of the Industrial Revolution and the agricultural Americas. With the decrease in immigration and the decline of the birth rate during the depression years, scholars suggested that the United States should prepare for a leveling-off of the population. But in recent years, the projections of the Census Bureau on population growth have been invalidated almost before their publication because of the unexpected increases. Again pundits prophesy that the population explosion will bring global misery. Among their predictions is the warning that colleges will not be able to cope with expanding enrollments. But new educational techniques and resources may be discovered that will solve this problem. The anticipated increase in enrollments, moreover, may not be fully realized if a war, serious depression, sharply increased tuition, or higher entrance standards prevent many youths from attaining a higher education. Because of the many unforeseeable factors that may impinge upon social phenomena, trend analyses range considerably in certainty of prediction: most long-range predictions represent mere estimates; short-term predictions possess greater certainty.

Evaluation of Descriptive Research

Descriptive research is the method of investigation that has been most commonly employed by educators. Popularity, however, is not proof of worth. Some descriptive studies increase our understanding of educational phenomena, but many studies are of limited value. In some respects, well-designed descriptive studies conform to the scientific method of research, but the complex nature of social science phenomena makes the full realization of this goal unattainable. Some of the problems that arise are concerned with [(1) a critical examination of the source materials, (2) technical terminology, (3) formulation of hypotheses, (4) observation and experimentation, and (5) generalization and prediction./

Critical Examination of Source Materials

Scientific inquiry requires the presentation of accurate facts that are verifiable by public tests of common perception. Some descriptive data measure up to this standard, but many of them are not established as precisely and objectively as the facts of physical science. Physical scientists are concerned with data on one level—the physical. Because educators may deal not only with physical phenomena, but also with diverse social, biological, or psychological phenomena, isolating causal factors that are of interest to them and measuring these variables precisely so as to establish relatively stable facts is often exceedingly difficult.

Obtaining reliable measurements for some social phenomena presents no problems. An investigator can ascertain that Johnny is a 100-pound male youth who has a 60-pound grip strength, and any competent observer can check and confirm these facts. But perplexing problems may arise if the researcher tries to obtain accurate information about the youth's attitudes toward Negroes or why the boy prefers fattening food. Johnny may deliberately conceal his motives and attitudes and give answers that he thinks are socially acceptable. His answers may reflect a reaction to a recent vivid experience rather than his customary attitude. His preference for fattening foods may be caused by one or several factors—family food habits, a desire to compensate for lack of success in athletics or intellectual activities, or physiological conditions. Disentangling these factors and determining in what proportion each one is responsible for his food choices may be a difficult if not an impossible task.

Descriptive studies cannot produce useful findings if the investigations are based on erroneous data. Yet, some researchers do not subject their source materials to a critical examination. They accept much information that appears in print or in official records at face value. This practice is dangerous, for records may be deliberately falsified or may include unintentional errors and printed materials may reflect the author's biases or may be based on secondhand rather than firsthand observations. Some researchers also forget that data collected from different sources, by different people, by different techniques, or at different times may not be comparable.

Technical Terminology

Descriptive research serves as a tool that is used to locate significant variables in the field. After the variables are identified, experimenters may study them under more rigorous conditions. Because descriptive researchers do the pioneer spadework upon which experimental researchers build, the variables in their studies may not be defined operationally with the degree of specificity that they are in experiments, their measuring instruments are often cruder, and many of their data are qualitative rather than quantitative in nature.

Sciences develop step by step. Since the social sciences are in a relatively primitive stage of their development, workers in the field have not devised a precise, well-developed, universally accepted vocabulary that can be employed to communicate with one another. Descriptive researchers initiate this search, but many investigators do not give sufficient attention to this problem. Different workers use different terms to describe the same phenomena. Investigators who employ the same terms do not always have the same meanings in mind. If two observers are seeking data about "cooperative behavior" of pupils, one may tabulate incidents of blind obedience to authority and the other incidents of critical-constructive participation. One worker may use the term "aggressive behavior" to refer to antisocial or delinquent acts, while another worker may use the same term to describe demonstrations of initiative and leadership. An absence of clearly assigned meanings for terms results in ambiguous communications, which cannot provide a solid foundation for scientific understanding.

Formulation of Hypotheses

The scientific method requires scholars to make intelligent guesses that will solve problems, and to test whether these guesses—hypotheses—present accurate explanations of phenomena. Many descriptive studies do not meet this requirement. When hypotheses are presented in descriptive studies, they are of a somewhat lower order than those found in explanatory studies. In the latter, the hypotheses offer general explanations of *why* certain phenomena behave as they do. Descriptive studies simply portray the facts—they describe *what* exists but do not account for why the present state of affairs has occurred. Descriptive studies may describe likenesses and differences between variables and establish rudimentary groupings of phenomena. Investigators may classify, order, and correlate data and describe relationships that appear to exist among variables, but they do not fully analyze and explain why these relationships exist. They do not put them to a crucial experimental test.

Descriptive studies range from weak status studies that do little more than ask questions and report answers, to interrelationship studies that present hypotheses which approach the level of explanatory hypotheses. Each type of study has utility in certain situations. Descriptive studies that obtain accurate facts about existing conditions or detect significant relationships among current phenomena and interpret the meaning of the data provide educators with practical and immediately useful information. Factual information about existing status enables members of the profession to make more intelligent plans about future courses of action and helps them interpret educational problems more effectively to the public. Pertinent data regarding the present scene may focus attention upon developments, conditions, and trends that might otherwise remain unnoticed. The data may convince citizens to keep pace with existing needs and to prepare for future events. Since educational conditions, processes, practices, and programs are changing constantly, up-to-date descriptions of what is taking place are needed.

If descriptive studies were employed only to obtain practical information that could be used to improve or to justify the immediate situation in a given school or community, they would not advance science. But some descriptive studies, particularly those that hypothesize relationships among and between variables, provide the factual foundations upon which higher levels of scientific understanding can be built. Compared with the natural sciences, research in education is of relatively recent origin. Many areas within the field have not been explored: numerous gaps in knowledge exist. Unless educators accumulate relevant facts about a situation, they cannot sense what is significant. A reservoir of information about the nature of educational phenomena must be collected, classified, and correlated before investigators can gain insights that will enable them to break through to higher levels of scientific understanding.

Descriptive research is sometimes disparaged because it provides the lowest level of scientific understanding—descriptions of what exists. Descriptive studies do not produce the grandiose scientific theories that form the apex of our hierarchy of knowledge. Indeed, some men classify descriptive studies as scholarly work, but do not consider them to be research. Educators, undoubtedly, have been too preoccupied with descriptive studies. The time has come to move on into more fundamental probes concerning the nature of the phenomena in the field. More experimental research is needed, but descriptive studies serve as useful exploratory tools.

The quality of descriptive research should be improved, however, for many studies are poorly conceived in design and lacking in depth and perspective. Rather than constructing well-thought-out hypotheses and collecting pertinent data to test them, many researchers merely make clerical tabulations of the available data on some subject. Their neat piles of data do not solve problems, for data that are not used to confirm or disconfirm a hypothesis concerning the nature of phenomena do not advance knowledge appreciably.

Hypotheses are more commonly stated in research papers

today than they were earlier in the century. Perhaps some statements taken from recent literature are the best means of illustrating the nature of descriptive hypotheses. In a study of permissiveness, permission, and aggression and the effect of adult presence or absence on aggression in children's play, Siegel and Kohn stated, "The hypothesis is that children under the two conditions will exhibit different session-to-session changes in aggression, in that aggression of the children under the adult-absent condition will tend to decrease in comparison to the aggression of the children under the adult-present condition, which will tend to increase" (121:134).

A study designed to explore the effect of personal values on pupils and teachers in the determination of school marks states that the investigator (10:28) examined the following three hypotheses:

1/
Among pupils of similar aptitude, age, and sex, the value patterns of those who receive high marks in a particular subject tend to have higher correlation with pupil value patterns considered ideal by the teacher who determines the marks than do the patterns of pupils who receive low marks in the subject.

2/
If aptitude, age, and sex are controlled, the value patterns of pupils with high scholarship averages in their several subjects will tend to have higher correlation with a composite value pattern determined by several teachers in the school than will patterns of pupils with low averages.

3/
In a Spearman two-factor pattern composed of a sample of teachers, a given number of high-achieving pupils, and the same number of low-achieving pupils in a particular high school, the loadings on the common factor for teachers and high-achieving pupils will tend to exceed loadings on this factor for low-achieving pupils.

The hypotheses that appear in some descriptive studies are ambiguously formulated, overgeneralized, or logically unsound. Furthermore, many research papers fail to include a thorough analysis of the problem and the assumptions on which the hypotheses are based so that the reader can determine how the researchers came to frame the hypotheses. Another common weakness of reports is the omission of the deductive elaboration of the hypotheses. The reports lead one to presume that the investigators tested the hypotheses directly rather than indirectly (according to step 4 of the Dewey stages of reflective thinking), through the deduced consequences of the hypotheses.

Observation and Experimentation

Whenever possible, social scientists test their hypotheses by experimentation: they manipulate the independent variable under controlled laboratory conditions and directly observe the results. But some social phenomena cannot be manipulated and subjected to controlled laboratory conditions. Observing the phenomena as they exist in the classroom, community, recreation center, or camp is the only way to examine and analyze the factors that are associated with their occurrence. Making observations in a dynamic, ongoing situation, however, is much more difficult than observing a few isolated variables in a rigidly controlled laboratory experiment. In some instances, moreover, descriptive researchers must rely on the observations made by others, which introduces the problem of checking the authenticity and credibility of secondhand information.

Workers who employ descriptive procedures may exercise every possible precaution when making observations so that confounding variables are eliminated and irrelevant factors do not bias their results, but at best, they can only approach experimental conditions. Because they cannot exercise the degree of control that experimenters can, descriptive researchers can never be certain that they have established cause-effect relationships. Correlation reveals association but does not prove causation. An investigator may ascertain that A is associated with the occurrence of B, but the question remains: Does A cause B, does B cause A, or is the association between A and B merely a reflection of a third factor that is operating? Descriptive researchers can only detect associations between variables, but this information is useful if it is used properly. Descriptive studies that discover the presence or absence of an association between variables serve as pilot projects. They screen out unpromising hypotheses and detect relationships between variables that experimenters can study profitably under more rigorously controlled laboratory conditions.

Generalization and Prediction

The goals of science are to explain, predict, and control conditions and events. Descriptive research contributes to science primarily by building a foundation of facts upon which explanatory hypotheses may be constructed and by checking the validity of existing theories. Science begins with descriptions of singular, unique events, but it does not remain on this primitive level of knowledge. Scientific workers endeavor to construct generalizations—hypotheses—that will explain why events occur. Rather than confining their attention to a particular isolated incident, they imaginatively structure broad generalizations that will account for the occurrence of many events and conditions. Their ultimate objective is to establish universal laws with predictive power that will enable man to control nature.

For the most part, descriptive research is temporally localized; hence, the findings of studies do not possess great predictive power. Most of the findings are applicable only within relatively short limits of time. Descriptive generalizations may help solve contemporary problems, but many of them have a limited useful life span. They do not survive because many social phenomena change from day to day and from one age to the next; they are not as stable as phenomena in the physical sciences. Some descriptive data, obviously, are more enduring than others. Data that relate to certain physical conditions of the school environment, such as location of buildings, or physical characteristics of a child, such as color of eyes, are quite stable. Data concerning some behavioral phenomena, such as intelligence or authoritarianism, are relatively more enduring than descriptions of attitudes, interests, desires, or opinions, which may be rather fleeting in nature. The transitory character of much knowledge collected in descriptive studies usually limits the relevance of the data to contemporary problems.

Many educators conduct studies that produce discrete bits of knowledge that are of local significance and do not advance scientific knowledge. If an investigator obtains data from a convenient sample of subjects, such as a cooperative class or a nearby school, the findings of his study have limited usefulness. The findings apply to the particular group of subjects that participated, but they cannot be generalized to a larger population. If a social scientist wishes to apply his findings to subjects or situations other than the specific ones included in his study, he must identify the population clearly and then randomly select a representative sample of subjects for his study.

Serious social scientists observe the niceties of sampling procedures in their inquiries, but despite their sincerity, they cannot establish such broad generalizations as do their colleagues in the natural sciences. Since cultures, communities, and schools differ from one another, and no culture is absolutely uniform in nature, descriptive data can mirror only particular aspects of specific event or conditions in a given setting.

"When social scientists seek generalizations about all human beings, rather than, say, about members of a specific culture or a specific organization, their sample is invariably nonrepresentative. No one has yet studied a representative sample of persons or behaviors from all cultures at all periods" (104:256–257). Chemists can be quite certain that one sample of pure magnesium is substantially like another, but educators can never claim that one child is exactly like all other children.

Social science workers are constantly plagued by the complexity of their phenomena. They are unable to abstract specific temporal and spatial characteristics from an event and generalize to all future occurrences of the event with any degree of preciseness. They find it almost an insurmountable task to forecast, for successful prediction rests upon the duplication of the past in the future. Rose states that

. . . as long as social science deals with social phenomena on the level at which they can be observed directly, it cannot find cause-and-effect laws that apply universally in all known and possible cultures. The explanation of this requires no metaphysics; it is simply based on the fact that one of the determinants of an individual's behavior, when it is of the mediating type, is his "apperceptive mass," the full range of experiences that he has had since birth and that is retained in his nervous system. To predict his physical movements at these times, the predictor would have to know everything that ever happened to him, and this is impossible. Further, no two individuals have had exactly the same past experiences, and therefore knowledge of how one individual acts is no sure guide to how another will act. This is to say that we may never be able to make perfectly accurate predictions about human behavior or to make propositions about human behavior that hold good universally, as we may be able to make for the behavior of turtles or rocks (104:158).

Educational phenomena involve far too many variables for researchers to spell out detailed laws. One cannot predict human behavior precisely, but neither can one be certain that life consists of random or accidental events. Descriptions of recurring patterns or regularities of human behavior enable investigators to make some reasonably reliable, limited predictions. Many predictions made by social scientists are more accurate than chance alone would allow. But these forecasts do not possess the universality, precision, or degree of accuracy that predictions do in the natural sciences. They are likely to be stated "When this happens, this *tends* to occur," or "If this happens, we can expect that to happen in 60 per cent of the cases." Evolving universal generalizations that permit highly accurate predictions may be the ideal, but even the physical scientists are less certain today than they once were of their ability to predict in certain areas except in terms of statistical probability.

11

Strategy of Experimental Research

When an educator engages in experimental research, he does not merely chronicle past events, determine the status of something, or observe and describe what exists. Through manipulating an experimental variable under highly controlled conditions, he strives to ascertain how and why a particular condition or event occurs. "Experimentation, as distinguished from observation, consists in the deliberate and controlled modification of the conditions determining an event, and in the observation and interpretation of the ensuing changes in the event itself" (143:618–619).

If science is to achieve its goal—explaining, predicting, and controlling behavior and events—causal connections among phenomena in a field must be discovered. From the previous chapter, you recall that causal-comparative studies are concerned with causality, and some carefully controlled investigations approach the level of experimental studies. But these ex post facto studies consist of postmortem examinations—systematic observations that are made after events have taken place. To determine whether studying in a quiet environment affects school marks, for example, an investigator locates pupils who have studied in a quiet environment and pupils who have not and compares their marks. In an experiment, on the other hand, the investigator manipulates purposively the experimental variable—study environment—and then observes what happens under controlled conditions: he assigns subjects to groups at random and tosses a coin to decide which group will study in a quiet room and which one will study in a noisy room, and after a reasonable period of time compares their scholastic performances.

In a causal-comparative study, the investigator never knows for certain whether having a quiet study environment or some associated factor causes the students to get high or low marks. If the students in the two groups received a distinctly different quality of parental guidance, their marks might have differed if they had all studied in the same environment. In an experiment, the effect of associated variables may also be mistaken for the effect of the experimental treatment, but the likelihood of making this mistake is not as great because the researcher can manipulate the experimental variable and can employ techniques that eliminate or control the effect of these associated variables.

Nature of Experimental Research

A number of steps are involved in experimental research. Unless all these procedures are executed expertly, the experimental testing process is valueless. The tasks that an investigator performs when he conducts an experimental study are:

1/
Surveying the literature relating to the problem.
2/
Identifying and defining the problem.
3/
Formulating a problem hypothesis, deducing the consequences, and defining basic terms and variables.
4/
Constructing an experimental plan that represents all the elements, conditions, and relations of the consequences, which may require that he (a) identify all nonexperimental variables that might contaminate the experiment, and determine how to control them, (b) select a research design, (c) select a sample of subjects to represent a given population, assign subjects to groups, and assign experimental treatments to groups, (d) select or construct and validate instruments to measure the outcomes of the experiment, (e) outline procedures for collecting the data, and possibly conduct a pilot or "trial run" test to perfect the instruments or design, and (f) state the statistical or null hypothesis.
5/
Conducting the experiment.
6/
Reducing the raw data in a manner that will produce the best appraisal of the effect which is presumed to exist.

7/
Applying an appropriate test of significance to determine the confidence one can place on the results of the study.

The first three of these tasks have been discussed in detail previously. The last two tasks involve a knowledge of statistics; hence, they are discussed in Chapters 13 and 14. This chapter is primarily concerned with the fourth task—designing the experiment and establishing the necessary controls. But before proceeding with that discussion, let us briefly review the relationship of the experiment to the problem and hypothesis.

Bases of an Experiment

Experimental research starts with the identification and rigorous logical analysis of the problem. The issues involved are sharpened by formulating hypotheses and deducing the consequences that are implied logically by them. A test situation is then devised to discover whether the consequences that should occur if the hypotheses are to be confirmed are observable.

Many students who are enthusiastic about conducting experimental studies are unaware of the precision that the analysis of problems and formulation of hypotheses requires. To them experimentation is a blind trial-and-error procedure: "If we try this, what will happen?" They have a nebulous notion about what they are testing, and their plans for observing what happens are equally indefinite. Sometimes they stumble upon fruitful explanations of causality by this procedure, but the chance of expending an enormous amount of effort without producing significant results is large. Conducting experiments to test crudely conceived hypotheses is a waste of time.

If a hypothesis and its deduced consequences are constructed properly, two factors are identified and defined clearly and unambiguously:

(1) an independent variable	and	(2) a dependent variable
Condition X	*is related to*	*Condition Y*

A hypothesis suggests that an antecedent condition (independent variable) is related to the occurrence of another condition, event, or effect (dependent variable). To test a deduced consequence of a hypothesis, an investigator attempts to control all conditions except the independent variable which he manipulates. Then he observes what happens to the dependent variable presumably because of the exposure to the independent variable. The dependent variable is the phenomenon that appears, disappears, or changes as the researcher applies, removes, or varies the independent variable. The independent variable is the factor that is manipulated purposively under observation to ascertain its relationship with the dependent variable.

Examples of Experiments

A botanist, for example, can contend that sunlight (independent variable) has an effect on plant growth (dependent variable). To test this hypothesis, he may obtain plants of the same species, cover each with a bell jar, and place one in a shaded place and the other in the sunlight. Thus, he manipulates the amount of sunlight the plants receive. His experiment will give him direct empirical evidence that exposure to the sun results in plant growth and the absence of the sunlight retards plant growth. The botanist may wish to broaden the experiment by setting out several like plants and shading the bell jars so that various intensities of light fall upon them in order to appraise how much various light conditions affect growth.

In education, an experimenter may vary some condition in the students' environment and observe its effect on achievement. He may hypothesize that children will learn to spell better if spaced practice is used rather than massed practice. The independent variable that he manipulates to test this hypothesis is the "spacing of practice." The dependent variable that experiences the effect of this manipulation is spelling mastery. During the experiment, the investigator attempts to keep all conditions the same for two groups of children except that one group studies spelling sixty minutes once a week and the other group has a practice session fifteen minutes a day the first four school days of each week. In other words, all conditions are held constant except the experimental variable—spacing of practice—which is manipulated. Consequently, any difference in the spelling mastery of these two groups at the close of the experiment can be attributed to the manipulation of the independent variable—spacing of practice.

Control of the Experiment

Experimental strategy is not simple; the investigator does not merely manipulate one variable to see what happens to another variable; an experimentation requires *controlled observation.*

Eliciting and controlling the expression of the independent variable may involve considerable effort. Identifying and controlling other variables that may affect the dependent variable is an equally difficult and important task. If the teacher who conducted the spelling experiment did not control the selection of the spelling words, the amount of time devoted to study, and the selection of the subjects, one group of students might have had easier words to spell, a longer total time to study, and a greater spelling mastery prior to the experiment than the other group. Consequently, at the conclusion of the experiment, the teacher would not know whether the manipulation of the independent variable—spacing of practice—or these other variables were responsible for the difference in the spelling mastery of the two groups.

How does the experimenter determine what variables can affect a dependent variable? Previous experience with the phenomena and a careful analysis of the problem will suggest some clues. An examination of experimental studies in the field will inform him about variables that other scholars have found to influence the dependent variable. Investigators who have studied sensorimotor skill, for example, have found little relationship between intelligence test scores and sensorimotor learning, but they have identified several other variables that are related to such skills: strength, speed, accuracy, endurance, agility, body size, reaction time, steadiness, balance, and control of voluntary movements. To discover whether a new teaching method will influence sensorimotor skill, an experimenter must control the variables that are known to be related to sensorimotor skill, so that their effect will not mask the possible effect of the new teaching method.

Purposes of Control

In an experiment, the investigator seeks to control variables for the following purposes: "(1) to isolate the determiners individually and in combinations; (2) to vary them as magnitudes either singly or in combinations; and (3) to describe quantitatively the extent of their expression and their interacting effects, again, either as single determiners or as combinations of determiners" (17:76).

Achieving Isolation/ To prevent a factor other than the independent variable from affecting the dependent variable, the researcher may remove the unwanted or interfering variable, or he may either keep constant its effect or equalize its presence in the experimental and control groups.

Achieving Changes in Magnitude/ An investigator may strive not only to isolate the independent variable, but also to ascertain how much effect it contributes. To achieve this objective, he must be able to vary the magnitude of the experimental variable. In a psychological study, for example, the experimenter may make observations for each degree of change in the independent variable—for example, intensity, pitch, or timbre of an auditory stimulus—to determine its effect on the dependent variable. In some studies, of course, he cannot seek this level of control because not enough is known about the independent variable to vary it through finely graded steps. When this condition exists, he investigates whether the presence or absence of a certain factor has any effect and leaves it for his successors to study the graduations of effect.

Achieving Quantitative Evaluation/ The ultimate goal of a researcher is to express the magnitude of the variable in quantitative terms. He wants to know not merely that one expression of a variable is larger or smaller than another, but precisely how much larger or smaller it is. If two variables are functionally related, he wants to state not merely that they are positively or negatively related, but rather the specific degree of relationship in terms of some numerical value.

Methods of Control

Researchers have devised a number of procedures to control variables. Brown and Ghiselli (17) suggest that controls fall into three broad categories: (1) physical manipulation, (2) selective manipulation, and (3) statistical manipulation. Sometimes direct physical manipulation is used to gain control with the same success in the social sciences as it is in the physical sciences. But because of the nature of educational phenomena, control must often be gained through the indirect methods of selection and statistical manipulation.

Physical Manipulation/ Various means of physical manipulation may be employed so as (1) to give all subjects the same exposure to the independent variable or (2) to control nonexperimental variables that affect the dependent variable. A *mechanical means* may be devised: an experimenter may soundproof or lightproof a room or blindfold subjects to screen out unwanted stimuli; use a one-way-vision screen to observe subjects so that his presence will not change or influence their behavior; employ a tachistoscope to present each subject with a specific number of words, numbers, pictures for brief intervals of duration; or construct a maze to study an ability to learn. *Electrical means* may be employed to effect control: an investigator may utilize constant-speed motors for driving various types of apparatus, such as the memory drum which presents materials through a slot in a machine while the drum revolves at selected speeds. *Surgical means* may be used to exercise control: an experimenter may remove glands from the body or destroy tissue in certain parts of the brain to determine their effects on behavior. *Pharmacological means,* such as changes of diet, drugs, or gland extracts can also be used to achieve control.

Selective Manipulation/ To make certain that the experimental findings do not merely measure the difference in the ways that the experimental and control subjects are treated, a researcher may endeavor to *hold conditions constant* for the two groups. All treatment sessions, for example, may be held in the same room and at the same time of day. The experimenters may be trained to follow the same procedures, to assume the same attitudes, to give instructions in the same way, and to use the same apparatus when working with all subjects.

Sometimes a researcher cannot hold conditions constant in the experiment; consequently, he resorts to techniques of balancing out, randomizing out, or counterbalancing unwanted variables that may affect dependent variable scores. To equalize or balance out the effect of differences in the abilities of teachers or the sensitivity of apparatus, an experimenter may randomly assign half of the experimental subjects and half of the control subjects to each teacher and to each piece of apparatus. To overcome differences in the subjects, he may pair subjects who are equal in respect to a given characteristic that might affect the dependent variable scores, such as intelligence, and randomly assign one member of each pair to the experimental group and the other member to the control group. The differences in subjects, teachers, and apparatus will affect the dependent variable scores, of course, but they will affect the scores of both groups. Consequently, the investigator can assume that the experimental findings are produced by the independent variable and not by these differences in the groups, teachers, or apparatus.

Some extraneous variables can be controlled through the selection of materials. Suppose that an experimenter wants to study the amount of time required to memorize materials of different lengths, such as a series of nonsense syllables. Something other than length of materials may affect the time required for learning. If the shorter units of materials are more difficult than the longer units, this condition may affect the amount of time required to master them. To control the unwanted factor of difficulty, the experimenter can select short and long learning units that are comparable in difficulty.

Statistical Manipulation/ When variables are not amenable to physical or selective manipulation, they may be controlled by statistical techniques. Statistical controls can achieve the same precision as other methods when they are employed to evaluate a variable's effect. Statistical techniques are particularly useful in a situation where multiple variables may be functionally related to a particular effect, as is often the case in education. Suppose that A, B, and C act conjointly on dependent variable Y. If only the relationship between A and Y is obtained, the findings are spurious, for A is partly a product of its interaction with B and C. Thus, some means must be found to hold B and C constant to determine the precise relationship between A and Y. Statistical procedures permit one to do this and thus to approximate the relative importance of the contribution of each variable to Y. Two of the most frequently used statistical procedures for effecting an analysis of multiple-variable situations are the method of partial correlation and the method of the analysis of variance. These methods are discussed in subsequent chapters and in advanced statistical texts.

Types of Factors to Be Controlled

Having briefly examined why and how a researcher tries to achieve control in an experiment, another question naturally arises: What does he try to control? Before examining arguments concerning this important question, you should become familiar with the communication system that is used in this chapter.

1/ Independent variable X.
The independent variable, which is often called the treatment, experimental, or antecedent variable, is represented by the symbol X.

2/ Dependent variable Y.
The dependent variable, which is often called the "criterion" or "predicted variable," is symbolized by the letter Y.

3/ Experimenter E.
The person who conducts the investigation or manipulates the experimental conditions is represented by the symbol E, and the plural is Es.

4/ Subject S.
The symbol for the living organism that is studied, the subject or respondent, is S, and the plural is Ss.

5/ Control and experimental groups.
The group that is exposed to X is the experimental group. The group that is not exposed to X, or is exposed to another X for comparison purposes, is the control group.

6/ Pretest T_1 and posttest T_2.
If a pretest T_1 is used in an experiment, it is administered before X is applied. A posttest T_2 is a test that subjects take after X is applied.

7/ Mean M.
To find the mean of a group (the average score), an experimenter adds the members' test scores and divides the sum by the number of members.

8/ Population (universe).
A population is a *whole*, all the units (subjects, objects, or events) in a group.

9/ Sample.
A sample consists of units that are selected from a given population. (Before reading further, master these terms and symbols. What do the symbols X, Y, E, S, T, and M represent?)

Selecting an experimental design is one of the most important decisions that an E makes.[1] If a design is valid, it will probably yield a truthful result and one that can be interpreted as such. There are two types of validity: internal and external.

Internal Validity/ When checking the internal validity of his design, an experimenter asks: Did the independent variable X really produce a change in the dependent variable? Before claiming that it did, he must make certain that some of the following extraneous variables have not produced an effect that can be mistaken for the effect of X.

1/ Contemporary history.
Sometimes the Ss experience an event—in or out of the experimental setting—besides the exposure to X, that may affect their dependent variable scores. If X is television instruction and the dependent variable is healthful practices of the students, the advent of an epidemic in the community rather than X may cause pupils to change some of their health practices. The simultaneous advent of the epidemic would be said to confound X. (An E uses the term "confound" to indicate that an effect can be attributed to two or more variables, and the portion due to each cannot be determined.)

1/ The author acknowledges his great indebtedness to the work of Campbell (22, 23, 24, 25), Campbell and Stanley (27), and their colleagues (26, 114). Much of the terminology and conceptual base of the following discussion on experimental design comes from these sources.

2/ Maturation processes.

Biological and psychological processes within the Ss may change during the progress of the experiment which will affect their responses. The Ss may perform better or worse on T_2 not because of the effect of X, but because they are older, more fatigued, or less interested than when they took T_1. Their age, fatigue, or interest would confound the interpretation of the effect of X.

3/ Pretesting procedures.

T_1 may serve as a learning experience that will cause the Ss to alter their responses on T_2 whether or not X is applied.

4/ Measuring instruments.

Changes in the testing instruments, human raters, or interviewers can affect the obtained measurements. If T_2 is more difficult than T_1, or a different person rates Ss on the rating scales, these factors rather than X can cause the difference in the two scores. Slight fluctuations in mechanical measuring instruments can also cause the difference. If the same person judges the performance of two groups in succession or the same groups before and after the application of X, his judgment may vary because he becomes more experienced and discriminating, or more fatigued and careless.

5/ Statistical regression.

In some educational research, particularly in remedial education, groups are selected on the basis of their extreme scores. When this selection procedure is employed, the effect of what is called "statistical regression" may be mistaken for the effect of X. Suppose that students who do exceptionally poor or exceptionally well on one test are selected to receive an experimental treatment. The mean (average score) of either of these groups will move toward the mean of the parent population on the second test whether or not X is applied. If the mean for the top ten Ss in a class is 90, the scores of these Ss will fan out on the retest—some will be higher and some will be lower—but the mean of the group will be almost inevitably lower. Similarly, the mean for the lowest ten Ss on the second test will be almost inevitably higher.

Upon retesting, low initial means go up toward the population mean and high initial means go down toward the population mean. Why? Regression toward the mean occurs because of random imperfections in measuring instruments. The less-than-perfect capacity of T_1 and T_2 to measure knowledge will cause a variation of Ss' performances. Pupils are likely to obtain somewhat similar scores on the T_1 and T_2, but their scores are likely to vary within a given range because there is a less-than-perfect correlation between the two tests. The more deviant (extreme) pupils' scores are from the population mean, the more they are likely to vary (see Figure 11.7). Random instability in the population may also account for regression toward the mean. Some subjects may obtain low scores on T_1 because they were upset or careless on that day. On the second test they may have better "luck," feel better, or strive harder to bring themselves up to their natural level. As a result, their higher scores will pull up the mean of their group on the second test.

6/ Differential selection of subjects.

If the experimental and control groups are exposed to X, a method of teaching, spelling, and afterward a test is given, the test results may reflect a pre-X difference in the two groups rather than the effect of X. Perhaps the experimental group could spell better than the control group before X was applied.

7/ Experimental mortality.

If a particular type of S drops out of one group after the experiment is under way, this differential loss may affect the findings of the investigation. Suppose that the Ss in the experimental group who receive the lowest T_1 scores drop out after taking the test. The remainder of the experimental group may show a greater gain on T_2 than the control group, not because of its exposure to X, but, because the low scoring Ss are missing.

8/ Interaction of selection and maturation, selection and history, etc.

When the experimental and control groups have the same T_1 scores, some other differences between them, such as intelligence, motivation, etc., rather than X may cause one of them to get higher T_2 scores. Because of this type of interaction, studies that compare volunteers (self-selected groups) with nonvolunteers must always be questioned. Suppose that an E locates forty children from impoverished homes who are poor readers, and twenty of them volunteer to participate in a cultural enrichment program. The volunteers may improve in reading more without X and benefit more from X than the nonvolunteers, because they are different initially—they are motivated more highly toward self-improvement to begin with.

External Validity/ Our discussion thus far has been confined to checking the internal validity of the design. An E gives this task primary consideration, but he is also concerned about external validity—the generalizability or representativeness of the experimental findings. Consequently, he asks: What relevance do the findings concerning the effect of X have beyond the confines of the experiment? To what subject populations, settings, experimental variables, and measurement variables can these findings be generalized?

When checking the design of an experiment, an E may ask: Can the findings be generalized to all college students? All students attending Harvard University? All Harvard freshmen? All Harvard freshmen who are enrolled in a particular course? Or must the findings be limited to the particular Harvard freshmen who participated in the experiment? An E can strengthen the external validity of his design if he describes the population to which the results will apply *before* he conducts the experiment. If he draws a random sample (see pages 205,

298) from this predetermined population (say, Harvard freshmen) and expose the sample to X, he can make the following generalization: The effect that X had on the sample population (fifty Harvard freshmen) will be the same for the population that the sample represents (all Harvard freshmen).

An investigator is concerned not only about the generalizability of his findings with respect to an S population, but also with respect to settings, independent variables, and measurement variables. Will the findings be representative of other geographical areas, sizes of schools, times of day, time of year, etc.? Will the findings provide information about situations in which one X, no X, variations of X, or more than one X is present? Will the findings be representative of situations in which one or several types of criteria measurement are used?

The representativeness of the setting that is selected for an experiment will determine how extensively the findings can be applied. If the findings of a study are derived from data that are obtained in a deprived rural area, an E cannot claim that they will hold true for wealthy metropolitan areas. If objective tests are used to measure the effect of a new teaching method, an E cannot claim that the same effect would have been observed if essay tests or oral participation had been used as the measuring instruments.

When examining the external validity of a design, the E checks the following threats to representativeness:

1/ Interaction effects of selection biases and X.
The characteristics of the Ss who are selected to participate in an experiment determine how extensively the findings can be generalized. A random sample of seventh-grade students from one school will not be representative of all seventh-grade students. The intelligence, socioeconomic status, or some other characteristic of these particular students may cause X to be more effective for them than for other seventh-grade students. If X is a new textbook, it may produce excellent results in Dort School where most students have high IQs. But an E cannot generalize that X will produce the same results in all seventh-grade classes, for the textbook may not be equally effective in Friar School where most students have low IQs.

2/ Reactive or interaction effect of pretesting.
Giving a pretest may limit the generalizability of the experimental findings. A pretest may increase or decrease the experimental Ss, sensitiveness to X: it may alert them to issues, problems, or events that they might not ordinarily notice. Consequently, these Ss may be no longer representative of the unpretested population from which they came. Suppose that fifty Harvard freshmen are given a racial-attitude test before and after they are exposed to X, a romantic film with a racial-prejudice theme. Their responses on T_2 may not reflect the effect of the film as much as the increased

sensitivity to racial prejudice that taking T_1 produced. The effect of the film for the experimental Ss may not be representative of its effect for Harvard freshmen who see the romantic film without being pretested.

3/ Reactive effects of experimental procedures.

The experimental procedures may also produce effects that limit the generalizability of the experimental findings. If the presence of observers and experimental equipment make pupils and teachers aware of the fact that they are participating in an experiment, they may alter their normal behavior. If they alter the very behavior that is being measured, the E cannot claim that the effect of X for the sample population will be the same for Ss who are exposed to X in nonexperimental situations.

4/ Multiple-treatment interference.

When the same Ss are exposed repeatedly to two or more Xs, the effects of the previous Xs are not usually erasable, hence, the findings may be generalized only to persons who experience the same sequence of treatments repeatedly. If Ss are exposed to three types of music throughout the day, they may be more productive when marching music is played; but they might not respond in the same way if marching music were played continuously.

Design with Minimal Control

A research design is to the E what a blueprint is to an architect. If the design is crudely conceived, the flawed product of the investigation will not be worthy of serious consideration. A well-developed design provides the structure and strategy that control the investigation and extract dependable answers to the questions raised by the problem hypotheses. The design suggests what observations to make, how to make them, what statistical tests are appropriate, how to analyze the quantitative data that are obtained, and what possible conclusions may be drawn from the statistical analysis. No one design solves all problems. The nature of the problem determines which basic design is most appropriate and how the design should be tailored to meet the needs of the investigation. In the following discussion, a simple design that provides minimal control is presented. This design will help you understand the advantages of the more rigorously controlled designs that are presented later.

One-group Pretest-Posttest Design (Design 1)

When this design is employed, the dependent variable is measured before the independent variable is applied or withdrawn, and then afterwards. The amount of change, if any, that has taken place is computed.

Design Procedures/ To ascertain whether a new teaching method will increase reading speed, for example, an E takes the following steps:

1/
Administers T_1 to measure the reading speed of a single group and obtains the mean for the group.
2/
Expose the Ss to X, the new teaching method, for a period of time.
3/
Administers T_2 to measure reading speed, and compares T_1 and T_2 means to ascertain what difference, if any, the exposure to X has made.
4/
Utilizes a statistical technique to ascertain whether the difference is significant.

The following is a paradigm for this design:

Pretest	Independent Variable	Posttest
T_1 Mean speed of reading for the group: 50 words per minute.	X	T_2 Mean speed of reading for the group: 80 words per minute.

$T_2 - T_1$ or $80 - 50 = 30$ wpm (the difference between the means that is caused presumably by X, the remedial teaching method).

Internal Validity/ The pretest in this design provides information that enables an E to ascertain how the Ss performed prior to the exposure to X and who dropped out of the experiment. If the same Ss take T_1 and T_2, *selection* and *mortality* variables are controlled.[2] But if some Ss drop out of the experiment, are absent from a testing or experimental session, or are replaced

2/ The following discussion will be easier to understand if you review periodically the section, "Types of Factors to Be Controlled," page 248 and check Table 11.1 on page 291.

by new Ss, these mortality factors rather than X may produce the difference in the test results. Consequently, the number and nature of the dropouts must always be checked carefully.

This design has many weaknesses. It does not enable an E to ascertain whether the difference between T_1 and T_2 scores is produced by X or by *history, maturation, pretesting, statistical regression, instrument variables,* or the *interaction of selection and maturation,* etc. If some Ss in the reading experiment are fitted with glasses between T_1 and T_2, this history variable rather than X may produce a difference in their scores. A *maturation* factor may also operate: the difference in the Ss' scores may be caused by the fact that they are older, more fatigued, less enthusiastic, or more accustomed to school routines when they take T_2 than when they take T_1.

Sometimes the *testing* practice or the motivation that is supplied by T_1 enables Ss to do better on T_2. In a weight-control study, a preliminary weigh-in may stimulate Ss to lose weight regardless of whether they are exposed to X, a therapeutic program. If Ss are asked about their personal practices or attitudes on T_1, they may answer honestly. After thinking about the significance of their replies, they may change their responses on T_2—not because of the effect of X, but because they wish to present themselves more favorably.

If the Ss are selected on the basis of extreme scores, *statistical regression* rather than X will almost invariably account for the difference in T_1 and T_2 results. Changes in the *measuring instruments* may also cause the differences. Knowledge of how well Ss did on T_1 may influence the judgment of the judge who rates them on T_2. This bias can be controlled if T_1 and T_2 are randomly shuffled so that the judge cannot tell which tests were taken first. If measurements of the dependent variable are taken from different types of records or tests, this difference may produce an effect that is inextricably confounded with the effect of X. Suppose that school accident reports are used to measure the effect of an experimental safety program. If accidents are reported on blank forms prior to the experiment and on carefully structured forms during the study, more accidents may be reported on the structured forms even though fewer accidents have occurred.

The one-group design does not satisfy the fundamental criteria for experimental methodology and should be used only for preliminary research when the independent variable is likely to produce a drastic effect, for this lessens the influence of extraneous variables; when the interval between T_1 and T_2 is of brief duration, for there is less opportunity for *history* and *maturation* to operate; and when the dependent variable is relatively stable, that is, when it is not apt to change unless a deliberate effort is made to bring about a change.[3]

Designs with Rigorous Control

During recent decades, educators have been under attack because their experiments were not carefully controlled. As a result, more rigorously controlled designs are now beginning to appear in the literature. No design can be endorsed unconditionally. Satisfying all internal and external validity requirements is almost an unattainable ideal, but competent investigators strive to satisfy as many as possible.

Control Group

To overcome difficulties that Design 1 presents, pioneer educators added the control group. By so doing, they provided the comparability that is required by science. The control group, which is not exposed to X, strengthens an E's conviction that the independent variable is solely responsible for the change in the dependent variable.

Suppose that Design 1, which requires no control group, is used, and the one group is exposed to X, a new reading method. If the T_2 mean is higher than the T_1 mean, the E wonders: Is this increase in reading ability caused by the new method or by the effects of *maturation, pretesting, history,* etc.?

To eliminate these doubts, suppose that the E assigns Ss to two groups and exposes only one group to X. Both groups will mature about the same amount and will experience the same pretesting practice and contemporary events during the experiment. Consequently, the E can conclude that the difference in their reading improvement is not caused by these factors, but presumably only by X, the reading method.

If the Ss are not randomly assigned to the two groups, however, the groups may differ, and these differences may produce effects that may be mistaken for the effect of X. The same thing may occur if the two groups experience different experimental conditions. Suppose that the Ss in an experimental reading group are more intelligent and have a better teacher, a more favorable class hour, and a quieter classroom than the Ss in

---

3/ Interaction of selection and maturation, etc., and factors threatening external validity also are present in this design. They are examined more conveniently under other designs later in the chapter.

the control group. These differences rather than X, the reading method, may be responsible for the experimental group's greater gain in reading achievement. Educators recognized this equivalency problem when they adopted the classical control-group experiment. They emphasized that the success of the experiment rested on one important assumption: *that the experimental and the control groups be equivalent in respect to all factors that may influence the dependent variable, except for the exposure to X.*

Random Assignment to Groups/ While seemingly strange, the best method of attaining experimental equivalency is through the use of simple randomization techniques.[4] To many people, the words "random" and "chance" suggest guesswork rather than scientific control. But randomization is not a haphazard or arbitrary method of assignment; it is a very systematic procedure. The *E* refrains from exercising direct control over the assignment of *Ss*, teachers, rooms, etc., because he may consciously or unconsciously choose the better ones for the experimental group. To avoid the introduction of biases toward the greater achievement of either group, he employs some randomization technique that gives each unit in a given population an equal chance of being placed in one of the comparisons groups. He may draw names out of a hat, flip a coin, employ published tables of random sample numbers (see page 298), or use some other known random procedure to assign *Ss* to experimental and control groups. Similarly, he should assign teachers, classrooms, equipment, and class periods strictly on a random basis. Randomization procedures do not remove extraneous variables, such as IQ or age, which may affect the dependent variable, nor do they control their presence. These extraneous variables still affect the inquiry, but the laws of chance rather than the personal bias of the *E* now operate. The validity of the assumption that random assignment will result in equivalent groups increases with the number of *Ss* used. The larger the number of *Ss*, the more equivalent or similar the groups will tend to be. If only a few *Ss* are selected, the more intelligent, older, or healthier ones may be assigned by chance to one group. If the groups are small, they are not likely to differ to any great extent, but the probability that differences will occur is greater than if the groups are large. To avoid confusing the effect of these differences with the effect of X, an E applies

4/ Randomization techniques have been recommended previously to select *Ss* from a population so as to obtain a representative sample of *Ss*. In an ideal experiment, random selection of *Ss* from a population and random assignment of *Ss* to groups is attained.

one of the *statistical tests of significance* that are explained in a subsequent chapter. These tests enable an E to ascertain whether the difference between performances of two randomly assigned groups is larger than can be expected to occur by chance for a sample of that size.

Statistical tests of significance provide a safeguard against attributing group differences to the effect of X. The possibility remains, however, that these group differences may mask the effect of X, particularly if the effect of X is small. To aid in removing this masking effect, analysis of covariance or matching procedures, which are described in the following paragraphs, may be used. If either of these techniques is used to make the experiment more sensitive—to gain statistical precision—it is used in addition to randomization and not as a substitute for randomization. If an E wants to keep intelligence from masking the effect that a programmed textbook X has on learning, he may pair Ss who have the same IQ scores and randomly assign the members of each pair to the experimental and control groups. Because his "equating technique" controls only one variable, IQ scores, he must randomize out other extraneous variables so that they will not differentially affect the comparison groups.

Matching with Random Assignment/ Because nature does an excellent job of matching identical twins, they may be used in some experiments in conjunction with a randomization technique. Because a sufficient number of twins is rarely available, matched Ss are used with validity in investigations but only in conjunction with randomization. The pairs of Ss are matched on their T_1 scores and/or on other variables that are known to have an effect on the dependent variable, such as IQ, age, sex, or socioeconomic background. Then one member of each pair is randomly assigned to the control group, and the other member to the experimental group.

Many difficulties may be encountered when matching techniques are employed. Determining which variables affect the dependent variable and which of these to use as a basis for matching often presents problems. If an E studies the reports of other investigators who were concerned with the same dependent variable, he may discover variables that have been demonstrated to affect the dependent variable. But obtaining accurate measurements of some relevant variables, such as emotional status, level of motivation, etc., for matching purposes may be difficult. Not uncommonly, moreover, extensive testing is required before a sufficient number of qualified pairs can be found. Finding enough Ss who are well matched on even two or three variables is difficult. In one study, *Ss* were matched on six variables from data collected from over 1,194 *Ss,* and only 23 matched pairs were found.

Random Assignment and Analysis of Covariance/ Because of the difficulties that arise when matching procedures are employed, educators are grateful for the development of procedures that enable them to control variation in the experimental and control groups through an *analysis of covariance*.[5] This statistical tool enables an *E* to adjust the T_2 mean scores to compensate for a lack of original equivalency between groups that is discovered when T_1 is given or that arises during the experiment.

"The era of exhaustive person-to-person matching appears now to be over" (142:334), for analysis of covariance achieves the same results without testing and discarding numerous *Ss* in search of matched pairs. Because it is so superior and efficient and involves no computional effort now that standard programs are available on computers, analysis of covariance is rapidly replacing the older, matching technique.

Fallacy of Matching without Random Assignment/ Until relatively recently, many educators assumed that the simple (1) matched-pair technique or (2) matched-group technique without random assignment would attain group equivalency. But these techniques almost inevitably create internal validity problems; hence, matching alone is no longer regarded as an acceptable procedure.

1/ Matched pairs

Matching equates groups in a few respects, but human beings vary in a multiplicity of ways. Many other variables beside the matched variables affect the dependent variable, and their effect may be mistaken for the effect of *X*. When an attempt is made to match *Ss* in two intact populations, the *Ss* who obtain extremely high or low scores will be few in number. Matching them closely will be difficult, and ignoring them will limit the population to which the findings of the study may be generalized. An insurmountable difficulty will arise, moreover, because the T_2 means of the residual matched groups will regress toward the means of their respective original populations.[6] The following illustration will reveal how this

5/ The use of this technique involves certain assumptions, such as that of homogeneity of regression.
6/ You will recall from our previous discussion concerning statistical regression (page 250) that when a group is retested, its T_1 mean will move toward the mean of the parent population whether *X* is applied or not.

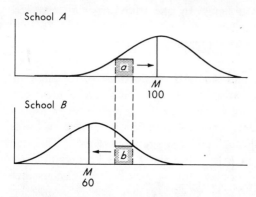

Figure 11.1/ Illustration of statistical regression: matched samples from dissimilar populations.

differential regression toward the mean will almost inevitably "un-equate" the matched groups.

Suppose that school A has a mean of 100 and school B has a mean of 60, and a sample group with a mean score of 80 is selected from each school population. These two sample groups, a and b, have matching mean scores of 80, but sample a is below the mean of school A, and sample b is above the mean of school B. Upon retesting, matched groups a and b will regress toward the means of their parent populations (see arrow in Figure 11.1). Hence, the mean score of sample a, the experimental group, will tend to rise and the mean score of sample b, the control group, will tend to drop whether X is applied or not. The findings of the study may merely reveal this differential degree of regression rather than any effect that is produced by X.

2/ Matched groups.

In the older, typical "experiment," when an educator found it diffi-cult to match subjects, he often attempted to *match groups.* He selected two groups that had about the same average possession of each relevant variable—the same mean scores—and a similar distribution pattern of scores around the mean. If intelligence was the matching variable, he found the mean IQ for two groups. If one group had an average IQ of 100 and the other of 110, he shifted Ss until both groups had an average IQ of 105. Since the IQs in one matched group may range widely about the average (80–130), and the IQs in the other group may have a narrow range of variation (98–115), he also used statistical procedures to ascertain how the scores were distributed. If they differed, he shifted Ss to make them similar.

This matched-group technique did not equate the groups, it merely made them appear superficially equal in a few respects. Regression to the mean would later take its toll. Nonmatched vari-ables could also create problems. If the groups were matched on two variables, such as IQs and skills, and the distributions of the scores about the means were made similar, the Ss could have different combinations of these capacities:

> Group X: Low IQs with high skills and high IQs with low skills.
>
> Group Y: High IQs with high skills and low IQs with low skills.

If these differences existed, they could affect the conclusions of the study.

The moral of these paragraphs is: Do *not* attempt to match Ss or groups without randomizing. Also, do not believe the results of those who do, except under rare circumstances which are not met in most educational research reports.

Randomized Control-group Pretest-Posttest Design (Design 2)

Because Designs 2, 3, and 4 require the utilization of a control group and random assignment of Ss to groups, they control many variables that other designs do not. Consequently, they are the most highly recommended experimental designs.

Design Procedures/ When employing Design 2, an E takes the following steps:

1/
Selects Ss from a population by random methods, if possible.
2/
Assigns Ss to groups and X to groups by random methods.
3/
Tests the groups[7] on the dependent variable, and finds the mean pretest score for the experimental group (T_{1_E} and for the control group T_{1_C}).
4/
Keeps all conditions the same for the groups, except for exposing the experimental Ss—but not the control Ss—to the independent variable for a stipulated time.
5/
Tests the groups on the dependent variable, and finds the mean posttest score[8] for each group, T_{2_E} and T_{2_C}.
6/
Finds the difference between the T_1 and T_2 means for each group, D_E and D_C.

7/ Sometimes Ss are pretested before they are assigned to groups.
8/ If the analysis of covariance technique is employed, the final mean scores are adjusted for pretest differences prior to step 6.

7/
Compares D_C and D_E to determine whether the application of X caused a significant change in the experimental group's scores as compared with the control group's scores.

8/
Applies an appropriate statistical procedure to ascertain whether the difference in the scores is sufficiently great to be a real difference, or whether it is only a chance occurrence.

Steps 2 to 6 may be depicted as follows:

Randomly Assigned*	Pretest	Treatment	Posttest
(R) Experimental Group	T_{1_E}	X	T_{2_E}
(R) Control Group	T_{1_C}		T_{2_C}
Experimental Group	$T_{2_E} - T_{1_E} = D_E$	(Difference between pretest and posttest mean scores.)	
Control Group	$T_{2_C} - T_{1_C} = D_C$	(Difference between pretest and posttest mean scores.)	

*/ In this text, whenever Ss and X are randomly assigned to groups the (R) placed before the group conveys this information.

This design may be extended to permit the study of two or more variations of the independent variable on a dependent variable. An E may study the effect of different amounts of a drug, different kinds of motivation, or different methods of instruction on performance. To ascertain the effect of teaching long division by two different methods, for example, one group may be exposed to X_a method, a second group to X_b method, and a third group to no X—no long division instruction.

(R) First group	$T_{1_{E_1}}$	X_a	$T_{2_{E_1}}$
(R) Second group	$T_{1_{E_2}}$	X_b	$T_{2_{E_2}}$
(R) Control group	T_{1_C}		T_{2_C}

If the E is merely interested in comparing the effects of two treatments, he may not use the no X control group, but it does give him an added measure of information for fuller interpretive purposes.

Internal Validity/ Design 2, generally speaking, controls the potential sources of internal invalidity. The effect of *intersession* developments—extraneous variables that arise between T_1 and

T_2—are balanced out by the presence of a randomized control group. The *contemporary historical* events and the changes in the *measuring instruments* that occur between T_1 and T_2 are experienced by all groups; hence, the effects of these variables are equalized and cannot be mistaken in the effect of X.

Additional precautions must be taken, however, to control *intrasession* conditions—differences that the experimental and control groups may experience when they are tested and treated separately. If a measuring instrument becomes less discriminating between the time that two groups take the *same* test, this factor may produce an effect that may be mistaken for the effect of X. If only one group takes T_2 in an overheated room late in the day, or is distracted by a troublesome student or the school band during a testing or treatment session, these factors may also affect the results of the experiment. If different teachers are in charge of the groups, differences in their personalities and proficiencies, in the way they administer the instructions, or in their convictions about the value of the treatment may influence the results. Many researchers, for example, make the mistake of selecting superior teachers for their experimental groups.

How does an E control intrasession conditions? He tests and treats Ss individually or in small groups, and randomly assigns Ss, times, and places to experimental or control conditions. Contemporary historical events, such as newspaper stories, a band practice, or cafeteria odors will affect the Ss, but they will affect a few Ss or several Ss in both groups approximately equally.

To control intrasession instrument differences, an E randomly assigns not only Ss but also mechanical instruments, teachers, observers, and raters to sessions—to a single session if possible. If a limited number of assistants or pieces of equipment are available, he assigns each one to an equal number of experimental and control sessions. Thus, if two pieces of equipment vary, or if one teacher is more proficient than the other, of if one observer rates higher or lower than other observers, these differences will affect experimental and control groups approximately equally. Ideally, an E does not let observers know which Ss receive what treatment, for this knowledge might influence their judgments, particularly if the observers believe that one treatment is better than the other.

Differential selection of Ss for comparison groups is controlled, because the randomization processes practically assure equivalency. If only a few Ss are selected, the groups may differ somewhat, but statistical tests of significance provide a safeguard against attributing these groups' differences to the effect of X.

An analysis of covariance or matching techniques may be employed to aid in removing the effect of group differences that might mask the effect of X. These techniques, of course, are used in addition to random assignment.

Maturation and *pretesting* are controlled by Design 2, for both groups should experience an equal effect of these variables. A comparison of the T_1 and T_2 data that this design provides makes it possible to ascertain whether *differential mortality* has taken place. When Ss drop out of an experiment, they may or may not drop out on a random basis. The Ss who fail to attend treatment or testing sessions may differ from those who do; they may be less healthy, less highly motivated, less responsive to the treatment; consequently, their absence may introduce a sampling bias.

Statistical regression is controlled by Design 2. If Ss are selected from extreme scorers in the same group and are randomly assigned to groups, statistical regression will take place. But the control group will regress as much as the experimental group. Consequently, the effect of regression cannot be confounded with X.

External Validity/ The discussion thus far has been concerned with the importance of checking internal validity. The E also worries about the external validity of the design—the generalizability or representativeness of the findings concerning the effect of X. He asks: Can extraneous variables interact with the experimental treatment and make the Ss unrepresentative of the population from which they were selected? Can the claim be made that the effect which X had on the Ss will be the same for other members of the population who did not participate in the experiment?

When Design 2 is used, giving a pretest may limit the generalizability of the experimental findings. An *interaction* of *pretesting* and X occurred in Cincinnati, for example, when the effect of a United Nations information publicity campaign was studied (130). Two equivalent samples of Ss were drawn from the city's population. One sample was interviewed before and after the campaign, and the other was interviewed only after.

	Interviewed	Campaign	Interviewed
Sample I	T	X	T
Sample II		X	T

When precampaign responses of sample I were compared with the postcampaign responses of sample II, there was very little difference between them. But, when sample I was reinterviewed after the campaign, the Es discovered that significant attitude and information changes had occurred. Apparently, the Ss in sample I had become interested in or sensitized to the United Nations as a result of the initial interview which made the publicity campaign effective for them and them only. An *interaction* of *pretesting* and X—initial interview and publicity campaign—had occurred. Do you see why it may be dangerous to generalize that the effect of X for a pretested sample will be the same for unpretested samples in the population? A researcher usually is not interested in generalizing only to pretested groups.

When Design 2 is used, an *interaction* of *selection* and X may occur. The cultural background, or some other characteristic of the Ss who are selected to participate in an experiment, may make the experimental treatment more effective for them than it would be for students elsewhere. An investigator must be particularly wary if a number of schools or Ss are asked to participate before some agree to cooperate. Volunteers are apt to differ from nonvolunteers. If the schools that participate are located in a scientific or university center where most parents are college graduates and where superior teachers are employed, an E cannot generalize that the findings of the experiment will hold for all schools in the country. Consequently, when designing a study, consideration should be given to reducing the number of Ss in a school and to increasing the number and types of schools participating in the experiment. Random selection—or at least a varied selection—of units from the population to which the E wishes to generalize as well as random assignment of Ss to groups is the ideal.

The *interaction* of X with other factors, such as *history,* may make it impossible to generalize the findings beyond the specific conditions of the experiment. If an experiment is conducted during a depression, a war, or a catastrophe in the community, these unique events may make Ss more responsive to X than they might be at other times. If an experiment is replicated in different time and place settings, and the hypothesized relations hold up in each instance, generalizations concerning the findings can be made with greater confidence.

The *reactive effects* of *experimental procedures* may hamper generalization. If Ss know that they are participating in an experiment, they may not react normally to X. Being singled out for special treatment often motivates Ss to put forth greater effort. Consequently, they perform better than nonexperimental Ss not because of the exposure to X, but because they want to justify the honor of being selected. Clues concerning the purpose of the experiment that are provided by test questions, experimental apparatus, or the behavior of the E may cause Ss to distort their responses to X. They may try to present themselves as favorably as possible, or they may try to be "good subjects" and help the E "prove what he wants to prove." An illustration of the reactive effects of experimental procedures is provided by what happened when college students were given dexedrine in an experiment. The Ss who thought they were given dexedrine had typical energizer-like reactions, but the Ss who thought they had received a barbituate showed a tendency toward barbituate-like reactions. It is interesting also to note that the percentage of such Ss responses dropped markedly when the Es knew what drug was being administered.

To minimize the reactive effect of experimental procedures, an effort should be made to keep the Ss and those who administer the treatments or tests unaware of the fact that an experiment is being conducted. If Ss cannot be kept ignorant of the experiment, members of both the experimental and the control groups should be made to feel equally singled out. More accurate data will be attained if Ss think they are getting identical treatments, or if they are at least unaware of which treatment they are receiving. The less conspicuous the experimental procedures are, the better. If an E can bury T_1 and T_2 in the routine school testing program, can assign Ss at random to groups without making them aware of it, and can have the regular teacher present X as a normal part of the instructional program, he can make generalizations concerning the findings of his study with greater confidence.

Randomized Solomon Four-group Design (Design 3)

Design 3 overcomes an external-validity weakness which exists in Design 2. The pretest in Design 2 may make the sample of Ss who participate in the experiment more or less sensitive to X than the unpretested members of the population. Consequently, one cannot generalize the experimental findings for the sample to the population.

Design Procedures/ To overcome the interaction of pretesting and X, Design 3 adds two unpretested groups (3 and 4) to the two groups in Design 2.

Group	Pretest	Treatment	Posttest	Difference*
1/ (R) Pretested	T_1	X	T_2	$1D = T_1, X, M, H$
2/ (R) Pretested	T_1		T_2	$2D = T_1, M, H$
3/ (R) Unpretested		X	T_2	$3D = X, M, H$
4/ (R) Unpretested			T_2	$4D = M, H$

* D, the difference between T_1 and T_2 mean scores represents the effects of various combinations of variables, such as: pretesting T_1, independent variable X, history H, maturation M. For group 4, for example, D represents the effect of maturation and history. To find the effect of X alone, subtract 4D from 3D. To find the effect of pretesting alone, subtract 4D from 2D. To find the effect of the interaction of pretesting and X, add 2D and 3D and subtract the sum from 1D.

Design 3 requires that the Ss be assigned at random to the four groups.[9] The random assignment of Ss makes it possible to assume that the pretest scores for groups 3 and 4 would have been similar to the pretest scores attained by groups 1 and 2.[10] But since groups 3 and 4 are not pretested, no interaction between X and the effects of T_1 can be reflected in their T_2 scores.

Design Validity/ Design 3 enables the E to control and to measure both (1) the *main effects* of *pretesting* and (2) the *interaction effects* of *pretesting* and X. Furthermore, he can measure the combined effects of *maturation* and *history,* if he compares the T_2 mean for group 4 with the T_1 means. This design actually amounts to doing the experiment twice (once with pretests and once without). Consequently, if the results of the "two experiments" are consistent, the E can have greater confidence in the findings than if the findings had not been replicated within the study.

Randomized Control-group Posttest-only Design (Design 4)

Design 4 consists of the last two groups in the Solomon design: the two unpretested groups.

9/ Supplementary matching procedures may be used with Designs 3 and 4. If matching is employed, the Ss are matched on some factor other than the dependent variable. If T_1 and T_2 are reading achievement tests, for example, the matching may be done on IQ scores, but not on reading scores.

10/ Campbell and Stanley suggest, however, that the assumed T_1 score should not be used when making a statistical analysis of the findings. They recommend other procedures (27:195).

Design Procedures/ This design is depicted as follows:

	Pretest	Treatment	Posttest
(R) Experimental Group		X	T_E
(R) Control Group			T_C

As in all rigorously controlled designs, prior to the application of X the Ss are assigned at random to the experimental and control groups. Why can the E omit the pretest? Because randomization techniques permit him to declare that at the time of assignment the groups were equal. The probability theory tells him to what extent the randomly assigned Ss in the two groups might have been expected to differ by chance on T_1, and the test of significance takes account of such chance differences.

After the Ss are assigned at random to groups, the experimental group is exposed to X, such as a film with a racial-prejudice theme, and the control group is not. During or after the exposure to X, the two groups are tested for the first time. Their scores are compared to ascertain the effect of X, and an appropriate test of significance is applied to determine whether this difference is greater than might have occurred by chance.

Design Validity/ Because a randomized control group is used and no T_1 is given, Design 4 controls—but does not measure—the main effects of *history, maturation* and *pretesting*. Design 4 is superior to Design 2 because no *interaction effect* of *pretesting* and X can occur. This feature, plus the fact that the design is less complicated and requires less effort than Designs 2 and 3, makes it worthy of consideration. The E does not have to administer T_1, and in many instances he can present X and T_2 simultaneously. Suppose that he wants to determine which of two letter formats is superior. If he presents two groups of parents with different persuasive appeals for cooperation on questionnaires, he can obtain T_2 data (replies) on the same questionnaires. Design 4 is particularly useful when pretests are unavailable, inconvenient, or too costly to obtain; when Ss anonymity must be kept; and when a pretest may interact with X.

When a limited sample of the population is available for the experiment (when there is some question about the genuine equivalency of the assignment to groups), Design 2 rather than

Design 4 should be employed, because the T_1 scores provide an added check on the sameness of the groups. If T_1 scores are available (if they have been accumulated as a routine part of the school testing program), Design 2 rather than Design 4 should be used. The additional T_1 information provided by Design 2 enables an E to make some types of analyses that he cannot make without it, and the special statistical tests that are available for Design 2 are more powerful than those that are available for Design 4.

Factorial Designs

Our discussion thus far has been confined to classical designs which require that an E vary a single X at a time and hold all other conditions constant. Because social and biological phenomena are complex, an educator cannot always fulfill these requirements. If he does fulfill them, he may prevent or ignore the simultaneous functioning of variables with which X interacts in normal situations. Since X may not produce the same effect independently as it does in conjunction with another X, findings concerning a single X may not be too significant.

Suppose that drugs A and B produce a slight healing effect when they are administered separately. When they are administered together, they produce a much greater healing effect than can be attributed to either drug acting alone. Information about the interaction of the drugs certainly is of much greater significance than information about the independent effect of each drug. Similar situations can arise in education. If a classical experiment reveals that democratic teachers have a greater effect on pupils' achievement than authoritarian teachers, the experiment has yielded valuable information. But suppose that a factorial design is used to study the effect that different types of teachers X_1 have on students of different levels of intelligence X_2. If the study reveals that democratic teachers have a greater effect on the learning of pupils with high IQs, and authoritarian teachers have a greater effect on the learning of pupils with low IQs, this information will be even more valuable to educators.[11]

11/ Contradictory findings are often reported in the literature. Suppose that two classical experiments, each utilizing the same design, are conducted. One reveals that democratic teachers are superior, and the other one reveals that authoritarian teachers are superior. Why do these reports differ? Perhaps Ss with high IQs were used in one experiment and Ss with low IQs in the other. A factorial design, such as the one above, in which the levels of intelligence are studied, would reveal the interaction that exists and would resolve what looks like a contradiction in the two reports.

Knowledge that is of vital importance to educators will elude them if they must limit research to the study of a single variable at a time. Education as a process involves a number of variables interacting simultaneously; hence, workers in the field need experiments that will allow them to look at the process more nearly as it occurs naturally.

Until relatively recently "the law of the single variable" tended to keep educators from investigating the interaction effects of váriables. R. A. Fisher overcame this obstacle when he developed factorial designs and the statistical techniques for their analysis. Factorial designs are extensions of Designs 2 and 4. They permit the E to manipulate two or more independent variables simultaneously (rather than in separate experiments) and to evaluate the effects of the variables independently.

Design Procedures/ Factorial designs of varying degrees of complexity have been developed. They may include two or more independent variables, and each one may be varied in two or more ways. The simplest factorial design is the 2 by 2 (2×2). In this design, the effects of two Xs (factors) are studied, each of which is varied in two ways (two levels or two values).

To illustrate, assume that we are interested in studying the effect of variations in teaching methods X_1 and variations in length of class periods X_2 on learning achievement. The variations of X_1 are lecture and discussion methods. The variations of X_2 are thirty-minute and fifty-minute class periods.

Since there are four possible combinations of variables, the Ss are assigned at random, each to one of the four experimental treatment groups. Group 1 is exposed to fifty-minute lecture periods, group 2 to thirty-minute lecture periods, group (3) to fifty-minute discussion periods, and group (4) to thirty-minute discussion periods (see Figure 11.2).

Six weeks later we measure the learning achievement (dependent variable) of each S, compute the mean score for each of the four groups, and record these scores in the appropriate squares (cells) in Figure 11.2. If the mean score for the fifty-minute lecture group is 59.0, for example, we record that score in the cell bearing the appropriate fifty-minute lecture label.

Since one of our objectives is to compare various combinations of these groups, we also obtain the mean scores for the pairs of groups that were exposed to the lecture method (1 and 2), the discussion method (3 and 4), the fifty-minute classes (1 and 3), and the thirty-minute classes (2 and 4). We place these mean scores beneath the columns or beside the rows of the groups that they represent. If the mean score for

(X_2) Length of class period

		Fifty minutes	Thirty minutes	Mean	Difference
	Lecture	(1) 59.0	(2) 58.0	58.5	−1.0
	Discussion	(3) 82.0	(4) 84.0	83.0	+2.0

(X_1) Method of teaching

Mean: 70.5   71.0   70.75

Difference: +23.0   +26.0   −3.0

Figure 11.2/ Illustration of a factorial design.

the two fifty-minute classes is 70.5, for example, we place that score beneath the column labeled fifty-minute classes.[12]

Design Information/ Our factorial design produces more information than we could obtain from two classical experiments. Two single X designs would enable us to answer two questions: What is the main effect of X_1 on the dependent variable? What is the main effect of X_2 on the dependent variable? The data from our 2×2 design enables us to answer these questions:

1/ What is the main (independent) effect of teaching method X_1 on achievement scores?
If we compare the mean score of the two lecture groups (58.5)[13] with that of the two discussion groups (83.0), the latter is noticeably higher (see Figure 11.2). Consequently, we suspect that the discussion method has a greater effect on learning achievement than the lecture method.

2/ What is the main effect of length of class X_2 on achievement scores?
The mean score for the two groups that had fifty-minute periods (70.5) and the mean score for the two groups that had thirty-minute periods (71.0) is almost identical. Obviously, the length of the class periods had little effect on the dependent variable.

3/ What is the interaction effect, if any, of teaching method and length of class periods on achievement scores?
This question forces us to determine whether the joint effect of particular variations of X_1 and X_2 on learning achievement is greater or less than can be attributed to either variable acting alone.

12/ $59.0 + 82.0 = 141$; $141 \div 2 = 70.5$
13/ $59.0 + 58.0 = 117$; $117 \div 2 = 58.5$

If there is an interaction, the effect that a teaching method has on learning will differ for thirty- and fifty-minute classes. If the discussion method, for example, is more effective with one length of class than it is with the other, there is an interaction. If there is no interaction, the effect of a teaching method on learning achievement will be the same for both lengths of classes. To summarize: (1) If there is an interaction, the effect of one X on the dependent variable will not be the same for both variations of the second X. (2) If there is no interaction, the effect of one X on the dependent variable will be the same for both variations of the other X.

Design Data Reveal No Interaction Effect/ Our data reveal no interaction between X_1 and X_2, for the effect of X_1 on learning achievement is approximately *the same* for both variations of X_2. The mean scores for the lecture method in the two lengths of classes are 59 and 58 and the mean scores for the discussion method are 82 and 84. The lack of interaction may be illustrated graphically, if we transfer the scores in Figure 11.2 to Figure 11.3. We note that the groups that were exposed to the discussion method performed better than those exposed to the lecture method.[14] Moreover, we can see that difference A (the difference between the mean scores of the lecture and discussion groups in fifty-minute classes) is practically the same as difference B (the difference between the mean scores of the lecture and discussion groups in thirty-minute classes). Whenever difference A and difference B are the *same,* i.e., when the lines

14/ In most factorial studies, the main effects are probably of the greatest interest to the E. Many times the interactions are not statistically significant. But knowledge of the lack of significance is important, for the E now knows that the discussion method of teaching is effective in and of itself. The importance of the main effects cannot be known, unless the interaction is specifically tested.

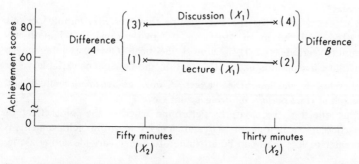

Figure 11.3/ Illustration of a lack of interaction between teaching methods and length of class period.

(X_2) Length of class period

		Fifty minutes	Thirty minutes	Mean	Difference
(X_1) Method of teaching	Lecture	(1) 59.0	(2) 77.0	68.0	+18
	Discussion	(3) 82.0	(4) 66.0	74.0	−16
Mean:		70.5	71.5	71.0	
Difference:		+23.0	−11.0		

Figure 11.4/ New means to illustrate interaction.

in Figure 11.3 are approximately parallel, it is unlikely that any interaction exists between the variables.

Another way to illustrate the absence of interaction is to compute the differences between the means of the groups. Return to Figure 11.2 and note that the difference between the means of the discussion and lecture groups is 23.0 for fifty-minute classes and 26.0 for thirty-minute classes.[15] Since these differences are not far apart, we suspect that there is no interaction present. The same conclusions can be reached by comparing the differences in the other direction; i.e., −1.0 and 2.0 are approximately the same—no interaction exists.

Design Data Reveal an Interaction Effect/ Our fictitious experiment revealed no interaction effect. But let us alter the data so that they will reveal an interaction effect, as illustrated in Figures 11.4 and 11.5. If we examine the main effect of teaching method, the mean score for the discussion groups (74.0) is higher than the mean score for the lecture groups (68.0). Hence, the discussion method appears to be somewhat superior. If we examine the interaction effect of teaching method X_1 and length of class period X_2, we note that the discussion method is superior in fifty-minute classes (82.0 − 59.0 = 23.0), but it is less effective than the lecture method in thirty-minute classes (66.0 − 77.0 = −11.0). Note the interaction effect as it is illustrated graphically in Figure 11.5. The lecture and discussion lines are *not parallel* as they were in Figure 11.3, for the two methods of teaching do not have the same effect on

15/ 82 − 59 = 23; 84 − 58 = 26

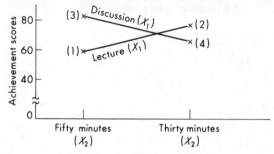

Figure 11.5/ Illustration of possible interaction.

achievement in fifty-minute and thirty-minute classes. Interaction between the independent variables exists, because the effect of one X on the dependent variable is not the same for both variations of the second X.

Design Extensions/ Factorial designs are not limited to the simple 2×2 designs. To these 2×2 designs, we may add no $-X$ and other X groups. It is possible to have 2×3 designs (two independent variables: one varied in two ways; the other varied in three ways), 3×3, $2 \times 2 \times 2$, etc. Suppose that we add one more X to our previous experiment: X_3 intelligence of the teacher, with two variations of it—high IQ and average IQ. We now have a $2 \times 2 \times 2$ design which requires eight treatment groups. This design can answer the following seven questions: What is the main (independent) effect on learning achievement of (1) X_1 (2) X_2 and (3) X_3? What is the interaction effect on learning achievement of (4) X_1 and X_2, (5) X_1 and X_3, (6) X_2 and X_3, and (7) X_1, X_2, and X_3?[16]

Factorial designs that are more sophisticated than this $2 \times 2 \times 2$ design can answer an even greater number of questions, but the more complex ones become unwieldly to handle. A $4 \times 3 \times 2$ design, for example, in which X_1 has four variations, X_2 has three variations, and X_3 has two variations, requires twenty-four treatment groups (see Figure 11.6), and a $6 \times 5 \times 4 \times 2$ design requires 240 groups.

An important characteristic of factorial designs is that several hypotheses can be tested simultaneously. Factorial designs have released educators from the bondage of classical designs. No longer must they conduct a series of single X experiments to answer questions about the effect that different Xs may have

16/ A two-variable interaction X_1 and X_2, is called a first-order interaction; a three-variable interaction X_1, X_2, and X_3 is called a second-order interaction.

(X_1) Method of teaching	(X_3) Sex	(X_2) Length of class period			
		30 min	40 min	50 min	60 min
Discussion	Boys				
	Girls				
Lecture	Boys				
	Girls				
Programmed learning	Boys				
	Girls				

Figure 11.6/ Illustration of a 4 x 3 x 2 design.

on learning achievement. Factorial designs permit them to conduct single experiments that will answer more complex questions, such as: What effect does X_1-type teacher have on learning achievement when using X_2-type methods in X_3-length classes with X_4-type students? With these tools in their possession, educators are in a much better position to grapple with phenomena encountered in the field.

Designs with Partial Control

If he can, an investigator utilizes a design that provides full experimental control through randomization. If this ideal cannot be realized, he may consider using a design that incorporates the most control that can be achieved under the existing conditions. If an E employs a partially controlled design, however, he must know what variables his design may fail to control, and he must carefully consider the likelihood that these variables rather than X may account for the experimental results. The more improbable it is that they do, the more "valid" is the experiment.

Nonrandomized Control-group Pretest-Posttest Design (Design 5)

The importance of obtaining equivalent experimental and control groups has been discussed previously. To achieve this equivalency, rigorously controlled designs, such as Designs 2, 3, and 4, require that Ss be assigned to comparison groups at random. Employing randomization procedures is not difficult, but upsetting class schedules, getting scattered Ss to participate, and obtaining a sufficiently large sample to ensure that the laws of chance will operate cannot always be done. Under some circumstances, therefore, an E may have to use preassembled groups, such as intact classes, for his experimental and control Ss.

Design Procedures/ The procedure for carrying out Design 5 is practically the same as that for Design 2, except for one important difference: In Design 5, the Ss are not assigned to groups at random. Preassembled groups that are as similar as availability permits are selected and are given pretests. The pretest mean scores and standard deviations[17] of the groups are compared to check their similarity.

The paradigm for Design 5 is the same as the one for Design 2, except that (R) is omitted to indicate the absence of random assignment to groups. If possible, however, some randomization technique is employed to determine which group will be exposed to X.

	Pretest	Treatment	Posttest
Experimental Group	T_{1_E}	X	T_{2_E}
Control Group	T_{1_C}		T_{2_C}

Internal Validity/ If similar groups are selected and their similarity is confirmed by the T_1 mean scores and standard deviations, this design controls several potential sources of internal invalidity. The presence of a control group enables the E to assume that the main effects of *history, pretesting, maturation,* and *instrumentation* will not be mistaken for the effect of X, for both the experimental and control groups will experience these effects. Differences in intrasession history and instrumentation which were discussed in Design 2 can arise, however, and they should be given serious consideration. The T_1 and T_2 data that are provided by this design make it possible to check whether the two groups differed in mortality.

The main source of internal invalidity for Design 5 is one that has not been discussed previously: an *interaction* of *selection* and *maturation,* an *interaction* of *selection* and *history,* etc., may take place. An E may select groups that are similar and that have approximately the same T_1 mean scores; but, in the absence of randomization, the possibility always exists that

17/ Standard deviation means the "spread" or "scatter" of the subject's scores about the mean.

other differences which distinguish the groups may be mistaken for the effect of X.

A selection-maturation interaction might be mistaken for the effect of X by a camp director, for example, if he used first-year campers for his experimental group and second-year campers for his control group. Suppose that the two groups had similar T_1 mean scores, and the first-year experimental group attained a higher T_2 mean than the second-year control group. The superior gain of the first-year group may not have been caused by X, but by the fact that the Ss were better adjusted to camp routines when they took T_2 than when they took T_1. Since members of the second-year group had minimal camp-life adjustments to make, their group would not exhibit a similar gain.

If the experimental Ss are self-selected—volunteer for exposure to X—and there is no comparable group of volunteers from the same population to serve as a control group, the possibility of a selection-maturation interaction is great. A group of volunteers is almost certain to be more highly motivated than a group of nonvolunteers; consequently, the assumption that the groups will progress uniformly becomes less likely. Suppose that an experimental group is composed of volunteer Ss who scored low on a spelling test, and the control group is composed of nonvolunteers from the same population (low-scoring Ss). If the experimental group exhibits the greater improvement in spelling after being exposed to X, a remedial program, the higher motivation of the volunteers rather than X may account for their greater improvement.

Statistical regression is a source of internal invalidity that can be avoided, but the possibility of its presence should be checked. You will recall that the T_1 mean of a sample group will move toward the population mean on T_2. The more deviant (extreme) a sample mean is from the population mean, the *more* it is likely to regress. In Figure 11.7, the population mean for University School is 110. Suppose that the class in University School with the low mean score of 80 serves as an experimental group in a remedial program, and the class with the mean score of 120 serves as the control group. You will note that the amount and direction of the regression of these two classes will differ. The experimental group regresses upward toward the population mean and may in consequence appear to be making greater progress than the control group, which regresses downward toward the population mean. Differential regression may be mistaken for, or may mask the effect of, X. (See data for University School in Figure 11.7.)

The mistake of comparing two groups with such dissimilar T_1 means is not commonly made by researchers. But some edu-

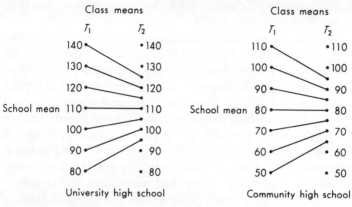

Figure 11.7/ Illustration of statistical regression.

cators do make the mistake of assuming that matching on T_1 scores established equivalent groups. Comparing matched Ss or matched groups that are drawn from populations that have different means is often responsible for introducing a regression effect in this design.

Suppose that an E introduces programmed learning in University School, which has a mean of 110, and uses Community School, which has a mean of 80, for comparison purposes. If he selects a class from each school that has a mean of 90 and compares the progress of these sample groups, the groups will be matched on T_1 means. But the experimental sample in University School with the mean of 90 is considerably below the mean of its parent population, and the control sample with a mean of 90 in Community School is above the mean of its parent population (see Figure 11.7). Since each sample will regress toward the mean of its parent population when retested, the University group will attain a higher mean on T_2 whether or not it is exposed to X. The mean of the University School sample will regress up, and the mean of the Community School sample will regress down. This regression effect in opposite directions might be mistaken for the effect of X.

When utilizing Design 5, every effort to rule out the possibility of differential recruitment of Ss must be made. But Campbell points out that, "In this popular design, the frequent effort to 'correct' for the lack of perfect equivalence by matching on pretest scores is *absolutely wrong* . . . as it introduces a regression artifact. Instead, one should live with any initial pretest differences, using analysis of covariance, gain scores, or graphic presentation" (23:7–8).

You will remember that analysis of covariance, which is done after T_2 is given, achieves the same results as matching without discarding or shifting any *Ss*. The *E* selects two intact groups, administers the experimental treatment, and then adjusts T_2 means to compensate for the lack of equivalency between the two groups. When the assumptions underlying analysis of covariance can be met, this is the most desirable tool to employ for Design 5.

External Validity/ When checking the external validity of this design—the representativeness of the findings—the same problems may arise that are encountered when Design 2 is used. But certain features of this design make it easier to overcome some of these problems.

An *interaction* of *selection* and *X* may occur. Because of particular characteristics of the *Ss* (sex, intelligence, socioeconomic status, etc.), *X* may be more effective for them than for other populations. But this problem can be overcome with this design more easily than it can with Design 2. School administrators are often reluctant to disrupt the school schedule to meet the requirements of Design 2, but they may cooperate with an *E* if he is willing to use intact classes for an experiment. Consequently, an *E* can obtain comparison groups for a wide variety of settings with Design 5 more readily than he can with Design 2, which enables him to generalize to a larger subject population.

The *reactive effects* of *experimental procedures* in Design 5 may also hamper generalization, but they may not be as reactive as those that must be employed when Design 2 is used. Conducting an experiment without the *Ss* being aware of it is easier when intact classes are used for comparison groups than when random samples are taken from classes and are assigned at random to treatment groups.

Counterbalanced Design (Design 6)

When random assignment of *Ss* is not possible and intact classes must be used, Design 6 may be employed to overcome some of the weaknesses in Design 5. This Counterbalanced Design, which is also known as a "rotation," "crossover," or "switchover design," is most commonly used when a limited number of *Ss* is available, no pretest is given, and more than one variation of *X* is tested.

Design Procedures/ In this design each group of *Ss* is exposed to each *X* (and, if necessary, no *X* situation) at different times during the experiment. To determine what effect four styles of type will have on reading-rate scores, for example, four groups

	Styles of type			
Replication	X_a	X_b	X_c	X_d
1	Group A	B	C	D
2	B	D	A	C
3	C	A	D	B
4	D	C	B	A
	Column mean score	Column mean score	Column mean score	Column mean score

Figure 11.8/ Illustration of a Counterbalanced Design.

of Ss are required. During the first replication of the design, group A reads X_a type, group B reads X_b type, group C reads X_c type and group D reads X_d type. Afterward, the mean reading-rate score for each group is computed, and the scores are recorded in the appropriate first-replication boxes (see Figure 11.8). Since four Xs are involved in the experiment, four experimental sessions are conducted. A different X (style of type) is presented to each group each time, and each X precedes and follows each other X an equal number of times.

After all the experimental sessions are completed, the column mean for each X is computed. A column mean represents the average reading rate for all groups when exposed to the X represented by the column heading. A comparison of these column mean scores reveals what effect the different styles of type have upon reading rate. Assuming that each unit of reading material was equally difficult, and there was no carry-over learning from one session to the next, the style of type that receives the highest mean reading-rate score is the best one to use.

Design Validity/ This design introduces a control that is lacking in Design 5. Because the nonrandomized groups in Design 5 are not equivalent in all respects, some difference in them, such as the superior intelligence of one group, may be mistaken for the effect of X. The Counterbalanced Design rotates out these Ss differences, and hence attains a kind of group equation. Since all Xs are administered to all groups, the results obtained for each X cannot be attributed to preexperimental differences in the groups. If one group is more intelligent than the others, each X will profit from this superiority.

Group differences that exist prior to the experiment may not be confounded with X in Design 6, but those that arise during the experiment may be. All groups may become more fatigued as an investigation progresses, but in each replication this fatigue factor will affect the mean score of each group and hence of each X. If one group becomes much more fatigued than the others, however, this *selection-maturation interaction* may be confounded with the effect of X. This type of interaction is less likely to occur in this design, however, than in Design 5. In Design 5, if just one group becomes excessively fatigued (selection-maturation interaction) or especially responsive to an extraneous event (selection-history interaction), this interaction effect may be mistaken for the effect of X. In a Counterbalanced Design, this mistake will not be made unless the interaction occurs during several replications—and in a different group each time—or is exceptionally strong on one occasion in one group.

This design presents one very serious problem in education: the effect of an exposure to one X may carry over and be combined with the measurements of the next X. In our previous experiment, for example, the experience of reading small type may enable Ss to read bigger type more rapidly than if they had not read small type beforehand. In a drug experiment, the effect of the first drug may remain in the body; consequently, measurements that are taken after the second drug is administered may represent the effect of both drugs. When the possibility of carry-over effects exists, sufficient time should elapse between replications to permit the effects from the previous treatment to dissipate. In many instances in educational research, however, the assumption that there is no residual or carry-over effect cannot be satisfied. The usefulness of the design, therefore, is limited.

One-group Time-series Design (Design 7)

This design is the same as Design 1, except that several measurements are taken before and after the introduction of X. The paradigm for Design 7 is as follows:

$$T_1 \quad T_2 \quad T_3 \quad T_4 \quad X \quad T_5 \quad T_6 \quad T_7 \quad T_8$$

Internal Validity/ Because multiple tests are given over a period of time, a time-series design controls more potential sources of internal invalidity than Design 1. Suppose that eye specialists using standard measuring techniques have appraised a group of Ss periodically over a span of four years, and they have

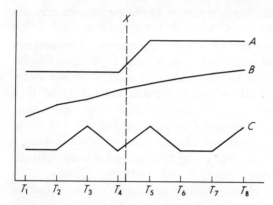

Figure 11.9/ Illustrative patterns of repeated measurements with the introduction of X.

found no appreciable change in the common eye impairment. On the same day all the Ss are given a recently discovered drug X, and within seventy-two hours their vision is normal. There is a possibility that something other than the drug may have caused the improvement in vision, but this possibility is not likely.

When employing Design 7, the justification for concluding that X caused a given effect *depends on the stability of the past performances or measurements*. In Figure 11.9, X may have caused the effect noted between T_4 and T_5 in test series A. But one cannot infer that X caused the increase that appears between T_4 and T_5 in B or C. Maturation rather than X may have caused the increase in B, for example, and random instability may have caused the fluctuation in C.

Multitesting provides this design with a great advantage over Design 1. If there is no appreciable difference in the first four T scores, the difference between the T_4 and T_5 scores is not likely to be caused by *maturation, testing,* or *regression*. Changes in the measuring *instruments* may occur over a period of time, but there is no reason why they should occur between T_4 and T_5 as opposed to earlier tests. If the record-keeping system is changed when X is introduced, however, or the raters know when X is introduced and have strong convictions concerning its potential effect, these changes and biases rather than X may account for the difference between the T_4 and T_5 scores.

Selection and *mortality* are controlled by this design if the same Ss participate in all phases of the experiment. *Contemporary history* variables provide the major internal-invalidity problem; hence, the possibility of their presence must be carefully checked. The difference between T_4 and T_5 scores may not be caused by X, for example, but the occurrence of an institutional event (dance, examination, etc.), seasonal or weather fluctuations, or cyclical variations (weekends, etc.). Suppose that an E checks library records for eight weeks to ascertain the effect of X—opening the stacks to all students after the fourth week. He may note a sharp increase in book withdrawals between T_4 and T_5 that is caused by the approach of final examinations rather than by the introduction of X.

External Validity/ The extent to which the findings of this design can be generalized depends upon the experimental conditions. An *interaction* of *pretesting* and X may occur. If achievement tests or other Ts that are commonly used in schools are employed, no problems will arise. Such tests are usually nonreactive, because the population to which one wishes to generalize also experiences them. Unique Ts, however, may make the Ss differ from the general population from which they came; consequently, the findings may apply only to Ss who take these specific pretests.

A *selection-X interaction* may occur when this design is used. An E may select Ss who have perfect attendance records over an extended period of time, or the repetition of unique Ts may cause absenteeism. Data obtained under either of these circumstances might not be representative of the effect of X for the general population, for students who avoid tests or have perfect attendance may differ from other students in respect to health, skills, interest in school, or other factors.

Control-group Time-series Design (Design 8)

This design utilizes a control group to overcome one of the weaknesses of Design 7: the failure to control history. If the control group fails to show a gain from T_4 to T_5 and the experimental group shows a gain, then the plausibility of *contemporary history* accounting for the X results is reduced greatly, for both groups have experienced these events. See the following paradigm:

Experimental group
$$T_{1_E} \quad T_{2_E} \quad T_{3_E} \quad T_{4_E} \quad X \quad T_{5_E} \quad T_{6_E} \quad T_{7_E} \quad T_{8_E}$$

Control group
$$T_{1_C} \quad T_{2_C} \quad T_{3_C} \quad T_{4_C} \qquad T_{5_C} \quad T_{6_C} \quad T_{7_C} \quad T_{8_C}$$

This design is also superior to Design 5, for it controls *selection-maturation interaction* to the extent that, if one group shows a greater rate of gain than the other, this accelerated gain would be revealed in the pre-X tests.

The multiple posttests that are employed in Designs 7 and 8 often provide vital information that a single posttest design would not reveal. In some instances, the long- and short-term effects of Xs vary not only in quality, but also in quantity. Suppose that an experiment is conducted to determine whether children achieve greater mastery of fractions by the "practice" or by the "understand" method. The former may produce greater initial gains, but the latter may produce less forgetting and greater long-term mastery.

Evaluation of Experimental Research

When the experimental method can be used to solve problems, it is the most satisfactory means of obtaining reliable knowledge. Knowledge of the past, descriptions of present status, pooled judgments, expert opinions, and hunches of skilled professional workers provide ideas and information that help men make educational decisions. Experimentation puts explanations concerning the relations among educational phenomena to an empirical test. The investigator manipulates the variables and observes the effect under rigorously controlled conditions. He describes his procedures so that other observers can check his findings under identical conditions. Experimentation serves as a high court of judgment; experimentation refines and sharpens the educational decision-making process.

To what extent have educators pursued experimental research? How successful have they been? Early in this century, members of the profession noted that natural scientists were taking giant strides of progress as a result of their experimental studies. A wave of enthusiasm for this type of research spread in educational circles, and many studies were initiated. Because of the nature of their subject matter, educators found that they had to hurdle many obstacles that did not hamper natural scientists; moreover, the experimental method could not be applied to some of their problems. Because progress was much slower than had been anticipated, the popularity of experimental studies waned.

During the past decade a constellation of events has spurred a revival of interest in educational research. Heated debates concerning the quality of education in this country and the initial impact of the knowledge and population explosions have alerted the public to the need for action. As a result of the extensive criticism of existing research, the provision of greater financial support, and the development of more sophisticated research tools, each year new experimental studies are being undertaken by educators. Many of these investigations conform closely to the scientific method of problem solving, but because of procedural weaknesses some of them are of limited value. The following discussion evaluates how well educational research measures up to the experimental standards in the natural sciences, identifies problems that impede progress, and delineates developments that are opening up exciting possibilities.

Formulation of the Problem

The scientific method of research requires a thorough analysis of a problem, the precise formulation of hypotheses, and a rigorous check on the assumptions and logical arguments underlying the experimental plans. Because these important responsibilities have often been neglected, severe attacks have been made on educational research studies. Griffiths contends, for example, that

. . . without doubt, the greatest weakness of research in educational administration is the lack of theory. Most studies in educational administration are done at the level of "naked empiricism." By this we mean that the researcher has an idea that a vaguely defined problem needs to be solved. He collects data through a questionnaire, survey, or some other method and attempts to find an answer by "looking at the data." By following this procedure we have amassed tons of data, but have come up with very few answers. The opposite of "naked empiricism" is research based on theory. By this is meant that the researcher starts with a well defined problem, a set of clearly stated assumptions, and from these assumptions he deduces by logico-mathematical methods a set of testable hypotheses. Theory is essentially a set of assumptions from which a set of empirical laws (principles) may be derived (65:16).

Griffiths's criticism of research in educational administration is applicable to many other areas within education.

When researchers conduct experimental investigations, they are less frequently guilty of collecting data aimlessly—without a theoretical orientation—than when they employ other research methods. Most experienced *Es* give consideration to the analysis of the problem and the formulation of hypotheses, and check the assumptions underlying their problems, but the quality of their work varies. Many novices, however, cannot accept the fact that designing an experiment can consume more time than conducting it. To them, planning an investigation to the finest detail—perhaps carrying out a pilot study—and removing all logical flaws and procedural imperfections before conducting any step of it is an unnecessarily burdensome task. They do not comprehend that conducting an experiment and writing a scholarly paper are not comparable undertakings. Once an experiment is put into motion, it must be run off exactly as planned; unlike a scholarly paper, an experiment cannot be patched up after it is under way.

Statement of Hypotheses/ The formulation and testing of problem hypotheses is one of the distinguishing characteristics of the scientific method. Hypotheses are the heart of scientific research—the working instruments of scientific reasoning. They are facilitating devices which give the facts obtained by the E a chance to confirm or disconfirm whether stipulated relationships among educational phenomena exist. Unfortunately, many Es are concerned primarily with experimental designs and statistical procedures, and give insufficient attention to the theoretical premises of their investigations. Many research reports are full of statistically significant findings that stand in such isolation of theoretical orientation that they contribute little or nothing to the advancement of science. Science makes great advances through experimental studies, but the experiment itself does not provide the intellectual thrust that pushes back the frontiers of knowledge. The experiment does not initiate discoveries; it tests ideas that are already born. The experimental design and statistical techniques merely check hypotheses that the researcher has developed or has derived from existing theories in the field. Thus, a brilliantly executed experiment is of little value if it tests a poorly conceived hypothesis.

Chain of Reasoning/ Scientific theories and hypotheses about the nature of things must be tested both logically and empirically. At the beginning of this century, in psychology "theory ranged far ahead of experiment and made no demand that propositions be testable. Experiment, for its part, was willing to observe any phenomenon, whether or not the data bore on theoretical issues. Today, the majority of experimenters derive their hypotheses explicitly from theoretical premises and try to nail their results into a theoretical structure" (37:674). Sophisticated educational researchers are beginning to take similar steps. They orient their experiments in theoretical propositions that exist in their field or in related fields, and through a chain of deductive reasoning set forth a justifiable set of inferences that lead step by step through the problem hypothesis to a statistical hypothesis. Once this logical chain of reasoning is forged, they begin to accumulate empirical evidence through experimental procedures. Finally, they utilize the process of inductive reasoning to relate the results of their tests of significance back to the problem hypothesis.

The informal, discursive discussions that appear in many research reports fail to bring this chain of deductive-inductive reasoning into proper focus. The necessity for a problem hypothesis is apparently not recognized, or confusion exists over the function of the problem hypothesis and the statistical hypothesis. The latter statement seems quite plausible, for many *Es* report the statistical, or null, hypothesis as if it were the problem hypothesis (see page 165). In many studies, the problem hypothesis is not presented in the formal "if-then" form. Readers must restate the problem in this form to check the logic of the arguments.

Researchers should make the arguments in their deductive-inductive chain of reasoning explicit in their research reports. To avoid finding fatal flaws in their reasoning at this stage of their work, they must always test the logical soundness of their investigative structure before they initiate any experimental procedures. By so doing, they may spot gaps or flaws in their chain of reasoning that need to be corrected. They may detect assumptions that their conclusions will be based upon which must be defended with additional logic or evidence or which require that they change their procedures.

Examination of Assumptions/ Experimental studies that are based on false assumptions cannot yield valid results, yet some *Es* fail to examine the assumptions underlying their hypotheses, procedures, and methods of analyzing the results. They assume, for example, that a given test will measure a particular ability of their *Ss,* without checking whether there is reliable evidence available to support their assumption. They apply statistical tests without satisfying the assumptions upon which the tests are based. Researchers are obligated to analyze critically the assumptions underlying every phase of their experimental plans, to eliminate those they cannot defend, and to recognize what implications the remaining ones have for the interpretation of their findings.

If assumptions are made manifest and are codified in research reports, they are readily available for critical inspection and cumulative development. Some educators are beginning to include such statements in their studies. To illustrate, one *E* in "An Experiment in Developing Critical Thinking in Children," stipulates that

. . . In the endeavor to set up criteria for the selection of content material and the development of teaching methods, the following assumptions were posited. . . .

1 That thinking is critical when it is essentially logical.
2 That logical thinking is no more than the application of the rules of logic to factual data in order to arrive at valid as well as true conclusions. It follows from this assumption that an individual's growth in the ability to do logical thinking must depend upon his acquiring a working knowledge of the basic rules of logic.
3 That children in the upper grades of the elementary school are, in general, mentally capable of acquiring the necessary understanding of logic and a proficiency in the use of its rules.
4 That the most effective way of helping children to acquire the necessary working knowledge of the principles of logic is through direct instruction.
5 That this direct instruction should consist of: *a.* Materials and learning content which embody the principles of logic. *b.* Teaching methods that provide full opportunity for the pupil to discover for himself these principles and to formulate them as generalizations (73).

Observation and Experimentation

Experimental research conforms to the scientific method of acquiring knowledge in that controlled observation is utilized to test hypotheses. But because of the complexity and nonuniformity of human phenomena, ". . . experiment in the social sciences is not possible in the same sense that it is in physics and chemistry where an experiment may be repeated an endless number of times under controlled and practically identical conditions. . . . But it is desirable to approach the methodology of the exact sciences in every way possible, recognizing that in so far as the experimenter falls short of such standards his results are defective" (127:228).

Question of Ethics/ Because educators use youngsters rather than inanimate elements and forces in their investigations, their freedom to exercise experimental control is somewhat limited. When they plan experiments, ethical questions such as the following may arise: Does the *S* have a moral right to know that he is part of an experiment? Is it ethical to use hidden microphones or other concealed methods of observation? Can *Es* add something to the diet or drinking water of *Ss* to study the effect without informing them? Do *Es* have the right to choose by a toss of a coin whether an *S* receives the experimental or the control treatment—especially if they strongly suspect that the experimental treatment may save lives? Do *Es* have the right to test hypotheses about stress, riots, sex, or suicides that may advance knowledge if there is a possibility that the experimental treatment may produce any physically or emotionally harmful effect? Researchers in the behavioral sciences must develop a sense of responsibility for the confidentiality of information and must be appropriately concerned about the invasion of privacy.

Quality of Tools/ Educators struggle not only with ethical problems but also with problems concerning the selection and use of research tools. Inappropriate, imprecise, or faulty apparatus and data collecting instruments may introduce inaccuracies in an experiment that will render it useless. Some *Es* are not as meticulous as they should be about selecting and maintaining the tools that they use to measure the influence of variables, to hold factors constant, to manipulate variables, and to amplify or magnify phenomena. Sometimes they report that the independent variable has produced an effect that has been caused by the improper functioning of apparatus. To avoid such foolish errors, experienced *Es* check and recheck their apparatus. They calibrate timers, gauges, and similar devices in terms of some criterion and examine equipment for wear of mechanical parts, faulty electrical contacts, and adequacy of lubrication.

Developing and selecting tools that possess the required validity, objectivity, and reliability are more difficult tasks than maintaining and utilizing them. Sometimes *Es* do not choose or cannot locate instruments that will produce the required kind and form of data. Sometimes they use tools that are not appropriate for testing the type of *Ss* that participate in an experiment. Quantifying findings also presents problems. It is not always possible to construct tools that will make accurate and sufficiently discriminating measurements. When competent observers use crude yardsticks to measure the same phenomenon, they do not always obtain identical measurements. The analysis and interpretation of data that are quantified grossly or structured inappropriately does not appreciably advance the understanding of educational phenomena.

Some of the problems that *Es* have struggled with for years are being overcome by revolutionary developments in experimental designs and statistical procedures. The construction of more powerful and more precise data-gathering and data-processing devices, such as computers, has opened up new frontiers of possibilities for the study of complex educational phenomena. Researchers are making more effective use of the traditional tools of their trade, and they are beginning to use the more sophisticated designs, statistical procedures, and research instruments. Creative minds are searching for additional ways to improve research techniques. Equally important, a concerted effort is being made to reduce the time gap between the discovery and utilization of tools.

Control of the Experiment/ Physical scientists conduct the majority of their experiments in the laboratory where they can maintain optimum conditions of control. Whenever possible, educators follow their example. But some problems, such as those concerning crowd behavior, cannot be re-created readily in the laboratory. When phenomena can be reproduced in the laboratory, human beings do not always react to X in the same way as they would in a normal situation. To overcome this, social scientists often test hypotheses in natural settings such as classrooms. They introduce as many controls as possible, but the number of extraneous variables that may affect the dependent variable increases in the nonlaboratory situation.

Because of the complexity of educational phenomena, discovering what variables to control and determining how to control them in any setting is extremely difficult. Educators may not be able to identify all the relevant extraneous variables that may affect the dependent variable. Unlike the physical scientists, they cannot remove many of the variables such as age, IQ, etc., that they do identify; consequently, they resort to a battery of other control techniques.

Through the use of a control group, they balance out or equalize the effect of some extraneous variables, such as history and pretesting. But the differences between the Ss in the two groups or the biases of the E who assigns Ss to groups may produce effects that may be mistaken for the effect of X. To overcome this problem, educators assign Ss to groups at random. Randomization techniques are invaluable equalizing tools; however, when a small number of Ss is assigned, the possibility always exists that by chance the groups may differ.

Matching groups on relevant variables enables educators to obtain pertinent information from a smaller number of Ss, but some Es make the mistake of assuming that matching alone equates the groups. Matching may remove the masking effect of the matched variable, but the presence of nonmatched variables and differential statistical regression may make the groups unequivalent. Matching plus random assignment to groups produces equivalency, but Es often have to engage in extensive testing to find a sufficient number of matched Ss. Fortunately, the development of analysis of covariance and computers has provided researchers with highly effective and useful tools that relieve them of the drudgery that is involved when the older matching techniques are employed.

Educators are acquiring a better understanding of how to control experiments, but in many instances they cannot manipulate human beings and class schedules to meet the requirements of the research designs that are most theoretically desirable.

When full experimental control cannot be achieved, they often use designs that provide partial control. No matter what design researchers use, they must be fully aware of the variables that remain uncontrolled. Table 11.1, which has been adapted from

Table 11.1/ Factors Jeopardizing the Validity of Experimental Designs

Sources of Invalidity	EXPERIMENTAL DESIGNS*							
	Little Control	Rigorous Control			Partial Control			
	1	2	3	4	5	6	7	8
Internal Validity								
Contemporary history†	−	+	+	+	+	+	−	+
Maturation processes	−	+	+	+	+	+	+	+
Pretesting procedures	−	+	+	+	+	+	+	+
Measuring instruments	−	+	+	+	+	+	?	+
Statistical regression	?	+	+	+	?	+	+	+
Differential selection of subjects	+	+	+	+	+	+	+	+
Experimental mortality	+	+	+	+	+	+	+	+
Interaction of selection and maturation, etc.	−	+	+	+	−	?	+	+
External Validity								
Interaction of selection and X	−	?	?	?	?	?	?	−
Interaction of pretesting and X	−	−	+	+	−	?	−	−
Reactive experimental procedures	?	?	?	?	?	?	?	?
Multiple-treatment interference						−		

* Names of Designs 1 to 8 are:
1/ One-group Pretest-Posttest
2/ Randomized Control-group Pretest-Posttest
3/ Randomized Solomon Four-group
4/ Randomized Control-group Posttest only
5/ Nonrandomized Control-group Pretest-Posttest
6/ Counterbalanced
7/ One-group Time-series
8/ Control-group Time-series

† NOTE: A plus symbol indicates control of a factor, a minus indicates lack of control, a question mark suggests there is some source for concern, and a blank indicates that the factor is not relevant.

Campbell and Stanley (27), presents a checkoff list for twelve potential sources of invalidity, to help the reader appraise how well certain designs control these factors.

When selecting an experimental design, an E encounters many perplexing problems and must make a number of difficult decisions. An ideal experimental design possesses both internal and external validity, but the conditions that are required to achieve each type of validity are often incompatible. The controls that are used to achieve internal validity may limit the representativeness of the findings. Taking a pretest, for example, may make the *Ss* unrepresentative of the parent population from which they were drawn. This occurred in the United Nations study that was conducted in Cincinnati. When faced with the dilemma of choosing between internal and external validity, an *E* must give internal validity prior consideration.

Generalization and Prediction

To advance knowledge appreciably in the field of education, researchers must understand the phenomena with which they are working. From carefully conducted descriptive studies they acquire a low level of understanding: an accurate account of what conditions, activities, and practices prevail in their field. Experimenters are not satisfied with finding out what exists; they seek a higher level of explanation. They probe the problem of causality: Why does this condition or event occur? What causes this particular effect? Until such knowledge is obtained, educators cannot expect to predict and control phenomena in their field with great success.

A scientist considers that he understands his phenomena when he can project the findings of a study to other *Ss* and situations. If a chemist applies an experimental stimulus to one pure sample of his phenomena, he can be relatively certain that all like samples will react in the same way. But because of the tremendous variability of people's minds, bodies, attitudes, and backgrounds, an educator cannot assume with full confidence that a stimulus which has been applied to one group of *Ss* will produce the same effect when it is applied to another group. Except when dealing with behavior that is practically unmodifiable among human beings, such as reflexes, a social scientist cannot project findings from one study to *all human beings*.

Samples of Subject and Nonsubject Populations/ Overgeneralizing experimental findings is a common error in educational research. The findings of a study in which young men in a Middle Western state teachers' college serve as *Ss* are, at best, applicable to similar males; they are not applicable to "ivy league," premedical, or high school males, or to female college students. Many educators pay too little attention to the external validity of their designs. An *E* cannot be expected to draw a sample that is representative of all children in this country for each experiment. With a little care, however, he can often select *Ss* in a manner that will make his findings applicable beyond the specific sample that participates in the experiment.

Since generalization is the goal of science, some critics suggest that an *E* should select representative samples from the

nonsubject populations as well as from the *S* populations to
which he wishes to generalize. If the experimental variable that
is being manipulated is "anxiety," these critics ask the following
questions: Will it be possible to generalize the findings to rural
as well as urban settings and to home as well as classroom
situations? Will the findings of the study be the same if *X* is
induced by electric shock or by verbal means? Will the findings
be the same if different types of experimental workers, teachers,
or observers are used—male and female, old and young, etc?
If the findings of the study are to have wide applicability,
the experimental design must incorporate a representative
sample—or at least a varied sample—of (1) the natural situations in which *X* is found, (2) the measurement variables,
(3) the tasks or learning materials, (4) the methods of administering the experimental treatment, and (5) the *Es*.

Generalizability of Research Designs/ Classical experimental
designs have helped educators gain valuable insights into their
phenomena, but the "law of the single variable" has impeded
the development of significant generalizations in our field. When
an *E* must isolate and vary one *X* at a time while holding constant the effects of all other variables, the effect that he observes
may not be generalizable to nonlaboratory situations. Educational phenomena are usually the product of many variables
operating simultaneously in the classroom, and a variable may
produce different effects when it interacts with different variables. Educators need to obtain more information about the
interaction of variables in the ongoing educational process.
This need has been met by the development of factorial designs
which make it possible to manipulate samples from a number
of populations (*Ss,* situations, tasks, *Es*) simultaneously.

Factorial designs are among the most important contributions
that have been made to research technique during this century,
but they also have limitations. In most instances, only a few
variables and levels of variables can be sampled, because obtaining and handling the number of groups that is required for
a complex design is too difficult. Restricting the number of variables, of course, restricts the representativeness of the research
findings. Some men (18,105) are working on other designs
to increase the generalizability of experimental studies. Educators should keep themselves informed of these developments
as they appear in the literature.

Accumulation of Reliable Knowledge/ At this point it may appear that the search for absolutely certain knowledge eludes
the researcher. Indeed it does, and the scientists of tomorrow

will fare no better. On the surface, the demand for certainty does not seem an unreasonable request with our modern know-how, but nevertheless it is impossible of realization. Inability to obtain certainty stems from the fact that experimental designs are imperfect; they are not capable of producing evidence that is universally certain. Experimentation produces statements of probability. According to the rules of logic, one is never fully justified in inferring universal statements from single or numerous observations, for any conclusions drawn in this manner may turn out to be false: no matter how many black crows one observes, the conclusion that *all* crows are black is not justified. In short, experimental statements are statistical inferences; they can only attain a degree of probability somewhere along a continuum between truth and falsity.

Certainty cannot be achieved through experimentation, but a competent researcher does everything practicable to reduce uncertainty. He uses a design that is technically as good as current knowledge and the given situation permit. He demonstrates the effect of the phenomena under consideration in as wide a variety of situations as possible, and states explicitly the degree of generality to which his hypothesis extends. His objective is to make the design as valid externally as is feasible without losing internal validity.

Through replication, conducting additional experiments with other Ss in similar situations, the original investigator and other investigators must ascertain how much confidence can be placed in the hypothesis. If the hypothesis is confirmed repeatedly, the probability that it is "true" is greatly strengthened, and this knowledge can become an established part of science. An increase in the generalizability of the original hypothesis can be sought through replicating the experiment with Ss in other settings and situations. Through such replications, educators can build cumulatively toward more comprehensive explanations of phenomena in their field.

In some physical sciences scholars are kept busy for years testing certain high-level hypotheses, theories, and laws; but for the most part educators have been able to achieve only low-level generalizations. Investigators in the field are working on a gigantic unfinished patchwork quilt. Through the replication of studies, some generalizations have become rather well-substantiated small patches of knowledge. Little work has been done with retesting other generalizations, or the results have been inconclusive. Some of the small patches of knowledge have been fitted into more comprehensive theoretical structures, but educators must keep integrating accumulated knowledge into generalizations of higher and higher levels.

12

Tools of
Research

Early in the planning stage of the research project, an investigator weighs the merits of various procedures for collecting evidence. After determining which approach yields the form and kind of data necessary to test his hypothesis adequately, he examines the available tools and chooses the ones that are most appropriate for his purpose. If the existing instruments do not meet his specific needs, he supplements or modifies them or constructs his own.

Note that the inquiry starts with the problem and that the nature of the hypothesis governs the selection of the tools. One does not master a single method of obtaining data—such as the questionnaire—and apply it to every problem that arises. Each tool is appropriate for acquiring particular data, and sometimes several instruments must be employed to obtain the information required to solve a problem. A researcher, therefore, must possess considerable knowledge about a wide variety of techniques and instruments. He must be familiar with the nature of the data that they produce; their advantages and limitations; the assumptions upon which their use is based; and the extent of their reliability, validity, and objectivity. Moreover, he must be very skilled in employing, constructing, and maintaining tools and interpreting the information they produce.

Sampling

Many problems in scientific research cannot be solved without employing sampling tools. Since most educational phenomena consist of a large number of units, an investigator cannot always interview, test, or observe each unit under controlled conditions. Sampling tools solve this dilemma, for they help a researcher select representative units from which he can gather data that permit him to draw inferences about the nature of the entire population. Sampling tools save time, money, and energy and provide a means of probing into problems that are too unwieldy to be tackled by conventional methods. No researcher can afford to be unfamiliar with sampling procedures and the pitfalls that may be encountered when utilizing them.

Construction of Samples

Sampling does not consist in collecting data casually from any conveniently located units. To obtain a representative sample, one systematically selects each unit in a specified way under controlled conditions. Several steps are involved in the process. A researcher must (1) define his population, (2) procure an accurate and complete list of the units in the population, (3) draw representative units from the list, and (4) obtain a sufficiently large sample to represent the characteristics of the population.

Defining the Population/ Conclusions cannot be drawn concerning a population until the nature of the units that comprise it is clearly identified. If a population is vaguely defined, one does not know what units to consider when selecting the sample. To obtain information about the average salary of university professors, for example, an investigator must define the specific population about which he intends to draw generalizations. Does he want to include professors of all ranks, in all schools—medicine, liberal arts, law—and in administrative positions? Certainly a salary generalization drawn from a population that includes administrators will differ from one that is confined to the lower-paid liberal arts professors. People are repeatedly deceived by institutional, political, and advertisers' reports, because they assume the generalizations presented were drawn from one population when they actually were drawn from another.

Listing the Population/ Once the population is clearly identified, the investigator obtains or constructs a complete, accurate, and up-to-date list (called a frame) of all the units in the population. This task may consume considerable time, and obstacles may arise that will prevent him from obtaining the required data. Suppose that he wishes to obtain information concerning the salaries of university professors in a specific geographical area. Institutions will have these records available, but they may be unwilling to reveal the information. In many instances the investigator may find that no tailor-made list of units in a population is available. Suppose that he wants a list of the unemployed experienced teachers living in Ohio or the boys who committed crimes in New York last year. No one agency keeps a record of all unemployed teachers. The courts may have information about juveniles, but their records may include neglected as well as delinquent children, and of course, they would not list unidentified criminals.

Many investigators produce disappointing results because they use available population frames without investigating the methods that were used to compile them, and without ascertaining whether all members of the population were included. Sometimes they select unit lists that are out of date, contain inaccuracies or duplications, or do not adequately represent the population. A classic example of this occurred in 1936 when telephone directories and automobile registrations were used to obtain a sample of how people would vote in the presidential election. On the basis of the data obtained from this sample, the prediction was made that Alfred Landon would be elected. What went wrong? Since the telephone directories and automobile registrations did not include the great number of voters in the lower economic brackets, a sample selected from these lists did not represent all members of the voting population.

Selecting a Representative Sample/ After defining a population and listing all the units, an investigator selects a sample of units from the list. Drawing a sample is a relatively simple task, but fatal mistakes are frequently made. If an investigator selects units that are conveniently at hand—the first twenty-five names on a list, the people who live in one block, the parents who attend a meeting, or the first four rows of students in the auditorium—these units may differ from the remaining units; hence, they may not be representative of the population. The slum dwellers living in one New York block are units in this metropolitan population, for example, but generalizations derived from data concerning their health, salaries, and dwellings certainly are not applicable to all citizens in the city. A "good" sample must be as nearly representative of the entire population as possible.

Obtaining an Adequate Sample/ Some samples are too small to represent the characteristics of the population. The IQ scores of two students selected as a sample from a population of 100 children, for example, are not likely to represent the average IQ of that group. But how large must a sample be to achieve an acceptable degree of reliability? No specific rules on how to obtain an adequate sample have been formulated, for each situation presents its own problems. If the phenomena under study are homogeneous, a small sample is sufficient. A few centimeters from a 1,000-gallon container of a particular chemical may be adequate. But, if the units under study are variable, as many educational phenomena are, a much larger sample is necessary. The greater the variability of the phenomena, the greater is the difficulty of obtaining an adequate sample. Increasing the size of the sample is of little value, of course, if units are not chosen in a way that ensures representativeness of the sample. In general, three factors determine the size of an adequate sample: the nature of the population, the type of sampling design, and the degree of precision desired. The researcher gives careful consideration to these factors and then selects the sampling design that will provide the desired precision at minimum cost.

Types of Sampling Designs

Several methods have been devised to select representative samples. The following discussion briefly describes random, stratified, double, and cluster sampling. Detailed explanations of these and other sampling techniques can be found in texts that are devoted to the subject.

Random Sampling/ The purpose and mechanics of drawing a random sample from a known population were discussed in Chapters 10 and 11. This method is reconsidered here merely for the sake of completeness and to refresh your memory. In random sampling, carefully controlled conditions are created to ensure that each unit in the population has an equal or known chance of being included in the sample. To prevent the investigator from biasing the results by exercising direct control over the choice of units, some mechanical device is employed to draw the sample. The names of all units may be placed in a fish bowl or on cards and shuffled thoroughly before the desired number of slips is drawn. If a small group is involved, a coin may be flipped to select the sample. Perhaps the best method is to employ a table of random numbers, such as those prepared by Fisher and Yates, Tippett, or Kendall and Babington-Smith. After assigning consecutive numbers to units of the population, one starts at any point on the table of random numbers and reads consecutive numbers in any direction (horizontally, vertically, or diagonally). When a number is read that corresponds with that written on a unit card, that unit is chosen for the sample. One continues to read until a sample of the desired size is obtained.

A random sample does not necessarily represent the characteristics of the total population, but when the choice of subjects is left to chance the possibility of bias entering the selection of the sample is reduced. By chance, of course, one could select a sample that did not accurately represent the total population. The more heterogeneous the units are and the smaller the sample, the greater is the chance of drawing a "poor" sample.

Stratified Sampling/ Since a random sample may by chance have an undue proportion of one type of unit in it, an investigator may use stratified random sampling to get a more representative sample. When employing this technique, he divides his population into strata by some characteristic and from each of these smaller homogeneous groups draws at random a predetermined number of units. To ascertain how people may vote on a public school issue, for example, he may subdivide a population into groups on the basis of known voting behavior—perhaps age, income, educational level, or religion. Stratified sampling, of course, is no better than simple random sampling unless one knows that a high correlation exist between certain groups of people and their voting behavior. *Proportional sampling* enables one to achieve even greater representativeness in the sample. This technique requires selection of units at random from each stratum in proportion to the actual size of the group in the total population. Hence, if 10 per cent of the voting population are college graduates, 10 per cent of the sample is taken from this stratum. Because proportional sampling improves representativeness, a researcher may use a smaller sample and thereby reduce the cost.

Double Sampling/ When employing a mailed questionnaire, double sampling is sometimes used to obtain a more representative sample. This precaution is taken when some randomly selected subjects do not return their questionnaires. The missing data will bias the results of the study, if the people who fail to reply to the query differ in some fundamental way from the other subjects in respect to the phenomena being studied. To eliminate this bias an investigator may draw a second sample at random from the nonrespondents and interview these people to obtain the desired information. This double-sampling technique enables him to check on the reliability of the information obtained from the first sample. Double or multistage sampling may also be used to "spot-check" data. After making a simple inexpensive survey of a large sample, an investigator may select another sample from this group for a more comprehensive investigation.

Systematic Sampling/ When a frame of a given population is available, a sample is sometimes drawn from fixed intervals on the list. Suppose that an investigator wants to select a sample of 50 names from a list of 500 school children, social agency cases, or factory workers. First, he divides 50 into 500 to determine what size of interval to use (in this case 10). Then, he picks a starting number at random from 1 to 10 (assume the number is 9) and selects each tenth name thereafter (thus, 9, 19, 29, . . .) until he has drawn the desired 50 names. If the names on the list are randomized at the beginning, this method is equivalent to the random-sampling technique.

But one must be wary of certain departures from randomness, such as a "trend." Suppose that children are listed by age in years and months and sample units are drawn at fixed intervals of 10. The estimated mean age of the group would vary from sample to sample depending on the beginning number selected at random. A group selected from intervals beginning at 2 would have a different mean age from one beginning with unit 10 on the list, for in the latter sequence each child would be older than his counterpart in the other sequence by eight ranks. Cyclical fluctuations are another factor that one must be on the alert to detect. If a list is kept of the number of college students utilizing the library each day, a biased sample will probably be obtained if every seventh day is chosen as a sample unit, for fewer students probably study in the library on Sundays than on weekdays.

Cluster Sampling/ In cluster sampling the sample unit contains groups of elements (clusters) instead of individual members or items in the population. Rather than listing all elementary school children in a given city and randomly selecting 15 per cent of these students for the sample, a researcher lists all the elementary schools in the city, selects at random 15 per cent of these clusters of units, and uses all the children in the selected schools as the sample. Rather than listing all the dwellings in a city, an investigator may list all the blocks in the city, select at random 7 per cent of these clusters of units, and include all the dwellings in the selected blocks in the sample. Observing clusters of units in a few schools is easier and less costly than observing randomly selected students scattered in many schools throughout the city. On the other hand, a cluster sample usually produces a larger sampling error than a simple random sample of the same size, for each cluster—such as a block in a given neighborhood—may be composed of units that are like one another, which reduces the representativeness of the sample.

Questionnaires

Questionnaires are widely used by educators to obtain facts about current conditions and practices and to make inquiries concerning attitudes and opinions. For some studies or certain phases of them, presenting respondents with carefully selected and ordered questions is the only practical way to elicit the data required to confirm or disconfirm a hypothesis.

Isolating specific questions for consideration tends to objectify, intensify, and standardize the observations that respondents make. Some subjects may not supply accurate answers, however, for they may suffer from faulty perception or memory or may not be able to express their impressions and ideas adequately in words. Respondents who are not free, willing, or qualified to divulge information may ignore certain questions or falsify their answers. Many people do not give thoughtful consideration to questionnaires; they fill out the forms carelessly or report what they assumed took place. Not uncommonly, respondents tailor replies to conform with their biases, to protect their self-interests, to place themselves in a more favorable light, to please the researcher, or to conform with socially accepted patterns. To obtain reliable data, therefore, a questionnaire must be carefully structured.

Methods of Presentation

Questionnaires may be presented to respondents in two ways: through the mails or in a face-to-face situation. In the latter case, a questionnaire is sometimes called a schedule, particularly if the interviewer fills out the query rather than the subject. Advantages and disadvantages are associated with both methods of contacting subjects.

Direct Contact/ Fewer partial responses and refusals to reply are obtained when the researcher personally presents the questionnaire, for he can explain the purpose and significance of the study, clarify points, answer questions, and motivate respondents to answer questions carefully and truthfully. But bringing a group together to fill out a questionnaire is often difficult, and meeting members individually may be excessively costly and time consuming; hence, questionnaires are usually sent through the mails.

Mailed Questionnaires/ Mailed questionnaires reach many people in widely scattered areas quickly and at a relatively low cost. The returns, unfortunately, do not bound back with equal celerity, and partial returns may introduce a bias that will render the obtained data useless. If nonrespondents are quite different from the respondents—less educated or less interested in the issue—they may not hold the same views as the respondents. If answers could be obtained from the nonrespondents, the findings of the study might be changed substantially. The mailed questionnaire has another limitation: a representative sample of data cannot be obtained if the population includes nonreaders.

Forms of Questionnaires

A researcher may cast questions in a closed, an open, or a pictorial form, and may utilize one type exclusively or a combination of them when structuring his questionnaire. The nature of the problem and the character of the respondents determine which form or forms will most likely supply the desired data.

Closed Form/ Closed-form or structured questionnaires usually consist of a prepared list of concrete questions and a choice of possible answers. To indicate his reply, a respondent marks "yes" or "no"; checks, circles, or underscores one or more items from a list of answers; or ranks a series of statements in the order of their importance (1, 2, 3, . . .). Sometimes he is asked to insert brief statements into blank spaces or on empty lines (How old were you on your last birthday? ————).

Closed-form questionnaries are easy to administer and fill out, help keep the respondent's mind riveted on the subject, and facilitate the process of tabulation and analysis. But they often fail to reveal the respondent's motives (why he answers as he does), do not always yield information of sufficient scope or depth, and may not discriminate between fine shades of meaning. Fixed alternative responses may make respondents take a stand upon issues about which they have no crystallized opinion or may force them to give answers that do not accurately express their ideas. The listed alternative answers may be placed in an order that encourages the respondent to reply in accordance with the researcher's wishes. If proper precautions are taken in constructing the questionnaire, these weaknesses can be somewhat overcome. To avoid biasing the results by placing the desired answers in the most conspicuous place, for example, items in a checklist may be randomized. Yes-no and true-false questions may be improved upon by inserting a third choice ("undecided," "don't know," or "no opinion"). When the investigator cannot provide a full range of choices in a checklist, he may resolve the difficulty by adding the statement "None of the above descriptions apply," or by leaving a blank in which the respondent may clarify, amplify, or qualify his answer.

Open Form/ Rather than forcing respondents to choose between rigidly limited responses, the open-form questionnaire permits them to answer freely and fully in their own words and their own frame of reference. This method of collecting data gives the subjects an opportunity to reveal their motives or attitudes and to specify the background or provisional conditions upon which their answers are based. Some disadvantages, however, are associated with the open-form questionnaire. When subjects have no clues to guide their thinking, they may unintentionally omit important information or fail to note sufficient details. If subjects are not highly literate and willing to give considerable time and critical thought to questions, they cannot provide useful data. If they are capable of providing a wealth of pertinent information, the task of categorizing, tabulating, and summarizing their many different, detailed, and complex answers may be extremely difficult and time consuming.

Pictorial Form/ Some questionnaires present respondents with drawings or photographs rather than written statements from which to choose answers, and the directions may be given orally. This form of questionnaire is a particularly suitable tool for gathering data from children and adults with limited reading ability. Pictures often capture the attention of respondents more readily than printed words, lessen subjects' resistance to responding, and stimulate their interest in the questions. Pictures may depict clearly some situations that do not lend themselves readily to verbal descriptions or may enable one to detect attitudes or to gather information that could not be tapped by other procedures. Pictorial techniques, however, possess at least two limitations: (1) they can only be used in situations involving distinguishable and understandable visual characteristics and (2) they are difficult to standardize, particularly when the pictures are photographs of human beings.

Construction of Questionnaires

Questionnaires are a popular research tool because every individual assumes that he knows how to ask questions. But asking questions that will obtain the precise data required to test a hypothesis is no easy task. A researcher is often amazed when respondents draw many different meanings from questions that he thought were perfectly clear. And he may prickle with resentment when colleagues point out biases in the wording or structuring of his questionnaire, which seems objective to him.

To obtain data about the income, marital status, or age of teachers, a researcher must ask specific rather than "shotgun" questions. Does he want to know the respondent's age on his last birthday, or in years and months at the present time? Does he want to know total income from all sources or only from teaching? Does he want to obtain salary information for the regular school session or also for summer school and evening classes? A question that merely asks a respondent to check whether or not he is married may need to be recast. To obtain more specific information, one might ask: Are you at present: Married_____ Single_____ Widowed_____ Divorced_____? Framing questions to obtain honest answers is an art. Note the difference in the following questions: Did you cheat on your school examinations? Did you ever engage in the commonplace practice of cheating on school examinations? Always_____ Usually_____ Sometimes_____ Infrequently_____ Never_____. Do you believe in the communistic policy of providing free college education for everyone? Should we provide everyone with a free college education? Did you exercise your American right to vote in the last school election? Did you vote in the last school election or for some reason were you unable to vote? Did_____ Did not_____.

Questionnaires have been subject to severe criticism, but many common weaknesses in them can be avoided if they are structured carefully and administered effectively to qualified respondents. The following discussion raises some pertinent questions concerning the use of this research tool. (Also see questions in Chapter 16.)

Establishing Rapport/ Is the study of sufficient importance to warrant asking busy people to answer the questions? Has permission to contact respondents been obtained from the highest authorities in the school, organization, or governing unit? Does the questionnaire or an accompanying letter explain clearly the purpose of the study, indicate that the investigation is sponsored by a reputable institution, arouse interest in contributing accurate information, and offer to provide respondents with a summary of the findings? Are respondents asked for any information that the researchers can easily obtain elsewhere?

Framing of Questions/ Has the researcher thoroughly explored his hypotheses, experiences, the literature, and other questionnaires so as to frame questions that probe the crucial issues in depth? Are the questions stated in crystal-clear, simple language and focused sharply on specific points? Are subordinate questions asked or is an exhaustive list of alternative choices provided so as to explore various aspects of a decision and to probe beneath vague, stereotyped, "don't know," or evasive answers? Are questions framed to elicit unambiguous answers (if possible, quantified answers—number of times per week rather than "sometimes," "often," or "always")?

Ordering of Questions/ Are items placed in a psychologically or logically sound sequence—simple, interesting, neutral questions preceding more difficult, crucial, or personal ones and those that establish a frame of reference or provide keys to recall before those asking for details? Is a smooth transition made from one group of questions to the next?

Designing the Directions and Format/ Are clear, complete directions given concerning the type and scope of information that is wanted, where to place the responses, and in what form? Are the categories, format, and directions designed to elicit accurate, unambiguous answers, to require a minimum of the respondent's time, to facilitate the tabulation and interpretation of data, and if possible, to permit the quantification of results?

Eliciting Honest Replies/ Are directions and questions worded and ordered so as to allay any fears, suspicions, embarrassment, or hostility on the part of the respondent? If personal questions are asked, is a guarantee of anonymity given, or is there assurance that the responses will be held in strict confidence? Are any questions colored or phrased so as to elicit replies that will support the researcher's beliefs? Are respondents asked for information concerning subjects about which they have little or no knowledge? Are specific questions asked in order to check the truthfulness of answers to general questions? Are parallel questions asked in order to check consistency of answers?

Interviews

Many people are more willing to communicate orally than in writing and, therefore, will provide data more readily and fully in an interview than on a questionnaire. Indeed, several advantages accrue from the friendly interaction in an interview that cannot be obtained in limited, impersonal questionnaire contacts. In a face-to-face meeting, an investigator is able to encourage subjects and to help them probe more deeply into a problem, particularly an emotionally laden one. Through respondents' incidental comments, facial and bodily expressions, and tone of voice, an interviewer acquires information that would not be conveyed in written replies. These auditory and visual cues also help him key the tempo and tone of the private conversation so as to elicit personal and confidential information and to gain knowledge about motivations, feelings, attitudes, and beliefs. Presenting questions orally is a particularly appropriate means for gathering information from children and illiterates.

Interviews vary in purpose, nature, and scope. They may be conducted for guidance, therapeutic, or research purposes. They may be confined to one individual or extended to several people who are closely associated with the individual, as in a case study. To solve some problems, a number of people with similar or different backgrounds are questioned once briefly or several times intensively. Sometimes interviews are repeated at intervals to trace the development of behavior, attitudes, or situations. Repeated interviews have been used, for example, to study the progressive reactions of voters toward presidential candidates during an election year. The following discussion describes several types of interviews.

Individual and Group Interviews

Most interviews are conducted in a private setting with one person at a time so that the subject feels free to express himself fully and truthfully. In some instances, however, group interviews produce more useful data. Varied viewpoints are obtained when qualified individuals with common or divergent backgrounds are brought together to explore a problem or to evaluate the merits of a proposition. The participants may not only present a wide range of information, but also may help one another recall, verify, or rectify items of information. Subjects may refrain from expressing some points before a group, however, that they might reveal in a private interview. One person (and not necessarily the best informed one), moreover, may dominate the discussion so that the viewpoints of the other participants are not explored thoroughly.

Structured Interviews

The structure of interviews varies as much as the number of participants. Some interviews are rigidly standardized and formal: the same questions are presented in the same manner and order to each subject and the choice of alternative answers is restricted to a predetermined list. Even the same introductory and concluding remarks are used. These structured interviews are more scientific in nature than unstructured ones, for the standardized approach introduces controls that permit the formulation of scientific generalizations. But the standardized interview also has certain limitations: collecting quantified, comparable data from all subjects in a uniform manner introduces a rigidity into the investigative procedures that may prevent the investigator from probing in sufficient depth.

Unstructured Interviews

Unstructured interviews are flexible; few restrictions are placed on respondents' answers. If preplanned questions are asked, the queries are altered to suit the situation and subjects. Sometimes subjects are encouraged to express their thoughts freely; only a few questions are asked to direct their discourse. In some instances, the information is obtained in such a casual manner that the respondents are not aware that they are being interviewed.

In an informal unstructured interview, one can penetrate behind initial answers, follow up unexpected clues, redirect the inquiry into more fruitful channels on the basis of emerging data, and modify categories to provide for a more meaningful analysis of data. Quantifying the accumulated qualitative data, however, may be difficult. Because of the nonuniform tactics that are employed in collecting the information, one usually cannot compare data from various interviews and derive generalizations that are universally applicable.

Nonstructured interviews are not ordinarily employed when one is testing and verifying hypotheses, but this informal approach is very helpful in the exploratory stage of research.

When an investigator is uncertain about what questions to ask or how to ask them, an informal interview may uncover the essentials of the problem and may help him select and formulate questions for standardized questionnaires and interviews. An unstructured interview may also provide insights into human motivation and social interaction that enable him to formulate fruitful hypotheses.

A researcher must be familiar with both structured and unstructured interview techniques, for he may employ both types during an investigation. Since many of the rules that apply to the formulation of questionnaires also apply to structured interviews, additional examples of the standardized approach are unnecessary. The methods of conducting the more informal interviews vary considerably. The following discussion will present two types of approaches: the nondirective depth interview and the focused interview.

Nondirective Depth Interview/ An unguided interview, which is almost psychoanalytical in character, is sometimes the most appropriate method for obtaining insights into hidden or underlying motivations; unacknowledged attitudes; personal hopes, fears, and conflicts; and the dynamic interrelatedness of responses. Rather than asking a number of direct or predetermined questions to obtain specific items of information, an investigator permits the subject to talk freely and fully concerning a particular issue, incident, or relationship. While the subject unfolds his story, the interviewer serves as a good listener who unobtrusively inserts a judicious "Hmm," "That is interesting," "Go on," or generalized question to stimulate the flow of conversation. When the interview is drawing to a close, the investigator may ask some direct questions to fill in the gaps and round out the discussion. By placing few restrictions on the direction of the discussion and encouraging a wide range of responses, the interviewer gets a natural and representative picture of the subject's behavior and gains an insight into the character and intensity of his attitudes, motives, feelings, and beliefs.

Focused Interview/ A focused interview is less diffused than a depth interview. The informant is asked to focus his attention upon a concrete experience that he has had. If he has seen a movie or read a book, for example, an effort is made to ascertain the specific effects that this experience has had upon him. To probe the attitudes and emotional responses of the subject, the interviewer analyzes the movie or book prior to meeting him; prepares appropriate questions to serve as a framework for the discussion; and during the interview, confines the conversation to these relevant issues. The respondent is permitted to express himself completely, but the interviewer directs the line of thought.

Conduct of an Interview

A successful interview is a dynamic interpersonal experience that is carefully planned to accomplish a particular purpose. Creating a friendly, permissive atmosphere, directing the discourse into the desired channels, encouraging the respondent to reveal information, and motivating him to keep presenting useful facts require a high degree of technical skill and competence. To evaluate the effectiveness of an interview, one must keep in mind many of the questions that were raised concerning questionnaires, as well as the following factors:

Preparing for the Interview/ Did the interviewer decide what areas of information to cover, and did he prepare appropriate questions to extract the desired data? Did he insert comments that made the respondent feel at ease and stimulated the flow of conversation? Did he find out as much as possible about the interests, beliefs, and backgrounds of the subjects so that he could gain their confidence, avoid antagonizing them, and "draw them out" about their experiences and special areas of knowledge? Did he obtain sufficient information to understand their frame of reference and interpret their replies as they were intended? Did he make a definite appointment for the interview at a time that was convenient for the subject? Did he conduct the interview in an environment in which the subject was at ease (usually in private) and in a setting where the most fruitful information could be obtained? Did he conduct a few preliminary interviews to detect weaknesses in his methods, questions, or recording system?

Establishing Rapport/ Was the interviewer pleasant, efficient, straightforward, and poised? Did he refrain from assuming an overly sentimental, solemn, or sympathetic attitude? Did he avoid adopting a superior, patronizing, clever, cunning, or "third-degree" manner? Did he dress appropriately? Did he use a suitable vocabulary and approach for working with the particular respondent?

Eliciting Information/ Was the interviewer an attentive, analytical listener who discerned when he should repeat or explain a question? Did he detect when answers were vague, contradictory, evasive, or deceptive? Did he introduce alternative or more penetrating questions to help respondents recall information, amplify statements, clarify their thinking, rectify facts, or give more concrete evidence? Did he pace the questions at the proper speed for the respondents? Did he ask general questions first and then sharpen the focus of succeeding questions? Did he follow up crucial clues provided by responses and stay with fruitful lines of questioning until he had extracted all the useful information? Did he inject courteous comments to redirect the interview into channels that were more pertinent to the inquiry? Did he sense when it was best to approach delicate matters and to probe for "depth materials"? Did he plan carefully the wording of such questions? Did his tone of voice, facial expression, or phrasing and timing of questions imply what answers he preferred? Did he avoid blaming or censuring the respondent and refrain from revealing that an answer shocked, annoyed, or displeased him? Did he seek the same information in different ways during the interview to check the honesty of responses? Did he check some replies against official records to determine whether they were accurate? Did he terminate the interview before the subject became tired?

Recording Data/ Did the interviewer use a schedule, a structured format, or a system that enabled him to record notes quickly and accurately? Did he make legible record of the exact (nonedited) words of the respondent during the interview or immediately afterward? Did he consider using a tape recorder that would free him during the interview, provide a means of verifying responses later, preserve the emotional and vocal character of replies, and help him avoid the omissions, distortions, modifications, and errors that sometimes are made in written accounts of an interview? Did the interviewer make notes concerning any behavior or conditions that he observed which did not conform with the respondent's replies? Did he make a record of significant emotional displays, hesitations, stammering, sudden silences or transitions, quickly corrected words, and obvious omissions?

Appraisal Instruments

In addition to interviews and questionnaires, researchers employ tests, scales, inventories, and other tools to obtain data. Hundreds of these instruments have been devised, and others are constantly being constructed. Some of them provide for a self-appraisal; others require that the assessments be made by an expert. *Mental Measurements Yearbook* and some research journals describe and evaluate many tests. These sources usually give the names of the publishers, the prices, and the grade level for which the tests are designed. Explanations of the techniques employed in constructing and evaluating tests appear in several measurement and evaluation texts. Because of the extensive literature in the field, this chapter can give only a brief description of some types of tools.

Instruments have been designed to measure[1] many different factors. Some appraise the *performances* and *potentialities* of the subjects. (1) Intelligence tests, for example, measure general mental abilities, and certain specialized tests assess a limited range of abilities, such as those required in mechanical comprehension or in the judgment of spatial relations. (2) Information and achievement tests measure the present level of mastery in a subject or skill that a person has attained as a result of instruction. Some tests measure proficiency in a specific area, such as typing, spelling, reading, or arithmetic. Other tests present educational achievement batteries that measure performance in several areas. (3) Aptitude tests predict the subject's ability to improve his performance with additional training in some particular academic or vocational field. Although based on present performance, these tests usually measure some areas in which the subject has not received specific training. Aptitude tests may appraise factors, such as mechanical skill, motor coordination, musical or artistic potential, or aptitude for medicine, engineering, languages, or stenography.

Tools are also available that measure the *preferences* and *behavior* of individuals. (1) Some instruments inventory the interest that subjects have in particular occupations or activities. (2) Other instruments ascertain the nature and dimensions of the attitudes and beliefs that individuals or groups hold concerning issues, activities, institutions, and segments of society. (3) A variety of tools assess emotional and social factors—the adjustment of a person to himself and to others. (4) Somewhat similar tests appraise aspects of a subject's behavior and conduct, such as his moral conduct, cooperativeness, friendliness, or leadership qualities.

Various techniques have been devised to determine the *environmental* and *physical* status of people and institutions. Some instruments measure aspects of the home: the socioeconomic status of the family, or the parent-to-parent, child-to-child, or parent-child relationships. Some survey instruments evaluate

---

1/ Measurement is a record of an observation. The recording is not a characteristic of the phenomenon observed, but a concept that is applied to an observation.

factors in a school, institution, or community, such as the number and quality of facilities, leadership services, and programs and practices. Medical and physical fitness tests assess the health status of individuals.

Appraisal instruments vary not only in respect to what they measure, but also in respect to how they obtain data. Information may be obtained through performance tests, inventories, scales, sociometric tools, projective techniques, or other means. The following discussion briefly describes several methods.

Tests

Pencil-and-paper tests and other special performance tests are commonly employed to measure subjects' abilities. Many considerations must be kept in mind when constructing these tests. After identifying the population for which the test is intended, the researcher defines the precise ability—breadth and depth—that is to be tested, analyzes all the factors that contribute to it, constructs test items to cover each one, and keeps the number in proportion to the contribution of the factor to the ability. He makes certain that the test items are of suitable difficulty for the subjects, present appropriate tasks for testing the specific performance, and conform to the rules that have been established for formulating various types of questions (multiple choice, matching, etc.). In addition, he may establish time limits for various phases of the test. After writing all the directions and test items clearly and concisely, and developing a format that makes the questions easy to read and to answer and the results easy to tabulate, the researcher administers his preliminary test draft to a group of subjects.

When the students have completed the test, he examines their responses and revises the directions that have caused confusion, corrects weaknesses revealed in the format, and eliminates or revises poor test items. After making the corrections, he rechecks to make certain that all aspects of the ability to be measured are still represented in proper proportion. The test constructor may also prepare norms to help users interpret whether their pupils are of average, above average, or below average level of ability. To establish norms, he draws a sample from the population for whom the test is intended, administers the final form of the test to these subjects, and constructs norms from the data collected.

One of the most important tasks a researcher performs when selecting or constructing a test or any other type of measuring instrument is to evaluate the objectivity, validity, reliability, and suitability of the appraisal tool. Before proceeding to the description of inventories, scales, and other measuring instruments, perhaps we should examine these evaluative criteria.

Objectivity/ <u>An objective test or scale is one that produces the same score regardless of who marks it.</u> To attain this quality in a test, researchers structure instruments that examiners can score without making subjective judgments. Examiners do not have to make subjective judgments if scoring keys are provided for true and false tests. If no guide is given for evaluating an essay test, on the other hand, the personal values and emphases of the examiner influence the scores that subjects obtain. The greater the degree of subjectivity that is involved in making judgments about the level of performance, the less objective is the test. To improve the objectivity of their tests, therefore, competent workers write specific directions to the observer or scorer and furnish scoring keys that allow no room for disagreement among scorers.

Validity/ An appraisal instrument that measures what it claims to measure is valid. A measuring instrument does not possess "all-purpose" validity. A test may be highly valid for use in one situation but invalid if used in another situation. Because an invalid test can serve no useful purpose, a researcher must present some evidence which provides confidence that a test measures the precise characteristics for which it was designed. When appraising the validity of a test for a specific study, an investigator may check one or more of the following types of validity: content validity, predictive validity, concurrent validity, and construct validity (3, 39).

1/ Content validity.
Content validity, which is also known as "logical," "sampling," or "curricular" validity, is most widely used in achievement testing. To establish content validity, the test constructor analyzes the content of the factor that he intends to appraise and structures a representative instrument to measure the various aspects of that content. To design a standardized algebra test, for example, he may examine many textbooks in the field and the courses of study and objectives prepared by the state departments of education and professional bodies. From these materials, he determines what content the test should cover and the proportion of it that should be devoted to various aspects of algebra. He may ask qualified experts to rate test items as to their importance and devise some method of pooling their judgments. When checking content validity, the test constructor alone and with the aid of others judges the extent to which the test items present a representative sample of the universe of

the content that the test is designed to measure. If an investigator wishes to determine whether a published test has content validity for his subjects, he compares the content of the course that his subjects have taken with the content of the test.

2/ Predictive validity.

Educators frequently are interested in using a test to predict some future outcome, such as success in school or in a job. A test that makes accurate forecasts concerning the future behavior for which it is designed possesses predictive validity. The basic procedure for determining predictive validity is (1) to administer the test, (2) to wait until the performance predicted by the test has occurred, and (3) to correlate the test scores and the actual performances the test is designed to predict. Suppose a scholastic aptitude test is designed to predict academic success in college during the freshman year. To determine the predictive validity of the test one would administer the test to a large random sample of first-semester senior high school students. After these students have completed their freshman year in college, one would correlate the predictions of the aptitude test with the academic grades the freshmen students received (criterion measure). The higher the correlation, the more effective the test would be as a predictor.

Two problems are associated with predictive validity. The prediction will only hold true in the situation in which it was validated or a similar situation. If the previous scholastic aptitude test were validated for a sample of junior college students, the same test might not make satisfactory predictions for students who plan to attend Princeton University. When developing a test that is to be used for predictive purposes, one may also discover that establishing the criteria to measure an outcome such as vocational success may be difficult. Establishing an unambiguous and agreed-upon criterion for teacher effectiveness, for example, is a vexing problem.

3/ Concurrent validity.

The procedure for establishing concurrent validity is the same as that for establishing predictive validity except that the outcome that is predicted is measured at approximately the same time as the predictor test is taken. If a new test is structured, for example, the scores that the students receive on the test may be correlated with the marks they recently received in the subject, ratings made by their teachers, or scores obtained on a similar test that has been validated which may be more expensive or more difficult to administer. Rather than waiting several years to ascertain whether a vocational interest test can predict success in a given occupation, an investigator may correlate the vocational interest test with the interest patterns of people who are successful in a given occupation or profession. Concurrent validity provides some immediate evidence of the usefulness of a test, but the fact that a test has concurrent validity does not guarantee that it has predictive validity.

4/ Construct validity.

Perhaps one of the most important types of validity to check is construct validity. A construct is an ability, aptitude, trait, or characteristic that is hypothesized to explain some aspect of human behavior, such as mechanical ability, intelligence, or introversion. Each such construct refers to a highly complex concept which is composed of many interrelated factors. Each construct may be exhibited in a number of situations, but no one observation may be regarded as a criterion of the construct.

When examining construct validity, the investigator is interested in understanding the nature of the properties being measured. Construct validity determines to what extent a test is consistent with a given theory or hypothesis under consideration—to what extent it taps what is implied by the theoretical definition.

Construct validation begins with defining the meaning of the construct, deducing certain consequences in a wide variety of situations that should and should not be observable if the construct that has been hypothesized does exist. The investigator then ascertains whether a given test shows that all these relationships between the construct and the predicted outcomes do hold. Cronbach suggests, for example, that "an investigator might define 'flexibility' in terms of the following expectations, among others: artists will be more flexible than nonartists; flexible persons will relearn a maze rapidly when the goal is shifted to a new position; flexible persons exposed to propaganda will shift their attitudes more rapidly than will nonflexible persons. He can then determine whether a certain test measures flexibility, so conceived, by investigating whether high scorers on the test exhibit the expected behaviors" (38:1554).

Construct validation is not merely an appraisal of the test alone, but also an assessment of the theory behind the test. If the predictions of the theory are borne out by the evidence obtained from the samples, all is well—at least for the present. Evidence has been obtained that confirms the hypothesis and indicates that the test does measure the relationships predicted by the hypothesis. If the predictions are not confirmed, the investigator assumes that one of the following possibilities accounts for this lack of verification: the test does not measure the construct; the hypothesis is incorrect or needs to be revised to conform with the evidence, or the experimental design did not test the hypothesis properly (39:295).

Reliability/ A test or scale is reliable if it consistently yields the same results when repeated measurements are taken of the same subjects under the same conditions. If a student receives a score of 110 on an intelligence test, for example, he should receive approximately the same score when an equivalent form of the test is given several weeks later. Three methods of measuring reliability are used: (1) the test-retest, (2) parallel-forms, and (3) split-half methods. In the first method, a group of subjects is given the same test twice and the resultant scores are correlated. If recall or the effect of practice will carry over from one testing to another, a parallel form of the test is constructed, the two forms are administered to the same subjects, and the agreement between the two test scores is determined. When the split-half method is used, the test is given only once, but items in it are divided randomly into halves, and the scores tabulated for each half are correlated.

Suitability/ When selecting a test, scale, or inventory, one must determine whether the instrument is suitable for his purpose. Will it obtain the type of data that he needs? Will it produce measurements that are sufficiently precise for his purposes? Will it be suitable for the age and type of subject and the time and locality in which he intends to use it? If two tests are equally reliable and valid, the instrument that is the cheaper, more easily and quickly scored, that is available in alternative forms, and that is accompanied by norms is usually preferable to its counterpart. Most publishers print manuals that give detailed information about the construction, reliability, and validity of standardized tests as well as the nature of the population upon which the norms are based. A prudent researcher carefully examines these explanations when he is searching for appropriate testing instruments. When conducting an investigation, he also remembers that the best tests available cannot yield reliable data if they are administered improperly or under undesirable and distracting conditions, scored incorrectly, or interpreted inaccurately.

Inventories

Inventories are instruments that attempt to "take stock" of one or more aspects of an individual's behavior rather than to measure in the usual sense. Unlike tests, inventories do not require subjects to perform at their maximum level. An inventory lists items relating to the factor being appraised, such as health practices or recreational activities, and requests subjects to indicate preferences or to check items that describe their typical behavior. The researcher evaluates the responses to obtain descriptions of certain fundamental predispositions of the subjects. Hundreds of inventories have been constructed to obtain information about interests, personality traits, social attitudes, social adjustments, study habits, and similar factors. Some commonly employed ones are the SRA Youth Inventory, the Strong Vocational Interest Blank, the Minnesota Multiphasic Personality Inventory, and the Washburne Social Adjustment Inventory.

Items are not placed in an inventory merely because the investigator strongly believes that they reflect the factor being measured. To validate an inventory, one demonstrates that the scores obtained on it agree highly with some other reliable device for measuring the factor under study. To measure interest in the teaching profession, for example, one may first list various interests that teachers seem to have. After presenting these statements to successful teachers and to people in other fields, the items upon which the teachers score high and other vocational groups score low are retained in the inventory.

Valid measurements are not obtained from an inventory, of course, if a subject gives false answers to make a desired impression or if he lacks sufficient insight into himself to make objective reports concerning his behavior. Some procedures have been devised to detect dishonest answers, and sometimes faking can be controlled by using items that do not readily reveal the nature of the factor being measured. The difficulty of validating inventories, however, limits their use as scientific instruments.

Scales

Many social science data cannot be measured in inches, grams, or similar standardized units that convey the same meaning to all people. But since measurement is the key to scientific advancement, workers in the field have striven to develop a number of scaling techniques that enable them to assign numerical values to their estimates of the magnitude of variables. Progress is being made in finding methods to transform qualitative data into quantitative measures that are more amenable to analysis and interpretation, but the work is still in a pioneer stage of development.

To construct valid, reliable, and objective scales, a researcher must overcome many obstacles. Describing the factor to be rated and identifying the characteristics that contribute to it may not be an easy task. Selecting representative items from the universe of items that contribute to the characteristics and differentiating clearly between various degrees of each characteristic so that the rater will know specifically what to evaluate when making each judgment may be difficult. The question of giving the proper weight to items may also arise.

The effectiveness of a rating scale depends in part, of course, upon the qualifications of the raters. Some people may not have sufficient knowledge about a factor to make discriminating observations and judgments. Not uncommonly, individuals check scale choices on the basis of inadequate evidence or merely guess, if they have had little or no opportunity to observe the factor being evaluated. Raters often suffer from a halo effect—they carry over a general impression gained from rating one factor to all factors that they rate. Some people rate everyone too severely or too leniently or refrain from checking items at either extreme of the scale. Because each rater tends to make judgments upon the basis of a slightly different frame of reference, pooled ratings are sometimes preferred.

Not all scales produce the same precision of measurement. Some of them are too primitive to be considered scientific instruments. In general, scales are divided into four types: nominal, ordinal, interval, and ratio. In _nominal scales_—the lowest level of scales—entities are placed in two or more categories which are given numbers merely to identify them; teaching methods, for example, may be labeled 1, 2, and 3, but these categories do not have an ordered relationship to one another. When an investigator wants to know whether entities vary in degree, he constructs an ordered scale. The crudest scale of this nature is the ordinal scale. _Ordinal scales_ place entities in a clearly defined rank order, but the distance between the intervals on the scale is unknown and not necessarily equal. If A, B, and C receive leadership scores of 15, 10, and 5, respectively, on an ordinal scale, one may say that A is superior to B in leadership and B is superior to C. One cannot claim that A is _as much_ superior to B as B is to C—that is, that the interval 10–15 is equal to the interval 5–10. To be able to state the latter, one must employ an interval scale.

An _interval scale_ not only places entities in a clearly defined order but also utilizes some means of attaining equidistant intervals of measurement. This scale permits one to say that the distance between A and B equals the distance between B and C, but it does not permit one to say that A with a score of 15 is thrice as good as C with a score of 5 and that B with a score of 10 is twice as good as C. To satisfy this requirement, one must employ a ratio scale. A _ratio scale_—the highest type of scale—possesses all the characteristics of an interval scale and in addition is characterized by an absolute zero which offers a consistent starting point for measurement. With such a scale, one can speak of relative amounts as well as difference in amount of any property or characteristic.

Many different methods of constructing scales have been devised. The following discussion provides a brief introduction to some of these techniques.

Rating Scale/ A rating scale ascertains the degree, intensity, or frequency of a variable. To construct such a scale, an investigator identifies the factor to be measured, places units or categories on a scale to differentiate varying degrees of that factor, and describes these units in some manner. No established rule governs the number of units that should be placed on a scale, but having too few categories tends to produce crude measures that have little meaning, and having too many categories makes it difficult for the rater to discriminate between one step and the next on the scale.

The description of the scale units may consist of (1) points, (2) numbers, or (3) descriptive phrases placed along a line:

(1) |　|　|　|　|　|　　　　or　　　(2)　1　2　3　4　5

or (3) *almost always, frequently, occasionally, rarely, almost never.*

Since these points, numerical symbols, and generalized terms do not necessarily carry the same measurement meaning to all people, more specific descriptive phrases may be presented to give the rater a clearer standard for judgment. In a Bogardus-type social-distance scale, for example, a subject may indicate how closely he is willing to associate with members of different ethnic groups, by checking statements that describe varying degrees of acceptability, such as: I would be willing to have an average member of various groups (1) as a mate, (2) as a personal friend, (3) as a neighbor, (4) as a fellow employee, (5) as a citizen of my country, (6) as a visitor to all parts of my country, or (7) as a visitor restricted to a limited area of my country.

Sometimes specimens of work are used to describe units on a scale. Samples of handwriting that represent various levels of merit, for example, may be placed on a continuum according to values determined by a jury. To rate a product, one matches it with the scale specimen that the product most nearly resembles. Man-to-man scales are similar to product scales, except that the bench marks on them are names of about three to five men. These men are known to the judges, and they possess varying degrees of a particular trait, say, leadership. Subjects are rated by matching them with the men on the scale that they most nearly resemble.

Scorecard/ A scorecard, which is frequently called a numerical rating scale, provides for the appraisal of a large number of items that contribute to the status or quality of some complex entity. Scorecards have been developed, for example, to evaluate school facilities, institutional programs, communities, textbooks, and the socioeconomic status of families. Each item on a scorecard is assigned a predetermined numerical value, and ratings are made by awarding all the points or some fraction thereof for the amount of the factor judged to be present. By combining all the ratings, one obtains a total score that indicates the overall evaluation of the object or condition observed. This technique is rather satisfactory when used to appraise physical facilities, but less effective when used to evaluate the program or quality of an institution. Certain intangibles in group activities seem to defy quantitative appraisal.

Rank-order Scale/ Rather than rating subjects, objects, products, or attributes on an absolute scale, a rank-order scale compares them with one another. This technique is especially useful for handling in a quantitative manner data that have not been precisely differentiated. Suppose an educator wishes to rate twelve teachers in respect to leadership ability. On a rank-order scale, he does not check a numerical symbol or descriptive phrase to indicate the degree of this quality that each possesses. Rather, he gives the teachers serial numbers to indicate how they rank in leadership in comparison with their colleagues. The teacher with the highest leadership qualities receives serial number 1; the next highest, serial number 2; and the lowest, serial number 12. Since more average teachers than extremely "good" or "poor" ones are found in most groups, detecting degrees of difference between the average teachers is often difficult. Rank-order scales, therefore, usually give a more reliable measure at the extremes of the scale than in the central portion.

Paired Comparisons/ In the method of paired comparisons, the subject is presented with a list of items, such as different ethnic groups, occupations, or recreational activities, and is asked to judge each item in turn with every other item in terms of which he prefers. A subject, for example, may be asked to underline which activity of the following pairs of activities he enjoys participating in the most:

football—tennis	baseball—tennis
baseball—checkers	pingpong—football
tennis—pingpong	tennis—checkers
football—baseball	pingpong—baseball
checkers—pingpong	checkers—football

The judgments of the subjects can be manipulated so that each activity can be assigned a scale value. This method, which may give more accurate results than the rank-order approach, is satisfactory when a small number of items is compared, but the procedure is too time consuming and laborious when a large number of comparisons is required.

Equal-appearing Intervals Scale/ The technique of equal-appearing intervals, which Thurstone utilized to establish attitude scale units, has become widely employed. In this method a hundred or more separate statements expressing various degrees of intensity of feeling toward a group, institution, object, or issue may be given to between fifty and a hundred judges. Each judge is asked to arrange the statements as objectively as possible into piles (usually seven to eleven) that appear to him to be equally spaced psychologically and to order the piles so that statements in the first pile represent the most favorable attitude toward the factor being evaluated, those in the center pile represent a neutral attitude, and those in the last pile represent the most unfavorable attitude. Afterward, the number of times that each statement is included in the several piles is tabulated, and each statement is assigned a score value based on the median position given to it by the judges. Statements that are too broadly scattered by the judges are discarded as ambiguous or irrelevant. To construct the final scale, somewhere between fifteen and forty of the remaining statements are selected to represent the different intensities of the attitude in question, and they are arranged in a random order. When taking the test, the subject checks only those statements with which he agrees, and his score is the median of the scale values for the statements.

Method of Summated Ratings/ The method of summated ratings, which dispenses with judges, was introduced by Likert. This method is as reliable as the Thurstone technique and somewhat simpler. The trial Likert test contains a large number of statements which indicate clearly a position for or against a particular issue. After each statement, subjects check one of several alternative answers, such as "strongly approve," "approve," "neutral," "disapprove," "strongly disapprove." The "arbitrary" or "sigma" methods may be used in scoring. The arbitrary method, which is sometimes preferred, will be explained because it is simpler. This method arbitrarily gives a weight of 1 to 5 to the alternative answers, and the same numerical values are always given to the responses that show the greatest favorableness toward the phenomena, for example:

"Exclude all Negroes from the city." strongly disapprove—weight of 5.

"Appoint a Negro to the school board." strongly approve—weight of 5.

Although the answers differ, they receive the same weight because they both reveal a favorable attitude toward Negroes. The total score for each subject is the sum of the values assigned to each item that he checked. Before constructing the final test, the investigator applies techniques that help him identify weak items. He eliminates those items that do not exhibit a substantial correlation with the total score or do not possess the power to discriminate consistently between people who receive high and low scores on the scale.

Sociometric Technique

In recent decades workers have been developing sociometric methods for obtaining data on social interaction among group members. In its simplest form, this technique involves asking each person in a group to select which other member he would prefer to associate with in a particular relationship or activity, for example, as a roommate or as a co-worker on a project. Sometimes subjects are asked to select second and third choices and to list the persons that they would reject. The choices may be plotted on a sociogram which presents each student's name within a circle or triangle and utilizes connecting lines (solid for acceptance and broken for rejection) and arrows to show the flow of interpersonal relationships. This network of acceptances and rejections reveals the star and mutual attractions in the group as well as the fringers and isolates; the sociogram depicts social subgroupings, cleavages, and cohesiveness. Sociometric data may also be presented on a matrix chart upon which all pupils' names are listed horizontally and vertically; first, second, third, and rejection choices (given and received) are plotted in the proper squares or cells; and the total acceptances and rejections for each subject is tabulated below.

A "guess-who" test is another device for detecting how persons in a group regard one another. The test presents a series of statements describing hypothetical people: "He is always cheerful and enthusiastic." "He is usually gloomy and complaining about something." Subjects are asked to write after each statement the name of the member in their group to whom it applies. The status of each member of the group can be judged by counting the frequency with which he is mentioned for various favorable and unfavorable descriptions.

Projective Techniques

Projective techniques are used to probe areas that cannot be reached easily by other means, or areas in which direct questions are apt to elicit distorted data. Instead of asking a subject for specific information, an investigator has him interpret or respond freely to ambiguous stimuli, such as inkblots, pictures, unfinished sentences, word associations, or lifelike dramatic roles. Through self-structured, spontaneous responses, the subject unconsciously reveals manifestations of his personality characteristics and organization. Only highly trained workers can interpret the implications of these responses, however, and scoring them is laborious. Projective techniques are difficult to validate, and many of the tools have not been standardized. Some weaknesses in them are being overcome, but much work remains to be done.

Observation

Interviews, questionnaires, and documentary sources are the only tools that can be used to obtain some data—particularly information about the personal lives of subjects, group activities from which outsiders are barred, and events that have occurred in the past. Direct observation, however, is the method that the researcher prefers to use when gathering data. A number of instruments and methods have been developed to help him focus his attention on specific phenomena, make objective and accurate observations, and systematize the collection of his data. In addition to the scorecards, rating scales, and various tests that have been discussed, some of the following techniques are commonly employed.

Checklists and Schedules

Researchers often construct checklists or schedules to facilitate the recording of data. These instruments list items (carefully defined, observable factors) that are relevant to the problem and, if possible, group them into categories. After each item, a space is provided for the observer to write a few descriptive words or to indicate the presence, absence, or frequency of the occurrence of the phenomena. These guides enable investigators to record many different observations rather quickly and to avoid overlooking relevant evidence. Checklists also tend to objectify the observations and provide for a uniform classification of data. Some lists are designed so that the researcher can arrive at a score that enables him to make comparisons with other data or to determine the general condition of an object or facility.

Time Sampling

The time-sampling technique requires that one record the frequency of observable forms of occurrences during a number of definite time intervals that are systematically spaced. Let us consider an uncomplicated example to illustrate this technique. If a teacher desires to ascertain the types of activity engaged in by John Adams, he records observable forms of behavior that this pupil exhibits during a specified five-minute interval in a history class each school day for a two-week period. Rather than recording everything the boy does, the teacher may wish to tabulate the occurrence or nonoccurrence of one objectively defined form of behavior, such as "the frequency of class participation." To obtain such data, he observes John Adams during one class period each day for two weeks and records each time that John contributed to the class discussion. The length of the observation interval depends upon the nature of the problem and such practical considerations as the availability of the subjects for the duration of the observation period. Research reveals that in general, several short, well-distributed observations provide a more typical picture of behavior than a few long periods of observation.

Time sampling is a valuable technique, because observable instances of behavior are quantified directly. If a series of observations are made on the same day, on successive days, or at any other stated intervals of time, a score is obtained that shows the number of times that the subject exhibited a particular form of behavior during each period and during the total number of periods. These obtained scores lend themselves readily to statistical treatment.

Behavioral Diaries and Anecdotal Records

Sometimes rather informal methods are employed to collect data. When a pupil is involved in a significant incident in the classroom, hall, or lunchroom, or is involved in some other concrete situation, an investigator may write a factual statement about what the subject said or did, note the date of the incident, and describe the situation in which it occurred. After accumulating a series of these direct observations of significant behavior over a period of time, an investigator may have sufficient data to gain considerable insight into the development and adjustment of the subject.

Anecdotal records are of little value, however, if observers are not able to report the relevant facts objectively. Some investigators make the mistake of accumulating only negative data; others record vague generalizations about the incident or a subjective interpretation of it rather than stating exactly what the subject said or did. Sometimes investigators generalize about the behavior of a subject before they have collected sufficient data. This technique's greatest liability is that considerable time is required to record, analyze, and interpret the data.

Mechanical Instruments

When several observers describe the same incident, their reports may vary because of their personal biases, selective perceptions, emotional involvements, or capricious memories. Mechanical instruments which are unaffected by such factors often obtain a more accurate record of an event. Motion pictures and sound recordings preserve details in a reproducible form so that the full account of an incident may be studied repeatedly and intensively by the investigator and also may be checked by other research workers. Films are used to analyze audience reactions, to make slow-motion analyses of complex activities that cannot be studied under normal conditions, and for many other purposes. Some mechanical instruments give a reliable account of what happened in a quantified form. Dynamometers, for example, measure the strength of the hand grip, and electromyographs record the frequency, intensity, and duration of the activity of a muscle. Rather than measuring the responses of subjects, some instruments control the stimulus source in an experiment. The episcotister, for example, regulates the intensity of light emanating from a source. Hundreds of mechanical instruments have been constructed, and the research worker should become familiar with those that are used in his field.

Although mechanical devices may produce more refined and reliable data than human observers, these instruments are subject to certain limitations. They can be employed more easily in controlled laboratory experiments than in studies conducted in a natural setting, such as a classroom. The presence of the instrument sometimes alters the behavior of the subjects and as a consequence the investigator does not get an accurate measure of their typical behavior. The money and time required to construct, utilize, or maintain an instrument may be prohibitive. Both crude and complicated instruments present problems, and of course, well-designed, precise instruments cannot yield reliable data if they are not properly employed and maintained. Also, classifying data collected by mechanical instruments in a manner that will reveal meaningful relationships is no easier than categorizing data obtained from less sophisticated tools.

Data Processing

Much of the mathematical and statistical drudgery that was once required to process research data has been eliminated by the electronic digital computer. In minutes this accurate, timesaving tool performs tasks that would take weeks or months to complete with conventional clerical and desk calculator tools. Most universities now have electronic computers, and these institutions usually grant free computer time to students working on their dissertations and to faculty members working on unsponsored research. Those individuals who plan a career in research—or even in teaching and administrative work—should become acquainted with the computer so as to capitalize on its potentialities. Practically all major research today is processed by electronic equipment and the implications and consequences that high-speed computers hold for tomorrow are far-reaching.

Research information is readied for computer processing by recording data on punched cards, punched paper tape, or magnetic tape which the machine can read. The tabulating card (IBM), which is used in the punched-card system, has eighty columns across the length of the card, and each column has twelve punching positions. The two punching positions at the top of the card—positions 12 and 11—(these two positions are not always numbered) are used for alphabetical and signal punches for accounting purposes. The ten positions below—indicated by the printed digits 0 through 9—are punched with the coded numerical data from which the necessary computations are made.

Perhaps you will gain some concept of data-processing procedures by examining a study conducted by Fox and Wedekind (58) which was designed to predict college applicants' freshman grade-point averages by curriculum (engineering or liberal arts) and by sex at the University of Pittsburgh. The investigators ascertained certain data concerning each applicant (sex, college curriculum, high school rank, and scholastic aptitude test scores) and had the information coded and punched in specific columns on IBM cards. In column 1, for example, digit 1 was punched for a male subject, and digit 2 for a female. In column 2, digit 1 or digit 2 was punched for a liberal arts student or an engineering student, respectively. The remaining information was punched in other specific columns.

After the data cards were punched, an explicit series of instructions (a program) were prepared to tell the machine what

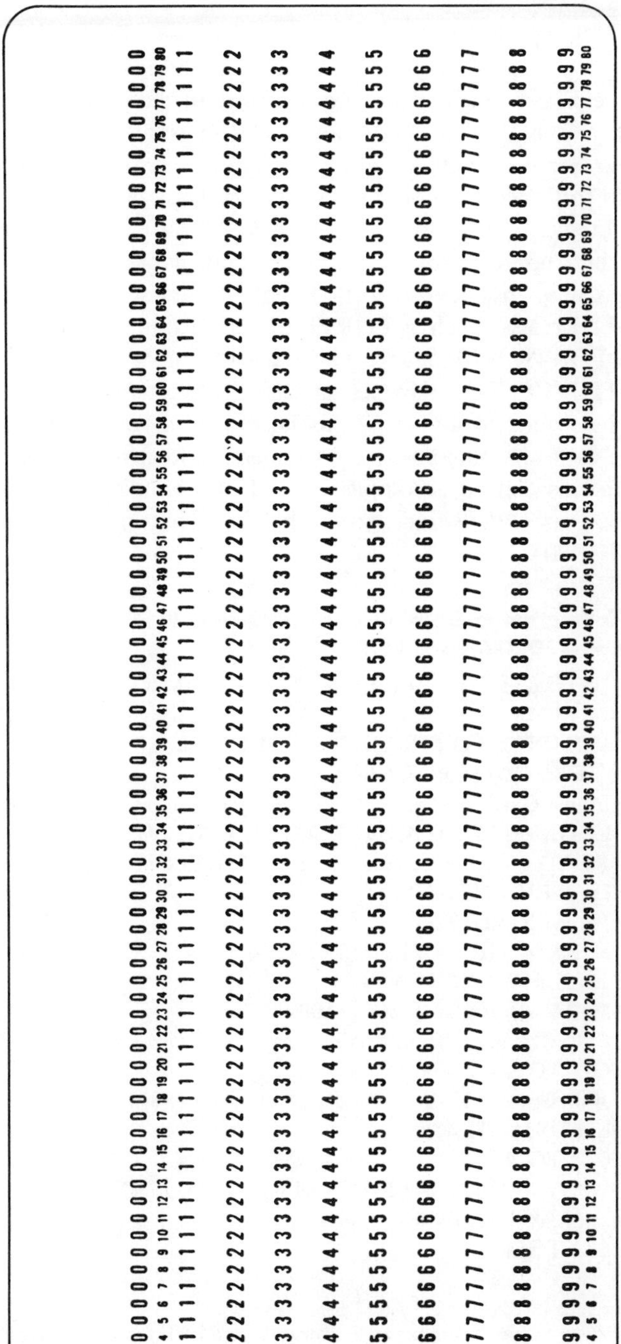

Figure 12.1 / IBM tabulating card.

operations to perform and how to perform them in order to analyze the data and to make the required computations to solve the problem. In most computing centers, programs for many operations, such as correlations, multiple correlations, *t* test, etc., are ready-made and available in the program library, such as the PEST.[2] If a ready-made program is available, the researcher need only submit properly punched data and control cards to the center in order to have the necessary computations executed.

When no ready-made program is available, the researcher writes one. Instructions to the computer are written in an artificial language,[3] such as FORTRAN (FORmula TRANslation). The FORTRAN language includes statements such as READ, WRITE, GO TO, PUNCH, and IF. These instructions tell the machine what to do—read this information, go to that instruction, write the outcome, etc. Innumerable logical and numerical operations can be accomplished with this simple language.

Fox and Wedekind wrote the following program for an IBM-7070.

7070 Program to Obtain Estimated Quality Point Averages.
Written in FORTRAN and PEST

```
*** ESTIMATED QPA, 59, 60 TO 61 ADM OF      5U)
                                              )PEST
 * COMPILE FORTRAN, PUNCH OBJECT,
     EXECUTE FORTRAN                          )
   Blank Card
 C ESTIMATED QPA, 59, 60 TO 61, L. W. FOX
 1 READ 101, ISEX, ISATV, ISATM, IHSR
   IF(ISEX)  200,200,2
 2 IF(ISEX-12)  3,5,6
 3 JQPA = 7164 + (123*ISATV) + (134*ISATM) +
     (22267*IHSR)
 4 JQPA = (JQPA + 500)/1000
   PUNCH 101, ISEX, ISATV, ISATM, IHSR, JQPA
   GO TO 1
 5 JQPA = -32370 + (102*ISATV) + (188*ISATM) +
     (21958*IHSR)
   GO TO 4
 6 JQPA = 35529 + (247*ISATV) + (75*ISATM) +
     (13058*IHSR)
   GO TO 4
```

2/ Pittsburgh Executive System for Tapes.
3/ Direct machine language is very complex. If a researcher learns FORTRAN or some other intermediary machine language, he can write his program in this language and a computer program called a compiler will translate the FORTRAN into an equivalent machine language program.

101 FORMAT (12,38H   415,)
200 END
    Blank Card
    Data
    Card with zero punched in columns 1 and 2

Note:/ In statements 3, 5, and 6, the asterisk (*) means multiplication.

Perhaps the following discussion will help you understand the basic FORTRAN statements 1 to 6. In statement 1 the computer reads in terms of the card format listed in 101 (which appears near the end of the set of instructions) the subject's sex and curriculum code, name, SATV score and SATM score (verbal and mathematics scholastic aptitude scores), and IHSR (high school rank). Immediately below is a brief statement—IF (ISEX) 200,200,2—which checks for error if the sex-curriculum code is negative or zero. In statement 2 the computer switches the data to the appropriate regression equation: statement 3 for liberal arts, males; statement 5 for engineering; or statement 6 for liberal arts, females. In this instance, let us assume the student is liberal arts, male; hence, the data are switched to statement 3. In statement 3 the predicted quality-point average is computed for liberal arts, male. In statement 4 a correction is made for the decimal point; then there is a PUNCH statement which punches a card with the same information as statement 1 plus the predicted quality-point average; an instruction to return to 1 follows. The next student's card is read and the process continues until all cards are processed.

Modern data-processing installations possess other units in addition to the computer. Some of the processing units and the functions they perform are as follows: The *key punch,* a punching machine that is actuated by the keyboard and operated much like a typewriter, perforates the card in the proper position of the column assigned to the data; the *verifying machine* determines whether the original punching of the card is accurate; the *reproducer* copies some of or all the data from one card to another; the *sorter* arranges the cards into specific categories; the *collator* assembles the cards that are alike in specific information; the *accounting* machine totals the data by columns and prints out the desired subtotals or totals; and the *interpreter* translates the perforations on the card into numerical or alphabetical symbols for visual identification.

13

WILLIAM J. MEYER

Descriptive
Statistics

Almost all empirical research requires some sort of statistical analysis so that the outcome of the study can be evaluated. Sometimes quite complex analyses are required for answering an empirical question while at other times a very simple straightforward analysis is sufficient. The choice of a specific statistic depends upon the question being asked in the study and upon the nature of the data. Viewed in these terms, *statistics are tools of research* and should not be conceived as the end product of research. Thus, if a simple measure of central tendency (mean, median, or mode) answers the question, there is little merit in performing more complicated analysis for the sake of window dressing—but the availability of electronic computers makes it too easy to overanalyze data.

The next two chapters introduce the basic terms and concepts involved in statistical analysis and provide some examples of the arithmetical operations involved in the various procedures. The materials developed in these chapters illustrate statistical methods for evaluating data derived from the various research strategies and methods described in Chapters 10 and 11. The reader will do well to relate the statistical procedures in these chapters to the materials in the earlier chapters.

Organizing the Data

Suppose the research problem required the administration of an achievement test to 92 eleventh-grade pupils. Recording each score as it appeared would make it very difficult to judge visually such things as the variability of the distribution or the average score. Thus, the first step after collecting the data is its organization into a meaningful form.

The Frequency Distribution

One useful system is to place the highest score at the top of a column, and then to place every other possible score, from the top score to the bottom, down the column. After recording the total range, the frequency of occurrence of each of the scores is tallied. The resulting table is called a "frequency distribution." Table 13.1 illustrates a typical frequency distribution where the column heading X is the notation for "raw score" and f is the symbol for "frequency."

The Class Interval/ The data arranged in a frequency distribution to the left of the line in Table 13.1 are easier to conceptualize than they would be if they were presented in random fashion; even so, they are difficult to grasp. Data may be presented in a more meaningful way by organizing them into class intervals of a width greater than 1. Scores are then tallied as they fall within each of the class intervals. To the right of the line in Table 13.1 is a reorganized frequency distribution using a class interval of 5. It is immediately apparent that this distribution presents a clearer picture of the subjects' performance on the test.

The width of the class interval may assume any value, dependent upon the variability of the data and the individual preferences of the investigator. Too coarse a grouping (large class interval), however, tends to mask the essential nature of the distribution and is a source of error in subsequent computational procedures. On the other hand, too fine a class interval often does not give the economy of space desired and does not reduce the labor involved in preparing the distribution over that for a class interval of size 1. A useful though arbitrary rule of thumb is to fix the number of intervals at some figure between 12 and 16, usually 15, and then determine the size of the class interval. This operation simply requires that the range be divided by the number of class intervals desired. The

Table 13.1/ Frequency Distribution of Achievement Test Scores of 92 Eleventh-grade Pupils

X	f	X	f	X	f	X	f
86	1	56		26		85–89	1
85		55	1	25		80–84	2
84		54	1	24		75–79	3
83		53	2	23	1	70–74	
82	1	52	1	22		65–69	4
81		51	1	21		60–64	10
80	1	50	1	20		55–59	5
79		49	1	19		50–54	6
78		48	1	18	1	45–49	8
77		47	1	$N = \overline{92}$		40–44	13
76	2	46	3			35–39	16
75	1	45	2			30–34	15
74		44	1			25–29	7
73		43	3			20–24	1
72		42	2			15–19	$\overline{1}$
71		41	4				$\overline{92}$
70		40	3				
69	1	39	6				
68	1	38	5				
67	1	37	2				
66	1	36	1				
65		35	2				
64	1	34	3				
63	3	33	3				
62	1	32	3				
61	2	31	1				
60	3	30	5				
59	2	29	4				
58	1	28	3				
57	1	27					

resulting dividend will, when rounded to the nearest whole number, give the interval size.[1]

One additional assumption is pertinent to the present discussion of class intervals. In using numbers in statistics, we assume that each number relates to a theoretical continuum. Such an assumption implies that the quantitative measures we make

1/ For the sake of consistency among investigators, a general rule to follow is to set the value of the lower limits of the interval as a multiple of the interval size. For example, in Table 13.1 the lower limits are 15, 20, 25, etc.

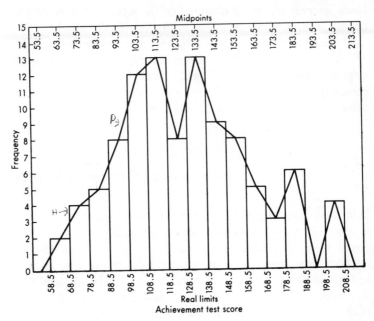

Figure 13.1/ Frequency polygon and histogram.

of any attribute can assume an infinite number of values. Sometimes this assumption leads to rather silly statistical statements, such as, "The average American family produces 2.15 children." We cannot always meet the requirements of a continuous series, but if it is assumed that any number is actually a point on a continuum, each number takes on a range of values. For example, the _real limits_ of the number 5 extend from 4.5 to 5.4999+, or 5.5. Applying this principle to the class interval 45–50 would mean that the real limits of the interval were 44.5 to 50.5.

Graphic Presentation of a Frequency Distribution/ It is often helpful to present a frequency distribution in graphic form. There are at least two types of such graphs: the _frequency polygon_ and the _histogram._ Figure 13.1 illustrates the basic difference in the construction of these graphs. The points marked off along the horizontal axis, or _abscissa,_ for the histogram are the upper and lower limits of each class interval. The points along the abscissa for the frequency polygon are the midpoints of each class interval. Frequencies are denoted on the vertical scale, or _ordinate,_ and are identical for each type of graph.

Each interval on the ordinate scale is actually 1 unit of frequency with a width equal to 1 interval on the abscissa. The total frequency is represented by the area under the polygon or histograph. The decision about the type of graph to use is largely a matter of personal preference; the polygon, however, generally provides a clearer picture when more than one distribution is to be plotted on the same set of axes.

Measures of Central Tendency

Whenever one wishes to evaluate the outcome of a study, it is crucial that the attributes of the sample that could have influenced it be described. When evaluating a study of learning methods, for example, one might wish to know the general intellectual ability of the subjects, their age, level of academic achievement, pretest performance, and posttest performance. Such information about the sample also provides a basis for determining the degree to which the data are generalizable. Three statistics, the *mode, median,* and *mean,* provide a means of describing the "typical" individual within a sample. These statistics are frequently referred to as "measures of central tendency."

The Mode

The measure or score which occurs *most often* in a frequency distribution is called the "mode." When a class interval is used, the mode is the midpoint of the interval with the largest number of cases. If two adjacent scores have the same frequency and they are the highest in the distribution, then the mode is the sum of the two scores divided by 2, or the arithemetical average of the two. Whenever there are two nonadjacent scores with the same frequency and they are the highest in the distribution, each score may be referred to as the "mode" and the distribution is *bimodal.*

Of the three measures of central tendency, the mode is the easiest to determine, involving for the most part an inspection of the frequency distribution. Unfortunately, it is also the least reliable because with successive samplings from the same population the magnitude of the mode fluctuates significantly more than the median or mean. It is possible, for example, that a change in just one score can substantially change the value of the modal score.

The Median

That point on a distribution below which 50 per cent of the cases fall is called the "median" P_{50}. The median is that point on a frequency distribution which divides the distribution exactly in half, so that half the observations are above it and half are below it. Consider this distribution of scores: 5, 9, 11, 16, 20, 21, 23. The N is an odd number and the median is 16. There are three scores below 16 and three scores above 16. Adding an additional score (4, for example) makes the $N = 8$, an even number. There are now two middle values, 11 and 16. The median is the arithmetical average of the two scores; $(11 + 16)/2 = 13.5$.

The procedure for determining the median when several subjects have the same score is somewhat more complicated. The data in Table 13.2 are arranged in group intervals of 5 where

Table 13.2/ Computation of the Median

X	f	Cf
85–89	1	92
80–84	2	91
75–79	3	89
70–74		86
65–69	4	86
60–64	10	82
55–59	5	72
50–54	6	67
45–49	8	61
40–44	13	53
35–39	16	40
30–34	15	24
25–29	7	9
20–24	1	2
15–19	1	1

many cases fall at each score. The following computational procedures apply for any group interval size.

1/
Determine the appropriate class intervals for the data and set up a frequency table (see Table 13.2).

2/

Since our concern is with the fiftieth percentile, we need to determine that score below which 50 per cent of the cases fall. To determine the exact number of cases up to the centile desired, multiply N, which is 92, by the value of the centile. In this case, 50 per cent of 92 is 46.

3/

Next to the frequency column make another column and label it Cf (cumulative frequency). Starting at the bottom, add the frequencies for each class interval, placing each successive sum in the next row.

4/

Examination of the Cf column shows that there are 40 cases between the interval 15–19 and the interval 35–39. But adding the frequency in the next step interval gives a sum greater than 46. Therefore, we know that the desired score is somewhere in the interval 40–44. The problem is to determine what proportion of the cases in that interval will give us the required 46.

5/

Six cases are needed from the next interval 40–44, the desired 46 less the 40 cases included below this interval. Since the frequency in the next interval is 13, we need 6/13 or 0.46 of these cases.

6/

The proportion of cases determined in step 5 is based on an interval width of 1, whereas our interval size is 5. Therefore, we must convert this proportion into units equal to the class interval by multiplying the proportion by 5; $0.46 \times 5 = 2.30$.

7/

Adding 2.30 to the bottom real limit of the interval 40–46, which is 39.5, gives the desired median score 41.80.

$$\text{Median} = 39.5 + 6/13 \ (5)$$
$$= 41.80$$

The median provides a satisfactory estimate of central tendency and is especially satisfactory when the frequency distribution contains a few extreme scores (scores which are far removed from the center of the distribution). The value of the median is not distorted by extreme scores, as is the mean, because it is not influenced by the *magnitude* of the deviant scores but only by the frequency with which such scores occur. Use of the mean in this situation would grossly distort the "true" average.

In terms of sampling fluctuation, the median is superior to the mode but less stable than the mean. For this reason, and because the median does not possess convenient algebraic properties, it is not used as often as the mean.

The Mean

The "mean" M is defined as the sum of all the scores ΣfX divided by the total number of scores N.

$$M = \frac{\Sigma fX}{N} \tag{1}$$

shows this definition in statistical shorthand. Thus, ΣfX means the sum of the products of each score multiplied by the frequency with which the score occurs, N is the number of scores or subjects, and M is the mean. When a calculator is available, formula (1) is an efficient method of computing the mean.

When the data are arranged in a frequency distribution with any class interval size, the arithmetic involved in the computation of the mean can be reduced by the use of deviations from an arbitrary origin (AO). Consider the following distribution of weights of nine 10-year-old boys: 85, 86, 87, 88, 89, 90, 91, 92, 93. Each score has a frequency of 1. We can compute the mean by use of formula (1); $\Sigma fX = 801$, which when divided by $N = 9$, gives a mean of 89. Since 85 is the lowest weight in the distribution, we can consider it as a base score from which all the other scores deviate. In this example, the score of 85 is the AO and its deviation score (x') is zero. The next-highest score of 86 deviates 1 step interval from 85 and thus has a deviation score of 1. A score of 87 deviates 2 step intervals from AO and thus has a deviation score of 2. Following the same procedure for each score gives the following distribution of deviation scores: 0, 1, 2, 3, 4, 5, 6, 7, 8. If we determine the mean of these deviations and then add the mean deviation to the base score of 85, we obtain the mean of the original distribution. Thus, $\Sigma X' = 36$ which, divided by $N = 9$, gives the mean deviation score of 4. The final step is to add 4 to the AO, $4 + 85 = 89$.

It does not matter where in the distribution the AO is located. In the previous example the AO could just as readily have been set at the score of 90. Now the distribution of deviations would include negative scores, $-5, -4, -3, -2, -1, 0, 1, 2, 3$, which, when summed algebraically, give a value for fx' of -9. Dividing by $N = 9$ gives a mean deviation score of -1. Subtracting from the AO of 90 gives the mean, 89.

When the data are arranged with a class interval larger than 1, as shown in Table 13.3, the same procedures are employed, with the exception that the midpoint of the interval is the AO. Thus, the scores in Table 13.3 should be viewed as progressing

Table 13.3/ Computation of the Mean Using Deviation Scores

X	f	x'	fx'
85–89	1	14	14
80–84	2	13	26
75–79	3	12	36
70–74	0	11	0
65–69	4	10	40
60–64	10	9	90
55–59	5	8	40
50–54	6	7	42
45–49	8	6	48
40–44	13	5	65
35–39	16	4	64
30–34	15	3	45
25–29	7	2	14
20–24	1	1	1
15–19	1	0	0
Total	92	..	525

from 17 to 22 to 27 to . . . to 87. The first step is the selection of the AO, which can be any class interval, and assigning it a deviation score value of 0. The AO selected in Table 13.3 is the bottom interval because it avoids the use of negative numbers.

The formula for obtaining the mean using deviation scores is

$$M = \text{AO} + i\frac{fx'}{N} \qquad (2)$$

where AO = arbitrary origin
  i = size of class interval
  fx' = sum of deviation score times frequency with which it occurs
  N = number of cases

Notice that each deviation score is multiplied by the frequency with which it occurs. These values are then summed and divided by N. The result, 5.71 in this example, is the mean of the deviation scores. This value means that the deviation score mean is 5.71 units above the AO in deviation units. But each deviation score unit is equal to 5 units of original scores. Therefore,

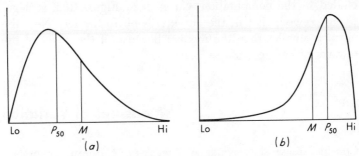

Figure 13.2/ (*a*) A positively skewed distribution and (*b*) a negatively skewed distribution. (Lo and Hi refer to scores.)

the next step is the conversion of the deviation mean into the original score units with a class interval of 5. This involves multiplying the deviation mean by the class interval size; $5(5.71) = 28.55$. The final step is adding the converted deviation mean to the midpoint of the AO:

$$M = 17 + 28.55 = 45.55$$

With the exception of the situation where extreme scores occur in the distribution, the mean is generally the best measure of central tendency. The value of the mean tends to fluctuate least from sample to sample and it possesses known mathematical relationships with other statistics. Thus, in most situations the mean is more likely to be used than either the mode or the median.

The mean can be conceptualized as a fulcrum such that the distribution of scores around it is in perfect balance. Since the scores above and below the mean are in perfect balance, it follows that the algebraic sum of the deviations of these scores from the mean is 0. Whereas the median counts each score, no matter what its magnitude, as only one score, the mean takes into account the absolute magnitude of the score. The median, therefore, does not balance the halves of the distribution except when the distribution is exactly symmetrical, in which case the mean and the median have identical values.

Another way of contrasting the median and the mean is to compare their values when the distribution of scores is not symmetrical. Curve *a* of Figure 13.2 is positively skewed; that is, the curve tails off to the right. In this case the mean is larger than the median because of the influence of the few very high scores. Thus these high scores are sufficient to balance off the several lower scores. The median does not balance the distribution because the magnitude (weight) of the scores is not included in the computation. Curve b of Figure 13.2 is negatively skewed; that is, the curve tails off to the left. Now the mean is smaller than the median because of the effect of the few very small scores.

Measures of Variation

Consider these statements: A 2-week-old full-term infant is 7 pounds underweight. A 22-year-old woman is 7 pounds underweight. The first statement seems almost ridiculous whereas the second is not unusual. The first statement is silly because we know that the variation in weight, in pound units, is quite small at 2 weeks of age. Weight variation at 22 years is substantially larger, so that being 7 pounds underweight is not unusual. In both instances our reactions were based on an implicit knowledge of the expected variation at each age.

Similarly, in considering the outcome of an experiment it is important to know how much variation occurred within the sample. This information is important for estimating how much variation to expect when a particular experimental procedure is used on another sample and for communicating the characteristics of the sample. For example, two groups with the same mean IQs but different ranges of ability may require quite different teaching methods. We shall now examine four methods for determining variability.

The Range

The range is the easiest technique for estimating variability, but unfortunately, it only provides a crude and unreliable estimation. It is determined by subtracting the lowest score from the highest score. The larger the difference the greater the spread of scores. A single score which is unusually high or low would lead the investigator to conclude that more variation exists than might actually be the case. For this reason the range is rarely reported in the research literature.

The Semi-interquartile Range

The semi-interquartile range is defined as the difference between the 75th percentile and the 25th percentile divided by 2. Since the two percentiles cut off the upper and lower 25 per cent of the distribution, it can be seen that it is less influenced by unusually high or low scores than the range. Actually the semi-interquartile range provides a good estimate of variability, but is not generally used because it does not enter into convenient algebraic relationships with other more advanced statistical techniques.

The Average Deviation

The average deviation (AD) is a more precise estimate of variability than the semi-interquartile range because its computation depends upon the deviation of all the individual scores from the mean. It is computed by subtracting each score in the distribution from the mean, summing the resulting deviations, and dividing by N. The problem is that the algebraic sum of the deviations around the mean is zero. Therefore, when computing the AD, the algebraic sign is disregarded. Consider the following distribution of scores: 6, 10, 8, 4, 14, 12. The mean of the distribution is 9.00. Subtracting 9.00 from each of the scores in the distribution gives the following deviation scores: -3, 1, -1, -5, 5, 3, which when summed are equal to zero. Disregarding the algebraic sign gives us a sum of deviations equal to 18; dividing by $N = 6$ gives an AD of 3. Notice that every score entered into the computation.

The AD can be interpreted as the average distance between the mean and the scores in the distribution. The larger the AD, the larger is the spread of scores, or variability, in the distribution and, therefore, the greater is the distance between the mean and the average deviation of all the scores. This technique provides a reasonably stable estimate of variation but because it lacks algebraic properties (disregarding the direction of the deviation), it cannot be used with other more advanced statistical techniques.

The Standard Deviation

A major objection to the use of the AD was the fact that the direction of the deviations of the scores from their mean is disregarded. This was necessary, it will be recalled, because the sum of the deviations of the scores around their mean is 0. It is possible to overcome this obstacle, however, by squaring the deviations and then summing the squared deviations. This procedure removes the negative numbers because when two negative numbers are multiplied the resulting product is a positive number; that is, -4 multiplied by -4 equals $+16$. Consider the distribution of deviations used as an illustration of the AD: -3, 1, -1, -5, 5, 3. Squaring each of these deviation scores gives us 9, 1, 1, 25, 25, 9. The sum of these deviations is 70. As in the case of the AD, this sum is divided by N, which is 6. The resulting number is 11.67 and is called the "mean square deviation," or the "variance," symbolized by s^2. The arithmetical operations performed in computing the variance may be written in statistical symbols:

$$s^2 = \frac{\Sigma x^2}{N} \tag{3}$$

where s^2 = variance
   Σx^2 = sum of the squared deviations of each score from its mean
   N = number of cases

The variance is a useful index of variation but it is a square rather than a linear measure. Converting the variance to a linear measure requires taking the square root of it, and this operation gives us the root mean square deviation or the *standard deviation s*. The formula for the standard deviation is

$$s = \sqrt{\frac{\Sigma x^2}{N}} \tag{4}$$

If we now take the square root of the variance, 11.67, we obtain the standard deviation which equals 3.42.

The essential term in formula (4) is Σx^2, which is the sum of the squared deviations around the mean and is frequently referred to as the "sum of squares." To compute the sum of squares by subtracting each score from its mean is tedious and provides too many opportunities for error. There are, fortunately, two more direct approaches available. Formula (4a) involves the original raw scores and requires a calculator:

$$\Sigma x^2 = \Sigma X^2 - \frac{(\Sigma X)^2}{N} \tag{4a}$$

where ΣX^2 is the sum of the squared scores and $(\Sigma X)^2$ is the sum of the scores, squared. Substitution of the obtained sum of squares into formula (4) gives the desired s.

As an example of the procedure, we will recompute the s used earlier in this section, using formula (4a) to determine Σx^2. The original scores were 6, 10, 8, 4, 14, 12. To obtain ΣX^2 we square each of these scores and sum: 36, 100, 64, 16, 196, 144. The term $(\Sigma X)^2/N$ is obtained by first summing original scores (this is done when computing the mean) and then squaring this sum. The sum of scores is 54 which, when squared, is 2,916. This number is then divided by $N = 6$ and the result is 486. The Σx^2 is equal to $556 - 486 = 70$ and is identical in value to the Σx^2 computed directly. The Σx^2 is then substituted in formula (4) to obtain s.

When a calculator is not available and the data are grouped into class intervals, it is possible to determine s by using deviations from an arbitrary origin. The data in Table 13.4 are the same as those in Table 13.3

Table 13.4/ Computation of the Standard Deviation Using Deviation Scores

X	f	x'	fx'	fx'^{2}
85–89	1	14	14	196
80–84	2	13	26	338
75–79	3	12	36	432
70–74	0	11	0	0
65–69	4	10	40	400
60–64	10	9	90	810
55–59	5	8	40	320
50–54	6	7	42	294
45–49	8	6	48	288
40–44	13	5	65	325
35–39	16	4	64	256
30–34	15	3	45	135
25–29	7	2	14	28
20–24	1	1	1	1
15–19	1	0	0	0
Total	92		525	3,823

with the additional column fx'^2.

Step 1/ Compute the sum of squares:

$$\Sigma x^2 = \left[\Sigma fx'^2 - \frac{(\Sigma fx')^2}{N} \right] i^2 \qquad (4b)$$

where $\Sigma fx'^2$ = sum of the products of fx' multiplied by x'
$\Sigma fx'$ = sum of the frequencies times the deviation from the arbitrary origin
i^2 = square of the class interval size

Step 2/ Compute s:

$$s = \sqrt{\frac{\Sigma x^2}{N}}$$

The following computation is based on the distribution shown in Table 13.4.

Step 1/

$$\Sigma x^2 = \left[3823 - \frac{(525)^2}{92} \right] (5)^2$$
$$= 827.08 \ (25)$$
$$= 20677.00$$

Step 2/

$$s = \sqrt{\frac{20677.00}{92 - 1}}$$
$$= 15.07$$

The bracketed portion of formula (4b) gives Σx^2 in interval units which must be transformed into score units. This transformation is achieved by multiplying the bracketed expression by the square of the width interval i^2.

Conceptualizing the s, or any of the measures of variation, is more difficult than understanding the concept of central tendency. From one point of view, however, the s is similar to the mean; that is, it represents the mean of the squared deviations. Taking the mean and the standard deviation together, a sample can be described in terms of its average score and in terms of its average variation. If more samples were taken from the same population it would be possible to predict with some accuracy the average score of these samples and also the amount of variation.

Another way of conceptualizing the s is to think in terms of units of distance. Unlike the mean, the median, and the mode, which are points on the distribution, the s is a unit of distance from the mean. In very large and normally distributed samples, these units include known proportions of the population. For example, the distance from the mean to 1 standard deviation above the mean includes approximately 34 per cent of the scores in the total distribution. The distance from 1 s below the mean to 1 s above the mean includes 68 per cent of the scores in the total distribution. Figure 13.3 shows the various percentages included within different units of distance. These percentages are theoretical and only rarely does it occur that the actual percentages from real data coincide with the theoretical.

The standard deviation is the most widely used estimate of

variation because of its known algebraic properties and its amenability to use with other statistics. It also provides a better estimate of variation in the population than the other indexes. Finally, the numerical value of the standard deviation is likely to fluctuate less from sample to sample than the other indexes.

Applications of the s

The s is extremely important in sampling theory (discussed in Chapter 14), in correlational analysis, in estimating reliability of measures, and in determining relative position of an individual within a distribution of scores and between distributions of scores. The present discussion focuses on the last of these applications, and the others are included in later sections of this and the succeeding chapter.

Suppose a sixth-grader obtains a raw score of 70 on both an arithmetic and a vocabulary test. Further assume that the means of the two distributions of test scores are 50, with an s of 10 for arithmetic and an s of 15 for vocabulary. It is impossible to determine from these data the relative standing of the child because the two test scores are derived from different score units. In general, it is not possible to compare any sets of measurements unless they are derived from identical units of measurement. One procedure for transforming sets of scores with different units of measurement is to convert them into standard deviation units. Such transformed scores are called "standard scores" and denoted by the symbol z.

As a basis for understanding z scores, consider the terms in

$$z = \frac{X - M}{s} = \frac{x}{s} \tag{5}$$

which is the computational procedure for determining standard scores. The term $X - M$ indicates that the mean is subtracted from each original score. Thus, if a score is equal to the mean, the deviation x is 0 and the resulting z score is also 0. Recall, however, that the sum of the deviations of the scores around their mean equals 0 and since, in formula (5), the deviation of each score around the mean is involved, it follows that the mean of a distribution of z scores is also 0. Next, consider the fact that each deviation x is divided by s. The effect of this procedure is to give the distribution of standard scores a standard deviation of 1, or unity. The illustrative distribution of scores used earlier in our discussion is converted into z scores in Table 13.5. The mean of the z scores was determined by summing each standard score and dividing by N. The s was computed by means of formulas (4) and (4a).

Table 13.5/ Transformation of Original Scores into z Scores

X	X − M = x	z = x/s	
6	−3	−0.88	$M = \dfrac{\Sigma z}{N} = \dfrac{0.00}{6} = 0.00$
10	1	+0.29	
8	−1	−0.29	
4	−5	−1.47	$s = \sqrt{\dfrac{\Sigma x^2}{N}} = \sqrt{\dfrac{6.04}{6}} = 1.00$
14	5	+1.47	
12	3	+0.88	
Σ 54	0	0.00	*3.42*

Since the z scores in Table 13.5 have a mean of 0 and an s of 1, it is possible to describe each score in terms of its distance from the mean. Thus, an original score of 10 is 0.29 standard deviation units above the mean, whereas an original score of 4 is 1.47 standard deviation units below the mean. The algebraic sign preceding each z score immediately indicates whether the original score is above the mean (signified by a plus sign) or below the mean (signified by a minus sign). Returning to the original problem concerning the sixth-grader's performance in arithmetic when compared to vocabulary, the computations of his z scores for each subject are

Arithmetic
$$z = \frac{70 - 50}{10} = 2.00$$

Vocabulary
$$z = \frac{70 - 50}{15} = 1.33$$

These scores indicate a higher relative standing in arithmetic than in vocabulary. It is also clear that he is above the mean in both subjects.

Variations of standard scores are used in reporting test scores, especially commercially published tests of achievement and aptitude. One of the difficulties with z scores is that they involve negative numbers and decimals. To overcome this difficulty, it is common to multiply standard scores by 10 (to enlarge the standard deviation from 1 to 10) and add 50 to the result. Since the mean of a distribution of z scores is 0, the

Work

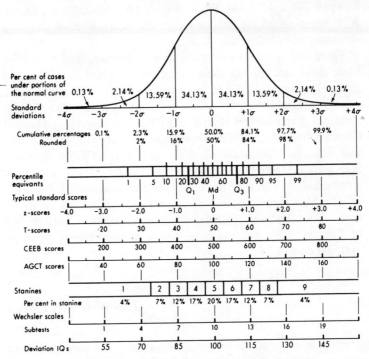

Figure 13.3/ Relationships among various types of derived scores.

effect of adding 50 is to expand the scale such that the mean is 50. This variation on a standard score is called a T score. The computations involved are shown by

$$T = 10\frac{X - M}{s} + 50 \qquad (6)$$

Suppose a score was exactly equal to the mean so that the expression $10\frac{X - M}{s}$ equals 0. In this case T equals 50. Now we will work out a T score for an original score of 4, taken from the distribution of original scores in Table 13.5. This score has a deviation of -5; dividing by $s = 3.42$ gives a z score of -1.47.

$$T = 10\frac{4 - 9}{3.42} + 50 = 10(-1.47) + 50 = -14.70 + 50.00$$
$$T = 35.30$$

Multiplying by 10 gives -14.70. Since this is a negative number, it is subtracted from 50 and the T score is 35.30. Using the same procedure we can compute T scores for each original score in Table 13.5: 41.20, 52.90, 47.10, 35.30, 54.70, 58.80. A T score of 35.30 indicates that the score is 1.47 standard deviation units below the mean.

There are several other variations of the standard score, the basic difference among them being the standard deviation and mean. In Figure 13.3 the relationship between some of these variations is shown. We will now examine briefly the College Entrance Examination Board (CEEB) and the Army General Classification Test (AGCT) system of standard scores. You will note that the standard score system for CEEB scores is 500 with a standard deviation of 100. The AGCT system of standard scores has a mean of 100 and a standard deviation of 20. Most intelligence scales yield IQs based on deviation units. The Wechsler Intelligence Scales (see the bottom line of Figure 13.3), for example, use a system with a mean of 100 and an s of 15.

The Normal Curve

Suppose it is possible to obtain measures on some particular trait or characteristic of man in which the sample comprised at least 1 million people. The resulting data are then organized in a frequency distribution, and finally a frequency polygon is constructed. The shape of this polygon can be almost anything, depending upon how the trait is distributed in the population. Thus we might find a U-shaped distribution, a J-shaped distribution, a bimodal distribution, or a normal distribution. With so many cases included in the sample, it is fairly certain that all the curves will be smooth, especially if the class interval is small.

Our concern will be with the normal distribution because much of the work in statistical inference relates to the normal curve. There is the additional fact that many traits usually measured in education distribute themselves normally, or nearly so. It should be understood, however, that the properties of the normal curve are theoretical and will not exactly fit data derived from actual experiments.

Properties of the Normal Curve

The normal curve is frequently described as bell-shaped because of its characteristic roundness at the top and inflections on each side (see Figure 13.4). The tails of the curve are

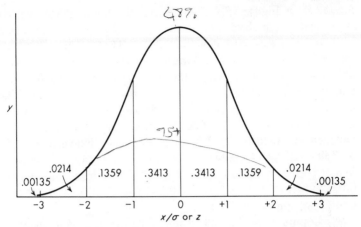

Figure 13.4/ Normal curve showing areas between ordinates at different values of x or z. (*From George A. Ferguson, Statistical Analysis in Psychology and Education, New York: McGraw-Hill Book Company, 1959, p. 81.*)

asymptotic to the base line; that is, the tails of the curve theoretically never touch the base line. A normal curve can be plotted by the following formula:

$$y = \frac{N}{s\sqrt{2\pi}} e - \frac{(x)^2}{2s^2} \tag{7}$$

where y = height of curve for any value of X
$\quad\quad \pi$ = 3.1416, a mathematical constant
$\quad\quad s$ = standard deviation of distribution
$\quad\quad e$ = 2.71828, a mathematical constant
$\quad\quad N$ = number of cases; also corresponds to the total area under the curve
$\quad\quad x$ = deviation of a score (x) from the mean

The height of the normal curve y can be determined for any value of X by substituting in formula (7).

Area under the Normal Curve/ In defining the terms used in formula (7), the comment was made with respect to N that it corresponds to the total area under the curve. In theoretical terms the area under the normal curve represents every possible event, score, or, in general terms, entity that exists in a population. Again theoretically, the possible number of such entities is infinite. Thus, when N relates to people, the curve assumes all possible people.

The area relationships under the normal curve are graphically presented in Figure 13.4. Notice that the abscissa (base line) is defined in standard score units ($z = x/s$) so that the mean is 0 and the standard deviation is 1.[2] The numbers between the ordinates (vertical lines) represent proportions of the total area under the curve. Thus, the area between 0 and $+1z$ includes approximately 34 per cent of the total area under the curve. A similar proportion exists between 0 and $-1z$, so that approximately 68 per cent of the area (or of the entities) is included between $\pm 1z$. The area included between $\pm 2z$ is $0.1359 + 0.3413 + 0.3413 + 0.1359 = 0.9544$, or approximately 95 per cent of the area. The area between $\pm 3z$ is $0.0214 + 0.1359 + 0.3413 + 0.3413 + 0.1359 + 0.0214 = 0.9972$, or almost all the area.

A commonly used practice derived from the relationship of the area under the normal curve involves estimating percentile ranks. In this situation, the area above or below any point on the base line is involved. Suppose, as an example, a student's z score on a nationally standardized achievement test was $+1.00$. The area between 0 and $+1z$ is approximately 0.34. The total area below the ordinate 0, which is actually the mean, must be 0.50 because the mean in a normal distribution cuts the distribution exactly in half. Thus the total area below the student's z score is $0.50 + 0.34 = 0.84$, which when multiplied by 100 shows that the student is as good as or better than 84 per cent of the people in a specific population. In turn, some 16 per cent performed better than he did.

This is another example of a student's achieving a z score of -2. In this case the area below $-2z$ is 0.022; multiplying by 100 places the student at the second percentile. The relationship between the various transformed standard scores and percentiles are shown in Figure 13.3.

The Table of the Normal Curve/ A property of the normal curve, noted in the last section, is that of continuity; that is, the curve is smooth and continuous. Because of this continuity it is possible to determine the area between ordinates for an infinite number of z-score values. These values have been tabled and appear in Table A of Appendix A. For the sake of convenience, one page of this table is reproduced in Table 13.6 and we shall now examine its properties.

Column A of the table contains standard score ($z = x/s$)

2/ It can be demonstrated that if scores are normally distributed around the mean, the distribution of the deviations around the mean is also normal.

Table 13.6/ Areas under the Normal Curve

A	B	C	D
z or x/s	Area: M to z	Area: q Smaller	y or Ordinate
1.50	0.43319	0.06681	0.1295
1.55	0.43943	0.06057	0.1200
1.60	0.44520	0.05480	0.1109
1.65	0.45053	0.04947	0.1023
1.70	0.45543	0.04457	0.0940
1.75	0.45994	0.04056	0.0863
1.80	0.46407	0.03593	0.0790
1.85	0.46784	0.03216	0.0721
1.90	0.47128	0.02872	0.0656
1.95	0.47441	0.02559	0.0596
2.00	0.47725	0.02275	0.0540
2.05	0.47982	0.02018	0.0488
2.10	0.48214	0.01786	0.0440
2.15	0.48422	0.01578	0.0396
2.20	0.48610	0.01390	0.0355
2.25	0.48778	0.01222	0.0317
2.30	0.48928	0.01072	0.0283
2.35	0.49061	0.00939	0.0252
2.40	0.49180	0.00820	0.0224
2.45	0.49286	0.00714	0.0198
2.50	0.49379	0.00621	0.0175
2.55	0.49461	0.00539	0.0154
2.60	0.49534	0.00466	0.0136
2.65	0.49598	0.00402	0.0119
2.70	0.49653	0.00347	0.0104
2.75	0.49702	0.00298	0.0091
2.80	0.49744	0.00256	0.0079
2.85	0.49781	0.00219	0.0069
2.90	0.49813	0.00187	0.0060
2.95	0.49841	0.00159	0.0051
3.00	0.49865	0.00135	0.0044
3.25	0.49942	0.00058	0.0020
3.50	0.49977	0.00023	0.0090
3.75	0.49991	0.00009	0.0004
4.00	0.49997	0.00003	0.0001

values computed by methods already described in this chapter. Column B, M to z, refers to the proportion of area between the mean (on Figure 13.4 the mean z score is 0) and the value of the z score. As a check on the comparability of the values shown in Figure 13.4 with those in Table 13.6, we shall determine from the tabled values the proportion of area between $\pm 2z$. We first enter column A of Table 13.6 and locate $z = 2.00$. The proportion of area indicated in column B is 0.47725. This figure is the proportion of area between M and either $+2z$ or $-2z$, but we want the area between $\pm 2z$. Since the curve is symmetrical we can multiply the value by 2; the result is 0.95450, or approximately 0.95, which is identical to the area derived from the curve. The same procedure gives the proportion of area between the mean and any z value.

In considering the meaning of the area proportions in column C, remember that an ordinate erected from any point along the base line divides the curve into two parts. An ordinate erected at the mean divides the curve exactly in half, but for all other values of z the curve is divided into two unequal parts. For example, in Figure 13.4, the area to the *left* of $z = +1$ is larger than the area to the *right*. Column C refers to the smaller of the two areas. Similarly, the area to the left of $z = -2$ is smaller than the area to the right. Suppose we wanted to know what proportion of area existed beyond a standard score of 1.95. Enter column A with $z = 1.95$ and move across to column C. The proportion of area beyond $z = 1.95$, then, is 0.02559. Because the curve is symmetrical the same area proportion exists for $z = -1.95$.

It is also possible to estimate percentile ranks using column C of the normal curve table. As an example, take $z = 1.95$. Since approximately $0.03 \times 100 = 3$ per cent of the area lies beyond this point and we know that the total area to the right of $z = 0$ is 0.50, then the proportion of area between $z = 0$ and $z = +1.95$ is $0.50 - 0.03 = 0.47 \times 100 = 47$ per cent. We also know that 50 per cent of the area lies *below* $z = 0$; therefore, $0.50 + 0.47 = 0.97 \times 100 = 97$th percentile. Now suppose $z = -1.50$. Column C shows a proportion of area of approximately 0.06; that is, 0.06 of the total area is below $z = -1.50$. $z = -1.50$ then corresponds to a percentile rank of $0.06 \times 100 = 6$th percentile.

Column D refers to the height of the ordinate for any z-score value along the base line. Although these values are of importance to understanding the mathematical properties of the normal curve, they are used infrequently in most statistical techniques.

Correlation

The discussion so far has been concerned exclusively with the distribution of a single variable. Very frequently, however, there is interest in examining the degree of *relationship* existing between two variables. For example, at the beginning of the school year when a teacher examines the distribution of IQ scores of her new students, she does so with the more or less implicit assumption that some relationship exists between intellectual ability and academic performance. (Of course, the more sophisticated teacher understands that this relationship is far from perfect and that an innumerable array of variables influences academic performance.) The teacher also uses this assumed relationship to *predict* the academic performance of the children in her classroom. Thus, knowing that a positive relationship exists between IQ and achievement, she anticipates (predicts) that those children with higher IQ scores will attain higher achievement scores than the children with the lower IQs.

Whenever two measurements for the same individual can be paired for all the individuals in a group, the degree of relationship between the paired scores is called the "correlation." The most widely used measure of the relationship between two variables is the *product moment correlation coefficient r.*

The Concept of Correlation

Suppose we have two measures, X and Y, on each of 10 children. The data are arranged, as shown in Table 13.7, such that the scores for the X variable are ordered from the highest to the lowest score. Data for the Y variable are arranged in three different ways corresponding to the column headings A, B, and C. The data in column A show that each subject attains the same score on both variables.[3] Thus the child with the highest score on X also has the highest score on Y; conversely, the child with the lowest score on X has the lowest score on Y. You will note that each score on X corresponds exactly with the Y score. When this occurs, there is a perfect relationship between the variables. The direction of this relationship is positive because an increase in value for the X scores results

---

3/ Situations where the same scores occur on both variables seldom, if ever, occur with real data. These data are intended only to serve as illustrations of possible relationships between two variables.

in a corresponding increase in the Y scores. As you shall see in the next section, a perfect positive relationship is indicated by a correlation coefficient r of $+1.00$, the maximum value.

Table 13.7/ Paired Scores for Three Levels of Correlation

Subject	A		B		C	
	X	Y	X	Y	X	Y
1	10	10	10	1	10	9
2	9	9	9	2	9	4
3	8	8	8	3	8	3
4	7	7	7	4	7	1
5	6	6	6	5	6	10
6	5	5	5	6	5	2
7	4	4	4	7	4	7
8	3	3	3	8	3	8
9	2	2	2	9	2	6
10	1	1	1	10	1	5

We can also represent the data in column A graphically, as shown in Figure 13.5a. Notice that the entries for this figure involve placing *two* scores, X and its corresponding Y, in each cell. The resulting distribution of scores is called a *bivariate frequency distribution* (see page 358 for a more detailed example) and shows the general trend of the scores. Graph a depicts a single line of dots because the relationship is perfect; that is, $r = 1.00$. A more typical distribution would show dots (scores) falling around an imaginary line, in which case the degree of relationship would be less than perfect.

The scores in column B of Table 13.7 show that the person obtaining the highest score on the X variable has the lowest score on the Y variable. Conversely, the lowest score on the X variable corresponds to the highest score on the Y variable. This relationship, shown in Figure 13.5b is called a "negative relationship." As in the case of the column A data, the relationship is perfect (maximal) and corresponds to an r of -1.00.[4] A more likely negative relationship would show a distribution of scores that varied around an imaginary straight line.

Column C of Table 13.7 shows paired scores between

4/ Again, perfectly related variables seldom, if ever, occur.

which the relationship is essentially nonexistent; that is, scores on the X variable are independent of scores on the Y variable. Figure 13.5c is a bivariate frequency distribution where

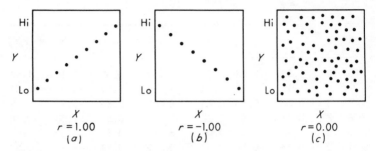

Figure 13.5/ Scatter Plots for Three Levels of Correlation.

$r = 0.00$. You will note that the scores fall all over the surface of the graph in such a way that a change in one variable is unrelated to the other variable.

The Product Moment Correlation r

The product moment correlation is an index of relationship that can take values from -1.00 to $+1.00$. The meaning of these values was shown in columns A and B of Table 13.7, where the means and standard deviations of the X and Y variables were identical. It is much more likely, however, that the means and standard deviations for each variable will be different. In that case, you will recall from the discussion of standard scores, the original scores are transformed into z scores so that the two variables have identical means and standard deviations. For each subject there are two z scores, one for the X variable and one for the Y variable. Using the paired z scores, the product moment correlation can be defined as the average product of the paired z scores divided by N. The definitional formula of r is

$$r = \frac{\Sigma z_x z_y}{N} \tag{8}$$

It can be shown algebraically that the maximum value of the term $\Sigma z_x z_y$ is attained when, for each pair of z scores, $z_x = z_y$. It can also be shown that when the z scores for each pair are identical, the sum of their products equals N.

We shall now compute r using formula (8) and the data for columns A and C in Table 13.7. The necessary computations are summarized in Table 13.8. The means and standard deviations for the X and Y variables are identical: $M = 5.5$, $s = 2.9$.

Table 13.8 / Computation of the Product Moment r Using Standard Scores

A					C				
X	Y	z_x	z_y	$z_x z_y$	X	Y	z_x	z_y	$z_x z_y$
10	10	1.53	1.53	2.34	10	9	1.53	1.19	1.82
9	9	1.19	1.19	1.43	9	4	1.19	−0.51	−0.61
8	8	0.85	0.85	0.73	8	3	0.85	−0.85	−0.72
7	7	0.51	0.51	0.27	7	1	0.51	−1.53	−0.78
6	6	0.17	0.17	0.04	6	10	0.17	1.53	0.26
5	5	−0.17	−0.17	0.04	5	2	−0.17	−1.19	0.20
4	4	−0.51	−0.51	0.27	4	7	−0.51	0.51	−0.26
3	3	−0.85	−0.85	0.73	3	8	−0.85	0.85	−0.72
2	2	−1.19	−1.19	1.43	2	6	−1.19	0.17	−0.20
1	1	−1.53	−1.53	2.34	1	5	−1.53	−0.17	0.26
Σ55	55	0.00	0.00	9.62	55	55	0.00	0.00	−0.75

The z scores for each variable were determined in the usual way [see formula (5), page 345]. The column headed $z_x z_y$ stands for the products of the z scores for the X and Y variables. The sum of the products of the paired z scores for the data in column A is 9.62. Dividing by $N = 10$ gives $r = 0.96$ (the r does not equal 1.00 because of rounding errors). The sum of the paired z scores for the data in column C is −0.75. Dividing by $N = 10$ gives $r = -0.07$.

Computation of r/ Fortunately, the product moment r can be computed without the tedious process of computing separate z scores. A variety of formulas exist for the computation of r, each of which is derived from the basic definitional formula. The following formula is used whenever a calculator is available:

$$r = \frac{N\Sigma XY - (\Sigma X)(\Sigma Y)}{\sqrt{N\Sigma X^2 - \Sigma X^2}\sqrt{N\Sigma Y^2 - \Sigma Y^2}} \tag{9}$$

For illustrative purposes we will compute the data in column C of Table 13.8 by using the raw scores. The terms ΣX and ΣY in formula (9) refer to the sums of the original scores for the X and Y variables, respectively; ΣX^2 and ΣY^2 are the sums of the squared scores for the X and Y variables; ΣXY is the sum of the products of the paired X and Y scores; N is the total number of pairs. Performing the required arithmetic results in the following sums: $\Sigma X = 55$, $\Sigma Y = 55$, $\Sigma X^2 = 385$, $\Sigma Y^2 = 385$, $\Sigma XY = 296$. Substituting in formula (9) we have

$$r = \frac{10(296) - (55)(55)}{\sqrt{10(385) - (55)^2}\ \sqrt{10(385) - (55)^2}}$$

$$= \frac{-0.65}{\sqrt{825}\ \sqrt{825}} = \frac{-0.65}{825}$$

$$= -0.07$$

The resulting r is identical to that obtained using formula (9).

Without a calculator, the operations involved in computing r from original data are time consuming. A more convenient arrangement is to organize the data in a bivariate frequency distribution, as shown in Table 13.9, and compute r using deviations from an arbitrary origin. Examination of the following formula:

$$r = \frac{N\Sigma x'y' - (\Sigma x')(\Sigma y')}{\sqrt{N\Sigma x'^2 - (\Sigma x')^2}\ \sqrt{N\Sigma y'^2 - (\Sigma y')^2}} \qquad (9a)$$

which is used in computing r from an arbitrary origin, shows that the only new term is $\Sigma x'y'$—the sum of the products of the paired deviations from an arbitrary origin.

The data shown in Table 13.9 are the scores of 92 sixth-grade pupils on the Verbal Scale of the Primary Mental Abilities Test (PMA), the X variable, and an achievement test score, the Y variable. Table 13.9 is arranged such that the columns (numbered 1 to 6) refer to the achievement scores and the rows (also numbered 1 to 6 at the bottom of the table) refer to the PMA scores. Column 1 and row 1 are the frequencies with which each score occurs; column 2 and row 2 are the deviations x' and y' from the arbitrary origin; column 3 and row 3 are the products of the deviation times the frequencies; column 4 and row 4 are the products of column 2 times column 3, and row 2 times row 3. These manipulations are already familiar from the discussion of the mean and the standard deviation. The entries in column 5 are the sums of the x' values for a constant y' value; the entries in row 5 are the y' values for a constant x' value. Thus for a y' value of 12, the sum of the x' values is $13 + 11 + 10 = 34$. For an x' value of 11, the sum of the y' values is $12 + 9 + 5 = 26$. The sum of the values in column 5 is actually the sum of fx' values (the sum of row 3 equals the sum of column 5) and the sum of the values in row 5 is actually the sum of fy' values (the sum of column 3 equals the

Table 13.9/ Bivariate Frequency

X = Verbal Ability (columns 5–6 through 31–32)
Y = Achievement (row intervals)

Intervals	5–6	7–8	9–10	11–12	13–14	15–16	17–18	19–20	21–22	23–24	25–26	27–28	29–30	31–32	(1) f	(2) y'	(3) fy'	(4) fy'^2	(5) $\Sigma x'$	(6) $y'\Sigma x'$
85–89														/	1	14	14	196	12	168
80–84													/		2	13	26	338	21	273
75–79										/	/	/		/	3	12	36	432	34	408
70–74															0	11	0	0	0	0
65–69							//				//	/	/	//	4	10	40	400	32	320
60–64			/			//		/	/		/				10	9	90	810	77	693
55–59					/	//	//	/			/		/		5	8	40	320	32	256
50–54		/			/	/	/	//	/				/	//	6	7	42	294	35	245
45–49					/		//	//	//						7	6	42	252	64	384
40–44			//	//	/		/		//			/			14	5	70	350	77	385
35–39		//	/	///	////			////	/						16	4	64	256	71	284

X = Verbal Ability

Y = Achievement

Intervals	5-6	7-8	9-10	11-12	13-14	15-16	17-18	19-20	21-22	23-24	25-26	27-28	29-30	31-32	(1) f	(2) y′	(3) fy′	(4) fy′²	(5) Σx′	(6) y′Σx′
30-34	/	/	//	//		/////	//	/	//						15	3	45	135	67	201
25-29	///	/	/				/	/							7	2	14	28	16	32
20-24		/													1	1	1	1	1	1
15-19					/										1	0	0	0	4	0
f (1)	4	5	7	7	10	12	11	11	7	1	5	3	5	4	92		524	3,812	543	3,650
x′ (2)	0	1	2	3	4	5	6	7	8	9	10	11	12	13		Σx′	Σy′	Σy′²	Σx′	Σx′y′
fx′ (3)	0	5	14	21	40	60	66	77	56	9	50	33	60	52	543					
fx′² (4)	0	5	28	63	160	300	396	539	448	81	500	363	720	676	4,279	Σx′²				
Σy′ (5)	9	18	31	28	46	66	65	56	35	13	49	26	49	33	524					
x′Σy′ (6)	0	18	62	84	184	330	390	392	280	117	490	286	588	429	3,650	Σx′y′				

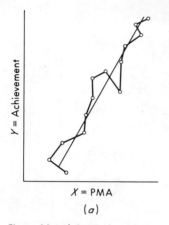

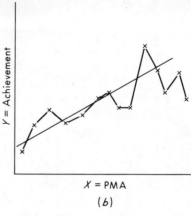

Figure 13.6a/ Regression of X on Y.

Figure 13.6b/ Regression of Y on X.

sum of row 5). The required $\Sigma x'y'$ is determined in column 6 by multiplying the paired values in columns 2 (the y' values) and 5. Similarly, row 6 is obtained by multiplying the paired values in rows 2 and 5. The sums of row 6 and column 6 should be identical.

Substituting the values derived in formula (9a), we obtain

$$r = \frac{92(3650) - (543)(524)}{\sqrt{92(4279) - (543)^2} \sqrt{92(3812) - (524)^2}}$$

$$= 0.58$$

Correlation and Accuracy of Prediction

An examination of the bivariate frequency distribution shows a tendency for high scores on the PMA to be associated with high scores on the achievement test. Similarly low scores on the PMA are associated with low achievement scores. Knowing that a child scored above average on the PMA, we would also expect him to score above average on the achievement. More specific prediction statements can be made than just "above average" if we know the magnitude of r and understand regression.

The Concept of Regression/ Suppose we determine, for each row, the mean PMA score and connect each of the points. The resulting line is uneven (see Figure 13.6a) but we can assume that with the addition of more cases the line would be straighter. This line depicts the rate of change of PMA scores as the achievement scores change and is known as the "regression of the X variable on the Y variable." We can also determine, for each column, the mean achievement score and connect each of the points. Again, the line is uneven (see Figure 13.6b) but it would straighten out with the addition of more cases. This line depicts the rate of change of achievement scores as the PMA scores change and is called the "regression of the Y variable on the X variable." These regression lines show that as each variable increases there is a proportional increase in the other variable.

Because of sampling errors, the means of the columns or rows rarely fall in a straight line. Thus, in constructing a regression line an attempt is made to fit the line to the existing means, that is, to develop a line which passes *near* all the means. The method used in fitting these lines to the data is called the "method of least squares." The formula for the regression of Y on X is

$$Y' = b_{yx}X + a \tag{10}$$

where $Y' = $ predicted score for a particular value of X
$\quad\quad b_{yx} = $ slope of line (that is, angle of line as it cuts Y axis)
$\quad\quad a = $ point where line cuts Y axis
The formula for the regression of X on Y is

$$X' = b_{xy}Y + a \tag{10a}$$

where $X' = $ predicted score for a particular value of Y
$\quad\quad b_{xy} = $ slope of the regression line (that is, the angle of the line as it cuts the X axis)
$\quad\quad a = $ point where line cuts Y axis
By means of algebraic manipulation it can be shown that formulas (10) and (10a) are equivalent to

$$Y' = r\frac{sy}{sx}(X - M_X) + M_Y \tag{11}$$

$$X' = r\frac{sx}{sy}(Y - M_Y) + M_X \tag{11a}$$

which are the equations used when predicting raw scores on one variable from a knowledge of raw scores on the second variable. If Y scores were predicted for each value of X, the resulting points on the bivariate distribution would form a straight line known as the regression of Y on X. A plotting of the predicted X scores for every value of Y would also form a straight line and would be the regression of X on Y.

Accuracy of Prediction

An examination of the bivariate distribution (Table 13.9) indicates that the scores in each of the columns and rows vary around their respective means. Suppose that there had been no variability in any of the columns or rows. Knowing the rate of change of one variable in relation to the other, it would be possible to predict a score for an individual that would be exactly correct; that is, no error would be involved. When the variability around each of the column and row means is zero, the correlation is equal to unity ±1, and perfect predictions are possible.

Correlations of unity rarely if ever occur with real data. The $r = 0.58$ between verbal ability and achievement is typical of the correlations obtained for similar problems. Again, the bivariate distribution will help in understanding the relationship between the size of r and accuracy of prediction. For example, a score of 47 on the achievement test is above the mean achievement test score $(M = 45.55)$. Since the correlation is positive, we automatically expect that a predicted PMA score will also be above the mean $(M = 16.30)$. Notice, however, that the range of scores on the PMA for achievement test scores in the interval 45–49 ranges from 13.5 to 31.5. Using formula (11a), the actual predicted score is 17.3. Thus, all scores other than 17.3 represent errors. The difference between a predicted score and the observed score is called an "error of estimate."

The Standard Error of Estimate/ Consider the situation where $r = 1.00$ so that all predictions will be exactly correct. It follows, then, that the sum of the deviations of the predicted from the observed score $(Y' - Y$ and $X' - X)$ will be 0, no error. The size of the sum of the deviations is dependent upon the standard deviation of scores within the columns or rows; the larger the standard deviation, the larger will be the sum of the deviations and, consequently, the smaller the value of r. The amount of error in a predicted score, then, is the standard deviation of the scores within the particular column or row.

Fortunately, the standard deviation of each column or row need not be computed. On the assumption that the column or row standard deviations are approximately equal, one measure of variability, called the "standard error of estimate," can be used. The formula for the standard error of estimate for predicting X from a knowledge of Y $(s_{x \cdot y})$ is

$$s_{x \cdot y} = s_x \sqrt{1 - r^2} \tag{12}$$

and the formula for the standard error of estimate for predicting Y from a knowledge of $X(s_{y \cdot x})$ is

$$s_{y.x} = s_y \sqrt{1 - r^2} \qquad (12a)$$

The standard error of estimate for predicting a PMA score from a knowledge of an achievement test score is determined from formula (12). This formula is used because we are predicting X from a knowledge of Y.

$$s_{y.x} = 17.1 \sqrt{1 - 0.58^2}$$
$$= 17.1(0.81)$$
$$= 13.8$$

We interpret $s_{x \cdot y}$ as a standard deviation. Thus the predicted PMA score is 17.3, and the standard error of estimate is 13.8. Recall, from our discussion of the normal curve, that 68 per cent of the cases (or area) falls between $\pm 1s$. Using this fact, we can say that if we made many predictions for an achievement score of 47, 68 per cent of the observed scores would fall between $\pm 1 s_{y \cdot x}$ (that is, between 33.2 and 60.8). In almost every instance the observed scores would fall between $\pm 3 s_{y \cdot x}$ (5.6 — 88.4).

Assumptions Underlying the Product Moment r

The product moment r is one of the most frequently used indexes of relationship, but this should not prompt the conclusion that it can be used indiscriminantly. The following assumptions about the basic data must be tenable:

1/
The nature of the relationship between X and Y must be *linear* as opposed to *curvilinear* or some other form. This means that in fitting regression lines to the data, a straight line provides the best description of the relationship. There are mathematical approaches to the determination of whether a linear relationship exists, but linearity can also be estimated from an examination of the bivariate frequency distribution.

2/
When using r and $s_{y.x}$ or $s_{x.y}$ for prediction purposes, the variability in the columns (rows) should be essentially equivalent.

Correlation among Ranks (Rho)

Many times in educational research it is not possible to obtain scores on one or more variables but it is possible to rank individuals on the variables. When this situation occurs the correlation is determined from the rank positions.

One example of a rank-correlation procedure is Spearman's rank-difference correlation technique (rho), as defined by

$$p = 1 - \frac{6\Sigma D^2}{N(N^2 - 1)} \tag{13}$$

The only new term in this formula is D, the difference between an individual's rankings on the two variables. The data in Table 13.10 are ranks based upon the scores of 13 students on two

Table 13.10/ Rank-order Correlation of Performance on Two Child Psychology Examinations*

Student	X_1	X_2	Rank 1	Rank 2	D	D²
A	20	53	7.5	11.0	−3.5	12.25
B	17	33	3.5	3.0	0.5	0.25
C	10	28	1.0	1.5	−0.5	0.25
D	11	28	2.0	1.5	0.5	0.25
E	27	60	12.5	13.0	−0.5	0.25
F	19	52	6.0	10.0	−4.0	16.00
G	20	47	7.5	7.0	0.5	0.25
H	24	40	10.5	4.0	6.5	42.25
I	27	44	12.5	6.0	6.5	42.25
J	18	43	5.0	5.0	0.0	0.00
K	21	54	9.0	12.0	−3.0	9.00
L	24	51	10.5	9.0	1.5	2.25
M	17	48	3.5	8.0	−4.5	20.25
Total					0.0	145.50

* These are error scores; therefore a low score indicates good performance.

examinations. Substituting in formula (13), we obtain

$$p = 1 - \frac{6(145.50)}{13(169 - 1)}$$
$$= 1 - 0.40$$
$$= 0.60$$

The rank-order formula and the formula for the product moment r are equivalent when only a single score appears in each class interval. This rarely occurs because scores accumulate in those intervals which are in the middle of the distribution. The effect of more than one score appearing in an interval is to reduce the estimate of relationship when compared with r. Nevertheless, the interpretation of *rho* is identical to that of r.

Multiple Correlation

The product moment r between verbal ability and achievement was 0.58. This is a typical value for this sort of problem and indicates that considerable error is involved in making predictions of achievement from an aptitude test score. A more accurate prediction might be possible if another test score were used in combination with verbal ability. When an investigator uses two or more variables in combination to predict a single variable, the multiple correlation is used. The notation for a multiple correlation is $R_{1.23 \cdots n}$, where the subscript 1 stands for the variable being predicted or the criterion variable and the remaining subscripts represent the predictor variables.

Before considering some of the statistical principles involved in multiple correlation, we shall first examine the logic involved in the technique. In attempting to improve $r = 0.58$ we would not (or should not) add just any variables to the prediction equation. Ideally, the second predictor variable should not be highly correlated with the first predictor variable, but it should be correlated with the criterion variable, achivement. In other words, the second predictor variable should add something that is *independent* of the first predictor variable and should still be correlated with the criterion variable. The discovery of such variables has proved very difficult because predictor variables are usually correlated with each other. It is possible, of course, to find predictor variables that are not correlated, but such variables usually do not correlate with the criterion.

Assuming, for the moment, that possible predictor variables are found, there is the problem of combining the variables so that the maximum correlation is obtained. One possibility is to combine the variables such that each contributes equally to the prediction of the criterion. This procedure is sensible only when it is known that each variable contributes equally to the criterion variable—a situation which does not often prevail. The more sensible procedure is to weight each predictor variable in accordance with its contribution to the criterion variable. Consider the situation where predictor A contributes more to performance on the criterion than variable B. We would predict a higher criterion score for somebody who scored higher on variable A than on variable B in this situation than if the reverse were true.

The Multiple Regression Equation/ The procedure by which the prediction of the criterion measure is maximized involves the differential weighting of the predictor variables. These optimal weights are called "beta weights" and are derived such that prediction errors are minimized. Unlike the prediction equation for r, which involves one predictor variable, two (or more) predictor variables are involved with multiple R. The assigned beta weights must minimize predictive errors for all combinations of predictor variables. It can be shown that the following do, in fact, minimize predictive errors in the two-predictor-variable problem:

$$\beta_2 = \frac{r_{12} - r_{13}r_{23}}{1 - r^2{}_{23}} \tag{14}$$

$$\beta_3 = \frac{r_{13} - r_{12}r_{23}}{1 - r^2{}_{23}} \tag{14a}$$

where r_{23} = product moment correlation between the two predictor variables

r_{12} = correlation between criterion variable and first predictor variable

r_{13} = correlation between criterion and second predictor variable

Suppose that to the verbal-ability variable we add reasoning ability as a second predictor variable. The relevant variables are X_1 = achievement, X_2 = verbal ability, and X_3 = reasoning ability, and the correlations between them are $r_{12} = 0.58$, $r_{13} = 0.36$, and $r_{23} = 0.42$. Substituting in formulas (14) and (14a), we obtain

$$\beta_2 = \frac{0.58 - 0.36(0.42)}{1 - (0.42)^2} = 0.52$$

$$\beta_3 = \frac{0.36 - 0.58(0.42)}{1 - (0.42)^2} = 0.15$$

Notice that β_2 is larger than β_3 because verbal ability correlates higher with the criterion than reasoning ability.

The Multiple Correlation $R_{1.23. \ldots n}$/ The multiple $R_{1.23}$ is the correlation between a criterion variable and the sum of two weighted predictors. The formula used for computing $R_{1.23}$ is

$$R_{1.23} = \sqrt{\beta_2 r_{12} + \beta_3 r_{13}} \tag{15}$$

By substituting the beta weights and correlations obtained in formula (15), we obtain a multiple correlation which is improved by 0.01:

$$R_{1 \cdot 23} = \sqrt{0.52(0.58) + 0.15(0.36)}$$
$$= 0.59$$

The additional labor has added very little to our ability to predict achievement. This occurred because the correlation between X_2 and X_3 indicates a considerable overlap between the two predictor variables, so that X_3 has little that is unique to contribute to the prediction equation. Suppose, however, that r_{23} is only 0.10. In this case β_2 is 0.55 and β_3 is 0.30, which, when substituted in formula (15), give an $R_{1 \cdot 23}$ of 0.65.

Prediction of the Criterion/ When the beta weights are determined, it is possible to predict scores on the criterion variable from a knowledge of the predictor variables. The equation for predicting a raw score from a knowledge of two predictor scores is

$$X' = \beta_2 \frac{s_1}{s_2} X_2 + \beta_3 \frac{s_1}{s_3} X_3 + \left(M_1 - \beta_2 \frac{s_1}{s_2} M_2 - \beta_3 \frac{s_1}{s_3} M_3 \right) \tag{16}$$

Using formula (16), we shall now predict an achievement score X' when the verbal ability score X_2 is 17.0 and the reasoning ability score X_3 is 13.4. From our earlier computations in this chapter, we already know: $\beta_2 = 0.52$, $\beta_3 = 0.15$, mean achievement $M_1 = 45.5$, the standard deviation of the achievement scores $= 28.7$, mean verbal ability score $M_2 = 16.3$, and the standard deviation of the verbal ability scores is 17.1. Formula (16) also requires the mean reasoning ability score M_3, which is 12.4, and the standard deviation is 14.5. Substituting these values in formula (16),

$$X' = 0.52 \frac{28.7}{17.1} 17.0 + 0.15 \frac{28.7}{14.5} 13.4$$
$$+ \left(45.5 - 0.52 \frac{28.7}{17.0} 16.3 - 0.15 \frac{28.7}{14.5} 12.4 \right)$$
$$= 45.2 + 45.4 - 14.3 - 3.7$$
$$= 72.6$$

Although $X' = 72.6$ seems to be much higher than the mean achievement score of 45.5, it is less than 1 standard deviation above the mean ($45.5 + 28.7 = 74.2$). This is consistent with the fact that both X_2 and X_3 are also less than 1 standard deviation above the mean. This seemingly high predicted achievement score occurs because of the large standard deviation of the achievement scores.

The Standard Error of Estimate/ When the multiple R is less than unity, we immediately know that errors of prediction will occur. As the magnitude of R increases, the deviation between the predicted score and the obtained score decreases. This relationship is identical to that which occurs with the product moment r. As was true with r, it is possible to determine the variability around the predicted score by means of the *standard error of estimate* $s_{1.23}$. The formula for $s_{1.23}$ is

$$s_{1.23} = s_1 \sqrt{1 - R_{1.23}^2} \tag{17}$$

Substituting in formula (17), we obtain

$$s_{1.23} = 28.7 \sqrt{1 - 0.59^2}$$
$$= 28.7\ (0.81)$$
$$= 23.2$$

Thus, for a predicted score of 72.6 we would expect that if many such predictions for $X_2 = 17.0$ and $X_3 = 13.4$ were made, 68 per cent of the obtained scores would fall between 49.4 and 95.8. Although the range of scores indicates that considerable error exists in such predictions, it should be noted that, for group predictions, more correct than incorrect predictions are made.

14

WILLIAM J. MEYER

Inferential Statistics

The preceding chapter described procedures for assessing the attributes of a sample. Frequently, however, the investigator is concerned with the generalizability of the data beyond the immediate sample. Stated somewhat differently, the investigator wishes to make inferences from the sample data to the population from which the sample was taken. This chapter is concerned with the degree to which such inferences from samples to populations are appropriate and with the degree of error that can be expected when such inferences are made. We shall also examine some of the statistical procedures used for assessing the outcome of experiments.

Sampling Theory

If all members of a *population* (*universe*), defined as *all* possible members of a specified group, were included in a study, there would be no need for inferential statistics because the statistical attributes of the group would be the population value. (The term "parameter" is sometimes used when referring to population values.) It is rarely possible to have available all members of a population, with the result that one is forced to take *samples* from the population. The statistics (*M, s*) derived from such samples are used to estimate the parameters of a population and are called "sample statistics." These sample statistics are used in conjunction with certain assumptions and statistical procedures to make *inferences* about the population. One basic assumption is that the members of the sample are ramdomly selected; that is, every member of the population has an equal chance of being included in the sample. In actual sample selection, randomization is rarely achieved so that the assumption is violated in most experiments. Because of the practical problems in obtaining a truly random sample, it is imperative that samples be at least representative of the population.

The Standard Error of a Statistic

In Chapter 13 we examined the concept of variability around the mean. In that discussion our concern was with the variability s of scores around the sample mean M. Suppose we had 1,000 samples, obtained the M and s for each one, and constructed a frequency polygon based on the 1,000 sample means. Assuming the measured attribute to be normally distributed in the population, the resulting polygon, called the "sampling distribution of the mean," would also be normally distributed. We shall designate the mean of this distribution of sample means as the population mean μ and its standard deviation as σ_m. Each of these sample means is an estimate of the population mean; since the population mean, in theory at least, represents a fixed value, differences between μ and M are considered to be *sampling errors*.

One way of understanding the concept of sampling errors is to deal directly with a small sampling distribution derived from a population where the theoretical mean is known. Let us suppose that a single coin is flipped ten times by each of twenty-five students and the mean number of heads is recorded. Further, suppose that 144 such means are derived, each involving 25 flips of the coin. The resulting distribution of means is presented in Table 14.1. We can compute the mean of the means M_m and the standard deviation of the distribution of means S_m using procedures described in Chapter 13, page 337. $M_m = 4.96$ and $s_m = 0.27$; these values are derived from actual sample statistics. Assuming the coin is perfectly balanced, we would expect that in 10 tosses of a coin, an average of 5 heads would occur. Thus the theoretically expected mean for the sampling distribution is 5 and our obtained M of 4.96 is a close estimate.

Now suppose we subtract M_m from each sample M. This operation gives us a distribution of deviations, or errors of sampling, which can be used to derive the standard deviation of

Table 14.1/ Mean and Standard Deviation of a Distribution of Mean Number of Heads Based on 144 Random Samples of Size 25

M	f	fM	fM²	
5.6	2	11.2	62.72	$M_m = \dfrac{714.0}{144}$
5.5	4	22.0	121.00	
5.4	6	32.4	174.96	$= 4.96$
5.3	10	53.0	280.90	
5.2	14	72.8	378.56	$s_m = 0.1\left[3550.84 - \dfrac{(714)^2}{144}\right]$
5.1	19	96.9	494.19	
5.0	13	65.0	325.00	$= 0.27$
4.9	22	107.8	528.22	
4.8	24	115.2	552.96	
4.7	10	47.0	220.90	
4.6	10	46.0	211.60	
4.5	7	31.5	141.75	
4.4	3	13.2	58.08	
Total	144	714.0	3550.84	

the sampling distribution. The standard deviation of a sampling distribution is called the "standard error." The standard deviation of a sampling distribution of means, such as in Table 14.1, is called the "standard error of the mean s_m." The s_m in our example is 0.27.

The Standard Error of the Mean/ The sampling distribution of the mean shown in Table 14.1 derives from an N of 144 samples. Variation around the mean of the distribution can be determined directly using any one of the formulas for standard deviation. The resulting s_m is 0.27.

Fortunately, the standard error of the mean, as well as other statistics, can be computed without an actual sampling distribution. If successive samples of the same size N are drawn from the same population, the resulting distribution of means has a standard deviation which is approximated by

$$s_m = \frac{s}{\sqrt{N}} \tag{1}$$

and is called the standard error of the mean, where s is the sample deviation and N is the sample size. The standard error of the mean is an estimate of the variation of the means based on the same size N.

We shall now estimate s_m using a sample with $N = 25$ (the sample size for each of the means in Table 14.1). Remember that each of the 25 subjects tossed the coin 10 times. The sample selected for this illustration has $M = 4.80$ and $s = 1.61$. Substituting these values in formula (1) we obtain

$$s_m = \frac{1.61}{\sqrt{25}}$$
$$= 0.29$$

which is fairly close to the empirically derived s_m of 0.27.

An examination of the relationships in formula (1) may be helpful. Notice that as the size of N increases, the size of s_m decreases; that is, the variation of the sample means around the population means decreases. This occurs because larger samples are less biased by extreme cases. Suppose the sample size of 25 was increased to 169 and maintained the s value of 1.61. The s_m would be 0.12, indicating less variation than had been the case.

Now we will hold N constant and vary s. Clearly, as s increases s_m increases. Consider the situation where s is quite large, say 20. This means that the average deviation from the sample mean is 20, which increases the likelihood that, for any one sample of size N, the mean will markedly deviate from the population mean. For $s = 16.0$ and $N = 25$, $s_m = 3.2$.

The Standard Error of the Product Moment Correlation s_r/ An obtained correlation between two variables derived from a particular sample represents an estimate of the population value of the correlation r. Successive samples of the same size N drawn from the same population will, therefore, vary around this population value. Estimates of the degree of variation are not as easily derived for r's because, depending upon the *sample size* and *population value* of r, the resulting sampling distribution of r may seriously depart from normality. Unless N is large (at least 30) and the population value of r is 0.50 or less, the sampling distribution will be skewed; the direction depending on the direction, plus or minus, of the correlation. If the foregoing conditions prevail, it is possible to estimate s_r by

$$s_r = \frac{1}{\sqrt{N - 1}} \tag{2}$$

When either one or both conditions are not present, an alternative equation is required which minimizes the effects of nonnormality. In order to understand this equation, it will first be necessary to understand why distributions of r's around large population r's $(0.60 - 1.00)$ are skewed. Essentially, this occurs because a product moment r has a fixed maximum value. Thus for an r of 0.90, the *possible* sample values can extend downward to negative values but up only to 1.00. Successive sample r's pile up between 0.90 and 1.00, producing a positively skewed distribution. If the population r is negative, the sampling distribution is negatively skewed. The solution is to normalize the distribution by transforming it such that the resulting values are essentially normal. The r to Z *transformation,* presented in Table B of Appendix A, serves to normalize the distribution. The standard error of Z is

$$s_Z = \frac{1}{\sqrt{N-3}} \tag{3}$$

Confidence Intervals/ As already noted, we usually do not know the population mean and must estimate it from a sample mean. Thus, it is not possible to know the exact value of the population mean but it is possible to specify an interval, with a known degree of confidence, within which the population mean lies. This interval is called a "confidence interval."

An understanding of confidence intervals can be derived from the area relationships for the normal curve. Recall that the area between $\pm 1s$ includes approximately 68 per cent of the total area under the curve. Since s_m is actually a standard deviation, it has the same relationship to the normal curve. For example, if a large number of samples of the same size N were obtained, we would expect, in theory, that 68 per cent of the sample means would fall between $\pm 1s_m$. Stated differently, we can say, with 68 per cent confidence, that the population mean falls between $\pm 1s_m$. If we wanted greater confidence, we could determine the interval for $\pm 2s_m$, which includes approximately 95 per cent of the sample means. In terms of our example based on one sample of $N = 25$, the 95 per cent confidence interval would be: $M = 4.96 \pm 2(0.27) = 4.42 - 5.50$. By using the 95 per cent confidence limits, we are also saying that 5 per cent of the time the population mean would not be included in the interval.

We shall now determine the 95 per cent confidence interval for the product moment r, where $r = 0.80$ and $N = 52$. Since r is greater than 0.50 we must transform it to Z (see page 372 for an explanation of this procedure). The Z value for $r = 0.80$ is 1.099 (see Table C of Appendix A). Next we determine the standard error of Z, which is computed by means of formula

(3), page 373: $s_z = 1/\sqrt{52-3} = 0.14$. We want the 95 per cent confidence interval so we add and subtract $0.14(2) = 0.28$ to $Z = 1.099$. The interval is $1.071 - 1.127$, but this is in Z values and we are interested in r. Thus we must convert the Z limits to r units, again using Table C of Appendix A. The transformed values are $0.79 - 0.81$, which is the 95 per cent confidence interval for r.

Tests of Significance

The discussion of inferential statistics has included so far the concepts of sampling distributions, sampling errors, and confidence intervals. Most research work in education, however, is concerned with comparisons of groups which have experienced different treatments, or with determining whether a treatment applied to a single group has induced a change in the group. Rather than estimating a population mean, most investigators are interested in determining whether observed differences between means can reasonably be ascribed to sampling error or whether the differences can be ascribed to treatment effects. If the observed differences between the means are attributable to sampling error, we can conclude that the means are chance fluctuations from the same population mean.

The Null Hypothesis H_0

Statistical tests of significance require a statistical hypothesis called the "null hypothesis." The null hypothesis states that *no difference exists between a sample statistic and a hypothetical population value or between two (or more) sample statistics.*

Let us now examine what is implied by statements which fit the definition of the null hypothesis. Recall that any sample statistic, which we will call for convenience θ, is an estimate of some population value θ_{pop}. These sample statistics vary around the population value with a variability equal to the standard error of the statistic. The null hypothesis implies that any observed discrepancy $\theta_{pop} - \theta$ is a chance occurrence and that the sample is actually from a population with the value θ_{pop}. When comparing two sample statistics, θ_1 and θ_2, we are estimating two population means, θ_{pop1} and θ_{pop2}. The null hypothesis states that the difference between the population means is zero; that is, the population means are equal. If, in fact, θ_{pop1} and θ_{pop2} are equal, any differences between θ_1 and θ_2 can be attributed to sampling error. However, if the two population means are not equal, the difference between θ_1 and θ_2 can be attributed to something other than sampling error.

The null hypothesis, that a particular deviation occurred by chance, is rejected when the probability of the event is 5 times in 100 (p = 0.05) or smaller. The smaller the level of significance required for rejecting the null hypothesis, the less chance there is that in fact it should have been accepted. Sometimes it happens that the null hypothesis is rejected when it should not have been. This is called a "type I error." Type I errors are more likely to occur when the level at which H_o is rejected is p = 0.05, called the "5 per cent level of significance," than when the level of significance is set at p = 0.01. Errors in the opposite direction can also occur. A *type II error* is said to occur whenever the null hypothesis is not rejected when in fact it should have been rejected. The more stringent the level of significance, the greater the probability of making a type II error.

Statistical Significance/ The concept of statistical significance refers to the probability of obtaining a difference between a population statistic and a sample statistic, or between two sample statistics.

The probability levels are determined by application of the area relationships under the normal curve (discussed in Chapter 13, page 348). Let us assume that the area under the normal curve represents the frequencies with which all the possible differences between an observed mean and a population mean can occur. What we have in effect is a hypothetical sampling distribution of deviations of sample means from a population mean. We already know that the standard deviation of this distribution (called the "standard error of the mean") can be estimated by means of the formula $s_m = s/\sqrt{N}$. If we now determine the deviation of the obtained sample mean from the population mean, $\mu - M$, we have x, the deviation. Dividing x by s_m gives us the already familiar standard score z. Thus the deviation of a sample mean from a population in standard score units is given by

$$z = \frac{\mu - M}{\dfrac{s}{\sqrt{N}}} \qquad (4)$$

An example that uses formula (4) may clarify the issue. Suppose we wish to determine whether a particular sample of 100 eleventh-graders with a mean IQ of 105 is from a population with a mean IQ of 100. The standard deviation is 16.00. By substituting in formula (4), we obtain

$$z = \frac{100 - 105}{16/\sqrt{100}} = 3.12 \qquad \text{Critical value}$$

Recall from our discussion of the normal curve that the column headed Area: q Smaller refers to the area to the right of the ordinate for a particular z value (or to the left of the ordinate if z is negative). See Figure 13.4 for a graphic description of this area. We can consider this area as a proportion of the total area. Entering Table A of Appendix A with $z = 3.12$, we find that the area to the right of the ordinate includes only 0.01 of the total possible area. This can also be interpreted as meaning that the obtained difference between the means will occur only once in 100 times. The value 0.01 is called the "level of significance" and means that the difference between $\mu = 100$ and $M = 105$ occurs by chance once every 100 times. Thus, we reject the null hypothesis and conclude that the sample is from a population whose mean IQ is something other than 100. In so doing we recognize that this could have been the one chance occurrence and that we have, therefore, committed a type I error.

The t Test of Significance

Throughout the discussion of hypothesis testing and the normal probability curve, the comment was made that the procedures assumed large samples. A large sample is comprised of 30 or more subjects. As the sample size decreases, the sampling distribution of a statistic becomes more and more peaked (leptokurtic) and the tails of the curve become somewhat higher than in a perfectly normal curve. In terms of hypothesis testing, this means that statistical significance will occur more often than is warranted. A z, for example, that is significant at the 0.05 level, when $N = 20$, may actually be significant at the 0.08 level. If the normal curve were used in this situation, an erroneous conclusion would have occurred.

Once the sample size drops below 30, the loss of even a single case influences the shape of the sampling distribution and, therefore, the accuracy of probability statements derived from the curve. In developing more accurate probability statements it was necessary to determine the sampling distribution for different sample sizes. These distributions were developed

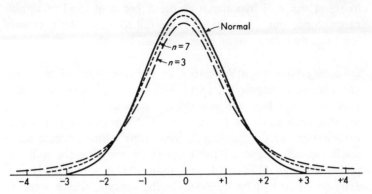

Figure 14.1/ Normal compared with t distribution for $n = 3$ and $n = 7$.

by R. A. Fisher and are called "t distributions" (see Table C of Appendix A). Figure 14.1 contrasts the t distributions for two sample sizes with that of the normal curve.

The t test is interpreted in precisely the same way as z, the only difference being that higher t values are required for rejecting the null hypothesis than are required for z.

Degrees of Freedom/ In the most general case, degrees of freedom (df) refers to the number of scores or frequencies permitted to vary around some constant or parameter. For example, suppose there are 10 scores in a distribution for which the mean is known. Since the sum of the algebraic deviations around the mean must equal 0, it follows that any 9 of the scores are free to vary in value but the tenth is not. Thus, when scores vary around a single parameter, 1 df is lost. The df in any situation can be determined by subtracting from the total number of cases N the number of restrictions imposed by fixed parameters.

As an example of the use of the t table (Table C of Appendix A), suppose the population IQ is 100, a sample IQ is 105, s is 15, and the sample size is 16. Substituting t for z in formula (4), and substituting the values in formula (4), we obtain

$$t = \frac{100 - 105}{15/\sqrt{16}}$$
$$t = 1.33$$

Since the sample size is 16 and the scores varied around only one mean, we know that the df is $16 - 1$ ($N - 1$), or 15. We enter Table C with 15 df and reading across to the column labeled 0.05 we note that a t of 2.131 is required in order to reject the null hypothesis at the 5 per cent level of significance. Since our t is only 1.33, we fail to attain the necessary level and therefore cannot reject the null hypothesis.

Estimating Population Variance / In the discussion of measures of variation (Chapter 13, pages 340 to 345), it was stated that s provides the best estimate of the population variation and, for this reason, is most widely used. Estimates of population variation are very important in hypothesis testing because a too small estimate increases the chances of rejecting the null hypothesis. When N is small (less than 30), it is less likely that extreme cases will be included in the sample, which leads to an underestimate of the population variance. A better estimate of the population variance is obtained when the sum of squares Σx^2 is divided by $N - 1$, the df, rather than by N. The effect of this correction is very slight when the sample size is large.

Comparing Two Sample Statistics

The t Test between Independent Means

Suppose an investigator is interested in the differential effectiveness of praise and blame on the discrimination learning of third-grade pupils. He has 50 subjects (Ss) available and randomly assigns them to the two groups. The children are given 40 learning trials and the number of correct responses is recorded. A summary of the data is presented in Table 14.2. The mean for the praise group is 20.12 while the mean for the blame group is 17.04, a difference of 3.08. We need to determine whether this difference should be attributed to chance alone (the null hypothesis) or whether it is reasonable to conclude that the praise and blame had differential effects on the learning task.

Recall that, in estimating the probability that a sample statistic departed by chance from a hypothetical population value, we estimated the variation of the sampling distribution of that statistic. In the present situation there are two sample statistics, each representing an independent estimate of the population value. If the experiment were repeated in exactly the same way 1,000 times, and if the means of the successive samples were normally distributed, the difference between the pairs of means for each of the 1,000 samples would also form a normal curve. If the treatments are, in fact, *not* differentially effective, the mean of this distribution of differences between the sample means will be approximately 0. In any one of the 1,000 experiments, the differences between the means will diverge more or less from 0 (in our illustrative experiment the discrepancy is 3.08), and we need to determine whether an observed discrepancy is statistically significant. Of course, the distribution of difference scores is theoretical, and we need not actually use 1,000 samples. The theoretical distribution of differences has a variation which is estimated by a statistic called the "standard error of the difference between independent means s_{DM}."

Table 14.2/ Number of Correct Responses in Forty Trials

Praise		Blame	
25	24	16	19
26	25	21	18
17	15	11	16
19	21	24	16
26	17	15	16
17	22	16	18
15	24	15	19
17	15	28	20
15	22	26	15
16	26	10	14
13	15	15	15
21	27	11	13
23		19	

The definitional formula for the standard error of the difference between independent means is

$$s_{DM} = \sqrt{\frac{s_1^2}{n_1} + \frac{s_2^2}{n_2} - 2r_{12}s_1s_2} \tag{5}$$

which includes the variance errors of M_1 and M_2. The formula also includes a product moment correlation whose value reflects the degree of relationship between pairs of subjects. When comparing two randomly selected samples, however, the assumption is made that r_{12} is 0; that is, there is no reason to assume a relationship between random pairs of subjects. Thus the formula for s_{DM} reduces to the square root of the sum of the variance errors of the sample means.

We shall now rewrite the definitional formula into computational form. Recall that the standard error of a single sample mean is given by $s/\sqrt{N}$, where s equals $\dfrac{\Sigma x^2}{N}$. *Combining the two* standard error terms, we obtain

$$s_{DM} = \sqrt{\frac{\Sigma x_1^2 + \Sigma x_2^2}{N_1 + N_2 - 2}\left(\frac{1}{N_1} + \frac{1}{N_2}\right)}$$

where Σx_1^2 and Σx_2^2 are the sums of squares around each sample mean. Notice that these sums of squares are pooled and divided by the total N minus 2 df (2 df are lost because the deviations are taken separately around each sample mean). This procedure is logical because now the estimate of the standard error of differences is based on the larger total N.

The difference between the sample means divided by the standard error of the difference gives us the familiar x/s, which is the t test. The formula for the t test between *independent means* is

$$t = \frac{M_1 - M_2}{\sqrt{\dfrac{\Sigma x_1^2 + \Sigma x_2^2}{N_1 + N_2 - 2}\left(\dfrac{1}{N_1} + \dfrac{1}{N_2}\right)}} \tag{6}$$

(handwritten: Unmatched pairs)   *(handwritten: df consists of all subjects minus 2)*

Returning to the experiment on the effects of praise and blame on discrimination learning, we shall now work out the necessary computations required in formula (6). The method for determining Σx^2 is identical to that in Chapter 13, pages 343 to 344, and will not be repeated here.

$$t = \frac{20.12 - 17.04}{\sqrt{\dfrac{484.64 + 460.96}{25 + 25 - 2}\left(\dfrac{1}{25} + \dfrac{1}{25}\right)}}$$

$$= \frac{3.08}{\sqrt{\dfrac{945.60}{48}\left(\dfrac{1}{25} + \dfrac{1}{25}\right)}} = \frac{3.08}{\sqrt{19.70(0.08)}} = \frac{3.08}{\sqrt{1.57}}$$

$$= 2.44$$
$$df = 48$$
$$p = 0.02$$

The resulting t is 2.44. Since the scores vary around two sample means (that is, since there are two parametric restrictions), 2 df are lost. Thus $50 - 2 = 48$ df. Enter Table C with 48 df. (Table C does not include an entry for 48 df so we shall make our judgement on the basis of 40 df, which is more conserva-

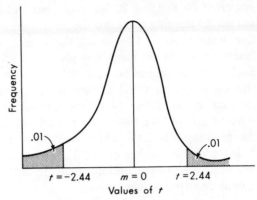

Figure 14.2/ Area relationships for $t = 2.44$, $df = 48$.

tive. If our t is significant with 40 df, we can be certain it is significant with 48 df.) At 40 df a t of 2.021 is necessary for significance at the 5 per cent level, and our t is larger. We can conclude, therefore, that the difference between the sample means did not occur by chance alone and that the group that received praise performed better than the group that received blame. Figure 14.2 shows these relationships graphically.

The t Test between Nonindependent (Correlated) Means

There are some experiments in which the experimenter attempts to control certain important variables rather than assuming that they will distribute themselves randomly within his groups. By introducing these controls he hopes to reduce the standard error of difference term in computing his t test. The more commonly used of these experimental designs is the _matched-pairs_ approach. In this design each subject in one group is matched as closely as possible on certain variables with a subject in the second group. The better the match and the more matching variables used, the greater is the reduction in the standard error term. Keep in mind, however, that the magnitude of the standard error term is a function of the sample size (the sample size in the case of matched pairs is the _number of pairs,_ not the number of Ss). The more matching variables added, the more difficult it becomes to develop large samples. This is an important consideration when deciding whether to use a matched-pairs design or a randomized design involving independent means.

Summarized in Table 14.3 are the number of correct

responses on the first 20 learning trials and the number on the second 20 learning trials, for the *same* subjects, in a discrimination learning task. Computing the means for the praise and blame groups in the usual way gives us 13.5 and 11.5, respectively. The difference between the means is 1.80. For demonstration purposes, we shall now compute t as if the scores in each column of Table 14.3 were different Ss; that is, randomly selected groups. We follow the procedures in formula (6) and the resulting t is 1.12, which with 18 df [using formula (6), N is the actual number of Ss 20], is *not* statistically significant. We must conclude, therefore, that the differences between the groups occurred by chance.

Table 14.3/ Analysis of Matched-pairs data

Praise	Blame
16	20
11	8
8	9
12	13
7	10
14	17
9	11
13	15
10	12
15	18

Recall, from the discussion of the standard error of the difference between independent means, that the definitional formula included a product moment r. We assumed r to be 0 because Ss were paired randomly. This assumption is not tenable in this problem because the pairs of scores are derived from the same Ss. Computing r we find a correlation of 0.89 between the two sets of scores, which we will now include in our computation. The resulting t is larger because the standard error term has been substantially reduced.

$$t = \frac{13.3 - 11.5}{\sqrt{\frac{82.5 + 148.10}{10 + 10 - 2}\left(\frac{1}{10} + \frac{1}{10}\right) - 2(0.89)(0.96)(1.29)}}$$
$$= 2.95$$

Although the larger t resulting from including the correlation term is desirable, there also occurs an undesirable loss of df. Thus, df in this problem is *not* $10 + 10 - 2 = 18$; rather, $df = 9$. This happens because the correlation shows that the pairs of scores are *not* free to vary. Knowing an individual's score on trials 1 to 20 we also know (within the limits of predictive error) his score in trials 21 to 40. Therefore, only one column of scores is free to vary and the df for that column is $10 - 1 = 9$.

Fortunately, the t between correlated means can be computed without using the r.

$$t = \frac{\bar{D}}{\sqrt{\dfrac{\Sigma d^2}{N(N-1)}}} \qquad (7)$$

is algebraically identical to the formula that includes the correlation term. We shall now reanalyze the same data using formula (7). The $\bar{D}$ in formula (7) is the mean of the difference scores computed by subtracting the scores of the praise group

Table 14.4/ Analysis of Matched-pairs Data

Subject	Praise	Blame	Difference	D^2
1	16	20	+4	16
2	11	8	−3	9
3	8	9	+1	1
4	12	13	+1	1
5	7	10	+3	9
6	14	17	+3	9
7	9	11	+2	4
8	13	15	+2	4
9	10	12	+2	4
10	15	18	+3	9
			18	66

from the scores of the blame group, as shown in Table 14.4. Algebraically summing these difference scores gives the same value, 1.80, as subtracting the means of the two groups. The next step involves squaring each difference score (see the last column of Table 14.4). The denominator term of formula (7) is the *standard error of the difference between correlated means*. Σd^2 is the sum of squares of the distribution of difference scores and is computed in the same way as Σx^2, as shown in Chapter 13, pages 383 to 384. The computations are

[handwritten: 342 to 344]

$$t = \frac{1.8}{\sqrt{\dfrac{0.33}{10(9)}}} = \frac{1.8}{0.61}$$

$$= 2.95$$
$$df = 9$$
$$P = 0.05$$

In this case, t is 2.95 which, with 9 df (the number of pairs, 10, minus 1) is significant at the 5 per cent level. Now we can reject the null hypothesis and conclude that performance during trials 21 to 40 is better than during trials 1 to 20; that is, learning occurred.

Including the correlation term in the standard error formula reduced the standard error to a point where the difference between the means is statistically significant. Remember that our concern here is with a distribution of differences between means, and this distribution will be *less variable* when a significant variable influencing the differences between means is controlled. Formula (7) is not only appropriate in the situation where the pairs of scores are for the same individual but also where Ss have been matched on some variable influencing performance on the experimental task. Statistically speaking, however, the procedure causes a loss in df that may not be offset by the amount of reduction in the standard error brought about by the matching variable. Generally speaking, randomized designs are preferred over matched-pair designs.

[handwritten: Over 30, reverse this.]

Multiple Group Comparisons

[handwritten margin: Analysis of variance. Compares means of three or more groups.]

An extension of the study on the effects of praise and blame would be the addition of a third group—a group receiving candy for correct responses. Subjects are randomly assigned to each of the three groups and we wish to compare performances of the groups. Comparisons of the three groups could be accomplished by computing three t tests, but this procedure violates certain basic principles of probability and is inefficient when many group comparisons are involved. Analysis of variance procedures allow one to test for significance of differences among several groups at one time.

Partitioning Sums of Squares

Consider Table 14.5, in which each entry is a score made by a subject in a particular experimental treatment group. M_A, M_B, and M_C are the means of each group. We can also determine the mean for all three groups combined, which is called the "grand

Table 14.5/ Entries in a Simple Analysis of Variance for Three Groups

A	B	C
X_{1a}	X_{1b}	X_{1c}
X_{2a}	X_{2b}	X_{2c}
X_{3a}	X_{3b}	X_{3c}
.	.	.
.	.	.
.	.	.
X_{na}	X_{nb}	X_{nc}
M_A	M_B	M_C

mean M." The *total sum of squares* Σx^2 is the sum of the squared deviations of each score around the grand mean and is the left-hand term in the following formula:

$$\text{Total} = \text{within} + \text{between}$$
$$\Sigma(X - M)^2 = \sum_{1}^{n}\sum_{a}^{c}(X - M_i)^2 + \Sigma n_i(M_i - M)^2 \tag{8}$$

The total sum of squares can be partitioned into two independent parts: the sums of squares of the group means around the grand mean, and the sums of squares of the individual scores within a group around the mean of that group. Formula (8) shows that the total sum of squares is equal to the sum of squares attributable to variation among subjects treated in the same way (the variation of each individual score within a group around the mean of that group), which is called the "within-groups sum of squares Σx_w^2," plus the sum of squares derived from the variation of each group mean around the grand mean, which is called the "between-groups sum of squares Σx_b^2."

As an illustration of the relationships among the sums of

squares, we have substituted numbers in place of the letters in Table 14.5. These numbers and the summary statistics of the data are shown in Table 14.6. Computation of the three sums of squares was accomplished by using formula (8). Observe that the computation of the total sum of squares involves subtracting each score from the grand mean 5.9 and squaring the result. Each squared deviation is summed; thus, $\Sigma x^2 = 91.7$. The within-groups sum of squares involves the summation of the deviations of each score around its mean. There are, then, three

Table 14.6/ An Illustration of Partitioning Sums of Squares

	Groups			
	A	B	C	
	7	4	5	Within-group $A\Sigma x^2 = \Sigma(3.8-7)^2 + (3.8-2)^2$
	2	9	7	$+ \cdots + (3.8-4)^2 = 22.8$
	5	6	10	Within-group $B\Sigma x^2 = (6.4-4)^2 + (6.4-9)^2$
	1	8	6	$+ \cdots + (6.4-5)^2 = 17.2$
ΣX	4	5	9	Within-group $C\Sigma x^2 = (7.4-5)^2 + (7.4-7)^2$
	19	32	37	$+ \cdots + (7.4-9)^2 = 17.2$
M	3.8	6.4	7.4	Sum of within $\Sigma x^2 = 22.8 + 17.2$
s^2	5.7	3.4	3.4	$+ 17.2 = 57.2$
s	2.4	1.8	1.8	Between-groups $\Sigma x^2 = \Sigma(5.9-3.8)^2$
Grand mean 5.9				$+ (5.9-6.4)^2 + (5.9-7.4)^2 = 34.5$

Total $\Sigma x^2 = \Sigma(5.9-7)^2 + (5.9-2)^2 + (5.9-5)^2$
$+ \cdots + (5.9-9)^2 = 91.7$

within-groups sums of squares: group $A = 22.8$, group B = 17.2, group $C = 17.2$. The three are summed: $\Sigma x_w^2 = 57.2$.[1] The between-groups sum of squares involves summing the squared deviation of each sample mean from the grand mean; $\Sigma x_b^2 = 34.5$. It can now be shown that $\Sigma x^2 = \Sigma x_w^2 + \Sigma x_b^2$, or $91.7 = 57.2 + 34.5$.

Estimating Population Variance

It is possible to obtain estimates of the population variance by dividing within-groups and between-groups sums of squares by the appropriate degrees of freedom. Since the total sum of squares is derived from variations around a single mean (the grand mean), only 1 df is lost. Thus the total df is $N - 1$.

[1] The logic of summing each within-groups Σx^2 is identical to that used in the standard error term of the t test [formula (6)] and will be further explained in the next section.

This can be partitioned into the *df* associated with the between-groups sums of squares, which is derived from the variation of the group means around a single mean (the grand mean), and the *df* associated with the within-groups sum of squares, which is derived from the variation of each individual score within a group around the mean of the group. The between-groups *df* is equal to the number of means r minus 1 $(r - 1)$. The *df* for Σx_w^2 is equal to the total number of subjects minus the number of groups $(N - r)$. Summarizing the *df* for each sum of squares, we have

$$N - 1 = N - r + r - 1$$

Total = within + between

From the discussion of Table 14.6, we know that $\Sigma x_w^2 = 57.2$. Dividing by $df = 15 - 3$ $(N - r)$ we obtain $s_w^2 = 4.7$, the within-groups variance. The between-groups sum of squares $\Sigma x_b^2 = 34.5$. Dividing by $3 - 1 = 2$ $(r - 1)$ we obtain $s_b^2 = 17.3$. Each of these values is an independent estimate of the population variance and is called a "mean square."

The Within-groups Variance/ The s_w^2 is an unbiased estimate of the population variance. In the previous section on partitioning sums of squares, the within-groups sums of squares were combined. Now we have seen that the combined Σx_w^2 are divided by $df = N - r$ to provide an unbiased estimate of the population s^2. This procedure is based on the assumption that a composite estimate of the population variation is superior to a single estimate because the composite is based on a larger $N = n_1 + n_2 + n_3$.

We might also view Σx_w^2 as reflecting the average variation within the samples used in the experiment. This variation can be thought of as uncontrolled variation; that is, variation among subjects which influence each subject's performance on the task. Consider the unlikely situation where, within each of three groups, each S has the same score; no variation exists within a group. Assuming that the single scores differ among the groups, one could conclude that the experimental treatments differed from one another and that each treatment was equally effective for those Ss on which it was used. Thus, in a real sense the within-groups variance can be thought of as an *error term*—a term reflecting uncontrolled variation.

The Between-groups Variance/ The s_b^2 is also an estimate of the population variance and is independent of s_w^2. It reflects the variation of the sample means around the population mean. Assuming that the sample means are equal (the null hypothesis), this variation provides an estimate of the population variation. If the means are not equal, the null hypothesis is untrue; then s_b^2 reflects the population variance plus the variance attributable to differences among the sample means.

In most experiments, one hopes for differences among the group means because such differences presumably reflect differences in treatment effectiveness. Because s_w^2 and s_b^2 are unbiased estimates of the population s^2, the investigator hopes that s_b^2 will be larger than s_w^2. If this occurs he knows that there are differences among the means. Under the terms of the null hypothesis, $s_b^2/s_w^2 = 1$; that is, $s_b^2 = s_w^2$.

The F Test of Significance

R. A. Fisher has shown that the ratio of the between-groups variance to the within-groups variance has a specific sampling distribution F. In other words, if we were to determine the ratio of the between-groups variance to the within-groups variance for 10,000 different samples of the same size N, we would obtain a distribution of Fs. It is from the F table (Table E of Appendix A) that we can determine the probability that observed differences among three or more sample means occurred by chance. We shall now work through a problem which demonstrates the computations involved and the interpretation of an F.

The data for the problem are summarized in Table 14.7.

Table 14.7/ Number of Correct Responses Made by Three Different Treatment Groups

	Praise	Blame	Candy	
	25	16	25	
	26	11	15	
	17	11	21	
	19	18	17	
	26	15	22	
	23	16	24	
	24	15	15	
	25	20	22	
	17	16	26	
	19	10	15	
$\Sigma X =$	221	148	202 =	571
$\Sigma X^2 =$	5,007	2,284	4,250 =	11,541

1 / Total sum of squares:

$$\Sigma x_t^2 = \Sigma X^2 - \frac{(\Sigma X)^2}{N}$$

$$(25)^2 + (26)^2 + (17)^2 + (19)^2 + \cdots$$

$$+ (15)^2 - \frac{(571)^2}{30} = 672.97$$

2 / Between-groups sum of squares:

$$\Sigma x_b^2 = \frac{(\Sigma X_A)^2}{N_A} + \frac{(\Sigma X_B)^2}{N_B} + \frac{(\Sigma X_C)^2}{N_C} - \frac{(\Sigma X)^2}{N}$$

$$= \frac{(221)^2}{10} + \frac{(148)^2}{10} + \frac{(202)^2}{10} - \frac{(571)^2}{30}$$

$$= 286.87$$

3 / Within-groups sum of squares:

$$\Sigma x_W^2 = \Sigma X_A^2 - \frac{(\Sigma X_A)^2}{N_A} + \Sigma X_B^2 - \frac{(\Sigma X_B)^2}{N_B}$$

$$+ \Sigma X_C^2 - \frac{(\Sigma X_C)^2}{N_C}$$

$$= 5,007 - \frac{(221)^2}{10} + 2,284 - \frac{(148)^2}{10} + 4,250 - \frac{(202)^2}{10}$$

$$= 386.10$$

A more convenient approach to the computation of the within-groups sum of squares is to subtract the sum of squares between groups from the total sum of squares:

$$672.97 - 286.87 = 386.10$$

The results of the analysis of variance are presented in Table 14.8. Allocation of df follows the model presented earlier in this chapter. The total number of df available is equal to $N - 1$ or $30 - 1 = 29$; the number of df attributed to the between-

Table 14.8 / Summary of the Analysis of Variance of the Three Treatment Groups

Source of Variance	Sum of Squares	df	Mean Square	F
Between treatments	286.87	2	143.43	10.03
Within groups (error)	386.10	27	14.30	
Total	672.97	29		

groups-sum of squares is $r - 1$ or $3 - 1 = 2$; and the number of within-groups df is equal to $N - r$ or $30 - 3 = 27$. Dividing the two sums of squares by their appropriate df results in the required variance estimates. Dividing the between-groups s^2 by the within-groups s^2 results in an F of 10.03. Entering the F table with 2 and 27 df we find that the required F for significance at the 5 per cent level is 3.35. Since the F is larger than that required we can reject the null hypothesis and conclude that the treatments produced differences among the groups. Inspection of the data suggests that the praise and candy groups are better than the blame group. When an analysis of variance is statistically significant, it is permissible to compare separate groups by means of t tests. Ryan (14) discusses the issues involved in this procedure.

Factorial Analysis of Variance

Suppose an experimenter believes that there are sex differences in performance on the discrimination task as well as differences attributable to the praise and candy. He has identified two factors: sex of subject and reward condition. Within each factor there are two levels: male and female, praise and candy. The factorial design requires that all combinations of levels within the factors be examined. Our illustrative example indicates that there are $2 \times 2 = 4$ (read 2 by 2) combinations: praise–male, praise–female, candy–male, and candy–female. The experiment requires, therefore, four groups. If there were three levels of reward and two levels for sex, the design would be a 3×2 factorial requiring six groups. Suppose we had *three factors,* each with two levels. The design would then be a $2 \times 2 \times 2$ factorial design requiring eight groups.

Partitioning Sums of Squares

In order to better understand the sources of variation in the factorial design, a simple example of a 2×2 design, where $N = 3$ for each of the four groups, is presented in Table 14.9. Levels A and B (column scores) will be labeled the "T factor," and levels C and D (row scores) will be labeled the "S factor." Notice that we can evaluate the differences between levels A and B of the T factor without regard to the S factor. Thus, the mean for level A is the sum of all the A scores divided by $N;$ $25/6 = 4.2$. The mean for level B is $37/6 = 6.2$. Similarly, we can test for differences between levels C and D of factor S by

Table 14.9/ An Example of a 2 × 2 Factorial Design

A		B	
C	D	C	D
5	4	3	9
2	7	6	7
1	6	4	8

ΣX 8   17   13   24
ΣX^2 30 101   61 194
M 2.6 6.3 4.3 8.0
Grand mean = 5.2

$$\Sigma x_t^2 = (5)^2 + (2)^2 + \cdots (8)^2$$
$$- \frac{(62)^2}{12} = 65.7$$

$$\Sigma x_b^2 = \frac{(8)^2}{3} + \frac{(17^2)}{3} + \frac{(13)^2}{3} + \frac{(24)^2}{3}$$
$$- \frac{(62)^2}{12} = 45.7$$

$$\Sigma x_w^2 = \Sigma x_t^2 - \Sigma x_b^2 = 65.7$$
$$- 45.7 = 20.0$$

disregarding factor T. The mean for level C is $2\frac{1}{6} = 3.5$ and the mean for level D is $4\frac{1}{6} = 6.8$.

Partitioning the sum of squares is similar to the procedure followed for the analysis of variance of three groups. We have the total sum of squares, the sum of the squared deviations from the grand mean of each subject's score; the between-groups sum of squares, the sum of the squared deviations from the grand mean of each group mean; and the within-groups sum of squares, the sum of the squared deviations of each score from its own mean for each group, and the summed results. Direct computation gives $\Sigma x_t^2 = 65.7$, $\Sigma x_w^2 = 20.1$, $\Sigma x_b^2 = 45.6$.

We shall now focus our attention on Σx_b^2. The computations in Table 14.9 involve taking each of the four group means and determining its squared deviation from the grand mean. Our interest, however, is not in the differences among the four groups but in the differences between A and B and between C and D. We shall now compute the sum of squares for the difference between A and B without regard to C and D. For A, we have $8 + 17 = 25$; for B, $13 + 24 = 37$:

$$\frac{(25)^2}{6} + \frac{(37)^2}{6} - \frac{(62)^2}{12} = 12.0$$

Computing the sum of squares for C and D regardless of A and B, we have for C, $8 + 13 = 21$, and for D, $17 + 24 = 41$:

$$\frac{(21)^2}{6} + \frac{(41)^2}{6} - \frac{(62)^2}{12} = 33.3$$

The total sum of squares between groups, however, is 45.7 and our total is 45.3. The remaining sum of squares is attributable to the interaction of variables T and S or, more commonly, the $T \times S$ interaction.

The Interaction Sum of Squares/ We shall first set up a 2×2 table and label each cell. The formula for computing the interaction sum of squares for Table 14.10 is

$$\left[\frac{(a + d) - (b + c)}{4n} \right]^2 \tag{9}$$

We will now substitute numbers in each cell and compute the interaction, as shown in Table 14.11. Computing the interaction sum of squares in this way is identical to subtracting from the total between-groups sum of squares the sum of squares attributable to variables T and S.

Table 14.10/ A 2 $\times$ 2 Interaction

	A	B
C	a	b
D	c	d

Table 14.11/ All Entries for a 2 $\times$ 2 Interaction

	A	B
C	8	13
D	17	24

$$\left[\frac{(8 + 24) - (13 + 17)}{4(3)} \right]^2 = .3$$

Obviously the $T \times S$ interaction of 0.3 represents a very small proportion of the total between-groups sum of squares. The fact that it is so small means that the difference between the means for A and B for level C is the same as the difference between A and B for level D; that is, any difference between A and B is independent of variable S. The difference between M_A and M_B for level C is $2.6 - 4.3 = -1.7$; the difference between M_A and M_B for level D is $6.3 - 8.0 = -1.7$.

Variance Estimates for a 2 $\times$ 2 Factorial/ From our earlier discussion of the analysis of variance we know that $N - 1 =$

total df, $N - r =$ within-groups df, and $r - 1 =$ between-groups df. Assigning df to the present problem we have total $df = 11$, within-groups $df = 8$, between-groups $df = 3$. Dividing $\Sigma x_w^2 = 20.0$ by $df = 8$ we obtain 2.5; dividing $\Sigma x_b^2 = 45.7$ by $df = 3$ we obtain 15.2. Since $F = \Sigma x_b^2 / \Sigma x_w^2$ we have $F = 6.1$. Entering Table E of Appendix A with 3 and 8 df, we find that $F = 4.07$ is required for significance at the 0.05 level. Since our F is larger, we can conclude that the differences among the four groups are statistically significant.

As noted earlier we are really interested in the differences between levels of variable T, variable S, and also the $T \times S$ interaction. We were able to break down the between-groups Σx_b^2, and we can also break down the total between-groups df of 3. Thus, for the difference between A and B we have 1 df; for C and D we also have 1 df. The remaining df of 1 is assigned to the interaction sum of squares; that is, $1 \times 1 = 1$. We can now summarize the analysis of this 2×2 factorial analysis of variance. As shown in Table 14.12, the

Table 14.12/ Summary of 2 × 2 Factorial Analysis of Variance

Source	Sum of Squares	df	Mean Square	F	p
Variable T	12.0	1	12.0	4.8	
Variable S	33.3	1	33.3	13.3	0.01
Interaction: $T \times S$	0.3	1	0.3	—	
Within-groups	20.0	8	2.5		
Total	65.7	11			

$F = 4.8$ for variable T is not statistically significant (for 1 and 8 df, F must be 5.32 for the 0.05 level); the $F = 13.3$ for variable S is statistically significant; the $T \times S$ interaction $F = 0.3$; the interaction is not statistically significant because F is less than 1.

We shall now return to our problem involving praise, blame, and candy. When the experimenter examines the data, he suspects that even though the praise and candy groups perform at the same level, the praise treatment is more effective with the girls in his sample. He decides to replicate the experiment using praise and candy as one independent variable and boys and girls as the second independent variable: that is, using a

Table 14.13/ Total Number of Correct Responses on a Discrimination Learning Task

PRAISE		CANDY	
Boys	Girls	Boys	Girls
20	30	20	20
21	37	10	22
12	30	16	13
14	38	12	23
21	39	17	12
18	32	30	19
19	32	22	14
12	39	27	19
14	36	32	18
20	38	22	14
$\Sigma X =$ 171	351	208	174
$\Sigma X^2 =$ 3047	12443	4810	3164

2×2 factorial design. The results are summarized in Table 14.13. The first computation is the total sum of squares and is identical to procedures previously used.

1/ Total sum of squares:

$$(20)^2 + (21)^2 + (12)^2 + (14)^2 + \cdots + (14)^2 - \frac{(904)^2}{40} = 3033.6$$

The second step involves determining the sum of squares between all the groups:

2/ Between-groups sum of squares:

$$\frac{(171)^2}{10} + \frac{(351)^2}{10} + \frac{(208)^2}{10} + \frac{(174)^2}{10} - \frac{(904)^2}{40} = 2167.8$$

We are not interested, however, in whether the groups are different but, instead, in the differences between the two independent variables, reward treatment and sex differences. We are also interested in the treatment $\times$ sex interaction. More specifically, we want to know whether praise and candy are differentially effective regardless of subject's sex, whether there are sex differences regardless of reward condition, and whether the two independent variables interact. The next two procedures show how to compute the sum of squares between reward conditions and sex, respectively:

3/ Between-rewards sum of squares:

$$\frac{(522)^2}{20} + \frac{(382)^2}{20} - \frac{(904)^2}{40} = 490.0$$

In step 3, all scores in the praise group are combined regardless of the subject's sex, and the same procedure is used with the blame group. In step 4, the praise and candy groups are combined for boys and girls separately:

4/ Between-sexes sum of squares:

$$\frac{(379)^2}{20} + \frac{(525)^2}{20} - \frac{(904)^2}{40} = 532.8$$

The within-groups sum of squares is obtained by subtracting the between-groups sum of squares from the total sum of squares:

5/ Within-groups sum of squares:

$$3033.6 - 2167.8 = 865.8$$

Procedures 3 and 4 give us the sum of squares for each independent variable taken separately. The variance is determined by dividing the sum of squares by df, which in each case is 1. The total df is equal to $N - 1$, or $40 - 1 = 39$. The within-groups df is $N - r$, or $40 - 4 = 36$. Adding the df for each independent variable gives us 2; adding the within-groups df gives us 38. There are, however, 39 df; thus, we must account for the additional df. The remaining df is associated with the interaction of the two independent variables.

The numerical value of the interaction is determined by subtracting from the between-groups sum of squares the between-sexes and the between-rewards sums of squares:

$$2167.8 - (532.8 + 490.0) = 1145.0$$

All the sums of squares necessary for completing the problem are now computed. As shown in Table 14.14, we next divide the sums of squares by the appropriate df to obtain the mean square. The F ratio is determined by dividing the mean squares for treatments, sex, and treatments $\times$ sex interaction by the within-groups mean square. Entering Table E with 1 and 36 df we find that an F of 4.11 is needed for significance at the

Table 14.14/ Summary of the Analysis of Variance of the Data in Table 14.13.

Source	Sum of Squares	df	Mean Square	F
Between treatments T	490.0	1	490.0	20.3
Between sexes S	532.8	1	532.8	22.1
$T \times S$ interaction	1145.0	1	1145.0	47.5
Within-groups	865.8	36	24.1	
Total	3033.6	39		

5 per cent level. We conclude, therefore, that the difference between the treatment groups is statistically significant and the praise group's performance is superior; that the difference between the sexes is statistically significant in favor of the girls; and that the interaction between the two variables is also statistically significant.

Interpreting the Interaction/ Inspection of the sum of scores for each of the four groups in Table 14.15 suggests that the female subjects are more influenced by the praise condition than by the candy condition, whereas the boys are more affected by the candy condition. Summarized in Table 14.15 are the

Table 14.15/ The Interaction of Treatments and Sex Variables

	Praise	Candy	Difference
Girls	35.1	17.4	17.7
Boys	17.1	20.8	—6.3
Difference	18.0	—3.4	

mean scores for each group along with the differences between them. Observe that the difference between the sexes for the praise condition is 18.0 but that the sex difference for the candy condition is negative, —3.4. The difference between the two reward conditions for the girls is 17.7 but the difference for the boys is in a negative direction, —6.3. The fact that these difference scores are grossly different and are also in opposite directions indicates the presence of an interaction.

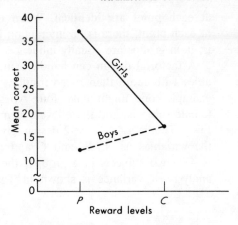

Figure 14.3/ Graphic Representation of a 2 x 2 interaction.

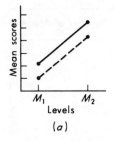

(a)

Figure 14.4a/ Levels.

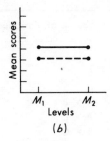

(b)

Figure 14.4b/ Levels.

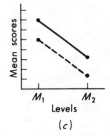

(c)

Figure 14.4c/ Levels.

The interaction is shown in Figure 14.3, in which the mean scores are plotted on the ordinate. The two treatment levels, *P* and *C,* are plotted on the abscissa. Notice that the line connecting the two means for boys is almost horizontal. The line connecting the two means for the girls is much steeper. These lines indicate that the difference between means *P* and *C* for boys is less than the difference between means *P* and *C* for the girls. Figure 14.3 shows that the girls perform better for praise than for candy, whereas the boys perform slightly better for candy than for praise.

Suppose that the lines connecting the two means are parallel. Figures 14.4a, b, and c show parallel lines where the direction of the differences between the means is varied. In Figure 14.4a, the two lines increase from a lower to a higher mean; Figure 14.4b shows two parallel horizontal lines; and Figure 14.4c shows two parallel lines where the lines decrease from a higher mean to a lower mean. The fact that the lines in all three figures are parallel indicates that the differences between the means at each point are identical. When the differences are similar at each point, there is no interaction between the variables; that is, both groups are equally influenced by each treatment.

A factorial design can handle a number of independent variables with more than two variations within each variable. For example, one might have four types of rewards, male versus female subjects, and three levels of motivation (high, moderate, low). This is a $4 \times 3 \times 2$ design, giving us 24 groups. Defining the variables as *A, B,* and *C* and assuming that the total *N* is 48 (two subjects in a group), the resulting summary of the analysis of variance is shown in Table 14.16. In addition to

Table 14.16/ Summary of an Analysis of Variance of a $4 \times 3 \times 2$ Factorial Design

Source of Variation	Degrees of Freedom
A	3
B	2
C	1
A × B	6
A × C	3
B × C	2
A × B × C	6
Within groups (error)	24
Total	47

testing for differences among the independent variables we can also test the statistical significance of the three 2-way interactions ($A \times B, A \times C,$ and $B \times C$) and the one 3-way interaction ($A \times B \times C$). Triple interactions show the effects of all three variables on the dependent variable.

Repeated-measures Analysis of Variance

Design 7, described in Chapter 11 (pages 281 to 283), includes the experimental situation where several measures are made on a subject over a period of time. A typical experiment involves a learning situation where scores are accumulated at defined intervals (scores for every 10 trials or scores within a one-minute interval). A plot of the means at each of these intervals provides a curve showing the *rate* at which a particular response is acquired. A horizontal curve indicates that no learning took place during the experiment, while a curve which rises over the experimental period indicates that learning did occur.

Partitioning Sums of Squares/ A highly simplified set of data is presented in Table 14.17, comprised of one group ($N = 5$) and three repeated measures, designated "trials." Thus we have a total of 15 measures. The *column* sums (ΣX, ΣX^2) are the scores of the five subjects on the first, second, and third

Table 14.17/ Repeated Measures for One Group

Subjects	1	2	3	Σ
1	2	4	5	11
2	1	3	6	10
3	3	2	4	9
4	1	3	6	10
5	3	3	4	10
ΣX	10	15	25	50
ΣX^2	24	47	129	502
M	2	3	5	

trials, respectively. As indicated by the trial means, there is improvement in performance over trials. The *row* sums are the total scores of each S over the three trials. Our task is to determine whether the increasing means represent a chance occurrence or whether the increase is statistically significant. The null hypothesis is that the line is a chance departure from a hypothetical *horizontal* line. Notice that the line connecting the means may increase or decrease; the null hypothesis is only concerned with the departure from the horizontal.

We begin partitioning the sums of squares by calculating the total Σx_t^2:

$$\Sigma x_t^2 = (2)^2 + (1)^2 + (3)^2 + \cdots + (4)^2 - \frac{(50)^2}{15} = 33.3$$

The next step is to determine the sum of squares associated with the trial means, which is computed as if they represented sample means. Thus, we have

$$\Sigma x_b^2 = \frac{(10)^2}{5} + \frac{(15)^2}{5} + \frac{(25)^2}{5} - \frac{(50)^2}{15} = 23.3$$

Next we consider the sums of the rows, paying particular attention to the variation among the sums for subjects. This is between-subject variation, which is a part of the total variation. Had the experimental treatment influenced each S in the same way, there would have been no variation among these sums. As it is, there is very little, as shown by the following computations:

$$\Sigma x_{Ss}^2 = \frac{(11)^2}{3} + \frac{(10)^2}{3} + \frac{(9)^2}{3} + \frac{(10)^2}{3} + \frac{(10)^2}{3} - \frac{(50)^2}{15} = 0.6$$

If we now add the sum of squares for trials and the sum of squares for subjects, we obtain $23.3 + 0.6 = 23.9$, which does not sum to the total sum of squares of 33.3. The difference of 9.4 is called the "subjects $\times$ trials interaction" and represents a pooling of the random variation of each S over the trials; that is, it sums, over all Ss, individual variation from trial to trial. For example, in Table 14.17, subject 3 drops one score unit between trials 1 and 2, and subject 4 improves 2 score units, but subject 5 remains even. Such variation is, in effect, unexplained and unique to the individual. In this sense it represents random error and is used in assessing statistical significance.

Estimating Variance/ As has been true before, we determine variance by dividing the sums of squares by the appropriate df. We are interested in determining the significance of the differences among trial means, and we must therefore determine the variance for trials. Since there are three trial means we know that df = number of trial means $T - 1 = 2$. The df for Ss is the number $Ss - 1$; $5 - 1 = 4$. Finally, df for the subjects $\times$ trials interaction is the product of df for Ss times df for trials: $4 \times 2 = 8$.

The F Test for Repeated Measures/ The analysis of variance is summarized in Table 14.18. Since the $T \times Ss$ interaction is the pooled fluctuation and thus represents chance errors, it is reasonable to determine whether this variation is the same as the variation associated with the trial means. The null hypothesis

Table 14.18/ Summary of Analysis of Variance for Repeated Measures

Source	Sum of Squares	df	Mean Square	F
Trials T	23.3	2	11.7	9.7
Subjects Ss	0.6	4	0.2	—
Interaction: $T \times Ss$	9.4	8	1.2	
Total	33.3	14		

states that the trials variance equals the $Ss \times$ trials variance, in which case $F = 1$. Table 14.18 shows that the trials $F = 9.7$, which for 2 and 8 df is statistically significant at the 0.01 level. Thus, we can conclude that the increase in means over trials is not a chance occurrence but represents a statistically reliable improvement. The F for Ss is less than 1, which indicates that the Ss are fairly uniform in their performance.

Repeated Measures with Two Treatments/ Most psychological and educational research is concerned with comparisons of performance curves for two or more groups which have received different experiences. In Figure 14.5 there are two learning curves which appear to rise at different rates of learning. The statistical procedures for assessing whether learning occurred or not and for determining whether two groups learned at differential rates will now be described (Figure 14.5 on p. 405).

Summarized in Table 14.19 are the results of a hypothetical experiment involving a reward variable (praise versus candy) and four intervals of time. The time intervals in this experiment are blocks of 10 trials where for each block of 10 trials the number of correct responses by each subject is determined. T_1, T_2, T_3, and T_4 refer to the blocks of trials, and the numbers immediately below are scores.

This experimental design involves a comparison between two independent samples (praise versus candy) and a comparison involving repeated measures on the same subject. We already know how to use analysis of variance involving a comparison of two groups (see pages 390 to 398), and the analysis of Table 14.17, summarized in Table 14.18, explained the procedures for a repeated-measures analysis of variance. The data in Table 14.19 require a combination of the two procedures. Two error terms (within-groups and $Ss \times$ trials) are involved in this analysis. The within-groups term is used to determine the signifi-

Table 14.19/ Number of Correct Responses for Each Treatment Group over Successive Trials

				Trials		
	S_s	T_1	T_2	T_3	T_4	Σ
Praise	1	3	7	8	10	28
	2	1	5	6	8	20
	3	2	4	3	9	18
	4	4	2	5	7	18
	5	1	3	7	10	21
Total		11	21	29	44	105
Candy	1	1	1	3	5	10
	2	3	4	5	6	18
	3	3	5	5	4	17
	4	2	1	2	7	12
	5	2	2	3	6	13
Total		11	13	18	28	70

cance of the difference between the two groups (praise and candy). The Ss $\times$ trials term is used to determine the significance of the differences between trials and also the interaction of trials $\times$ groups. The latter interaction term involves a comparison of the two groups over trials; that is, the interaction is concerned with the *rates* of learning for each group.

1/ We shall now partition the sums of squares in the same manner as before. The first step is to determine the total sum of squares:

$$(3)^2 + (1)^2 + (2)^2 + \cdots + (10)^2 - \frac{(175)^2}{40} = 253.40$$

2/ Next we determine the sum of squares attributable to differences among the subjects. This involves summing the total score for each S, and using these scores in the analysis. Between-subjects sum of squares:

$$\frac{(28)^2}{4} + \frac{(20)^2}{4} + \frac{(18)^2}{4} + \frac{(18)^2}{4} + \cdots + \frac{(13)^2}{4} - \frac{(175)^2}{40} = 59.15$$

3/ We can also determine the sum of squares between trials. The sums involved include the scores for all Ss on each trial, regardless of the group. Between-trials sum of squares:

$$\frac{(22)^2}{10} + \frac{(34)^2}{10} + \frac{(47)^2}{10} + \frac{(72)^2}{10} - \frac{(175)^2}{40} = 137.70$$

4/ The between-groups sum of squares involves the total scores for each group, which is the sum of scores for subjects. Between-groups sum of squares:

$$\frac{(105)^2}{20} + \frac{(70)^2}{20} - \frac{(175)^2}{40} = 30.65$$

5/ The within-groups sum of squares can be obtained by subtraction. We have the between-Ss sum of squares, which is the variation among Ss. Part of this variation is attributable to the variation between groups. Thus, there is variation among Ss because of the different experimental treatments. If now we subtract the sum of squares for between groups from the sum of squares between Ss, we obtain the within-groups sum of squares:

$$28.50 = 59.15 - 30.65$$

6/ The $Ss \times$ trials interaction sum of squares consists of the pooled variation over trials for each individual S. In effect, the curves presented in Figure 14.5 are based on averages for all the Ss, so that no one curve may look like the average curve. From our previous discussion of the $Ss \times$ trials interaction, we concluded that such individual variation represented uncontrolled or chance variation. But in that situation we had only one treatment group, whereas our present problem includes two treatment groups. In this case we *cannot* conclude that all the $Ss \times$ trials variation is chance because part of the variation may have been caused by the two treatments. Thus, after computing the $Ss \times$ trials sum of squares, we will be able to take out a part attributable to the interaction of trials $\times$ groups. The necessary computations are total sum of squares minus subject sum of squares minus trials sum of squares equals subjects $\times$ trials sum of squares:

$$253.40 - 59.15 - 137.70 = 56.55$$

7/ Before computing the groups $\times$ trials interaction sum of squares, we need to determine the total amount of variation existing among the trial means regardless of treatment group. This sum of squares is called the *between-cells* sum of squares and is computed as follows:

$$\frac{(11)^2}{5} + \frac{(21)^2}{5} + \frac{(29)^2}{5} + \cdots + \frac{(28)^2}{5} - \frac{(175)^2}{40} = 181.80$$

8/ We can now take from the between-cells sum of squares the sum of squares attributable to the treatment groups and the sum of squares attributable to trials:

$$181.80 - 30.65 - 137.70 = 13.45$$

9/ It is now possible to obtain the corrected $Ss \times$ trials interaction. This term will serve as a basis for determining the significance of the trials differences and the interaction of trials $\times$ groups. We shall refer to this term as the "pooled $Ss \times$ trials error." Subject $\times$ trials sum of squares minus rewards $\times$ trials sum of squares equals pooled $Ss \times$ trials error:

$$56.55 - 13.45 = 43.10$$

We have now completed the computations necessary for evaluating a repeated-measures analysis involving two treatment groups. The next step is to estimate the variance, which involves dividing each sum of squares by the appropriate df. As before, we shall first determine the total df. Observe, from Table 14.19, that there is a total of 40 scores (4 trials times 10 Ss). Total $df = N - 1$; $40 - 1 = 39$. The between-groups df is the number of groups r minus 1; $2 - 1 = 1$. The df for within groups is equal to the total number of Ss minus the total number of groups $(N - r)$; $10 - 2 = 8$.

Table 14.20/ Summary Analysis of Variance Repeated-measures Design

Source of Variation	Sum of Squares	df	Mean Square	F
Treatment	30.65	1	30.65	8.61*
Within-groups error	28.50	8	3.56	
Trials	137.70	3	45.90	25.50†
Treatments $\times$ trials	13.45	3	4.48	2.49
Pooled $Ss \times$ trials error	43.10	24	1.80	
Total	253.40	39		

* Significant at 0.05.
† Significant at 0.01.

So far we have accounted for $N - r + (r - 1)$ $[(10 - 2) + (2 - 1)]$ equals 9 df out of a total of 39 df. The remaining df are accounted for in the following way: the $Ss \times$ trials interaction has 30 df (the number of Ss multiplied

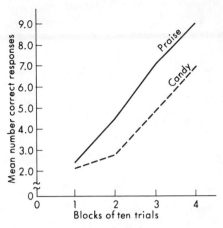

Figure 14.5/ Learning curves for different reward conditions over trials.

by the trials df, which is the number of trials minus 1); $10(3) = 30$; the $Ss \times$ trials consists of the trials sum of squares with 3 df and the interaction of trials $\times$ groups, which is obtained by multiplying the trials df by the groups df, $3 \times 1 = 3$. The df for pooled $Ss \times$ trials error is $30 - 3 - 3 = 24$.

We are now ready to compute the F tests. Summarized in Table 14.20 is the analysis of variance for the data in Table 14.19. The difference between each treatment group is determined by dividing the mean square for treatments by the within-groups mean square: $30.65/3.56 = 8.61$. Entering Table E of Appendix A with 1 and 8 df, we find that F is significant at the 0.05 level. This means that the difference between the groups is statistically significant. The F for trials is obtained by dividing the mean square for trials by the mean square for pooled $Ss \times$ trials error: $45.90/1.80 = 25.50$. Entering Table E with 3 and 24 df, we find F is significant at the 0.01 level. This means that, for both groups *combined*, the curve is not horizontal. Examination of Figure 14.5 shows that performance improves over trials and the F means that improvement is not a chance occurrence. The treatments $\times$ trials F is obtained by dividing the mean square for treatments $\times$ trials by the mean square for pooled $Ss \times$ trials error: $4.48/1.80 = 2.49$. Entering Table E with 3 and 24 df, we see that the interaction is not statistically significant. This means that the two curves in Figure 14.5 are parallel and that any fluctuation between the lines occurred by chance.

Summarizing the results of the analysis of variance, we can

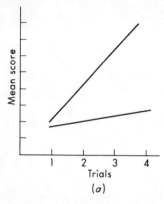

Figure 14.6a/ Trials.

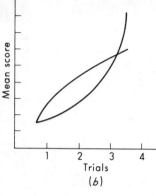

Figure 14.6b/ Trials.

conclude that the praise group made more overall correct responses than the candy group; that both groups combined improved their performance over trials; and that the rates of improvement for the two groups were essentially parallel.

For illustrative purposes, Figures 14.6a and b show two sets of curves in which a statistically significant trials × groups interaction might have occurred. Figure 14.6a illustrates the situation where one group learns very rapidly and the second group improves very little. Figure 14.6b shows a situation where one group starts off faster than the second but the second group exceeds the performance of the first group by the third trial and continues to improve on the fourth trial. It should be clear that a significant trials × groups interaction only tells whether the interaction is significant; it does not describe the nature of the interaction. The interpretation almost always requires drawing the curves and comparing the shapes of the curves.

The Chi-square Test of Significance

There are many occasions in educational research where the investigator is interested in testing a hypothesis that a certain *proportion* of a population exhibits a particular attribute. He selects a sample from the population and determines the proportion possessing the attribute and the proportion not possessing the attribute. The significance test is determined in terms of the probability that the observed proportion is a chance departure from the expected proportion. The test of significance is called "chi square" (χ^2).

The Sampling Distribution of χ^2

An example of a problem in which the χ^2 test of significance is appropriate might involve classifying pupils into three achievement categories, high, average, and low. Suppose this classification was made on a group of 20 children. We must further develop a hypothesis about the proportion of sixth-grade children expected in each of the three categories. For illustrative purposes, we shall hypothesize that 25 per cent of the population falls in the high category, 50 per cent in the average category, and 25 per cent in the low category. Thus for a sample of 20 Ss we would expect 5 Ss in the high category, 10 Ss in the average category, and 5 Ss in the low category. We will call these hypothesized frequencies "expected frequencies." We next administer an achievement test. All children with scores below a preset score are placed in the low category and all children with scores above a preset score are placed in the high category. Those children with scores between the high and low cutoff scores are placed in the average category. The observed frequencies are: four children in the low category, nine in the average category, and seven in the high category. We can determine whether the discrepancies between the observed and theoretical frequencies were chance discrepancies by using

$$\chi^2 = \sum \frac{(O - E)^2}{E} \tag{10}$$

where O is the observed frequency and E is the expected frequency.

Summarized in Table 14.21 are the computations required for our example. Observe that three chi squares are computed, one for each discrepancy between O and E. Summing (Σ) the individual chi-squares gives $\chi^2 = 1.2$. Table D of Appendix A has the χ^2 values required for significance at the 0.05 and

Table 14.21/ Computation in Computing Chi Square

	O	E	O–E	(O–E)²	$\frac{(O-E)^2}{E}$
Low	4	5	−1	1	0.2
Average	9	10	−1	1	0.2
High	7	5	2	4	0.8
Total					Σ1.2

0.01 levels. The χ^2 values at 0.05 and 0.01 vary in accordance with the degrees of freedom, which are dependent upon the number of categories. Thus, in our example there are frequencies in each of three categories. Once the frequencies for two categories are known, the third category must equal the difference between the sum of the frequencies in the two categories minus the total N. Our problem then has 2 df, the two categories free to vary. Table D shows that $\chi^2 = 1.2$ is not statistically significant. This means that our hypothetical proportions of 25 per cent, 50 per cent, and 25 per cent are tenable.

A further examination of Table D shows that as the df increase, the magnitude of χ^2 required for significance at the 0.05 or 0.01 level also increases. To understand why this happens, we shall add four more categories to our example problem, giving us a total of seven categories. Computing χ^2 for seven categories by using formula (10) means that four additional $(O-E)^2/E$ ratios are summed to give the total χ^2 and therefore increases the total χ^2 value. Thus, the magnitudes of a distribution of χ^2 vary according to the number of categories free to vary, that is, the degrees of freedom. As the discrepancies between the observed and expected frequencies increase and as the df increases, there is an increase in the value of χ^2. The tabled values for each df take into account the fact that χ^2 has a greater probability of being large as the df increase. Thus, the probability values for varied df are comparable.

Applications of χ^2

The χ^2 test of significance can be used in a variety of situations where categories are adequately defined and where there is a basis for determining theoretical or expected frequencies. In actual research use, the number of categories is usually quite small because of the difficulty of reliably differentiating people into finer and finer categories. Two of the more frequently used applications of χ^2 are presented in this section.

The $k \times l$ Contingency Table/ In many studies it is possible to categorize Ss on two dimensions simultaneously. Thus, a person may possess a B.A. degree and have an income over $10,000 per year or a person may have a B.A. degree and blue eyes. Both examples suggest a relationship between the categories; that is, having a B.A. degree *may* be associated, in the general population, with incomes over $10,000, or it may be associated with blue eyes. In the $k \times l$ contingency table, where k is columns and l is rows, we seek to determine whether two variables, each with more than two categories, are significantly associated.

Summarized in Table 14.22 are the results of a study of attitudes towards merit raises among teachers in each of five age categories. Twenty teachers in each age group were interviewed and their attitudes were classified as "favorable," "neutral," or "unfavorable."

Table 14.22/ Attitudes toward Merit Raises*

Age	Favorable	Neutral	Unfavorable	
21–25	15(8.6)	2(3.6)	3(7.8)	20
26–30	11(8.6)	4(3.6)	5(7.8)	20
31–35	9(8.6)	5(3.6)	6(7.8)	20
36–40	5(8.6)	5(3.6)	10(7.8)	20
41–45	3(8.6)	2(3.6)	15(7.8)	20
	43	18	39	100

* Numbers in parentheses are expected frequencies.

The computation of χ^2 requires expected frequencies for each cell of the table. Without any theoretical basis for assuming that the proportion of favorable, neutral, or unfavorable reactions will change with age, we must assume that a proportionate number of $Ss,$ from our total N of 100, will fall in each category. Thus, the first computation is the determination of the expected frequencies for each cell. Since our row totals are all 20, the computations are simplified because the expected frequencies for the columns will all be the same. The expected frequency for the cell 21–25 $\times$ Favorable is determined by multiplying the sum of the column frequency (43) by the sum of the row frequency (20) and dividing the product (860) by 100: 860/100 = 8.6. Thus 8.6 is the expected frequency for every cell in the Favorable column. The expected frequency for the Neutral column is obtained as follows: $18 \times 20/100 = 360/100 = 3.6$. The expected frequencies for the Unfavorable column can be obtained either by the above procedure $(39 \times 20/100 = 780/100 = 7.8)$ or by subtraction: $20 - 8.6 + 3.6 = 7.8$. You can use subtraction because the expected frequencies *must* sum to 20. We now have the observed and expected frequencies necessary for computing χ^2 by formula (10). The computations are summarized in Table 14.23, where it can be seen that $\chi^2 = 24.4$.

Before determining the level of significance, we must decide on the number of df. This can be done by examining Table

Table 14.23 / Computation of χ^2 for a 5×3 Contingency Table

Favorable				Neutral				Unfavorable			
O	E	$\frac{(O-E)^2}{E}$	χ^2	O	E	$\frac{(O-E)^2}{E}$	χ^2	O	E	$\frac{(O-E)^2}{E}$	χ^2
15	8.6	$(6.4)^2/8.6$	4.7	2	3.6	$(1.6)^2/3.6$	0.7	3	7.8	$(4.8)^2/7.8$	2.9
11	8.6	$(2.4)^2/8.6$	0.7	4	3.6	$(0.4)^2/3.6$	0.0	5	7.8	$(2.8)^2/7.8$	1.0
9	8.6	$(0.4)^2/8.6$	0.0	5	3.6	$(1.4)^2/3.6$	0.5	6	7.8	$(1.8)^2/7.8$	0.4
5	8.6	$(3.6)^2/8.6$	1.5	5	3.6	$(1.4)^2/3.6$	0.5	10	7.8	$(2.2)^2/7.8$	0.6
3	8.6	$(5.6)^2/8.6$	3.6	2	3.6	$(1.6)^2/3.6$	0.7	15	7.8	$(7.2)^2/7.8$	6.6
Total			$\Sigma 10.5$				$\Sigma 2.4$				$\Sigma 11.5$

$\Sigma\chi^2 = 10.5 + 2.4 + 11.5 = 24.4$

14.22 and understanding that, when summing rows, only two cells can vary and the third is fixed. When summing columns, only four cells can vary and the fifth is fixed. Thus there are $4 \times 2 = 8$ cells that can vary so there are 8 df. A convenient rule for determining df with any size of contingency table is $(k\text{-}1)$ $(l\text{-}1)$ or $(3\text{-}1)$ $(5\text{-}1) = 8$. Entering Table D with $\chi^2 = 24.4$, $df = 8$, we see that the χ^2 is significant at the 0.01 level. Reexamining Table 14.22 shows that the younger teachers react favorably to the merit raise system whereas older teachers react unfavorably. Thus, there is a relationship between age and attitude toward merit raises.

Fourfold Classification/ The χ^2 test of significance is frequently used in the situation where there are two variables, each categorized in two ways. For example, we might ask a sample of 60 men and 40 women how they feel about prohibition. We classify their responses into two categories: favorable and unfavorable. The observed frequencies are summarized in Table 14.24.

Table 14.24/ Sex Differences in Attitudes toward Prohibition*

	No	Yes	Σ
Men	40 (30)	20 (30)	60
Women	10 (20)	30 (20)	40
Σ	50	50	100

* Numbers in parentheses are expected frequencies.

We need to determine the expected frequencies without any theoretical basis for deriving them. We shall now examine the logic involved in determining these expected frequencies.

Table 14.25 is a fourfold contingency table where each cell is defined by a letter. The sums of the rows are given by $A + B$ and $C + D$. The column sums are given by $A + C$ and $B + D$. Under the terms of the null hypothesis, the total frequency of *favorable* responses $B + D$ can be pooled; that is, they represent two estimates of the frequency of favorable attitudes. Dividing the sum by N gives the estimate of the proportion of favorable attitudes existing in the population. Similarly the sum

Table 14.25/ A Fourfold Contingency Table

	No	Yes	
M	A	B	A + B
W	C	D	C + D
	A + C	B + D	N

$A + C$ divided by N gives an estimate of the population proportion unfavorable to prohibition. Having determined these proportions we now compute the expected frequencies.

$$E_A = \frac{A + C}{N}$$

$$E_B = \frac{B + D}{N}$$

$$E_C = \frac{A + C}{N}$$

$$E_D = \frac{B + D}{N}$$

We shall now apply these formulas to the data in Table 14.22. The computation of the expected frequencies is

$$E_A = \frac{40 + 10}{100} = 0.5(60) \qquad E_B = \frac{20 + 30}{100} = 0.5(60)$$
$$= 30 \qquad\qquad\qquad = 30$$
$$E_C = \frac{40 + 10}{100} = 0.5(40) \qquad E_D = \frac{20 + 30}{100} = 0.5(40)$$
$$= 20 \qquad\qquad\qquad = 20$$

Computation of χ^2 now follows in the usual way according to formula (10), with the modification of the correction for continuity required whenever 1 df is available.

$$\chi^2 = \frac{(40 - 30)^2}{30} = 3.33 \qquad \chi^2 = \frac{(10 - 20)^2}{20} = 5.0$$
$$\chi^2 = \frac{(20 - 30)^2}{30} = 3.33 \qquad \chi^2 = \frac{(30 - 20)^2}{20} = 5.0$$
$$\Sigma\chi^2 = 16.6$$

The resulting χ^2, with 1 df, is larger than that required for significance at the 5 per cent level, so we may reject the null hypothesis and conclude that sex differences exist in attitudes toward prohibition. Examination of the contingency table indicates that women have more favorable attitudes toward prohibition than men do.

There is an alternative method for computing χ^2 for a 2×2 contingency table. The necessary computations are

$$\chi^2 = \frac{N(AD - BC)^2}{(A + B)(C + D)(A + C)(B + D)} \tag{11}$$

The letters in formula (11) refer to the cells in the contingency table, as shown in Table 14.25. Thus, $A = 40$, $B = 20$, $C = 10$, and $D = 30$. Substituting in formula (11),

$$\chi^2 = \frac{100(1200 - 200)^2}{(60)(40)(50)(50)}$$
$$= 16.6$$

The df is 1 because as soon as the frequency for one cell is known the remaining three are fixed. Entering Table D with $\chi^2 = 16.6$ and 1 df we find that the χ^2 is significant at the 0.01 level. Again, we may conclude that there are sex differences in attitudes toward prohibition.

15

Writing the Research Report

A knowledge of the rules and principles involved in writing a research report will help you write better theses, dissertations, term papers, and professional articles and will enable you to read research publications more easily and more discriminatingly. Because a lack of technical writing skills will handicap your professional growth, you should master the fundamentals now and strive to perfect your skills throughout your career.

Format of the Report

Because research reports are read by busy professional people, a rather formal and uniform method of presenting them has evolved. Most graduate schools, research institutions, and professional journals publish a report format that they expect investigators to follow. To avoid having a report rejected or returned for extensive revisions because of improper makeup, a researcher should study the required format and adhere to it meticulously. The requirements at various institutions differ, but all formats are somewhat similar to the following outline which embraces three main divisions: the preliminaries, the body of the report or text, and the reference matter. Each main division may consist of several sections.

I. Preliminary Materials
   A. Title Page
   B. Approval Sheet (if any)
   C. Preface and Acknowledgments
   D. Table of Contents
   E. List of Tables (if any)
   F. List of Figures (if any)
II. Body of the Report
   A. Introduction
      1. Statement of the Problem
      2. Analysis of Related Studies
      3. Assumptions Underlying the Hypotheses
      4. Statement of Hypotheses
      5. Deduced Consequences
      6. Definition of Terms
   B. Method of Attack
      1. Procedures Employed
      2. Sources of Data
      3. Data-gathering Instruments
   C. Presentation and Analysis of Evidence
      1. Text
      2. Tables (if any, are usually incorporated into the text)
      3. Figures (if any, are usually incorporated into the text)
   D. Summary and Conclusions
      1. Brief Restatement of Problem and Procedures
      2. Findings and Conclusions
III. Reference Materials
   A. Bibliography
   B. Appendix (if any)
   C. Index (if any)

Preliminary Materials

Several pages of preliminary material are presented prior to the body of a report in a dissertation. The title page, which appears first, contains the following information: (1) title of the study, (2) full name of the candidate and his previous academic background, (3) name of the faculty and institution to which the report is submitted, (4) degree for which the report is presented, (5) year when the degree is to be conferred. These items, which are illustrated in the sample title page shown on page 416, are centered between the margins of the page and no terminal punctuation is used. The title is typed in capital letters, but usually only the initial letters of principal words are capitalized in other items. If the title extends beyond one line, it is double-spaced and placed in an inverted pyramid style. Vague or broad generalizations and ambiguous or unnecessary words are not acceptable in titles. A title should contain key words or phrases that give a clear and concise description of

TITLE OF DISSERTATION

by
Candidate's Full Name

Previous Degrees, Institutions, and Years of Graduation
A. B., University of California, 1960
M.A., University of Wisconsin, 1963

Submitted to the Graduate School of the University
of Pittsburgh in partial fulfillment of the
requirements for the degree of
Doctor of Philosophy

Pittsburgh, Pennsylvania
1966

the scope and nature of the report. The key words should make it easy for bibliographers to index the study in the proper category

If the institution requires an approval sheet, a page of the dissertation allots space for the adviser's signature and his name is typed below. Sometimes the names of all faculty committee members are presented on this page. A preface, if included, usually contains a brief statement of the purpose and scope of the report. In addition, thanks may be expressed to those who gave the writer substantial guidance or assistance, but a long list of effusive acknowledgments is not in good taste.

TABLE OF CONTENTS

The table of contents, which occupies a separate page or pages, gives the reader a bird's-eye view of the report and enables him to locate quickly each section of it. The chapter headings are usually typed in capital letters and their subdivisions in small letters with the initial letter of the principal words capitalized. These headings appear in the exact words and order that they are in the report, and each is followed by the correct page citation. The relationship between main headings and subtopics is shown by proper indentation and capitalization. If possible, the headings are confined to one line of space, and parallel gram-

LIST OF TABLES*

Table	Page
1. Mean Length of Sentence in Spoken Language as Shown in Twelve Investigations	26
2. Mean Number of Words per Sentence in Written Composition by Age and School Grade	32
3. Mean Number of Words per Sentence in Written Compositions by Intelligence and Sex	38

(*a*)

* The list of tables always begins on a new page.

LIST OF ILLUSTRATIONS*

Figure	Page
1. Grades of Mental Deficiency	15
2. Clinical Types of Mental Deficiency	20
3. Incidence of Mental Deficiency in the United States	25

(*b*)

* The list of illustrations always begins on a new page.

matical structure is used for the same value of headings. Following the table of contents are separate pages for the list of tables and the list of illustrations. The information for each item in these lists includes (1) number, usually arabic, of the table or figure, (2) exact title, and (3) number of page on which it appears in the body of the report. These preliminary materials are illustrated on the sample pages shown on pages 417 and 418. A research report that appears in a periodical does not ordinarily present these preliminary materials; the body of the report, moreover, may be condensed, and some sections, unfortunately, may be omitted to save space.

Body of The Report

The kernel of the study, the data and their analyses, follows the preliminary materials. This body of the report contains four logical divisions: (1) an introduction, (2) the method of attack, (3) the presentation and analysis of evidence, and (4) the summary and conclusions.

Introduction/ The first chapter serves as an orientation to the investigation. In the introduction the researcher states and analyzes the nature of the problem and reviews the related studies. His resume of the literature does not present a chronological list of abstracts that the reader must dissect to discover how they relate to the present problem, but rather points up the issues involved in the investigation and reveals the importance of the undertaking. In the review, the researcher brings together the results of the existing research, shows how the studies are related, and indicates where gaps or weaknesses exist that have given rise to the present study. The significance of the problem and the need for conducting the investigation become evident when the problem is placed in this wider framework of knowledge.

After reviewing the background of the problem and delimiting the precise points that he will investigate, the writer presents his hypotheses, the deduced consequences, and the assumptions on which the hypotheses are predicated. He then defines the terms that are essential to the study or are used in a restricted or unusual manner. This information gives the reader a clear concept of the scope of the investigation, the precise solution or explanation offered for the problem, and the evidence sought to test it.

Method of Attack/ When describing the procedures employed in the investigation, the researcher gives an accurate, detailed description of how the work was done as well as all of the information that the reader needs to judge the validity, adequacy, and suitability of the methods and instruments employed. His objective is to provide an explanation that will enable the reader to repeat the investigation—reproducing the exact conditions of the original study—to check the findings. This explanation, generally speaking, is rather extensive, and thus is placed in a chapter by itself. Since the findings of a study can be no better than the tools and methods used to solve it, scholars usually examine this section of the report with extreme care.

The kinds of procedural information presented depend on the nature of the study. An investigator may present the types of data gathered; the number and kinds of subjects—sex, age, previous experience, or any distinguishing characteristics that could affect the results of the investigation; how and on what basis the subjects were selected; when, where, and how the data were collected; the number of subjects who did not complete or did not participate in all parts of the study and why; the exact method of executing the experiment—experimental controls, how variables were manipulated, uncontrolled factors that may have affected the results and their possible implications; and verbal or written directions given to subjects. An account of the pilot study may be given. To assist other investigators, the researcher may explain any methods that were employed and abandoned because they proved to be inadequate or valueless.

Well-known data-gathering instruments and readily available apparatus are described briefly and references are listed to reveal where more detailed discussions may be found. But if new apparatus or instruments or variations of an old one are employed, detailed descriptions and drawings of them and clear explanations of how they were used are given. After describing the investigative instruments, the researcher explains the procedures employed to calibrate those that require it and tells what was done to determine the validity and reliability of the tools. Before presenting the results of his findings, the researcher checks to make certain that he has not omitted any essential information concerning his procedures that the reader must possess to follow or to comprehend the rest of the report.

Presentation and Analysis of Evidence/ The presentation and analysis of the data constitute a vital part of the study, for these materials represent the researcher's contribution to the advancement of knowledge. Because of the wide variety of studies and kinds of data that exist, no specific directions can be given for organizing this section of the report. The analysis of the data may be covered in one or more chapters, which may consist of tables, figures, and paragraphs of discussion that point out important aspects of the data. Raw data may be recorded in the most convenient form for collecting; but in the body of the report, data relevant to each hypothesis must be classified in ways that reveal the pertinent information required to confirm or disconfirm the hypothesis. In many studies, the raw evidence is subjected to specific statistical treatments and the values that are obtained rather than the raw evidence are reported in the study. When this procedure is followed, the treatment to which the data were subjected is clearly specified.

In the analysis of the data, the researcher points out the important facts that the collected evidence reveals and notes their relationships. He does not repeat all the detailed information that is in the tables and graphs, but rather interprets what the facts mean—their causes and effects and whether they confirm or disconfirm the hypothesis. Extracting the meaning from the data is one of the most difficult and most delightful phases of an investigation. If more than one explanation can be given for a particular fact, the researcher discusses all explanations, not merely the one he favors. After drafting an explanation, he examines the data for exceptions, tries to account for them, and restates his explanation if necessary. Any uncontrolled factors that may have affected the results, and their possible implications, are discussed. If the results of the investigation are in agreement or disagreement with other studies, this fact is pointed out and possible explanations are given for any differences. When stating the results of the study, careful qualifications are included that stipulate the precise condition or limits to which the conclusions apply.

When presenting and analyzing data, the researcher exercises caution. To check his work, he asks questions, such as the following: Are these data a product of any errors in observations or computation? Have I confused facts with opinions? Have I drawn a conclusion from unrepresentative data? Have I omitted or ignored evidence because it did not conform to my hypothesis? Have I assumed that B is the effect of A merely because it follows A? Have I assumed that because A and B resemble each other in some respects they must resemble each other in another respect? Have I assumed that something is true merely because an important man has said it is so? To what extent could chance factors have influenced my results?

Summary and Conclusions/ In the summary, the researcher briefly reviews the procedures, findings, and entire evolvement of the problem. The important points in the study are brought together in the summary, but not all the evidence upon which they are based is repeated. The conclusions are stated precisely and related directly to the hypotheses that were tested; the conclusions reveal whether the conditions that were deduced to be observable if the hypotheses offered an adequate explanation of the phenomena being studied were observable. The conclusions announce whether the findings of the study confirmed or disconfirmed the hypotheses. If the conclusions modify an existing theory, this fact is discussed. If the investigation raised any questions that suggest areas for further research, this information is presented tersely.

The summary and conclusion chapter is the most widely read part of a study because it recapitulates the information that has been presented in the previous sections of the report. Most readers scan the summary first to obtain an overview of the problem and to determine its usefulness to them. If the study is pertinent to their purposes, they examine the remaining chapters.

In addition to the summary, some institutions require a candidate to submit an abstract of 600 words or less to fulfill requirements for a degree. This abstract may be included in the formal report or may be published subsequently in *Dissertation Abstracts* or some other source. Some research journals also print a brief abstract in distinctive type at the beginning of each report. An abstract does not serve as a substitute for the summary and conclusion chapter, but rather as a synopsis that gives pertinent information which enables a scholar to judge whether he wishes to read the complete work.

Reference Materials

The bibliography, which will be discussed in detail later in this chapter, follows the main body of the report. An appendix, if included, follows the bibliography. The investigator does not merely dump leftover products of the study in the appendix; rather, he presents relevant supporting materials that are too unwieldly to be placed in the body of the dissertation, such as questionnaires, form letters, evaluation sheets, checklists, courses of study, long quotations, raw data, documents, and interview forms. The items in the appendix are grouped, labeled, lettered, and listed in the table of contents. If a study is complex, of major importance, or to be published in book or monograph form, the researcher also prepares an alphabetized index which follows the appendix.

Style of Writing

To avoid making unnecessary, time-consuming revisions of his report, a researcher should study the report format and style manual recommended by his professor or editor. Several style manuals are available to choose from if he is specifically granted the right to select his own (28,34,47,48,90,135,137). After adopting a style manual, he must adhere to it throughout the report, for switching from one acceptable style of writing to another is not permissible.

Mastering the methods of reporting research is important, for an outstanding scientific investigation is of little value if the findings are not communicated effectively to others. Accomplishing this feat is somewhat different from writing a nontechnical composition. Entertaining, amusing, or persuading the reader is not the objective of the researcher, nor does he merely discuss his opinions concerning a problem or suggest solutions and argue on the basis of general observations. A researcher presents a hypothesis, explains the procedures employed to test it, cites the factual data collected, and announces whether they confirm or disconfirm the hypothesis. A clear, objective, logical presentation and analysis of the evidence rather than an emotionalized argument or diverting descriptions are required in a scientific report.

A research report is not ordinarily read by laymen, but rather by well-informed individuals with more than a passing interest in the topic. These experts scrutinize the report systematically. They search for flaws in the chain of reasoning, and for assertions that are not supported by the evidence. They question interpretations placed upon the data and the accuracy of the footnotes. They may even check the results by repeating the experiment. A research report must stand the test of critical scholarship supplied by other investigators.

Organization

Spewing a disordered jumble of raw facts into a report form not only fails to convey information to the reader, but usually indicates that the author has not grasped the significance of his materials. Meaning cannot be derived easily from chaotic masses of isolated items. Data must be grouped and ordered into logical, attractive patterns before they can convey clear messages. Only through arduous intellectual effort can a researcher organize facts so that they deliver the precise ideas he has in mind.

A writer does not insert a blank sheet of paper in a typewriter and compose a report as he would a family letter. The final draft of a report is the end product of a process that begins in the initial stages of an investigation. When first exploring the literature and pondering upon his potential problem, a researcher notices that certain topics recur and seem to be related to it. If he jots down several of these items, the relationship between a few isolated facts may snap suddenly into focus and enable him to group them under one heading. After scanning several source materials, the investigator identifies some major topics, organizes them into a crude outline, and thereafter files his notes under these categories. While refining his hypothesis and doing more reading and more observing, he may note and correct weaknesses in his outline, such as gaps that exist, materials that are not in the most logical order, topics that are in poor proportion, or items that need to be combined or omitted. An outline is not a rigid instrument that is constructed accurately in one draft, but rather a map that is continuously being improved upon. Even in the most primitive stage of development, an outline serves a useful purpose. With each successive revision, it becomes a more reliable instrument.

What dictates the items and the order in an outline? The report format required by the institution provides the general framework. The hypotheses serve as guides for structuring the specific arguments—the procedures employed, the evidence collected, and the conclusions reached. But within each argument, materials must be ordered in terms of time, place, cause and effect, similarities and contrasts, or some other basis. After all the arguments are structured, they must be placed in a logical order.

Before writing the first draft of his dissertation, a researcher once again reviews the institutional format requirements and remodels sections of his outline that do not conform to it. He also makes certain that items in the outline are directly related to his hypotheses, and checks whether the items are placed in the most logical order. After extending the outline so that it includes both the main topics and the subtopics, he may also write topic sentences for the paragraphs that will come under them. When the outline seems satisfactory, he asks competent colleagues and his adviser to examine it critically for weaknesses.

Most researchers make detailed outlines, but some people find that they can write more spontaneously if they do not. This type of worker immerses himself in his subject, takes notes, and mentally structures information into orderly patterns as he reads and observes. After getting a good grasp of the materials, he records his ideas quite quickly. But he may outline these written materials afterward to check whether he has presented topics in the most logical order and has given them proper emphasis.

An outline also helps the researcher construct chapter titles and section headings. Doing this work carefully is important, for headings give readers an overview of the materials, help them find their way around in the report, and make it easier for them to grasp meanings. Headings cannot accomplish these objectives, of course, unless they are sufficiently specific to suggest the contents of the succeeding paragraphs. When writing headings, one should use the same grammatical structure and style of capitalization for items on the same level.

Right.
Chapter
  I. Format of the Report
 II. Style of the Report
III. Typing of the Report
Wrong.
Chapter
  I. Format of the Report
 II. Style manuals are selected with care
III. Typing

Language

Words—the writer's communication tools—are selected and ordered to inform the reader about the investigation rather than to impress him with rhetorical flourishes. Encrusting a report with polysyllabic words, technical jargon, involved sentences, and profuse quotations tends to smother the reader's interest and to prevent him from receiving the intended message. Since a pompous, pedantic presentation blocks rather than increases understanding, an able writer gives a simple, straightforward account of what took place in his study and makes every effort to prevent misinterpretations from arising. He defines unfamiliar terms or uses them in a context from which their meaning can be inferred, and refrains from employing a term in one sense at one point in his argument and in a different sense in another. If obscure theories are mentioned in a report, he gives a brief description of them. If a graph or drawing will make the written discussion easier to understand, he constructs one.

A formal rather than a colloquial style is employed when writing research reports. But formal writing need not drain all spontaneity and individuality from ideas and press them into prim, plodding prose passages. A lucid, lively account of an investigation can be produced if a writer uses vivid, varied and accurate means of expression and prunes all hackneyed, extraneous, and vague words from his report. Familiar, concrete nouns arouse clearer mental images than planned profundities. Brisk, active verbs hold the readers' attention better than the plodding passive voice.

Proportion and Emphasis

To achieve proper proportion and emphasis in a report, a writer keeps revising his outline until he has placed all topics of equal importance on the same level. He refrains from stating main ideas in a few terse sentences and elaborating upon minor points. When revising a report, he deletes treasured words and sentences that give too much weight to minor topics and adds supporting evidence and illustrations to expand underdeveloped major topics. To avoid burying significant ideas under masses of rhetorical trivia, he places topic sentences where they quickly capture the reader's attention, puts key words or phrases at the beginning or end of sentences, and utilizes numbers, italics, or warning words to signal that statements are important.

Unity and Clarity

To achieve unity and clarity in his report, a researcher selects homogeneous items from his notes, states the ideas in coherent sentences, places these sentences in a logical sequence, and weaves them into paragraphs that in turn are logically related. Again and again he examines sentences, paragraphs, and chapters to determine whether like ideas have been placed in juxtaposition and whether one idea leads naturally to the next. After transposing misplaced items, combining similar ideas, culling unnecessary and repetitive materials, and correcting vague or weak reference of pronouns to their antecedents, he again checks the flow of his manuscript. He asks: Have I shown the connection between ideas, so that the reader can easily follow the arguments? Have I used transitional words, sentences, and paragraphs that will alert the reader to changes in the road ahead and lead him gently from point to point?

Other Style Problems

Many other questions concerning style arise during the writing of a report. This text cannot cover all of them, but the following paragraphs discuss some common ones.

Since a research report is a formal and objective account of an investigation, it is written in the third person. Personal pronouns—I, me, we, you, our, and us—are not used. Abbreviations are not usually employed *in the textual materials,* but they may be used in footnotes, bibliographies, appendixes, and tables. In dissertations "per cent" is spelled out, but some journals permit the use of the symbol % in tables and even in the textual discussion.

Numbers of less than 100, round numbers, and numbers that begin sentences are spelled out; fractions are spelled out unless they are part of a longer number. If small and large numbers appear in a series, figures are used for all of them. Although there are some exceptions, numbers of four digits or more usually have commas to point off thousands. The letters or numbers that enumerate items in a paragraph are enclosed in parentheses; either letters or numbers may be used, but not both forms in the same report.

Simplified spelling is not acceptable in research reports. Punctuation conforms to good usage and is consistent. The past tense is used when referring to what the researcher or other investigators have done. The present tense is used when referring the reader to tables that are presently before him and when mentioning general truths and well-established principles. Not all style books present exactly the same rules, but, as has been stated previously, after a style has been selected, it must be followed consistently throughout the report.

Construction of Tables and Figures

Tables and figures that are accurately compiled, properly arranged, easily read, and correctly interpreted may convey information more effectively than many paragraphs of written description. Since a large number of graphic procedures have been devised, the following discussion can only point out some general rules governing their construction. More detailed explanations are presented in textbooks devoted to the subject (28,47,48,90,135,137).

Tables

When collecting data, the researcher may use the most convenient method of recording information, such as listing pupils' names alphabetically and placing varied information about the pupils in columns bearing the appropriate labels. But he may have to reorder these data later so as to make comparisons on the basis of sex, age, schools, or geographical areas. If possible, of course, an investigator devises a plan to collect the original data in a tabular form that will force the desired answers into clear focus. Learning how to pattern data so as to bring out significant information is of utmost importance. Through the use of a table, a researcher may help readers spot important details, see relationships, get a concise overview of the findings, or grasp the significance of data much more quickly and easily than through many pages of prose explanation.

Content/ Simplicity and unity are essential in the construction of tables. A complex table followed by an explanation which extends for several pages may confuse rather than enlighten the reader. While flipping back and forth from pages of discussion to the table, the thread of the argument may be lost. If several comparisons of distinctly different kinds are incorporated in one table, or if like comparisons are separated into many different tables, a reader may become bewildered. A well-constructed table, like a well-written paragraph, consists of several related facts that are integrated to present *one main idea*.

A well-constructed table is self-explanatory; it is complete and sufficiently clear to be understood without reading the textual explanation. Conversely, the textual discussion explains the generalizations that can be derived from the table and the relevancy of the information in a manner that enables the reader to grasp the main ideas without examining the table. In the textual discussion, the writer refers to the table by number (and page if necessary) rather than by the less specific phrase, "see the following table."

Not all statistical materials are placed in formal tables. A simple statistical statement, such as the following may be inserted directly in the body of a paragraph: "Of the 376 children, 120 had received no Salk vaccine shots, 136 had received one, and 120 had received two." A few facts may be organized into an informal pattern and woven into the textual material by an introductory sentence followed by a colon, for example:

The teachers were about evenly divided in their choice of retirement plans:

	Women	Men	Total
Plan A	20	19	39
Plan B	16	18	34
Total	36	37	73

The table of contents in the dissertation does not list these informally presented statistical statements.

TABLE 3.—NUMBER OF PUBLIC ELEMENTARY- AND SECONDARY-SCHOOL
TEACHERS IN SERVICE, 1947-48 THRU 1956-57 [a]

Year	Number of elementary-school teachers	Percent change from previous year	Number of secondary-school teachers	Percent change from previous year	Total	Percent change from previous year
1	2	3	4	5	6	7
1947-48	578,226 [b]	.....	319,746 [b]	.....	897,972 [b]	.....
1948-49	594,047 [b]	+2.7%	330,289 [b]	+3.3%	924,336 [b]	+2.9%
1949-50	586,276	−1.3	318,163	−3.7	904,439	−2.2
1950-51	604,131	+3.0	323,486	+1.7	927,617	+2.6
1951-52	627,285	+3.8	329,173	+1.8	956,458	+3.1
1952-53	653,573	+4.2	339,010	+3.0	992,583	+3.8
1953-54	661,900	+1.3	362,848	+7.0	1,024,748	+3.2
1954-55	690,987	+4.4	389,342	+7.3	1,080,329	+5.4
1955-56	718,772	+4.0	408,329	+4.9	1,127,101	+4.3
1956-57	751,490	+4.6	426,560	+4.5	1,178,050	+4.5
Change from 1947-48 to 1956-57.	+173,264	+30.0%	+106,814	+33.4%	+280,078	+31.2%

Source: Columns 2, 4, and 6 from: National Education Association, Research Division. *Advance Estimates of Public Elementary and Secondary Schools for the School Years,* 1947-48 thru 1956-57.
[a] See footnote to Table 2.
[b] Includes principals and supervisors.

Figure 15.1/ A table. (*From Research Division of NEA, "The Postwar Struggle to Provide Competent Teachers," Research Bulletin 35 (October, 1957), 107.*)

Placement/ A table never precedes but rather follows, as closely as possible, the first reference to it in the report. A table that will not fit into the remaining space on the page is placed on the next page at the end of the first paragraph. A table that covers more than half a page is usually centered on a page by itself. Long, detailed tables that interrupt the continuity of the discussion may be put in the appendix. If all tables are typed on separate pages, they will not have to be recopied each time the report is revised; when the final draft of the report is assembled, the original tables can be inserted in the proper places.

Numbers and Captions/ Tables are numbered consecutively throughout the report, including those that appear in the appendix. Many styles of constructing tables are acceptable, but consistency of style is required. One style that may be used conforms to the following pattern. The word "table," followed by its number, is placed alone on the first line and the heading or title two lines below it. Both items are typed in full capital letters, arabic numerals are used, and no end punctuation is necessary. A title more than one line long is single-spaced and typed to form an inverted pyramid. An effective heading describes precisely what the table contains; to aid the reader, the key descriptive word is placed near the beginning of the title. In parentheses below the title, information may be placed that the reader must possess when he scans the data, such as the unit of measurement (in thousands of dollars) or source of data (1967 Budget of Pittsburgh Public Schools). Sometimes the source is placed just beneath the table, as it is in Figure 15.1, which presents a slightly different but equally acceptable style.

In tables, the captions (column headings) and stubs (row labels) should be brief yet accurate and complete. Captions should be parallel in grammatical structure; common abbreviations may be used, but other abbreviations are avoided if possible. Long captions may be typed broadside so as to be read up from the bottom of the page. Writers employ different capitalization styles; some capitalize only the initial letter in the first word, and proper nouns and adjectives.

To facilitate locating items referred to in the table, the columns may be numbered (sometimes in parentheses) below the column captions (see Figure 15.1). Units of measurement may be given following the column caption or below the horizontal line beneath the caption. Figure columns are aligned on the right, but if decimals are used, the decimals are aligned. When no data are available, the omission is indicated by dots or dashes, or by leaving the space blank, rather than by a zero—which represents a value of zero rather than an omission. Table footnote references are noted by standard typewriter characters—*, **, ***—or by superscript lower-case letters—[a,b,c]. Table footnotes are placed just below the horizontal line at the bottom of the table rather than at the bottom of the page.

Size/ Tables should be no larger than the pages of the manuscript or publication. Folding tables into the copy is unsatisfactory and should be avoided if possible. If tables will not fit into the normal pages—lengthwise, crosswise, or spread across two facing pages—they may be reduced in size by photocopying them or using smaller print. If a table extends beyond a page in length, the word "table" and the number are repeated, followed by the word "continued," at the top of the succeeding pages. (For example, Table 3—Continued.) The title is omitted on the continued table, but all other captions are repeated. If a table covers two facing pages, the full heading is placed on the top of the first page and only the word "table" and the number, followed by the word "continued," appear on the top of the opposite page.

Rulings/ Rulings or lines are used only if they make the table easier to read. A double or heavy horizontal line may be placed above the column captions, a single one below them, and another below the last row of items in the table. Vertical rules and additional horizontal ones may be added if they break up the data into logical groups or make the arrangement simpler to use. Rulings are not used on the sides of tables.

Figures

Some ideas may be communicated more effectively by figures than by written or tabular presentations. A drawing of a piece of apparatus or a flow chart that traces channels of authority may clarify points that would otherwise require several pages of textual explanation. Presenting data in a graph or chart form may reveal important trends or relationships that a reader might not grasp when examining complex statistical data. Figures do not replace word descriptions, but they may help a researcher explain and interpret complicated instruments and data to the reader.

Types/ The commonest forms of figures used in reports are line graphs, bar graphs, pie charts, area or volume charts, component or belt charts, pictorial charts, flow charts, maps, diagrams of apparatus, and photographs. A number of reference books explain in detail the methods of presenting these figures, the advantages and disadvantages of utilizing each type, the pitfalls to avoid, and the rules governing their construction (28,47,63,90,135,137). The following discussion merely suggests some general rules for constructing figures.

Purpose/ Figures are not introduced merely to convey simple concepts or to make the report more interesting. A drawing or graph is used only if it snaps important ideas or significant relationships into a sharp focus for the reader more quickly than other means of presentation. Complex, confused, or carelessly prepared figures may be less effective communicators than words. A well-constructed figure weaves a few pertinent related facts together to present one main idea. It is simple and uncluttered with unneccessary details. Concise captions, labels, and legends are placed on the figure to describe the nature of the data and to interpret the information presented.

Number and Captions/ Illustrative materials are labeled with the word "figure" or "fig." and are numbered consecutively throughout the report with arabic numbers. The word "figure" and its number are usually placed below the illustration. The title for the illustration may be placed either (1) after the figure number, (2) at the top of the illustration, or (3) within the figure. The caption may be typed or lettered in full capital letters and in an inverted pyramid form with no terminal punctuation, or as an ordinary sentence in paragraph, underhung, or block form. The advice given previously about the placement of tables in the text and references to them in the written discussion also applies to figures.

Acknowledgment of Indebtedness

A research worker acknowledges his indebtedness to other authors not only as a matter of honesty and courtesy, but also as a means of confirming his work and indicating the quality and thoroughness of his investigation. To many readers, the footnotes and bibliography in a report, which gives clues concerning the related literature in the field, are as important as the textual materials. When writing a doctoral dissertation, therefore, or an article for a professional journal, or a term paper, one should include all the information that readers will need to locate the source materials with a minimum of effort. Sources of all quoted materials and important works that were used in preparing the report must be fully identified in accordance with the style rules that have been designed to transmit such information. Mastering these rules is one more basic skill for a writer.

Quotations

Laymen often joke about the array of quotations and footnotes found in research reports, and their barbs are not always unwarranted. Interlarding a report indiscriminately with quotations and footnotes is a cultural affectation that some inexperienced writers assume to conceal shoddy workmanship. Pasting numerous quotations into an authority-laden mosaic does not create an acceptable research report, for strings of these passages are dull and difficult to read. They reveal that the author is little beyond the note-taking stage of his work. A research report is a creative effort—a synthesis of what the investigator has read, observed, thought, and mentally ordered into new patterns—rather than a mere compilation of other men's work. A researcher may use quotations, but he uses them sparingly and purposively rather than as a crutch for a lazy mind.

Art of Quoting/ If an author paraphrases rather than quotes materials, his discussion usually moves more directly and forcefully toward his objective. To credit the original author of an idea that is borrowed but not quoted directly, the writer places a footnote superscript at the end of the statement and the appropriate documentation in the footnote.

When an investigator cannot rephrase a law, formula, or idea as concisely, accurately, or effectively as the original author, he uses a direct quotation. Whenever possible he selects a short quotation or strips the chaff from a longer one and plants the kernel in his own sentence. To avoid introducing quotations repeatedly with "Mr. X says," he places the introductory phrase within or at the end of the quotation.

Mechanics of Quoting/ The rules for presenting short and long direct quotations differ. A short quotation is enclosed in quotation marks, double-spaced, and incorporated in the paragraph. A quotation that appears within a short quotation is enclosed in single quotation marks. The arabic reference numeral to the footnote is typed half a space above and after the phrase or sentence quoted, and after the punctuation mark if it comes at the end of the sentence. Long quotations—four or more typewritten lines—are usually set off in separate single-spaced paragraphs that are indented in their entirety, and no quotation marks are necessary. Quotations within long quotations are set off by full quotation marks. Exceptionally long quotations may be placed in the appendix. A quotation that occurs in a footnote is single-spaced, enclosed in quotation marks, and indented in paragraph style.

In the previous discussion on taking notes (see Chapter 6), the text stressed the importance of checking for accuracy when duplicating quoted material. An explanation was also given of the method writers use to denote omissions in a quotation—ellipses—and to introduce corrections or explanations—brackets. Perhaps mention should be made of some other mechanics. If the first word of a quotation is grammatically linked to what precedes it in the sentence, the word is not capitalized even though it was capitalized in the original sentence. For example: (1) We agree with Dr. Jones that "measurement is essential in research." (2) Dr. Jones stated, "Measurement is essential in research." Questions may also arise concerning the end punctuation in quotations. Only one punctuation mark accompanies the terminal quotation marks: (1) a period or comma is placed inside closing quotation marks, (2) a colon or semicolon is placed outside quotation marks, (3) an interrogation or exclamation point is placed inside if it belongs to the quoted matter and outside if it is a part of the whole sentence.

Footnotes

Footnotes serve various purposes: (1) Some give source references for direct quotations or paraphrased material, (2) some provide cross references to materials appearing in other parts of the report, (3) some indicate sources that contain substantiating evidence, and (4) some explain or elaborate upon a point in the textual discussion. The last type should be kept to a minimum. Many editors insist that if something is important enough to be said, it should be placed in the body of the text.

Citation of Footnotes/ Several methods for inserting footnotes have been devised. The traditional procedure is to place at the bottom of the page all footnotes for citations appearing on that page. The footnotes are separated from the text by a short line—twenty spaces—drawn from the left margin one space below the written discussion. Beneath this line a double space is left before the first footnote is typed; the footnotes are single-spaced with double spaces between them. Each footnote is indented as in a paragraph and preceded by a superscript numeral that corresponds to the reference numeral used in the textual material. The first word of the footnote follows the reference superscript numeral; no punctuation or space is necessary (see page 435). If the text consists of tables, mathematical materials, or formulas, an asterisk or some symbol other than a number is selected to identify a footnote. The writer either numbers footnotes consecutively throughout the report, or begins anew on each page or in each chapter, depending upon the institutional requirements.

If a report is to be published, authors may employ other methods of inserting footnotes to facilitate the work of the printer. They may place the footnote immediately following the textual reference on the page and separate this source information from the rest of the paragraph by typing unbroken lines above and below it. To conserve space and to cut printing costs, some publishers prefer to have a coded reference to a source placed immediately after and in alignment with a direct quotation. A bibliographical code similar to the one used in this book, i.e., (16:24–25), may be employed. Many research journals use an author and date of publication code, i.e., (Jones, 1966). You will find examples of the latter in Appendix I. If an investigator uses the author-date method, he can omit or add references to a bibliography at any time without renumbering all the entries and making the necessary changes throughout the text. This method of citation is especially applicable for materials that appear in research journals where no quoted materials appear.

Abbreviations in Footnotes/ To save time and space, full bibliographical information is presented in the footnotes the first time that a reference is made to a source; thereafter, abbreviations are used to identify it. The abbreviation *ibid.* is employed when the succeeding references to a work *immediately* follow the first full citation (see sample footnotes 16 to 18). If references to *other works intervene* between the first and later citations to the same work, the abbreviation *loc. cit.* or *op. cit.* is used. If the reference is to the same page, *loc. cit.* is used; otherwise *op. cit.* and the volume, if necessary, and page number are given (see sample footnotes 20 and 22). The author's last name precedes these abbreviations, but his first name is added if more than one author cited in the report has the same last name. After the second work by the same author is cited, an abbreviated or full title must be given in each subsequent citation to make unmistakably clear which of his works is meant (see sample footnote 24). Some writers always use the abbreviated title instead of *op. cit.* and *loc. cit.* The terms *ibid., op. cit.,* and *loc. cit.* are followed by periods to denote that they are abbreviations, and they are underscored to indicate italics. The following samples of footnotes illustrate the use of these abbreviations:

[16] Alice W. Heim, "Adaptation to Level of Difficulty in Intelligence Testing," *British Journal of Psychology,* 46 (August, 1955), p. 211.

[17] *Ibid.* [same work, same page as above]

[18] *Ibid.,* p. 214. [same work as 16, but page 214]

[19] Robert A. Jackson, "Prediction of the Academic Success of College Freshmen," *Journal of Educational Psychology,* 46 (May, 1955), p. 296.

[20] Heim, *loc. cit.* [refers to 16, exactly the same page]

[21] Samuel F. Klugman, "Agreement between Two Tests as Predictors of College Success," *Personnel and Guidance Journal,* 36 (December, 1957), p. 255.

[22] Heim, *op. cit.,* 220. [refers to 16, but page 220]

[23] Alice W. Heim, *The Appraisal of Intelligence.* London: Methuen and Co., 1954, p. 169. [second work by Heim is introduced]

[24] Heim, "Adaptation in Intelligence Testing," *op. cit.,* p. 223. [repetition of title indicates which Heim work is meant]

A number of other abbreviations appear in research reports. Many of them are in Latin, although some are now being replaced by English terms. If a researcher is not familiar with these abbreviations, he cannot interpret the footnotes in many source materials and cannot utilize these shorthand devices when writing his report. Thus, in addition to the symbols above, a researcher should master the following common communication symbols:

anon. anonymous

Bk., Bks. book(s)

c. or *ca.* about (approximate date, *c.* 1245)

cf. compare (cf. *ante* p. 16, compare above; cf. *supra,* compare any preceeding material; cf. *post* p. 26, compare below; cf. *infra,* compare any subsequent material)

Ch., Chap., Chaps. chapter(s)

col., cols. column(s)

e.g. for example

ed., edd. edition(s)

ed., eds. editor(s); edited by

et al. and others (author Jones *et al.* stated)

et seq., et seqq. and the following (16 *et seq.,* page 16 and the following page)

f., ff. and the following page(s) (pp. 3 f., page 3 and the following page; pp. 3 ff., page 3 and the following pages)

i.e. that is

id., idem the same as before (the same person)

l., ll. lines(s) (ll. 8–12, lines 8 to 12)

mimeo. mimeographed

MS, MSS manuscript(s)

n., nn. footnote(s) (n. 10, nn. 1–6)

N.B. please note; mark well

n.d. no date (given for a publication)

n.n. no name

n.p. no place

N.S. New Series; New Style (of dating, since 1752)

No., Nos. number(s)

O.S. Old Series; Old Style (of dating, before 1752)

p., pp. page(s)

passim here and there (discussed in various places in the work)

Pt., Pts. part(s)

q.v. (quod vide) which see (used to suggest consulting a work, now replaced by English "see")

rev. revised, revision

Sec., Secs. section(s)

trans. translator; translated by

viz. namely

Vol., Vols. volume(s)

vs., vss. verse(s)

Bibliography

The bibliography should give a clear, complete description of the sources that were used when preparing the report. Some bibliographies classify entries under headings such as Books, Periodicals, Newspapers, Reports, Public Documents, and Miscellaneous, but most of them arrange items in a single alphabetized list. The latter method must be adopted and items must be numbered consecutively if, instead of page footnotes, the cross-reference system of citations from the body to the bibliography of the report is used, as is done in this text.

Style of Citing/ Bibliographical items are usually listed alphabetically by authors' surnames, but a chronological arrangement is used in some studies. When the author's name is not given, the work is listed under the name of the school system, institution, or agency that prepared the report (see Bibliography 137). When no clue of authorship is available, the work is listed under the first important word of the title (see Bibliography, 90). To make the author's name stand out, the first line of each entry is typed flush with the margin and the remaining lines are indented. Double spacing or single spacing with double spaces between entries is used.

No universally accepted style for constructing a bibliography exists. The researcher adopts one that is approved by his advisor or publisher and uses it consistently..The following samples present a simple and workable style:

1/ For a book.
Surname of author, given name or two initials, *Title Taken from Title Page* [underlined]. Edition if more than one, volume if more than one, place of publication: publisher, date on title page or copyright date.

2/ For an article.
Surname of author, given name or two initials, "Title of Article," *Name of Periodical* [underlined]. Volume of periodical (month, day, year), beginning page.

3/ For a newspaper.
Name of Paper [underlined], month, day, year, section of paper, page. [If author and title are given, they precede name of paper.]

4/ For unpublished materials [speeches, letters, mimeographed materials, etc.].
Surname of author, given name or initials, "Title of Material," nature of material and where it is available or was presented,[1] date.

Sometimes the above bibliographical style is also used for footnotes, except that the regular paragraph indention rather than the underhung style is employed and the exact page of the quotation is given. But most institutions require further

1/ For example: Unpublished Ph.D. dissertation, University of Pittsburgh.
Paper read before the annual convention of the Educator's Club, New York City.
Minutes of the Wayne Township Board of Education, Wayne, Michigan.
Letter to the writer from Dr. John Dewey, Teachers College, Columbia University.

changes in footnotes; they stipulate that the author's given name must appear first, and some recommend a different form for the punctuation and placement of items (see page 435). In some institutions, additional information is also required in the bibliography. As the last item in each entry, the total number of pages in the source is listed to give the reader some concept of the comprehensiveness of the work. Brief annotations summarizing the contents, strengths, weaknesses, biases, or unique contributions of sources may also be required. The annotations are single-spaced and separated from the rest of the entry by a double space.

Aids for Citing/ A competent researcher uses the same style for like items throughout his bibliography and rechecks each item in every entry for accuracy and completeness. When uncertain about how to write an entry, he consults a style book. Different types of bibliographical entries, of course, present different problems. An examination of the bibliography in this text and the following general rules will answer some common questions.

1/
When two or more works by the same author are listed, an unbroken line about six spaces in length, followed by a comma, is sometimes substituted for his name after the first entry. The titles of his works are alphabetized under his name. Publications of which he is coauthor follow those of which he is sole author.
2/
If a book has two or three authors, the second and third authors' names are written in the normal order (see Bibliography, 4, 9). If there are more than three authors, the name of the first is given, followed by "et al." or "and others" (see Bibliography, 70).
3/
An editor or compiler is indicated by placing the proper abbreviation in the parentheses following the name (see Bibliography, 14).
4/
When identifying the place of publication, the name of the city is sufficient if it is well known; otherwise the name of the state or the complete address is added.

Preparation of the Report

When preparing a report you will adopt the patterns of working that are most suitable for you. But acquiring some knowledge of how others have solved common writing, revising, and typing problems may help you improve your system.

Drafting and Revising the Report

Some parts of a report, such as the review of the literature, may be written fairly early in an investigation, but most of the writing is done after the hypotheses have been tested. The researcher collects data and organizes them into tables, graphs, or some other form that brings out relationships. He classifies his notes and places them in the order that they appear in his outline. Then, while examining the data and notes, he writes paragraphs of explanation and interpretation for each section of the report, composes transitional statements or paragraphs that lead the reader from one point to the next, and drafts the conclusions.

Even at this stage of the work, an investigator may reorder points in the outline to achieve a more logical presentation or smoother transitions. Thus, in all but the final copy of a report, he types each paragraph on a separate page so that sufficient room is left to make corrections or revisions. By so doing, he may rewrite materials, add paragraphs, or shift items from one section of the report to another without retyping entire pages or chapters of contiguous materials.

Writing is arduous work. The prolonged process of composing, reordering, adding, deleting, and polishing is taxing. Successful writers redraft their reports many times before they are satisfied with the results, and their faculty advisors or editors may make many additional suggestions for improvements. Revising a report usually consumes many more hours than writing the original draft.

A beginner has much to learn before he can write effectively. You may make better progress if you form the following work habits:

1/
Set aside regular hours for writing and observe your schedule faithfully.
2/
Choose an environment that is conducive to work and make certain that the necessary reference books, dictionaries, and files are at hand.
3/
To overcome the difficulty of getting started at each writing session, stop writing early each day and spend a few minutes organizing materials and listing the things to do the following day.

4/

After working for a few days, set the draft aside and return later to read it critically.

5/

Since items in a report do not have to be written in a consecutive order, compose a rough draft of a section whenever sufficient insight into the materials has been gained.

6/

Concentrate on communicating information when writing. Do not let minor problems interrupt the flow of thought and block progress—skip over them and return later to find the proper word, devise a deft transition, check a fact, or insert an illustration.

7/

When bogged down in a particular paragraph or section of a report, reread the preceding materials and the outline to regain perspective.

8/

Ask colleagues to read the report and point out any gaps, weaknesses, or ideas that are not clearly communicated.

9/

Allot generous amounts of time for making unhurried, thorough revisions.

Typing the Report

Before typing the report, the researcher should reread the institutional requirements. The style manual usually stipulates that white bond paper of the proper size and weight be used; quite commonly $8\frac{1}{2}$ by 11 inches and a 20-pound-weight stock is required for the first copy and a lighter-weight stock for the carbon copies. The style manual gives special directions for the headings, tables, figures, footnotes, quotations, bibliography, and appendix. The regulations for spacing, indention, alignment of numbers, and margins (left one and a half inches, right one inch, top and bottom one and a quarter inches is common) should also be checked. A typewriter with large (pica) type is usually recommended, and the same one, or at least the same style and size of type, should be used throughout the report. The use of an electric typewriter or Varityper is permissible in some institutions. A nongreasy, fresh, black carbon paper, a medium-inked typewriter ribbon, and clean type are necessary to produce a clear, dense copy.

Before typing the final draft of a report, the researcher reads the manuscript critically, searching for inaccurate statements, ambiguous passages, omissions, and inconsistencies. After making an exacting examination to locate errors in quotations, footnotes, tables, figures, paragraphing, sentence structure, headings, mathematics, spelling, style, proper names, or bibliography, he marks the copy to provide the typist with the necessary directions for producing a satisfactory typescript. The time spent in checking the above details is well invested, for ultimately the researcher alone—and not the typist, the sponsor, or the publisher—is held responsible for the contents of the report.

A term paper or a master's thesis may be typed personally, but a doctoral dissertation should be prepared by a professional typist who has had considerable experience in doing such work. When the final typed copy of the report is completed, proofreading it with the greatest care is necessary. Proofreading and correcting a page before removing it from the typewriter is a prudent practice. A few erasures may be made to correct a copy, but crossing out or inserting words or sentences and typing over letters are not permissible. If revisions necessitate retyping, care should be taken to equalize the materials which are inserted and deleted so that the last line on the page comes out even. If such care is not taken, one may have to retype the rest of the chapter and renumber the remaining pages of the report.

Every page in a report receives a number. Small Roman numerals are centered at the bottom of the preliminary pages, except on the title page, where the number "i" counts as a page but does not appear. Hence, the numbering begins with "ii" on the next page. Arabic numerals are placed on the top right-hand corner of all other pages, with the exception of the first one in each new chapter, which is numbered in the center at the bottom.

When typing any draft of an investigation, a researcher should make one or two carbon copies. The second copy is valuable if he loses the first one, wants to use copies both at home and at the office, or has to refer to the manuscript while his adviser or colleagues are examining the original draft. Filing the duplicate and first copies in separate places gives added protection against loss through fire and other means. Making duplicate copies of the early drafts of a report is a matter of personal choice, but many publishers and all dissertation committees require that at least two copies of the final draft be submitted.

16

Evaluation and Publication of Research

The preceding chapters have acquainted you with the objectives of researchers, some of the skills and knowledges they must acquire, and the methods they use to locate and tackle problems. Gaining an insight into the intricacies of scientific investigations is important, for society cannot make the most satisfactory progress if time, money, and energy are expended on faulty work. Neither can society advance if reliable findings concerning education are not widely disseminated to scholars and the general public for critical examination and appropriate application. This chapter, therefore, will discuss the evaluation and publication of research reports.

Evaluation

Because an educator cannot possibly read the hundreds of studies that appear in print each year, and certainly does not want to apply the findings of faulty investigations, he must learn how to screen out unworthy ones. When engaging in research himself, he must be able to evaluate not only every aspect of his predecessor's investigations, but also his own study. No universally accepted yardstick has been designed for measuring research reports, but the following questions suggest some items to check before undertaking a study, during the investigation, and when the study is completed.

Title of the Research Project

1/
Does the title precisely identify the area of the problem?

2/
Is the title clear, concise, and descriptive enough to permit the study to be indexed in its proper category?

3/
Are superfluous words such as "a study of" or "an analysis of" and catchy, misleading, and vague phrases avoided?

4/
Do nouns serve as the key words in the title?

5/
Are the principal words placed at the beginning of the title statement?

Preliminary Materials

1/
Does the report contain a title page, approval sheet, preface or acknowledgments, table of contents, list of tables, and list of figures?

2/
Are the mechanical features of the above materials in accord with the required style manual?

3/
Are all necessary items included in each section and proper headings provided where necessary?

4/
Do the captions that appear in the table of contents and list of tables and figures correspond exactly with the captions and page citations they refer to in the text? Is the same grammatical structure and style of capitalization used for captions on the same level?

Description and Statement of the Problem

1/
Has a thorough analysis been made of all the facts and explanations that might possibly be related to the problem, and have the relationships between these factors been explored thoroughly?

2/
Are the arguments that were used to isolate the pertinent variables, explanations, and relationships logically sound?

3/
Does the statement of the problem encompass and agree with all the relevant facts, explanatory concepts, and relationships that the analysis indicated had a bearing on the problem?

4/
Are all the problem elements expressed in an orderly system of relationships?

5/

Does the statement of the problem appear early in the study? Is it clearly labeled? Are unnecessary words, such as "the purpose of this study," avoided?

6/

Is the problem statement expressed succinctly and unambiguously in a grammatically correct interrogative or declarative sentence?

Scope and Adequacy of the Problem

1/

Does the problem meet the scope, significance, and topical requirements of the professor, institution, or periodical for which it was prepared?

2/

Is the problem sufficiently delimited to permit an exhaustive treatment, yet sufficiently significant to warrant investigating it?

3/

Does the problem possess potential value in helping to solve theoretical or practical educational problems? Does it refine, verify, revise, or extend the findings of existing research in respect to either content or method?

Review of the Literature

1/

Has a thorough review been made of all the literature dealing with the variables under investigation?

2/

Have previous studies been evaluated in regard to the adequacy of their sample, faulty techniques, and unwarranted conclusions?

3/

Has the background of the earlier studies been developed to show that the existing evidence does not solve the immediate problem adequately?

4/

Does the review of the literature merely present studies in a chronological order and force the reader to assimilate the facts and draw conclusions concerning the relationship of the cited studies to the problem? Or does the review establish a theoretical framework for the problem, preferably as a series of postulates? Does it bring together pertinent data and theories and weave them into a network of relationships—a series of postulates—that point up relevant issues, reveal gaps in knowledge, and prepare the way for the logical leap to hypothesis construction?

Statement of Assumptions

1/

Are the assumptions on which the hypotheses are predicated made explicit for the critical inspection of the reader?

2/
Is the statement of the assumptions and the explanation of the theoretical framework within which the investigator intends to work presented in a logical and inclusive chain of reasoning?

3/
Are the assumptions properly labeled, codified, and inserted in the report?

Statement of Hypotheses and Deduced Consequences
1/
Are the hypotheses in agreement with all the known facts and compatible with well-attested theories?

2/
Do they explain more facts that are relevant to the problem than any rival hypotheses?

3/
Are the hypotheses testable?

4/
Are the deduced consequences logically implied by the hypotheses?

5/
Are the hypotheses and their deduced consequences expressed in clear, precise terms so that they leave no question about the factors to be tested?

6/
Are the hypotheses and their deduced consequences clearly labeled and placed early in the report?

7/
Will the hypotheses aid in the prediction of facts and relations that were previously unknown?

Definition of Terms
1/
Are the important variables and terms defined in clear and unequivocal language?

2/
Are the definitions formulated in operational terms?

3/
In the body of the report, are the terms and concepts used consistently as defined?

4/
Is the "definition of terms" section of the report labeled clearly and placed early in the study?

5/
Is unnecessary technical jargon avoided?

Method of Attack

Since each problem is unique, the means of attacking investigations vary accordingly. The following discussion raises some questions concerning considerations that are common to many problems.

General Considerations

1/

Can one collect the quantity and quality of data necessary to investigate the problem? Are the necessary tools, techniques, and subjects available? Does any known source of data exist, and can one gain access to it? Does the researcher possess the language, mathematical, and specialized skills necessary to obtain the data?

2/

Is an accurate, detailed explanation of the method, techniques, and tools used to test the deduced consequences given early in the report? Are the reasons for choosing them made clear? Is this information brought together in one section of the report and properly labeled? Can another worker replicate the study from a description of the procedures cited in the report?

3/

Do the reported procedures adequately and correctly represent the particular factors, conditions, and relationships of the consequences to be tested?

4/

Do these procedures collect the evidence with a minimum of effort or are equally effective but simpler ones available?

5/

Will these methods, tools, and techniques produce relevant, reliable, valid, and sufficiently refined data to justify the inferences drawn from them?

6/

Is locating or devising more refined data-gathering techniques necessary in order to obtain deeper insights into the phenomena?

7/

Are the assumptions that underlie the use of the data-gathering devices fully met in this study?

8/

Have the procedural errors and inadequacies that existed in previous studies been eliminated, the weaknesses of the present study been pointed out, and the procedures that were first employed and then abandoned because they proved worthless been discussed?

9/

Does the report describe where and when the data were gathered?

10/

Does the report describe precisely the number and kind of subjects, objects, and materials used in the investigation and indicate whether and why any of them did not participate in all parts of the investigation?

11/

If a pilot study or pretest was conducted, does the investigator explain the procedures or instruments that were employed and does he cite the reasons for refining the methodology?

12/
Are copies of the oral and written directions and the printed forms and questionnaires used in the investigation included in the report?

General Considerations in Descriptive Studies

1/
Is the research design adequate, in scope, depth, and precision, to obtain the specific data required to test the hypothesis, or will the design produce a haphazard, superficial, indiscriminate collection of data?

2/
Has every possible precaution been taken to establish observational conditions, frame questions, design observation schedules, record data, and check the reliability of witnesses and source materials so as to avoid collecting data that are the product of perceptual errors, faulty memory, deliberate deception, and unconscious bias?

3/
Are the specific items the observer is to note when describing a condition, event, or process clearly identified, and is a uniform method provided for recording precise information?

4/
Are the standards employed to classify, compare, and quantify the data valid?

5/
Are the categories for classifying data unambiguous, appropriate, and capable of bringing out likenesses, differences, or relationships?

6/
Does the report admit instances encountered where the elusive quality of descriptive phenomena makes it difficult to obtain and interpret data?

7/
Does the study reflect an analysis of surface conditions, or does the investigation probe into the interrelationships or causal relationships?

General Considerations in Historical Studies

1/
Is the report based upon primary sources? If some secondary sources are used, do they contribute the "less significant" data rather than the crucial evidence for the solution of the problem?

2/
Has more than one independent, reliable eyewitness been found to support the alleged facts?

3/
Has an investigation been made to check the witnesses' trustworthiness, competence, biases, motives, and position at the time of observation, as well as to check how and when they recorded their observations?

4/

Have the source materials been examined critically for authenticity and credibility?

5/

Are words and statements from earlier documents correctly interpreted? Is there any evidence to indicate that conceptions of later times have been read into them?

6/

When necessary, has advice been sought from experts in auxiliary fields to determine the authenticity of data?

7/

Have the sources been assigned to a particular author, time, or place?

General Considerations in Experimental Studies

1/

Is the design clearly formulated? Will it answer the questions that the hypothesis raises? Does the design provide the controls required to obtain valid answers?

2/

Have all potential sources of threats to internal and external validity been checked carefully?

3/

Is the investigator in a position where he can control the manipulation of the independent variable, or is he in an ex post facto research situation where he can only observe a phenomenon and search back for variables that may have contributed to its occurrence?

4/

If the subjects in the experimental group are self-selected (they chose to take a class, go to college, take a remedial treatment), has consideration been given to what this will do to the equivalency of the groups?

5/

Have the number and character of the subjects who dropped out of the experiment been checked carefully?

6/

Have the groups in the experiment been divided into subgroups (sex, IQ, etc.), if pertinent information can be extracted from such data?

7/

If a matching or analysis of covariance technique is employed to remove the masking effect of specific variables, do these variables have a known effect on the dependent variable?

8/

Have any assumptions underlying the use of statistical techniques been violated?

9/

Are the null hypotheses rigorously defined? Are they related to the problem hypotheses?

10/
Was the level of significance necessary for the rejection of the null hypothesis specified prior to the collection and analysis of the data?

Sampling
1/
Does the report describe with precision the population that is involved in the study? Does the sample come from this population?
2/
Is the method of drawing the sample clearly specified?
3/
Do the control and experimental groups come from the same population, and were they selected in the same manner?
4/
Were randomization techniques employed to select subjects from the population?
5/
Were randomization techniques used to assign subjects, teachers, observers, equipment, rooms, etc., to treatment groups?
6/
Is the sample sufficiently large and drawn in a manner to represent the characteristics of the population?
7/
To what subject populations and nonsubject populations (settings, experimenters, teachers, tasks, measurement variables) can the findings be generalized? Has the investigator overgeneralized his findings?
8/
Did the pretest, the behavior of the experimenter, or the fact that the subjects knew they were participating in the experiment, affect their responsiveness to the independent variable, and make them unrepresentative of the population from which they came?

Instrumentation
1/
Is the investigator familiar with the rules to be observed, the conditions to be met, and the operations to be performed when utilizing the various measures, scales, tests, and instruments?
2/
Do the instruments possess the reliability and validity (content, predictive, concurrent, or construct) required for the research purpose? Are the instruments and test norms appropriate for the sample of subjects in the study (age, ability, sex, etc.)?
3/
Are the tests appropriate for the time available for administration and conditions under which they are to be administered (size of room or group, abilities of test administrators, scorers, or interpreters)?

4/

Do the judges who are to rate the phenomena possess the necessary background and information? Are they predisposed in a given direction concerning the phenomena? Is the basis on which they are to make judgments clearly specified?

5/

Are there any items or factors in the testing instruments that might limit the extent or type of the subject's responses?

Questionnaires and Interviews

1/ Content of questions.

a. Is each question necessary?

b. Is each question sharply delineated to elicit the specific responses required as data?

c. Do the questions cover the decisive features of the needed data?

d. Do any questions ask for information that the respondents do not possess?

e. Are more concrete questions required to obtain an accurate description of the respondent's behavior?

f. Are more general questions required to elicit prevailing attitudes or overall facts?

g. Are the questions colored by personal or sponsorship biases, loaded in one direction, or asked at the improper time?

h. Does each question present a sufficient number of alternative answers to permit the respondent to express himself properly and accurately?

2/ Wording of questions.

a. Is each question short and simple and written in unambiguous, understandable, and nontechnical language?

b. Are any questions misleading because of the absence of important alternative choices, poorly constructed alternatives, improper order, or an inadequate frame of reference?

c. Are stereotyped, prestige-carrying, or superlative words and phrases used that bias the response?

d. Are the questions framed so that they annoy, embarrass, or anger the respondents and cause them to falsify their answers?

e. Would a more or less personalized wording of the questions better elicit the desired information?

3/ Sequence of questions.

a. Do initial questions "set the stage" for those that follow and aid in the recall of ideas, or do they make subsequent topics inappropriate and embarrassing?

b. Are the questions grouped, ordered, and located so as to arouse interest, to maintain attention, and to avoid resistance?

c. Are follow-up questions or "probes" necessary?

4/ Form of responses.

a. Should the responses be obtained in a form requiring a check, a word or two, a number, or a free answer?

b. What is the best type of check question to ask—dichotomous, multiple-choice, or scale?

c. Should a distinction of degree be made when rating items by employing an ordinal, interval, or ratio scale?

d. Are the directions concise and clear, located next to the point of application, and made easy to follow by the inclusion of properly placed blank spaces, columns, or boxes? Are any illustrations necessary?

e. Is the instrument structured to facilitate the tabulation of data?

f. Are the multiple-choice responses arranged randomly to reduce the likelihood of systemic errors?

g. Was a random sample of nonresponding subjects checked to determine whether their answers differed from those who did respond?

5/ Pretesting the instrument.

a. Was the questionnaire pretested?

b. Was a clear explanation of the purpose of the study and the specific intent of each question given during the pretesting period?

c. After redrafting the wording of the proposed instrument, was the reliability of the responses checked?

Collection and Presentation of Data

1/

Did the researcher decide how he would order and break down his data early in his investigation?

2/

Are the classification categories sufficiently comprehensive and specific? Are any unnecessary data presented? Is the amount of data collected adequate? Are the methods employed to treat data appropriate?

3/

Was the interviewer, observer, or scorer biased because he had access to information about the previous behavior of subjects?

4/

Were precautions taken to collect and record data objectively and accurately? Were procedures and results checked for errors made when observing phenomena, making mathematical computations, selecting or carrying out experimental or statistical procedures, or copying quotations, dates, names, or any data?

5/

Were source materials examined critically for authenticity and credibility? Are sources given for theories and facts taken from other reports so that the reader can examine them himself? Are all source materials paraphrased accurately?

6/

Are drawings, charts, diagrams, graphs, tables, or photographs used when they can convey ideas most effectively?

7/

Do the tables and figures conform to the rules for constructing "good" ones? Do they present the evidence accurately—without distortion or misrepresentation?

8/

Are line symbols rather than color variations used to identify lines on a graph if the report is to be reproduced by photographic processes?

9/

Does the textual presentation conform to recognized standards of formal English and to the prescribed style and format? Is the discussion unambiguous? Are transitional words, sentences, and paragraphs inserted to clarify the relationship between items?

10/

Was the level of statistical significance reported for findings that involved comparisons between groups or relationships between variables?

Analysis of Data

1/

Is the evidence collected to test each deduced consequence of a hypothesis adequately and logically analyzed?

2/

Is the analysis objectively stated and free from mere opinion and personal prejudices?

3/

Have broad generalizations been made without sufficient evidence to support them? Are the generalizations carefully qualified?

4/

Does the analysis contain any contradictions, inconsistencies, or misleading, vague, or exaggerated statements?

5/

Does the researcher confuse facts with opinions and inferences?

6/

Does the researcher omit or ignore evidence that does not agree with his hypothesis?

7/

Is attention called to unpredicted relations as well as the hypothesized relations in the data?

8/

Does the research relate the findings to previous research and, if possible, carry the inferences concerning relationships in the data to a higher level of generalization or theory?

9/

Are uncontrolled factors that may have affected the results discussed?

10/

Have any weaknesses in the data been honestly admitted and discussed?

Summary and Conclusions

1/

Are the summary and conclusions concisely and precisely stated?

2/
Are the conclusions justified by the data gathered?
3/
Are the conclusions qualified to show the limits (nature of sample, methods, etc.) within which they apply?
4/
Do the summary and conclusions recapitulate the information presented in previous sections of the report, or has the mistake been made of introducing new data?
5/
Are the conclusions stated in terms that make them verifiable?
6/
Does the researcher state specifically what empirically verifiable evidence has been produced to confirm or disconfirm the hypothesis?
7/
Does the researcher make a concluding statement in which he accepts or rejects the hypothesis?
8/
Does the study report any new questions that arose that should be investigated?

Bibliography and Appendix
1/
Do the style, content, and arrangement of the bibliography meet the requirements of the audience for which the report was written?
2/
Are all entries in the bibliography placed in the proper order?
3/
Does each entry contain all the necessary items of information, and are the items ordered properly, spelled correctly, and punctuated accurately?
4/
Is all cumbersome or voluminous supporting material—test forms, raw data, personal communications—located in the appendix? Has any unnecessary material been placed in the appendix?
5/
Are the items in the appendix grouped in homogeneous sections with appropriate headings?

Report Format and Style
1/
Is the report neat, attractive, and divided into appropriate sections or chapters?
2/
Is the report ordered according to the format required by the professor, institution, or periodical?
3/
Are concise, descriptive headings used?

4/

Is the report free from padding with irrelevant words, phrases, quotations, statistics, examples, and other data that are not essential for accuracy, clarity, or completeness?

5/

Are concrete familiar words, short direct sentences, and the active voice used whenever possible?

6/

Has an approved style been followed consistently throughout the report? Has a careful check been made of spacings, margins, quotations, footnotes, tables, figures, bibliography, appendixes, headings, abbreviations, capitalization, punctuation, indentions, and the enumeration of items?

7/

Are the drawings and graphs prepared in the proper manner to ensure satisfactory reproduction?

8/

Are major topics developed insufficiently or are minor ones over-expanded?

9/

Does the report require an index?

Abstract

1/

Does an abstract accompany the report?

2/

Is the abstract prepared in accordance with the institution's or periodical's standards for style and form?

3/

Does the abstract cover the principal points: statement of problem, hypotheses, procedures, results, and conclusions?

4/

Is the abstract under the maximum number of words in length?

Publication

Researchers must know not only how to evaluate reports, but also how to get them published. After devoting months to investigations and accepting the assistance of faculty members, librarians, and colleagues, researchers are professionally obligated to observe the academic tradition of publishing their findings. If they do not disseminate their findings to other scholars, their discoveries cannot possibly benefit mankind. Aside from research reports, educators often have other important ideas, data, questions, criticisms, and problems that should be communicated to others for the betterment of the profession. But they cannot get any article printed in professional journals and books unless they know something about publishers and the procedures involved in preparing manuscripts for them.

Types and Standards of Publishers

Various agencies publish the work of researchers. Professional associations print many studies in an abstract form in their journals every year. Some professional organizations and philanthropic foundations produce monographs of outstanding scientific investigations, and university presses print a few studies of special merit. In *Dissertation Abstracts,* The University Microfilms, Ann Arbor, Michigan, publishes the doctoral dissertation abstracts that many universities require candidates to submit. From time to time, other agencies publish pertinent reports in their area of interest.

Most publishers do not offer remuneration for reports; indeed, some journals require a payment for publication privileges. Because an increasing number of investigations are undertaken each year, journal space is at a premium today. The rising costs of publication, moreover, prohibit the reproduction of many studies in their entirety. One attempt to solve this problem has been made by establishing a private nonprofit organization, the American Documentation Institute (ADI).[1] After depositing the basic data with the ADI, a researcher submits his report to a journal without including the long tables and other items on which his analysis is based. In a footnote to his report, he indicates that a microfilm or photocopy of the complete material may be obtained from the ADI for a nominal fee.

Since the nature, style, and quality of reports accepted by various journals differ, a researcher must evaluate journals to determine which one publishes the type and level of study he has to submit. After selecting a reputable journal, he should become thoroughly familiar with the editor's manuscript criteria. These criteria may be printed in the journal periodically, but if they are not, an examination of a few issues will reveal the editor's preferences in regard to the nature, length, and organization of articles as well as footnotes and bibliographical style. To ignore these manuscript requirements is most imprudent. Writing a 1,000-word report for a journal that limits articles

1/ Auxiliary Publication Project, Photoduplication Service, Library of Congress, Washington, D.C.

to 600 words or neglecting to follow the required organizational pattern can lead only to a rejection slip or a request for drastic revisions.

Preparation for Publication

Writing for publication sometimes requires considerable work in addition to the preparation of the original dissertation. A candidate does not have many prepublication duties if his study is reproduced on microfilm or microcards, which is a common practice. He may have to recast his study somewhat before publishing it—in monograph form, which is sometimes done, or in book form, which is rarely done. If he writes an abstract of his study or presents his findings in a journal article, he has to compress the contents of his entire report into relatively few pages.

An abstract, for example, may be limited to 600 words. Thus, a researcher must strip the key ideas from his original manuscript—largely from the summary and conclusions and express them in clear, crisp sentences. He also revises his format and style to conform with the publisher's requirements. Preparing a report for a journal involves somewhat similar tasks, but more pages may be devoted to the discussion. Because a doctoral dissertation contains considerable substance, the contents may be divided to produce two or more journal articles of eight to fifteen double-spaced pages in length. Descriptions of masters' theses are usually confined to a single journal article a few pages in length.

After pruning and polishing a report to meet the exacting requirements of editors, the author numbers the pages consecutively from start to finish and fastens them together with paper clips. Then he slips them unfolded into an envelope and sometimes adds a piece of cardboard that is slightly larger than the material for protection—particularly if photographic prints or drawings intended for halftone reproductions are included. After inserting a letter in the envelope which explains that the article is being submitted for possible publication, he mails it to the editors. To protect himself against loss, he insures the mailed manuscript and places a carbon copy of it in his files.

Before a report is published, the author may have to obtain written permission to use quotations, graphic materials, and speeches from the copyright holders. His letters requesting authorization to reproduce material must identify each item precisely and explain how it is to be employed. Replies to these letters must be kept in the author's or publisher's files for later reference in case questions arise. A copyright may also have to be obtained for the report itself, particularly if it is in book form. This task is usually performed by the publisher, but an author may reserve the right to apply to the Register of Copyrights, Library of Congress, and obtain it for himself.

Reviews and Revisions

When editors receive a manuscript, they may send the author a brief note of acknowledgment, but aside from that they do not communicate with him for several weeks. In the interim, qualified specialists review the article and decide whether to accept it, reject it, or request that certain revisions be made. A manuscript may be rejected for several reasons—because the work lacks merit, is unsuitable for the particular journal, or is similar to a backlog of articles accepted previously by the publisher. A report that is rejected for the last reason may be submitted to another publisher, but no editor will accept a manuscript that contains fundamental weaknesses.

A conditionally accepted report is returned to the author with suggestions for improvements. The editors may recommend that certain points be expanded or omitted, question the accuracy of statements, point out passages that need clarification, suggest changes in organization and literary form, or note inconsistencies in style. Requests for revisions should challenge rather than discourage the author. Learning to write requires a long apprenticeship, and continuous criticism by qualified men is a prod that stimulates progress. Not all the editor's suggestions have to be accepted, but each one should be given serious consideration.

When making changes in the manuscript, the insertions are printed or written legibly. Insertions are never placed in the margin, for the margins are reserved for instructions to the printer. To indicate an insertion, a caret ($\wedge$) is placed at the proper point in the copy and the additional material is written horizontally in the space above—never below—the caret. Long insertions may be typed on small slips of paper and taped to the margin of the copy near the line containing the caret. Material that is to be shifted to another page may be crossed out, retyped, and inserted in the proper place or the material may be circled and labeled "tr. to p. 16." If the latter is done, the place where it belongs is indicated on page 16 by inserting a caret in the proper place and above it the note, "tr. from p. 5." When material is to be deleted and none added, the unwanted characters are merely crossed out. Revisions of a few sentences in length may be typed on small slips of paper and pasted over deleted materials in the copy.

Galley and Page Proofs

After returning the revised manuscript to the editor, several months may elapse before the author receives the galley proofs of his article and the cut dummies (if any) of the engraver's proofs. The galley proofs are long sheets of paper that contain about three normal pages of print and no illustrations or page numbers. The author compares the galley proofs with his manuscript and corrects any errors. This proofreading task is exacting work that must be done with scrupulous care. An author does not merely scan the article to make certain that the copy makes sense. To detect inaccuracies or omissions, he checks each character, letter, word, and line. If possible, he follows the galley proof as someone slowly reads aloud from the manuscript. The reader spells out all proper names and technical terms and reads out punctuation marks, italics, paragraph breaks, decimal points, prime marks, and other departures from ordinary type. Particular attention is given to tables, figures, dates, and quotations. Proofreading is done twice if time permits, for the second reading is almost certain to reveal additional errors.

Because a printer does not look for corrections in the body of the galley proof unless he sees a proofreader's mark in the margin, an author must study these standard symbols until he can automatically apply and interpret them. When correcting a galley proof, he communicates his ideas to the editor and printer by placing the appropriate symbol in the left or right margin, whichever is nearer the error, and on the same line as the error. When more than one error appears on a line, the corrections are written consecutively from left to right and separated one from another by a slanted line. All notes or queries to the editor or printer are circled to indicate that they are not to be set in type. To restore something that has been crossed out, a row of dots is placed under the deleted material and in the margin the delete sign is crossed out and "stet" (let it stand) is added. When proofreading, the writer utilizes a number of other symbols in much the same manner. Some of the standard symbols are given below.

When checking the cut dummies of the engraver's proofs, an author makes certain that no figure has been placed upside down and that no items have been omitted. In the margin of the galley proof, he indicates near which passage the printer is to place a figure. (For example, he writes in the margin of galley 5, "Insert Fig. 2 here" and then jots the number of that galley, "gal. 5," below Fig. 2 in the cut dummy.) Before return-

Insertions, Deletions, Spacing

ℐ //	Delete words or ~~the~~ letters mar/ked.
the/h	Insert the word or⋀letter in ṭe margin.
#	Insert space between⋀words.
◡	Close up sp͡ace.

Paragraphing and Punctuation

¶	⋀Make new paragraph.
No ¶	No paragraph—run in or on.
⊙	Insert period. (Sixty children participated⋀)
⋏//	Insert comma. (Smith⋀John⋀and Valois, Jean)
ᐱ/ᐱ	Insert quotation marks. (Explain the⋀mechanism⋀of the mind.)
ᐱ	Insert apostrophe. (The teachers equipment was good.)
-/ or =/	Insert hyphen. (ten⋀volume encyclopedia)

Type

⋀2	Insert inferior figure or letter subscript. (HSO_4)
2ᐯ	Insert superior figure or letter superscript. (Lee[1] and Ogg⋀ conducted studies.)
Caps	SET IN capitals.
Cap	capital letter required.
lc	Use lower-Ȼase letter.
ital.	Set in italic type.
9	Turᵁ a reversed letter.
X	Replace broken type.
lf	Set in (lightface) type.
bf	Set in boldface type.

Position

tr //	Transpose of order words or letters.
⌐‾⌐	Elevate letters or words. (John ⌐and⌐ Mary)
⌐‗⌐	Lower letters or words. (John ⌐and⌐ Mary)
ctr	]Center on page or line.[
⌐	Move to right._]
⌐	[_Move to left.
//	Align type vertically.
═══	Straighten line horizontally. (He gr͞e͞eted the cro͞wd.)

Miscellaneous

1942 / ?	Query to author. (In 1952 Hitler delivered the speech.)
stet	Let all words above dots ~~in sentence~~ stand as they are.
sp	Spell out. (Tests were given to 20 children.)
⊥	Push down a space that prints.
⌐	Mark off or break; start new line.

ing the galley and engraver's proofs to the publisher, the writer must answer all the printer's and editor's queries and supply any missing materials, captions, or credit lines. An editor usually writes a lengthy query on a small colored piece of paper and attaches it to the side of the galley. He writes a brief query in the margin of the galley and after the suggested change places a slanted line and circled question mark. To accept a change, the author crosses out the question mark; to reject it, he crosses out the whole query.

Making alterations in the galley proofs other than the correction of printer's errors is extremely expensive. Merely inserting a word may require resetting the type for the rest of the paragraph. Because the writer may have to pay the charges for these alterations, he should endeavor to submit a perfect manuscript. If changes in the galley proof are necessary, making deletions and additions so that they fill the same amount of space as the original materials will hold costs to a minimum.

After the editor and author have carefully checked the galley proofs, they return them to the printer. He corrects all the marked items and then breaks the type into page lengths, inserts the footnotes, places the illustrations where they belong, and adds the chapter titles, running heads, and page numbers. Copies of the page proofs and the dead galley proofs are then sent to the editor, who examines them to determine whether all the errors have been corrected and no new errors have been introduced as a result of the resets or addition of new materials. Journal page proofs are not usually sent to the author for an additional check, but book page proofs are. Some duties, such as inserting the page numbers for cross-reference citations and preparing an index, cannot be performed until one has the page proofs. Upon receiving either the galley or page proofs, the author should give them immediate attention and return them promptly, or he will upset the production schedules of editors and printers.

The rewarding moment comes when a researcher first reads his report in print. The publication of a book or article climaxes a prolonged period of cooperative effort on the part of the author, editors, and printers. After an article is submitted, several months may pass before it is published, and a book may be in production for a couple of years. Because many would-be authors do not realize how much work is involved in transforming a manuscript into print, they fail to allot sufficient time for this task. When manuscripts are returned to them, they resent reviewers' criticisms, revise materials reluctantly, or become too discouraged to continue writing. If their articles are accepted, they often do a superficial job of proofreading and disregard the editor's concern about meeting deadlines and printing schedules.

The exacting process of preparing a manuscript for publication may seem burdensome, but these revisions and checks are essential for the production of a worthwhile report. Maintaining a high level of performance in this final stage of one's work is of utmost importance, for a carefully conducted investigation may be disregarded by other scholars if the public account of it is poorly prepared. Since one is judged for years by the quality of his printed report, a researcher should expend the effort necessary to publish a work that meets the highest standards of scholarship.

Appendix A.
Tables

Table A/ Normal Curve Functions

z or x/σ	Area: m to z	Area: q Smaller	y or Ordinate
0.00	0.00000	0.50000	0.3989
0.05	0.01994	0.48006	0.3984
0.10	0.03983	0.46017	0.3970
0.15	0.05962	0.44038	0.3945
0.20	0.07926	0.42074	0.3910
0.25	0.09871	0.40129	0.3867
0.30	0.11791	0.38209	0.3814
0.35	0.13683	0.36317	0.3752
0.40	0.15542	0.34458	0.3683
0.45	0.17364	0.32636	0.3605
0.50	0.19146	0.30854	0.3521
0.55	0.20884	0.29116	0.3429
0.60	0.22575	0.27425	0.3332
0.65	0.24215	0.25758	0.3230
0.70	0.25804	0.24196	0.3123
0.75	0.27337	0.22663	0.3011
0.80	0.28814	0.21186	0.2897
0.85	0.30234	0.19766	0.2780
0.90	0.31594	0.18406	0.2661
0.95	0.32894	0.17106	0.2541
1.00	0.34134	0.15866	0.2420
1.05	0.35314	0.14686	0.2299
1.10	0.36433	0.13567	0.2179
1.15	0.37493	0.12507	0.2059
1.20	0.38493	0.11507	0.1942
1.25	0.39435	0.10565	0.1826
1.30	0.40320	0.09680	0.1714
1.35	0.41149	0.08851	0.1604
1.40	0.41924	0.08076	0.1497
1.45	0.42647	0.07353	0.1394

Table A/ Normal Curve Functions (Continued)

z or x/σ	Area: m to z	Area: q Smaller	y or Ordinate
1.50	0.43319	0.06681	0.1295
1.55	0.43943	0.06057	0.1200
1.60	0.44520	0.05480	0.1109
1.65	0.45053	0.04947	0.1023
1.70	0.45543	0.04457	0.0940
1.75	0.45994	0.04056	0.0863
1.80	0.46407	0.03593	0.0790
1.85	0.46784	0.03216	0.0721
1.90	0.47128	0.02872	0.0656
1.95	0.47441	0.02559	0.0596
2.00	0.47725	0.02275	0.0540
2.05	0.47982	0.02018	0.0488
2.10	0.48214	0.01786	0.0440
2.15	0.48422	0.01578	0.0396
2.20	0.48610	0.01390	0.0355
2.25	0.48778	0.01222	0.0317
2.30	0.48928	0.01072	0.0283
2.35	0.49061	0.00939	0.0252
2.40	0.49180	0.00820	0.0224
2.45	0.49286	0.00714	0.0198
2.50	0.49379	0.00621	0.0175
2.55	0.49461	0.00539	0.0154
2.60	0.49534	0.00466	0.0136
2.65	0.49598	0.00402	0.0119
2.70	0.49653	0.00347	0.0104
2.75	0.49702	0.00298	0.0091
2.80	0.49744	0.00256	0.0079
2.85	0.49781	0.00219	0.0069
2.90	0.49813	0.00187	0.0060
2.95	0.49841	0.00159	0.0051
3.00	0.49865	0.00135	0.0044
3.25	0.49942	0.00058	0.0020
3.50	0.49977	0.00023	0.0009
3.75	0.49991	0.00009	0.0004
4.00	0.49997	0.00003	0.0001

Table B/ Transformation of r to z_r*

r	z_r	r	z_r	r	z_r	r	z_r	r	z_r
0.000	0.000	0.200	0.203	0.400	0.424	0.600	0.693	0.800	1.099
0.005	0.005	0.205	0.208	0.405	0.430	0.605	0.701	0.805	1.113
0.010	0.010	0.210	0.213	0.410	0.436	0.610	0.709	0.810	1.127
0.015	0.015	0.215	0.218	0.415	0.442	0.615	0.717	0.815	1.142
0.020	0.020	0.220	0.224	0.420	0.448	0.620	0.725	0.820	1.157
0.025	0.025	0.225	0.229	0.425	0.454	0.625	0.733	0.825	1.172
0.030	0.030	0.230	0.234	0.430	0.460	0.630	0.741	0.830	1.188
0.035	0.035	0.235	0.239	0.435	0.466	0.635	0.750	0.835	1.204
0.040	0.040	0.240	0.245	0.440	0.472	0.640	0.758	0.840	1.221
0.045	0.045	0.245	0.250	0.445	0.478	0.645	0.767	0.845	1.238
0.050	0.050	0.250	0.255	0.450	0.485	0.650	0.775	0.850	1.256
0.055	0.055	0.255	0.261	0.455	0.491	0.655	0.784	0.855	1.274
0.060	0.060	0.260	0.266	0.460	0.497	0.660	0.793	0.860	1.293
0.065	0.065	0.265	0.271	0.465	0.504	0.665	0.802	0.865	1.313
0.070	0.070	0.270	0.277	0.470	0.510	0.670	0.811	0.870	1.333
0.075	0.075	0.275	0.282	0.475	0.517	0.675	0.820	0.875	1.354
0.080	0.080	0.280	0.288	0.480	0.523	0.680	0.829	0.880	1.376
0.085	0.085	0.285	0.293	0.485	0.530	0.685	0.838	0.885	1.398
0.090	0.090	0.290	0.299	0.490	0.536	0.690	0.848	0.890	1.422
0.095	0.095	0.295	0.304	0.495	0.543	0.695	0.858	0.895	1.447
0.100	0.100	0.300	0.310	0.500	0.549	0.700	0.867	0.900	1.472
0.105	0.105	0.305	0.315	0.505	0.556	0.705	0.877	0.905	1.499
0.110	0.110	0.310	0.321	0.510	0.563	0.710	0.887	0.910	1.528
0.115	0.116	0.315	0.326	0.515	0.570	0.715	0.897	0.915	1.557
0.120	0.121	0.320	0.332	0.520	0.576	0.720	0.908	0.920	1.589
0.125	0.126	0.325	0.337	0.525	0.583	0.725	0.918	0.925	1.623
0.130	0.131	0.330	0.343	0.530	0.590	0.730	0.929	0.930	1.658
0.135	0.136	0.335	0.348	0.535	0.597	0.735	0.940	0.935	1.697
0.140	0.141	0.340	0.354	0.540	0.604	0.740	0.950	0.940	1.738
0.145	0.146	0.345	0.360	0.545	0.611	0.745	0.962	0.945	1.783
0.150	0.151	0.350	0.365	0.550	0.618	0.750	0.973	0.950	1.832
0.155	0.156	0.355	0.371	0.555	0.626	0.755	0.984	0.955	1.886
0.160	0.161	0.360	0.377	0.560	0.633	0.760	0.996	0.960	1.946
0.165	0.167	0.365	0.383	0.565	0.640	0.765	1.008	0.965	2.014
0.170	0.172	0.370	0.388	0.570	0.648	0.770	1.020	0.970	2.092
0.175	0.177	0.375	0.394	0.575	0.655	0.775	1.033	0.975	2.185
0.180	0.182	0.380	0.400	0.580	0.662	0.780	1.045	0.980	2.298
0.185	0.187	0.385	0.406	0.585	0.670	0.785	1.058	0.985	2.443
0.190	0.192	0.390	0.412	0.590	0.678	0.790	1.071	0.990	2.647
0.195	0.198	0.395	0.418	0.595	0.685	0.795	1.085	0.995	2.994

* Reprinted, by permission, from Allen L. Edwards, Statistical Methods for the Behavioral
Sciences, New York: Holt, Rinehart and Winston, Inc., 1954.

Table C/ Critical Values of t*

	Level of Significance for Two-tailed Test					
df	0.10	0.05	0.025	0.01	0.005	0.0005
	Level of Significance for One-tailed Test					
	0.20	0.10	0.05	0.02	0.01	0.001
1	3.078	6.314	12.706	31.821	63.657	636.619
2	1.886	2.920	4.303	6.965	9.925	31.598
3	1.638	2.353	3.182	4.541	5.841	12.941
4	1.533	2.132	2.776	3.747	4.604	8.610
5	1.476	2.015	2.571	3.365	4.032	6.859
6	1.440	1.943	2.447	3.143	3.707	5.959
7	1.415	1.895	2.365	2.998	3.499	5.405
8	1.397	1.860	2.306	2.896	3.355	5.041
9	1.383	1.833	2.262	2.821	3.250	4.781
10	1.372	1.812	2.228	2.764	3.169	4.587
11	1.363	1.796	2.201	2.718	3.106	4.437
12	1.356	1.782	2.179	2.681	3.055	4.318
13	1.350	1.771	2.160	2.650	3.012	4.221
14	1.345	1.761	2.145	2.624	2.977	4.140
15	1.341	1.753	2.131	2.602	2.947	4.073
16	1.337	1.746	2.120	2.583	2.921	4.015
17	1.333	1.740	2.110	2.567	2.898	3.965
18	1.330	1.734	2.101	2.552	2.878	3.922
19	1.328	1.729	2.093	2.539	2.861	3.883
20	1.325	1.725	2.086	2.528	2.845	3.850
21	1.323	1.721	2.080	2.518	2.831	3.819
22	1.321	1.717	2.074	2.508	2.819	3.792
23	1.319	1.714	2.069	2.500	2.807	3.767
24	1.318	1.711	2.064	2.492	2.797	3.745
25	1.316	1.708	2.060	2.485	2.787	3.725
26	1.315	1.706	2.056	2.479	2.779	3.707
27	1.314	1.703	2.052	2.473	2.771	3.690
28	1.313	1.701	2.048	2.467	2.763	3.674
29	1.311	1.699	2.045	2.462	2.756	3.659
30	1.310	1.697	2.042	2.457	2.750	3.646
40	1.303	1.684	2.021	2.423	2.704	3.551
60	1.296	1.671	2.000	2.390	2.660	3.460
120	1.289	1.658	1.980	2.358	2.617	3.373
∞	1.282	1.645	1.960	2.326	2.576	3.291

* Abridged from Table III of R. A. Fisher and F. Yates, Statistical Tables for Biological, Agricultural, and Medical Research, Oliver & Boyd, Ltd., Edinburgh, by permission of the authors and publishers.

Table D/ Distribution of χ^2*

n	P = 0.99	0.98	0.95	0.90	0.80	0.70	0.50
1	0.00016	0.00063	0.0039	0.016	0.064	0.15	0.46
2	0.02	0.04	0.10	0.21	0.45	0.71	1.39
3	0.12	0.18	0.35	0.58	1.00	1.42	2.37
4	0.30	0.43	0.71	1.06	1.65	2.20	3.36
5	0.55	0.75	1.14	1.61	2.34	3.00	4.35
6	0.87	1.13	1.64	2.20	3.07	3.83	5.35
7	1.24	1.56	2.17	2.83	3.82	4.67	6.35
8	1.65	2.03	2.73	3.49	4.59	5.53	7.34
9	2.09	2.53	3.32	4.17	5.38	6.39	8.34
10	2.56	3.06	3.94	4.86	6.18	7.27	9.34
11	3.05	3.61	4.58	5.58	6.99	8.15	10.34
12	3.57	4.18	5.23	6.30	7.81	9.03	11.34
13	4.11	4.76	5.89	7.04	8.63	9.93	12.34
14	4.66	5.37	6.57	7.79	9.47	10.82	13.34
15	5.23	5.98	7.26	8.55	10.31	11.72	14.34
16	5.81	6.61	7.96	9.31	11.15	12.62	15.34
17	6.41	7.26	8.67	10.08	12.00	13.53	16.34
18	7.02	7.91	9.39	10.86	12.86	14.44	17.34
19	7.63	8.57	10.12	11.65	13.72	15.35	18.34
20	8.26	9.24	10.85	12.44	14.58	16.27	19.34
21	8.90	9.92	11.59	13.24	15.44	17.18	20.34
22	9.54	10.60	12.34	14.04	16.31	18.10	21.34
23	10.20	11.29	13.09	14.85	17.19	19.02	22.34
24	10.86	11.99	13.85	15.66	18.06	19.94	23.34
25	11.52	12.70	14.61	16.47	18.94	20.87	24.34
26	12.20	13.41	15.38	17.29	19.82	21.79	25.34
27	12.88	14.12	16.15	18.11	20.70	22.72	26.34
28	13.56	14.85	16.93	18.94	21.59	23.65	27.34
29	14.26	15.57	17.71	19.77	22.48	24.58	28.34
30	14.95	16.31	18.49	20.60	23.36	25.51	29.34

* Abridged from Table IV of Fisher and Yates, Statistical Tables for Biological, Agricultural, and Medical Research, Oliver & Boyd, Ltd., Edinburgh, by permission of the authors and publishers.

Table D/ Distribution of χ^2 (Continued)

n	0.30	0.20	0.10	0.05	0.02	0.01	0.001
1	1.07	1.64	2.71	3.84	5.41	6.64	10.83
2	2.41	3.22	4.60	5.99	7.82	9.21	13.82
3	3.66	4.64	6.25	7.82	9.84	11.34	16.27
4	4.88	5.99	7.78	9.49	11.67	13.28	18.46
5	6.06	7.29	9.24	11.07	13.39	15.09	20.52
6	7.23	8.56	10.64	12.59	15.03	16.81	22.46
7	8.38	9.80	12.02	14.07	16.62	18.48	24.32
8	9.52	11.03	13.36	15.51	18.17	20.09	26.12
9	10.66	12.24	14.68	16.92	19.68	21.67	27.88
10	11.78	13.44	15.99	18.31	21.16	23.21	29.59
11	12.90	14.63	17.28	19.68	22.62	24.72	31.26
12	14.01	15.81	18.55	21.03	24.05	26.22	32.91
13	15.12	16.98	19.81	22.36	25.47	27.69	34.53
14	16.22	18.15	21.06	23.68	26.87	29.14	36.12
15	17.32	19.31	22.31	25.00	28.26	30.58	37.70
16	18.42	20.46	23.54	26.30	29.63	32.00	39.25
17	19.51	21.62	24.77	27.59	31.00	33.41	40.79
18	20.60	22.76	25.99	28.87	32.35	34.80	42.31
19	21.69	23.90	27.20	30.14	33.69	36.19	43.82
20	22.78	25.04	28.41	31.41	35.02	37.57	45.32
21	23.86	26.17	29.62	32.67	36.34	38.93	46.80
22	24.94	27.30	30.81	33.92	37.66	40.29	48.27
23	26.02	28.43	32.01	35.17	38.97	41.64	49.73
24	27.10	29.55	33.20	36.42	40.27	42.98	51.18
25	28.17	30.68	34.38	37.65	41.57	44.31	52.62
26	29.25	31.80	35.56	38.88	42.86	45.64	54.05
27	30.32	32.91	36.74	40.11	44.14	46.96	55.48
28	31.39	34.03	37.92	41.34	45.42	48.28	56.89
29	32.46	35.14	39.09	42.56	46.69	49.59	58.30
30	33.53	36.25	40.26	43.77	47.96	50.89	59.70

Table E/ 5 Per Cent (Roman Type) and 1 Per Cent (Bold-face Type) Points for the Distribution of F^*

Degrees of Freedom for Greater Mean Square

Degrees of Freedom for Lesser Mean Square	1	2	3	4	5	6	7	8	9	10	11	12	14	16	20	24	30	40	50	75	100	200	500	∞
1	161 **4052**	200 **4999**	216 **5403**	225 **5625**	230 **5764**	234 **5859**	237 **5928**	239 **5981**	241 **6022**	242 **6056**	243 **6082**	244 **6106**	245 **6142**	246 **6169**	248 **6208**	249 **6234**	250 **6258**	251 **6286**	252 **6302**	253 **6323**	253 **6334**	254 **6352**	254 **6361**	254 **6366**
2	18.51 **98.49**	19.00 **99.01**	19.16 **99.17**	19.25 **99.25**	19.30 **99.30**	19.33 **99.33**	19.36 **99.34**	19.37 **99.36**	19.38 **99.38**	19.39 **99.40**	19.40 **99.41**	19.41 **99.42**	19.42 **99.43**	19.43 **99.44**	19.44 **99.45**	19.45 **99.46**	19.46 **99.47**	19.47 **99.48**	19.47 **99.48**	19.48 **99.49**	19.49 **99.49**	19.49 **99.49**	19.50 **99.50**	19.50 **99.50**
3	10.13 **34.12**	9.55 **30.81**	9.28 **29.46**	9.12 **28.71**	9.01 **28.24**	8.94 **27.91**	8.88 **27.67**	8.84 **27.49**	8.81 **27.34**	8.78 **27.23**	8.76 **27.13**	8.74 **27.05**	8.71 **26.92**	8.69 **26.83**	8.66 **26.69**	8.64 **26.60**	8.62 **26.50**	8.60 **26.41**	8.58 **26.35**	8.57 **26.27**	8.56 **26.23**	8.54 **26.18**	8.54 **26.14**	8.53 **26.12**
4	7.71 **21.20**	6.94 **18.00**	6.59 **16.69**	6.39 **15.98**	6.26 **15.52**	6.16 **15.21**	6.09 **14.98**	6.04 **14.80**	6.00 **14.66**	5.96 **14.54**	5.93 **14.45**	5.91 **14.37**	5.87 **14.24**	5.84 **14.15**	5.80 **14.02**	5.77 **13.93**	5.74 **13.83**	5.71 **13.74**	5.70 **13.69**	5.68 **13.61**	5.66 **13.57**	5.65 **13.52**	5.64 **13.48**	5.63 **13.46**
5	6.61 **16.26**	5.79 **13.27**	5.41 **12.06**	5.19 **11.39**	5.05 **10.97**	4.95 **10.67**	4.88 **10.45**	4.82 **10.27**	4.78 **10.15**	4.74 **10.05**	4.70 **9.96**	4.68 **9.89**	4.64 **9.77**	4.60 **9.68**	4.56 **9.55**	4.53 **9.47**	4.50 **9.38**	4.46 **9.29**	4.44 **9.24**	4.42 **9.17**	4.40 **9.13**	4.38 **9.07**	4.37 **9.04**	4.36 **9.02**
6	5.99 **13.74**	5.14 **10.92**	4.76 **9.78**	4.53 **9.15**	4.39 **8.75**	4.28 **8.47**	4.21 **8.26**	4.15 **8.10**	4.10 **7.98**	4.06 **7.87**	4.03 **7.79**	4.00 **7.72**	3.96 **7.60**	3.92 **7.52**	3.87 **7.39**	3.84 **7.31**	3.81 **7.23**	3.77 **7.14**	3.75 **7.09**	3.72 **7.02**	3.71 **6.99**	3.69 **6.94**	3.68 **6.90**	3.67 **6.88**
7	5.59 **12.25**	4.74 **9.55**	4.35 **8.45**	4.12 **7.85**	3.97 **7.46**	3.87 **7.19**	3.79 **7.00**	3.73 **6.84**	3.68 **6.71**	3.63 **6.62**	3.60 **6.54**	3.57 **6.47**	3.52 **6.35**	3.49 **6.27**	3.44 **6.15**	3.41 **6.07**	3.38 **5.98**	3.34 **5.90**	3.32 **5.85**	3.29 **5.78**	3.28 **5.75**	3.25 **5.70**	3.24 **5.67**	3.23 **5.65**
8	5.32 **11.26**	4.46 **8.65**	4.07 **7.59**	3.84 **7.01**	3.69 **6.63**	3.58 **6.37**	3.50 **6.19**	3.44 **6.03**	3.39 **5.91**	3.34 **5.82**	3.31 **5.74**	3.28 **5.67**	3.23 **5.56**	3.20 **5.48**	3.15 **5.36**	3.12 **5.28**	3.08 **5.20**	3.05 **5.11**	3.03 **5.06**	3.00 **5.00**	2.98 **4.96**	2.96 **4.91**	2.94 **4.88**	2.93 **4.86**
9	5.12 **10.56**	4.26 **8.02**	3.86 **6.99**	3.63 **6.42**	3.48 **6.06**	3.37 **5.80**	3.29 **5.62**	3.23 **5.47**	3.18 **5.35**	3.13 **5.26**	3.10 **5.18**	3.07 **5.11**	3.02 **5.00**	2.98 **4.92**	2.93 **4.80**	2.90 **4.73**	2.86 **4.64**	2.82 **4.56**	2.80 **4.51**	2.77 **4.45**	2.76 **4.41**	2.73 **4.36**	2.72 **4.33**	2.71 **4.31**
10	4.96 **10.04**	4.10 **7.56**	3.71 **6.55**	3.48 **5.99**	3.33 **5.64**	3.22 **5.39**	3.14 **5.21**	3.07 **5.06**	3.02 **4.95**	2.97 **4.85**	2.94 **4.78**	2.91 **4.71**	2.86 **4.60**	2.82 **4.52**	2.77 **4.41**	2.74 **4.33**	2.70 **4.25**	2.67 **4.17**	2.64 **4.12**	2.61 **4.05**	2.59 **4.01**	2.56 **3.96**	2.55 **3.93**	2.54 **3.91**
11	4.84 **9.65**	3.98 **7.20**	3.59 **6.22**	3.36 **5.67**	3.20 **5.32**	3.09 **5.07**	3.01 **4.88**	2.95 **4.74**	2.90 **4.63**	2.86 **4.54**	2.82 **4.46**	2.79 **4.40**	2.74 **4.29**	2.70 **4.21**	2.65 **4.10**	2.61 **4.02**	2.57 **3.94**	2.53 **3.86**	2.50 **3.80**	2.47 **3.74**	2.45 **3.70**	2.42 **3.66**	2.41 **3.62**	2.40 **3.60**

12	4.75 **9.33**	3.88 **6.93**	3.49 **5.95**	3.26 **5.41**	3.11 **5.06**	3.00 **4.82**	2.92 **4.65**	2.85 **4.50**	2.80 **4.39**	2.76 **4.30**	2.72 **4.22**	2.69 **4.16**	2.64 **4.05**	2.60 **3.98**	2.54 **3.86**	2.50 **3.78**	2.46 **3.70**	2.42 **3.61**	2.40 **3.56**	2.36 **3.49**	2.35 **3.46**	2.32 **3.41**	2.31 **3.38**	2.30 **3.36**
13	4.67 **9.07**	3.80 **6.70**	3.41 **5.74**	3.18 **5.20**	3.02 **4.86**	2.92 **4.62**	2.84 **4.44**	2.77 **4.30**	2.72 **4.19**	2.67 **4.10**	2.63 **4.02**	2.60 **3.96**	2.55 **3.85**	2.51 **3.78**	2.46 **3.67**	2.42 **3.59**	2.38 **3.51**	2.34 **3.42**	2.32 **3.37**	2.28 **3.30**	2.26 **3.27**	2.24 **3.21**	2.22 **3.18**	2.21 **3.16**
14	4.60 **8.86**	3.74 **6.51**	3.34 **5.56**	3.11 **5.03**	2.96 **4.69**	2.85 **4.46**	2.77 **4.28**	2.70 **4.14**	2.65 **4.03**	2.60 **3.94**	2.56 **3.86**	2.53 **3.80**	2.48 **3.70**	2.44 **3.62**	2.39 **3.51**	2.35 **3.43**	2.31 **3.34**	2.27 **3.26**	2.24 **3.21**	2.21 **3.14**	2.19 **3.11**	2.16 **3.06**	2.14 **3.02**	2.13 **3.00**
15	4.54 **8.68**	3.68 **6.36**	3.29 **5.42**	3.06 **4.89**	2.90 **4.56**	2.79 **4.32**	2.70 **4.14**	2.64 **4.00**	2.59 **3.89**	2.55 **3.80**	2.51 **3.73**	2.48 **3.67**	2.43 **3.56**	2.39 **3.48**	2.33 **3.36**	2.29 **3.29**	2.25 **3.20**	2.21 **3.12**	2.18 **3.07**	2.15 **3.00**	2.12 **2.97**	2.10 **2.92**	2.08 **2.89**	2.07 **2.87**
16	4.49 **8.53**	3.63 **6.23**	3.24 **5.29**	3.01 **4.77**	2.85 **4.44**	2.74 **4.20**	2.66 **4.03**	2.59 **3.89**	2.54 **3.78**	2.49 **3.69**	2.45 **3.61**	2.42 **3.55**	2.37 **3.45**	2.33 **3.37**	2.28 **3.25**	2.24 **3.18**	2.20 **3.10**	2.16 **3.01**	2.13 **2.96**	2.09 **2.89**	2.07 **2.86**	2.04 **2.80**	2.02 **2.77**	2.01 **2.75**
17	4.45 **8.40**	3.59 **6.11**	3.20 **5.18**	2.96 **4.67**	2.81 **4.34**	2.70 **4.10**	2.62 **3.93**	2.55 **3.79**	2.50 **3.68**	2.45 **3.59**	2.41 **3.52**	2.38 **3.45**	2.33 **3.35**	2.29 **3.27**	2.23 **3.16**	2.19 **3.08**	2.15 **3.00**	2.11 **2.92**	2.08 **2.86**	2.04 **2.79**	2.02 **2.76**	1.99 **2.70**	1.97 **2.67**	1.96 **2.65**
18	4.41 **8.28**	3.55 **6.01**	3.16 **5.09**	2.93 **4.58**	2.77 **4.25**	2.66 **4.01**	2.58 **3.85**	2.51 **3.71**	2.46 **3.60**	2.41 **3.51**	2.37 **3.44**	2.34 **3.37**	2.29 **3.27**	2.25 **3.19**	2.19 **3.07**	2.15 **3.00**	2.11 **2.91**	2.07 **2.83**	2.04 **2.78**	2.00 **2.71**	1.98 **2.68**	1.95 **2.62**	1.93 **2.59**	1.92 **2.57**
19	4.38 **8.18**	3.52 **5.93**	3.13 **5.01**	2.90 **4.50**	2.74 **4.17**	2.63 **3.94**	2.55 **3.77**	2.48 **3.63**	2.43 **3.52**	2.38 **3.43**	2.34 **3.36**	2.31 **3.30**	2.26 **3.19**	2.21 **3.12**	2.15 **3.00**	2.11 **2.92**	2.07 **2.84**	2.02 **2.76**	2.00 **2.70**	1.96 **2.63**	1.94 **2.60**	1.91 **2.54**	1.90 **2.51**	1.88 **2.49**
20	4.35 **8.10**	3.49 **5.85**	3.10 **4.94**	2.87 **4.43**	2.71 **4.10**	2.60 **3.87**	2.52 **3.71**	2.45 **3.56**	2.40 **3.45**	2.35 **3.37**	2.31 **3.30**	2.28 **3.23**	2.23 **3.13**	2.18 **3.05**	2.12 **2.94**	2.08 **2.86**	2.04 **2.77**	1.99 **2.69**	1.96 **2.63**	1.92 **2.56**	1.90 **2.53**	1.87 **2.47**	1.85 **2.44**	1.84 **2.42**
21	4.32 **8.02**	3.47 **5.78**	3.07 **4.87**	2.84 **4.37**	2.68 **4.04**	2.57 **3.81**	2.49 **3.65**	2.42 **3.51**	2.37 **3.40**	2.32 **3.31**	2.28 **3.24**	2.25 **3.17**	2.20 **3.07**	2.15 **2.99**	2.09 **2.88**	2.05 **2.80**	2.00 **2.72**	1.96 **2.63**	1.93 **2.58**	1.89 **2.51**	1.87 **2.47**	1.84 **2.42**	1.82 **2.38**	1.81 **2.36**
22	4.30 **7.94**	3.44 **5.72**	3.05 **4.82**	2.82 **4.31**	2.66 **3.99**	2.55 **3.76**	2.47 **3.59**	2.40 **3.45**	2.35 **3.35**	2.30 **3.26**	2.26 **3.18**	2.23 **3.12**	2.18 **3.02**	2.13 **2.94**	2.07 **2.83**	2.03 **2.75**	1.98 **2.67**	1.93 **2.58**	1.91 **2.53**	1.87 **2.46**	1.84 **2.42**	1.81 **2.37**	1.80 **2.33**	1.78 **2.31**
23	4.28 **7.88**	3.42 **5.66**	3.03 **4.76**	2.80 **4.26**	2.64 **3.94**	2.53 **3.71**	2.45 **3.54**	2.38 **3.41**	2.32 **3.30**	2.28 **3.21**	2.24 **3.14**	2.20 **3.07**	2.14 **2.97**	2.10 **2.89**	2.04 **2.78**	2.00 **2.70**	1.96 **2.62**	1.91 **2.53**	1.88 **2.48**	1.84 **2.41**	1.82 **2.37**	1.79 **2.32**	1.77 **2.28**	1.76 **2.26**
24	4.26 **7.82**	3.40 **5.61**	3.01 **4.72**	2.78 **4.22**	2.62 **3.90**	2.51 **3.67**	2.43 **3.50**	2.36 **3.36**	2.30 **3.25**	2.26 **3.17**	2.22 **3.09**	2.18 **3.03**	2.13 **2.93**	2.09 **2.85**	2.02 **2.74**	1.98 **2.66**	1.94 **2.58**	1.89 **2.49**	1.86 **2.44**	1.82 **2.36**	1.80 **2.33**	1.76 **2.27**	1.74 **2.23**	1.73 **2.21**

* Reprinted, by permission from G. W. Snedecor, Statistical Methods, 5th ed., Ames, Iowa: Iowa State College Press, 1956, pp. 246–249.

Appendix B.

An Example of Constructing a Theoretical Framework

In the past much research work was devoted to isolated studies. To advance the frontiers of knowledge, strong pleas have been made in recent years for the development of theoretical frameworks or models in various areas of knowledge that will stimulate, guide, and integrate research work. A study made of the characteristics of teachers serves as an example of one attempt to do this.

Over the years, information relative to teacher characteristics has been accumulated in an unsystematic manner with little attention given to building a theory of teacher behavior. Ryans[1] and his associates have taken steps in this direction. He states that his proposals "do not constitute a complete inventory of all assumptions required for a theory of teacher behavior. Nor is any particular claim made at this point for theoretical rigor. But if in the area of teacher behavior there are advantages in resolving and systematizing our thinking, a starting point is necessary regardless of how tentative it may be."

To develop a systematic theory, Ryans defined the term "teacher behavior," stated the two major assumptions necessary for a theory of teacher behavior, and listed a number of implications or subassumptions (postulates) relating to each of them. From this theoretical framework he proceeded to make several

1/ David G. Ryans, *Characteristics of Teachers*. Washington, D.C.: American Council on Education, 1960, pp. 13–26.

propositions concerning teacher behavior in general terms that researchers could convert into exact and testable hypothesis form.

Definition

Teacher behavior may be defined simply as the behavior, or activities, of persons as they go about doing whatever is required of teachers, particularly those activities which are concerned with the guidance or direction of the learning of others.

Basic Assumptions and Subassumptions

Assumption I: Teacher behavior is a function of situational factors and characteristics of the individual teacher. In setting out to formulate some theory of teacher behavior, the basic assumption might well be expected to bear resemblance to formulations made for similar purposes in connection with learning theory and personality theory. Indeed, in behavior theory, some expression of faith in the reliability, or consistency, of behavior is required. In the present case the basic assumption may be summarized in the proposition that teacher behavior is a resultant of (*a*) certain situational factors and (*b*) certain organismic conditions, and their interaction—or, simply, that teacher behavior is a function of certain environmental influences and the learned and unlearned characteristics of the individual teacher. . . .

Postulates

Postulate I-A: Teacher behavior is characterized by some degree of consistency. One implication of the basic assumption is that teacher behavior (and social behavior, with which education deals) is characterized by some degree of unformity; that, as Mill put it: ". . . there are such things in nature as parallel cases, that what happens once will, under sufficient degree of similarity of circumstances, happen again. . . ." We are stating simply that teacher behavior (a particular kind of behavior of a particular teacher) is not haphazard or fortuitous, but instead is consistent, or reliable, and therefore is capable of being predicted.

Postulate I-B: Teacher behavior is characterized by a limited number of responses. Another implication of the basic assumption (and perhaps it is so fundamental to scientific theory that it is unnecessary to state it explicitly with respect to teacher behavior) is expressed by Keynes' Postulate of Limited Independent Qualities, which states that: ". . . objects in a field over which our generalizations extend, do not have an infinite number of independent qualities; . . . their characteristics, however numerous, cohere together in groups of invariable connections, which are finite in number. . . ." Accordingly, the number of responses the individual teacher is capable of making, and the number of stimulus situations and organismic variables that may affect a teacher's behavior, are limited. This assumption is important if we hope to predict teacher behavior. It presents the researcher with a "tolerable" problem.

Postulate I-C: Teacher behavior is always probable rather than certain. All human behavior, characterized as it is by variability rather than by *complete* uniformity or consistency, must always be considered in the light of probability instead of from the standpoint of invariable cause-effect relationships. The error component resulting from such variability will inevitably be present in any assessment that is attempted of either (*a*) situational or stimulus conditions, (*b*) organismic conditions (genetic bases, past experience, motivation), or (*c*) teacher behavior (the dependent variable, or criterion). Behavior can be predicted only with varying degrees of probability.

Postulate I-D: Teacher behavior is a function of personal characteristics of the individual teacher. Teacher behavior is determined in part by the teacher's personal and social characteristics (e.g., in the intellectual, emotional, temperamental, attitudinal, and interest domains), which have their sources in both the genetic (unlearned) and experiential (learned) backgrounds of the individual. Knowledge of such characteristics contributes to prediction, within limits, of teacher behavior.

Postulate I-E: Teacher behavior is a function of general features of the situation in which it takes place. Teacher behavior is determined, in part, by general features of the situation in which it has its setting—features which may be observed to be common to situations of a general class and which, therefore, may be distinguished from the unique features of specific teaching situations. Information about such relevant features assists in the prediction, within limits, of teacher behavior.

Postulate I-F: Teacher behavior is a function of the specific situation in which it takes place. Finally, teacher behavior is determined, in part, by unique features of the particular situation in which it has its setting at a particular time. These features vary from situation to situation and contribute to the aspect of teacher behavior which is, to an extent, unique to the particular situation.

Assumption II: Teacher behavior is observable. When we attempt to study teacher behavior, we also make the assumption that teacher behavior may be identified objectively, either by direct observation or by indirect approaches that provide correlative indices of teacher behaviors. Examples of the indirect approaches are the assessment of pupil behavior, the use of tests of teacher abilities and knowledge, and the use of interviews or inventories to elicit expression of teacher preferences, interests, beliefs, and attitudes.

Several implications of this assumption may be noted here in the form of the following postulates.

Postulate II-A: Teacher behaviors are distinguishable. If teacher behaviors are observable, it follows that those with certain features must be capable of being identified and described so as to be distinguished from other teacher behaviors. Some behaviors have certain characteristics in common, which constitute generic or core components that may be abstracted to facilitate (*a*) communication of generalized descriptions of those behaviors, and (*b*) the identification of such behaviors in individual teachers. Teacher behaviors can be distinguished under observation.

Postulate II-B: Teacher behaviors are classifiable qualitatively and quantitatively. A second aspect of the assumption of the observability of teacher behavior is that teacher behaviors are classifiable, both qualitatively and quantitatively. A class, or category, of teacher behaviors is simply a grouping of specific behaviors which have many resemblances to one another and relatively few *important* differences. When we find such behavioral analogues, we take them as an indication that still other resemblances may exist, since resemblances in nature tend to go together in fairly large groups (Postulate of Limited Independent Qualities). When behaviors have been grouped together in the light of their resemblances, it becomes possible to abstract the general class description from the descriptions of specific manifestations and thereby provide the basis for a "concept" of teacher behavior of a certain kind and permit greater common understanding of the behavior.

Teacher behaviors that are similar, that have certain resemblances or common elements, may be classified in the same qualitative category. Within any given category, these behaviors may be further assigned to subclasses, which may be treated quantitatively. This is to say that teacher behaviors are subjectable to measurement—albeit approximate measurement. These quantitative subclasses may be of either of two types: (1) those permitting enumeration, or counting, only, or (2) those characterized by continuity and varying as a metric (exemplified at the lowest level of refinement by ordinal subclasses and at successively more refined levels by equal-interval and equal-ratio subclasses). . . .

Postulate II-C: Teacher behaviors are revealed through overt behavior and also by symptoms or correlates of behavior. Teacher behaviors may be revealed, or may be observed, either (1) by the representative *sampling* of specific teacher acts or behaviors, or (2) by specific signs, or indicators, or *correlates,* of the behavior under consideration.

In sampling behavior, we assume that the performance of the individual during the behavior sample is approximately (and at some level of probability) representative of the larger aspects, or universe, of his behavior. In judging behavior from signs or correlates, it is assumed that a behavior can be inferred or estimated approximately, in probability terms, from observed correlates of that behavior—from phenomena that are known to have been associated with that behavior in the past.

Some Propositions and Hypotheses

From the standpoint of the Teacher Characteristics Study, the foregoing definition and basic assumptions, together with their implications, provide a theoretical framework and starting point from which the researcher might reasonably proceed to propositions regarding teacher behavior—propositions that may be employed as hypotheses and tested against empirical data.

The number of descriptive classifications and specific propositions which might be generated with regard to teacher behavior is almost limitless, although we probably would not be interested in all such hypotheses even if it were possible to assemble them. Some classifications and some hypotheses seem more relevant than others. No doubt many of them could be incorporated in existing research designs and tested to determine their probable acceptability. . . .

Tests of a number of hypotheses about teacher classroom behaviors and other teacher characteristics were attempted by the Teacher Characteristics Study, and a major portion of this volume is given to reporting the data that were collected for these tests. It is not appropriate to list in this chapter—which deals with general theory of teacher behavior and problems related thereto—all the propositions of hypotheses which guided the research of the project. However, to illustrate the kind of propositions which may grow out of the basic assumptions and postulates stated earlier, a few of those to which the staff of the Teacher Characteristics Study gave attention are listed below.

Proposition: General classes of teacher classroom behaviors fall into relatively homogeneous clusters characterized by substantial intercorrelation of behaviors within a cluster. Teacher behavior *in toto* may be described in terms of a limited number of such major clusters of behaviors.

Proposition: The major clusters or families formed by teacher behaviors have the characteristics of *dimensions.* Individual teachers, in their manifestations of a particular behavior pattern, vary along a continuum between two behaviorally describable poles.

Proposition: Reliable estimates of teacher behavior constituting a major cluster (positions along a major dimension) may be obtained through assessments derived from the observations of trained observers.

Proposition: The classroom behavior of a teacher with respect to a major dimension, as represented by assessments made by trained observers, is characterized by substantial stability over considerable periods of time.

Propositions: The extent of intercorrelation among major dimensions of teacher behavior varies for different subpopulations of teachers, such as elementary teachers and secondary teachers.

Proposition: Correlates scales may be developed, using paper-and-pencil responses of teachers as indicators which will permit the indirect estimation of various kinds of teacher characteristics such as social attitudes, educational viewpoints, verbal ability, and emotionality.

Proposition: Teacher characteristics of the type described in the preceding proposition, as revealed by *correlates* in the form of paper-and-pencil responses of teachers to questions about their preferences, activities, and the like, are consistent and stable over substantial periods of time.

Proposition: Different subpopulations of teachers, classified according to grade level and subject matter taught, differ significantly in teacher characteristics.

Proposition: Certain teacher characteristics vary with the age of the teacher.

Proposition: Certain teacher characteristics are correlated with grades or marks earned by the teacher when in college.

Proposition: Certain teacher characteristics are related to the earlier youth activities of the teacher.

For some of these propositions there is considerable evidential support. For others considered by the Teacher Characteristics Study, lack of statistical corroboration or, equally often, absence of adequate controls, indicates that rejection, or at least suspended judgment, is in order. These findings are discussed in later chapters.

Appendix C.

An Example of Hypothesis Construction

The problem of constructing hypotheses often perplexes students, and most examples in the literature are too complex for them to understand. Perhaps the following article,[1] which informally explores a problem area in mental health and proposes several hypotheses, will provide a general understanding of the process. The article is written primarily for classroom teachers and does not present as rigorous an analysis of the problem and as precise statements of the hypotheses as the researcher employs. But it does reveal the types of explorations and explanations that investigators make in the early stages of problem evolvement.

Most classroom teachers are concerned about the mental health of their students for at least two reasons: they know that the level of interpersonal adjustment of the student has an effect on his level of academic learning, and they accept the *health* of the student as being important in its own right. This discussion of group mental health—the mental health of children in the classroom group—is intended especially for the classroom teacher. His job is essentially that of a group worker; and as such, he needs to have the understandings and skills essential to hygienic group management.

What follows, then, is an attempt to explore three questions which appear to be basic to an understanding of classroom mental health:

1/ Allen Menlo, "Mental Health within the Classroom Group," *School of Education Bulletin, University of Michigan,* 31 (May, 1960) : 121.

1/
What differentiates a mentally healthy from a mentally unhealthy classroom—at least, as far as experience appears to indicate?
2/
What kinds of things tend to influence the level of mental health in the classroom—at least, as far as human relations research appears to indicate?
3/
What hypotheses, then, can be drawn regarding the management of mental health in the classroom—at least, as far as they sound psychologically reasonable?

Question 1 asks how we can assess the level of mental health in a classroom. Practically, the question asks for an identification of those dimensions along which one must observe in order to evaluate or judge the level of mental health within the classroom group. Four dimensions are suggested.

The amount of acceptance or rejection within the group. This refers to the extent of positive or negative affect in the classroom, or the degree of friendly versus unfriendly atmosphere. This is the kind of thing teachers find out by doing a sociometric study on how much class members like each other, how much they think others like them, how much they like the teacher, how much they think the teacher likes them, and how much the teacher actually likes them. The assumption here is that the predominance of accepting attitudes and behaviors is healthier than the predominance of rejecting ones.

The amount of cooperative action or aggression within the group. This refers to the extent of active or passive movement with or against others, or the degree of helping versus force, threat, coercion, or harm. Teachers find this out when they ask students questions on how much they perceive themselves, other children, and the teacher as either being pushed around or pushing others around. The assumption here is that the predominance of cooperative actions is healthier than the predominance of aggressive actions.

The amount of involvement in or withdrawal from the class process. This refers to the extent of active or passive movement toward or away from others, or the degree of participation versus self-isolation and escape. Teachers assess this when they look for how much children appear to be, or feel they are, a part of the classroom experience. Here the assumption is that the presence of student involvement is healthier than the presence of withdrawal.

The amount of feeling of comfort or anxiety in the class. This refers to the extent of feelings of "at ease" or tension, or the degree of calm versus nervous feelings and behaviors. One way teachers evaluate this is by providing opportunities for students' expressions of happiness or unhappiness with respect to class procedures, other students, the teacher, and the general class situation. The assumption is that a predominance of feelings of comfort is healthier than one of anxiety.

Question 2 calls for a definition of the conditions which may influence a classroom group toward the manifestation of these symptoms. The findings of several studies strongly indicate a causative relationship between the exposure of human beings to certain conditions and their resultant demonstration of certain behaviors and attitudes consistent with the four sets of symptoms mentioned above. Specifically, these relationships are as follows:

When communication is cut off between people, they tend to develop misperceptions, misunderstanding, and even hostilities regarding and toward each other. When communication is open, people tend to develop realistic perceptions and positive feelings between each other.

When people have a perception of shared objectives, a feeling of cohesiveness, and see each other in a "good light" their contacts tend to produce accepting and mutually supportive attitudes and behaviors toward each other. People's contacts under conditions of uncommon objectives, lack of a spirit of "we-ness," and seeing each other's "poorer" side tend to produce unaccepting, nonsupportive attitudes and behaviors toward each other.

A highly restrictive style of leadership control tends to produce aggressive, scapegoating, and drop-out types of behaviors and attitudes among people. Less restrictive leadership control tends to produce cooperative, noncritical, and stay-in types of behaviors and attitudes.

People tend to get more involved in an experience when they participate in the planning of it, have opportunity to express their feelings about it, hear others' feelings about it, and have some active responsibility in carrying it out. People tend to resist those experiences in which they have no share in the planning, expression of feelings, or responsibility for implementation.

People tend to be attracted toward and feel more involved in activities which they see as having good chances of satisfying their own needs. People tend not to be attracted toward and not feel involved in activities which they see as having a poor chance of satisfying their own needs.

People tend to feel comfortable and secure in situations when they perceive themselves as having value and perceive others as representing friendly forces toward them. People tend to feel uncomfortable and insecure in situations when they perceive themselves as having minimal value and perceive others as representing unfriendly forces toward them.

The answers to the first two questions have described, thus far, the manifestations of healthy versus unhealthy socioemotional dynamics in a classroom group and have indicated the conditions which may be partially or wholly causative to these manifestations.

Question 3 is about the implications of all this for the teacher as a practitioner of hygienic group management. These implications follow in the form of hypotheses which are derived, more or less directly, from the foregoing material. These hypotheses are either partially or wholly untested and will probably remain unsubstantiated until teachers at various levels begin to research them within their own classes and schools. In the absence of experimental evidence, the teacher should find it interesting to test these hypotheses with his own classroom teaching-learning experiences.

Hypothesis A. Teachers who jointly plan classroom procedures and learning activities with their students contribute more to the mental health of students than do teachers who refrain from planning with their students.

Hypothesis B. Teachers who provide their students with opportunities for emotional ventilation and expression of feelings about what goes on in class, their peers, their teacher, and themselves contribute more to the mental health of students than teachers who do not make provisions for this.

Hypothesis C. Teachers who make maximum use of student services for leadership in the classroom contribute more to the mental health of students than teachers who give all or most of the services themselves.

Hypothesis D. Teachers who maintain flexible, uncrowded agenda of activity and subject matter in their classrooms contribute more to the mental health of students than teachers who keep crowded agenda.

Hypothesis E. Teachers who build motivation to learn by interpersonal cooperation in their classrooms contribute more to the mental health of students than teachers who build motivation by interpersonal competition.

Hypothesis F. Teachers who accept, and help their students accept, a wide range or variation in behavior and attitudes in their classrooms contribute more to the mental health of students than teachers who are, and help their students be, critically evaluative of individual differences in behavior and attitude.

The problem of maintaining good mental health in the classroom is one in which teachers are gaining more understanding and skill. Administrative and supervisory personnel are also becoming more intelligently familiar with the needs and the techniques, and their support, encouragement, and assistance do much to help the teacher accomplish his purposes.

Appendix D.

An Example of Deducing the Consequences

Deducing the consequences of a hypothesis and discovering whether they are observable through appropriate tests is an important responsibility of the researcher. If factual affirmation can be found for one consequent, a hypothesis gains some support. If factual evidence can be found to support several entailed consequences, the cumulative evidence considerably strengthens the confirmation of the hypothesis. Since students often have difficulty in grasping the process of deducing consequences, the following discussion[1] of Newton's "theory" of the composition of white light may provide a helpful illustration.

Observing the colored spectrum which appears when sunlight is refracted in a crystal, Newton conceived the hypothesis that white light is a mixture of rays differing in refrangibility, and that the different colors of the spectrum correspond to the different degrees of refrangibility. This hypothesis entailed a number of consequents. We can represent the matter in this way:

If white light is a mixture of rays differing in refrangibility, and *if* the different colors of the spectrum correspond to the different degrees of refrangibility.

then (1) rays of different colors cannot come to a focus at the same distance from the lens (and this explains the "blurred" images seen through earlier telescopes);

1/ W. H. Werkmeister, *An Introduction to Critical Thinking.* Lincoln, Nebraska: Johnsen Publishing Company, 1957, p. 585.

then (2) for each color there must be a definite and specific amount of refraction and the refrangibility of every color must be constant;

then (3) mixing in a due proportion all the primary colors should produce white light;

then (4) the rainbow can be explained as the result of refraction;

then (5) the "permanent colors of natural bodies" are the result of the reflection of light rays.

Here we have a hypothesis which entails at least five groups of consequents. If all of them are supported by the facts—and, through a series of ingenious experiments, Newton could show that this is the case—then the hypothesis may be said to be confirmed or verified beyond reasonable doubt.

Appendix E.

An Example of
a Presentation of
a Problem

Many students raise questions concerning the logical chain of reasoning that runs through the review of the literature, the theoretical orientation of the problem, and the statement of specific problem hypotheses. These excerpts from a study concerning "Classroom Behavior and Underachievement"[1] may provide some helpful insights.

The low scholastic performance of a substantial number of high-ability students is a continuing concern of parents and educators at all levels. The number of studies that have identified and contrasted the characteristics of the underachiever and the matched achiever is impressive. Shaw and McCuen (1960) concluded that underachievement can be identified in the early elementary-school years and increases with age, and Frankel (1960) found that it continues to increase through the senior high school. Battle (1957), Frankel (1960), Spaulding (1960), and Fink (1962) reported significant differences between achievers and underachievers in values, goals, self-concepts, and other psychological factors. Bruner and Caron (1959) and Pierce (1960) found that high and low achievers differ significantly in their patterns of motivation, perceptions, and cognitive structuring, with sex differences so striking that the data for boys and girls were interpreted separately. How family

1/ Hugh V. Perkins, "Classroom Behavior and Underachievement," *American Educational Research Journal*, 2 (January, 1965): 1.

This research was supported by Public Health Service Grant MH 07344-01 and by the General Research Board and the Computer Science Center of the University of Maryland. The author gratefully acknowledges the contributions made to this study by Richard M. Brandt, Arianna Claypool, Angus McDonald, Jr., and Johanna C. Van Looy.

values and training patterns, social class, and ethnic origin influence motivation and performance is discussed by Strodtbeck (1958), Rosen and D'Andrade (1959), Frankel (1960), and Pierce (1960).

The purpose of the present study was to identify those student-behavior, learning-activity, teacher-behavior, and teacher-role variables that are related to a lack of academic achievement among high-ability fifth-grade pupils. The development of instruments for measuring these variables is described in an earlier article (Perkins, 1964). These instruments are reproduced in Table 1.

Rationale and Hypotheses

The rationale of this study is based upon the following propositions drawn from perceptual, developmental, personality, and learning theory: (1) An individual responds to a situation in accordance with the way he perceives it; (2) Areas, events, and activities that have special significance for an individual are those that facilitate or threaten his maintenance and enhancement of self; (3) Behaviors that are reinforced tend to be repeated.

It is reasonable to assume that underachievers and achievers differ in the kinds of behavior they find self-enhancing and reinforcing and therefore differ in behavior. This leads to the general hypothesis that underachievers and achievers differ significantly in the proportion of classroom time spent in certain kinds of behavior and to the following two specific hypotheses:

1 Compared with achievers, underachievers spend a significantly greater proportion of their classroom time (a) intent on work in another academic area (WOA), (b) intent on nonacademic work (WNA), and (c) withdrawing (WDL).
2 Compared with underachievers, achievers spend a significantly greater proportion of their classroom time (a) reading or writing (REWR), (b) highly involved in learning activity (HIAC), and (c) working with peers (SWP).

On the other hand, since human-development theory stresses the need of *every* child to relate himself to significant adults, peers, and the situation, there are certain kinds of behavior in which underachievers and achievers will spend about the same proportions of time. The specific hypothesis is as follows:

3 Underachievers and achievers do not differ significantly in the proportion of classroom time spent (a) listening and watching (LISWAT), (b) interacting with the teacher (SWT), or (c) engaging in friendly nonwork interaction with peers (SF).

Also included in this study is a theory of sex differences leading to the following specific hypothesis:

4 Compared with boys, girls spend more classroom time in language activities (REWR) and in social interaction (SWP, SWT, SF); whereas boys are more highly active (HIAC), more involved in other academic and in nonacademic areas (WOA, WNA), and more withdrawn (WDL).

Finally, group-dynamics theory and studies of teacher interaction lead to the following specific hypothesis:

5 Learning activities, work-oriented student behavior, and the teacher roles and kinds of behavior that facilitate learning are positively and significantly related to academic achievement. Those kinds of teacher and student behavior that are less facilitative of learning are negatively associated with academic achievement.

Appendix F.

An Example of Criticism of a Theory

When a new theory, "Movement and Meaning," was developed by Ellfeldt and Metheny,[1] the investigators made the following comments concerning the theory:

> The somatic [bodily] or structural aspects of [human] movement have been studied by many investigators; but the significance of the human ability to conceptualize the sensory or perceptual aspects of movement has received little attention; and the questions relating to human meanings and values in this conceptualization of the structural-perceptual experience of movement-kinesthesia[2] have scarcely been raised (p. 264).
>
> The central problem of this study was the development of a tentative general theory about the meaning of human-movement kinesthesia as a somatic-sensory experience which can be conceptualized by the human mind (p. 265).

The investigators identified the essential elements common to *all* forms of human movement—structural, perceptual, and

---

1/ Lois Ellfeldt and Eleanor Metheny, "Movement and Meaning: Development of a General Theory," *Research Quarterly,* 29 (October, 1958): 264.

2/ Kinesthesia is derived from *kinein* (to move) and *aisthēsis* (perception); the sense whose end organs lie in the muscles, tendons, and joints and are stimulated by bodily tensions; the muscle sense.

conceptual—and developed a vocabulary to refer to these elements:

Kinestruct: n. A dynamic somatic form constructed by body masses in motion.

Kinescept: n. A sensory form created by kinesthetic perception of a kinestruct.

Kinesymbol: n. A conceptual form which is an abstraction of the significance or import of a kinestruct and its kinescept within the socio-psycho-somatic context of a situation (p. 268).

Using this vocabulary, the relationships among these elements were analyzed in relation to the process of human thought.

From this analysis, a tentative general theory of the meaning inherent in human-movement kinesthesia was formulated.

The theory that Ellfeldt and Metheny developed, like all other theories, was not constructed for an eternity. After a theory·is formulated, it is submitted to other scholars for examination. After analyzing the theory or conducting studies to validate it, other scholars may reject the theory or suggest clarifications, revisions, or extensions that will lead to the formulation of a more acceptable theory. To illustrate, shortly after Ellfeldt and Metheny published their theory, "Movement and Meaning," Hubbard[3] examined it and offered the following criticism:

The new theory of "movement and meaning" though interesting, has several weaknesses. A basic fallacy occurs in the concept of kinesthetic feedback as presented in the statement that "the kinescept provides a sensory record . . . even while it is controlling or guiding the response" (p. 269). The kinesthetic input, or kinescept, is a *result* of the muscular action causing the movement and of the movement. Thus, kinesthesis is an inherent error-sensing mechanism. But the assumption that kinesthesis senses errors in the output in time to alter the action which produces it is highly questionable in the case of fast, skilled movements.

As a simple example, the skilled typist may sense that a wrong key was struck and stop to check visually. Very rarely does the typist block the stroke in time to prevent the error or in time to prevent additional letters appearing. Whether recognition of the wrong key being struck results from a discrepancy between the material being transcribed and the "kinesymbol" or a discrepancy between the "kinesymbol" leading to and the "kinescept" leading from the stroke is a moot question. The important point is that the error initiated tends strongly to occur and that feedback rarely

3/ Alfred W. Hubbard, "Comments on the Article by Lois Ellfeldt and Eleanor Metheny, 'Movement and Meaning: Development of a General Theory,'" *Research Quarterly,* 30 (May, 1959): 244.

occurs in time to prevent the error. Error prevention, when it does occur, is in terms of a temporary blockage of production. In sport, dance, or piano playing where the situation requires continued production, the error may be noted, but the general process proceeds.

Kinesthesis may be error-sensing, but not error-correcting, in fast movements because of an inherent characteristic of the neuromuscular system. In fast, skilled movements, and especially those involving large segments of the body, the segment outruns the impressed force of the muscle, or muscles, initiating the movement. Thus, control is inherent in the combination of muscular forces initiating the stroke. Even though error is sensed as the movement is being executed, the error results unless the stroke is checked by an antagonist. Then it must be returned and restarted. Compensation for errors sensed through kinesthesis can sometimes be made in subsequent strokes of serial movement patterns. The result may be partially saved. And, of course, errors can be corrected in subsequent executions of the skill. In general, though, kinesthetic input is like a follow-through—it may indicate what went wrong but not in time to prevent it.

A second major weakness of the new theory is the suppression or disregard of the vital part other sensory inputs have in shaping skilled motor performance. The definitions (p. 268) establish a hierarchy from action to concepts based on kinesthesis, but kinesthesis without touch, pressure, and vision would be a relatively sterile sense. The quality, meaning, and effectiveness of motor performance depends on visible effects. Vision generally provides the basic feedback concerning the external effect of our actions. Vision also provides a basis for comprehending the action of others. Many "kinesymbols" originate in visual perception—seeing and trying are normal. Visual analysis of motor performance by skilled observers (coaches) often locates the source of motor errors and leads to better performance—and probably better "kinesymbols"—through discourse and demonstration.

Kinesthesis, touch, and pressure inputs accompany the production of action and precede the visible effect. A performer can predict the visible result from these inputs—once he learns to interpret them. He may "feel" the difference between two performances, but he cannot perceive good movement kinesthetically until he produces it. He cannot predict the outcome of performance from the "feel" during production until he determines what cues from kinesthesis, touch, and pressure correlate with good performance. Otherwise, old errors feel good. Obviously, vision is necessary to keep abreast of play in competition with opponents. But an individual executing a thoroughly practiced routine in gymnastics or figure skating, where he has only himself to control, might conceivably operate on the basis of cues from kinesthesis, touch, and pressure. He can, but partial or complete deprivation of vision produces considerable decrement in performance (1). This suggests that kinesthesis, even with touch and pressure, is not a sufficient basis for controlling previously well "kinesymbolized" skills.

A ·third weakness may be simply overstatement for emphasis. Statements that "a kinestruct can never be described in detail," that "the 'feel of a movement' can never be described in words," and that "conceptualizations of kinesthetic perception cannot be expressed in the symbols of any other sensory conceptualizations" are highly questionable. "He raised his arm" is concise and presumably sufficiently descriptive for the occasion. Describing any movement "in detail" is infinitely complicated and probably useless. Dynamic forms can be described, although precise description may confuse the uninitiated. Incidentally, human movement is compounded from discrete muscle impulses rather than "continuous changes in tension in every muscle fiber of the body." The "feel of movement" can be shared. Prefacing statements with "it should feel as though" directs attention to kinesthetic, touch, and pressure sensations and, by directing a person to try for this feel, often bears fruit. The "kinesymbol," "kinescept," and "kinestruct" may be unexpressed operationally, but this does not mean that they are unexpressable or uncommunicable. Speaking is a motor response and thinking is done in terms of subovert movements. We translate words into action and action into words. We verbalize visual concepts, visualize verbal concepts, and express ideas with movements. And if a dancer can communicate concepts without discourse, discourse might communicate concepts without large, somatic movements—granting that both might miss the point in translation and both translations might result in jargon.

Finally, "recognizing that the kinestruct and its kinescept are both kinesymbols" and that these "cannot be expressed in the symbols of any other sensory conceptualization" makes all action and errors kinesymbolic and untouchable. Automatic feedback control of kinestructs by kinescepts makes action reflex and errors immutable since the movement is a motor image of the symbolic pattern. Thus, in trying to summarize the authors' position, but with no intention of distorting their meaning by injudicious quotation, we seem to find that movement has an untouchable origin and an immutable nature which presents physical education with an unsolvable problem and which makes any claims of teaching or training people in motor skills presumably fraudulent. The general theory (p. 272) might be rephrased to state that human movement is meaningful action based on the meaning of movement. This does not summarize the extensive findings concerning movement, perception, and their relations, but it at least leaves the door open for learning—*Alfred W. Hubbard, University of Illinois, Urbana, Illinois.*

Bibliography

1 Graybiel, Ashton, *et al.,* "Russian Studies of Vision in Relation to Physical Activity and Sports." *Research Quarterly* **26:**480–85; Dec. 1955.

Appendix G.

An Example of Psychological Theory

Examples of the development of fairly complex hypotheses stated with some degree of precision are difficult to locate in educational literature. Admittedly, there are some relatively simple statements, but to find more sophisticated presentations one must turn to other fields. The following illustration from the field of psychology[1] presents a theory of error which includes four postulates. Note the care that has been given to the definition of terms, the statement of the postulates, and the deductions derived from one of them.

Definitions

Error: A response other than that appropriate to the motor set present, where this response is appropriate to other parts of the stimulus complex.

Response: Observable striated muscular behavior by the individual.

Motor set: Bodily orientation for the performance of a given behavior, inferred jointly from the instructions given by the experimenter or subject to himself and the physical orientation of the person. We can to some extent get at it by asking the subject what he intends or intended to do, or by setting up an objective criterion

1/ R. B. Ammons, "Errors: Theory and Measurement," Kentucky Symposium: *Learning Theory, Personality Theory, and Clinical Research.* New York: John Wiley & Sons, Inc., 1954, p. 142.

for determining whether or not the physical orientation would allow the performance of the task.

Appropriate response: The response which the individual says he intends or intended to make and for which he is physically oriented is the appropriate response to the motor set. Appropriate responses to other parts of the stimulus complex are those which would be most frequently made if those parts of the stimulus complex were dominant.

Stimulus complex: Various components which make up the stimulus such as stimuli from motor set, specific drive stimuli, and external stimuli. Any of these can be changed relatively independently, changing the stimulus complex.

Dominance of a component of the stimulus complex: A drive stimulus is more dominant as the drive becomes stronger. When the subject is asked to describe a situation, a particular stimulus component is dominant to the extent that it is mentioned earlier in his description. Frequently, this dominance must be inferred from the past history of the individual. The report may not be accurate from the point of view of the experimenter, as in the case of the individual who has always hated a sibling and now reports that his emotion is one of love and affection, yet behaves as if he hated her. . . .

Drive stimuli: Those stimuli characteristically noted by the human organism in connection with hunger, thirst, sex frustration, fear, anxiety, etc. One could infer the presence of such stimuli in terms of strength of drive.

External stimuli: Environmental energies which affect the receptors of the organism. When the organism is oriented in such a way that the receptor can be affected by the energy and the energy is sufficient to stimulate the receptor, stimulation is normally assumed to take place.

Strength of the response tendency: Latency of the response, physical strength of the response, and probability of the response occurring in the presence of or closely following the presence of a given stimulus complex.

Stimulus similarity: Stimulus complexes are similar to the degree that they contain similar components and are relatively less separated along the various discriminable continua.

Strength of drive: Might be the self-rating of the individual or might be inferred from the past history of the individual with respect to the time since drinking, time since eating, number of times a pleasant or unpleasant consequence has followed a particular stimulus complex, etc. Thus drive stimuli can be associated with primary or secondary drives as conceived of by Hull. Emotions are considered to be drives.

Reward: The satisfaction of some need, goal-object consumption, or avoidance of noxious stimulation. . . .

Postulates

Postulate 1: To any stimulus component or complex, there are a number of possible responses. The strengths of the response tendencies differ. Thus there is present a "strength" hierarchy of responses to any given stimulus component or complex. . . .

Postulate 2: The more similar a stimulus component or complex is to another given stimulus component or complex which has regularly elicited a response in the past, the stronger the response of this kind now elicited by the new stimulus. . . .

Postulate 3: The stronger the drive, the stronger the response.

Postulate 4: The components of a given stimulus complex may in isolation elicit different responses. When the components are combined in the stimulus complex, the greater the dominance of a given component and the greater the strength of a given response tendency associated with it, the more likely the stimulus complex is to elicit this response.

Deductions

Deduction 4a: If a response has been regularly elicited under a low drive and is now elicited with a high drive of the same kind present, we will observe an increase in "errors," providing the strongest response tendencies to the motor set and the drive are different and that to the motor set is dominant.

Deduction 4b: If a response has been regularly elicited under one drive, and the drive is changed to another without altering the other stimulus components (especially motor set), there will be more errors, providing the appropriate dominant response to the drive-stimulus component from the original drive was the same as that to the motor set, but that to the new drive stimulus is different from that to the motor set, the motor set staying the same.

Deduction 4c: To the extent that a single stimulus component dominates the total stimulus complex, the successive responses given by an individual will be more similar to each other.

Strong emotion leads to stereotypy of responses, as does instruction induced "motor set," and the "same" physical stimulation. In free association, problem areas will be talked about more frequently than other areas. In the case of errors, we find that certain kinds are quite frequent, i.e., certain types of slips of the tongue and certain kinds of accidents in the accident-prone person. These errors should indicate the life areas in which the person has problems and thus be of diagnostic value to the clinician.

Deduction 4d: Other stimulus conditions being approximately equal, if one arouses a feeling about an error he should get real-life responses associated with a similar set, emotion, or drive more quickly than if no feeling is aroused. . . .

Appendix H.

An Example of a Model

In recent literature of the behavioral sciences, the term "model" has become quite fashionable.[1] As more and more investigators use the term, it has taken on wider and more varied meanings. In general, it entails finding a structure that enables one to present concepts in such a way that researchers can gain useful insights into their phenomena.

Guilford and Merrifield have constructed a model to organize intellectual factors into a system. They define model as a "set of constructs specified in such a way that their formal connections are evident."[2] They depict the structure of intellect in the form of a three-dimensional rectangular solid as seen below, and carefully define their terms.[3]

The constructs in this model are the individual abilities, i.e., the cells in the three-dimensional matrix. The formal connections between the constructs are deducible from the categories with the three variables of classification: operation, content, and product. These three are considered as formally independent, so that no combination of operation, content, and product is logically excluded from the system.

1/ May Brodbeck, "The Philosophy of Science and Educational Research," *Review of Educational Research,* 27 (December, 1957): 436.
2/ J. P. Guilford and P. R. Merrifield, *The Structure of Intellect Model: Its Uses and Implications.* Reports from the Psychological Laboratory, University of Southern California, 24 (April, 1960), p. 13.
3/ *Ibid.,* p. 13.

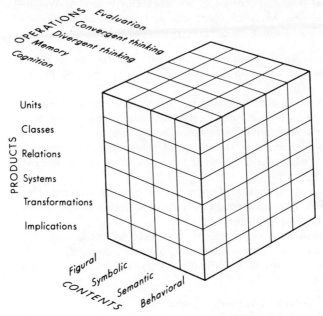

Fig. A.

The investigators do not consider the model to be perfect and the positions of the factors in it to be permanently fixed. They expect that additional empirical evidence may lead to some changes. They point out that[4]

A model is used as a theory when connections between its constructs and the empirical world are hypothesized. The acceptance of a theory depends upon the verification of such hypotheses. For the structure-of-intellect model to be supported as theory requires two types of verification. First, previously found factors must be confirmed as distinct from each other, when interpreted in terms of their location in the model. Second, new factors must be hypothesized from the model, and their separate existences verified.

At present the investigators are testing "whether unknown unique abilities that are predicted by the model do, in fact exist as distinguishable entities."[5] The model has been used "as a basis for a rough consideration of problems of curriculum in education, in relation to teaching of reading, and as a basis for a systematic orientation with respect to psychological tests."[6]

4/ *Ibid.*, p. 13.
5/ *Ibid.*, p. 2.
6/ *Ibid.*, p. 3.

Definitions/ The major concepts are labeled in Figure A. We shall begin with the kinds of operations and end with the kinds of products, also defining the parameters themselves.

Operations/ Major kinds of intellectual activities or processes; things that the organism does with the raw material of information.[7]

Cognition: Discovery, awareness, rediscovery, or recognition of information in various forms; comprehension or understanding.

Memory: Retention of information in any form.

Divergent production: Generation of information from given information, where the emphasis is upon variety of output from the same source.

Convergent production: Generation of information from given information, where the emphasis is upon achieving unique or conventionally accepted or best outcomes.

Evaluation: Reaching decisions or making judgments concerning the goodness (correctness, suitability, adequacy, desirability) of information in terms of criteria of identity, consistency, and goal satisfaction.

Contents/ General varieties of information.

Figural content: Information in concrete form, as perceived or as recalled in the form of images. The term "figural" implies some degree of organization or structuring.

Symbolic content: Information in the form of signs, having no significance in and of themselves, such as letters, numbers musical notations, etc.

Semantic content: Information in the form of meanings to which words commonly become attached, hence most notable in verbal thinking; involved in doing verbal tests, where the things signified by words must be known.

Behavioral content: Information, essentially non-verbal, involved in human interactions, where awareness of the attitudes, needs, desires, intentions, thoughts, etc. of other persons and of ourselves is important.

Products/ Results from the organism's processing of information.

Units: Relatively segregated or circumscribed items of information having "thing" character.

Classes: Aggregates of items of information grouped because of their common properties.

Relations: Recognized connections between units of information based upon variables that apply to them.

Systems: Organized or structured aggregates of items of information; complexes or interrelated or interacting parts.

Transformations: Changes in existing or known information or in its use, as in production.

Implications: Extrapolations of information, in the form of expectancies, predictions, antecedents, and consequents.

7/ "Information" is defined in a later section of this report as "that which the organism discriminates."

Appendix I.

An Example of
a Research
Report

Research reports are written in a formal style. The division of the contents may vary somewhat depending on the nature of the problem and the requirements of the institution or publisher, but all research reports conform to the same general pattern.[1] Below is the study which was discussed in Chapter 8.

The relationship of lateral dominance to reading achievement has been the subject of recurring study for many years. Three important theoretical formulations have guided much of this research. Dearborn (1931) found that a preponderance of the children who were referred to a reading clinic were left-eyed, or lacked ocular and manual dominance, or had mixed dominance. He believed these conditions to be associated with reading difficulty because it seems logical that people who have them will tend to approach a word from the wrong direction.

Monroe (1932) suggested that in moving the eyes to the right, as is required in reading, the left field of vision is obstructed by the bridge of the nose, and consequently the development of left-to-right eye movements may be more difficult for the left-eyed child. She also suggested that a child who has opposite eye-hand dominance may prefer different directional movements for eye and hand, and therefore find the complex hand-eye coordinations necessary in space perception difficult.

Harris (1957) found mixed hand preference much more com-

1/ Irving H. Balow and Bruce Balow, "Lateral Dominance and Reading Achievement in the Second Grade," *American Educational Research Journal,* 1 (May, 1964): 139.

mon in a clinical group of disabled readers than in the general school population. He suggested that this lack of consistent hand preference may be the result of a special maturational difficulty or slowness.

Balow (1963), working with 302 first-grade children, studied the effect on three measures of reading achievement of these various types and degrees of hand and eye dominance, singly and in interaction: strong, moderate, and mixed hand dominance; normal, crossed, and mixed dominance; and directional confusion. He reasoned that if these characteristics are associated with reading disability, they are also associated with reading achievement in the first grade. Yet, he found no combination of hand dominance and eye dominance, hand-eye dominance and knowledge of right and left, or strength of dominance and knowledge of right and left significantly associated with reading achievement.

The problem considered in this study is whether the dominance anomalies specified by Dearborn, Harris, and Monroe are significantly associated with reading achievement in the second grade.

Procedure

The sample of first-grade children selected by Balow (1963) was retested in the second grade and constituted the sample for this study. The original sample was obtained by listing the first-grade teachers in a middle-class suburb of St. Paul, Minnesota, and assigning a number to each. A table of random numbers was then entered to select 13 teachers. The sample consisted of all children in the classrooms of these 13 randomly selected teachers. Of the original 302 children, 250 were still in the district and completed all the tests. The *Harris Tests of Lateral Dominance* were again administered to those children in the sample who had not established a consistent directional preference in the first grade. Dominance retesting was completed in October and November. The *Gates Advanced Primary Reading Tests* (Word Reading and Paragraph Reading) were administered in February and were used as measures of reading achievement. The IQ scores were secured from the *Lorge-Thorndike Intelligence Tests, Level 1,* which had been administered to these children in the first grade.

Four comparisons were made, all children being utilized in each comparison. The analysis of covariance, with IQ used as a covariate, was used for the tests of significance.

Results

The 250 children were classified according to their hand-eye dominance as follows: normal—those having hand preference and eye preference on the same side of the body; crossed—those having hand preference and eye preference on opposite sides of the body; and mixed—those having mixed hand preference according to the *Harris Tests of Lateral Dominance*. If the views of Dearborn,

Harris, and Monroe are valid, the crossed-dominance group and/or the mixed-dominance group should achieve significantly below the normal group in reading achievement.

Table 1 shows the number in each group, the mean raw scores on word reading and paragraph reading, and the mean average grade-equivalent scores on the two tests. Each row of mean scores in Table 1 was tested by the analysis of covariance, with IQ used

Table 1/ Mean Scores for Children Classified According to Hand-Eye Dominance

	Normal Dominance	Crossed Dominance	Mixed Dominance
Word reading	31.76	30.08	29.78
Paragraph reading	21.26	20.17	20.96
Average grade equivalent	4.12	3.96	3.98
N	140	87	23

as an adjusting variable, to determine whether the effect of hand-eye dominance is significant. The largest F ratio (for the word-reading results) was 1.898, which with 2 and 246 degrees of freedom is not significant at the .05 level. The first null hypothesis was therefore accepted. We conclude that in the population of second-grade children of which this sample was representative there is no significant relationship between reading achievement and hand-eye dominance.

To test the second hypothesis, the 250 children were classified according to strength and direction of hand dominance (strong, moderate, or mixed, right or left, as determined by the dominance tests). If mixed dominance, as Harris and Dearborn contend, is an important factor in reading disability, the mixed group in our classification should achieve less than the other two groups. Table 2 shows the number in each group, the mean raw scores on word

Table 2/ Mean Scores for Children Classified According to Strength and Direction of Hand Dominance

	Strong Right	Moderate Right	Mixed	Moderate* Left
Word reading	31.09	31.06	29.78	31.75
Paragraph reading	20.70	20.74	20.96	22.38
Average grade equivalent	3.99	4.07	3.98	4.25
N	86	125	23	16

* The sample included only two children with strong left dominance. They were included in the moderate left group.

reading and paragraph reading, and the mean average grade-equivalent scores on the two tests.

Each row of mean scores in Table 2 was tested by the analysis of covariance to determine whether strength of hand dominance or direction of dominance (right or left) is significantly associated with reading achievement. The largest F ratio (.567) was found between adjusted means for the word-reading test and is not significant at the .05 level. The second null hypothesis was accepted. We conclude that in the underlying population neither strength nor direction of hand dominance is significantly associated with reading achievement.

To test the third hypothesis, the children were classified according to strength and direction of eye preference. According to Dearborn and Monroe, the left-eyed child is more likely to have difficulty in learning to read. Table 3 shows the number in each group, the mean raw scores on word reading and paragraph reading, and the mean average grade-equivalent scores for the two tests.

The mean score differences in each row in Table 3 were tested

Table 3/ Mean Scores for Children Classified According to Strength and Direction of Eye Dominance

	Strong Right	Moderate Right	Mixed	Moderate Left	Strong Left
Word reading	31.47	29.65	35.47	30.97	29.10
Paragraph reading	21.11	19.39	24.53	20.91	19.76
Average grade equivalent	4.10	3.82	4.54	4.08	3.86
N	114	31	19	35	51

for significance, using the analysis of covariance. The largest F ratio (1.871) was found for the paragraph-reading scores. This value of F is not significant at the .05 level; hence the hypothesis of no difference in achievement between eye-dominance groups was accepted. The data provide no adequate basis for asserting that in the underlying population either strength or direction of eye dominance is significantly associated with reading achievement.

To test the fourth hypothesis, children who had established consistent hand dominance at entrance to first grade were classified in the early-dominance group and those who had not were classified in the late-dominance group. Table 4 shows the number in each classification, the mean raw scores for word reading and paragraph reading, and the mean average grade-equivalent scores. The third column shows the same summary values for the mixed group (who are included in the late-dominance classification). The differences between these groups are smaller than in any of the previous classifications and including the mixed group under late dominance has not appreciably affected the mean scores of that group.

The mean scores of the two groups in Table 4 were compared using the analysis of covariance. The largest F ratio (.154) could well have occurred by chance; hence the null hypothesis was accepted. We conclude that establishing consistent hand dominance by the time of entrance into first grade has no significant beneficial effect on reading achievement and failing to establish consistent

Table 4/ Mean Scores for Children Classified According to Time of Establishing Hand Dominance

	Early Dominance	Late Dominance	Mixed
Word reading	30.92	31.11	29.78
Paragraph reading	20.79	20.95	20.96
Average grade equivalent	4.04	4.03	3.98
N	151	99	23

hand dominance until later has no significant retarding effect on reading achievement.

Discussion and Conclusions

Having the dominant hand and eye on the same side of the body, on opposite sides of the body, or having mixed hand dominance has no significant effect on reading achievement in the second grade. This conclusion adds to the evidence casting doubt upon the validity of the theoretical formulations of Dearborn, Harris, and Monroe when these formulations are extended to randomly selected school children instead of clinic cases of reading disability.

Strength of hand dominance and direction of hand dominance have no significant effect on reading achievement in the second grade.

In this group of 7-year-old children, 9.2 per cent manifested mixed hand dominance. In Harris' group (1957), 18 per cent were classified as mixed hand dominant. Inasmuch as the children in this study average well above the norm in reading achievement, the possibility does exist that in a more nearly average group of children there might be a greater proportion with mixed hand dominance and that mixed hand dominance might be significantly related to reading achievement.

Neither left-eye dominance, mixed eye dominance, nor strength of eye dominance has a significant facilitating or depressing effect on reading achievement in the second grade.

Establishing consistent hand dominance prior to first grade, during the first grade or second-grade years, or not at all, is not significantly related to reading achievement in the second grade.

Lateral dominance does not seem to be a fruitful area for seeking out determiners of individual differences in reading achievement.

References

1 Balow, Irving H. "Lateral Dominance Characteristics and Reading Achievement in the First Grade." *Journal of Psychology* 55: 323–28; April 1963.
2 Dearborn, Walter F. "Ocular and Manual Dominance in Dyslexia." *Psychological Bulletin* 28: 704; November 1931.
3 Harris, Albert J. "Lateral Dominance, Directional Confusion, and Reading Disability." *Journal of Psychology* 44: 283–94; October 1957.
4 Monroe, Marion, *Children Who Cannot Read*. Chicago: University of Chicago Press, 1932. 205 pp.

Bibliography

1 Alexander, Carter, and Arvid J. Burke, *How to Locate Educational Information and Data,* 4th ed. New York: Bureau of Publications, Teachers College, Columbia University, 1958.

2 American Association for Health, Physical Education and Recreation, *Research Methods in Health, Physical Education, and Recreation.* Washington, D.C.: 1959.

3 American Psychological Association et al., "Technical Recommendations for Psychological Tests and Diagnostic Techniques," *Psychological Bulletin, Supplement,* 51 (1954): 1.

4 Anderson, John E., and J. T. Cohen, "The Effect of Including Incomplete Series in the Statistical Analysis of Longitudinal Measurements of Children's Dental Arches," *Child Development,* 10 (June, 1939): 145.

5 Angell, James R., "The Organization of Research," *Journal of Proceedings and Addresses of the Association of American Universities.* Chicago: The University of Chicago Press, 1919.

6 Ausubel, D. P., *Theory and Problems of Adolescent Development.* New York: Grune & Stratton, Inc., 1954.

7 Balow, Irving H., and Bruce Balow, "Lateral Dominance and Reading Achievements in the Second Grade," *American Educational Research Journal,* 1 (May, 1964): 139.

8 Barton, Mary N., *Reference Books: A Brief Guide for Students and Other Users of the Library.* Baltimore: Enoch Pratt Free Library, 1962.

9 Barzun, Jacques, and Henry F. Graff, *The Modern Researcher.* New York: Harcourt, Brace & World, Inc., 1957.

10 Battle, Haron J., "Relation between Personal Values and

Scholastic Achievement," *Journal of Experimental Education,* 26 (September, 1957): 27.

11 Berelson, Bernard, *Content Analysis in Communication Research.* New York: The Free Press of Glencoe, 1952.

12 Bierstedt, Robert, "A Critique of Empiricism in Sociology," *American Sociological Review,* 14 (October, 1949): 584.

13 Block, Marc, *The Historian's Craft.* New York: Alfred A. Knopf, Inc., 1953.

14 Bloom, Benjamin S. (ed.), *Taxonomy of Educational Objectives: The Classification of Educational Goals.* New York: Longmans, Green & Co., Inc., 1956.

15 Borg, Walter R., *Educational Research: An Introduction.* New York: David McKay Company, Inc., 1963.

16 Brickman, William, W., *Guide to Research in Educational History.* New York: New York University Press, 1949.

17 Brown, Clarence W., and Edwin E. Ghiselli, *Scientific Method in Psychology.* New York: McGraw-Hill Book Company, 1955.

18 Brunswik, Egon, "Representative Design and Probabilistic Theory in a Functional Psychology," *Psychological Review,* 62 (May, 1955): 193.

19 Bryant, Lawrence C., and John H. Deloach, "Status of Music in Negro High Schools in South Carolina," *Journal of Research in Music Education,* 12 (Summer, 1964): 177.

20 Burt, Cyril, "Review: A Young Girl's Diary," *The British Journal of Psychology, Medical Section* 1 (July, 1921): 353.

21 Butts, R. Freeman, *The American Tradition in Religion and Education.* Boston: Beacon Press, 1950.

22 Campbell, Donald T., "Factors Relevant to the Validity of Experiments in Social Settings," *Psychological Bulletin,* 54 (July, 1957): 297.

23 Campbell, Donald T., "Quasi-Experimental Design," supported in part by Project C-998, with the Office of Education, U.S. Department of Health, Education and Welfare. Evanston, Ill.: Northwestern University, mimeograph, n.d.

24 Campbell, Donald T., "Administrative Experimentation, Institutional Records and Nonreactive Measures," in *Research Seminar on Teacher Education,* Report on Cooperative Research Project. Evanston, Ill.: Northwestern University, mimeograph, 1963, p. 75.

25 Campbell, Donald T., "From Description to Experimentation: Interpreting Trends as Quasi-experiments," in C. W. Harris (ed.), *Problems in Measuring Change.* Madison, Wis.: The University of Wisconsin Press, 1963, p. 212.

26 Campbell, Donald T., and K. N. Clayton, "Avoiding Regression Effects in Panel Studies of Communication Impact," Department of Sociology, *Studies in Public Communication.* Chicago: The University of Chicago, 1961, p. 99.

27 Campbell, Donald T., and J. C. Stanley, "Experimental and Quasi-experimental Designs for Research on Teaching," in N. L. Gage (ed.), *Handbook of Research on Teaching.* Chicago: Rand McNally & Company, 1963.

28   Campbell, W. G., *Form and Style in Thesis Writing.* Boston: Houghton Mifflin Company, 1954.

29   Chiappetta, Michael, "Historiography and Roman Education," *History of Education Journal,* 4 (Summer, 1953) : 149.

30   Cochran, W. G., and Gertrude M. Cox, *Experimental Designs.* New York: John Wiley & Sons, Inc., 1957.

31   Cohen, A. K., *Delinquent Boys: The Culture of the Gang.* New York: The Free Press of Glencoe, 1955.

32   Cohen, Morris, R., and Ernest Nagel, *An Introduction to Logic and Scientific Method.* New York: Harcourt, Brace & World, Inc., 1934.

33   Conant, James B., *On Understanding Science.* New Haven, Conn.: Yale University Press, 1947.

34   Cordasco, Franesco, and Elliott S. M. Gatner, *Research and Report Writing.* New York: Barnes & Noble, Inc., 1955.

35   Corliss, Leland M., "Analysis of Recorded Prevalence, Amount of Medical Care, and Follow through on Organic Heart Disease in 95,000 Pupils," *The Journal of School Health,* 35 (January, 1965) : 1.

36   Corotto, Loren V., "The Prediction of Success in Initial College Mathematics Courses," *The Journal of Educational Research,* 56 (January, 1963) : 268.

37   Cronbach, Lee J., "The Two Disciplines of Scientific Psychology," *American Psychologist,* 12 (November, 1957) : 671.

38   Cronbach, Lee J., "Validity," in Chester W. Harris (ed.), *Encyclopedia of Educational Research.* New York: The Macmillan Company, 1960.

39   Cronbach, Lee J., and Paul Meehl, "Construct Validity in Psychological Tests," *Psychological Bulletin,* 52 (1955) : 281.

40   Culbertson, Jack, and Stephen P. Hencley, *Educational Research: New Perspectives.* Danville, Ill.: The Interstate Printers and Publishers, Inc., 1963.

41   Dewey, John, *How We Think.* Boston: D. C. Heath and Company, 1933.

42   Dewey, John, *Logic: The Theory of Inquiry.* New York: Holt, Rinehart and Winston, Inc., 1938.

43   Diaz, A. J. (ed.), *Guide to Microforms in Print, 1962.* Washington, D.C.: Microcards Edition, 1962.

44   Dimitroff, Lillian, "A Quantitative-Qualitative Analysis of Selected Social Science Generalizations in Social Studies Textbooks in the Intermediate Grades," *Journal of Educational Research,* 55 (November, 1961) : 135.

45   Dollard, John, and Neal E. Miller, *Personality and Psychotherapy.* New York: McGraw-Hill Book Company, 1950.

46   Draper, Andrew S., *Origin and Development of the Common School System of the State of New York.* Syracuse, N.Y.: C. W. Bardeen, Publisher, 1903.

47   Dugdale, Kathleen, *A Manual of Form for Theses and Term Papers.* Bloomington, Ind.: Indiana University Bookstore, 1962.

48 Dugdale, Kathleen, *A Manual on Writing Research*. Blooming-ton, Ind.: Indiana University Bookstore, 1962.
49 Durkheim, Emile, *Suicide* (translated by John A. Spaulding and George Simpson). London: Routledge & Kegan Paul, Ltd., 1952.
50 Eaton, Allen, and S. M. Harrison, *A Bibliography of Social Surveys*. New York: Russell Sage Foundation, 1930.
51 Edwards, Newton, and H. G. Richey, "The School in Ameri-can Society," *Review of Educational Research*, 28 (February, 1958): 29.
52 Eells, Walter C., "First American Degrees in Music," *History of Education Quarterly*, I (March, 1961): 35.
53 Ellfeldt, Lois, and Eleanor Metheny, "Movement and Mean-ing: Development of a General Theory," *Research Quarterly*, 29 (October, 1958): 264.
54 Fell, Sister Marie Léonore, *The Foundations of Nativism in American Textbooks, 1783–1860*. Washington, D.C.: The Catholic University of America Press, 1941.
55 Filby, Yasuko, "Teaching Machines: A Review of Theory and Research," *Nordisk Psykologi*, 13 (1961): 209.
56 Fine, Bernard J., "Introversion-Extraversion and Motor Ve-hicle Driver Behavior," *Perceptual and Motor Skills*, 16 (February, 1963): 95.
57 Finley, Carmen J., and Jack M. Thompson, "A Comparison of the Achievement of Multi-graded and Single-graded Rural Ele-mentary School Children," *The Journal of Educational Research*, 56 (May–June, 1963): 471.
58 Fox, Lawrence W., and Carl E. Wedekind, "Studies of Pre-dicted Quality Point Average and Cross Validation Based on the Freshman Classes Entering the University of Pittsburgh in Fall of 1959 and the Fall of 1960." Pittsburgh, Pa.: Office of Institute Planning, The University of Pittsburgh, 1961.
59 Gage, N. L., *Handbook of Research on Teaching*. Chicago: Rand McNally & Company, 1963.
60 Galilei, Galileo, *Dialogues Concerning Two New Sciences*. Evanston, Ill.: Northwestern University Press, 1946.
61 Geiger, George, "Values and Social Science," *Journal of Social Issues*, 6 (no. 4, 1950): 8.
62 Good, Carter V., *Introduction to Educational Research*. New York: Appleton-Century-Crofts, Inc., 1963.
63 Good, Carter V., and Douglas E. Scates, *Methods of Research*. New York: Appleton-Century-Crofts, Inc., 1954.
64 Gottschalk, Louis, *Understanding History*. New York: Alfred A. Knopf, Inc., 1956.
65 Griffiths, Daniel E., *Research in Educational Administration*. New York: Bureau of Publications, Teachers College, Columbia University, 1959.
66 Gross, Neal, W. S. Mason, and A. W. McEachern, *Explora-tions in Role Analysis*. New York: John Wiley & Sons, Inc., 1958.

67 Henderson, Robert W., *Ball, Bat and Bishop*. New York: Rockport Press, Inc., 1947.

68 Hockett, Homer C., *Introduction to Research in American History*. New York: The Macmillan Company, 1932.

69 Hodnett, Edward, *The Art of Problem Solving*. New York: Harper & Row, Publishers, Incorporated, 1955.

70 Hopper, Robert L., et al. "Interdisciplinary Research in Educational Administration," *Bulletin of Bureau of School Service*, vol. 26, no. 2. Lexington, Ky.; University of Kentucky, December, 1953.

71 Hug-Hellmuth, Hermine (ed.), *A Young Girl's Diary*. New York: Thomas Seltzer, 1923.

72 Hull, Clark L, *Mathematico-Deductive Theory of Rote Learning*. New Haven, Conn.: Yale University Press, 1940.

73 Hyram, George H., "An Experiment in Developing Critical Thinking in Children," *Journal of Experimental Education*, 26 (December, 1957): 125.

74 Jevons, W. Stanley, *The Principles of Science*. London: Macmillan & Co., Ltd., 1924.

75 Johnson, Allen, *The Historian and Historical Evidence*. New York: Charles Scribner's Sons, 1930.

76 Johnson, Palmer O., and R. W. B. Jackson, *Modern Statistical Methods*. Chicago: Rand McNally & Company, 1959.

77 Jones, Harold E., *Development in Adolescence*. New York: Appleton-Century-Crofts, Inc., 1943.

78 Kagan, Jerome, and Howard A. Moss, *Birth to Maturity: A Study in Psychological Development*. New York: John Wiley & Sons, Inc., 1962.

79 Kemp, William W., "The Support of Schools in Colonial New York by the Society for the Propagation of the Gospel in Foreign Parts," *Contributions to Education*, no. 56. New York: Bureau of Publications, Teachers College, Columbia University, 1913.

80 Kerlinger, Fred N., *Foundations of Behavioral Research*. New York: Holt, Rinehart and Winston, Inc., 1964.

81 Knox, Ronald (trans.), *The Autobiography of St. Thérèse of Lisieux*. New York: P. J. Kenedy & Sons, 1958.

82 Krathwohl, David R., et al., *Taxonomy of Educational Objectives Handbook II: Affective Domain*. New York: David McKay Company, Inc., 1964.

83 Krug, Josef, "Kritische Bemerkungen zu dem' Tagebuch eines halbwüchsigen Mädchens," *Zeit schrift für Angewandte Psychologie*, 27 (July, 1926): 370.

84 Larrabee, Harold A., *Reliable Knowledge*. Boston: Houghton Mifflin Company, 1945.

85 Leonard, Fred E., and George B. Affleck, *A Guide to the History of Physical Education*. Philadelphia: Lea & Febiger, 1947.

86 Lindquist, E. F., *Design and Analysis of Experiments in Psychology and Education*. Boston: Houghton Mifflin Company, 1953.

87 McAshan, Hildreth H., *Elements of Educational Research*. New York: McGraw-Hill Book Company, 1963.

88 McGuigan, F. J., *Experimental Psychology*. Englewood Cliffs, N.J.: Prentice-Hall, Inc., 1960.

89 McNemar, Q., *Psychological Statistics*. New York: John Wiley & Sons, Inc., 1955.

90 *A Manual of Style,* revised and enlarged. Chicago: The University of Chicago Press, 1949.

91 Marx, Melvin, H., *Theories in Contemporary Psychology*. New York: The Macmillan Company, 1963.

92 Massanari, K. L., "Public Opinion as Related to the Problem of School District Reorganization in Selected Areas in Illinois," *Journal of Experimental Education,* 17 (June, 1949): 389.

93 Mill, John S., *A System of Logic*. New York: Harper & Brothers, 1846.

94 Mitzel, Harold E., "A Behavioral Approach to the Assessment of Teacher Effectiveness." New York: Office of Research and Evaluation, Division of Teacher Education, mimeograph, 1957.

95 Mussen, Paul H. (ed.), *Handbook of Research Methods in Child Development*. New York: John Wiley & Sons, Inc., 1960.

96 Muuss, Rolf E., *Theories of Adolescence*. New York: Random House, Inc., 1964.

97 NEA, Research Division, "Teaching Assignments and Time Schedules," *Research Bulletin,* 29 (February, 1951): 10.

98 NEA, Research Division, "Growth in School Enrollments," *Research Bulletin,* 36 (December, 1958): 124.

99 Northrop, F. S. C., *The Logic of the Sciences and the Humanities*. New York: The Macmillan Company, 1949.

100 Porter, Rutherford B., "A Comparative Investigation of the Personality of Sixth-grade Gifted Children and a Norm Group of Children," *The Journal of Educational Research,* 58 (November, 1964): 132.

101 Powell, Marvin, and Jerry Bergem, "An Investigation of the Differences Between Tenth-, Eleventh-, and Twelfth-Grade 'Conforming' and 'Nonconforming' Boys," *The Journal of Educational Research,* 56 (December, 1962): 184.

102 President's Committee on Education beyond the High School, *Second Report to the President*. Washington, D.C.: Government Printing Office, 1957.

103 Report of the Committee on Historiography, *Theory and Practice in Historical Study*. New York: Social Science Research Council, 1946.

104 Rose, Arnold M., *Theory and Method in the Social Sciences*. Minneapolis: The University of Minnesota Press, 1954.

105 Roy, S. N., and R. Gnanadesikan, "Some Contributions to ANOVA in One or More Dimensions: I and II," *Annals of Mathematical Statistics,* 30 (June, 1959): 304.

106 Russell, Bertrand, *An Outline of Philosophy*. London: George Allen & Unwin, Ltd., 1927.

107 Ryan, T. A., "Multiple Comparisons in Psychological Research," *Psychological Bulletin,* 56 (January, 1959): 26.

108 Ryans, David G., *Characteristics of Teachers.* Washington, D.C.: American Council on Education, 1960.

109 Salmon, Wesley C., *Logic.* Englewood Cliffs, N.J.: Prentice-Hall, Inc., 1963.

110 Scates, Douglas E., "The Conceptual Background of Research," in *The Conceptual Structure of Educational Research,* Chicago: The University of Chicago Press, 1942.

111 Scates, Douglas E., "Fifty Years of Objective Measurement and Research in Education," *Journal of Educational Research,* 41 (December, 1947): 241.

112 Schlesinger, A. M., "History," in W. Gee (ed.), *Research in the Social Sciences.* New York: The Macmillan Company, 1929.

113 Schramm, Wilbur, "Television in the Life of the Child—Implications for the School," in *New Teaching Aids for the American Classroom.* Washington, D.C.: U.S. Department of Health, Education, and Welfare, 1962.

114 Schutz, Richard E., Ellis B. Page, and J. C. Stanley, *Curriculum Guide for A Course in Educational Media Research,* Project no. B-236. Washington, D.C.: U.S. Department of Health, Education, and Welfare, October, 1962.

115 Searles, Herbert L., *Logic and Scientific Methods.* New York: The Ronald Press Company, 1948.

116 Sellitz, Claire, et al., *Research Methods in Social Relations.* New York: Holt, Rinehart, and Winston, Inc., 1962.

117 Seybolt, Robert F., "The S.P.G. Myth: A Note on Education in Colonial New York," *Journal of Educational Research,* 13 (February, 1926): 129.

118 Shores, Louis, *Basic Reference Sources: An Introduction to Material and Methods.* Chicago: American Library Association, 1954.

119 Shuttleworth, Frank K., *The Physical and Mental Growth of Girls and Boys Aged Six to Nineteen in Relation to Age at Maximum Growth,* Monograph of the Society for Research in Child Development, 1939.

120 Sidman, Murray, *Tactics of Scientific Research.* New York: Basic Books, Inc., Publishers, 1960.

121 Siegel, Alberta, E., and L. G. Kohn, "Permissiveness, Permission and Aggression in Children's Play," *Child Development,* 30 (March, 1959): 131.

122 Siegel, Sidney, *Nonparametric Statistics.* New York: McGraw-Hill Book Company, 1956.

123 Smith, Mildred M., "An Analysis of Stories in Basal Readers with Cultural Settings Outside Continental United States," *Studies in Education 1959,* Thesis Abstract Series, School of Education, Indiana University, 11 (1960): 259.

124 Smith, H. L., and E. A. O'Dell, *Bibliography of School Surveys and of References on School Surveys,* bulletin of the School of Education, vol. 8, nos. 1, 2. Indiana University, 1931.

125 Smith, H. L., and E. A. O'Dell, *Bibliography of School Sur-*

veys and of References on School Surveys, bulletin of the School of Education, vol. 14, no. 3. Indiana University, 1938.
126 Solomon, Richard L., "An Extension of Control Group Design," *Psychological Bulletin,* 46 (no. 4, 1949): 137.
127 Spahr, Walter E., and Rinehart J. Swenson, *Methods and Status of Scientific Research.* New York: Harper & Brothers, 1930.
128 Stanley, Julian C., "Controlled Experimentation in the Classroom," *Journal of Experimental Education,* 25 (March, 1957): 195.
129 Stanley, William O., and B. Othanel Smith, "The Historical, Philosophical, and Social Framework of Education," *Review of Educational Research,* 26 (June, 1956): 308.
130 Star, Shirley A., and Helen M. Hughes, "Report on an Educational Campaign: The Cincinnati Plan for the United Nations," *American Journal of Sociology,* 55 (January, 1950): 389.
131 Stogdill, Ralph M., *Individual Behavior and Group Achievement.* Fair Lawn, N.J.: Oxford University Press, 1959.
132 Taba, Hilda, and Elizabeth Noel, *Action Research.* Washington, D.C.: Association for Supervision and Curriculum Development, 1957.
133 Thorndike, Edward L., "The Nature, Purposes and General Methods of Measurements of Educational Products," in *The Measurement of Educational Products,* seventeenth yearbook, part II. Chicago, Ill.: National Society for the Study of Education, 1918.
134 Thucydides, *The History of the Peloponnesian War* (translated by H. Dale). London: G. Bell & Sons, Ltd., 1912.
135 Turabian, Kate L., *A Manual for Writers of Term Papers, Theses, and Dissertations.* Chicago: The University of Chicago Press, 1960.
136 U.S. Department of Commerce, Bureau of Census, *Illustrative Projections of the College-age Population, by States: 1958–1973,* Current Population Reports, ser. P-25, no. 132. Washington, D.C.: Feb. 20, 1956.
137 *U.S. Government Style Manual,* rev. ed. Washington, D.C.: Government Printing Office, 1959.
138 U.S. Office of Education, *National Survey of Secondary Education,* bulletin no. 17. Washington, D.C.: 1932.
139 U.S. Office of Education, *National Survey of the Education of Teachers,* bulletin no. 10. Washington, D.C.: 1933.
140 Van Dalen, D. B., "A Differential Analysis of the Play of Adolescent Boys," *Journal of Educational Research,* 41 (November, 1947): 204.
141 Wade, Durlyn E., "Teacher Load and Class Size in High School English," *Journal of Secondary Education,* 40 (February, 1965): 51.
142 Walker, Helen M., "Methods of Research," *Review of Educational Research,* 26 (June, 1956): 323.
143 Werkmeister, W. H., *An Introduction to Critical Thinking.* Lincoln, Nebr.: Johnsen Publishing Company, 1948.
144 Wilson, G. M., and C. O. Dalrymple, "Useful Fractions," *Journal of Educational Research,* 30 (January, 1937): 341.

145 Winchell, Constance, M., *Guide to Reference Books,* 7th ed. Chicago: American Library Association, 1951. Supplements: 1950–1952, 1953–1955, 1956–1958, and 1959–1962.
146 Woody, Thomas, "Of History and Its Methods," *Journal of Experimental Education,* 15 (March, 1947): 175.
147 Wylie, R. C., *The Self-concept.* Lincoln, Nebr.: University of Nebraska Press, 1961.
148 Young, Pauline V., *Scientific Social Surveys and Research.* Englewood Cliffs, N.J.: Prentice-Hall, Inc., 1956.
149 Zoolalian, Charles H., "Factors Related to Differential Achievement among Boys in Ninth-Grade Algebra," *The Journal of Educational Research,* 58 (January, 1965): 205.

Name Index

Subject Index